**Language in Mind**   gravity
                       foot-fee...

a chair : a man-made object designed
to ~~symbolise~~ recognise, and pander to human motives
for being seated.

_Oxygen and food as inputs_

are fractals present in the cosmos,
as well as in synapses?

---

P.337. Theory of mind — working models — empathy.
        Fodor 1979 'The Language of thought'
P.346  The culturally mediated (re-presented) mind.
P.375  Jackendoff tries to analyze consciousness.
P.387  Pre-linguistic constructs = rigid → reduced re-modelling
        by language.
P.390  Excellent examples of child's early spatial encounters.
P.401. Gravity: non-linguistically cognated but beyond recollection.
        It took Isaac to realise what he already 'knew.'
P.412. Babies stare longer at the familiar?!! Does averted gaze
        mean fear of the unknown? This does not sound right.
        Perhaps the sparking of rutted synapses = pleasure. Yes.

P.466.  He admits the investigator of language uses his
        own language — with all its arrogant assumptions
        and pre-conceived (!) notions. He is stirring a trifle.
P.495. (Lucy) Language can influence languageless thought???
P.496. (Slobin) 2 word utterances — universally the same semantics.
P.496. (Slobin) The pre-lexical prevails for years?
P.496/7. Tone-through-bone not considered. Hormone soup.
P.497. Scientists trying to unravel grammar! They fail!
P.498. Continues the special case of deaf kids born 2 the hearing.
P.500. The problem of interpretation of attention and
        gestures re-surfaced!
P.516  The ~~ergative~~ more pervasive than first appears!
P.516 (Dubois) 1987 ergatives underpin all languages.

PS16 Nutty Klaxon uncle and baby's distress.

PS17 When adults are asked to view a scene, they focus on the patient. When asked to _talk_ about the scene, this bias is lost! An ergative remnant from cause/effect learned in the womb?!.

PS18. The above is lost, because the parent arrogantly assumes that s/he is the actor and the baby, the patient. The baby fights this wilfully, but should lose.

# Language in Mind
Advances in the Study of Language and Thought

edited by Dedre Gentner and Susan Goldin-Meadow

A Bradford Book
The MIT Press
Cambridge, Massachusetts
London, England

This book was set in Sabon on 3B2 by Asco Typesetters, Hong Kong.
Printed and bound in the United States of America.

Library of Congress Cataloging-in-Publication Data

Language in mind ; advances in the study of language and thought / edited by Dedre Gentner and S. Goldin-Meadow.
   p.   cm.
"A Bradford book."
Includes bibliographical references and index.
ISBN 0-262-07243-2 (hc. : alk. paper)—ISBN 0-262-57163-3 (pbk. : alk. paper)
1. Psycholinguistics. 2. Cognition. I. Gentner, Dedre. II. Goldin, Susan.
P37 .L357   2003
401′.9—dc21                                                   2002029578

10 9 8 7 6 5 4 3 2

# Contents

# Contributors

Lera Boroditsky
Department of Brain and Cognitive
Sciences
Massachusetts Institute of Technology

Melissa Bowerman
Max Planck Institute for
Psycholinguistics

Soonja Choi
Department of Linguistics and
Oriental Languages
San Diego State University

Eve V. Clark
Department of Linguistics
Stanford University

Jill G. de Villiers
Department of Psychology
Smith College

Peter A. de Villiers
Department of Psychology
Smith College

Suzanne Gaskins
Department of Psychology
Northeastern Illinois University

Silvia P. Gennari
Department of Linguistics
University of Maryland

Dedre Gentner
Department of Psychology
Northwestern University

Susan Goldin-Meadow
Department of Psychology
University of Chicago

Giyoo Hatano
Human Development and Education
Program
University of the Air

Jennifer L. Hendry
Department of Psychology
University of Southern Mississippi

Mutsumi Imai
Faculty of Environmental Information
Keio University

Kayoko Inagaki
Faculty of Education
Chiba University

Stan A. Kuczaj, II
Department of Psychology
University of Southern Mississippi

Barbara Landau
Department of Cognitive Science
Johns Hopkins University

Stephen C. Levinson
Max Planck Institute for
Psycholinguistics

John A. Lucy
Committee on Human Development
University of Chicago

Barbara C. Malt
Department of Psychology
Lehigh University

Reiko Mazuka
Department of Psychology
Duke University

Edward Munnich
School of Education
University of California, Berkeley

Webb Phillips
Department of Brain and Cognitive
Sciences
Massachusetts Institute of Technology

Lauren A. Schmidt
Stanford University

Dan I. Slobin
Department of Psychology
University of California, Berkeley

Steven A. Sloman
Department of Cognitive and
Linguistic Sciences
Brown University

Elizabeth S. Spelke
Department of Psychology
Harvard University

Michael Tomasello
Max Planck Institute for Evolutionary
Anthropology

# Acknowledgments

This book is the culmination of the efforts of many people. We are particularly grateful for the early and generous support of the MIT Press, which made the book possible. Our job as editors was greatly aided by the excellent work of our copy editor, Anne Mark, and by Thomas Stone, Sandra Minkkinen, and the rest of the staff at the MIT Press.

The original impetus for this book was a workshop on language and thought sponsored by the Cognitive Science Program at Northwestern University in spring 1998 at which the editors and many of the authors were present. The ideas that emerged during the workshop made it clear that a new movement was building. Many of these ideas have been incorporated into this book.

We thank Northwestern University for its support of the Cognitive Science workshop program. Dedre Gentner's work on this book was supported in part by a sabbatical fellowship at the Center for Advanced Study in the Behavioral Sciences, through a grant from the William T. Grant Foundation, award number 95167795. Her research related to the book was supported by NSF award number 21001/REC-0087516 and by NSF award number SBR-9720313/5-27481. Susan Goldin-Meadow's work on the book was supported in part by a fellowship from the John Simon Guggenheim Memorial Foundation and the James McKeen Cattell Fund. Her research related to the book was supported by NIH grant number R01 DC00491.

Finally, we thank Michelle Osmondson of Northwestern University for her help in editing, and Kathleen Braun of Northwestern University for masterminding the entire process of assembling the book.

# I

# Introduction

# Whither Whorf

Dedre Gentner and Susan Goldin-Meadow

For the last two decades, the hypothesis that language can influence thought—generally known as the *Whorfian hypothesis*—has been in serious disrepute. Admitting any sympathy for, or even curiosity about, this possibility was tantamount to declaring oneself to be either a simpleton or a lunatic. The view of most language researchers is well expressed by Pinker (1994, 65): "Most of the experiments have tested banal 'weak' versions of the Whorfian hypothesis, namely that words can have some effect on memory or categorization. Some of these experiments have actually worked, but that is hardly surprising." Devitt and Sterelny (1987, 178) express this skepticism even more strongly: "[T]he argument for an important linguistic relativity evaporates under scrutiny. The only respect in which language clearly and obviously does influence thought turns out to be rather banal: language provides us with most of our concepts." The latter quotation exemplifies the rather schizophrenic way in which the Whorfian question has been viewed. The language-and-thought question is dismissed as banal and unimportant, yet in the same breath it is stated (almost in passing) that language provides us with most of our concepts—a view far stronger than that of even the most pro-Whorf researchers.

Whorf was not the first to express the idea that language influences thought. For example, Humboldt (1836) viewed language as the formative organ of thought and held that thought and language are inseparable (see Gumperz and Levinson 1996a; Lucy 1996, for reviews). Whorf's own views were somewhat more subtle than is generally realized. Along with his well-known strong conjecture:

We dissect nature along lines laid down by our native language. The categories and types that we isolate from the world of phenomena we do not find there because they stare every observer in the face; on the contrary, the world is presented in a kaleidoscope flux of impressions which has to be organized by our minds—and this means largely by the linguistic systems of our minds. (1956, 213)

he also considered weaker views:

My own studies suggest, to me, that language, for all its kingly role, is in some sense a superficial embroidery upon deeper processes of consciousness, which are necessary before any communication, signaling, or symbolism whatsoever can occur ... (1956, 239)

Nonetheless, the hypothesis that has come to be known as the Whorfian hypothesis, or alternatively the *Sapir-Whorf hypothesis*, states that (1) languages vary in their semantic partitioning of the world; (2) the structure of one's language influences the manner in which one perceives and understands the world; (3) therefore, speakers of different languages will perceive the world differently.

Why would anyone ever come up with the hypothesis that the language we speak shapes the thoughts we think? Consider a plausible scenario. When retelling an event, speakers of Turkish are required by their language to indicate whether they themselves actually witnessed that event (Aksu-Koç and Slobin 1986). Of course, the speaker knows whether she witnessed the event. However, she may not be interested in conveying this bit of information to the listener. Speakers of English have the option (which they often exercise) of leaving out whether they actually witnessed the event they are retelling—speakers of Turkish do not. After many years of routinely marking whether they witnessed an event, it is possible that Turkish speakers will tend to encode whether an event has been witnessed, whether or not they are talking. That is, Turkish speakers may habitually attend to this feature of the world much more than English speakers do. In other words, their way of viewing the world may have been altered just by becoming speakers of Turkish as opposed to English. This is the kind of reasoning that underlies the Whorfian hypothesis.

This strong Whorfian position was widely embraced in the 1950s and 1960s, drawing experimental support from Brown and Lenneberg's (1954) studies, which showed a positive relation between the codability of

English color terms (speakers' agreement on the names of colors) and people's ability to retain and recognize a given color from an array. The idea was that color terms influence the way in which people partition the color space, and hence their perception of color, whether or not they are talking. Other work on color within English (e.g., Lantz and Stefflre 1964) also seemed to support the hypothesis. But soon afterward Rosch published her influential paper showing that the Dani people in New Guinea, despite possessing only 2 basic color terms (dark and light), as opposed to 11 in English, nonetheless behaved on cognitive tasks as though their color categories resembled the English system ([Rosch] Heider 1972). Rosch found that the Dani's similarity groupings accorded better with English basic color terms than with their own linguistic groupings. Further, when asked to learn new categories, the Dani found the task easier when the categories were grouped around English focal colors. The implication was that the perception of color—and which colors are considered focal—is determined by the biology of human color perception and not by the language learned.

These negative findings ushered in a period of extreme skepticism concerning the possibility of linguistic influences on thought (e.g., Clark and Clark 1977; Devitt and Sterelny 1987; Pinker 1994). This skeptical view dovetailed nicely with strong zeitgeists in adjoining fields. In linguistics, the Chomskian emphasis on universals of grammar, coupled with the view that language is a separate system from general cognition and with a de-emphasis of the semantic arena, discouraged any search for a relation between language and cognition. Within cognitive psychology, there was a strong sense that concepts come first and that language merely names them: nouns name persons, places, or things; verbs name actions and events; adjectives name modifying concepts; and so on. In cognitive development, the Piagetian influence favored the same direction of influence—from thought to language. The dominant position of cognitive psychologists in the last few decades has been that (1) human conceptual structure is relatively constant in its core features across cultures, and (2) conceptual structure and semantic structure are closely coupled. Note that this view allows for no variation in semantic structure across cultures. The same view can be seen in cognitive linguistics, where the coupling between language and cognition has been taken to be strong enough to allow semantic structure to serve as a window on conceptual structure. One lucky implication of this view for cognitive researchers was that the semantic structure of any given language—say, English—could serve as a guide to universal conceptual structure.

Strangely enough, even during this period, when discussions of language and thought were about as respectable as discussions of flying saucers, the position was enjoying a revival in folk theories of politically correct speech. Terms like *senior citizens*, *hearing impaired*, and *learning disabled* were assiduously used instead of terms like *old*, *deaf*, and *dumb*. Interestingly, academicians—even while rejecting the hypothesis in their work—joined others in our culture in behaving as though they believed that language could shape thought. Consider the example of *chairman*, now replaced by the term *chair* (suggesting that we, perhaps rather oddly, prefer the risk of confusing a human with an inanimate object over the risk of gender-specific labeling). Presumably the male-oriented label came about because men were the typical occupants of leadership positions; in this sense, our language reflected the state of the world. But why do we think it so important to change the term now? We seem to believe that calling the position *chairman* potentiates a gender bias, and that calling it *chair* can subtly change our perceptions so that we will be less likely to assume that the position should be filled by a male. Insisting upon the word *chair* seems to reflect a folk belief that changing our language can contribute to changing our cognition. Yet despite embracing—or at any rate acquiescing to—this folk belief in their personal behavior, most cognitive researchers continued to find the language-and-thought hypothesis unworthy of serious consideration in their professional life.

Recently things have changed. After decades of neglect, the language-and-cognition question has again become an arena of active investigation. Why? At least three themes can be identified. First was the brilliant work of Talmy, Langacker, Bowerman, and other language researchers who, beginning in the 1970s, analyzed the semantic systems of different languages and demonstrated convincingly that important differences exist in how languages carve up the world. For example, English and Korean offer their speakers very different ways of talking about joining objects. In English, placing a videocassette in its case or an apple in a bowl is described as putting one object *in* another. However, Korean makes a distinction according to the fit between the objects: a video-cassette placed in a tight-fitting case is described by the verb *kkita*, whereas an apple placed in a loose-fitting bowl is described by the verb *nehta*. Indeed, in Korean, the notion of fit is more important than the notion of containment. Unlike English speakers, who say that the ring is placed *on* the finger and that the finger is placed *in* the ring, Korean speakers use *kkita* to describe both situations since both involve a tight-fitting relation between the objects (Choi and Bowerman 1991).

This evidence of substantial variability in how languages partition the world has profound consequences. It means that at least one—if not both—of the two core assumptions held by cognitive psychologists and linguists is wrong. If semantics varies crosslinguistically, then one cannot maintain that conceptual structure is universal and that seman-tic structure reflects conceptual structure. One could simply adopt the assumption that semantic structure and conceptual structure are inde-pendent of one another, leaving the universal view of cognition intact. However, faced with this dichotomy, a number of researchers have taken the alternative route of exploring ways in which semantic structure can influence conceptual structure.

The second theme developed from a set of theoretical arguments. These include the revival of Vygotsky's (1962) case for the importance of language in cognitive development, Hunt and Agnoli's (1991) influential review paper making the case that language influences thought by in-stilling cognitive habits, Miller and Stigler's (1987) research on cross-linguistic differences in number systems and their influence on learning arithmetic, and Lucy's (1994) research on the cognitive effects of classi-fier grammars.

The third important trend was a shift away from the focus on color to the study of domains such as space, which offer much richer possi-bilities for cognitive effects. Spatial relations are highly variable cross-linguistically (e.g., Bowerman 1980, 1989, 1996; Brown 1994; Casad and Langacker 1985; Levinson and Brown 1994; Talmy 1975, 1985). This suggests the possibility of corresponding cognitive variability. Fur-ther, spatial relational terms provide framing structures for the encoding of events and experience. They play a more interesting cognitive role than color names. Finally, spatial relations, like color concepts, are amenable to objective testing in a more direct way than, say, people's concepts of justice or causality. The work of Levinson's group demonstrating cognitive differences that follow from differences in spatial language—specifically, from the use of absolute spatial terms (analogous to *north-south*) versus egocentric terms (e.g., *right/left/front/back*)—has been extremely influential in attracting renewed interest to the Whorfian question, either arguing for the effect (Levinson 1996, 1997; Levinson and Brown 1994; Pederson 1995) or against it (Li and Gleitman 2002). Interestingly, there has continued to be a line of research on color, the bête noir of the Whorfian hypothesis (Kay and Kempton 1984; Lucy and Shweder 1979). Davidoff, Davies, and Roberson (1999) have recently produced counterevidence to Rosch's claims, based on a reanalysis of her results and on further work with another New Guinea tribe.

These themes coalesced in 1991 with the Wenner-Gren Foundation Symposium in Jamaica on the topic of rethinking linguistic relativity. Its direct result was an influential volume edited by Gumperz and Levinson (1996b), and its indirect result was to spark a renewed look at issues of language and thought. One important outcome of this symposium was Slobin's "thinking for speaking" hypothesis: that language influences thought when one is thinking with the intent to use language and that this influence is not at all trivial. Variants of this idea had been considered before; for example, Pinker (1989, 360) states that "Whorf was surely wrong when he said that one's language determines how one conceptualizes reality in general. But he was probably correct in a much weaker sense: one's language does determine how one must conceptualize reality when one has to talk about it." However, Slobin was the first to focus closely on the idea of "thinking for speaking" and to delineate its implications. This version is more cautious than the grand view that language determines the way in which we perceive the world; but for that very reason it is more palatable, and perhaps more conducive to empirical testing. Moreover, it invites close consideration of the processes by which speakers link cognition and language. It also spurs related questions, such as whether speaking and comprehending are equivalent in their opportunities for linguistic influences on thought and whether language influences thinking when one is talking to oneself (a link with Vygotsky's inner speech).

The purpose of this volume is not to settle the question of language and thought—which in any case we suspect is not one question but several—but to make it clear that the question (or questions) are worth asking and to encourage theoretical and empirical research. This time around we come equipped with better analyses of the linguistic distinctions and a better understanding of the relevant psychological processes and methods for testing them. Theories and experiments are being advanced at a rapid pace. A strong sign of the health of this arena, as is clear from the chapters in this volume, is that there are now close debates on specific issues. Current research continues to find mixed results, again as demonstrated in this volume. But the depth and precision of questions has increased dramatically since the early investigations.

The topics dealt with here range broadly; they include space, number, motion, gender, theory of mind, thematic roles, and the nature and function of objects versus substances. There are even two separate chapters that raise the ante on language and cognition enough to be titled "What Makes Us Smart? Core Knowledge and Natural Language" (Spelke) and "Why We're So Smart" (Gentner). The fields represented span a broad spectrum of cognitive science: cognitive psychology, cognitive development, linguistics, anthropology, and animal cognition.

To begin, theoretical chapters by Clark, Levinson, and Tomasello introduce the relevant questions from different perspectives. The remaining chapters fall into three broad (and overlapping) categories based on their questions and methods: *language as lens, language as tool kit,* and *language as category maker.* The answers are far from uniform.

Under the theme *language as lens,* the question posed is whether the language we acquire influences how we see the world. This view is closest to the classical "Whorfian hypothesis" that the grammatical structure of a language shapes its speakers' perception of the world. On the affirmative side, Boroditsky, Schmidt, and Phillips argue that gender assignments, long thought to be purely grammatical, have subtle but pervasive effects on how people think about objects. A more neutral position is taken by Slobin, who argues for limited effects of the semantics of motion verbs on how people talk about—and to some extent how they think about—motion events. On the negative side, Munnich and Landau find that distinctions in spatial language do not predict deviations in spatial representation. Also on the negative side, Malt, Sloman, and Gennari tested two possible claims of the language-and-thought hypothesis and found evidence for neither. One was that manner-path differences in the way actions are lexicalized would predict which aspects of events are likely to be retained for later recognition; the other was that nonlinguistic similarity groupings of artifact categories would reflect the semantic categories found in different languages.

Under the theme *language as tool kit*, the question posed is whether the language we acquire augments our capacity for representation and reasoning. This theme harks back to Vygotsky's view that "... learning to direct one's own mental processes with the aid of words or signs is an integral part of the process of concept formation" (Vygotsky 1962, 59; quoted in Kuczaj, Borys, and Jones 1989). All the authors in this section argue in the affirmative. Gentner suggests that relational language augments the human ability to engage in relational thought. Kuczaj and Hendry argue that teaching symbolic systems to chimpanzees leads to gains in their cognitive abilities. Inagaki and Hatano discuss linguistic and conceptual factors that influence inductive projection between animals and plants. De Villiers and de Villiers argue that acquiring the ability to use complement clauses fosters the development of theory of mind and thus the ability to pass false-belief tasks. Spelke suggests that language plays a role in providing conceptual links between initially separate modules.

Under the theme *language as category maker*, the question posed is whether the language we acquire influences where we make our category distinctions. On the affirmative side, Bowerman and Choi suggest that the acquisition of spatial semantics in a language influences infants' early categorization of spatial relations, and Lucy and Gaskins argue for the influence of classifier typology on the development of nonverbal classification. Imai and Mazuka take a more neutral stance, arguing for a limited role for linguistic typology and an important role for universal ontological knowledge on early individuation. Finally, Goldin-Meadow finds evidence for a possible universal starting point—namely, the ergative construction—that all humans may experience before learning language. Goldin-Meadow's findings point to thought before language and thus have a non-Whorfian feel. But how can the ergative construction be so basic and at the same time be so difficult for speakers of nonergative languages to fathom? Perhaps it's because the nonergative languages that most of us speak have irrevocably altered our ergative starting point and thus, in Whorfian fashion, have influenced how we think.

There are some interesting connections among the views taken here. First, in the *language as lens* chapters, some authors dismiss language as simply a mediator of cognition, arguing that when parallels between language and thought are found, it is merely because language is used covertly in the task (in other words, the task is really a language task and thus not a good test of the Whorfian hypothesis). The chapters in the *language as tool kit* section take issue with the "merely" in this claim. They suggest that such covert uses are a manifestation of the usefulness of language in the cognitive arsenal. However, both views agree that language is a powerful mediator of cognition when we speak—and much of our lives is spent in language-related activities. We learn not just by direct experience but also by hearing or reading about the state of affairs, so at least in this sense language has the potential to shape our conceptions of the world.

Another contrast is that whereas the *language as lens* view tends to focus on obligatory elements of language, the *language as tool kit* view encompasses specific content words, such as relational terms, and special-purpose constructions such as the complement clause construction. Also, tests of the *language as lens* hypothesis tend to involve cross-linguistic comparisons; indeed, all of the chapters in this section have taken this tack. In contrast, tests of the *language as tool kit* hypothesis can also be carried out within a language, by comparing outcomes when different sets of symbolic terms are made available to populations: for example, to primates (Kuczaj and Hendry), to children (Gentner), or to deaf individuals learning language late in life (de Villiers and de Villiers). Tests of the *language as category maker* view are often crosslinguistic, comparing speakers of languages that draw the boundaries between categories in different places (Bowerman and Choi, Lucy and Gaskins, and Imai and Mazuka). However, it can also be informative to examine populations that have never been exposed to language on the assumption that these populations offer us a pre-language view of thought (Goldin-Meadow).

Finally, a developmental issue that emerges primarily in the last section of the book is the chicken-and-egg question: which comes first, the concept or the linguistic term? Scholars like Bowerman have for some time challenged the long-standing view that concepts come first and language merely names them. This question clearly calls for a developmental perspective and, indeed, each of the chapters in the *language as category maker* section examines categories over developmental time.

In the past, empirical tests of the language-and-thought question have not proven convincing to either side in the debate. We suggest this stalemate has come about, in part, because the language-and-thought question is not one question but many. Whether language has an impact on thought depends, of course, on how we define language and how we define thought. But it also depends on what we take to be the criterion for "having an impact on." Language can act as a lens through which we see the world; it can provide us with tools that enlarge our capabilities; it can help us appreciate groupings in the world that we might not have otherwise grasped. As illustrated in this book, exploring these and other possibilities requires comparisons across languages and domains, as well as comparisons across thinkers who have and have not been exposed to language. From such an agenda, we are unlikely to get a yes-or-no answer to the whole of Whorf's thesis. But if we have delineated a set of more specific questions for which the answer is no to some and yes to others, we will have achieved our goal.

## References

Aksu-Koç, A., and Slobin, D. I. (1986). A psychological account of the development and use of evidentials in Turkish. In W. Chafe and J. Nichols (Eds.), *Evidentiality: The linguistic coding of epistemology* (pp. 185–201). Norwood, NJ: Ablex.

Bowerman, M. (1980). The structure and origin of semantic categories in the language-learning child. In M. L. Foster and S. Brandes (Eds.), *Symbol as sense* (pp. 277–299). New York: Academic Press.

Bowerman, M. (1989). Learning a semantic system: What role do cognitive predispositions play? In M. L. Rice and R. L. Schiefelbusch (Eds.), *The teachability of language* (pp. 133–168). Baltimore: Brookes.

Bowerman, M. (1996). Learning how to structure space for language: A cross-linguistic perspective. In P. Bloom, M. A. Peterson, L. Nadel, and M. F. Garrett (Eds.), *Language and space* (pp. 385–436). Cambridge, MA: MIT Press.

Brown, P. (1994). The INs and ONs of Tzeltal locative expressions: The semantics of static descriptions of location. *Linguistics, 32*, 743–790.

Brown, R., and Lenneberg, E. H. (1954). A study in language and cognition. *Journal of Abnormal and Social Psychology, 49*, 454–462.

Casad, E. H., and Langacker, R. W. (1985). "Inside" and "outside" in Cora grammar. *International Journal of American Linguistics, 51*, 247–281.

Choi, S., and Bowerman, M. (1991). Learning to express motion events in English and Korean: The influence of language-specific lexicalization patterns. *Cognition, 41*, 83–121.

Clark, H. H., and Clark, E. V. (1977). *Psychology and language: An introduction to psycholinguistics* (pp. 515–558). New York: Harcourt Brace Jovanovich.

Davidoff, J., Davies, I., and Roberson, D. (1999). Colour categories in a Stone-Age tribe. *Nature, 398*, 203–204.

Devitt, M., and Sterelny, K. (1987). *Language and reality: An introduction to the philosophy of language.* Oxford: Blackwell.

Gumperz, J. J., and Levinson, S. C. (1996a). Introduction to part I. In J. J. Gumperz and S. C. Levinson (Eds.), *Rethinking linguistic relativity* (pp. 21–35). Cambridge: Cambridge University Press.

Gumperz, J. J., and Levinson, S. C. (Eds.). (1996b). *Rethinking linguistic relativity.* Cambridge: Cambridge University Press.

Heider, E. R. (1972). Universals in color naming and memory. *Journal of Experimental Psychology, 93*, 10–20.

Humboldt, W. von (1836). *On language: The diversity of human language-structure and its influence on the mental development of mankind* (P. Heath, Trans.). Cambridge: Cambridge University Press (1988).

Hunt, E., and Agnoli, F. (1991). The Whorfian hypothesis: A cognitive psychology perspective. *Psychological Review, 98*, 377–389.

Kay, P., and Kempton, W. (1984). What is the Sapir-Whorf hypothesis? *American Anthropologist, 86*, 65–79.

Kuczaj, S. A., II, Borys, R. H., and Jones, M. (1989). On the interaction of language and thought: Some thoughts and development data. In A. Gellatly, D. Rogers, and J. Slaboda (Eds.), *Cognition and social worlds* (pp. 168–189). Oxford: Oxford University Press.

Lantz, D., and Stefflre, V. (1964). Language and cognition revisited. *Journal of Abnormal and Social Psychology, 69*, 472–481.

Levinson, S. C. (1996). Relativity in spatial conception and description. In J. J. Gumperz and S. C. Levinson (Eds.), *Rethinking linguistic relativity* (pp. 177–202). Cambridge: Cambridge University Press.

Levinson, S. C. (1997). From outer to inner space: Linguistic categories and non-linguistic thinking. In J. Nuyts and E. Pederson (Eds.), *Language and conceptualization* (pp. 13–45). Cambridge: Cambridge University Press.

Levinson, S. C., and Brown, P. (1994). Immanuel Kant among the Tenejapans: Anthropology as applied philosophy. *Ethos, 22,* 3–41.

Li, P., and Gleitman, L. (2002). *Turning the tables: Language and spatial reasoning. Cognition, 83,* 265–294.

Lucy, J. A. (1994). *Grammatical categories and cognition.* Cambridge: Cambridge University Press.

Lucy, J. A. (1996). The scope of linguistic relativity: An analysis and review of empirical research. In J. J. Gumperz and S. C. Levinson (Eds.), *Rethinking linguistic relativity* (pp. 37–69). Cambridge: Cambridge University Press.

Lucy, J. A., and Shweder, R. A. (1979). Whorf and his critics: Linguistic and nonlinguistic influences on color memory. *American Anthropologist, 81,* 581–618.

Miller, K. F., and Stigler, J. W. (1987). Counting in Chinese: Cultural variation in a basic cognitive skill. *Cognitive Development, 2,* 279–305.

Pederson, E. (1995). Language as context, language as means: Spatial cognition and habitual language use. *Cognitive Linguistics, 6,* 33–62.

Pinker, S. (1989). *Learnability and cognition: The acquisition of argument structure.* Cambridge, MA: MIT Press.

Pinker, S. (1994). *The language instinct.* New York: Morrow.

Talmy, L. (1975). Semantics and syntax of motion. In J. Kimball (Ed.), *Syntax and semantics* (Vol. 4, pp. 181–238). New York: Academic Press.

Talmy, L. (1985). Lexicalization patterns: Semantic structure in -lexical forms. In T. Shopen (Ed.), *Language typology and syntactic description: Vol. 3. Grammatical categories and the lexicon* (pp. 57–149). New York: Cambridge University Press.

Vygotsky, L. S. (1962). *Thought and language.* Cambridge, MA: MIT Press. (Original work published 1934.)

Whorf, B. (1956). *Language, thought, and reality: Selected writings of Benjamin Lee Whorf* (J. B. Carroll, Ed.). Cambridge, MA: MIT Press.

# II

## Position Statements

# 1

# Languages and Representations

Eve V. Clark

## 1.1 Introduction

Although we use language every day to talk about experience, language itself is far from being an exact representation of our experience. When we understand and produce language, we always have to take into account the fact that language does *not* offer us exact maps of the experiences we may wish to recount to someone or interpret from someone else. As Slobin has pointed out:

Language evokes ideas: it does not represent them. Linguistic expression is thus not a straightforward map of consciousness or thought. It is a highly selective and conventionally schematic map. At the heart of language is the tacit assumption that most of the message can be left unsaid, because of mutual understanding (and probably mutual impatience). (1979, 6)

Add to this the fact that what is conventionally schematic in one language may not be so in another. Effectively, Slobin here echoes Whorf:

Users of markedly different grammars are pointed by their grammars towards different types of observations and different evaluations of externally similar acts of observation.... ([1940] 1956, 221)

Whorf in turn follows Boas, who pointed out that those elements in a language that are obligatory—the grammatical categories—are what determine "those aspects of language that *must* be expressed" (1938, 127). In short, what is *obligatory* in each language can differ, so that speakers only express part of whatever they have in mind (Boas 1911).

What this implies is that speakers will select different details, different aspects, from their representations of each scene or event, depending on what language they are speaking. In some languages, they must always indicate the time of the event being reported relative to the time of speech; in others, they must attend to internal properties of the event (whether it has been completed or remains incomplete, whether it involves iteration or not, and whether it represents permanent or temporary characteristics); in still others, whether the speaker personally experienced the event being reported or whether the facts and details are known from hearsay; whether the objects and activities being reported are visible to the speaker or not, or whether they are close to the speaker, to the addressee, or to some third person; in still others, they must always attend to the gender of each nominal used to designate a participant in an event. What is obligatory in one language can be entirely absent from another (e.g., gender in German vs. English; aspect in Polish vs. Hebrew; speaker's source of knowledge—direct or hearsay—in Turkish or Bulgarian vs. Greek or Arabic; and so on).

## 1.2   Representations for Language

What are the cognitive consequences of all this? Does absence from the grammatical repertoire of a language mean absence from all conceptual representations? The answer to this, I argue, is no. When we represent the actions we do in putting on shoes versus putting on a coat, our representations are likely to be highly similar regardless of whether we speak Japanese (and must therefore choose which of two distinct verbs to use for these two activities) or speak English (and rely on just one verb for both actions). In the same way, if we *call to mind* a sequence of events, we can typically also call up many details about their relative internal and external timing (sequence, completeness, overlap, unfinished elements, etc.) even though there may be no ready way to express these details in our language. But if we are planning to *tell* someone else about this sequence of events, then we need attend only to those properties of the events that must be encoded in the language we use (Slobin 1996a). The same goes for *thinking about* versus *talking about* motion. If we demonstrate an action to someone else, we usually include in our gestures details that mark the manner in which the action was performed, but when we talk about the same episode, we may or may not include information about manner, depending on the language we use (e.g., Slobin 1996b; see also McNeill 1998). This suggests that the nature of the representation we draw on and the details we have to take into account will differ with what we are doing—here, for instance, remembering versus recounting.

Do we therefore set up and store multiple representations? Or just a single representation with every possible detail included so we can select whatever it is we need on each occasion when we call up that representation with a particular goal or purpose in mind? But selecting the relevant information from such a representation could take time. Having representations for talking instead could be one factor that streamlines our skill in retrieving and organizing just those grammatical elements we need when we plan and then produce an utterance. And this would imply that we call on other, more elaborated (or simply different) representations for other purposes.

In fact, even for language, we probably draw on multiple representations. First, as we listen to someone speaking, we need to be able to recognize the words and expressions from the *acoustic* information we perceive. So we need to have the appropriate representations of words stored, for example, so we can identify the same word uttered on different occasions and by different speakers. For production, though, we need instead a detailed set of *articulatory* directions so we can produce the target words and expressions when we wish to say them ourselves. These representations for understanding versus speaking require that we store very different kinds of information for use in the processes of comprehension versus production (Clark 1993). We need further linguistic representations for the graphemic forms that can be used to represent language. We must represent the *visual* shapes of letters, for instance, so we can recognize them in different fonts and in different handwritings. And we need representations of the *motor* programs we rely on in writing those same letters ourselves. The representations needed for language use in a literate society comprise at least these, and maybe more. We clearly include very different kinds of information in our representations for listening versus talking, on the one hand, and for reading versus writing, on the other.

## 1.3   Representations for Events

How do we represent events? When we say we remember something or that we are thinking about something, what information do we call up?

What about when we categorize some experience without talking about it? Or make a mental comparison between this occasion and another remembered from a long time ago? We can clearly draw on any and all information that we have represented in memory about the relevant events. But do we draw on one single all-purpose representation of each event? Or do we draw just on the representation that we might need for present purposes? Notice that the information we might need about one event in order to compare it to another might not be the same as the information we would need if we planned to talk about that same event, and the information we would need for talking about the event in language A could be different in a variety of ways from what we would need in language B. (And many speakers are multilingual.)

The same event, I suggest, could be represented in a variety of ways in memory. We can store it from the perspective of more than one participant (or even of onlookers); we can include various amounts of detail; and we can connect one or more of these representations to other representations already in memory. This would all suggest that we don't rely on just one representation of a specific event for all we do in remembering that event, thinking about it, comparing it to another event, reading about it, or recounting it to someone else. It's important to keep this in mind because it is all too easy to allude to *the* representation in memory for event X, when in fact *which* representation we actually call up on each occasion probably depends very much on whether we are daydreaming, trying to reconstruct some detail, planning to tell someone about a specific episode, or simply remembering that one episode was very similar to another, remembered from a different occasion. In short, it seems likely that we rely on multiple representations much of the time, and then draw on the one with the relevant amount of detail for the current purpose.

## 1.4 Perspective and Lexical Choice

Languages differ not only in their grammatical structure and in the precise repertoire of obligatory distinctions speakers must make in each utterance, but also in the range of lexical choices available (just how the lexicon maps onto each conceptual domain) and which range of conceptual perspectives speakers can therefore make use of. Where a language has terms for four or five taxonomic levels for plants and animals, for example, speakers will have more options in deciding which level of categorization is the appropriate one when giving specific instructions, telling a story, or writing a report. Each lexical choice marks the conceptual perspective that the speaker has chosen to take on that referent for that occasion (e.g., Clark 1997; Schober 1998), but speakers of different languages will have different numbers of options available in different domains.

These differences in the lexicon, and in the grammar too, reflect some of the historical differences among languages. Each community of speakers has its own history that has helped shape both lexicon and grammar over time. We trace close relations among languages by tracking cognates in their lexicons and by looking at typological patterning in grammatical structures (e.g., Croft 1990; Greenberg 1966). But while differences in grammatical structure require the speakers of each language to take into account somewhat different combinations of grammatical features as they think—and plan—*for speaking*, these differences affect only what is represented for linguistic expression. Keeping track of details for speaking is not the same as remembering an event, or thinking about connections among certain events. It is only when speakers put something *into words* that they must encode just those grammatical distinctions that are obligatory for their language, and those, I suggest, are "given" or present because of the habits of thought we develop for each language.

The point is this: If people think for speaking, they must have represented those grammatical distinctions that are obligatory for the language they are using. If instead, they are thinking for understanding what someone said and computing all the implicatures in arriving at an interpretation—versus thinking for remembering, thinking for categorizing, or one of the many other tasks in which we call on the representations we may have of objects and events—then their representations may well include a lot of material not customarily encoded in their language. It seems plausible to assume that such conceptual representations are nearer to being universal than the representations we draw on for speaking.

*Use morse or texting.*

Where do these conceptual representations come from? They are most likely built up from what infants and young children find salient in their early organization of conceptual categories and relations. As a result, languages, or rather their speakers, probably draw quite heavily from the universals of the most general representations in selecting grammatical distinctions to encode. This would explain, for instance, why young children at times try to express distinctions not conventionally made in the language they happen to be being exposed to, distinctions that *are* made in other languages (see Clark 2001; Clark and Carpenter 1989).

## 1.5    Some Consequences

What follows from this view of thinking and speaking? First, we should expect to find a considerable range from one language to the next in the grammatical distinctions that are obligatory, just as there is a range in what receives lexical encoding in different languages. Speakers of each language come to encode any obligatory distinctions as a matter of course whenever they speak that language. And a major part of acquisition is learning which grammatical details are obligatory. But this doesn't tell us anything about how being speakers of Hebrew, of Navajo, of Mandarin, or of Spanish will affect how people think about the world at large when they are *not* using language. That is, distinctions that are encoded grammatically, like aspect or gender, should probably have little or no effect on tasks that have no linguistic basis.

Second, we should find that in tasks that require reference to representations in memory that don't make use of any linguistic expression, people who speak very different languages will respond in similar, or even identical, ways. That is, representations for nonlinguistic purposes may differ very little across cultures or languages. Of course, finding the appropriate tasks to check on this without any appeal to language may prove difficult. The point is that if we make use of different representations depending on whether we are using our language or not, the fact of being a speaker of a particular language (or languages) cannot be said to limit or restrict how we represent the world around us. It will only shape what we are obliged to include when we talk (Slobin 1996a).

Overall, this view underlines the need for more precision when we characterize the range of representations we can draw on, the kinds of conceptual and perceptual tasks where we make use of them, and any differences there may be between representations for speaking and those we can draw on for other kinds of cognitive tasks.

## Note

Preparation of this chapter was supported in part by the National Science Foundation (SBR97-31781) and the Spencer Foundation (199900133).

## References

Boas, F. (1911). Introduction. *Handbook of American Indian languages* (Bureau of American Ethnology, Bulletin 40, Part 1). Washington, DC: Government Printing Office.

Boas, F. (1938). Language. In F. Boas, *General anthropology* (pp. 124–145). New York: Heath.

Clark, E. V. (1976). Universal categories: On the semantics of classifiers and children's early word meanings. In A. Juilland (Ed.), *Linguistic studies offered to Joseph Greenberg on the occasion of his sixtieth birthday: Vol. 3. Syntax* (pp. 449–462). Saratoga, CA: Anma Libri.

Clark, E. V. (1993). *The lexicon in acquisition.* Cambridge: Cambridge University Press.

Clark, E. V. (1997). Conceptual perspective and lexical choice in acquisition. *Cognition, 64,* 1–37.

Clark, E. V. (2001). Emergent categories in first language acquisition. In M. Bowerman and S. C. Levinson (Eds.), *Language acquisition and conceptual development* (pp. 379–405). Cambridge: Cambridge University Press.

Clark, E. V., and Carpenter, K. L. (1989). The notion of source in language acquisition. *Language, 65,* 1–30.

Croft, W. (1990). *Typology and universals.* Cambridge: Cambridge University Press.

Greenberg, J. H. (1966). *Language universals.* The Hague: Mouton.

McNeill, D. (1998). Speech and gesture integration. In J. M. Iverson and S. Goldin-Meadow (Eds.), *The nature and function of gesture in children's communications* (pp. 11–28). San Francisco: Jossey-Bass.

Schober, M. F. (1998). Different kinds of conversational perspective-taking. In S. Fussell and R. J. Kreuz (Eds.), *Social and cognitive approaches to interpersonal communication* (pp. 145–174). Mahwah, NJ: Erlbaum.

Slobin, D. I. (1979). *The role of language in language acquisition.* Invited Address, 50th Annual Meeting of the Eastern Psychological Association, Philadelphia.

Slobin, D. I. (1996a). From "thought and language" to "thinking for speaking." In J. J. Gumperz and S. C. Levinson (Eds.), *Rethinking linguistic relativity* (pp. 70–96). Cambridge: Cambridge University Press.

Slobin, D. I. (1996b). Two ways to travel: Verbs of motion in English and Spanish. In M. Shibatani and S. Thompson (Eds.), *Grammatical constructions: Their form and meaning* (pp. 195–219). Oxford: Oxford University Press.

Whorf, B. L. (1956). Linguistics as an exact science. In J. B. Carroll (Ed.), *Language, thought, and reality: Selected writings of Benjamin Lee Whorf* (pp. 220–232). Cambridge, MA: MIT Press. (Original work published in 1940. *Technology Review, 43*, 61–63, 80–83.)

# 2

# Language and Mind: Let's Get the Issues Straight!

Stephen C. Levinson

## 2.1 Introduction

Current discourse on the topic of language and mind is at about the intellectual level of a chat show on the merits of democracy. Ideological nonsense, issued by famous scholars, fills the air, even the scientific journals. Serious scholars tend to leave well enough alone, since such exchanges reveal a banal underlying lack of analysis. It is as if the topic of "Whorfianism" is a domain where anybody can let off steam, go on mental holiday, or pounce upon an ideological enemy. This is a pity, because the issues are deeply relevant to understanding our place in nature, and how we should understand our unique language capacity. Further, the issues are entirely open to careful analysis and empirical investigation, using the normal methods of the linguistic and psychological sciences.

In this chapter, I try to spell out in the simplest terms what the underlying issues are (but see Levinson 1996, 1997a, 2000, 2001, in press, for deeper discussion). We have to establish some kind of sensible mode of discourse before empirical results can be appreciated for what they are. As I outline at the end of the chapter, there is an accumulated body of such results, but first we had better try to establish the foundations for rational discourse.

## 2.2 The Doctrine of Simple Nativism and Its Coevolutionary Alternative

There is a widespread presumption in the cognitive sciences that language is essentially innate. All the other species have innate communication systems, so why not humans too? Of course, languages don't all

*but that's Perhaps they do — not the whole story.*

sound alike, but that's a matter of superficial clothing. Underneath, it's the very same flesh and blood. There are two basic tenets to the doctrine. The first holds that the syntax of language is fundamentally universal and innate, a view of course associated with Chomsky. The second (of central interest to this chapter) holds that the semantics is given by an innate "language of thought," a view ably defended by Fodor (1975). Put them together and one has the widespread presumption, which I will dub *Simple Nativism*, which curiously enough is not generally associated with any adaptational or evolutionary argument for language (see Levinson 2000). The central property of Simple Nativism is the claim that all the major properties of language, the object of study, are dictated by inbuilt mental apparatus. The observable variation is simply "noise," and nothing much can be learned from it. Protagonists of this view can be found across the cognitive sciences, including linguists like Jackendoff (see Landau and Jackendoff 1993), cognitive psychologists like Pinker (1994) or Gleitman (see, e.g., Li and Gleitman 2002), and the so-called evolutionary psychologists like Tooby and Cosmides (1992).

Despite its prominence, this doctrine is peculiar. First, it is impossible to reconcile with the facts of variation across languages. Second, it is a theory of innate (thus biological) endowment outside biology. There is no biological mechanism that could be responsible for providing us with all the meanings of all possible words in all possible languages—there are only 30,000 genes after all (about the number of the most basic words in just one language), and brain tissue is not functionally specific at remotely that kind of level. Third, it misses the most fundamental biological specialization of our species: the species has coevolved with culture—we cannot survive without it, but with it we have evolved a method of adapting to new ecological niches with much greater rapidity than our genome.

This last point is worth developing a little further. Human evolution has been shaped by the development of two distinct types of information transfer across generations, genetic and cultural, with systematic interactions between them (Durham 1991). Just look at the evolution of our hands and the progression of the tools to be found in the archaeological record. Language is an obvious central part of this gene-culture coevolution—it is culture, responding to its particular ecological niche,

*dexterity is more likely by natural selection*

that provides the bulk of the conceptual packages that are coded in any particular language. The contents of language, and much of its form, are thus largely the products of cultural tradition—but at the same time those cultural elements are constrained in many different ways by the biological nature of the organism, particularly its learning capacity. Rather precise information about this kind of interaction has now been provided by the study of infant speech perception. Infants are highly sensitive to the initial speech sounds around them, and they seem to have an innate fine-grained categorical system of perception shared with monkeys and other mammals. But by six months after birth infants have done something no monkey can do: they have warped this system of categories into line with the local language they are hearing around them. In that short time, they have acquired a cultural acoustic landscape. It is hard to escape the conclusion that human infants are "built" to expect linguistic diversity and have special mechanisms for "tuning in" to the local variety (Kuhl and Meltzoff 1996, 1997). We can expect to find exactly the same sort of interaction between prelinguistic perceptual distinctions and linguistically variable semantic distinctions. Thus, Choi et al. (2000; see also McDonough, Choi, and Mandler, in press; Bowerman and Choi, this volume) have shown that 9-month-old infants have equal facility to make, for example, English versus Korean spatial distinctions, while by 18 months they are tuned into the local language-specific distinctions. By the time we reach adulthood, just as we find alien language distinctions hard to hear, so English-speaking adults have lost the ability to make Korean distinctions even in nonlinguistic implicit categorization. Infants, unlike monkeys, are preadapted for cultural variation, for discovering the local system and specializing in it.

This alternative coevolutionary account, with psychology and cultural variation locked in mutual adaptation, is much better suited than Simple Nativism to understanding linguistic and cultural variation. It makes us think differently about what the biological endowment for language must be like. Instead of expecting that endowment to predict all the interesting properties of observable languages, we need rather to think about it as a learning mechanism wonderfully adapted to discerning the variability of culturally distinctive systems—a mechanism that simultaneously puts limits on the variation that those systems can throw at it. On this account, the essential properties of language are divided between two inheritance systems, biological and cultural, and the long-term interactions between them.

Simple Nativism has blocked sensible and informed discussion of the relation between language and thought for decades. Once the facts about linguistic diversity are properly appreciated, it will be clear that Simple Nativism ceases to be of any real interest.

## 2.3   Linguistic Variation

Simple Nativists hold that linguistic categories are a direct projection of universal concepts that are native to the species:

> Knowing a language, then, is knowing how to translate mentalese into strings of words and vice versa. People without a language would still have mentalese, and babies and many nonhuman animals presumably have simpler dialects. (Pinker 1994, 82)

Learning a language is on this view simply a matter of learning the local projection, that is, finding the local phonetic clothing for the preexisting concepts. Or as Li and Gleitman (2002, 266) put it:

> Language has means for making reference to the objects, relations, properties, and events that populate our everyday world. It is possible to suppose that these linguistic categories and structures are more or less straightforward mappings from a preexisting conceptual space, programmed into our biological nature: Humans invent words that label their concepts.

Hence, they hold, "the grammars and lexicons of all languages are broadly similar."

The view just sketched is simply ill informed. There is no sense of "broad" under which "the grammars and lexicons of all languages are broadly similar." If there were, linguists could produce a huge range of absolute linguistic universals—but they cannot do so. As Greenberg (1986, 14) has put it, either language universals are trivial ("All spoken languages have vowels"), or they are conditional generalizations with statistical generality. It is fundamentally important to cognitive science that the true range of human language variation is not lost sight of.

It may be useful to review some of the fundamental parameters of variation. Natural languages may or may not be in the vocal-auditory channel—they can be shifted to the visual-manual one, as in sign languages. When they are broadcast in an acoustic medium, they may have as few as 11 or as many as 141 distinctive sounds or phonemes (Maddieson 1984). Languages may or may not have morphology, that is, inflection or derivation. Languages may or may not use constituent structure (as in the familiar tree-diagrams) to encode fundamental grammatical relations (Austin and Bresnan 1996; Levinson 1987). Thus, they may or may not have syntactic constraints on word or phrase order. Languages may or may not make use of such basic word class distinctions as adjective, adverb, or even, arguably, noun and verb (Mithun 1999, 60–67). If they do, the kind of denotation assigned to each may be alien from an English point of view. Languages force quite different sets of conceptual distinctions in almost every sentence: some languages express aspect, others don't; some have seven tenses, some have none; some force marking of visibility or honorific status of each noun phrase in a sentence, others don't; and so on and so forth. Linguists talk so often about universals that nonlinguists may be forgiven for thinking that they have a huge list of absolute universals in the bag; but in fact they have hardly any that have even been tested against all of the 5%–10% of languages for which we have good descriptions. Almost every new language that is studied falsifies some existing generalization—the serious comparative study of languages, and especially their semantic structures, is unfortunately still in its infancy.

I emphasize the range of linguistic variation because *that's the fundamentally interesting thing* about language from a comparative point of view. We are the only known species whose communication system is profoundly variable in both form and content (thus setting aside, e.g., minor dialects in bird song form; Hauser 1997, 275–276). So we can't have the same kind of theory for human communication that we have for bee or even monkey communication; fixed innate schemas are not going to give us a full explanation of language. Of course, the human innate system must be superbly equipped to expect and deal with the variation—and so it is. This is what Kuhl (1991) has so nicely shown in the realm of speech sounds, as noted above: infants, unlike monkeys, are built to specialize early in the local sound-system.

Let us now pursue the subject of special interest to this chapter: semantic variation across languages. Take the spatial domain. On first principles, this is a conceptual domain where we would least expect major semantic variation; after all, every higher animal has to be able to find its way home, and mammals share a great many specialized anatomical and neurophysiological systems dedicated to telling them where they are and where things are with respect to them. So if the Fodor, Pinker, or Gleitman story is correct anywhere, it should be so here: spatial categories in language should be direct projections of shared innate conceptual categories. But it turns out that there is not the slightest bit of evidence for this.

We may take a few simple examples of spatial concepts where universal agreement on spatial categories has been expected. Let us start with deixis, often presumed universal in all essentials. It has been supposed that all languages have demonstratives that make at least a contrast between 'this' and 'that', but even spoken German seems to falsify that (some German dialects arguably have no demonstratives at all, but only articles). And for languages that do have two demonstratives, it turns out that there are at least four semantic types; more generally, research shows almost as many semantic distinctions in demonstratives as languages investigated (Meira and Dunn, in preparation). Likewise, it has been supposed that all languages make a basic distinction between 'come' and 'go' verbs. But in fact not all languages handle this distinction in lexical verbs (instead, e.g., using 'hither', 'thither' particles), and, when they do, there is tremendous variation in exactly what is coded. Typically, but not always, 'go' has no deictic coding, merely pragmatically contrasting with 'come', and the 'come' verb may or may not entail arrival at the deictic center, and may or may not allow motion continued beyond this center (Wilkins and Hill 1995).

Next, let us turn to the subdomain of so-called topological spatial relations. These are relations of contact or propinquity (like English *on*, *at*, *in*, *near*), which, following Piaget and Inhelder (1956), have been taken to be the simplest kind of spatial relation. Landau and Jackendoff (1993) have suggested that closed-class spatial expressions in languages are highly restricted in conceptual type, referring only to "the very gross geometry of the coarsest level of representation of an object—whether

it is a container or a surface" (p. 227). On the basis of English prepositions, they confidently make universal claims of the following sort: no
language will have spatial relators expressing specific volumetric shapes
of ground objects—for example, there will be no preposition or closed-
class spatial relator *sprough* meaning 'through a cigar-shaped object'
(p. 226). But the Californian language Karuk has precisely such a spatial
prefix, *-vara* 'in through a tubular space' (Mithun 1999, 142)! The whole
set of claims is based on woeful ignorance of the crosslinguistic facts.

Still, however rich the rest of the semantic distinctions, it could be that
every language encodes a notion precisely like English *on* and *in*. Not so:
many languages fractionate these notions and indeed have much more
specific notions, like 'in a hemispherical container' versus 'in a cylindrical
container'. Tzeltal makes many such distinctions in spatial predicates
(Brown 1994). But perhaps we simply need to qualify the claim: if a
language encodes spatial relations in prepositions (or postpositions), then
every such language encodes a notion precisely like English *on* or *in*. This
is not remotely true either. In current work, Sergio Meira and I have
mapped the adpositions (prepositions or postpositions) of a dozen languages of different stocks onto exactly the same set of 70 spatial scenes,
each scene depicting a subtype of a topological relation.[1] What emerges
quite clearly is that there is no basic agreement on what constitutes an
'in' scene, a spatial relation of containment, or any other basic topological relation. It is simply an empirical matter that spatial categories are
almost never the same across languages, even when they are as closely
related as English and Dutch.

Finally, we have also surveyed a wide sample of languages for the
kinds of coordinate systems or frames of reference they use for describing the location of objects widely separated from a reference object
(Levinson, in press). In these situations, some kind of angular specification on the horizontal plane is called for—as in 'The ball is behind the
tree'. It turns out that although languages vary greatly in the detailed
geometry employed, there are three main families of solutions: an egocentric (or more accurately viewpoint-dependent) *relative* system (as
in the 'The ball is left of the tree'), a geocentric *absolute* system (as in
'The ball is north of the tree'), and an object-centered *intrinsic* system
(as in 'The ball is at the front of the truck'). These three are all polar

coordinate systems and constitute the best claim for universals in the spatial domain. But there are some important caveats. First, not all languages use all three systems. Rather, they form an inventory from which languages must choose at least one—all combinations are possible, except that a relative system entails an intrinsic system. That means there are languages without words for 'left' or 'right' directions, but where all spatial directions must be specified in terms of cardinal directions like 'east' (so one has to say things like 'Pass the northern cup', 'There's a fly on your northern leg', etc.). Second, as mentioned, the local instantiation of any one system may be of a unique kind. Consider for example relative systems, which if fully developed involve a 'left', 'right', 'front', 'back' set of distinctions. Now, these distinctions are very variously mapped. They involve a projection of viewer-centered coordinates onto a landmark object, so that, for example, the ball can be said to be behind the tree. In English, this projection involves a reflection of the viewer's own left-right-front-back coordinates onto (in this case) the tree, so the tree's *front* is the side facing us, and its *back* is the side away from us, but its *left* and *right* are on the same side as the viewer's. In Hausa and many other languages, this projection involves translation, so 'left' and 'right' remain as in English, but 'front' and 'back' are reversed ('The ball is behind the tree' means it is between the viewer and the tree). In some dialects of Tamil, the projection involves rotation, so 'front' and 'back' are like in English, but 'left' and 'right' are reversed. And so on and so forth—there is plenty of semantic variation. Although the choices between different frames of reference are limited, they are quite sufficient to induce the very strongest "Whorfian" effects, as described below (and see Levinson 1996; Pederson et al. 1998).

To sum up: the Simple Nativist idea (as voiced by Pinker and Gleitman) that universal concepts are directly mapped onto natural language words and morphemes, so that all a child-learner has to do is find the local name as it were, is simply false. There are vanishingly few universal notions, if any, that every language denotes with a simple expression. Even the renowned case of the color words only substantiates this fact: languages vary substantially in the number of color words they have, and what they actually denote (Kay and McDaniel 1978; Kay, Berlin, and Merrifield 1991). A term glossed as 'red' may—according to the standard theory—actually include brown, yellow, and related hues, and 'black' may include blue and green. But some languages have at best only incipient color words (Levinson 2000), and this has required substantial weakening of the standard theory (Kay and Maffi 1999). There is really no excuse for continued existence of the myth of a rich set of lexically packaged semantic universals. Removing that myth opens the way for entertaining seriously a heretical idea.

## 2.4   The Very Thought: Could the Language We Speak Influence the Way We Think?

There is an ideological overtone to Simple Nativism: the independence of thought from language opens up to us the freedom of will and action ("[S]ince mental life goes on independently of particular languages, concepts of freedom and equality will be thinkable even if they are nameless" Pinker 1994, 82). So Whorfianism and linguistic determinism *have* to be impossible! This moral imperative is beside the point, not only because we are not in the preaching business, but also because, despite some incautious language, no one, not even Whorf, ever held that our thought was in the infernal grip of our language. Whorf's own idea was that certain grammatical patterns, through making obligatory semantic distinctions, might induce corresponding categories in habitual or non-reflective thought in just the relevant domains (see Lucy 1992b for careful exposition). Now that idea, generalized also to lexical patterns, seems neither anti-American nor necessarily false. More generally still, it seems fairly self-evident that the language one happens to speak affords, or conversely makes less accessible, certain complex concepts. There are languages with no or very few number words, and without a generative system of numerals—it seems unlikely that the speakers of such a language would ever entertain the notion 'seventy-three', let alone that of a logarithm, and certainly their fellows would never know if they did. As mentioned, there are languages that only use cardinal direction terms for spatial directions, where one must constantly be able to unerringly locate the center of a quadrant at, say, 15 degrees east of north—speakers of such languages can be shown to have a developed sense of direction of a different order of magnitude from speakers of languages that lack such constant reference to geocentric coordinates (Levinson, in press). If they didn't have such competence, they couldn't communicate; the language affords, even requires, certain underlying computations (see section 2.5). In this sort of way, languages can differentially impede, facilitate, or require underlying mental operations.

In this section, I want to show that the web of theoretical commitments we already have in the linguistic and psychological sciences seem to converge on the presumption that speaking specific languages does indeed have cognitive consequences for the speakers of those languages.

First, take the simple question "Do we think the same way that we speak?" Making various classical assumptions (e.g., accepting the notion of a *representation*), this question can reasonably be rendered as the more specific "Are the representations we use in serious nonlinguistic thinking and reasoning the very same representations that underlie linguistic meanings?" The answer, I have shown (Levinson 1997a), has to be no. The reasons are various, but conclusive: semantic representations have to be decoupled from conceptual representations to allow for various properties of linguistic meaning like deixis, anaphora, very limited lexica, linearization, and so on, which are clearly not properties of conceptual representations. Besides, there are many different kinds of conceptual representation, from the imagistic to the propositional. But there are also quite persuasive arguments to the effect that though linguistic and nonlinguistic representations are distinct, there must be at least one level of conceptual representation that is closely aligned to a semantic level; otherwise, we couldn't transform the one into the other with the facility we have, as shown by the speed of language encoding and comprehension. Further, any semantic distinctions must be supported by the underlying conceptual distinctions and processes that are necessary to compute them (if you have a lexical concept 'seven'—and not all languages do—you had better be able to count to 7 if you are going to use it correctly). So, overall, that level of conceptual representation is close to, but not identical to, a level of semantic representation.

Our next simple question is, "Do all humans think alike?" Given that there are multiple representation systems (for vision, touch, smell, etc.), many of them specialized to the sensory modalities, and given that many human sensory experiences are basically similar (given the world we all inhabit), there is no doubt that there is a broad base of "psychic unity" in the species. But we are interested in the more abstract representations in which we think and reason, which are closest to language. We can transform the basic question then into the more specific "Is the conceptual representation system closest to semantic representation universal in character?" The answer to that question is—perhaps surprisingly— almost certainly no. The answer can be derived from both first principles and empirical investigation. Here I concentrate on the reasoning from first principles, postponing the empirical arguments to the following section.

Why must the conceptual representations closest to semantic representations be nonuniversal? Because languages vary in their semantic structure, as we saw in section 2.3. Simply put, the fact is that there are few if any lexical concepts that universally occur in all the languages of the world; not all languages have a word (or other expression) for 'red' or 'father' or 'in' or 'come' or even 'if'. Now the consequences of that basic fact are easily enough appreciated. Let us pursue a *reductio*. We have established that semantic representations map fairly directly, but not exactly, onto the closest level of conceptual representation (CR). Assume now that CR is universal. Then, allowing for some slippage, semantic representations (SR) must be roughly universal too. But they are not. Therefore, we must abandon the assumption that CR is universal.

Approaching the problem from the other direction, we know that languages code different concepts at the lexical level. Now assume—as Fodor and many psychologists do—that corresponding to a lexical item is a single holistic concept (Fodor, Fodor, and Garrett 1975). Further assume, as they do, that SR and CR are coextensive. Then, since we think in CR, users of different languages think differently. So, it follows that "nondecompositionalists" (i.e., those who do not think that lexical concepts decompose into subconcepts) are implicit Whorfians—a fact that they do not seem to have appreciated.[2]

Linguists tend to be decompositionalists—they tend to think that lexical concepts are complex, composed out of atomic concepts. Naturally, they are not always so naive about semantic variation as the psychologists. But they think they can escape the immediate Whorfian consequence: languages encode different concepts at the lexical level, but they "compose" those semantical concepts from a universal inventory of atomic concepts. Even assuming that SR and CR are closely related, as seems to be the case, it no longer seems to follow that different languages require different conceptual relations, or that speaking a language would induce different ways of thinking: both SR and CR could be universal at the level of conceptual primes or primitives. So we can cook our varied semantic cakes out of the same old universal flour and sugar.

Though I am sympathetic with the decompositional move, it is hardly the intellectual triumph that it may seem. Suppose I hypothesize a universal inventory of 20 or 100 primes, and now I come across a language that has words that won't decompose into those primes. What will I do? Add to the universal inventory the features we need for that language, of course. So what makes them universal? At least one language uses them! How would you falsify such a theory? There isn't any way to falsify a theory of universals that consists in an augmentable list of features that any one language may freely select from. It's the weakest possible kind of theory—it would need to be supplemented with a theory that tells us why *just those features* and no others are in the inventory, and we are in no position to do that because we have as yet no idea of the real extent of semantic variation.

But there's another problem with decomposition. Psycholinguistic evidence shows that when words are activated, the concept as a whole is activated, not little bits of it. And the psychologists have compelling evidence that we don't think at that atomic level—we think at the macro-level of conceptual wholes, the level reflected in lexical concepts. The reasons for this lie partly in properties of short-term memory, the major bottleneck in our computing system. For short-term memory is limited to, say, five chunks at a time, while not caring a jot about how complex the underlying chunks are—or, put another way, what they can be decomposed into (Miller 1956; Cowan 2001). We don't have to think about a *hundred* as 'ten tens' when doing mental arithmetic, or *aunt* as 'mother's sister, or father's sister, or father's brother's wife, or mother's brother's wife' when greeting Aunt Mathilda. Composing complex concepts gives enormous power to our mental computations, and most of those complex concepts are inherited from the language we happen to speak. So the linguists are wrong to think that lexical decomposition will let them off the Whorfian hook. Sure, it allows them to hold a remoter level of universal concepts, and it might help to explain how we can learn complex cultural concepts, but the conceptual level closest to the semantic representations, and the level in which we compute, seems likely to be heavily culture specific.

So, given the facts of semantic variation, and what we know about mental computation, it is hard to escape the conclusion that, yes, the ways we speak—the kinds of concepts lexically or grammatically encoded in a specific language—are bound to have an effect on the ways we think. And this conclusion is going to be general over all the different kinds of theory scholars are likely to espouse: noncompositional or compositional representational theories, and equally of course connectionist theories, where activation patterns are a direct reflection of input patterns.

## 2.5   The Issues in the Light of Empirical Evidence

So now at last we might be prepared to accept the idea that it is worth empirically investigating the kinds of influence a specific language might have on our mental coding of scenes and events, our nonlinguistic memory and inference. In fact, there is already a quite impressive body of evidence that demonstrates significant effects here. I will review a few examples, concentrating on our own work.

Curiously enough, the color work in the tradition of Berlin and Kay (1969), which has been taken to indicate simple universals of lexical coding, has also yielded evidence for the impact of linguistic categories on memory and perceptual discriminations. As noted above, the lexical universals are of a conditional sort; for example, if a language has just three color words, one will cover the "cool" range (black, green, blue), another the "warm" range (red, yellow, orange), and another the "bright" range (white, pink, pale blue, etc.) (see Kay and McDaniel 1978). So it is easy to find languages that differ in their color coding. Lenneberg and Roberts (1956) had earlier shown that having specific terms for, say, 'yellow' versus 'orange', helped English speakers memorize colors, compared to Zuni speakers who have no such lexical discrimination. Lucy (1981) showed similar effects for Yucatec versus Spanish versus English speakers, and Davidoff, Davies, and Roberson (1999) did the same for English versus Berinmo. Kay and Kempton (1984) explored the effects of linguistic coding on perceptual discriminability and found that if a language like English discriminates 'blue' and 'green', while another like Tarahumara does not, English speakers but not Tarahumara speakers will exaggerate the perceptual differences on the boundary. This suggests that our visual perception may be biased by linguistic categorization just as our auditory perception clearly is by the specific phonemes in a language (which is why of course late second language learners have difficulty perceiving and producing the alien speech sounds).

Turning to our own work, in a large-scale long-term collaborative enterprise involving two score researchers, we have researched linguistic differences in the spatial domain. Our goals have been first, to understand the linguistic differences here, and second, to then explore the relation of those linguistic differences to nonlinguistic cognition. I have already outlined above some of the quite surprising linguistic differences to be found across languages; in general, it is hard to find any pair of spatial descriptors with the same denotation across languages (see, e.g., Levinson and Wilkins, in press). In the subdomain of frames of reference, we have pursued the nonlinguistic correlates in detail. The following is a synopsis of much detailed work (see Levinson 1996, 1997b, in press; Pederson et al. 1998; and references therein).

As mentioned above, languages make different use of the three basic frames of reference. Some languages, like English or other European languages, employ the relative frame of reference (involving left/right/front/back terms projected from a viewpoint) along with the intrinsic (involving properties of the landmark or reference object, e.g., its intrinsic top, back, sides, etc.). Other languages, like Tzeltal or Arrernte, use no relative frame of reference, but instead supplement an intrinsic system with an absolute one—that is, a cardinal-direction type system. In languages like these, speakers can't say 'Pass me the cup to your left', or 'Take the first right', or 'He's hiding behind the tree'—the relevant spatial expressions simply don't exist. Instead, they have to say 'Pass me the cup to the west', or 'Take the first turn to the south', or 'He's hiding east of the tree', as appropriate. Such cardinal-direction systems are actually quite diverse (e.g., they may have arbitrary directions unrelated to the earth's poles) and are always different from the English speaker's use of map coordinates (e.g., in the English system there is no linguistic convention about how many degrees on either side of grid-north still constitutes 'north', and English speakers only use this system on a geographic scale).

We made the following predictions. First, speakers of languages with absolute coordinates should have a better sense of direction than speakers of relative languages: they not only have to know where, say, 'south' is at any one moment (otherwise they couldn't speak the language), but they also need to know, for example, that place B is south of A, because they may have a verb 'go-south' properly used for any motion from A to B. We transported people from three absolute communities to novel locations and got them to point to a range of other locations at varying distances. They can do this with remarkable accuracy, but speakers of relative languages cannot (Levinson, in press). We have also examined unreflective gesture while speaking: for absolute speakers, gestures to places are geographically accurate; for relative speakers, are not. Second, we supposed that speakers of absolute languages would have to maintain internal representations of space in terms of fixed bearings, rather than egocentric coordinates. That is because if memories were coded in egocentric coordinates, there would be no way to describe them in the relevant language: there is no translation algorithm from egocentric coordinates to geocentric ones, or vice versa (you can't get from the description 'The knife was north of the fork' to the description 'The knife was left of the fork', or vice versa). Since one might want to talk about any observed situation, it had better be memorized in coordinates appropriate to the language. To test this, we invented a rotation paradigm, with which it is possible to distinguish nonlinguistic mental coding in any of the frames of reference. For example, subjects see an arrow on a table pointing to their left, or south. They are now rotated 180 degrees and are asked to place the arrow on another table so it is just as before. If they point it to their left, they thought about it in terms of egocentric coordinates; if to their right (i.e., south), in geocentric coordinates. This paradigm allows examination of different psychological capacities, and we designed a battery of tests exploring recognition memory, recall, and inference of different kinds, all conducted under rotation. The tasks were carried out in four relative and six absolute language communities. The results are quite startling: overwhelmingly, subjects follow the coding pattern in their language when performing these entirely nonlinguistic tasks (Levinson 1996, in press).

We find these results to be convincing evidence that linguistic coding is both a facilitator of a specific cognitive style and a bottleneck, constraining mental representations in line with the output modality. It seems that preferred frames of reference in language deeply affect our mental life. They affect the kind of mental coding of spatial relations in memory, and the way in which we reason about space, since the different frames of reference have different logical properties (see Levinson 1996). They affect the kinds of mental maps we maintain (as shown by the navigation experiments mentioned above), even the kind of mental imagery we use when we gesture. These are anything but superficial correlates of a mode of linguistic coding.

In a recent paper, Li and Gleitman (2002) try to resist these conclusions and reassert a Simple Nativist perspective. They carried out one simplified version of one of our tasks with an American student population and claimed that they could induce absolute or relative coding by manipulating the conditions of the task. First, the task yielded a relative result indoors, but a mixed relative/absolute result outdoors. Second, by placing salient landmarks or spatial cues at alternate ends of the stimulus and response tables, subjects could be made to construct the response in line with the landmark cue. Li and Gleitman conclude that we all think equally in relative or absolute frames of reference; it just depends on the conditions under which one coding system or another becomes more appropriate. Unfortunately, their results are either not replicable (the outdoors condition) or betray a misunderstanding of the nature of the three frames of reference (the landmark cues condition). When they used salient spatial cues on the stimulus and response tables, what they were actually doing was invoking a response in the intrinsic frame of reference, not the absolute one. We showed this by reproducing their experiment and introducing a new condition: subjects were now rotated 90 degrees instead of 180 degrees (Levinson et al. 2002). If you see a row of animals headed leftward, or south, on table 1 toward a jug, and are then rotated to face table 2 at 90 degrees, and are asked to place the animals just as they were (with an emphasis on remembering which animals were in which order), a response that preserves them heading left or heading south or heading toward the jug can easily be distinguished. English- or Dutch-speaking subjects will place the animals so they are heading either left (relative) or toward the jug (intrinsic), not south (absolute). That's because English and Dutch offer both the relative and intrinsic frames of reference—although the relative is dominant, as can be shown by increasing the memory load (e.g., by adding to the number of animals), whereupon the relative is selected over the intrinsic. In short, pace Li and Gleitman, the evidence remains that the frames of reference used in people's language match those used in their nonlinguistic cognition.

There are many other results that support the idea that linguistic coding has an effect on nonlinguistic cognition. Special mention should be made of the work of John Lucy (1992a; see also Lucy and Gaskins, this volume), which demonstrates that the original ideas of Whorf can be verified—namely, the idea that grammatical patterning with semantic correlates may have an especially powerful effect on implicit categorization. English has obligatory number marking (singular vs. plural) on countable nominals, while Yucatec has only optional number marking, mostly only on animates. Following the hypothesis that this insistent number marking in English might have nonlinguistic effects, Lucy showed that English speakers are better at remembering number in nonlinguistic stimuli. In work with Suzanne Gaskins, he has gone on to show that this lack of number marking in Yucatec is associated with nominals whose semantics are unspecified for quantificational unit (Lucy and Gaskins 2001). They tend to denote not bounded units, but essence or "stuff"; thus, the term used for 'banana' actually denotes any entity made of banana-essence (e.g., the tree or the leaf or the fruit). On sorting tasks, Yucatec speakers behave differently than English speakers: English speakers tend to sort by shape or function, Yucatec speakers by the material out of which things are made. The suggestion is that the pattern in the grammar has far-reaching correlations with implicit mental categories.

## 2.6  Conclusion

Where are we? I have tried to establish that (1) languages vary in their semantics just as they do in their form, (2) semantic differences are bound to engender cognitive differences, (3) these cognitive correlates of semantic differences can be empirically found on a widespread basis. As a consequence, the semantic version of Simple Nativism ought to be as dead as a dodo. But it isn't.

Why not? One reason is that its proponents think they have an argument that it *just has to be right,* so no negative evidence will be seriously entertained! The argument of course is a learnability argument. Consider what the poor child has to do: find the meaning corresponding to some acoustic signal—the child must segment the signal, find the word forms, and then hypothesize the meanings. Suppose, as Fodor, Pinker, and Gleitman hold, that the child is already provided with the relevant conceptual bundles; then all she has to do is map strings of phonemes to ready-made conceptual bundles. This is already difficult, since there are lots of those bundles. Now, suppose the picture was radically different, and the child had to construct the bundles—not a chance! Even worse, suppose that the child has not only to construct the possible meanings for words, but even to figure out how the adults *think,* since they think differently in different cultures. Now the child first has to learn the local cognitive style, and then construct the relevant meanings in line with the cognitive style, before finally being in a position to map the acoustics onto the meanings. The picture is hopeless—Simple Nativism just has to be right!

We can disarm this argument (but see Levinson 2001 for the full counterargument). First, the Fodorean picture doesn't really help. If languages only label antecedently existing concepts, the set of those concepts must include every possible concept lexicalizable in every possible language—a billion or more to be sure. So how will knowing that the needle is already in the haystack help the child find the one correct concept to match to a particular acoustic wave? Second, the picture of the child thumbing through her innate lexicon to find the right antecedently existing concept is surely absurd in the first place; once the lexicon gets to any size at all, it will be much easier to construct the concept than to find it. What the child is going to do is try and figure out what those peculiar adults or elder siblings are really preoccupied with. She will use every clue provided to her, and there are plenty. And some of the most valuable clues will be provided in many different ways by the fact that the adults *think* in a way tightly consistent with the semantics of the language they speak. For example, suppose the adults speak a language where the relative frame of reference predominates. Every aspect of the environment will reflect that fact—the way doors or books open, the arrangement of things (knife always to the right of the fork, socks in the left drawer), the nature of gesture (pointing to the side the referent was on when they were looking at it, not where it actually is from here now), the preferred side of the sidewalk they choose to walk on. In contrast, suppose the adults speak a language where the absolute frame of reference predominates. Now they won't care about preserving egocentric constancies; they will only care that one sleeps with one's head always to the north, builds windbreaks to the east, and, when pointing, points in the veridical direction. A thousand little details of the built environment and, more importantly, the conduct of interaction (see Tomasello, this volume) will inform the discerning toddler again and again till she gets the message. It is just *because* we think in line with how we speak, that the clues are not all in the language but are distributed throughout the context of language learning. This new picture doesn't banish the puzzles of how children perform the incredible feat of learning a language, but one thing is certain: it doesn't make it any *more* of an impossible feat than it was on the old picture given to us by the Simple Nativists.

So the overall message is that Simple Nativism has outlived its utility; it blocks a proper understanding of the biological roots of language, it introduces incoherence into our theory, it blinds us to the reality of linguistic variation and discourages interesting research on the language-cognition interface. As far as its semantic tenets go, it is simply false—semantic variation across languages is rich in every detail. We don't map words onto antecedently existing concepts, we build them according to need. That's why cognitive development in children exists, and why the history of science shows progress. The reason we have a developed vocabulary (instead of the limited repertoire of other animals) is that we have found it helps us to *think*. How it does that is explained by that foundational cornerstone of cognitive psychology, Miller's (1956) theory of recoding as a method of increasing computational power by getting around the bottleneck of short-term memory (see Cowan 2001 for an update). Linguistically motivated concepts are food for thought.

## Notes

1. The scenes were devised by Melissa Bowerman, with additions by Eric Pederson, and are available as the stimulus set Topological Relations Picture Series of the Max Planck Institute for Psycholinguistics, Nijmegen. For a preliminary report, see the Annual Report 2001, Max Planck Institute for Psycholinguistics (⟨http://www.mpi.nl⟩).

2. Fodor himself adopts the only way out of this dilemma, which is to say that every lexical concept in every language that ever has been and ever will be is already sitting there in our heads. So Cro-Magnon man already had the notions 'neutrino' and 'piano', but probably hadn't gotten around to giving them phonetic form!

## References

Austin, P., and Bresnan, J. (1996). Non-configurationality in Australian Aboriginal languages. *Natural Language and Linguistic Theory, 14*, 215–268.

Berlin, B., and Kay, P. (1969). *Basic color terms: Their universality and evolution*. Berkeley and Los Angeles: University of California Press.

Bowerman, M., and Levinson, S. C. (Eds.). (2001). *Language acquisition and conceptual development*. Cambridge: Cambridge University Press.

Brown, P. (1994). The INs and ONs of Tzeltal locative expressions: The semantics of static descriptions of location. *Linguistics, 32*, 743–790.

Choi, S., McDonough, L., Mandler, J., and Bowerman, M. (2000, May). *Development of language-specific semantic categories of spatial relations: From prelinguistic to linguistic stage*. Paper presented at the workshop "Finding the Words." Stanford University.

Cowan, N. (2001). The magical number 4 in short-term memory: A reconsideration of mental storage capacity. *Behavioral and Brain Sciences, 24*, 87–114.

Davidoff, J., Davies, I., and Roberson, D. (1999). Colour in a Stone-Age tribe. *Nature, 398*, 203–204.

Durham, W. (1991). *Coevolution*. Stanford, CA: Stanford University Press.

Fodor, A. J. (1975). *The language of thought*. New York: Crowell.

Fodor, J. D., Fodor, J. A., and Garrett, M. F. (1975). The unreality of semantic representations. *Linguistic Inquiry, 6*, 515–531.

Greenberg, J. 1986. On being a linguistic anthropologist. *Annual Review of Anthropology, 15*, 1–24.

Hauser, M. (1997). *The evolution of communication*. Cambridge, MA: MIT Press.

Kay, P., Berlin, B., and Merrifield, W. (1991). Biocultural implications of systems of color naming. *Journal of Linguistic Anthropology, 1*, 12–25.

Kay, P., and Kempton, W. (1984). What is the Sapir-Whorf hypothesis? *American Anthropologist*, *86*, 65–79.

Kay, P., and Maffi, L. (1999). Color appearance and the emergence and evolution of basic color lexicons. *American Anthropologist*, *101*, 743–760.

Kay, P., and McDaniel, C. K. (1978). The linguistic significance of the meanings of basic color terms. *Language*, *54*, 610–646.

Kuhl, P. (1991). Perception, cognition and the ontogenetic and phylogenetic emergence of human speech. In S. E. Brauth, W. S. Hall, and R. J. Dooling (Eds.), *Plasticity of development* (pp. 73–106). Cambridge, MA: MIT Press.

Kuhl, P., and Meltzoff, A. N. (1996). Infant vocalizations in response to speech: Vocal imitation and developmental change. *Journal of the Acoustical Society of America*, *100*, 2425–2438.

Kuhl, P. K., and Meltzoff, A. N. (1997). Evolution, nativism and learning in the development of language and speech. In M. Gopnik (Ed.), *The inheritance and innateness of grammars* (pp. 7–44). New York: Oxford University Press.

Landau, B., and Jackendoff, R. (1993). "What" and "where" in spatial language and spatial cognition. *Behavioral and Brain Sciences*, *16*, 217–238.

Lenneberg, E., and Roberts, J. (1956). *The language of experience: A study in methodology*. Memoir 13. Indiana University Publications in Anthropology and Linguistics. Baltimore, MD: Waverly Press.

Levinson, S. C. (1987). Pragmatics and the grammar of anaphora. *Journal of Linguistics*, *23*, 379–434.

Levinson, S. C. (1996). Frames of reference and Molyneux's question: Cross-linguistic evidence. In P. Bloom, M. Peterson, L. Nadel, and M. Garrett (Eds.), *Language and space* (pp. 109–169). Cambridge, MA: MIT Press.

Levinson, S. C. (1997a). From outer to inner space: Linguistic categories and non-linguistic thinking. In J. Nuyts and E. Pederson (Eds.), *Language and conceptualization* (pp. 13–45). Cambridge: Cambridge University Press.

Levinson, S. C. (1997b). Language and cognition: The cognitive consequences of spatial description in Guugu Yimithirr. *Journal of Linguistic Anthropology*, *7*, 98–131.

Levinson, S. C. (2000). Language as nature and language as art. In R. Hide, J. Mittelstrass, and W. Singer (Eds.), *Changing concepts of nature and the turn of the millennium* (pp. 257–287). Vatican City: Pontifical Academy of Science.

Levinson, S. C. (2001). Covariation between spatial language and cognition, and its implications for language learning. In M. Bowerman and S. C. Levinson (Eds.), *Language acquisition and conceptual development* (pp. 566–588). Cambridge: Cambridge University Press.

Levinson, S. C. (in press). *Space in language and cognition: Explorations in cognitive diversity*. Cambridge: Cambridge University Press.

Levinson, S. C., Kita, S., Haun, D., and Rasch, B. (2002). Re-turning the tables: Language affects spatial reasoning. *Cognition, 84,* 155–188.

Levinson, S. C., and Wilkins, D. (Eds.). (in press). *Grammars of space.*

Li, P., and Gleitman, L. (2002). Turning the tables: Language and spatial reasoning. *Cognition, 83,* 265–294.

Lucy, J. (1981). Cultural factors in memory for color: The problem of language usage. Paper presented at AAA.

Lucy, J. (1992a). *Grammatical categories and cognition: A case study of the linguistic relativity hypothesis.* Cambridge: Cambridge University Press.

Lucy, J. (1992b). *Language diversity and thought: A reformulation of the linguistic relativity hypothesis.* Cambridge: Cambridge University Press.

Lucy, J., and Gaskins, S. (2001). Grammatical categories and the development of classification preferences: A comparative approach. In M. Bowerman and S. C. Levinson (Eds.), *Language acquisition and conceptual development* (pp. 257–283). Cambridge: Cambridge University Press.

Maddieson, I. (1984). *Patterns of sounds.* Cambridge: Cambridge University Press.

McDonough, L., Choi, S., and Mandler, J. (in press). Understanding spatial relations: Flexible infants, lexical adults. *Cognitive Psychology.*

Meira, S., and Dunn, M. (in preparation). *Typological study of exophoric demonstratives.*

Miller, G. A. (1956). The magical number seven, plus or minus two: Some limits on our capacity for processing information. *Psychological Review, 63,* 81–97.

Mithun, M. (1999). *The languages of Native North America.* Cambridge: Cambridge University Press.

Pederson, E., Danziger, E., Wilkins, D., Levinson, S., Kita, S., and Senft, G. (1998). Semantic typology and spatial conceptualization. *Language, 74,* 557–589.

Piaget, J., and Inhelder, B. (1956). [1948] *The child's conception of space.* London: Routledge and Kegan Paul.

Pinker, S. (1994). *The language instinct.* New York: Morrow.

Tooby, J., and Cosmides, L. (1992).The psychological foundations of culture. In J. H. Barkow, L. Cosmides, and J. Tooby (Eds.), *The adapted mind* (pp. 19–136). Oxford: Oxford University Press.

Wilkins, D., and Hill, D. (1995). When 'GO' means 'COME': Questioning the basicness of basic motion verbs. *Cognitive Linguistics, 6,* 209–259.

# 3
## The Key Is Social Cognition

Michael Tomasello

## 3.1  Introduction

Surveying human evolution and history, it is difficult to find a good analogy to language. But the closest might be money. Economic activities—in the broad sense of people exchanging goods and services with one another—antedate the invention of money by many millennia, and economic activities do not absolutely require money. But the invention of money as a symbol for exchanges, and its historical development into more complex forms such as paper and electronic money, is clearly responsible for some new forms of economic activity. Certainly, modern economies could not exist as they do without something resembling the monetary symbol systems currently in use.

Let's try another, more cognitive analogy. Basic quantitative skills are possessed by all mammals and even some bird species, and so they assuredly do not rely on written symbols and notations. But when human beings invented written symbols and notations to help them count and calculate, all of a sudden they began to count and calculate in some new and more complex ways. And it is well known that some notation systems enable certain kinds of calculations that others do not. For example, it is basically impossible to imagine doing algebra or calculus (not to mention long division) with Roman numerals; something like Arabic numerals, based on the place value system (and with a zero), is required for modern mathematics.

The way human beings behave and think thus changes when symbols, including linguistic symbols, become involved. Money and mathematics are two good examples, but the analogy to language is not perfect.

Spoken language is more basic than these. In many ways, minted money and Arabic numerals are more like written language than spoken language—and indeed, historically the invention of written symbols for speech, mathematical activities, and economic activities were closely intertwined. Ontogenetically, human beings acquire competence with a spoken language much earlier than with written symbols, and this happens in close concert with their earliest understandings of many aspects of their physical and social worlds.

I have a specific hypothesis about how language transforms cognitive activity during human ontogeny. (Perhaps the hypothesis may be extended to human evolution, but that is another story.) It is based on the conviction that the two main functions of language—for communication and for cognitive representation—are closely interrelated. The key is the nature of uniquely human social cognition and how it enables the learning and use of linguistic symbols for purposes of interpersonal communication beginning in the second year of life. Gradually, these interpersonal instruments are internalized and used intrapersonally, becoming the major representational medium for certain kinds of human cognition. The hypothesis is thus explicitly Vygotskian in spirit, but I am focusing on much younger children than Vygotsky ([1934] 1962, 1978) and, I would argue, on much more fundamental aspects of human cognition.

## 3.2   Joint Attention as Social Cognition

All primate species cognitively represent the world. They recall where things are located after significant delays, they anticipate impending events, they use spatial detours and shortcuts creatively (cognitive mapping), they categorize novel objects on the basis of perceptual similarity, and they solve novel problems on the basis of mental trial-and-error or "insight" (Tomasello and Call 1997). These activities all involve the ability to cognitively represent the world in the sense that past sensorimotor experiences can be preserved and, in some cases, actively *re*-presented and consulted as a guide for behaviors such as navigation, search, or problem solving.

*a pointer (?)*
*meercats*
*shoals of fish.*
*monkeys + the nut anvil.*

Before they begin to use language, human infants cognitively represent the world in many of these same kinds of ways, and—importantly—in no others. However, socially and communicatively, the prelinguistic infant is doing things that other primate species are not. Specifically, she is both following into adults' attention to outside objects and events—for example, by following their pointing gestures or imitating their actions on objects—and actively directing their attention to outside objects and events —for example, by pointing and showing objects and events to others. No other species on the planet points to or shows objects and events to its conspecifics in these ways. This is a fact with far-reaching implications for our understanding of language and its relation to human cognition.

*attention*
*behaviour*
*? ?*
*Do*
*? ignore ?*

Carpenter, Nagell, and Tomasello (1998) followed longitudinally the emergence of nine different "joint attentional" behaviors, along with the emergence of linguistic skills, in infants from 9 to 15 months of age. The joint attentional behaviors included both those in which the infant followed into the adult's behavior or attention (e.g., gaze following, imitation of actions on objects) and those in which the infant directed the adult's attention via such actions as pointing and showing. Language comprehension and production were also assessed. The relevant findings were as follows: (1) All nine of the nonlinguistic joint attentional behaviors emerged in individuals as a group (mostly within a three- to four-month time window). (2) These behaviors emerged in a predictable order: first, behaviors that involved the infant checking that the adult was attending; next, those in which the infant followed adult attention to outside objects and events; and finally, those in which the infant actively directed adult attention to outside objects and events. (3) There was a very strong correlation between infants' ability to engage in joint attentional activities with their mothers and the emergence of language comprehension and production.

Carpenter, Nagell, and Tomasello (1998) argued for two key theoretical points relevant to the current discussion. First, they argued that the reason that all of these joint attentional behaviors emerge together is that they all represent—each in its own way—manifestations of infants' newfound understanding of other persons as intentional agents, like themselves, whose attention to outside objects can be followed into,

*What about contented gurgling, alone in a pram.*

directed, and shared. Other primate species do not understand others of their species in this same way, and so they do not engage in this complex of joint attentional activities. Second, Carpenter, Nagell, and Tomasello argued that the reason linguistic skills emerge on the heels of these joint attentional activities—and strongly correlate with them—is that language is itself a form of joint attentional activity. The infant's first comprehension of language is nothing other than her emerging understanding of utterances as indications of other persons' intention that she join them in attending to something. The infant's first production of language is nothing other than her emerging ability to express her own communicative intention that other persons join her in attending to something. Simply said, language is about sharing and directing attention, and so it is no surprise that it emerges along with other joint attentional skills.

*language as an attn. strategy?*

It is worth pausing for a moment to note that theories of language development that neglect these joint attentional skills have basically no explanation for why language emerges when it does. Prelinguistic infants, and many animal species, are able to (1) perceive outside entities, (2) perceive discrete vocal sounds, and (3) associate sounds with visual experiences. So why can they not learn a piece of language? The reason is that associating sounds with experiences is not language. It is simply associating sounds with experiences—in much the way that a pet dog associates the sound "Dinner!" with the experience of food. Learning a piece of language requires that the learner understand that the other person is making this sound in order to direct her attention to something on which he, the speaker, is already focused. Theories that do not appreciate the essential, indeed constitutive, role of this kind of social cognition in the process of language acquisition simply cannot explain why most children begin learning language only after their first birthday and not earlier.

And so, the first point is that language is acquired as a joint attentional activity for sharing and directing the attention of other persons. The social-cognitive ability that enables such activities—the understanding of other persons as intentional agents like the self—is specific to human beings and emerges reliably at around 9 to 12 months of age in human ontogeny.

*a noun directs attention to an object*
*category label*

### 3.3 Organizing Cognition for Purposes of Linguistic Communication

What makes skills of linguistic communication different from other joint attentional skills, of course, is the fact that the language the child is learning antedates her arrival on the scene. Each of the world's 6,000+ languages is a collection of symbols and constructions that some community of people has created over historical time for purposes of sharing and directing the attention of one another. What is so mind-boggling about languages is the unbelievable number of different ways each one of them has accumulated for accomplishing these tasks.

To concretize the discussion, let us focus on the process of establishing a topic by means of what philosophers call an "act of reference"—in this case, to a single individual object in the world. One could imagine a language in which this was done with proper names only. That is, just as we refer to highly familiar people, places, and things with proper names such as Bill, Fluffy, Disneyland, and Big Bertha (a golf club), so we might refer to each object in the world with its own proper name. But presumably this would at some point overtax human memory. Consequently, individuals typically have proper names for only a few hundred or perhaps thousand especially familiar persons, places, and things in the world (a different set for different individuals), and in addition they use many thousands of category labels (common nouns). To use these category labels to direct another person's attention to an individual object (in cases in which its identity is in question), they must then use some further means of specification, either linguistic (e.g., *the X in my room*) or nonlinguistic (e.g., pointing).

It is an astonishing property of these category labels that they are used to refer to objects from many different perspectives depending on both the communicative context and the communicative goals of the speaker. As just a sampling, common nouns embody attentional construals based on such things as (1) granularity-specificity (*thing, furniture, chair, desk chair*), (2) perspective (*coast, shore, beach, vacation lot*), and (3) function (*father, lawyer, man, American*) (Langacker 1991).

Then, once a speaker and a hearer have established shared attention to a particular X, they can make future references to it in the same context with some short, all-purpose, easy-to-use symbol like *it*.

*chair: a man-made object designed to symbolize and founder to human motives for sitting*

*I don't know ⊗ any man that did not come from the womb of a woman.*

The outcome is that an individual language user looks at a particular tree and, before drawing the attention of her interlocutor to that tree, must decide, based on her assessment of the listener's current knowledge and expectations (and her own communicative goal), whether to use *that tree over there, the oak, that hundred-year-old oak, the tree, the bagswing tree, that thing in the front yard, the ornament, the embarrassment, that one, that, it,* or any number of other expressions. In terms of the new information being communicated, when the speaker wants to predicate (focus the hearer's attention on) something about the tree, she must decide if the tree *is in, is standing in, is growing in, was placed in,* or *is flourishing in*—or whatever—the front yard. And in the construction chosen to unite topic and focus, many more specific perspectives arise as the speaker attempts to highlight or downplay specific referents (e.g., *A tree is in the yard* vs. *In the yard is a tree*)—and even more than that when multiple participants are involved, as in *He broke the vase, The vase broke, It was him that broke the vase, It was the vase that got broken,* and on and on. Finally, based on categories of consistent functions in constructions, speakers may actually construe things in ways other than their "normal" ontological class. For example, the speaker can conceptualize objects as actions (as in *He porched the newspaper*), actions as objects (as in *Skiing is fun*), and attributes as objects (as in *Blue is my favorite color*). Ultimately, users of a language become able to conceptualize all kinds of abstract situations in terms of concrete metaphorical construals—for example, *Love is a journey, The office is pressing on me,* or *My spirits are high* (Lakoff 1987).

The main point is that decisions to construe a referent or predication in one way rather than another possible way are not made on the basis of the speaker's direct goal with respect to the object or activity involved; rather, they are made on the basis of her goal with respect to the listener's interest and attention to that object or activity. The speaker knows that the listener, as a user of the same language, shares with her the same range of choices for construal; these are in the form of the myriad perspectives that are symbolized in the known, but on this occasion not chosen, symbols and constructions in the shared language. Human linguistic symbols are thus both *intersubjective*—(both users know, and each knows that the other one knows, the range of possibilities) and

adjective = attribute

*perspectival* (any one symbol embodies one way, out of these many simultaneously available ways, that a situation may be construed for a given communicative purpose). It is difficult to think of how or why, in the absence of linguistic communication, a child or adult might choose to construct all of the many different perspectives on things that are routinely symbolized in human languages.

## 3.4   New Forms of Thinking

The specific developmental hypothesis is this. As the young child internalizes a linguistic symbol or construction—as she culturally learns the human perspective embodied in that symbol or construction—she cognitively represents not just the perceptual or motoric aspects of a situation, but also one way, among other ways of which she is also aware, that the current situation may be attentionally construed by "us," the users of the symbol. The intersubjective and perspectival nature of linguistic symbols thus creates a clear break with straightforward perceptual or sensorimotor cognitive representations. It removes them to a very large extent from the perceptual situation at hand, and in ways much more profound than the fact that they can stand for physically absent objects and events (and other simple forms of spatiotemporal displacement). Rather, the intersubjective and perspectival nature of linguistic symbols actually undermines the whole concept of a perceptual situation, by layering on top of it the multitudinous and multifarious perspectives that are communicatively possible for those of us who share a certain set of linguistic symbols.

This is the major sense in which, as I proposed initially, the communicative and cognitive functions of language are inextricably intertwined (see also Tomasello 1999). But it must be emphasized that acquiring skills of linguistic communication does not magically create new cognitive skills and representations out of nothing. Acquiring a language in the first place requires the whole panoply of basic primate cognitive skills of perception, categorization, memory, relational understanding, problem solving, and so on. In addition, it requires the uniquely human form of social cognition—understanding other persons as intentional agents like the self—without which there could be no humanlike forms of cultural or symbolic activity at all. But then, in my hypothesis, as these skills are used to acquire a historically evolved set of linguistic symbols and constructions, children begin to think in some fundamentally new ways.

This is not the end of the ontogenetic story, of course. We might also go on to somewhat older children and examine how they internalize their entire symbolic and linguistic dialogues with other persons in Vygotskian fashion. In Tomasello 1999, I attempted to show how this "second stage" of internalization leads young children to engage in such qualitatively new forms of cognitive activity as multiple classifications of objects and events, metaphorical construals of abstract situations and events, dialogic thinking, and reflecting on one's own thinking. I also attempted to show that the internalization process is not something mystical, as some seem to believe; rather, it is simply the normal process of cultural learning from others when the activity being learned is one that involves perspective taking. Reflecting on one's own thinking derives from internalization in the special case of an activity in which another person takes a perspective on you and your cognitive activities—as in so-called instructed learning (Tomasello, Kruger, and Ratner 1993).

But all of this is a booster rocket on top of the primary reality that emerges at the end of infancy: the intersubjective and perspectival forms of symbolic communication that children engage in with other persons—and the internalization of these into the kind of flexible and powerful cognitive representations characteristic of, and characteristic only of, the species *Homo sapiens*.

## 3.5   Linguistic Cognition

*We may say that thinking is essentially the activity of operating with signs.*
Ludwig Wittgenstein

*We have no power of thinking without signs.*
Charles Sanders Peirce

*Only in terms of gestures as significant symbols is the existence of mind or intelligence possible.*
George Herbert Mead

*Thought is not merely expressed in words; it comes into existence through them.*
Lev Vygotsky

These four thinkers have thought as much about thinking as anyone. What could they possibly mean by saying, essentially, that thinking is only possible with symbols? They presumably do not mean that a chimpanzee or human infant using a tool is not thinking in any way, but only that these nonlinguistic creatures are not thinking in the same way as symbolic creatures; there exist forms of cognitive activity in which they cannot engage. In my terms, perhaps what these four thinkers mean is that intersubjective and perspectival symbols that are learned and used in communicative interactions with other symbol users create the possibility of examining things from many different perspectives simultaneously, for anticipating the differing perspectives of other persons on things, and indeed for reflecting on one's own thinking from different perspectives as well. It is these kinds of thinking in which nonsymbolic creatures are unable to engage. They are unable because they do not possess the representational medium within which to conduct such dialogic and multilogic forms of mental activity; that is to say, they do not possess the representational medium that emerges as human infants begin to symbolically communicate with their fellow creatures at around 1 year of age.

Some might object to this proposal by claiming that a prelinguistic child or nonhuman primate may construe an object or situation in more than one way: one time a conspecific is a friend and the next time an enemy; one time a tree is for climbing to avoid predators and the next time it is for making a nest in. In these different interactions with the same entity, the individual is certainly deploying its attention differentially depending on its goal at that moment—taking different perspectives, if you will. But shifting attention sequentially in this manner as a function of the goal of the moment is not the same thing as knowing simultaneously a number of different ways in which something might be construed. Does a chimpanzee or a prelinguistic human infant understand that this object in front of her is simultaneously an orange, a piece of fruit, a meal, an object, a gift from a friend, a sphere, and a temptation—among other things? Does a chimpanzee or a human infant understand that this event occurring in front of her is simultaneously a fight, a chase, a social interaction, an act of retribution, an act of aggression, a tragedy, and an impending murder—among other things? If she does not, what does this imply about how she can think about, and cognitively represent, the objects and events taking place around her?

Since Whorf 1956, the language-cognition question has focused on whether learning one language, rather than another language, affects nonlinguistic cognition. The acid test is whether learning one language rather than another language leads to some discernible difference in how individuals behave in nonverbal tasks that assess their perception of colors, or of space, or of object shapes (Gumperz and Levinson 1996). What I am talking about here—by invoking nonhuman primates, prelinguistic infants, and the like—is something different, and indeed at the moment I am agnostic about the Whorfian question in particular. What I am talking about is what Slobin (1991) calls "thinking for speaking." From this perspective, there is no privileging of nonlinguistic cognition as somehow the real thing—which we then see if language affects. From this perspective, it is preferable to simply say that cognition takes many forms depending on many factors, and one form—which is unique to the human species after 1 or 2 years of age—is linguistic cognition in which individuals structure their thinking by means of one or another historically evolved collection of intersubjective and perspectival symbols and constructions. Language does not affect cognition; it is one form that cognition can take.

To summarize, the three main claims made in this chapter—which together justify its title—are as follows:

1. The evolution of linguistic communication in the human species and the acquisition of language by human children rest crucially on uniquely human skills of social cognition. These skills enable individuals both to read the communicative intentions of others, as embodied in their symbolic behaviors, and to culturally learn those symbolic behaviors themselves.

2. When used in acts of communication, these social-cognitive skills serve to create intersubjectively understood and perspectivally based linguistic symbols, which can be used to invite other persons to construe phenomena from any one of many simultaneously available perspectives. Internalizing such acts of symbolic communication creates especially flexible and powerful forms of cognitive representation, and these then, later in ontogeny, enable metaphorical, dialogic, and reflective thinking.

3. Communicating with other persons linguistically thus leads human beings to conceptualize things and events in the world in myriad different complex ways. Without these communicative activities, human beings would have no reason to conceptualize things and events in these ways, and so they simply would not do it.

## Note

Thanks to Heide Lohmann for thoughtful comments on an earlier version of this chapter.

## References

Carpenter, M., Nagell, K., and Tomasello, M. (1998). Social cognition, joint attention, and communicative competence from 9 to 15 months of age. *Monographs of the Society for Research in Child Development, Volume 255.*

Gumperz, J. J., and Levinson, S. C. (Eds.). (1996). *Rethinking linguistic relativity.* Cambridge: Cambridge University Press.

Lakoff, G. (1987). *Women, fire, and dangerous things: What categories reveal about the mind.* Chicago: University of Chicago Press.

Langacker, R. (1991). *Foundations of cognitive grammar.* (Vol. 2.) Stanford, CA: Stanford University Press.

Slobin, D. (1991). Learning to think for speaking: Native language, cognition, and rhetorical style. *Pragmatics, 1,* 7–26.

Tomasello, M. (1999). *The cultural origins of human cognition.* Cambridge, MA: Harvard University Press.

Tomasello, M., and Call, J. (1997). *Primate cognition.* Oxford: Oxford University Press.

Tomasello, M., Kruger, A. C., and Ratner, H. H. (1993). Cultural learning. *Behavioral and Brain Sciences, 16,* 495–552.

Vygotsky, L. (1962). *Thought and language.* Cambridge, MA: MIT Press. (Original work published 1934.)

Vygotsky, L. (1978). *Mind in society: The development of higher psychological processes* (M. Cole, Ed.). Cambridge, MA: Harvard University Press.

Whorf, B. (1956). *Language, thought, and reality* (J. B. Carroll, Ed.). Cambridge, MA: MIT Press.

# III

Language as Lens: Does the Language We
Acquire Influence How We See the World?

# 4

# Sex, Syntax, and Semantics

Lera Boroditsky, Lauren A. Schmidt, and Webb Phillips

## 4.1 Introduction

Speakers of different languages must attend to and encode strikingly different aspects of the world in order to use their language properly (Sapir 1921; Slobin 1996). For example, to say that "the elephant ate the peanuts" in English, we must include tense—the fact that the event happened in the past. In Mandarin, indicating when the event occurred would be optional and couldn't be included in the verb. In Russian, the verb would need to include tense, whether the peanut-eater was male or female (though only in the past tense), and whether said peanut-eater ate all of the peanuts or just a portion of them. In Turkish, one would specify whether the event being reported was witnessed or hearsay. Do these quirks of languages affect the way their speakers think about the world? Do English, Mandarin, Russian, and Turkish speakers end up thinking about the world differently simply because they speak different languages?

The idea that thought is shaped by language is most commonly associated with the writings of Benjamin Lee Whorf. Whorf, impressed by linguistic diversity, proposed that the categories and distinctions of each language enshrine a way of perceiving, analyzing, and acting in the world. Insofar as languages differ, their speakers too should differ in how they perceive and act in objectively similar situations (Whorf 1956). This strong Whorfian view—that thought and action are entirely determined by language—has long been abandoned in cognitive science. However, definitively answering less deterministic versions of the "Does language shape thought?" question has proven very difficult. Some studies have claimed evidence to the affirmative (e.g., Boroditsky 1999, 2001; Bowerman 1996; Davidoff, Davies, and Roberson 1999; Imai and Gentner 1997; Levinson 1996; Lucy 1992; Slobin 1996); others, evidence to the contrary (e.g., [Rosch] Heider 1972; Li and Gleitman 2002).

## 4.2    Thinking for Speaking

In part, the "Does language shape thought?" question has been difficult to answer because it is so imprecise. A different phrasing has been suggested by Slobin (1996), who proposed replacing *language* and *thought* with *speaking*, *thinking*, and *thinking for speaking*. One advantage of this substitution is that it allows us to distinguish between what are often called linguistic and nonlinguistic thought. Basically, cognitive processes involved in accessing and selecting words, placing them in grammatical structures, planning speech, and so on, are all instances of thinking for speaking. Thinking for speaking differs from one language to another. For example, when planning to utter a verb, English speakers never need to worry about grammatical gender agreement between the verb and the subject of the sentence. By contrast, Russian speakers do need to worry about this, and so their thinking for speaking will necessarily be different from that of English speakers.

## 4.3    Beyond *Thinking for Speaking*

A further question to ask is whether the habits that people acquire in thinking for speaking a particular language will manifest themselves in their thinking even when they are not planning speech in that language. What if people are performing some nonlinguistic task (i.e., a task that can be accomplished through some nonlinguistic means) or thinking for a different language? For example, are native Russian speakers more likely to notice whether all or only some of the peanuts were eaten even when they're speaking English? One way to rephrase the "Does language shape thought?" question is to ask, "Does thinking for speaking a particular language have an effect on how people think when not thinking for speaking that same language?"

Further, how (through what cognitive mechanisms) can thinking for speaking a particular language exert influence over other types of thinking? Are some cognitive domains more susceptible to linguistic influence than others, and if so, why? For example, early work on color showed striking similarity in color memory among speakers of different languages despite wide variation in color terminology (Heider 1972; but see Davidoff, Davies, and Roberson 1999; Kay and Kempton 1984; Lucy and Shweder 1979). However, research into how people conceptualize more abstract domains like time has uncovered striking crosslinguistic differences in thought (Boroditsky 1999, 2001). Why would there be such strong evidence for universality in color perception, but quite the opposite for thinking about time? One possibility is that language is most powerful in influencing thought for more abstract domains, that is, ones not so reliant on sensory experience (Boroditsky 1999, 2000, 2001). While the ability to perceive colors is heavily constrained by universals of physics and physiology, the conception of time (say, as a vertical or a horizontal medium) is not constrained by physical experience and so is free to vary across languages and cultures (see Boroditsky 2000, 2001, for further discussion).

In this chapter, I consider an extreme point along this concrete-abstract continuum: the influence of grammatical gender on the way people think about inanimate objects. Forks and frying pans do not (by virtue of being inanimate) have a biological gender. The perceptual information available for most objects does not provide much evidence as to their gender, and so conclusive information about the gender of objects is only available in language (and only in those languages that have grammatical gender). This chapter examines whether people's mental representations of objects are influenced by the grammatical genders assigned to these objects' names in their native language.

## 4.4  Grammatical Gender

Unlike English, many languages have a grammatical gender system whereby all nouns (e.g., the words that refer to penguins, pockets, and toasters) are assigned a gender. Many languages only have masculine and feminine genders, but some also assign neuter, vegetative, and other more obscure genders. When speaking a language with grammatical gender, speakers are required to mark objects as gendered through definite articles and gendered pronouns, and often they need to modify adjectives or even verbs to agree in gender with the nouns. Does talking about inanimate objects as if they were masculine or feminine actually lead people to think of inanimate objects as having a gender? Could the grammatical genders assigned to objects by a language influence people's mental representations of objects?

### 4.4.1   Why Might Grammatical Gender Be Taken as Meaningful?

A priori, there are reasons to think that people would not take grammatical gender as meaningful. First, the assignment of grammatical gender to object names often appears to be semantically arbitrary. As Mark Twain noted in *A Tramp Abroad*, "In German, a young lady has no sex, while a turnip has.... [A] tree is male, its buds are female, its leaves are neuter; horses are sexless, dogs are male, cats are female ... tomcats included." Second, the grammatical genders assigned to names of particular objects vary greatly across languages (Braine 1987).[1] For example, the name for the sun is feminine in German, masculine in Spanish, and neuter in Russian. The name for the moon, on the other hand, is feminine in Spanish and Russian, but masculine in German.

But there are also reasons to think that people *would* take grammatical gender as meaningful. Since many other grammatical distinctions reflect differences that are observable in the world (the plural inflection, for example), children learning to speak a language with a grammatical gender system have no a priori reason to believe that grammatical gender doesn't indicate a meaningful distinction between types of objects. Indeed, many adult philosophers throughout history have thought that grammatical gender systems reflected the essential properties of objects, and even took a considerable amount of pride in the thought that the natural genders of objects were captured in the grammatical subtlety of their language (see Fodor 1959 for a history). Children learning a language may make similar (though perhaps less patriotically minded) hypotheses. Further, since most children grow up learning only one language, they have no opportunity to perform the comparative linguistics necessary to discover the seemingly arbitrary nature of grammatical gender assignment. For all they know, the grammatical genders assigned by their language are the true universal genders of objects.

### 4.4.2 How Could Grammatical Gender Affect Meaning?

How might people's representations of objects be affected by the grammatical gender of their labels? One possibility is that in order to efficiently learn the grammatical gender of a noun to begin with, people focus on some property of that noun's referent that may pick it out as masculine or feminine. For example, if the word for "sun" is masculine in one's language, one might try to remember this by conceiving of the sun in terms of what are perceived as stereotypically masculine properties like powerful and threatening. If the word for "sun" is feminine, on the other hand, one might focus on its warming and nourishing qualities.

Even after the grammatical genders of nouns are learned, language may influence thought during thinking for speaking (Slobin 1996). When speaking a language with grammatical gender, speakers often need to mark objects as gendered through definite articles (e.g., *le* and *la* in French), refer to objects using gendered pronouns (e.g., if the word for "fork" is masculine, a speaker might say the equivalent of *He is sharp*), and alter adjectives or even verbs to agree in gender with the nouns (e.g., in Russian, verbs in the past tense must agree in gender with their subject nouns). Needing to refer to an object as masculine or feminine may lead people to selectively attend to that object's masculine or feminine qualities, thus making them more salient in the representation.

### 4.4.3 Does Grammatical Gender Affect Meaning?

So, does talking about inanimate objects as if they were masculine or feminine lead people to think of them as masculine or feminine? Preliminary evidence suggests that it may (Jakobson 1966; Konishi 1993; Sera, Berge, and del Castillo 1994). In one early study, Russian speakers were asked to personify days of the week (reported in Jakobson 1966). They consistently personified the grammatically masculine days of the week (Monday, Tuesday, and Thursday) as males, and the grammatically feminine days of the week (Wednesday, Friday, and Saturday) as females, though they could not explicitly say why they did so.

In another study, German and Spanish speakers rated a set of nouns on the dimension of potency (a dimension highly associated with masculinity) (Konishi 1993). Half of the nouns were grammatically masculine in German and feminine in Spanish, and the other half were masculine in Spanish and feminine in German. Both German and Spanish speakers judged the word for "man" to be more potent than the word for "woman." Interestingly, they also judged nouns that were grammatically masculine in their native language to be more potent than nouns that were grammatically feminine. This was true even though all of the test nouns referred to objects or entities that had no biological gender (including names of inanimate objects, places, events, and abstract entities).

Converging evidence comes from a series of studies in which Spanish speakers were asked to rate pictures of objects as masculine or feminine (Sera, Berge, and del Castillo 1994). Spanish speakers consistently classified pictured objects in accordance with their grammatical gender in Spanish. The effect was more pronounced when the pictures were accompanied by their Spanish labels. The grammatical gender consistency effect also showed up when subjects were asked to attribute a man's or a woman's voice to each picture. Finally, Sera, Berge, and del Castillo found that by about second grade, Spanish-speaking children assigned voices to objects in accordance with the grammatical gender of their labels.

### 4.4.4   Limitations of Previous Evidence

Although results of these studies are suggestive, there are serious limitations common to these and most other studies of linguistic determinism. First, speakers of different languages are usually tested only in their native language. Any differences in these comparisons can only show the effect of a language on thinking for that particular language. These studies cannot reveal whether experience with a language affects language-independent thought such as thought for other languages or thought in nonlinguistic tasks.

Second, comparing studies conducted in different languages poses a deeper problem: there is simply no way to be certain that the stimuli and instructions are truly the same in both languages. This problem remains even if the verbal instructions are minimal. For example, even if the task is nonlinguistic, and participants are asked simply their language's equivalent of "Which one is the same?", one cannot be sure that the words used for "same" mean the same thing in both languages. If in one language the word for "same" is closer in meaning to "identical," while in the other language it is closer to "relationally similar," speakers of different languages may behave differently, but only because of the difference in instructions, not because of any interesting differences in thought. There is no sure way to guard against this possibility when tasks are translated into different languages. Since there is no way to know that participants tested in different languages are performing the same task, it is difficult to deem the comparisons meaningful.

Finally, in all of the tasks described so far, participants were asked to provide some subjective judgment (there were no right or wrong answers). Providing such a judgment requires participants to decide on a strategy for completing the task. When figuring out how to perform the task, participants may simply make a conscious decision to follow the grammatical gender divisions in their language. Evidence collected from such subjective judgments cannot reveal whether gender is actually part of a person's conceptual representation of an object, or whether (left with no other criterion for making the subjective judgment) the person just explicitly decided to use grammatical gender in answering the experimenter's questions.

Showing that experience with a language affects thought in some broader sense (other than thinking for that particular language) requires observing a crosslinguistic difference on some more covert measure in a non-language-specific task. The studies described in this chapter do just that. People are tested in tasks where the purpose of the experiment is covert or where the task requires participants to provide a correct answer (i.e., not a subjective judgment). Further, Spanish and German speakers are tested in English (and sometimes in nonlinguistic tasks), allowing us to assess the effects of people's native language on their thinking more generally (not just thinking for that same language). Finally, a series of studies shows that crosslinguistic differences in thought can be produced just by grammatical differences and in the absence of other cultural factors.

So, does talking about inanimate objects as if they were masculine or feminine actually lead people to think of inanimate objects as having a gender? Could the grammatical genders assigned to objects by a language influence people's mental representations of objects?

## 4.5   Grammatical Gender and Memory

To investigate this, Boroditsky, Schmidt, and Phillips (2002) taught a group of Spanish and German speakers proper names for 24 objects (e.g., an apple may have been called *Patrick*) and then tested their memory for these object-name pairs. The experiment was conducted entirely in English, and all objects were chosen to have opposite grammatical genders in Spanish and German. For both Spanish and German speakers, half of the time the gender of the proper name assigned to an object was consistent with the grammatical gender of the object's name (in their native language), and half of the time it was inconsistent. All of the participants were native speakers of either Spanish or German, but both groups were highly proficient in English.

The prediction was that German speakers would be better at remembering a proper name for "apple" if the name was *Patrick* than if it was *Patricia*, and the opposite should be true for Spanish speakers (because the word for "apple" is masculine in German, but feminine in Spanish). As predicted, Spanish and German speakers' memory for object-name pairs (e.g., apple-Patricia) was better for pairs where the gender of the proper name was consistent with the grammatical gender of the object name (in their native language) than when the two genders were inconsistent. Since theobject names used in this study had opposite grammatical genders in Spanish and German, Spanish and German speakers showed opposite memory biases: for those objects for which Spanish speakers were most likely to remember female names, German speakers were most likely to remember male names (and vice versa). Further, a group of native English speakers (similar in age and education to the Spanish and German speakers) were tested in the same task. They were able to correctly remember the object-name pairs as well as Spanish and German speakers did for consistent pairs, and better than they did for inconsistent pairs. This suggests that Spanish and German speakers' previous language experience actually interfered with their ability to remember object-name pairs when the pairs happened to be conceptually inconsistent in gender. Since both groups performed the task in English, it appears that the semantic representation of gender (once it has been established) is not language specific. Objects do appear to have conceptual gender, and this gender is consistent with the grammatical gender assigned by language.

But what does it mean for a turnip to be conceptually feminine or for a toaster to be conceptually masculine? How does gender actually make its way into the representations of objects? As suggested earlier, one possibility is that, depending on grammatical gender, different (stereotypically masculine or feminine) aspects of objects may become more or less salient in the representations of those objects. For example, if the noun that names a toaster is masculine, then perhaps its metallic and technological properties may become more salient; but if the noun is feminine, then perhaps its warmth, domesticity, and ability to provide nourishment are given more importance.

## 4.6   Grammatical Gender and Object Descriptions

To test whether grammatical gender really does focus speakers of different languages on different aspects of objects, Boroditsky, Schmidt, and Phillips (2002) created a list of 24 object names that had opposite grammatical genders in Spanish and German (half were masculine and half feminine in each language), and then asked a group of native Spanish speakers and another group of native German speakers to write down the first three adjectives that came to mind to describe each object on the list. The study was conducted entirely in English, and none of the participants were aware of the purpose of the study. The question was whether the grammatical genders of object names in Spanish and German would be reflected in the kinds of adjectives that Spanish and German speakers generated. All of the participants were native speakers of either Spanish or German, but both groups were highly proficient in English. Since the experiment was conducted entirely in English (a language with no grammatical gender system), this is a particularly conservative test of whether grammatical gender influences the way people think about objects.

After all of the adjectives provided by Spanish and German speakers were collected, a group of English speakers (unaware of the purpose of the study) rated the adjectives as describing masculine or feminine properties of the objects ($+1$ = feminine, $-1$ = masculine). The adjectives were arranged in alphabetical order and were not identified as having been produced by a Spanish or a German speaker.

As predicted, Spanish and German speakers generated adjectives that were rated more masculine for items whose names were grammatically masculine in their native language than for items whose names were grammatically feminine. Because all object names used in this study had opposite genders in Spanish and German, Spanish and German speakers produced very different adjectives to describe the objects. For items that were grammatically masculine in Spanish but feminine in German, adjectives provided by Spanish speakers were rated more masculine than those provided by German speakers. For items that were grammatically masculine in German but feminine in Spanish, adjectives provided by German speakers were rated more masculine than those provided by Spanish speakers.

There were also observable qualitative differences between the kinds of adjectives Spanish and German speakers produced. For example, the word for "key" is masculine in German and feminine in Spanish. German speakers described keys as *hard, heavy, jagged, metal, serrated,* and *useful,* while Spanish speakers said they were *golden, intricate, little, lovely, shiny,* and *tiny*. The word for "bridge," on the other hand, is feminine in German and masculine in Spanish. German speakers described bridges as *beautiful, elegant, fragile, peaceful, pretty,* and *slender,* while Spanish speakers said they were *big, dangerous, long, strong, sturdy,* and *towering*.

These findings once again indicate that people's thinking about objects is influenced by the grammatical genders their native language assigns to the objects' names. A further question is whether differences in language per se lead to differences in thought, or whether other cultural differences act as intermediary causal factors. For example, the way objects are personified in fairy tales or in poetry may depend on the grammatical genders of their names. Further, grammatical genders might affect the design of artifacts such that German bridges may differ from Spanish bridges in a way consistent with grammatical gender.

## 4.7   Separating Effects of Language and Culture

To test whether grammatical gender in a language can indeed exert a causal power over thought (without intermediary cultural factors), Boroditsky, Schmidt, and Phillips (2002) taught native English speakers about a soupative/oosative distinction in the fictional Gumbuzi language. Participants were shown drawings of 4 males and 4 females along with 12 inanimate objects and were taught which would be soupative (preceded by *sou*) and which oosative (preceded by *oos*) in Gumbuzi. The soupative/oosative distinction always corresponded to biological gender (all females were in one category and all males in the other) but also extended to inanimate objects. A given subject might have learned that pans, forks, pencils, ballerinas, and girls are soupative, while pots, spoons, pens, giants, and boys are oosative. Which objects were designated as grammatically masculine and which feminine was counterbalanced across subjects such that each object was assigned to the same grammatical category as biological females for half of the subjects, and assigned to the same grammatical category as males for the other half.

After subjects had mastered the oosative/soupative distinction, they were shown all the pictures again one at a time (unlabeled) and asked to generate adjectives to describe the objects. These adjectives were then independently rated as depicting masculine or feminine properties of the objects.

As predicted, English speakers produced more masculine adjectives to describe objects when they (i.e., their names) belonged to a grammatical category with biological males than when the same objects belonged to a grammatical category with biological females. Just as with the Spanish and German speakers, there was also an observable *qualitative* difference between the adjectives produced for an item when it was grammatically grouped with males than when it was grouped with females. For example, when the violin was grammatically feminine in Gumbuzi, English speakers described a picture of a violin as *artsy, beautiful, beautiful, creative*, *curvy*, *delicate*, *elegant*, *interesting*, *pretty*, and *wooden*. When it was grammatically masculine, English speakers described it as *chirping*, *difficult*, *impressive*, *noisy*, *overused*, *piercing*, *shiny*, *slender*, *voluptuous*, and *wooden*. It appears that just differences in grammar, with no concomitant differences in culture, are enough to influence how people think about objects.

These findings suggest that people's ideas about the genders of objects can indeed be influenced by the grammatical genders assigned to those objects in a language. But all of the studies described so far have included some linguistic component in the tasks (albeit the linguistic component was in a language other than the one producing the effects). Subjects were asked either to remember names for objects or to produce adjectives in response to words or pictures. Could grammatical gender have an effect even if no words were used in a study?

## 4.8   Grammatical Gender and Picture Similarity

Several recent studies have investigated the effects of grammatical gender in tasks involving no words, only pictures (Boroditsky, Schmidt, and Phillips 2002). In one study, Spanish and German speakers rated the similarity of pairs of unlabeled pictures depicting objects and people. All of the objects were chosen to have opposite grammatical genders in Spanish and German, and the picture of each object was compared to pictures of several biological males and females. Even in this non-linguistic task (involving no labels and no verbalization in any language), Spanish and German speakers produced similarity ratings consistent with the gender assignments of their native language. Both Spanish and German speakers rated an object more similar to a person when the grammatical gender of the object matched the biological gender of the person than when the genders did not match. This was true even though participants were instructed and tested in English and all of the objects had opposite grammatical genders in Spanish and German. The same differences were obtained even when Spanish and German speakers made their similarity judgments while performing a verbal interference task (shadowing randomly generated letter strings).

Further, a group of Spanish/German bilinguals was tested in the same task. The degree to which a subject's pattern of similarity scores corresponded to either the Spanish or the German grammatical gender system was well predicted by that person's relative skill in Spanish versus German as well as by other aspects of linguistic experience such as whether the person was born in a Spanish- or German-speaking country, how much earlier the person started learning one language versus the other, and how many years the person had spoken the two languages.

In another set of studies, English speakers were taught the Gumbuzi oosative/soupative grammatical distinctions as described earlier, and were then asked to rate the similarity of pairs of pictures depicting people and objects that were either in the same grammatical category or in different grammatical categories in Gumbuzi. Just as was observed with Spanish and German speakers, pairs of items that were in the same grammatical category were rated more similar than items that came from different grammatical categories. Just as before, the effects did not go away when subjects made the similarity ratings while performing a verbal interference task. These findings once again suggest that learning new grammatical categories can shape the way people think about objects (in this case demonstrated as an increase in the perceived similarity of pictures).

## 4.9   But *How* Does Language Affect Thought?

Beyond demonstrating that learning linguistic categories can affect people's descriptions of objects or similarity ratings, it is important to consider *how* learning such categories can have this effect. One possibility is that in order to make sense of the grammatical categories they encounter in language (or in the laboratory), people deliberately look for similarities between items assigned to the same grammatical category. If a meaningful and consistent set of similarities is discovered, these similarities can then be stored (or perhaps the features that are relevant to the similarity can be made more salient in the representation). This would explain both the increased within-category similarity (Boroditsky, Schmidt, and Phillips 2002) and the bias in descriptions observed in the earlier studies. This type of mechanism is supported by recent findings suggesting that comparison leads to an increase in similarity (so long as the items being compared make it possible to discover meaningful similarities) (Boroditsky 2002; see also Gentner and Namy 1999; Loewenstein and Gentner 1998).

However, there might also be a more mundane explanation for all this. Perhaps people give higher similarity ratings to items assigned to the same grammatical category not because they have discovered or highlighted their similarities, but simply because these items share a new common feature—the name of the category they belong to. That is, maybe just the fact that both items are called "oosative" or "soupative" is enough to produce the increase in within-category similarity. To test this explanation, Boroditsky, Schmidt, and Phillips (2002) taught a new group of subjects a new variation on the oosative/soupative distinction in Gumbuzi. Instead of being based on biological gender (thus making it possible to carry out a meaningful set of consistent comparisons), the categories were made arbitrary with regard to gender. Unlike the old Gumbuzi categories that included either 4 instances of males or 4 instances of females, the new arbitrary categories included a mix of males and females in each category. As before, subjects were trained until they could categorize the objects perfectly into oosative and soupative, and then they were asked to rate similarity between pairs of pictures that were either in the same category or in different categories. Although these subjects had the same proficiency with the categories as the subjects in the old studies, and although (just as before) all objects in a category shared the same category name (oosative or soupative), there was no increase in similarity for within-category comparisons. It appears that (at least in these studies) just sharing a category name is not sufficient to significantly increase the similarity between two objects. Only when a category is meaningful, somehow interpretable beyond rote memorization, does the similarity of items within a category increase.

So it appears that linguistic categories can influence people's thinking by encouraging them to carry out comparisons that they wouldn't have otherwise carried out (or perhaps wouldn't have carried out as often or with the same goals in mind). In the process of carrying out these comparisons, people may discover meaningful similarities between objects or perhaps make comparison-relevant features more salient in the representations. Clearly, many parts of this proposal remain to be specified and tested. One prediction made by this view is that after learning a meaningful category, people should be faster and/or better able to name similarities between category members because they have already carried out the comparisons and may have stored the similarities. Some preliminary evidence suggests that this is indeed the case (Boroditsky, Schmidt, and Phillips 2002). After being taught the Gumbuzi oosative/soupative categories (the gender-based versions), subjects were asked to name similarities between as many person-object pairs as they could in a period of five minutes (a time period far too short to complete all pairs). Answers such as *oosative*, *soupative*, *masculine*, and *feminine* were excluded from all analyses (only five of these were produced across all subjects). When the pairs consisted of items from the same category, people were able to generate more similarities than when the pairs contained items from different categories. These findings suggest that learning to group objects into meaningful categories does encourage the discovery or at least the highlighting of their similarities.

## 4.10  So, Does Language Shape Thought?

The results reviewed in this chapter demonstrate that a grammatical distinction in language has the power to bias people's memory, their descriptions of words and pictures, their assessments of picture similarities, and their ability to generate similarities between pictures. This is true even though people perform tasks in a language different from the one they learned the distinction in, perform tasks involving no words (just pictures), or perform tasks where the point of the experiment is covert (e.g., the adjectives task). Previous evidence also suggests that the same grammatical distinction affects people's decision making (e.g., assigning voices to animated characters), personification of nouns (as in the Russian days of the week), and ratings of object characteristics (e.g., potency). In short, speakers of different languages behave differently in a host of tests in ways that are consistent with the distinctions made in their language. But does all this evidence mean that language affects thought? In particular, does it mean that linguistic categories (e.g., a noun's being grammatically feminine or masculine) actually alter nonlinguistic representations? Perhaps linguistic categories simply get recruited covertly for all these tasks, so even though speakers of different languages may exhibit different patterns in behavior, linguistic and nonlinguistic representations remain truly separate, and everybody's nonlinguistic representations are in fact the same.

This is an interesting possibility, and a difficult one to rule out empirically. For example, Boroditsky, Schmidt, and Phillips (2002) attempted to disable people's linguistic faculties by asking them to shadow speech while they performed the similarity-rating tasks described earlier. If effects of grammatical gender disappeared under these conditions, then we might have been able to infer that grammatical categories had not affected nonlinguistic representations. Instead, it would seem that language affected thinking in this case because people covertly invoked linguistic representations in a set of seemingly nonlinguistic tasks. But it turned out that tying up the linguistic faculties had no effect on the results (the effects of grammatical gender were equally strong when subjects were shadowing speech as when they were not). Can we now conclude that grammatical gender definitely does affect people's nonlinguistic representations? This seems premature. Perhaps the shadowing task simply did not disable all of the aspects of language that could have been covertly recruited for the task. Perhaps some different, more complex verbal interference task would have changed the results. Several other tasks could be tried, but as long as the verbal interference does not get rid of the effect of language on thought, there will always be doubt about whether or not all of the necessary linguistic faculties were properly interfered with. There seems to be no sure way to disable all linguistic processes (and this is in no small part due to the difficulty of deciding on what counts as linguistic and nonlinguistic processing in the first place).

Fortunately, being able to discriminate between these two possibilities is not necessary here. Regardless of which possibility is correct, it appears that language plays an important role in thinking. Whether people's native language is covertly involved in all manner of seemingly nonlinguistic tasks (even despite verbal interference, in nonlinguistic tasks, and in tasks conducted in other languages), or whether aspects of grammar are able to influence nonlinguistic representations directly, it appears that thinking involves a collaboration between many different linguistic and nonlinguistic representations and processes. This means that the private mental lives of speakers of different languages may differ dramatically—and not only when they are thinking for speaking their particular language, but in all manner of cognitive tasks.

## 4.11   Conclusions

A body of evidence suggests that people's thinking about objects can be influenced by aspects of grammar that differ across languages. A series of studies found effects of grammatical gender on people's descriptions of objects, their assessments of similarity between pictures of objects, and their ability to remember proper names for objects. Another set of studies showed that differences in thought can be produced just by grammatical differences and in the absence of other cultural factors. It is striking that even a fluke of grammar (the arbitrary designation of a noun as masculine or feminine) can have an effect on how people think about things in the world. Considering the many ways in which languages differ, our findings suggest that the private mental lives of people who speak different languages may differ much more than previously thought.

## Notes

This research was funded by an NSF Graduate Research Fellowship to the first author. Partial support was also provided by NIMH research grant MH-47575 to Gordon Bower. We would like to thank Michael Ramscar, Herbert H. Clark, Eve Clark, Barbara Tversky, Gordon Bower, Dan Slobin, and Steven Pinker for helpful comments on earlier versions of the chapter and insightful discussions of this research, and Jill M. Schmidt for her indispensable work in assembling the stimuli.

1. Despite wide variation in the assignment of grammatical genders, speakers across languages do share some common beliefs about the genders of objects. For example, when asked to classify names or pictures of objects into masculine and feminine, English and Spanish speakers tend to judge natural objects as more feminine and artifacts as more masculine (Mullen 1990; Sera, Berge, and del Castillo 1994). It is also interesting that English speakers make consistent judgments about the genders of objects, despite the lack of a grammatical gender system in English (Sera, Berge, and del Castillo 1994). Finally, English speakers'

intuitions about the genders of animals correspond well with the grammatical genders assigned to those animals' names in Spanish, German, and Russian (Boroditsky and Schmidt 2000). Clearly, further studies involving non-Indo-European languages are necessary to assess the generality of these findings.

# References

Boroditsky, L. (1999). First-language thinking of second-language understanding: Mandarin and English speakers' conceptions of time. *Proceedings of the Cognitive Science Society*, *21*, 84–89.

Boroditsky, L. (2000). Metaphoric structuring: Understanding time through spatial metaphors. *Cognition*, *75*, 1–28.

Boroditsky, L. (2001). Does Language Shape Thought? Mandarin and English speakers' conceptions of time. *Cognitive Psychology*, *43*, 1–22.

Boroditsky, L. (2002). Comparison and the development of knowledge. To appear in *Cognition*.

Boroditsky, L., and Schmidt, L. (2000). Sex, syntax, and semantics. *Proceedings of the Cognitive Science Society*, *22*, 42–47.

Boroditsky, L., and Schmidt, L., and Phillips, W. (2002). *Can quirks of grammar affect the way you think? Spanish and German speakers' ideas about the genders of objects.* Manuscript submitted for publication.

Bowerman, M. (1996). The origins of children's spatial semantic categories: Cognitive versus linguistic determinants. In J. J. Gumperz and S. C. Levinson (Eds.), *Rethinking linguistic relativity* (pp. 145–176). Cambridge: Cambridge University Press.

Braine, M. (1987). What is learned in acquiring word classes: A step toward an acquisition theory. In B. MacWhinney (Ed.), *Mechanisms of language acquisition* (pp. 65–87). Hillsdale, NJ: Erlbaum.

Choi, S., and Bowerman, M. (1991). Learning to express motion events in English and Korean: The influence of language-specific lexicalization patterns. *Cognition*, *41*, 1–3, 83–121.

Davidoff, J., Davies I., and Roberson, D. (1999). Colour categories in a Stone-Age tribe. *Nature*, *398*, 203–204.

Fodor, I. (1959). The origin of grammatical gender I. *Lingua*, *8*, 1.

Gentner, D., and Imai, M. (1997). A cross-linguistic study of early word meaning: Universal ontology and linguistic influence. *Cognition*, *62*, 169–200.

Gentner, D., and Namy, L. (1999). Comparison in the development of categories. *Cognitive Development*, *14*, 487–513.

Heider, E. (1972). Universals in color naming and memory. *Journal of Experimental Psychology*, *93*, 10–20.

Imai, M., and Gentner, D. (1997). A cross-linguistic study of early world meaning: Universal ontology and linguistic influence. *Cognition, 62*, 169–200.

Jakobson, R. (1966). On linguistic aspects of translation. In R. A. Brower (Ed.), *On translation* (pp. 232–239). New York: Oxford University Press.

Kay, P., and Kempton, W. (1984). What is the Sapir-Whorf hypothesis? *American Anthropologist, 86*, 65–79.

Konishi, T. (1993). The semantics of grammatical gender: A cross-cultural study. *Journal of Psycholinguistic Research, 22*, 519–534.

Levinson, S. C. (1996). Frames of reference and Molyneux's question: Cross-linguistic evidence. In P. Bloom, M. Peterson, L. Nadel, and M. Garrett (Eds.), *Language and space* (pp. 109–169). Cambridge, MA: MIT Press.

Li, P., and Gleitman, L. (2002). Turning the tables. *Cognition, 83*, 265–294.

Loewenstein, J., and Gentner, D. (1998). Relational language facilitates analogy in children. *Proceedings of the Cognitive Science Society, 20*, 615–620.

Lucy, J. (1992). *Grammatical categories and cognition: A case study of the linguistic relativity hypothesis*. Cambridge: Cambridge University Press.

Lucy, J., and Shweder, R. (1979). Whorf and his critics: Linguistic and non-linguistic influences on color memory. *American Anthropologist, 81*, 581–618.

Mullen, M. K. (1990). Children's classification of nature and artifact pictures into female and male categories. *Sex Roles, 23*, 577–587.

Sapir, E. (1921). *Language*. New York: Harcourt, Brace, and World.

Sera, M., Berge, C., and del Castillo, J. (1994). Grammatical and conceptual forces in the attribution of gender by English and Spanish speakers. *Cognitive Development, 9*, 261–292.

Slobin, D. (1996). From "thought and language" to "thinking for speaking." In J. J. Gumperz and S. C. Levinson (Eds.), *Rethinking linguistic relativity* (pp. 70–96). Cambridge: Cambridge University Press.

Twain, M. (1880). *A tramp abroad*. Leipzig: Bernhard Tauchnitz.

Whorf, B. (1956). *Language, thought, and reality: Selected writings of Benjamin Lee Whorf* (J. B. Carroll, Ed.). Cambridge, MA: MIT Press.

# 5

# Speaking versus Thinking about Objects and Actions

Barbara C. Malt, Steven A. Sloman, and Silvia P. Gennari

## 5.1   Introduction

A strong version of the Whorfian hypothesis is that the influence of language on thought is obligatory or at least habitual; that is, thought is always, or under most circumstances, guided by language. This version is reflected in proposals such as that a person whose language does not include a subjunctive tense will have trouble thinking counterfactually (Bloom 1981); that a person whose language highlights specific qualities of a named object with a classifier particle will notice those qualities more (Carroll and Casagrande 1958); that a person whose language has only a few color terms will discriminate colors less well than someone whose language has more color terms (Brown and Lenneberg 1954); that a person whose language uses vertical metaphors to talk about time will think about time differently than someone whose language uses horizontal metaphors (Boroditsky 1999). In all these cases, it is assumed that the nonlinguistic cognitive processes of a person who speaks a particular language are closely and habitually, if not inextricably, linked to the form or content of the language.

Other versions, however, suggest different forms of the relation between language and thought. Slobin (1996a), for instance, suggests that language influences thought primarily in "thinking for speaking"; that is, language will influence the processing of an event when talking about it because language forces a segmentation of the event compatible with the devices the language has for expressing it. Others have variously suggested that language may provide a means of integrating sources of information that cannot be integrated in other representational systems

(Hermer-Vazquez, Spelke, and Katsnelson 1999), that language provides a source of information that can be drawn on in decision making (Kay and Kempton 1984), or that language helps encode information in and retrieve it from memory ([Rosch] Heider 1972; Heider and Olivier 1972). In all cases, language influences thought but only under specific and limited circumstances.

In keeping with such views, we suggest that at the lexical level, language and thought need not closely or commonly mirror each other. On the linguistic side, naming—of objects, events, or other entities—is a communicative process and is therefore sensitive to influences such as a language's history and the particular history of a speaker and addressee. The vocabulary of each language changes over time and is shaped by a variety of forces such as cultural needs, contact with other languages, and sound changes, which drive meaning shifts including broadening, narrowing, differentiation, and reinterpretation of individual word meanings, and which can add words to or delete words from the language's lexicon (e.g., Hock and Joseph 1996; Keller 1994). Such factors contribute to how many choices of names for an entity a speaker has and which is dominant. Speakers must also choose a name, out of the possible names, that they know their addressee will be able to use to pick out the intended referent. This choice must take into account the addressee's knowledge base, what the addressee will assume the speaker knows he or she knows, and specific shared experiences in which speaker and addressee may have established a use of a particular term to pick out a particular kind of object (e.g., Brennan and Clark 1996; Clark 1996; Clark and Wilkes-Gibbs 1986). Speakers must also assess the situation to determine the level of specificity needed and choose a name that will convey as much information as is needed but not more (Brown 1958; Grice 1975). What name a person uses for an entity on any particular occasion is thus influenced by the set of names his or her language makes available for that domain and the pattern of application of names to entities that the language has evolved, by the goals of the particular communication, and by the common ground of the speaker and addressee.

On the nonlinguistic side, though, these influences are not directly relevant to the general conceptual system and the various processes that draw on it. The encoding in and retrieval of information from memory, the use of the information in problem solving and decision making, the perception of similarity among entities, the classification of a new entity by recognizing its relation to some set of familiar entities, and so on, are not in themselves about communication. There is no functional reason why the encoding or use of information about entities by a single individual in a noncommunicative context must be sensitive to language history, Gricean considerations, or shared linguistic knowledge between sets of individuals. Thus, the potential exists for naming and nonlinguistic processes to proceed without a direct and obligatory or habitual influence of the first on the second.

Of course, it is possible that the names are indirectly but powerfully relevant to nonlinguistic processes. Much work at the lexical level (e.g., the early work on color names; see also Boroditsky 1999; Levinson 1996a,b) has hypothesized that they are. This work has assumed that in some way, the names that people give entities permanently or habitually influence how they encode, retrieve, compare (etc.) those entities. However, the mechanisms supporting such an influence remain unspecified. To take the case of color terms, the version of the hypothesis in which the influence of language on thought is obligatory and permanent—the version that drove the classic research on color (see Lucy 1992, 1996)— suggests that a language's color vocabulary somehow determines color perception: the colors actually look different to people with different color vocabularies. Consideration of possible mechanisms for such an effect suggests, though, that this is a priori not likely. Such a mechanism would violate virtually all theories of color perception; phenomena such as color constancy have been modeled by focusing exclusively on the optical array generated by a three-dimensional configuration of a scene. It seems likely that any effect of color names on performance in color tasks must come from higher processes. For instance, the number of named values on a dimension might influence the amount of attention to that dimension or might create richer or poorer retrieval cues for the colors in a memory task. If a person speaks a language that names only "light" versus "dark," he or she may pay less attention to hue variation than someone whose language has contrastive names for more of the hue continuum, and so that person may perform poorly when asked to pick out a previously presented color from an array of color chips. Likewise, a person whose language has few color names may be less able to use names as a way to help remember the hue of a color. In either case, when working with colors that are physically present, the person may be no less able to discriminate among them than someone with a richer color vocabulary.

This brief consideration of specific mechanisms for a linguistic influence on color perception suggests an effect of names on performance in color tasks but a limit on the nature of the possible influence. The available empirical evidence is consistent with this suggestion (Berlin and Kay 1969; Kay and McDaniel 1978; though see Roberson, Davies, and Davidoff 2000). These findings raise the possibility that a mirroring relation in the domain of color is not obligatory, and perhaps not even habitual, but may depend on task-processing demands. (See also Jackendoff and Landau 1991 and Hermer-Vazquez, Spelke, and Katsnelson 1999 on the relation of task demands to language-mediated responses in the domain of spatial cognition and spatial terms.) We propose that a useful step for thinking about the relation of naming to thought more generally is likewise to put forward assumptions about the nature of linguistic and nonlinguistic representations and the processes that operate on them. Doing so makes it possible to generate hypotheses about when an influence of language on thought should be found and when it should not.

Our assumptions are as follows (Malt et al. 1999). At the conceptual level, entities (objects, events, etc.) are represented as points in multidimensional feature space. They tend to form clusters in this space (Rosch and Mervis 1975). No fixed boundaries separate these clusters, and so conceptual categories are only implicitly defined. Further, the clusters formed may vary depending on feature weightings imposed by different contexts and task demands (Medin, Goldstone, and Gentner 1993), so there is no fixed conceptual structure. At the linguistic level, names are associated with points in the space with varying degrees of strength, with the strength of the name generally varying in proportion to the similarity of the entity to other entities in a cluster. Because names are explicitly represented, the linguistic categories are explicit, although their boundaries are fuzzy.

Under these assumptions, the probability that an entity is called by a given name will generally reflect its centrality to a cluster of entities associated with the name. However, additional complexity in how names are chosen can arise in several ways. We assume that similarity is exemplar based (e.g., Brooks 1978, 1987; Medin and Schaffer 1978). This type of similarity metric allows that chains of entities sharing a common name may come into existence such that entities at one end of a chain may have few features in common with those at the other end (Heit 1992; Lakoff 1987). In addition, the association mechanism allows experience with names for entities to alter the strength of association of a name with that entity, independent of the similarity of the entity to other entities associated with the name.

We have previously suggested that crosslinguistic variation in naming patterns for artifacts (Malt et al. 1999; Sloman, Malt, and Fridman 2001) will arise because (1) since different artifacts enter different cultures at different times, the exemplar-based similarity processes will produce different patterns as a given language extends its set of names to new exemplars, and (2) non-similarity-based influences on naming such as a marketer's motivation to bestow one name or another will add to the crosslinguistic diversity. Our simple model suggests that crosslinguistic variation in naming patterns will exist even for domains that are more constant in their instantiation across cultures (e.g., color, motion, and space). These domains are like artifacts in that their linguistic categories are not assigned from scratch by each new speaker of the language, but are transmitted across generations of speakers. If cultures have either random starting points or motivated variation in which entities they first attend to and name, phenomena similar to those for artifacts may occur as a result of the exemplar-based categorization process. A culture names certain points in space and then extends these names in various ways or introduces new names depending on what else needs to be named and what other things are similar within the set already named. The result will be that different cultures will generate different clusters and chains of entities sharing names. As with artifacts, non-similarity-based processes may also influence names within these domains. Cultural need or lack of need to distinguish sets of entities as the language continues to evolve is itself a non-similarity-based influence, and contact with other languages may influence how many different names are available for linguistic discrimination within a domain. Thus, naming patterns even for domains that are universal in human experience are likely to show crosslinguistic variation.

In contrast, conceptual groupings are not transmitted from generation to generation in our view, but are formed to serve the demands of a particular task and are based on perception of features relevant to that situation. Of course, conceptual knowledge is culturally transmitted, but this knowledge is not about groupings per se; rather, it is about the nature of specific objects or types of objects. In those cases where cultures differ in their understanding of the nature of objects, groupings formed by perceivers of the objects from different cultures may vary correspondingly. However, we suggest that the understanding of most everyday entities is determined largely by features such as size and shape, functional role (for artifacts), behavior (for animals), and so on, that are perceived similarly by members of most or all cultures (see, e.g., Berlin 1992; Hunn 1997; Malt 1995 on cross-cultural similarities in classification of plants and animals). We therefore hypothesize that conceptual groupings of entities, as opposed to linguistic ones, will tend to be universal and independent of the naming pattern used by a particular language.

Given that conceptual knowledge has names linked to it, though, and names serve to indicate linguistic category boundaries, we must consider whether differences in the patterns of names for speakers of different languages lead to differences in the representation of the entities in conceptual space—thereby answering the question of the relation between conceptual and linguistic clusters by indicating an enduring distortion of the conceptual space to reflect linguistic categories, as proposed in strong versions of the Whorfian hypothesis. Our assumption that there are no fixed boundaries or clusters in conceptual space, but only those created by the demands of a particular context, suggests that there is not, and that there is no single answer to the question of the relation between concepts and linguistic categories. Tasks that activate names along with nonlinguistic information are likely to show influences of name similarity on response patterns because the names, in this case, are part of the information available to draw on in executing the task. The names themselves may also feed back to the conceptual feature space to activate certain features more than others (e.g., in feature induction; Gelman 1988). But given that people differentially weight features depending on context and task demand, and that names are only one piece of information among many, our assumptions suggest that when the task does not activate names, universal responses can be found.

Our working model thus suggests the following predictions about crosslinguistic variability in naming and its relation to nonlinguistic knowledge and task performance: (1) Crosslinguistic variability will exist in naming patterns across a wide range of domains. (2) Conceptual knowledge is not necessarily closely tied to linguistic categories; it may be universal. (3) Nevertheless, all domains potentially will show an influence of linguistic categorization on performance in nonlinguistic tasks. Specifically, linguistic categorization will influence performance of linguistically mediated tasks; no such influence will occur if the task context does not explicitly invoke names or if names do not provide a useful basis for decisions.

We now summarize two studies that test our predictions. The first, discussed in more detail in Malt et al. 1999, examines naming and similarity judgments for a set of containers by speakers of English, Spanish, and Chinese. We test both whether naming varies across cultures and whether similarity judgments are influenced by naming differences or are the same across cultures. The second study, discussed in more detail in Gennari et al. 2002, takes as a starting point an analysis of verbs of motion that establishes linguistic differences in how simple actions are lexicalized in Spanish versus English. We use this difference to ask whether the linguistic differences produce habitual differences in the perception of similarity and the storage in memory of simple motion events.

## 5.2 Artifacts

Casual observation suggests that names for some artifacts in a given language do diverge from what the object's features, by themselves, would dictate as the likely name for the object. For instance, a plastic container for holding drinks, having a straw and in the shape of Mickey Mouse, can be called a water *bottle*, but a plastic container for holding drinks, having a straw and in the shape of a bear, can be called a juice *box* (see figures 2 and 3 in Malt et al. 1999). Neither resembles the usual appearance of things called *bottle* or *box*; only the bottle has the usual function of its namesake; and the two are similar enough in physical and functional features that it is hard to see how the features alone would result in different names for the two. The labels standardly given to these objects seem to be influenced by the history of what other objects they evolved from and what the manufacturer wanted to convey to consumers about possible uses through the name. If each culture has its own history of human-made objects and names for them, then differences across languages in naming patterns are likely to arise. Anecdotal evidence likewise supports this idea; for instance, Americans call a stuffed easy chair and a wooden kitchen chair by the same name, but Chinese give the stuffed seat the same name as sofas. In addition, Kronenfeld, Armstrong, and Wilmoth (1985), looking at 11 drinking vessels, found that Americans, Japanese, and Israelis grouped the vessels by name in different ways.

The first goal of this study was thus to see whether such crosslinguistic diversity in naming patterns would show up in a domain other than that used by Kronenfeld, Armstrong, and Wilmoth and under more systematic examination of names for a much larger set of objects. Given such diversity, we could then ask the second question: would groups of people who have different naming patterns for the objects show differences in their perception of similarity among the objects? If similarity and naming are closely linked, then they should. In contrast, if naming and similarity are dissociable, then speakers of languages with different name boundaries might nevertheless provide comparable similarity judgments.

### 5.2.1   Method

The materials consisted of a set of 60 photographs of ordinary objects found in homes, grocery and drug stores, and so on. They represented as wide a range of objects likely to be called *bottle* or *jar* in English as we could find (e.g., an aspirin bottle, a baby bottle, a peanut butter jar, a mustard jar), along with some others not likely to be called by those names but sharing substantial properties with them (e.g., a milk jug, a margarine tub). Figure 5.1 illustrates three stimulus objects; see also figure 5 of Malt et al. 1999. The range of objects allowed us to

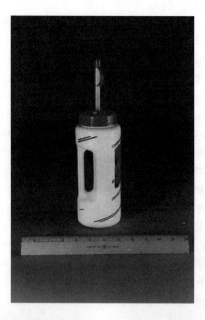

**Figure 5.1**
Examples of stimulus objects. Manufacturer information has been removed from the labels for publication purposes. Participants saw color photographs with full label information.

make a sensitive test of any difference in naming boundaries in the three languages.

These photographs were shown to 76 native speakers of American English, 50 native speakers of Mandarin Chinese, and 53 native speakers of Argentinean Spanish. The participants first sorted the objects into piles on the basis of similarity and then named the objects in their native language. Participants were asked to focus on the overall qualities of each object, including physical or functional features or both, and to put into piles the objects that seemed very similar to them. We will focus on results for this "overall" sort here, but each group also carried out separate sorts based on physical or on functional features as well, and the results of both lead to the same conclusions as those for overall similarity. For the naming task, participants were asked to give whatever name seemed best or most natural to them. Each participant was tested in his or her native language. Instructions for Chinese and Spanish speakers were translated from the English versions.

### 5.2.2   Results and Discussion

As table 5.1 shows, the naming patterns across the three languages had some clear commonalities; for instance, all the objects called *jar* by English speakers were also within a single category for both Spanish and Chinese speakers—but they also had some distinct differences. English speakers divided the objects by name into three main groups of approximately the same size: *jar*, *bottle*, and *container*. The remaining 10 objects fell into four smaller categories. Chinese speakers, in contrast, grouped most of the objects into one very large category. They used a second category name for 10 objects and placed the remaining 10 in three additional categories. Spanish speakers had the largest number of different name categories, but 28 of the objects received a single name, *frasco* (or its diminutive, *frasquito*). The remaining objects were spread across fourteen additional names. Notably, the categories of one language were not neat subsets or supersets of the categories of others (see also Malt, Sloman, and Gennari 2001). For instance, the large Spanish category *frasco* encompassed 6 of the objects that English speakers called *bottle* and 3 that they called *container*, but the remaining objects that

**Table 5.1**
English, Chinese, and Spanish linguistic categories, with Chinese and Spanish described in terms of their English composition. (After Malt et al. 1999.)

| English | N | Chinese | N | English composition |
|---|---|---|---|---|
| Jar | 19 | Ping2[a] | 40 | 13 bottles, 8 containers, 19 jars |
| Bottle | 16 | Guan4 | 10 | 2 bottles, 3 containers, 5 cans |
| Container | 15 | Tong3 | 5 | 1 bottle, 1 container, 3 jugs |
| Can | 5 | He2 | 4 | 3 containers, 1 box |
| Jug | 3 | Guan3 | 1 | 1 tube |
| Tube | 1 | | | |
| Box | 1 | | | |

| | | Spanish | N | English composition |
|---|---|---|---|---|
| | | Frasco/ Frasquito | 28 | 6 bottles, 3 containers, 19 jars |
| | | Envase | 6 | 2 bottles, 4 containers |
| | | Bidon | 6 | 1 bottle, 2 containers, 3 jugs |
| | | Aerosol | 3 | 3 cans |
| | | Botella | 3 | 3 bottles |
| | | Pote/ Potecito | 2 | 2 containers |
| | | Lata | 2 | 2 cans |
| | | Tarro | 2 | 2 containers |
| | | Mamadera | 2 | 2 bottles |
| | | Gotero | 1 | 1 bottle |
| | | Caja | 1 | 1 box |
| | | Talquera | 1 | 1 container |
| | | Taper | 1 | 1 container |
| | | Roceador | 1 | 1 bottle |
| | | Pomo | 1 | 1 tube |

[a] The number in the Chinese names refers to tone.

they called by these names were spread across ten of the remaining Spanish categories.

We derived a judgment of the similarity of each pair for each group of speakers by determining how many times, across members of the group, the objects of the pair were sorted into the same pile. When pairs are frequently put into the same pile, we assume they are perceived as highly similar, and when they are rarely put into the same pile, we assume they are perceived as low in similarity. A matrix was constructed for each language group, representing all possible pairwise similarity judgments for the group. Correlations of the matrices between groups were quite high, $r = .91$ for two (English speakers with Chinese speakers and Spanish speakers with Chinese speakers) and $r = .94$ for the other (English speakers with Spanish speakers). This result indicates that the three groups were judging similarity in much the same way, and it implies that perception of similarity among the objects was quite constant across the groups.

Although the preceding observations give an intuitive feel for differences between naming and similarity, they do not provide a basis for directly comparing the extent of commonality or divergence among the languages in naming versus similarity. To better evaluate the differences among groups, we used the cultural consensus model (CCM) of Romney, Weller, and Batchelder (1986). Applying this model to both the naming and the similarity data allows the two to be compared using a common measure. The idea of the model is to represent the relations among the responses of all participants regardless of group. The representation is then analyzed using a principal components analysis to see if its underlying structure embodies group differences. If no differences obtain between groups, then only a single factor should emerge and all participants should load positively on it. If differences do obtain between groups, then factors should emerge that distinguish the groups.

We considered only factors that accounted for significant variance (factors with eigenvalues greater than 1). For naming, three such factors emerged, and all three distinguished the Chinese, Spanish, and English speakers, indicating that they do indeed apply different linguistic category boundaries to the objects. For sorting, a very different pattern emerged. Only a single factor accounted for significant variance, and all

118 participants loaded positively on it. In other words, the individuals tested did not sort the objects in language-specific ways despite their very different linguistic category boundaries.

Thus, the CCM analyses show significant group differences for naming, but none for sorting. Although the three groups have different linguistic categories, their similarity judgments were largely convergent. This result is consistent with that suggested by more informal examination of the naming data and the correlations between similarity matrices. It demonstrates a dissociation between naming and similarity and argues that the different naming patterns across languages do not necessarily or habitually impose differences in how speakers of the languages perceive relations among the objects.

### 5.3  Motion Events

It is important to set our findings with artifacts in the broader context of linguistic and nonlinguistic categorization in other domains. Because artifacts are constructed by humans to meet specific human needs, they vary substantially over time and across cultures and potentially in the groupings that may have existed at various times and been salient or important enough to be distinguished by name. It could be argued that this domain is one that is particularly likely to allow influences on naming that are distinct from those governing nonlinguistic groupings and to show culture-specific patterns of naming.

In contrast to their differing experiences with artifacts, people in all cultures presumably experience a nearly identical three-dimensional existence in space and exhibit a highly similar range of motions through that space (with the exception of some culture-specific forms of dance, etc.). We have argued that there is likely to be linguistic diversity even in domains such as this, in which exposure to the exemplars of the domain are more nearly universal. Analysis of verb lexicalization patterns across languages supports this point for motion, as we will discuss. The linguistic variation observed in this domain may have more potential to influence thought in a permanent or at least habitual way than it does for artifacts. It is not the result of idiosyncratic cultural differences in what exemplars have been invented, or what speakers have been exposed to, or what marketing experts in a particular culture have chosen to create for the culture. The particular variation we examine here, in the nature of the information encoded in the verb, shows two main patterns across many languages and so could be argued to reflect two equally viable ways of linguistically encoding universal experience. As such, these patterns are possibly more closely linked to salient alternative ways of thinking about events and may more readily influence the way speakers of the languages think about them. This domain thus provides a different, and arguably stronger, test of our expectation that there will be a dissociation between linguistic and conceptual representations. We also test our expectation that there is, nevertheless, the potential for task performance to be influenced by linguistic knowledge across all domains. We tested these ideas by looking at how speakers of Spanish and English name and conceptualize simple motion events.

Motion verb meanings can be decomposed into conceptual components such as path (the direction of the movement), the figure/agent of the movement, and the manner of movement (e.g., walking vs. running). However, languages differ in the way they lexicalize these components, especially for culminated motion events (i.e., actions involving a change of state or location) (Aske 1989; Jackendoff 1990; Levin and Rappaport Hovav 1992; Slobin 1996a,b; Talmy 1985). In languages like English and other Germanic languages, motion verbs normally encode manner of motion (e.g., *clamber, stride, creep, slip, sneak, stroll*). They use particles and prepositional phrases to indicate path and the endpoint of the trajectory (*in/out, into the house, out of the house*). In contrast, in languages like Spanish and other Romance languages, Turkish, and Hebrew, motion verbs typically express path and the endpoint of the trajectory (in Spanish, *entrar* 'enter', *salir* 'exit', *subir* 'ascend', *bajar* 'descend'), using adverbial phrases only optionally to express manner (*entra caminando* '(he) enters walking'). Although certain manner distinctions are encoded (*caminar* 'walk' vs. *correr* 'run'), Spanish does not systematically encode manner like English. Thus, to talk about culminated events, English speakers typically encode both manner (in the verb) and path (in an adverbial phrase), while Spanish speakers encode path in the verb and tend to omit manner considerations.

Given this evidence for linguistic variation in the domain of motion, we can ask if these differences in the ways English and Spanish speakers typically use and hear verbs to describe motion events have consequences for their nonlinguistic cognitive processes. In the experiment, we compared English and Spanish speakers' linguistic descriptions of simple motion events (a person walking into a room, a person running out of a room, etc.) to their subsequent performance on both recognition memory and similarity judgments. We also investigated the effect of language mediation on recognition and similarity judgments when participants have not generated overt linguistic descriptions of the events. If the differences in how English versus Spanish speakers label motion affects what properties of an event they focus on, we would expect differences in perceived similarity and in recognition confusions between stimuli that differ in path versus in manner: if Spanish speakers encode primarily path while English speakers encode both manner and path, Spanish speakers should tend to view actions with shared path as more similar than English speakers do, and they should show more confusion in memory for stimuli that share path and differ only in manner. If this influence is obligatory or habitual, we should see the language difference regardless of whether speakers have generated overt linguistic descriptions. If the influence of language on performance depends on its specific role in the task, we would expect to see an effect of language only when verbal labels for the events have been given.

### 5.3.1   Method

Participants were 47 native speakers of Argentinean Spanish and 46 native speakers of American English. All the Spanish speakers used Spanish exclusively in their daily activities and none considered themselves fluent in English. All the English speakers used English as their primary language.

The stimuli consisted of digitized short films, comprising 108 motion events. Only culminated events were included since continuous events or activities such as running and jumping are lexicalized in the same way in English and Spanish. The films were organized in a set of 36 target films and a set of 72 alternates, 2 for each of the target events, giving a total of 36 triads. Within a triad, all videos depicted a similar event. The target video showed a motion event (e.g., an agent walking into a room) and the two alternates portrayed variations in either the manner or the path dimension. In the same-path alternate, the manner of movement was changed while path was kept the same (e.g., the agent striding into the room). In the same-manner alternate, the direction or path was altered while manner was held constant (e.g., the agent walking out of the room). Figure 5.2 shows frames corresponding to one triad.

Three different groups of participants for each language made recognition memory and similarity judgments after encoding target events presented on a computer screen. In the shadow condition, participants were asked to simultaneously repeat nonsense syllables compatible with both English and Spanish phonology while viewing the 36 target films. This condition was designed to minimize linguistic processing by loading verbal working memory. In the free encoding condition, participants simply watched the target videos. In the naming first condition, participants were instructed to describe the event as they viewed each film. Before a participant's descriptions were recorded, four examples were provided that suggested the general form of the desired descriptions (e.g., "What happens in the clip? He walks into the room."). In all conditions, encoding was followed by a retention interval of 10 to 20 minutes involving an unrelated task to make recognition harder.

After distraction, participants gave recognition memory judgments to all 108 clips by indicating as quickly as they could whether or not they had seen the video by pressing a key on the keyboard. Similarity judgments were then collected for all 36 triads. On each trial, participants were shown the target clip first followed by the two alternates, and they selected the clip that they believed was most similar to the target. In a final phase, participants gave verbal descriptions of each video that they had not already described (i.e., all the clips for shadow and free encoding participants; only alternates for naming first participants). The purpose of this task was to allow us to check that the expected typological linguistic differences were present.

### 5.3.2    Results and Discussion

**5.3.2.1    Comparison of Linguistic Differences**    To verify the predicted linguistic differences between Spanish and English, the linguistic descriptions given for each video were analyzed separately for each language. English speakers usually named the target event (e.g., agent *runs in*) with

(a)

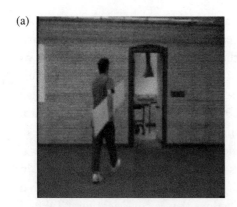

(b)

(c)

**Figure 5.2**
Example of a triad. (*a*) The agent carries the board into the room. (*b*) The agent drags the board into the room. (*c*) The agent carries the board out of the room. (After Gennari et al. 2002.)

the same verb as the same-manner alternate (e.g., agent *runs out*) and the same-path alternate with a different verb (e.g., *walk in*). In contrast, Spanish speakers usually named the target event with the same verb as the same-path alternate (e.g., *entra* 'enters') and the same-manner alternate with a different verb (e.g., *sale* 'exits'). Overall, 89% of the English verbs were manner verbs, and 89% of the Spanish verbs were path verbs. Looking at the entire verbalizations (including adverbial phrases), Spanish speakers expressed manner less often than English speakers, mentioning it in only 71% of cases despite the salience of this element in the videos. These results thus verify that each language has a preferred pattern of describing the stimuli's actions that is consistent with Talmy's (1985) typology.

**5.3.2.2 Recognition Memory Performance** If the language spoken influences the way that speakers of a language think about events, then recognition memory should reflect language differences. Because Spanish focuses more heavily on path than English, Spanish speakers can be expected to pay more attention to path than English speakers. Spanish speakers should therefore have a higher ratio of false alarms on same-path alternates relative to same-manner alternates than English speakers do.

Table 5.2 shows the mean number of false alarms for each alternate type in all conditions and languages. Contrary to the prediction, no sig-

**Table 5.2**
Mean false alarms as a function of item type and encoding condition. (From Gennari et al. 2002.)

| Item type | Encoding condition | | |
| --- | --- | --- | --- |
| | Shadow | Free encoding | Naming first |
| *English* | | | |
| Same-path item | 12.75 | 7.13 | 6.79 |
| Same-manner item | 13.38 | 7.73 | 4.79 |
| *Spanish* | | | |
| Same-path item | 13.25 | 9.00 | 6.94 |
| Same-manner item | 12.62 | 9.00 | 5.38 |

nificant differences were obtained across languages. Taking the relative probability of false alarming to the same-path alternate over the same-manner alternate as the dependent variable, only encoding condition had a significant effect, and this effect was due entirely to a difference, for English only, between the free encoding and naming first conditions: there was a slightly higher ratio of confusions on same-path relative to same-manner for the naming first condition. This across-condition difference in English is not what would be expected from the linguistic pattern. If anything, naming first should increase the proportion of same-manner confusions, because the verb lexicalizing the actions in the naming first condition expressed manner. Overall, recognition performance does not support the idea that the linguistic differences in how the Spanish and English languages encode motion influences recognition memory for motion events for speakers of the two languages.

Although encoding condition had only a minimal effect on the ratio of false alarms to the two types of alternates, it did influence overall performance. Performance was best in both languages for the naming first condition, in which participants gave overt linguistic labels to the events at the time of perceiving them. It was worst in both languages for the shadow condition, in which linguistic encoding was actively blocked. This pattern is compatible with the idea that labeling the entities to be remembered is a useful strategy for performance in the memory task. Language appears to influence memory here in that giving the action a label allows the label to serve as a useful retrieval cue.

**5.3.2.3 Similarity Judgments**  To investigate whether the two groups show differences in their similarity judgments related to language differences, we determined whether the same-path or same-manner alternate was selected as more similar to the target event for each item and participant. We then calculated the probability of selecting the same-path alternate for each language and condition. If Spanish speakers focus more on path than English speakers do, Spanish speakers should show a higher probability of same-path choices.

The results are shown in figure 5.3. There was no overall language effect. However, there was a main effect of encoding condition and a significant interaction between language and condition.

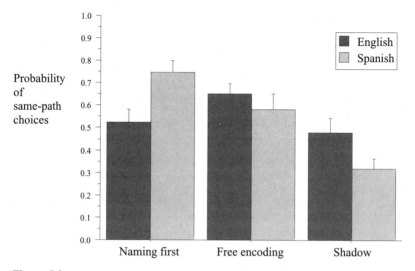

**Figure 5.3**
Probability of same-path similarity choices in the similarity task as a function of language and encoding condition. (From Gennari et al. 2002.)

The absence of a main effect of language reflects the fact that speakers did not, in general, show the pattern of responding predicted by their language biases: Spanish speakers did not show a consistently stronger preference for same-path choices than English speakers. The most striking aspect of the data is that for Spanish speakers, same-path choices increased from the shadow condition to free encoding to naming first. This pattern is not consistent with the idea that language has an obligatory or habitual influence on nonlinguistic processing. It is, however, consistent with the idea that when explicit linguistic labels are involved in encoding, those labels can influence later responses. In this case, it appears that overtly labeling the events primarily with verbs that encode path (as Spanish-speaking participants did in the naming first condition) caused these speakers to judge events that shared path as more similar than events that did not. The fact that the free encoding condition, which allowed linguistic encoding but did not demand it, was intermediate in path-based similarity choices compared with the naming first and shadow conditions is also consistent with this idea.

English speakers, in contrast to Spanish speakers, showed no clear pattern related to encoding condition. The results across conditions differed significantly only in the comparison between the free encoding and shadow conditions, where the free encoding condition had a higher probability of same-path choices. Same-path choices were also slightly higher for the free encoding condition than for the naming first condition, though not significantly so. The pattern for English speakers may result from a combination of two factors. In the naming first condition, a small general nonlinguistic preference for same-path choices may have been counteracted by a labeling effect that drew attention more equally toward manner. In the shadow condition, a preference for same-path choices may have been counteracted by the difficulty of encoding path (which requires attention to and integration of a more extended sequence of frames; Bingham 1995; Bingham, Schmidt, and Rosenblum 1995) relative to manner (Todd 1983) under heavy secondary task demands. This explanation for performance in the shadow condition is consistent with the surprising fact that Spanish speakers, in the shadow condition, actually made more same-manner than same-path choices, at odds with both their language's bias and the possibility of a general nonlinguistic preference for same-path choices in this task. Spanish speakers' performance in the memory task was particularly poor relative to that of English speakers in this task, suggesting that the shadowing task was especially taxing for them and may have reduced encoding of path in this condition. In sum, the pattern for the English speakers does not support a close link between their linguistic bias toward manner and their similarity judgments. The pattern of choices is consistent with an influence of linguistic bias only in the naming first condition, although our account suggesting this influence remains speculative.

**5.3.2.4 Summary**  We found no effect of language in the recognition memory task for both linguistic and nonlinguistic encoding and no effect of language in the similarity task after nonlinguistic encoding. We did find a linguistic effect in the similarity task after verbal encoding, especially for Spanish speakers, an effect that conformed to language-specific patterns. We also found that memory performance for speakers of both languages improved with linguistic encoding. These results suggest that (1) as we found with artifacts, linguistic and nonlinguistic performance were dissociable, but (2) language-specific regularities made available in the experimental context can be incorporated into a strategy to make similarity judgments, and (3) language may, more generally, serve as a useful tool in tasks like memory retrieval.

## 5.4　General Discussion

### 5.4.1　Summary

These investigations have demonstrated a dissociation between naming and perceived similarity for artifacts. Specifically, the linguistic categories for a set of common containers varied across speakers of English, Spanish, and Chinese, yet speakers of the different languages clustered the objects by similarity in essentially the same ways. The data also showed a dissociation for motion events. When encoding of actions was nonlinguistic, verbs of motion behaved like artifacts: speakers of English and Spanish showed the same pattern of similarity judgments and false alarms in memory for previously viewed action clips despite describing the clips linguistically in different ways. These results are consistent with our predictions that all domains will exhibit variability in linguistic categorization across cultures but that nonlinguistic conceptual performance will not necessarily follow suit.

The motion events study also suggests that the extent to which language influences nonlinguistic performance depends on whether the nonlinguistic task draws on language as a mediator. That is, a linguistic effect was apparent in the similarity task after verbal encoding, an effect that conformed to language-specific naming patterns. No such effect was found in recognition memory.

We conclude that, at the lexical level, language and thought need not closely reflect one another. The data rule out a strong version of the Whorfian hypothesis at the lexical level. Instead, the data are consistent with the view that language affects thought only under restricted conditions. Specifically, we argue that language affects thought when it is used as a tool for thought (see also Gentner and Loewenstein 2002). A correspondence between linguistic differences and nonlinguistic performance for speakers of different languages will be observed when the task allows use of language to encode stimuli, and when performance is evaluated using a measure that is sensitive to the information provided by the linguistic encoding.

### 5.4.2 Evolutionary Issues

We suggested that a dissociation between naming on the one hand and similarity judgments and recognition on the other would arise because naming is a communicative process responsive to pressures such as a language's history and the particular history of speaker and addressee. As a result, the categories defined by the names given to entities and those defined by purely conceptual clusters may diverge. Although our argument is not rooted in considerations about the evolution of the cognitive systems themselves, it is compatible with Clark's (1996) point that language evolved to facilitate communication, not thought. Keller and Keller (1996) likewise note that vision and visual representations evolved long before language did, and Hermer-Vazquez, Spelke, and Katsnelson (1999) hint at the same point with regard to spatial and general conceptual knowledge. This substantial dissociation in evolutionary sequencing suggests that conceptual representations should not be so closely tied to and shaped by language that they cannot be readily separated. As Keller and Keller point out, linguistic and nonlinguistic sources of information need to be integrated in the performance of many tasks (see also Hermer-Vazquez, Spelke, and Katsnelson 1999), but that fact does not imply that nonlinguistic modes of thought should be dominated by linguistic information (see also Jackendoff 1996).

### 5.4.3 Developmental Issues

A widespread assumption in language acquisition research is that children learn word meanings as a mapping of words to the conceptual categories by which they partition the world. The correspondence is also assumed to work in the other direction: the properties, functions, and relations of objects are learned, in part, through the guidance offered by word learning (e.g., the distinguishing features of pine and oak trees are normally learned in order to be able to name them correctly). We do not deny some correspondence, or its central importance to learning. Indeed, our data show substantial correspondence between similarity and naming clusters. Our conclusion, however, is that the correspondence is not perfect, suggesting that children must be learning something beyond a simple mapping between words and similarity clusters, a conclusion consistent with our view that objects can be grouped differently by different conceptual tasks. In acquiring the linguistic categories, children must also be learning the naming conventions of their particular language, including where names may deviate from those suggested by similarity clusters. They must also ultimately take into account these deviations in making inductions about objects on the basis of their names.

A particularly intriguing piece of language acquisition research to consider in relation to our findings was conducted by Bowerman (1996a,b; see also Bowerman and Choi, this volume). Parallel to our findings for artifacts, Bowerman has found that languages label spatial relations in substantially different ways. For instance, the relations described by speakers of English as a Band-Aid *on* a leg, a ring *on* a finger, and a picture *on* a wall are labeled separately as *op*, *om*, and *aan*, respectively, by speakers of Dutch. Further, these discrepancies arise in part because the languages differ substantially in which dimensions of a spatial relation they use as the basis for the linguistic grouping. Korean, for instance, distinguishes tight versus loose fit of one object within another in a way that crosscuts the English categories of *into* and *out of*. Because all humans have similar bodies existing in the same three-dimensional space, space is a domain for which universal conceptualization has been suggested (e.g., Clark 1973; see Bowerman 1996a,b). The fact of crosslinguistically divergent naming patterns in this domain is therefore in itself quite interesting and bolsters our argument that all domains will show diversity in linguistic categorization.

The linguistic data by themselves do not address the question of whether the conceptualization of the domain is truly universal or is influenced by the linguistic differences. Bowerman has found that children learning a given language use their first spatial words to express relations similar to those that adult speakers of the language do, showing that they grasp the language-specific meanings of the spatial terms early in acquisition. There is little evidence of a phase in which the children resist the peculiarities of their language, making shared mistakes as they try to apply the labels to some common prelinguistic conceptualization. She concludes that the children do not seem to bring to the language-learning task strong universal assumptions about the similarity of spatial relations.

This observation implies that language might itself serve as the guide to the child's conceptualization of spatial relations, and that children do not have a language-independent shared perception of the relations, contrary to the arguments we have made for our domains. However, the evidence is not definitive (and Bowerman herself remains neutral on this point; but see Bowerman and Choi, this volume). Indeed, as Bowerman notes, there is ample evidence that children have an understanding of spatial relations before they acquire names for them. Because those prelinguistic spatial concepts cannot be influenced by names not yet learned, it seems logically necessary that children do have some shared prelinguistic conceptualization of spatial relations. Young children may simply not perceive spatial relations as falling into strong similarity clusters, and so they may have no difficulty distributing them into linguistic categories in a variety of different ways. Alternatively, even if children do have strong notions of what spatial relations resemble each other, these clusters may not interfere with learning linguistic categories. Our own data imply that children acquiring Spanish, Chinese, and English must learn substantially different linguistic groupings of artifacts that are perceived similarly (at least by adults). Perhaps the multidimensional nature of the entities (artifacts or spatial relations), along with children's inclination to accept labels provided by the adult language "expert" (Mervis 1987) (and their good memory), allows children to acquire linguistic groupings based on whichever dimensions their language highlights without substantial interference from nonlinguistic groupings.

Even if young children do not exhibit strong prelinguistic groupings of spatial relations, it is possible that older children or adults develop stronger notions of the resemblances among spatial relations. It remains an empirical question whether such notions are influenced by the naming patterns that have been learned at that point, or whether they would be shared across speakers of different languages. To address this issue, it would be necessary to get measures of the perceived similarity among different examples of spatial relations (using depictions such as those provided in Bowerman 1996a,b) for speakers of different languages. We predict, of course, that speakers of different languages will share perception of similarity.

### 5.4.4  Relation to Recent Studies of Adult Cognition

There has been a recent surge of studies exploring aspects of the Whorfian hypothesis in adult cognition. Although we cannot discuss most of them here, work by Billman (Billman and Krych 1998; Billman, Swilley, and Krych 2000) is particularly closely related to our own. Billman manipulated the labels used to describe motion events for native speakers of English. Either events were labeled out loud for participants, or participants were primed to generate particular kinds of labels themselves. Some events received path labels (e.g., *exiting*) and some received manner labels (e.g., *skipping*). Billman then tested whether the participants made more mistakes at recognizing path or manner foils as a function of the type of verb label used at encoding. The predicted interaction was obtained. Because explicit linguistic encoding was involved in this paradigm, the results are consistent with our expectation that a language effect can emerge under such circumstances.

Billman's results do contrast with ours in showing an effect of verb type on recognition memory; we found no such effect, even with explicit labeling, on memory performance. (The effect that we found occurred in similarity judgments.) However, Billman's recognition test occurred one full day after encoding, whereas ours occurred within the same experimental session. The longer delay may have in some way caused Billman's participants to rely more heavily on the verbal encodings at test. Her encoding manipulation could also be considered more explicit than ours in that a single (presented or generated) verb was the main linguistic encoding for each stimulus (with some variation for the generated cases), and each participant received only one of the two types of verbs. We merely asked our participants to describe the videos, with their differing native languages yielding the verb type manipulation. As a result, Billman's participants may have been much more consciously aware of the verb label as part of the to-be-remembered event than ours were. In addition, our participants more often produced information about path or manner not lexicalized in the main verb by using adverbial phrases.

These phrases (in the naming first condition) may have helped guide memory along with the verbs and reduced the impact of the verb difference. Billman's results establish that a verb type effect can be seen in recognition memory under some circumstances. However, since we are interested in the effect of differences in linguistic patterns during ordinary language use, our paradigm may better address that situation.

We have focused our discussion to this point on work that is compatible with ours, but we must also note that other recent work has produced results that are not so readily compatible. Boroditsky (1999) found that native speakers of Mandarin and of English seem to think about time using different conceptual metaphors, in ways that correspond to the expression of time in their respective languages. Levinson (1996a, b, this volume) found that the Tzeltal language describes spatial orientation (what English speakers would label as *in front of*, *to the right of*, etc.) in radically different terms from English, and that Tzeltal speakers perform differently in a variety of spatial tasks, including some seemingly not closely linked to linguistic encoding. For instance, Levinson (1996b) suggests that speakers of Tzeltal have difficulty actually perceiving the difference between right- and left-oriented letters (e.g., *b* vs. *d*) even when both are physically present for comparison. It is not yet clear how language exerts its influence on performance in the tasks involved in these pieces of research (see Levinson 1996a for discussion of some of the issues involved). Whether the explanation ultimately will be compatible with our view remains to be seen. Such issues can only be resolved by formulating them in terms of explicit models of task performance (see also Jackendoff 1996).

## Note

This work was supported by NIMH grant MH51271 to Barbara Malt and Steven Sloman and an American Philosophical Society sabbatical fellowship to Barbara Malt. We thank Dedre Gentner and Susan Goldin-Meadow for helpful comments on a previous draft of the chapter.

## References

Aske, J. (1989). Path predicates in English and Spanish: A closer look. *Proceedings of the Berkeley Linguistics Society*, *15*, 1–14.

Berlin, B. (1992). *Ethnobiological classification: Principles of categorization of plants and animals in traditional societies*. Princeton, NJ: Princeton University Press.

Berlin, B., and Kay, P. (1969). *Basic color terms: Their universality and evolution*. Berkeley and Los Angeles: University of California Press.

Billman, D., and Krych, M. (1998). Path and manner verbs in action: Effects of "skipping" or "exiting" on event memory. *Proceedings of the Cognitive Science Society, 20*, 156–161.

Billman, D., Swilley, A., and Krych, M. (2000). Path and manner priming: Verb production and event recognition. *Proceedings of the Cognitive Science Society, 22*, 615–620.

Bingham, G. (1995). Dynamics and the problem of visual event recognition. In R. F. Port and T. van Gelder (Eds.), *Mind as motion: Explorations in the dynamics of cognition* (pp. 403–448). Cambridge, MA: MIT Press.

Bingham, G., Schmidt, R., and Rosenblum, L. (1995). Dynamics and the orientation of kinematic forms in visual event recognition. *Journal of Experimental Psychology: Human Perception and Performance, 21*, 1473–1493.

Bloom, A. H. (1981). *The linguistic shaping of thought: A study in the impact of language on thinking in China and the West*. Hillsdale, NJ: Erlbaum.

Boroditsky, L. (1999). First-language thinking for second-language understanding: Mandarin and English speakers' conceptions of time. *Proceedings of the Cognitive Science Society, 21*, 84–89.

Bowerman, M. (1996a). Learning how to structure space for language: A cross-linguistic perspective. In P. Bloom, M. A. Peterson, L. Nadel, and M. F. Garrett (Eds.), *Language and space* (pp. 385–436). Cambridge, MA: MIT Press.

Bowerman, M. (1996b). The origins of children's spatial semantic categories: Cognitive versus linguistic determinants. In J. J. Gumperz and S. C. Levinson (Eds.), *Rethinking linguistic relativity* (pp. 145–176). Cambridge: Cambridge University Press.

Brennan, S. and Clark, H. H. (1996). Conceptual pacts and lexical choice in conversation. *Journal of Experimental Psychology: Learning, Memory, and Cognition, 22*, 1482–1493.

Brooks, L. (1978). Nonanalytic concept formation and memory for instances. In E. Rosch and B. Lloyd (Eds.), *Cognition and categorization* (pp. 169–211). Hillsdale, NJ: Erlbaum.

Brooks, L. (1987). Decentralized control of cognition: The role of prior processing episodes. In U. Neisser (Ed.), *Concepts and conceptual development: Ecological and intellectual factors in categorization* (pp. 141–173). New York: Cambridge University Press.

Brown, R. W. (1958). How shall a thing be called? *Psychological Review, 65*, 14–21.

Brown, R. W., and Lenneberg, E. H. (1954). A study in language and cognition. *Journal of Abnormal and Social Psychology, 49,* 454–462.

Carroll, J. B., and Casagrande, J. B. (1958). The function of language classifications in behavior. In E. E. Maccoby, T. M. Newcomb, and E. L. Hartley (Eds.), *Readings in social psychiatry* (pp. 18–31). New York: Holt, Rinehart and Winston.

Clark, H. H. (1973). Space, time, semantics, and the child. In T. E. Moore (Ed.), *Cognitive development and the acquisition of language* (pp. 27–64). New York: Academic Press.

Clark, H. H. (1996). Communities, communalities, and communication. In J. J. Gumperz and S. C. Levinson (Eds.), *Rethinking linguistic relativity* (pp. 324–358). Cambridge: Cambridge University Press.

Clark, H. H., and Wilkes-Gibbs, D. (1986). Referring as a collaborative process. *Cognition, 22,* 1–39.

Gelman, S. A. (1988). The development of induction within natural kind and artifact categories. *Cognitive Psychology, 20,* 65–95.

Gennari, S. P., Sloman, S. A., Malt, B. C., and Fitch, W. T. (2002). Motion events in language and cognition. *Cognition, 83,* 49–79.

Gentner, D., and Loewenstein, J. (2002). Relational language and relational thought. In J. Byrnes and E. Amsel (Eds.), *Language, literacy, and cognitive development* (pp. 87–120). Mahwah, NJ: Erlbaum.

Grice, H. P. (1975). Logic and conversation. In P. Cole and J. Morgan (Eds.), *Syntax and semantics: Vol. 3. Speech acts* (pp. 41–58). New York: Academic Press.

Heider, E. R. (1972). Universals in color naming and memory. *Journal of Experimental Psychology, 93,* 10–20.

Heider E. R., and Olivier, C. (1972). The structure of the color space in naming and memory for two languages. *Cognitive Psychology, 3,* 337–354.

Heit, E. (1992). Categorization using chains of examples. *Cognitive Psychology, 24,* 341–380.

Hermer-Vazquez, L., Spelke, E. S., and Katsnelson, A. S. (1999). Sources of flexibility in human cognition: Dual-task studies of space and language. *Cognitive Psychology, 39,* 3–36.

Hock, H. H., and Joseph, B. D. (1996). *Language history, language change, and language relationship: An introduction to historical and comparative linguistics.* Berlin: Mouton de Gruyter.

Hunn, E. (1977). *Tzeltal folk zoology: The classification of discontinuities in nature.* New York: Academic Press.

Jackendoff, R. (1990). *Semantic structures.* Cambridge, MA: MIT Press.

Jackendoff, R. (1996). The architecture of the linguistic-spatial interface. In P. Bloom, M. A. Peterson, L. Nadel, and M. F. Garrett (Eds.), *Language and space* (pp. 1–30). Cambridge, MA: MIT Press.

Jackendoff, R., and Landau, B. (1991). Spatial language and spatial cognition. In D. J. Napoli and J. A. Kegl (Eds.), *Bridges between psychology and linguistics: A Swarthmore festschrift for Lila Gleitman* (pp. 145–169). Hillsdale, NJ: Erlbaum.

Kay, P., and Kempton, W. (1984). What is the Sapir-Whorf hypothesis? *American Anthropologist, 86,* 65–79.

Kay, P., and McDaniel, C. K. (1978). The linguistic significance of the meanings of basic color terms. *Language, 54,* 610–646.

Keller, C. M., and Keller, J. D. (1996). Imaging in iron, or thought is not inner speech. In J. J. Gumperz and S. C. Levinson (Eds.), *Rethinking linguistic relativity* (pp. 115–132). Cambridge: Cambridge University Press.

Keller, R. (1994). *On language change: The invisible hand on language.* London: Routledge.

Kronenfeld, D. B., Armstrong, J. D., and Wilmoth, S. (1985). Exploring the internal structure of linguistic categories: An extensionist semantic view. In J. W. D. Dougherty (Ed.), *Directions in cognitive anthropology* (pp. 91–113). Urbana: University of Illinois Press.

Lakoff, G. (1987). *Women, fire, and dangerous things: What categories reveal about the mind.* Chicago: University of Chicago Press.

Levin, B., and Rappaport Hovav, M. (1992). The lexical semantics of verbs of motion: The perspective from unaccusativity. In I. Roca (Ed.), *Thematic structure: Its role in grammar* (pp. 247–269). Berlin: Mouton de Gruyter.

Levinson, S. C. (1996a). Frames of reference and Molyneux's question: Cross-linguistic evidence. In P. Bloom, M. A. Peterson, L. Nadel, and M. F. Garrett (Eds.), *Language and space* (pp. 109–169). Cambridge, MA: MIT Press.

Levinson, S. C. (1996b). Relativity in spatial conception and description. In J. J. Gumperz and S. C. Levinson (Eds.), *Rethinking linguistic relativity* (pp. 177–202). Cambridge: Cambridge University Press.

Lucy, J. A. (1992). *Language diversity and thought: A reformulation of the linguistic relativity hypothesis.* Cambridge: Cambridge University Press.

Lucy, J. (1996). The scope of linguistic relativity: An analysis and review of empirical research. In J. J. Gumperz and S. C. Levinson (Eds.), *Rethinking linguistic relativity* (pp. 37–69). Cambridge: Cambridge University Press.

Malt, B. C. (1995). Category coherence in cross-cultural perspective. *Cognitive Psychology, 29,* 85–148.

Malt, B. C., Sloman, S. A., and Gennari, S. P. (2001). *Universality and language-specificity in object naming.* Manuscript submitted for publication.

Malt, B. C., Sloman, S. A., Gennari, S., Shi, M., and Wang, Y. (1999). Knowing versus naming: Similarity and the linguistic categorization of artifacts. *Journal of Memory and Language, 40,* 230–262.

Medin, D. L., Goldstone, R. L., and Gentner, D. (1993). Respects for similarity. *Psychological Review, 100,* 254–278.

Medin, D. L., and Schaffer, M. M. (1978). Context theory of classification learning. *Psychological Review, 85*, 207–238.

Mervis, C. B. (1987). Child basic categories and early lexical development. In U. Neisser (Ed.), *Concepts and conceptual development: Ecological and intellectual factors in categorization* (pp. 201–233). Cambridge: Cambridge University Press.

Roberson, D., Davies, I., and Davidoff, J. (2000). Color categories are not universal: Replications and new evidence from a Stone Age culture. *Journal of Experimental Psychology: General, 129*, 369–398.

Romney, A. K., Weller, S. C., and Batchelder, W. H. (1986). Culture as consensus: A theory of culture and informant accuracy. *American Anthropologist, 88*, 313–338.

Rosch, E., and Mervis, C. B. (1975). Family resemblances: Studies in the internal structure of categories. *Cognitive Psychology, 7*, 573–605.

Slobin, D. (1996a). From "thought and language" to "thinking for speaking." In J. J. Gumperz and S. C. Levinson (Eds.), *Rethinking linguistic relativity* (pp. 70–96). Cambridge: Cambridge University Press.

Slobin, D. (1996b). Two ways to travel: Verbs of motion in English and Spanish. In M. Shibatani and S. Thompson (Eds.), *Grammatical constructions: Their form and meaning* (pp. 195–219). Oxford: Clarendon Press.

Sloman, S. A., Malt, B. C., and Fridman, A. (2001). Categorization versus similarity: The case of container names. In U. Hahn and M. Ramscar (Eds.), *Similarity and categorization* (pp. 73–86). Oxford: Oxford University Press.

Talmy, L. (1985). Lexicalization patterns: Semantic structure in lexical forms. In T. Shopen (Ed.), *Language typology and syntactic description: Vol. 3. Grammatical categories and the lexicon* (pp. 57–149). Cambridge: Cambridge University Press.

Todd, J. T. (1983). Perception of gait. *Journal of Experimental Psychology: Human Perception and Performance, 9*, 31–42.

# 6

## The Effects of Spatial Language on Spatial Representation: Setting Some Boundaries

Edward Munnich and Barbara Landau

### 6.1 Introduction

When people say that language and thought are intimately related, they are right. At bottom, the meanings that are expressed by languages must in some way reflect conceptual entities and relationships that are important in human cognition. Foundational concepts—such as space—allow us to talk about the world around us and our experiences in it, and spatial language must have evolved so that we can do so. In this sense, spatial language must *reflect* aspects of our spatial knowledge, following its skeletal structure. Perhaps more controversial is the question of what effect language has on thought. Language is a powerful representational medium that is acquired early in life and, indeed, is the major medium by which we communicate our knowledge to others. However, many have further speculated that the power of language may go beyond mere communication of knowledge: it might actually change the way we think, either by allowing only certain concepts to be expressed or, more extremely, by modulating the form and/or content of our knowledge. The latter hypothesis is consistent with the conclusion reached by Benjamin Lee Whorf (1956), who suggested that because of the intimate relationship between language and thought, speakers of different languages would have different ways of conceptualizing the world (see Lee 1996). In this chapter, we will be considering the hypothesis that language affects thought in the context of one domain: spatial knowledge. Applied to this domain, the hypothesis predicts that learning how one's language encodes space should permanently alter the nature of one's spatial thought. More specifically, we will consider the hypothesis that the

*or disused?*

foundational *nonlinguistic* spatial representations upon which the language of space stand will be permanently changed.

The idea that such linguistic experience might cause reorganization of nonlinguistic spatial knowledge has recently taken on new prominence in the face of discoveries that languages vary quite widely in how they encode space (Bowerman 1996; Levinson 1996; Lucy 1992). For example, the English word *on* encodes a relationship that is encoded by two separate words in German (and other languages): German *an* refers to instances of support involving attachment, such as "the painting ON the wall" or "the tab ON the soda can," whereas *auf* refers to support that can occur without attachment, as in "the cup ON the table." English (among other languages) does not draw this particular distinction in its inventory of basic spatial terms; hence, English differs from German in the way these particular spatial relations are lexically encoded.

In other cases, English makes distinctions not found in the basic spatial lexicon of other languages. For example, English obligatorily distinguishes between relationships in which one object is "on" another and relationships in which one object is "above" the other. However, both of these relationships can be encoded by the single term *ue* (*-ni*) (literally, 'top (-locative)') in Japanese. Finally, there are cases where the spatial distinctions that are made in English appear to be orthogonal to the distinctions made by other languages. Bowerman and Choi (1994) point out that the Korean verb *kkita* translates roughly as English *put on*, but only in the sense of putting a cap on a pen and other "tight-fit" relationships. English also uses *put on* to encode "loose-fit" relationships such as putting a book on a table or a blanket on a bed, but here Korean must use a separate verb, *ppusta*. While the meaning of *kkita* can be expressed paraphrastically in English, there is no single morpheme in English that captures all of and only its meaning. Thus, what appears to be an unquestionably natural encoding to English speakers may be relatively unnatural in the lexicon of another language, and vice versa. For some theorists, such widespread variation has called into question the nature (or even existence) of spatial semantic universals and has suggested instead that the character of one's native spatial language may shape the character of one's nonlinguistic spatial representations.

The hypothesis that learning a particular language causes changes in *nonlinguistic* spatial cognitive structures is a strong one, as it makes claims both about the role of language in the development of spatial cognition and about the malleability of nonlinguistic spatial representations. But it is a claim that has proven difficult to test. One reason is that the most general form of the hypothesis—that spatial language changes spatial cognition—is simply too general to be testable. Clearly, we must define what we mean by "language," what we mean by "spatial cognition," and what qualifies as "change," before we attempt to discover whether differences in language play a role in shaping thought. To the extent that different investigators have conceptualized these notions differently, studies of whether language changes thought are the equivalent of the three blind men exploring different parts of an elephant. The highly charged nature of exchanges in this literature may be caused, in part, because of different implicit conceptualizations of what "counts" as an effect of language on thought.

In this chapter, we will limit our discussion to the effects that learning a native language may have on the structure of one's nonlinguistic representation of space. Crosslinguistic differences in spatial coding are substantial enough that they could plausibly cause changes in spatial thought: for the native speaker, these differences are engaged over the long term, every time a speaker uses some aspect of spatial language. Although it is possible to examine effects within a single language, we believe that some of the strongest tests of the "language changes thought" hypothesis should be found in crosslinguistic studies that compare the spatial representations of individuals who have spent a lifetime speaking different languages. Simply put, if one's native language encodes distinction A but not distinction B, then engaging that distinction over and over again as one talks about space should ultimately allow the encoding of distinction A but not B when one engages in *nonlinguistic* tasks as well.

We hope to shed light on the effects of linguistic experience by comparing and contrasting two different kinds of effects. The first is the effect of linguistic experience on the organization of *linguistic* representations. Abundant evidence shows powerful effects of this kind. Learning a native language results in significant reorganization of the speaker's phonological, syntactic, and semantic representations. These effects are deep, permanent, and hard to undo later in development. They clearly demonstrate that one system of knowledge—linguistic representation—is modulated by the experience of learning one's native language. The second kind of effect we will consider is the effect of learning a language on the organization of *nonlinguistic* representations. This kind of effect is most likely the one that people have in mind when they speak of effects of language on "thought." However, the evidence here is decidedly mixed, in part because of the absence of precise definitions of what aspects of nonlinguistic thought could or should be affected by linguistic experience. To take an extreme example, it is unlikely that anyone would argue that crosslinguistic differences in the color lexicon should lead to differences in the absorption spectra of the rods and cones. But where *should* the effects take place? Should they occur in direct perceptual matching of colors, in memory for colors over a period of minutes, days, or weeks, in communication to others about colors, or what?

In this second arena, where researchers have sought effects on nonlinguistic representations, we will review evidence that is largely negative. There are now several clear and compelling cases showing the *absence* of effects of learning a native language on modulating nonlinguistic knowledge. These cases have the advantage that the nonlinguistic effects are carefully operationalized, so that, with these negative findings, we can gain a solid sense of what kinds of capacities are left unaffected by having learned different languages. Such cases allow us to explore the boundaries of the kinds of positive effects one might expect, and they thereby shed light on the general issue of where we might expect language to cause changes in nonlinguistic cognitive systems.

Our chapter is organized as follows. First, we present evidence that linguistic experience causes changes in linguistic organization. This evidence consists of well-documented cases in which crosslinguistic differences have been shown to shape young children's linguistic representations during an early period of learning. These changes appear to occur during particular time periods in development ("sensitive periods") and are remarkably hard to "undo" in adulthood. We offer these as clear examples of reorganizational effects, and we use several of their characteristics as indices of significant change. Next, we present evidence that linguistic experience does *not* cause changes in *nonlinguistic* organization. The cases we consider include the widely studied domain of color, as well as a number of other cases that fall broadly within the domain of spatial language and spatial cognition. These include (1) memory for names for spatial locations compared with nonlinguistic memory for the same spatial locations, (2) object naming compared with nonlinguistic judgments of object similarity, and (3) the language of motion events compared with nonlinguistic judgments of similarity among motion events. Finally, we consider several cases in which investigators have concluded that linguistic experience *does* affect cognition. After careful consideration, we conclude that the effects reported in these studies are relatively shallow and may not in fact reflect changes in nonlinguistic representations. In other words, these findings may be the exceptions that prove the rule: when a task directly involves language, its solution is bound to be affected by linguistic experience.

## 6.2   Linguistic Experience Causes Reorganization of Linguistic Representations

It is obvious that language learning involves the acquisition of distinctions that are specific to the native language. What is less obvious is the nature of the mechanisms that underlie this change. Because infants must be prepared to learn any language, they must be capable of learning any distinction that is encoded in any of the at least 5,000 human languages. At the same time, because they typically learn just one language at a time, children must either permanently discard or learn to ignore the distinctions that are irrelevant to their language. These basic facts have allowed researchers to ask about the timeline within which children learn their native language distinctions and the mechanisms of this learning— in particular, whether the distinctions that are irrelevant to their native language are lost to them forever.

### 6.2.1   Spatial Semantics
One striking source of evidence for change in linguistic representations is the domain of spatial language. It has long been assumed that spatial

language is rooted in spatial concepts that are shared universally by humans. Indeed, there are substantial similarities in the stock of spatial terms that crop up across languages (Talmy 1983; Landau and Jackendoff 1993). Because universal spatial concepts are thought to serve as the foundation for spatial language, it is further assumed that children's first spatial words map onto the spatial concepts they have already acquired. From this perspective, the same spatial concepts should be expressed by children regardless of the cultural or linguistic environment in which they are raised.

However, recent research has also uncovered a surprising degree of crosslinguistic diversity in the semantics of spatial terms. And this diversity is subtle: although it seems intuitively obvious that a spatial relationship of, say, "containment" should be expressed by all languages in their basic lexicon, there is substantial variation in the way languages do encode even such a fundamental relationship.

Bowerman (1996) has described some of this variation, as illustrated in figure 6.1. As one example, English uses the preposition *in* to denote the relationship of "an apple IN a bowl" but uses *on* to refer to the relationship of "a cup ON a table" or "a door ON a cupboard." In contrast, other languages show very different groupings of the same physical spatial relationships: Spanish uses a single preposition (*en*) for all three relationships, while Dutch has three separate prepositions (*op*, *aan*, and *in*, respectively) for the three senses. This example highlights the fact that the crosslinguistic differences occur because the concepts underlying a single term in a language can be quite different from each other. These differences can be quite subtle, as evidenced by the difficulty that we have in capturing the "meaning" of a term such as *on* or *in* in English. Although we might want to claim that the meaning of *on* is 'gravitational support' (as in the the relationship of "a cup ON a table"), the term can be used in contexts where gravity is irrelevant to the relationship (e.g., "a fly ON the ceiling"). Attempts to capture the meanings of individual spatial terms in English have historically encountered such difficulties, and the meanings of even simple spatial terms have remained elusive (Bennett 1975; Clark 1973; Herskovits 1986; Lakoff 1987).

Even broader differences exist between Korean and English. Bowerman and Choi (1994) have shown that verbs of joining and separating in

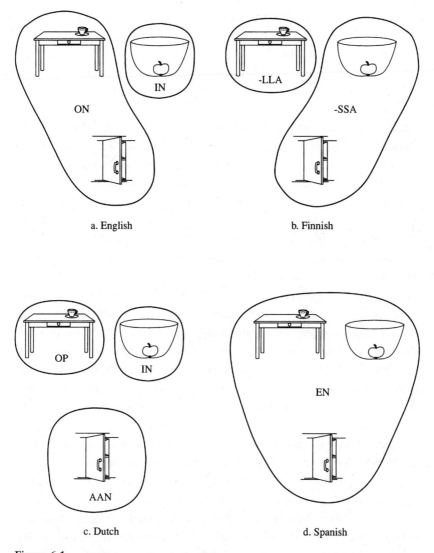

**Figure 6.1**
Different languages express the same spatial relationships quite differently. (From Bowerman 1996.)

Korean are organized in part by a property that is not encoded as a distinction between spatial prepositions: "tightness of fit." For example, one can use the same verb (*kkita*, roughly 'to fit tightly') for putting a piece INTO a puzzle and for putting the top ON a pen. This verb contrasts with a different one that describes other containment events such as putting cars INTO a box (*nehta*, roughly 'to put loosely in or around'). The distinction based on tightness of fit thus crosscuts the distinction between containment (*in*) and support (*on*) made in English. Again, the crosslinguistic differences reflect the fact that each language selects a slightly different set of distinctions that it considers mandatory in the encoding of spatial relationships.

Given such crosslinguistic differences, Bowerman and Choi (1994) have raised the important question of how and when children learn the distinctions pertinent to their native language. If universals in nonlinguistic spatial cognition serve as the principal guides for the acquisition of spatial language, then one might expect that the same meanings would be expressed early in language learning, despite differences in the target native language. For example, all children might first express the category of "containment" relationships with a single term and make the same kinds of distinctions between this type of relationship and others. Alternatively, if learning spatial language is not principally guided by a single group of universal nonlinguistic spatial concepts, one might predict that children's earliest expressed spatial meanings would vary in accordance with the target language being learned and that even quite subtle distinctions would be learned early in development.

Bowerman and Choi (1994) evaluated these possibilities by examining young children's production of spatial terms when they were invited to talk about relationships brought about by the actions of separating and joining objects. They examined the production of 18- to 24-month-old children who were growing up in Dutch-, Korean-, and English-speaking families, as well as adult native speakers of these languages. Their results showed that, by the age of 24 months, children's patterns of production strongly reflected the distinctions made by adults. For example, children learning English used the verb-preposition complex *put on* to describe events in which a person dons a hat, shirt, or shoe. In contrast, children learning Korean distinguished among these different events, by using a different verb depending on which piece of clothing was donned. This evidence strongly supports the idea that children acquire the semantic distinctions pertinent to their language during an early period of language learning. At the same time, all children's productions—regardless of the language being learned—respected certain coarse cut lines. For example, no child used a single verb to express both a relationship involving joining and one involving separation of objects or surfaces. This suggests that children approach the acquisition of spatial terms with some fundamental predispositions—such as the tendency to avoid collapsing two relationships that are direct spatial opposites of each other. Finally, Bowerman and Choi mentioned intriguing evidence that suggests a particular mechanism by which different spatial-semantic concepts might be formed from early experience. The Dutch word *uit* means 'out' and is commonly used in contexts similar to those where English speakers use *out*—for example, to express the relationship "to take something OUT of a container." Dutch, however, also uses *uit* in the context of removing one's shoes (and other articles of clothing): for example, *trek je jas/schoen UIT* 'take your coat/shoe OUT'. When adult native Dutch speakers are asked why they use *uit* in this context, they are often surprised and cannot make the connection between this usage and the predominant use of *uit* in the language, suggesting that *uit* may be a homonym in Dutch, with two separate meanings. Dutch children, however, see no problem in using *uit* for removing clothing, taking objects out of containers, and a host of actions intermediate to these two. Their generalization of *uit*, therefore, is very broad. In fact, it is much broader than the corresponding pattern for *out* among children learning English, where a contrast is made between taking things *out of* containers but taking clothes *off* the body. Bowerman and Choi suggest that it might be the use of a single term *uit* in broadly different contexts that leads children to assume that generalization should be quite broad, in a sense "filling in" the intermediate space by inference (for discussion and additional supporting evidence, see Landau and Shipley 2001).

The lesson from Bowerman and Choi's work is that subtle semantic categories are formed very early in language learning. These categories do not map transparently onto categories derivable from perceptual or motor experience (though see Mandler 1996 for another view). Rather, they appear to depend on both initial predispositions about the organization of lexical categories (e.g., do not collapse directly opposing spatial relationships) and specific evidence gleaned from hearing adult uses. What Bowerman and Choi show, then, is that linguistic categories—in this case, spatial semantic categories—are learned early in life, and that learning depends on experience that is specifically linguistic. What the results do not tell us, however, is whether these newly learned lexical categories were constructed from nonlinguistic spatial categories (cognitive, perceptual, or sensorimotor) and whether the acquisition of the former categories somehow changes the organization of the latter. Because Bowerman and Choi did not compare children's linguistic productions with their performance on nonlinguistic tasks, these findings do not address the question of whether the acquisition of spatial language changes spatial thought.[1]

### 6.2.2  Phonology

A somewhat different—and perhaps more instructive—case involves phonology. The physical sound stream can be processed at a number of levels, including the acoustic, phonetic, and phonemic levels. Each language selects from a universal inventory of phonetic contrasts those that will be phonemic—that is, relevant to the meanings of the words in that particular language. Because infants must be capable of learning any human language, it stands to reason that their brains would be sensitive to all possible distinctions. Indeed, it appears that infants go through a stage of being "universal listeners": regardless of their own native language, they are capable of distinguishing a wide range (perhaps all) of the consonants that occur in the world's languages (e.g., Aslin et al. 1981; Best, McRoberts, and Sithole 1988; Streeter 1976; Trehub 1976; Tsushima et al. 1994; Werker et al. 1981; Werker and Lalonde 1988; Werker and Tees 1984).

An example of this early universality is that Werker and Tees (1984) —using a conditioned head-turn paradigm—found that 6- to 8- month-olds from English-speaking environments were sensitive to a change between a dental /t/ and a retroflex /t/, which is a phonemic contrast in Hindi but not in English. That is, infants were able to distinguish phonemes that occur in a language they had never heard and that their parents could not distinguish. Within the next few months, however, a significant reorganization takes place in infants' capacity to discriminate among syllables that are phonemically different in their native language (Werker 1995). By 10–12 months, infants show the capacity to discriminate syllables containing phonemic contrasts in their native language, but no longer those of other languages. The same English-learning infant who could, at 6–8 months, discriminate between dental and retroflex /t/'s can no longer do so. This language-specific pattern remains in place throughout life.

Given the compelling nature of this change in discriminative capacity, one can ask whether it affects nonlinguistic processing: does linguistic experience change the way the mind processes acoustic stimuli in nonlinguistic modes as well? In an early interpretation of the infancy findings, Tees and Werker (1984) suggested that the capacity to discriminate nonnative phonemic contrasts declines within the first year of life and, at that point, is permanently lost. This interpretation was consistent with two kinds of evidence. First, infants appear to lose the capacity to make nonnative phonemic distinctions. Second, adults find it difficult or impossible to discriminate among syllables embodying nonnative phonemic contrasts. Loss of such discriminative capacity would certainly be consistent with the idea that linguistic experience has deep and permanent effects on nonlinguistic representation.

The hypothesis of permanent loss was soon rejected, however. Several groups have discovered that there are circumstances under which adults can discriminate phonetic contrasts that do not map onto phonemic contrasts in their native language. In one experiment, Werker and Logan (1985) tested the capacity of adult English speakers to discriminate between syllables that included contrasts that are not phonemic in English. They found that when tokens of two contrasting nonnative phonemes were presented with interstimulus intervals (ISI) of 500 ms or less, adults were able to discriminate them as well as they discriminated English phoneme contrasts. However, when ISIs were extended to 1500 ms, participants could only discriminate English phonemic contrasts; they could no longer discriminate the nonnative contrasts. This suggested that there are at least two different modes of processing the same stimulus. With shorter ISIs, people might be processing in an "acoustic" or "phonetic" mode, which need not engage only phonemic contrasts. But with longer ISIs, they might be processing in a linguistic mode, which mandatorily engages phonemic contrasts.

Best, McRoberts, and Sithole (1988) have provided additional evidence that the ability to distinguish sounds outside of linguistic contexts remains intact, despite loss of the ability to distinguish nonnative phonemes. In particular, adults are able to discriminate contrasts that are not phonemic in their native language, provided that the contrasts lie well outside their native language's phonemic system. These researchers found, for example, that adult English speakers could discriminate different types of clicks, which provide a phonemic contrast in Zulu but not in English. This suggests that it is the competition between native and nonnative phonemic contrasts that causes difficulty in distinguishing nonnative phonemes. Absent competition—that is, for those nonnative phonemes that are unlike any native phonemes—underlying acoustic information can still be recruited in making a distinction.

From this body of research, we can conclude that linguistic experience reorganizes one's representation of sounds for the purposes of language processing, but this experience does not lead to permanent loss of the capacity to process nonnative contrasts. That is, linguistic experience changes the mental representations serving language, but not those serving nonlinguistic domains. As with the spatial semantic domain, it is clear that native distinctions are acquired quite early in life, as the child learns his or her native language. The evidence from phonology also clearly indicates that our capacity to discriminate acoustic and phonetic contrasts in a *nonlinguistic* mode remains despite the effects of profound *linguistic* reorganization.

## 6.3   Linguistic Experience Does *Not* Cause Reorganization of Nonlinguistic Representations

Perhaps an area such as acoustic processing is not a domain in which we should expect an effect of language on nonlinguistic representation: one could argue that only areas of "higher" cognition should be affected. We therefore now turn to several areas that provide excellent test cases for the proposition that language changes the nature of people's nonlinguistic representations. In each case, people's crosslinguistic differences in language tasks have been compared to their performance in nonlinguistic tasks. The question is whether differences observed in the language tasks are reflected by isomorphic differences in the nonlinguistic tasks. We begin with the classical studies of color naming and color memory by [Rosch] Heider and Olivier (1972), which set the standard in searching for the effects of language on thought. We then consider several different cases that echo the basically negative outcomes documented in Heider and Olivier's studies.

### 6.3.1 Color

One of the staples of anthropological-linguistic research is the domain of color. Crosslinguistic variation in the distribution of color terms across the dimensions of hue, saturation, and brightness was first systematically documented by Berlin and Kay (1969), and this analysis remains the standard to which most investigators refer. Berlin and Kay observed that the number of "basic" color terms varies over languages from approximately 2 to 12, with English at the upper end, having 11 terms. From a Whorfian perspective, the discovery of such crosslinguistic variation raised the intriguing question of whether long-lived differences in the range of color terms of a native language could eventually lead to differences in nonlinguistic processes governing the perception of color.

Heider and Olivier (1972) set out to test this hypothesis by comparing patterns of naming color chips with patterns of memory for the same color chips, among people who were native speakers of two radically different languages: English-speaking Americans, who have 11 basic color terms, and the Dani of Irian Jaya (Indonesian New Guinea), who have only 2. Heider and Olivier argued that one could determine whether linguistic differences had an impact on nonlinguistic representations only by creating the right experimental test. Their linguistic measure would be the distribution of naming across a wide range of color chips, varying in hue and brightness, all at low saturation, avoiding the highly saturated hues that serve as universal focal areas for colors. Their "nonlinguistic" measure would be one in which participants would view a color patch, and then, after a 30-second unfilled interval, pick that same patch from an array containing highly similar colors from the initial array. Heider and Olivier were careful to point out that they did not know, in advance, whether verbal and/or visual coding would be used in this task. They pointed out that both were available, in principle, though they hoped that the task would be sufficiently difficult that there would be errors in memory. The critical measure would be a comparison of the language and the memory data, in order to determine "whether the verbal code would interact with the visual to influence the nature of memory errors" (p. 339).

It did not. Heider and Olivier found, first, that the distribution of *names* across the color space varied just as predicted by the anthropological studies. That is, English speakers used roughly 11 basic terms to divide up the color space, and Dani speakers used 2 terms, dividing the same space in quite a different manner. But the comparison of memory results for the two language groups did not differ: both groups showed virtually identical patterns of confusion in memory between adjacent colors, unaffected by the presence (for the English speakers) or absence (for the Dani speakers) of linguistically marked boundaries.

In their discussion of the results, Heider and Olivier point out that it would have been quite possible for the visual memory to be biased by the verbal code, resulting in memory differences across the language groups. In fact, this was the pattern they predicted:

Such interaction could have resulted from various mechanisms: Since the visual image appears more "labile" than the verbal item, the verbal code might have become a fixed reference point for the image; that is, as the memory image faded or changed over time, it might have changed along lines "laid down" by the concurrent verbal code. Or the verbal code might have set limits for imagery changes; for example, an image tagged "mola" by a Dani S might have shifted in any direction so long as it remained within the color space recognized as "mola" by that S. Or the verbal code might have caused a "bias" at the point of response only. By any of these mechanisms, colors which were closer to each other in the name structure should have been more often confused with each other in recognition.... We did not find such an effect. (pp. 351–352)

They conclude, "Descriptively, we can say that 'mental' visual images, at least of colors, like 'perception itself' (Gibson 1967), do not appear easily changed by language" (p. 352).

Recently, Heider and Olivier's findings have been disputed, in a modified replication and extension of their study by Roberson, Davies, and Davidoff (2000). We disagree with Roberson, Davies, and David-off's interpretation of their results and believe that they are not necessarily incompatible with Heider and Olivier's conclusions. We discuss our objections in detail in section 6.4. For now, we rest with Heider and Olivier's conclusion that the representation of color in memory, for the purposes of later recognition, is not easily changed by substantial variation in the structure of the color lexicon.

### 6.3.2   Spatial Location

The recent renewal of interest in language and thought can be traced, in part, to the discovery of striking crosslinguistic differences in the domain of space—a domain long viewed as a primary example of the importance of nonlinguistic cognitive universals in structuring language (see, e.g., Clark 1973). However, as we have discussed, recent discoveries of substantial crosslinguistic differences in spatial language have led to speculation that, rather than cognition shaping language, the forces might actually work in the opposite direction: differences in one's native spatial language could shape one's nonlinguistic representations.

Munnich, Landau, and Dosher (2001) sought to test this hypothesis by examining two prongs of the debate. On the one hand, the strong evidence for universals in spatial language (Talmy 1983; Landau and Jackendoff 1993) suggests that there should be structural parallels between spatial terms and their nonlinguistic encoding. To the extent that all languages engage a universal system of spatial cognition, we should observe common structures in spatial terms and memory for location, both within a language and across languages. On the other hand, the strong evidence for crosslinguistic differences in the encoding of space raises the possibility that some aspects of spatial memory might be shaped by lifelong engagement of certain spatial distinctions in one's native language. As Heider and Olivier argued, perhaps as the visual image fades (within a very short period of time, we now know), the encoding of location might become "anchored" or "biased" or even straightforwardly translated into a verbal code, which would then change the content of the memory.

Munnich, Landau, and Dosher were fortunate that part of the work had already been done for them. Hayward and Tarr (1995) had conjectured that spatial language and spatial memory might share some aspects of spatial structure. They tested this idea by engaging adult speakers of English in a naming task and a memory task. Both tasks used the same stimuli, in which a target figure (a circle) was presented in one of 48 locations around a reference object (a computer). In the naming task, participants were asked to fill in a blank to complete the sentence that described the spatial relationship between figure and reference object (e.g., "The circle is ____ the computer"). In the memory task, participants were briefly presented with an array containing the target figure and reference object. Next, they saw a visual mask. Finally, a test array appeared in which the relationship between figure and reference object was either the same as the original, or different—in which case the figure object was translated by small amounts.

Hayward and Tarr's results showed remarkable parallels in spatial structure between the naming and memory tasks. In the naming task, speakers produced basic spatial terms (such as *above, below, left,* and *right*) most often when the figure object was located along one of the four principal axes extending from the reference object. Use of these terms declined as the figure object was located farther from these axes. In the memory task, Hayward and Tarr found that participants' memory for location of the figure object was best when it lay along one of these same axes, suggesting that the principal axes organized both language and memory (but see Crawford, Regier, and Huttenlocher 2000 for a different interpretation).

These results suggest a homology between spatial language and spatial cognition, at least in the case of native English speakers. From this evidence, however, it is impossible to infer a causal sequence: nonlinguistic spatial structures could serve as the support upon which spatial language is built; alternatively, learning spatial language (which appears to respect such axial structure) could have shaped the nature of memory. The causal sequence requires an experimental design analogous to that used by Heider and Olivier—one in which native speakers of different languages are tested in both naming and memory, and the patterns of performance are compared. Munnich, Landau, and Dosher (2001) carried out just such experiments.

Their first experiment was designed as a semireplication of Hayward and Tarr's study, incorporating the requirement of a crosslinguistic comparison. Native adult speakers of English and Japanese were tested in either a naming task or a memory task. English and Japanese were chosen because they share substantial aspects of spatial terminology, but also differ in significant ways. For example, English, Japanese, and Korean have terms that are the equivalent of English *above*, *below*, *left*, and *right*, and one might conjecture that these terms should show roughly the same spatial distribution. If the homology uncovered by Hayward and Tarr applies universally, then one might predict further that the same spatial structures would show up across language groups in *both* the naming and memory tasks. At the same time, English distinguishes between contact and noncontact relationships along these axes, whereas Japanese and Korean do not. As shown in figure 6.2, English obligatorily contrasts *on* with *above*, but the basic spatial terms of Japanese and Korean do not make this contact/noncontact distinction. If these crosslinguistic differences change the structure of nonlinguistic memory, then one would predict that a contact/noncontact distinction

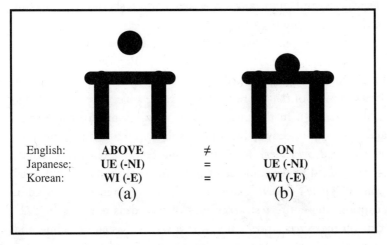

**Figure 6.2**
English displays an obligatory contrast between relationships expressed by *above* and *on*, as shown. However, Japanese and Korean do not display such an obligatory contrast in their basic spatial terms.

**Figure 6.3**
The basic stimuli used by Munnich, Landau, and Dosher (2001) consisted of a target figure (a circle) presented in one of 72 locations around a square reference object. English and Japanese speakers were asked to either *name* the target figure's location or *remember* its location for a later test.

would show up in the naming task for English but not Japanese or Korean speakers, and—crucially—the same pattern should occur for the two groups in the memory task.

Stimuli were closely modeled after those of Hayward and Tarr; an example is shown in figure 6.3. In the naming task, English- and Japanese-speaking participants were asked to fill in a sentence describing the spatial relationship of the figure to the reference object (i.e., "The circle is _____ the square"). In the memory task, participants from the same language groups were shown the target display, which was presented for 500 ms, followed by a mask for 500 ms, and finally a test array, which participants judged as the same as or different from the first. The visual mask was designed to prevent low-level visual persistence. As an additional caution, the entire test array was displaced as a whole by 1/2″ (1.27 cm) on the screen, preventing any low-level visual encoding and ensuring that the task would have to be solved using memory.

In the naming task, both language groups showed the predicted dense use of basic spatial terms along the principal axes of the reference object.

Both language groups also showed similar axial structure in the memory task, confirming the prediction that language and memory share a universal base. The results of the two tasks were not identical, however. For example, the naming task showed quite sharp, categorical use of the basic terms: the terms were used most densely along the principal axes of the reference object, but fell off quickly just outside these axes. The categorical nature of the basic spatial terms was also shown in the dense distribution of the terms all along the axes, with no effect of distance from the reference object (at least with the stimuli used). In contrast, the memory task showed a more *graded* advantage for locations along the axes, with the highest accuracy along the axes and a smooth decline as the figure object was located farther away from the axes. In addition, there was a hint of an advantage in locations that were aligned with the reference object's edges, suggesting that axial structure might not be the only organizing factor in the memory task. Further, the graded structure of memory was shown in effects of distance from the reference object: locations closer to the reference object were remembered more accurately than locations farther away from it.

What did not show up in this first experiment was the anticipated difference between English and Japanese terms distinguishing between contact and noncontact. This was probably due to the two-dimensional planar appearance of the stimuli: even many English-speaking participants avoided the term *on* and used *above* for locations that were in contact with the upper edge of the reference object. In order to better test for this critical distinction, Munnich, Landau, and Dosher carried out a second experiment, using illustrations of balls, tables, and other real objects whose possible force-dynamic relationships with the reference object would be absolutely clear (see figure 6.4). In this experiment, Munnich, Landau, and Dosher tested adults whose native language was either English or Korean. As is the case in Japanese, the Korean basic lexicon does not distinguish obligatorily between relationships of contact and noncontact along the reference object's axial extensions. Observing arrays such as a ball ON a table as opposed to a ball ABOVE a table would surely elicit the lexical distinction among English speakers, but not Korean speakers. The key question was whether this linguistic difference

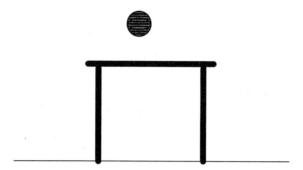

**Figure 6.4**
Munnich, Landau, and Dosher (2001) used pictures of balls, tables, and other real objects to suggest possible force-dynamic relationships that could engage the *on/above* distinction in English.

—if it emerged—would be correlated with parallel differences in the memory task.

As predicted, the results of the naming task revealed clear distinctions between the distributions of basic lexical items used by English and Korean speakers. All English speakers consistently invoked the *on/above* distinction (figure 6.5(a)). In contrast, only half of the Korean speakers (5 out of 10) ever mentioned contact in their descriptions of scenes that portrayed contact. In addition, those who used contact terms did so only occasionally. That is, the contact/noncontact distinction is not carried by the basic lexicon: although it can, of course, be encoded by Korean, it is not mandatory. In contrast, the distinction is mandatory in English: it would be ungrammatical to use the term *above* for a ball located ON a table, or the term *on* for a ball floating in the air ABOVE a table.

What, then, of the memory task? The results revealed that the contact/noncontact distinction was equally important for both language groups. The two groups did not differ in memorial accuracy for any of the test locations (figure 6.5(b)), showing that, whether the linguistic distinction is made or not made on a regular basis over a lifetime of use, the structure of memory remains the same. The results echo those of Heider and Olivier (1972) in the domain of color. The representation of location in memory is not affected by differences in the contrasts made by different languages, even if they are engaged over an entire lifetime.

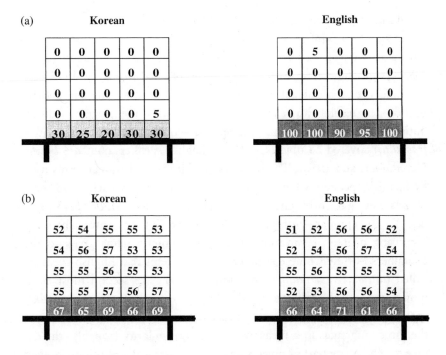

**Figure 6.5**
Results from Munnich, Landau, and Dosher's (2001) experiment 2: (*a*) the naming task, measuring percentage of responses in which contact terms were used, and (*b*) the memory task, measuring percentage correct. The reference object (table) is drawn at the bottom of each set of results, and percentages are given for each location in which the target figure object appeared.

### 6.3.3 Objects

A third case has recently been reported for the domain of objects. Like color and spatial location, the domain of objects would intuitively appear to be one in which universal aspects of perception and cognition collaborate to serve up "natural" categories, such as classes of artifacts, natural kinds, and subsets of these. Lexical items in different languages might then be mapped onto these natural categories, yielding great similarity across languages and cultures in the kinds of things that deserve to be named. Indeed, there is strong evidence for universals in naming.

However, there are also surprising and subtle differences, even in the domain of artifacts. Malt et al. (1999; see also Malt, Sloman, and

Gennari, this volume) examined one type of artifact—containers—and found significant differences in the distribution of names across individual items. Malt et al. carried out a naming task in which adult native speakers of Chinese, Spanish, and English provided words for 60 diverse containers (e.g., a one-gallon milk jug, a peanut butter jar, and a baby bottle). The results showed surprising variation in the range and distribution of names. For example, the Spanish word *frasco* (or its diminutive *frasquito*) covered 28 objects; of these, English speakers named 6 *bottle*, 3 *container*, and 19 *jar*. The second and third most frequent terms used by Spanish speakers were *envase* and *bidon* (6 objects each), and these objects were named by English speakers as *container* (6), *bottle* (3), and *jug* (3). The comparison between Chinese and English showed the same surprising degree of variation. The most common name given to the containers (40) by Chinese speakers spanned items that English speakers called *bottle* (13), *container* (8), and *jar* (19). The second most common name used by Chinese speakers (10) spanned objects that English speakers called *container* (3), *bottle* (2), and *can* (5). Correlations among the three languages in a measure of naming similarity (roughly, the degree to which any pair of objects have similar name distributions) ranged from .35 to .55. The presence of these positive but relatively modest correlations indicates some similarity in the distribution of names. However, the correlation across languages is clearly far from perfect—as predicted by the authors' informal analyses of everyday usage of different container names across the three languages. The absence of strong positive correlations indicates that there is substantial crosslinguistic variation in the distribution of names across the same exemplars of common containers.

What is the relationship between these differences in naming and people's nonlinguistic representations of these objects? Malt et al. next carried out sorting tasks to test whether crosslinguistic differences observed in naming would be reflected in a nonlinguistic context. That is, they asked whether the different groups of native speakers would sort the same objects according to the boundaries of their linguistic categories. If so, one would expect similarity between the results of the naming and sorting tasks *within* each language group, and differences in the structures obtained from both types of task *between* the language groups.

Malt et al. asked participants to sort on three different criteria. People were instructed to carry out a physical sort based on the "physical qualities of each container; that is, what it looks like, what it's made of, and so on." They were also instructed to carry out a functional sort based on the "function or use of each container, that is, how it contains the substance that is in it (in a stack; in separate pieces, as a single solid; as a liquid; with pouring capability, etc.)." Finally, people were instructed to carry out an overall sort based on "the overall qualities of each container ... focus[ing] on any feature of the container including what it looks like, what it's made of, how it contains the substance that is in it ... or any other aspect of the container that seems important or natural" (p. 240).

Analyses of the sorting data—using methods parallel to those used for the naming data—revealed substantial similarity across language groups in the judged similarity of the objects, whether the sort was done on the basis of physical, functional, or overall similarity. Sorts based on overall similarity resulted in correlations ranging from .91 to .94 across the three groups of speakers, sorts based on physical similarity resulted in correlations ranging from .82 to .89, and sorts based on functional similarity resulted in correlations ranging from .55 to .79. These correlations are all substantially higher than those emerging from the naming data, and they indicate that the nonlinguistic sorting instructions engaged a different kind of similarity metric from that used in the naming task. Whatever the nature of this similarity metric, it clearly was shared across groups of speakers who named the objects quite differently from each other.

In a final set of analyses, Malt et al. carried out multidimensional scaling analyses for each set of results, as well as correlations across the analyses, to determine whether the nonlinguistic sorting results were good predictors of the naming results, and whether this held more strongly within a language group than between language groups. The results showed moderate correlations between sorting by overall similarity and naming, and between sorting by physical similarity and naming within language groups. However, as Malt et al. point out, these correlations were far from perfect; in fact, most of the predictive power in these correlations was due to the overall similarity in nonlinguistic sorting across language groups. This indicates that, although there is some relationship between nonlinguistic similarity judgments and naming, the relationship is not one of identity. In other words, naming engages more than judged similarity among objects. Interestingly, the correlations between sorting by functional similarity and naming were overall low to moderate, which is consistent with the idea that function plays only a moderate role in object naming (Landau, Smith, and Jones 1997; Malt and Johnson 1992).

Malt et al.'s findings have obvious relevance to the hypothesis that language shapes thought. By this hypothesis, the substantial differences in how languages carve up the humble domain of containers should have a powerful effect on the organization of this domain in nonlinguistic tasks as well. Yet Malt et al.'s findings indicate that, if anything, the reverse is true: despite significant, long-lived differences in how speakers of English, Spanish, and Chinese name containers, they still appear to share perceived physical similarities among the objects. Thus, as Malt et al. state, "[t]he data do imply that linguistic categories cannot be the only determinant of perceived similarity among these objects. The magnitude of our correlations suggest[s] that linguistic categories are not even the primary determinant of perceived similarity.... [I]f anything,... perception of the similarity among objects remains relatively constant despite wide variation in linguistic category boundaries" (p. 258).

Thus, we see again that, despite striking crosslinguistic differences in the semantic structure of an everyday domain, there is no evidence that language shapes thought.

### 6.3.4   Motion Events

The final case we will present is that of motion events, for which crosslinguistic differences have been amply documented (Berman and Slobin 1994; Talmy 1985, 1991). Talmy was the first to systematically describe these differences as ones in which languages appear to parse motion events somewhat differently. According to his analysis, all languages encode the motion event in terms of certain key components. These include the figure object (often the thing that moves), the motion the figure object undergoes, the path the figure object moves along, and the ground or reference object, which serves as the locational anchor for the figure object. In Talmy's much-cited example *The boat floated into the cave*, the *boat* represents the figure, *float* represents the motion, *into* represents the path, and *the cave* represents the reference object.

As Talmy describes, this parsing in English actually divides the perceived scene into certain components that are, in principle, separable. For example, the verb *float* represents specifically the manner of motion, or the way in which the boat moves into the cave. Although this seems completely natural to English speakers, it is not the only way to parse the event, and different languages actually take advantage of other options. For example, Spanish speakers tend to parse the event into figure and reference objects, as in English, but the complex of motion-manner-path is parsed somewhat differently: Spanish encodes the motion together with the path, with the verb *entrar* 'go into', and leaves the manner to be expressed as a separate word, the adverb *flotando* 'floating'. Talmy reviews the evidence that languages can select among different possible event parsings and concludes that certain components can be conflated, whereas others remain distinct across all languages. The components that are most commonly conflated include motion-manner, motion-path, and motion-figure (examples in English include motion-plus-manner verbs such as *roll, run, float, slide*; motion-plus-path verbs such as *enter, exit, climb*; and motion-plus-figure verbs such as *rain, spit*). As Talmy points out, these linguistic choices appear to be typological tendencies; that is, different languages show different biases for conflating these elements.

The facts about Spanish (and other languages) have led many investigators to ask the natural question whether consistent, long-lived usage of these conflation patterns might change people's representation of motion events. One approach has been to ask whether the hypothesized crosslinguistic differences in conflation patterns are reflected in the way that different speaker communities *linguistically* encode motion events. Do language groups systematically vary in what they emphasize in descriptions of motion events? There is now a variety of evidence showing that they do. When speakers of different languages (such as English and Spanish) observe the same motion events and then describe them, their descriptions—that is, their parsing of the event using language—tends to follow the bias shown by their language as a whole (Berman and Slobin 1994; Billman and Krych 1998; Gennari et al. 2000; Malt, Sloman, and Gennari, this volume). For example, English speakers tend to use manner-of-motion verbs, and they express the path separately in a prepositional phrase, whereas Spanish speakers tend to use verbs that conflate motion and path, and they express the manner of motion separately.

But does this difference in the *linguistic* representation also have the effect of changing *nonlinguistic* representations of motion events? Gennari et al. (2000) investigated this claim by comparing English and Spanish speakers' linguistic descriptions of motion events with their recognition of the same events, as well as their similarity judgments for target and distractor events. All participants were shown short video clips depicting motion events in which the manner of motion and path varied, in order to highlight the differences between English and Spanish. One group was asked to describe the event as they viewed it (describe-first). A second group was neither encouraged to describe nor prevented from describing the event to themselves as they viewed it (free encoding). A third group carried out a shadowing task while they viewed the event, in order to prevent any linguistic encoding while they viewed the event (shadowing). After viewing the events, all participants were given a recognition task, a similarity task, and a description task. In the recognition task, participants were asked to decide which of two motion events was one they actually saw. Targets were mixed with lures that either (1) preserved manner and changed path or (2) preserved path and changed manner. For example, one target was a scene of a man CARRYING a board INTO a room, and the corresponding lures were (1) a man CARRYING a board OUT OF the room (preserving manner changing path) and (2) a man DRAGGING a board INTO a room (changing manner, preserving path). In the similarity task, the target event was shown, followed by two events (presented simultaneously) from which the participant was to judge which was more similar to the target. Again, lures varied whether manner of motion or path was changed. Finally, in the description task, all participants were asked to verbally describe the events.

The comparisons considered by Gennari et al. are instructive, not only for their specificity about what would "count" as an effect of language on thought, but also for their usefulness in examining interactions that might occur between linguistic and nonlinguistic tasks. The results showed, first, the expected crosslinguistic differences in the way speakers linguistically encoded the events: English speakers tended to assign the same verb to actions sharing manner, and Spanish speakers tended to assign the same verb to actions sharing path. Moreover, English speakers tended to mention manner more often than Spanish speakers, and Spanish speakers tended to mention path more often than English speakers. But these strong linguistic differences—expected on the presumption that learning a language changes one's *linguistic* representations—were not reflected in the results of the nonlinguistic tasks. In the recognition task, there were no differences between speaker groups in the tendency to false-alarm to same-path versus same-manner lures. And in the similarity task, there were no differences among speaker groups in the tendency to match manner versus path lures to the target *except* under the describe-first condition. That is, when Spanish speakers were asked to verbally describe the event as the first part of the procedure, they then tended to choose events with the same path as "more similar" to the target event. English speakers showed no bias at all. The other encoding conditions (shadowing, free encoding) showed either no effects at all, or effects that went counter to the patterns predicted if one's native language shapes one's nonlinguistic representations.

Thus, Gennari et al.'s findings join the other negative findings we have reviewed, suggesting that lifelong experience speaking a given language does *not* lead to changes in corresponding nonlinguistic representations. These findings also point out that lifelong experience speaking a language *does* lead to changes in the way that one linguistically encodes events, much as in the domains of color, location, and object. Finally, Gennari et al.'s findings provide insight into the circumstances under which one *might* see effects of native language on performance in a non-linguistic task. When Spanish speakers had already encoded the motion event linguistically, they tended to judge similarity more in terms of path components than did English speakers. This suggests that effects of language might emerge in putatively nonlinguistic tasks *when the participant has encoded the event linguistically.*

We now turn to several findings that suggest positive effects of language on thought. We argue that these tasks fail to rule out linguistic mediation and that their results, therefore, have no bearing on the debate over effects of language on nonlinguistic cognition.

## 6.4    Some Exceptions That Prove the Rule

### 6.4.1    Color

Heider and Olivier's work on color naming and memory provided one of the clearest disconfirmations of the Whorfian hypothesis. However, the generality of the findings has recently been challenged by Roberson, Davies, and Davidoff (2000; Davidoff, Davies, and Roberson 1999), who carried out a replication of Heider's work with a different culture: the Berinmo of Papua New Guinea. Unlike the Dani, whose color lexicon has two basic terms, the Berinmo use five color terms to carve up the spectrum. In both cases, the relatively small number of color terms means that neighboring color categories are collapsed under a single name, and the question is whether this pattern of linguistic usage will affect nonlinguistic measures of memory as well. If naming does affect memory, then color categories in memory should show the same structure as color categories in naming.

The importance of Roberson, Davies, and Davidoff's study is that the Berinmo color lexicon partitions the spectrum differently from both Dani and English. Dani collapses neighboring categories such that one term (corresponding to *warm*) covers the range labeled *yellow, orange,* and *red* in English, and another term (corresponding to *cool*) covers the range labeled *blue* and *green* in English. In other words, the Dani categories form supersets of the English categories. Berinmo partitions the spectrum somewhat differently. For example, the Berinmo term *nol* covers exemplars that span a region encompassing hues called *green* and hues called *blue* in English. The Berinmo term *wor* covers exemplars that span a region encompassing some hues called *green* in English as well as some called *yellow* or *orange.* Therefore, the Berinmo could in principle have nondistinctive color categories that cross the lexically determined boundaries of English. The hypothesis that language affects thought predicts that color memory should follow the cut lines of the language— which differ considerably between English and Berinmo.

Roberson, Davies, and Davidoff measured color naming and color memory among Berinmo and English speakers, using the methods of Heider and Olivier. They report that the fit between Berinmo color naming and Berinmo color memory is better than the fit between Berinmo color memory and English color memory, and thereby conclude that the Berinmo language provides the best predictor of Berinmo memory. They regard this as consistent with the Whorfian hypothesis and inconsistent with the findings of Heider and Olivier.

But their study and analyses are far from conclusive. There are both logical and methodological problems. Carrying out a replication of Heider and Olivier's experiment, Roberson, Davies, and Davidoff asked Berinmo speakers to name color chips (naming task), and they also asked them to remember the color chips for later recognition (memory task); as in Heider and Olivier's memory task, participants viewed a color chip and then waited 30 seconds, after which they were asked to select the same (remembered) color from the total set of 40 color chips. The data were analyzed as in Heider and Olivier's study, by carrying out separate multidimensional scaling solutions for the two tasks: the naming task measured how often the same name was used for different color chips, and the memory task measured the number of times a given chip was remembered as a different chip (i.e., error patterns). These multidimensional scaling solutions were then compared for goodness of fit, which represents the similarity of the two spaces derived from naming and from memory.

The key tests of the Whorfian hypothesis are these. First, if lifelong use of different color lexicons alters nonlinguistic color memory, then one would expect a good fit between naming and memory *within* a single culture—regardless of how the lexicon is structured. This is because the Whorfian hypothesis predicts that color memory should match color naming. On this first measure, Roberson, Davies, and Davidoff report a good fit between Berinmo naming and Berinmo memory (i.e., a low stress value of 0.158), and they also report that this is close to the value found by Heider and Olivier for the Dani data (low stress value of 0.126). According to Heider and Olivier's report, the minimum stress value is 0 (for identical configurations) and the maximum stress value is 0.667 (for completely unrelated configurations). English speakers also showed a relatively good fit between naming and memory tasks: Heider and Olivier had reported a stress value of 0.212, and Roberson, Davies, and Davidoff report a stress value of 0.172. These values indicate that patterns of color naming and color memory are similar within each culture.

The second test concerns the goodness of fit for configurations *across* cultures. Obviously, if the lexicons are quite different but memory is similar, then there would be a better fit for memory between the two cultures than there would be for naming (i.e., the stress value for memory across cultures should be lower than the stress value for naming). Heider and Olivier reported a trend in this direction, with a stress value of 0.194 for a comparison of *naming* configurations of Dani speakers and English speakers, and a stress value of 0.161 for a comparison of *memory* configurations of these groups, supporting the existence of universal color categories for memory despite differences in color categories in language. The analogous values reported by Roberson, Davies, and Davidoff went in the opposite direction: the stress value for naming between Berinmo speakers and English speakers was reported to be significantly *lower* (0.166) than the stress value for memory between the two groups (0.256). Roberson, Davies, and Davidoff argued that this pattern provides evidence for an influence of language on color memory, in accord with the Whorfian hypothesis.

This presents a puzzle. If language shapes memory, memorial structures should be about as similar across languages as are the linguistic structures from which they arose. But then why would these memorial structures be even further apart than the linguistic structures? To account for the additional variation in memory, consider that Berinmo speakers performed worse than English speakers overall on the memory task. One possibility is that Berinmo and English speakers each derive their memorial categories from their linguistic categories, but the Berinmo speakers have generally poorer memory than the English speakers; this would account for the lower overall accuracy of Berinmo speakers and contribute to the variation between the two groups in the memory task. In this case, the Whorfian account might survive. However, consider that Heider and Olivier reported a similar discrepancy between Dani and English speakers in their memory task. These two groups already showed a better fit in their memory than in their naming, and if generally poorer memory among Dani speakers led to some additional variation between Dani and English speakers in the memory task, it might have masked some of the similarity of the two groups' memorial structures. If that were so, an even stronger case might be made for universals in color memory based on Heider and Olivier's results.

Roberson, Davies, and Davidoff contend that the poor memory of Berinmo and Dani speakers relative to English speakers cannot be explained by a general deficit in memory for the former groups. As evidence, they point to a memory span task on which Berinmo and English speakers performed comparably. The results of this task notwithstanding, we find it quite plausible that Berinmo or Dani speakers who received little formal education would differ from English-speaking university students in some general aspects of memory. Whether this is the case or not, however, Roberson, Davies, and Davidoff need to offer some explanation for the fact that the disparity they found in memory across language groups was not equal to, but actually greater than, the disparity in naming.

A more important issue arises from Roberson, Davies, and Davidoff's explanation of the discrepancy in memory between language groups. They account for this in the following way: "Participants of both nationalities in the present experiment overtly used naming to assist memory during the retention interval.... Berinmo speakers tended to repeat a single word, such as 'nol, nol, nol,' during the retention interval, even if they used modifiers in the naming phase of the experiment" (p. 377). In other words, during the retention interval between target and test—which lasted 30 seconds—people apparently verbally encoded the colors and rehearsed the color names, conferring an advantage on those who had more color terms at their disposal—that is, the English speakers. In fact, we contend that this type of explicit linguistic mediation likely also plays a role in the other five experiments that Roberson, Davies, and Davidoff report (not discussed in this chapter). As a result, their tasks would not tap nonlinguistic representations of color and *cannot* provide evidence to support the hypothesis that language changes *nonlinguistic* thought.

Note that the same criticisms could have been raised if Heider and Olivier had found parallels between the color lexicon and color memory. They also used a 30-second retention interval, and they also reported that people remembered the colors in part by repeating their names to themselves. However, Heider and Olivier correctly rejected this as an account for their results: since explicit verbal mediation stacks the deck in favor of crosslinguistic *differences* in memory, it was surprising that they still found a high degree of uniformity in memory across language groups. The fact that Roberson, Davies, and Davidoff did not replicate Heider and Olivier's finding of universality in memory does not negate the latters' findings, but it does point to the need for further study of this issue. As for Roberson, Davies, and Davidoff's argument that their results support the Whorfian hypothesis, it appears that only a weak form of this hypothesis is supported. The Berinmo results reflect linguistic encoding of color chips, which—specifically *because* they are linguistically encoded—shows effects of language experience. By contrast, in order to support the contention that linguistic experience shapes non-linguistic cognition, the possibility of such verbal encoding will need to be specifically ruled out.

### 6.4.2   Spatial Location

Another widely cited line of research—this time, in the domain of spatial cognition—has been argued to show that language changes thought. Brown and Levinson (1993) report variation in the kinds of reference system used by speakers of Dutch and Tzeltal. In Dutch, terms corresponding to English *above*, *below*, *left*, and *right* are appropriate for use with object- or environment-centered frames of reference, whereas terms corresponding to English *north*, *south*, *east*, and *west* are appropriate only for use with geographic frames of reference. The same system is found in English. Different terms are used, depending on which frame of reference the speakers adopts. For example, in English the position of a particular bicycle may be described either as *to the north of the tree*, using an "absolute" (i.e., geographic) system, or *to the left of the tree*, using a "relative" (i.e., object- or environment-centered) system. However, these different reference systems are generally used in different contexts. For small layouts, it is unacceptable to use the geographic system, hence the oddity of *The bowl is to my east*, compared to *The bowl is to my left*. Generally, the geographic reference system in English—and in Dutch—is reserved for relationships between objects at least the size of bicycles and trees. In contrast, speakers of Tzeltal, a Mayan language spoken in Chiapas, Mexico, use an "absolute" system in all cases except where two objects are contiguous. Thus, the native speaker of Tzeltal would find it perfectly natural to state the equivalent of *The bowl is to my north*.

Brown and Levinson asked whether these differences in the use of reference frames might affect the way people encode spatial relationships in *nonlinguistic* tasks. For example, if Dutch speakers reserve the absolute frame of reference for large layouts, but Tzeltal speakers use it for a much larger variety of layouts, then there might be differences in the ways these different groups encode location in nonlinguistic tasks. Brown and Levinson specifically asked whether speakers of Tzeltal might be more inclined to use the absolute frame of reference to encode tabletop arrays, whereas speakers of Dutch might be inclined to use the relative frame of reference.

To test this, Brown and Levinson administered a variety of tasks that could be carried out according to either an absolute or a relative frame of reference. All of the tasks required people to observe the locations of objects—such as a cone, a cube, and a cylinder displayed in a row from left to right on a table. In one task, participants turned 180 degrees to view a different array made up of one object they had seen before and one new object. Finally, in all tasks, participants turned 180 degrees to face a response table on which they were asked to reconstruct the original array, choose an array that matched it, or—in the experiment in which participants turned twice—make an inference about the relative locations of objects viewed on the two tables (see figure 6.6 for an example). In these tasks, rotation reverses the relative frame of reference: what was to the left before turning around is now to the right, and vice versa. However, the same rotation does not affect the absolute frame of reference: north remains north, and south remains south. Therefore, responses reflect whether people have encoded the original array in a relative or absolute frame of reference. Those who have encoded the objects according to a relative frame of reference would recreate or

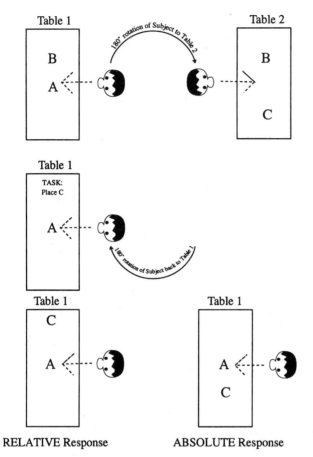

RELATIVE Response          ABSOLUTE Response

**Figure 6.6**
Layout of experiment testing people's nonlinguistic encoding of spatial relation-ships using either "relative" or "absolute" frame of reference. (From Levinson 1996.)

choose an array that reverses the absolute order of the objects, so that the northmost object becomes the southmost object; on the other hand, those who have encoded the objects according to an absolute frame of reference would recreate or choose an array that maintains the north-south order of the objects.

Across tasks of this kind, Brown and Levinson report that each language group responded in a manner consistent with the dominant frame of reference in that language: Tzeltal speakers showed a bias toward responses corresponding to the absolute frame of reference, whereas Dutch speakers showed a bias toward responses corresponding to the relative frame of reference. Brown and Levinson conclude that the frame of reference dominant in a participant's language biases the conceptual encoding employed by that person in nonlinguistic tasks. Extending these studies, Pederson and colleagues (Pederson et al. 1998) obtained similar results across a variety of languages.

Brown and Levinson, and Pederson et al., take the strong view that linguistic experience has shaped thought—specifically, that biases in linguistic encoding of space change the nature of nonlinguistic spatial encoding. However, we believe there are at least two alternative explanations for their findings. First, studies by Li and Gleitman (2002) have shown that both dominant ways of encoding spatial location—claimed by Brown and Levinson to be caused by differences in linguistic encoding —can be easily elicited among native English speakers. Li and Gleitman carried out a replication of several Brown and Levinson–style tasks, but included conditions in which the external environment for the task varied. The nature of the environment had strong effects on which frame of reference was recruited for encoding location in the nonlinguistic tasks. For example, Li and Gleitman carried out the same experiments either in a very plain room with blinds drawn over a window, in the same room with blinds up—exposing a view of a familiar street—or outdoors. The fewer the external landmarks, they reasoned, the more difficult it would be to use landmarks, pushing participants toward using a relative frame of reference. In contrast, a richer visual environment should encourage people to encode location using landmarks and therefore bias them toward using an absolute frame of reference. These were in fact the patterns that emerged, suggesting that people are rather flexible in their choice of reference frames and that these choices are partly mediated by the nature of the immediate physical environment. As Li and Gleitman point out, these findings should come as no surprise to anyone familiar with the literature on spatial cognition in animals: depending on the richness of the spatial environment, animals navigate using a body reference system or a reference system centered on aspects of the environment (see Gallistel 1990 for review). In the case of humans, Li and Gleitman's findings show that the Tzeltal pattern uncovered by Brown and Levinson readily extends to native English speakers, suggesting that the nature of the environment trumps any effects of language in determining the frame of reference that is used.

Li and Gleitman's work suggests that Brown and Levinson's findings are not due exclusively to long-term effects of language experience that have shaped nonlinguistic spatial cognition. At the same time, the findings are not immune to another criticism: to the extent that language does play a role in determining the frame of reference, it is possible that the tasks developed by Brown and Levinson are actually solved by using language. Careful inspection of these tasks shows that none of them has been carried out in such a way as to rule out the use of verbal encoding. In both Brown and Levinson's and Pederson et al.'s tasks, people are asked to look at a scene, to rotate themselves 180 degrees, and to then match or recreate the array. If it takes even several seconds for participants to turn around and assume their new position—facing the response table—this would be plenty of time to verbally encode and rehearse the locations of the objects. The locations participants rehearse would naturally be encoded in either the relative or absolute frame of reference, according to the language they speak. If so, then the task is a linguistically mediated one, and its results cannot be used to argue for or against the shaping of nonlinguistic spatial representations by language. Of course, these arguments apply to Li and Gleitman's experiments as well. But since they found effects of environment that were independent of language, the prospect of linguistic mediation does not lessen the impact of their results. Given the strong possibility that Brown and Levinson's task is mediated by language, we again conclude that there is no evidence that differences in linguistic experience shape nonlinguistic spatial cognition.

### 6.4.3 Space and Time

We review one final set of studies, which has been argued to show clear and incontrovertible effects of language on thought. Boroditsky (2001) has argued that language might affect thought by setting up a kind of mental model (our term) that can be used to solve problems (i.e., "thinking"). Her example concerns spatial metaphors, which are widely used across languages to discuss time, such as when one talks about "the good times ahead of us" or "moving deadlines back." Boroditsky points out that "horizontal" metaphors for time (e.g., ones using *ahead/behind* and their equivalents) are natural in English and other languages, but some languages, such as Mandarin, also use "vertical" metaphors to describe absolute time. Specifically, *shang* 'up' refers to events that are earlier in time, while *xia* 'down' refers to events later in time; that is, time proceeds in a downward direction. So Mandarin speakers say the equivalents of *Nixon is up from Clinton* or *Tuesday is down from Monday*.

If there are real differences in thought that are engaged when speakers use so-called horizontal or vertical metaphoric language, then these differences should affect problem solving. Boroditsky tested this hypothesis by comparing the ease with which native English speakers and native Mandarin speakers solve problems that depend on using spatial and temporal metaphoric language. She predicted that if people were primed with a *spatial* judgment task (horizontal or vertical) and then were given a *temporal* verification task, the nature of the prime should either facilitate or inhibit the temporal judgment. For example, people were primed by viewing scenes containing objects aligned either horizontally or vertically and then were asked to judge the truth of statements about these spatial configurations (e.g., *X is behind/above Y*). Following this set of priming trials, people were asked to judge the truth of a statement about a *temporal* relationship that used either terms engaging a horizontal model (*before/after* in English and their equivalents in Mandarin) or terms that engage a nonspatial model in English, but a vertical one in Mandarin (*earlier/later* and their correspondents in Mandarin).

Boroditsky found that native English speakers responded faster after horizontal priming than after vertical priming, regardless of whether they were asked about before/after or earlier/later relationships. In contrast, native Mandarin speakers who were given horizontal primes responded faster to before/after temporal statements whereas native Mandarin speakers who were given vertical primes responded faster to earlier/later temporal statements. Boroditsky concluded that "metaphorical language plays an important role in shaping abstract thought" (p. 24).

Does this mean that linguistic experience changed the nature of non-linguistic thought? In our view, the answer is a qualified no. Specifying exactly what has changed, and how it has changed, is critical. We interpret Boroditsky's results this way: the difference in the mental model or spatial schema that is naturally induced by using certain linguistic terms (and that varies over languages) has consequences for problem solving *because these same mental models or spatial schemas are used while solving the problem.*

Has Boroditsky shown an effect of language on nonlinguistic representations? We do not think that her results can be interpreted this strongly. Her task requires people to engage in linguistic processing in order to respond. Therefore, it could not show an effect on nonlinguistic representation. But what the results do show is that different kinds of mental models can be linked to different sets of lexical items (which are language dependent). Further, when these mental models are engaged for the purposes of problem solving (in this case, linguistic problem solving), they will inevitably reflect the effects of the language itself. In this sense, we interpret Boroditsky's results to be consistent with those of Brown and Levinson, which also show that linguistically mediated problem solving is affected by differences in linguistic experience. It is worth pointing out that Boroditsky also found that the response to priming shown by Mandarin speakers could be induced in native English speakers, by brief and simple training. This kind of flexibility suggests that any changes in "thought" are relatively superficial and that they constitute habitual tendencies rather than permanent changes. From this perspective, they are quite different kinds of effects from those seen in studies of the reorganization of language following different kinds of linguistic experience (see section 6.2).

## 6.5   Final Thoughts

The body of work we have reviewed points to the following conclusions. First, language experience has strong, incontrovertible effects on the representation of language. These effects are permanent, and they are diffi-cult if not impossible to alter through training later in life. Second, language-specific experience does not appear to affect nonlinguistic representations. That is, the nonlinguistic base that exists separately from language is not shaped by linguistic experience. Support for this conclusion comes from the representation of color, objects, and spatial location; in none of these have we found evidence for genuine, perma-nent changes in people's nonlinguistic representations resulting from differences in language experience. Thus, we conclude that there are boundaries below which language does not affect "thought"—at least in the sense of permanently reconfiguring nonlinguistic representations.

Yet the idea that "language affects thought" is still widely endorsed. How could it be that such a compelling idea—one that feels intuitively right to so many people—can receive such little empirical support?

One possibility is that we have not looked hard enough. Perhaps there are findings we are not aware of, which do show compelling effects of language on nonlinguistic representation. Perhaps, in our attempt to set up particular standards for proving change in nonlinguistic representa-tion, we have ended up circumscribing our review in such a way as to rule out the possibility of any "real" effects. Or perhaps our criteria have resulted in our missing some important ways in which language might reconfigure thought. The reader is invited to articulate better standards by which to decide what does or does not constitute an effect of language on thought.

Finally, we note that, despite our strong conclusions, we also believe that many unanswered questions remain about the possible ways in which language might affect cognition by providing a powerful tool of encoding. Such effects might include the capacity to represent more powerful and/or complex concepts, the capacity to manipulate complex concepts with ease, or the capacity to use linguistically mediated schemas (such as spatial ones) in the service of complex problem solving. These are certainly possibilities; but in our view, they represent effects of lan-guage on linguistically mediated representation, not permanent changes in the nature of nonlinguistic representation itself.

Although we have tried, in this chapter, to provide some sense of the boundaries beyond which researchers should not expect effects of lan-guage on cognition, it clearly remains important to understand the role that language does play in cognition. In addition to building theory, such understanding would have extremely important practical implications. For instance, educators in scientific and technical fields, as well as designers and engineers who are concerned with human factors, use spatial language to direct people's attention to the most important details in diagrams. Their success in doing so hinges on understanding both the power and the risk associated with language. If different linguistic structures engage different kinds of spatial schemas, for example, and if these structures vary from language to language, then speakers of different languages might approach solving spatial problems quite differently. In the extreme, it might be possible for a given language to facilitate solving one problem, while leading in the wrong direction for solving another problem. Even though our underlying nonlinguistic spatial representations may be the same regardless of the language we speak, the potential for language to guide problem solving is enormous. Thus, we would be well advised to consider the potential of language for mediating understanding as well as misunderstanding.

## Notes

The preparation of this chapter was supported in part by grant 9808585 from the National Science Foundation and grant FY99-1270 from the March of Dimes to Barbara Landau.

1. Note that Bowerman (1996) herself takes a neutral stand with respect to whether the Bowerman and Choi findings might suggest an effect of language on thought.

## References

Aslin, R., Pisoni, D., Hennessy, B., and Perey, A. (1981). Discrimination of voice onset time by human infants: New findings and implications for the effect of early experience. *Child Development*, 52, 1135–1145.

Bennett, D. (1975). *Spatial and temporal uses of English prepositions: An essay in stratificational semantics*. London: Longman.

Berlin, B., and Kay, P. (1969). *Basic color terms: Their universality and evolution*. Berkeley and Los Angeles: University of California Press.

Berman, R., and Slobin, D. (1994). *Relating events in narrative: A crosslinguistic developmental study*. Hillsdale, NJ: Erlbaum.

Best, C., McRoberts, G., and Sithole, N. (1988). The phonological basis of perceptual loss for non-native contrasts: Maintenance of discrimination among Zulu clicks by English-speaking adults and infants. *Journal of Experimental Psychology: Human Perception and Performance, 14*, 345–360.

Billman, D., and Krych, M. (1998, August). *Path and manner verbs in action: Effects of "skipping" or "exiting" on event memory.* Paper presented at the meeting of the Cognitive Science Society, Madison, WI.

Boroditsky, L. (2001). Does language shape thought? Mandarin and English speakers' conceptions of time. *Cognitive Psychology, 43*, 1–22.

Bowerman, M. (1996). Learning how to structure space for language: A cross-linguistic perspective. In P. Bloom, M. Peterson, L. Nadel, and M. Garrett (Eds.), *Language and space.* Cambridge, MA: MIT Press.

Bowerman, M., and Choi, S. (1994, November). *Linguistic and nonlinguistic determinants of spatial semantic development.* Paper presented at the Boston University Conference on Language Development, Boston, MA.

Brown, P., and Levinson, S. C. (1993). *Linguistic and nonlinguistic coding of spatial arrays: Explorations in Mayan cognition.* Working Paper 24. Nijmegen: Max Planck Institute for Psycholinguistics, Cognitive Anthropology Research Group.

Clark, H. (1973). Space, time, semantics, and the child. In T. E. Moore (Ed.), *Cognitive development and the acquisition of language.* New York: Academic Press.

Crawford, L., Regier, T., and Huttenlocher, J. (2000). Linguistic and non-linguistic spatial categorization. *Cognition, 73*, 209–235.

Davidoff, J., Davies, I., and Roberson, D. (1999). Colour categories in a Stone-Age tribe. *Nature, 398*, 203–204.

Gallistel, C. R. (1990). *The organization of learning.* Cambridge, MA: MIT Press.

Gennari, S., Sloman, S., Malt, B., and Fitch, W. (2000, March). *Language processing and perception of motion events.* Poster presented at the CUNY Conference on Human Sentence Processing, La Jolla, CA.

Gibson, E. (1967). *Principles of perceptual learning and development.* New York: Appleton-Century-Crofts.

Hayward, W., and Tarr, M. (1995). Spatial language and spatial representation. *Cognition, 55*, 39–84.

Heider, E., and Olivier, D. (1972). The structure of the color space in naming and memory for two languages. *Cognitive Psychology, 3*, 337–354.

Herskovits, A. (1986). *Language and spatial cognition: An interdisciplinary study of the prepositions of English.* Cambridge: Cambridge University Press.

Lakoff, G. (1987). *Women, fire, and dangerous things.* Chicago: University of Chicago Press.

Landau, B., and Jackendoff, R. (1993). "What" and "where" in spatial language and spatial cognition. *Behavioral and Brain Sciences, 16*, 217–238.

Landau, B., and Shipley, E. (2001). Labelling patterns and object naming. *Developmental Science, 4*, 109–118.

Landau, B., Smith, L., and Jones, S. (1997). Object shape, object function, and object name. *Journal of Memory and Language, 38*, 1–27.

Lee, P. (1996). *The Whorf theory complex: A critical reconstruction.* Amsterdam: John Benjamins.

Levinson, S. (1996). Frames of reference and Molyneux's question: Cross-linguistic evidence. In P. Bloom, M. Peterson, L. Nadel, and M. Garrett (Eds.), *Language and space.* Cambridge, MA: MIT Press.

Li, P., and Gleitman, L. (2002). Turning the tables: Language and spatial reasoning. *Cognition, 83*, 265–294.

Lucy, J. (1992). *Grammatical categories and cognition.* Cambridge: Cambridge University Press.

Malt, B., and Johnson, E. (1992). Do artifact concepts have cores? *Journal of Memory and Language, 31*, 195–217.

Malt, B., Sloman, S., Gennari, S., Shi, M., and Wang, Y. (1999). Knowing versus naming: Similarity and the linguistic categorization of artifacts. *Journal of Memory and Language, 40*, 230–262.

Mandler, J. (1996). Preverbal representation and language. In P. Bloom, M. Peterson, L. Nadel, and M. Garrett (Eds.), *Language and space.* Cambridge, MA: MIT Press.

Munnich, E., Landau, B., and Dosher, B. (2001). Spatial language and spatial representation: A cross-linguistic comparison. *Cognition, 81*, 171–208.

Pederson, E., Danziger, E., Wilkins, D., Levinson, S., Kita, S., and Senft, G. (1998). Semantic typology and spatial conceptualization. *Language, 74*, 557–589.

Roberson, D., Davies, I., and Davidoff, J. (2000). Colour categories are not universal: Replications and new evidence from a Stone-Age culture. *Journal of Experimental Psychology: General, 129*, 369–398.

Streeter, L. (1976). Language perception of 2-month-old infants shows effects of both innate mechanisms and experience. *Nature, 259*, 39–41.

Talmy, L. (1983). How languages structure space. In H. Pick and L. Acredolo (Eds.), *Spatial orientation: Theory, research, and application.* New York: Plenum.

Talmy, L. (1985). Lexicalization patterns: Semantic structure in lexical forms. In T. Shopen (Ed.), *Language typology and syntactic description: Vol. 3. Grammatical categories and the lexicon.* Cambridge: Cambridge University Press.

Talmy, L. (1991). Path to realization: A typology of event conflation. *Proceedings of the Berkeley Linguistics Society, 17*, 480–519.

Tees, R., and Werker, J. (1984). Perceptual flexibility: Maintenance or recovery of the ability to discriminate non-native speech sounds. *Canadian Journal of Psychology*, *34*, 579–590.

Trehub, S. (1976). The discrimination of foreign speech contrasts by infants and adults. *Child Development*, *47*, 466–472.

Tsushima, T., Takizawa, O., Sasaki, M., Shiraki, S., Nishi, K., Kohno, M., Menyuk, P., and Best, C. (1994). *Discrimination of English /r-l/ and /w-y/ by Japanese infants 6–12 months: Language-specific developmental changes in speech perception abilities.* Paper presented at the International Conference on Spoken Language, Yokohama, Japan.

Werker, J. (1995). Exploring developmental changes in cross-language speech perception. In L. Gleitman and M. Liberman (Eds.), *Language: An invitation to cognitive science* (Vol. 1, 2nd ed.). Cambridge, MA: MIT Press.

Werker, J., Gilbert, H., Humphrey, K., and Tees, R. (1981). Developmental aspects of cross-language speech perception. *Child Development*, *52*, 349–353.

Werker, J., and Lalonde, C. (1988). Cross-linguistic speech perception: Initial capabilities and developmental change. *Developmental Psychology*, *24*, 672–683.

Werker, J., and Logan, J. (1985). Cross-language evidence for three factors in speech perception. *Perception and Psychophysics*, *37*, 35–44.

Werker, J., and Tees, R. (1984). Cross-language speech perception: Evidence for perceptual reorganization during the first year of life. *Infant Behavior and Development*, *7*, 49–63.

Whorf, B. (1956). *Language, thought, and reality* (J. B. Carroll, Ed.). Cambridge, MA: MIT Press.

# 7

# Language and Thought Online: Cognitive Consequences of Linguistic Relativity

Dan I. Slobin

## 7.1 Introduction

The voluminous literature on linguistic relativity has concerned itself primarily with the search for influences of particular languages on non-linguistic cognition *in situations in which language is not being used, overtly or covertly*. This represents a long tradition in which anthropologists, psychologists, and linguists have sought to relate grammatical and semantic systems of a language to the worldview or epistemology or culture of the community of speakers of the language. For example, Lucy has proposed a set of requirements for studies of linguistic relativity. He stipulates that such research "should assess the cognitive performance of individual speakers *aside from explicitly verbal contexts* and try to establish that any cognitive patterns that are detected also characterize *everyday behavior outside of the assessment situation*" (Lucy 1996, 48; emphasis added). In this view, "cognition" is seen as a collection of concepts and procedures that come into play regardless of whether an individual is engaged in verbal behavior—speaking, listening, or verbal thinking. Such research is directed toward what Lucy calls "an independent cognitive interpretation of reality" (Lucy 2000, xii). A rather different approach to "cognition" is provided by investigators who concern themselves with language *use* and cultural *practice*. For example, Gumperz and Levinson, introducing *Rethinking Linguistic Relativity* (1996, 8), underline the importance of "theories of use in context," including formal semantic theories (e.g., Discourse Representation Theory, Situation Semantics) and pragmatic theories (Relevance Theory, Gricean theories), along with research in sociolinguistics and linguistic anthropology. In this chapter, I begin with the fact that human beings spend a large portion of their time engaging in linguistic behavior of one sort or another; that is, we are creatures that are almost constantly involved in preparing, producing, and interpreting verbal messages. Accordingly, research on linguistic relativity is incomplete without attention to the cognitive processes that are brought to bear, *online*, in the course of using language.

## 7.2  Thinking for Speaking

In research on narrative productions across languages, it has become clear to me that "we encounter the contents of the mind in a special way when they are being accessed for use" (Slobin 1987, 435). That is, there is a process of "thinking for speaking" in which cognition plays a dynamic role within the framework of linguistic expression:

The activity of thinking takes on a particular quality when it is employed in the activity of speaking. In the evanescent time frame of constructing utterances in discourse, one fits one's thoughts into available linguistic forms. A particular utterance is never a direct reflection of "objective" or perceived reality or of an inevitable and universal mental representation of a situation. This is evident within any given language, because the same situation can be described in different ways; and it is evident across languages, because each language provides a limited set of options for the grammatical encoding of characteristics of objects and events. "Thinking for speaking" involves picking those characteristics that (a) fit some conceptualization of the event, and (b) are readily encodable in the language. (Slobin 1987, 435)

The online effects of language on thought processes have been noticed by psychologists, although not seen as centrally important to the classical issues of language and cognition. For example, Pinker (1994, 58) writes that "there is no scientific evidence that languages dramatically shape their speakers' ways of thinking" and that the Sapir-Whorf hypothesis is "wrong, all wrong" (p. 57). But he has also noted:

Whorf was surely wrong when he said that one's language determines how one conceptualizes reality in general. But he was probably correct in a much weaker sense: one's language does determine how one must conceptualize reality when one has to talk about it. (Pinker 1989, 360)

In Levelt's (1989) production model, the "Conceptualizer" sends a "preverbal message" to the "Formulator." Levelt considers semantic differences between languages in this model:

A final issue to be raised is whether messages must, to some degree, be *tuned* to the target language. Will a message for an English Formulator have to differ from one that is fed into a Dutch Formulator, merely because of language-specific requirements? The answer ... is positive: Using a particular language requires the speaker to think of particular conceptual features. (Levelt 1989, 71)

Pinker, Levelt, and others, however, stress that online thinking while speaking is an encapsulated process, with no consequences beyond speech time. Comparing particular English and Dutch verb constructions, Pinker concludes that "it seems unlikely that the Dutch conceive of [the under-lying meanings] differently from us, except at the moment that they have to express them in words" (1989, 358). And Levelt, comparing deictic terms across languages, concludes, "It is highly unlikely ... that English and Dutch speakers *perceive* distance to ego differently than Spanish and Japanese speakers. But when they prepare distance information for ex-pression, English and Dutch speakers must represent that information in their messages in a bipartite way, whereas Spanish and Japanese speakers must use a tripartite code" (1989, 103–104). In brief, thinking-for-speaking effects are weak, not dramatic, and have no further impli-cations for perception or conceptualization of objects and events.

It is, of course, exceptionally difficult to determine how people "really" represent situations to themselves; furthermore, "weak, undramatic" effects are not without scientific interest. I wish to argue that serious study of *language in use* points to pervasive effects of language on selec-tive attention and memory for particular event characteristics. As I've argued in greater detail elsewhere (Slobin 1996a, 2000), whatever effects language may have when people are not speaking or listening, the mental activity that goes on while formulating and interpreting utterances is not trivial or obvious, and it deserves our attention.

Utterances are not verbal filmclips of events. An event cannot be fully represented in language: linguistic expression requires schematization of some sort. Every utterance represents a selection of characteristics, leav-ing it to the receiver to fill in details on the basis of ongoing context and background knowledge. Part of the background is a knowledge of what is obligatory or typical of the language being used. If I tell you about my "friend" in English, you will expect that sooner or later you will discover the sex of the friend, because you know that third-person pronouns in English indicate gender. If I go on and on to refer only to "my friend" or "they," you will begin to suspect that I have reason to conceal the person's gender. However, if we have the same conversation in a language that has no gendered pronouns, such as Turkish or Chinese or Hungarian, you probably will not have such suspicions. When speaking English, my thinking for speaking—my Conceptualizer—is tuned to gender and its communicative significance, and your "listening for thinking" is similarly tuned. We are not concerned with real-world cognition here, but with the ongoing construction of mental representations. Our basic cognition of gender does not change when we switch languages, as far as I know, although our social and cultural cognition may well change. Communication is embedded in culture, and much of culture is carried— indeed, constructed—by language. Therefore, the definition of cognition should not be restricted to phenomena of the physical world alone. Imagine, for example, that the political balance in the United States shifts, and Spanish becomes the official language. Americans now would have to know—in every encounter—who is *tú* and who is *Usted*. That is, the language would force our attention to fine points of status and intimacy that we have not had to resolve in using the universal English *you*. (I leave it to the reader to decide if such a demonstration of linguistic relativity would count as "dramatic." However, consider the ways in which the language of personal pronouns, honorifics, and discourse markers shapes social cognition and interaction across human societies.)

These are, of course, thought experiments. And one can argue that it is trivially obvious that a speaker or listener has to attend to those semantic features that are encoded in the grammatical and lexical elements of a particular language in order to learn and use that language. I propose that more rigorous demonstrations are possible, showing widespread "ripple effects" of habitual attention to linguistically encoded event characteristics. Several criteria are required for thinking-for-speaking research. I'll use the label *thinking for speaking*, but the framework embraces all forms of linguistic production (speaking, writing, signing) and reception (listening, reading, viewing), as well as a range of mental processes (understanding, imaging, remembering, etc.). Thus, there will also be examples of "thinking for translating," "listening for understanding," "reading for imaging," and so forth. Thinking-for-speaking research has the following characteristics:

*[handwritten marginal note: the 'language of art and architecture'?]*

1. The research addresses a *selection of languages* and a *semantic domain* that is encoded with some frequency in all of the languages.

2. The semantic domain is encoded by *special grammatical constructions or obligatory lexical selections* in at least some of the languages under comparison.

3. The domain is relatively *more codable* in some of the languages to be compared.

4. The research addresses a selection of *discourse situations* in which the semantic domain is regularly accessed.

Point 2 ensures that the domain is one that is *habitually* encoded in some of the languages. However, it allows for habitual encoding either by grammatical means (morphological elements, construction types) or by obligatory lexemes, such as the compass-point terms or landmark terms used for spatial orientation in many languages (Levinson 1996a,b, in press; Pederson et al. 1998). "Obligatory" is taken to mean that the dimension in question cannot be regularly referred to without the expression in question. Point 3 is concerned with relative "codability" of the domain—that is, ease of expression of the relevant categories. A more codable expression is more *accessible* in psycholinguistic terms; that is, it is short, and/or high frequency, and generally part of a small set of options in a paradigm or small set of items. Thus, a concept expressed by a single verb is more codable than a phrase or clause (e.g., *run* vs. *while running*); a concept expressed by one of a small set of terms in a closed set (such as *uphill, downhill, across*) is more codable than one expressed by choices from a larger and more open set (such as *to your left, to my left, toward town, in front of the tree*, etc.). Note also that grammatical constructions (Goldberg 1995) can provide codable means of expression, such as the English caused-motion construction.

## 7.3 Descriptions of Motion Events

My "parade case" of thinking for speaking is the encoding of motion events.[1] This is a semantic domain that is important in all languages, and it is one that exhibits distinctive types of lexicalization patterns cross-linguistically. The essence of a motion event is change of location—in

Talmy's terms, *path*. Following Talmy (1991, 2000), languages tend to encode the path of motion in one of two ways: either in a verb (*enter*, *exit*, etc.) or in an associated particle or "satellite" (*in*, *out*). A simple example is provided by English and French:

(1)  a.  The dog went *in*to the house.
     b.  Le chien est *entré* dans la maison.
         'The dog *entered* the house.'[2]

English "frames" path by means of a satellite (*in*); French "frames" path by means of a verb (*entrer*). English is a *satellite-framed* language (S-language); French is a *verb-framed* language (V-language). Path is highly codable in both languages. However, the languages differ in codability with regard to another dimension of motion events—*manner* of motion:

(2)  a.  The dog *ran* into the house.
     b.  Le chien est entré dans la maison *en courant*.
         'The dog entered the house *by running*.'

Manner is highly codable in English, because it is carried by the main verb. Every clause requires a verb, and it is just as easy to say *go in* as *run in*. I will argue that English speakers get manner "for free" and make widespread communicative and cognitive use of this dimension. In French, by contrast, manner is an adjunct—an optional addition to a clause that is already complete. French speakers indicate manner when it is at issue, but otherwise do not mention it. I will try to show that, as a consequence, they are less sensitive to this dimension overall.

The typological distinction between S- and V-languages is quite widespread, apparently independent of language family, geographical area, and culture. In the research summarized here, the two types of language are represented by the following sample:

*Satellite-framed (S-languages)*

*Germanic:*   Dutch, English, German, Icelandic, Swedish, Yiddish

*Slavic:*   Polish, Russian, Serbo-Croatian, Ukrainian

*Finno-Ugric:*   Finnish, Hungarian

*Sino-Tibetan:*   Mandarin Chinese

*Verb-framed (V-languages)*

*Romance:*    French, Galician, Italian, Portuguese, Spanish

*Semitic:*    Moroccan Arabic, Hebrew

*Turkic:*    Turkish

*Basque*

*Japanese*

*Signed languages:*    American Sign Language, Sign Language of the Netherlands

The claims made for English and French above hold for all of these languages (except for signed languages, where path and manner are expressed simultaneously, and both dimensions appear to be accessible and cognitively salient). S-languages allow for an economical expression of manner of motion in the main verb of a clause. Apparently as a consequence, these languages make habitual use of manner verbs when encoding motion events, and have developed large lexicons with many fine-grained distinctions of manner, in comparison with smaller and less differentiated manner lexicons in V-languages. One can say that the semantic space of manner of motion is "highly saturated" in S-languages, in comparison with V-languages. For example, French *bondir* doesn't distinguish between the manners of motion encoded in English by *jump*, *leap*, *bound*, *spring*, *skip*, *gambol*; Spanish *escabullirse* can be translated as *creep*, *glide*, *slide*, *slip*, *slither*. A detailed study of 115 English manner-of-motion verbs found only 79 French counterparts, many of them of low frequency in comparison with English manner verbs (Jovanović and Kentfield 1998). By contrast, a similar study of Russian and English showed these two S-languages to be comparably saturated on this dimension (Dukhovny and Kaushanskaya 1998).

On the basis of comparing a number of S- and V-languages, across a range of age and discourse types, I hypothesize a set of cognitive consequences of differential encoding of manner of motion:

If a language provides fine-grained, habitual, and economical expression of manner of motion:

• References to manner of motion will occur frequently, across genres and discourse contexts.

• Manner-of-motion verbs will be acquired early.

• The language will have continuing lexical innovation in this domain, including extended and metaphorical uses.

• Speakers will have rich mental imagery of manner of motion.

• Manner of motion will be salient in memory for events and in verbal accounts of events.

In brief, the proposal is that habitual, online attention to manner has made it especially salient in S-language speakers' conceptualizations of motion events.

## 7.4   Salience of Manner of Motion

Languages of both types, satellite- and verb-framed, have verbs of manner of motion, but we have already seen that V-languages tend to have fewer such verbs. In addition, such verbs occur less frequently in speech and writing in V-languages. (For convenience, these verbs will be referred to simply as *manner verbs* from here on.) Greater frequency of use of terms that encode a semantic domain probably indicates that the domain is salient and conceptually articulated in the minds of speakers. Various sorts of evidence point to this conclusion, and I will schematically summarize findings from a range of published and unpublished studies.[3]

### 7.4.1   Ease of Lexical Access

When asked to list manner verbs in a one-minute time frame, English speakers listed far more verbs than French speakers, in terms of both tokens per individual and types per group of informants. In addition, French speakers found it hard to limit themselves to manner verbs, listing nonmanner verbs such as *descendre* 'descend, go down' and *traverser* 'cross, traverse'; English speakers showed no such intrusions. Furthermore, when English speakers were asked to list *all* types of motion verbs, only 13% were nonmanner verbs. Many of the manner verbs that were listed are highly expressive, making fine-grained distinctions that are often not present in V-languages. For example, the following verbs were provided five or more times by a group of 70 undergraduates from the University of California at Berkeley: *crawl, dance, drive, fly, hop, jog, jump, leap, mosey, prance, run, saunter, shuffle, skip, sprint, walk.* Overall, this group produced 107 different manner verbs.[4] As shown in note 4, these verbs are sufficiently accessible to be elicited in one minute, indicating that the underlying concepts are readily available to English speakers. Such results indicate that manner of motion is a salient lexical domain for English speakers.[5]

### 7.4.2 Conversational Use

Similar crosslinguistic differences in attention to manner appear in spontaneous conversation. Intransitive verbs of human motion were checked in two-hour transcripts of conversations in Spanish and Turkish, both V-languages. The vast majority of verbs were simple path verbs, with no manner (97% of tokens in Spanish, 98% in Turkish). In both languages, the only manner verbs used were equivalents of *walk* (*caminar* and *pasear* in Spanish; *yürümek* in Turkish). In comparable British and American samples, 34 types of manner verbs were used, again indicating the salience of manner in English.[6]

### 7.4.3 Use in Oral Narrative

Narratives have been elicited in a large number of languages, from ages 3 through adulthood, using a wordless picture book, *Frog, Where Are You?* (Mayer 1969). (Research on "the frog story" in five languages is summarized in Berman and Slobin 1994; Strömqvist and Verhoeven, in preparation.) Using this method, semantic content and plot structure are controlled across languages and ages. Again, S-language speakers—at all ages—use manner verbs more frequently (tokens) and with greater lexical diversity (types). For example, consider data from three unrelated V-languages—Spanish, Turkish, and Hebrew—in comparison with three different S-languages—English, Mandarin, and Russian (Hsiao 1999; Özçalışkan and Slobin 1999). Narrators were children in the age range 3–11 and adults. The figures in table 7.1 show the proportion of manner verbs out of all motion verbs in the narratives, followed by the mean number of manner verbs used by adults.

Although there are differences within the two typological groups, it is clear that S-language speakers use manner verbs more frequently when

**Table 7.1**
Use of manner-of-motion verbs in frog-stories

| Language | Percentage of manner verb use (all ages combined) | Mean number of manner verbs per narrator (adults) |
|---|---|---|
| *V-languages* | | |
| Spanish | 20 | 3 |
| Turkish | 25 | 4 |
| Hebrew | 30 | 4 |
| *S-languages* | | |
| English | 45 | 7 |
| Mandarin | 62 | 11 |
| Russian | 69 | 16 |

describing events in the frog story. It is possible to talk about manner of movement in all of these languages, but apparently this dimension is a more regular part of thinking for speaking in S-languages.[7]

### 7.4.4   Use in Written Narrative

**7.4.4.1   Thinking for Writing**   The same patterns of attention to manner in S- and V-languages are found in novels across a range of languages. One might assume that writers of creative fiction would be relatively free of the sorts of linguistic constraints presented by typological differences in lexicalization patterns. Yet attention to manner of motion varies regularly with the type of language, apparently independent of obvious cultural factors of literary tradition and areal contact. In ongoing studies of "thinking for writing," my students and I have been examining novels written in several V-languages—Spanish, French, Turkish, Hebrew—in comparison with S-language novels in English, German, and Russian. Overall, S-language novels have greater type and token frequencies of manner verbs in situations in which human movement is described. For example, the figures in table 7.2 show the rates of use of manner verbs in describing self-motion of characters in novels in several languages. Percentages show the proportion of verbs of human movement that are manner verbs.[8] One might think that novelists writ-

**Table 7.2**
Use of manner-of-motion verbs in novels

| Language | Percentage of manner verb use |
|---|---|
| *V-languages* | |
| Spanish | 19 |
| Turkish | 21 |
| *S-languages* | |
| English | 41 |
| Russian | 56 |

ing in V-languages would have recourse to other means of drawing attention to manner of movement, in addition to manner verbs. Consider, for example, adverbs of manner (*slowly, quietly*), descriptions of motor behavior and body condition (*not looking where he went; sweating heavily and exhausted*), descriptions of inner states (*agitated, joyful*), descriptions of environmental conditions that affect manner of movement (*the snow was thick; the road was muddy*). To be sure, novelists do use such additional means of providing information about manner of movement. But even when all of these options are considered, the large relative differences between the two language types remain unchanged. S-language writers, overall, give their readers more information—explicit and inferential—about the manners in which their protagonists move about (Özçalışkan and Slobin 2000b).

**7.4.4.2 Thinking for Translating** Translators working between the two language types face problems in dealing with manner. For example, in a sample of novels translated from English into Spanish, only 62% of the original English manner verbs appeared in the translation, while in translations from Spanish to English, 95% of the original Spanish manner verbs were retained (Slobin 1996b, plus more recent data).[9] In fact, English translators generally *add* manner descriptions, apparently finding the Spanish original too bland for English readers: 100% of Spanish nonmanner motion verbs were replaced by manner verbs in English translations. Compare the following solutions to translation problems in the two directions:

(3)  a.  *English to Spanish*

He *stomped* from the trim house ... →

*Salió* de la pulcra casa ...

'He *exited* from the trim house ...'

b.  *Spanish to English*

... luego de diez minutos de asfixia y empujones, llegamos al pasillo de la entrada

'... after ten minutes of asphyxiation and pushes, *we arrived* at the entryway' →

... after ten minutes of nearly being smothered or crushed to death, we finally *fought our way* to the exit

These examples are typical of translations between English and Spanish, as well as translations between English and Turkish—quite a different sort of language, but demonstrating the same V-language characteristics. Note that in (3b), the English translator has not only added manner of motion (*llegar* 'arrive' → *fight one's way*), but also increased the vividness of the description overall (*asfixia y empujones* 'asphyxiation and pushes' → *nearly being smothered or crushed to death*). This is not a whim of an individual translator, but rather a quite general interest in manners of action in S-languages. Consider, for example, English verbs of manner of speaking (*whisper, murmur, scream, yell, shout, bellow,* etc.) or verbs of manner of object destruction (*shatter, crumble, crumple, rip, shred, smash,* etc.). More broadly, there may be thinking-for-speaking effects across a number of domains, reflecting widespread attention to manner of acting—at least in English, and probably in other S-languages as well.

### 7.4.5  Building Semantic Domains in Acquisition

Brown (1958), in describing early lexical acquisition, aptly referred to words as "lures to cognition." In the "Original Word Game," the child "must discover the stimulus attributes governing the tutor's verbal behavior" (p. 210). Bowerman has long argued that language guides the child to form language-specific semantic categories:

I argue that children are prepared from the beginning to accept linguistic guidance as to which distinctions—from among the set of distinctions that are salient to them—they should rely on in organizing particular domains of meaning. (Bowerman 1985, 1285)

With regard to manner of motion, the two language types differ in drawing the child's attention to this domain overall, as well as to semantic distinctions within the domain. In acquiring an S-language, in contrast to a V-language, the child has to pay attention to semantic dimensions that distinguish the many types of manner verbs that are encountered in the input. Children learning S-languages employ a large manner verb lexicon in the preschool period. For example, British, American, and Australian preschoolers (age 2–5) in the available CHILDES corpora for English use the following 32 types of verbs of manner of self-movement: *bump, chase, climb, crawl, creep, dance, float, flop, fly, hike, hop, jog, jump, march, paddle, pounce, race, roll, run, rush, scoot, skip, slide, slip, sneak, step, swim, tread, trip, trot, walk, wiggle.* By contrast, Spanish, French, and Italian preschoolers in CHILDES corpora use a limited set of such verbs, almost all of them relatively "nonexpressive" in relation to English—mainly the equivalents of *climb, dance, fly, jump, run, swim, walk* (Chouinard 1997; Mucetti 1997). That is, while S-language children are learning to distinguish expressive nuances of manner—such as *hop* versus *jump*, or *hike, jog, race, run, trot*—V-language children are learning broad categories of basic types of motor patterns, such as *run* versus *walk*. As a consequence, it seems reasonable to conclude that S-language children have been guided by their native language to pay attention to manner of motion and to construct a set of systematic semantic categories in this domain.

This conclusion is echoed by Levelt, who has written about the development of the Conceptualizer and the Formulator in childhood:

In learning the language, the speaker (the child) must surely have realized that the language requires him to attend to certain perceptual or conceptual features when he encodes a message.... But although conceptualizing and grammatical encoding *are* interacting for the language-acquiring child, the mature speaker has learned what to encode when preparing a message for expression. He knows by experience whether his language requires a category of medial proximity, number, tense, object shape, or whatever is needed, and he will select the appropriate information in building his preverbal messages. It is no longer necessary for the Conceptualizer to ask the Formulator at each occasion what it likes as input.... The language-specific requirements on semantic structure have become represented in the Conceptualizer's procedural knowledge base. (Levelt 1989, 104–105)

Thus, the child begins by "listening (and watching) for understanding," gradually learning to think for speaking. In the end, thinking for speaking becomes automatized, yet still relative to the particular language. Language-specific patterns can be established quite early, as shown in the work by Choi and Bowerman (1991; also Bowerman and Choi 2001) on very young children's differing spatial concepts in Korean and English, as well as in the frog-story research, where differences in narrative style between speakers of S- and V-languages are clearly present in the preschool period.[10]

Note, also, that both the lexicon and the grammar are at play in thinking for speaking, although traditional Sapir-Whorf discussions focus on obligatory grammatical distinctions. Gumperz and Levinson (1996) underline the cognitive effects of acquiring both systems of language:

[I]f one is to speak a language which makes certain distinctions obligatory, one simply *must* have categorized experience in appropriate ways (i.e., have noticed how states or events were structured on the relevant parameters) (p. 33).... [T]he lexical level can also have deep cognitive effects, by requiring distinctions to be noticed and memorized at the time of experience, in case the need arises for later description. (p. 11)

We will return to the latter point, which leads from thinking for *present* speaking to thinking for *potential* speaking. But first, there are several more indications of the salience of manner of motion in S-languages.

### 7.4.6 Innovative and Expressive Uses of Manner-of-Motion Verbs

The history of English verbs shows that manner of motion was already an elaborated semantic domain in Old English, with many new verbs being added ever since. For example, the *Oxford English Dictionary* lists the following as intransitive verbs of human motion that were innovated in the nineteenth century: *barge, clomp, cruise, dodder, drag oneself, ease, goose-step, hustle, leapfrog, lope, lunge, lurch, meander, mosey, race, sashay, scoot, scurry, skitter, smash, stampede, stomp, waltz, zip.* Clearly, this is a domain that continually attracts the attention of English speakers.

It is also a domain that plays an important role in reporting events—in the news media, novels, and conversations. Newspapers in English-speaking countries make use of such verbs for vivid reporting, as in the following examples:

(4)  "Sometimes the gunfire drives them to *flee* again, *crawling* under the coiled wire at the back of the compound and *scaling* the hillside in search of some other place to hide." (*New York Times*)

(5)  "Although there have been thousands of aftershocks, yesterday's was big enough to send frightened people *scurrying* out of their homes to safe, open spaces." (*San Francisco Chronicle*)

Not only are manner verbs used to provide graphic descriptions of motion, but they also serve to provide evaluations of the person who is moving, as in the following examples:

(6)  "Solomon Moss had never applied for a loan before and he had no idea of what to expect when he walked into Louhen's Quick Cash here. He bit his lip, *waltzed* up to the counter and asked to borrow $100." (*Washington Post*)

(7)  "Dalia Itzik [Labor Party member of the Knesset], who wore a short, tight, very secular suit ... *sashayed* past." (*New York Times*)

In these examples, the writer uses manner verbs to call forth particular images of moving figures, relying on the reader to access a conceptualization of the type of motion suggested—and thereby an evaluation of the moving figure as well. It is also common to use the manner-verb lexicon metaphorically, to add an evaluative dimension to descriptions of various sorts of nonliteral motion and change of state. For example, two countries are reported as "*shambling* into a confrontation"; a political campaign "*stumbles* on roadblocks"; prices can "*drift*," "*soar*," "*lurch*," or "*plunge*." The force dynamics of bodily movement serve as metaphors for political and economic events (Narayanan 1997), drawing upon fine-grained categories established in the minds of S-language speakers. Similar expressive and metaphorical uses of manner verbs are found in news reports and novels in other S-languages, such as Mandarin (Yu 1998) and Dutch; however, they are relatively infrequent in Turkish (Özçalışkan 2002) and other V-languages.

### 7.4.7   Mental Imagery

Such differences in extended uses of manner verbs suggest another online cognitive effect of language, which we might call "reading/listening for imaging." Most experimental research on linguistic relativity has dealt with language *production,* but many conceptual effects of language occur in the course of *reception.* We receive a great deal of our information about events through news reports, personal narratives, and hearsay. In all of these situations, verbal cues alone provide information for building up a mental representation of the event in question. Users of S-languages are habitually exposed to more elaborate and vivid descriptions of motion—actual and metaphorical. And it may well be that their mental imagery for described events—in comparison with users of V-languages —contains more information about manners of movement and change of state, along with the evaluative conclusions that can be drawn from such information.

Suggestive evidence for this proposal comes from reading accounts of the same event in newspapers written in different languages. For example, it is my impression that events reported in English and Dutch seem to be more active, dynamic, or violent than reports of the same events in French, Spanish, or Turkish. These impressions have been confirmed by native speakers of those languages. For example, compare the following three reports of an attempt by French troops to block a Greenpeace demonstration against a French nuclear test in the Pacific:

(8)   *English*

"Squads of troops ... *stormed* the Greenpeace flagship Rainbow Warrior.... 15 commandos *clambered* on board.... Greenpeace defied warnings not to *breach* the 12-mile exclusion zone to *power* across the lagoon in Greenpeace dinghies." (*The Guardian* [London])

(9)   *French*

"Les commandos de marine *arraisonnent* le Rainbow Warrior....
Le Rainbow Warrior est passé à la offensive dès l'aube,
*franchissant* la limite des eaux territoriales françaises ..."
'The marine commandos *take control of* the Rainbow Warrior....
The Rainbow Warrior switched over to the offensive at dawn,
*crossing* the limits of French territorial waters ...' (*Le Figaro* [Paris])

(10) *Spanish*

"Pero cada vez que una embarcación se atreve a *atravesar* la zona de exclusión ..."

'But each time that an embarkation dares to *cross* the exclusion zone ...' (*ABC* [Madrid])

While all changes of location are given with manner verbs in English (*storm*, *clamber*, *breach*, *power*), the two Romance languages use no manner verbs, and they devote less attention to movement overall. These differences hold up across a sample of news stories in these languages.

A small experiment (Slobin 2000) has begun to confirm the impression that there are major differences in mental imagery between speakers of S- and V-languages. I gave English and Spanish speakers passages to read from novels, later asking them to report mental imagery for the protagonist's manner of movement. The examples were from Spanish novels, in which manner verbs were not used, but in which the author had provided information about the nature of the terrain and the protagonist's inner state, allowing for inferences of manner. English speakers were given literal translations of the Spanish texts. For example, in a selection from Isabel Allende's *La casa de los espíritus* (*The House of the Spirits*), the following information was provided as part of a long paragraph:

(11) *Spanish original*

"Tomó sus maletas y echó a *andar por el barrial y las piedras de un sendero* que conducía al pueblo. *Caminó* más de diez minutos, agradecido de que no lloviera, porque *a duras penas podía avanzar con sus pesadas maletas* por ese camino y comprendió que la lluvia lo habría convertido en pocos segundos en un lodazal intransitable."

*English version*

"He picked up his bags and started to *walk through the mud and stones of a path* that led to the town. He *walked* for more than ten minutes, grateful that it was not raining, because *it was only with difficulty that he was able to advance along the path with his heavy suitcases*, and he realized that the rain would have converted it in a few seconds into an impassable mudhole."

Not surprisingly, almost all English speakers reported mental imagery for the manner in which the protagonist moved, using manner verbs such as *stagger, stumble, trudge*, as well as more elaborate descriptions, such as "he dodges occasional hazards in the trail," "he rocks from side to side," and "slowly edges his way down the trail." Surprisingly, only a handful of Spanish speakers from Mexico, Chile, and Spain provided such reports. The vast majority reported little or no imagery of the manner of the protagonist's movement, although they had clear images of the muddy, stony path and the physical surroundings of the scene. They reported having seen a series of static images or still pictures ("more like photographs"). Bilinguals tested in both languages systematically reported more mental imagery for manner of motion, and less for physical surroundings, when reading in English, in comparison with Spanish.

In current dissertation research at the University of California at Berkeley, Kyung-ju Oh has presented English and Korean speakers with a series of videoclips to label. In the clips, the same person is performing various activities, including moving in different manners. As expected, English speakers provide more manner verbs than Korean speakers. In a surprise memory task, subjects are asked to compare their memory of each clip with a standard clip of the same actor walking at a normal rate. English speakers, but not Korean speakers, accurately identify the length of stride and degree of arm swing in the original clips, as compared with the standard—although these details of manner did not occur in their labeling of the clips. This may be the first clear evidence of differential attention to *perceived* manner of motion on the basis of native language.

### 7.4.8   Salience of Paths and Landmarks

The differences between S- and V-languages are also reflected in relative attention to path segments and landmarks—that is, sources, goals, and other objects encountered along a trajectory (Slobin 1997). I will not summarize these patterns here, but will simply emphasize that lexicalization patterns play a role in determining the degree of attention to *all* event components, resulting in specific forms of narrative style and mental imagery that characterize event descriptions in the two language types. Briefly, V-language narratives are more concerned with establishing the physical and emotional settings in which people move, often allowing both path and manner to be inferred, whereas S-language narratives attend to both manner of movement and successive path segments. As one consequence, it seems that V-language speakers conceive of manners of motion as activities that take place in specified geographical regions, while S-language speakers "seem to conceive of manner and directed motion as *a single conceptual event,* making it difficult to have a mental image of one without the other" (Slobin 2000, 132; see also Ohara 2000).

### 7.4.9 Language and Thought Online in the Domain of Motion Events

To summarize, a large collection of different kinds of data strongly suggests that users of S- and V-languages attend differently to the components of motion events while producing or interpreting linguistic communications about motion. For S-language speakers, manner is an inherent component of directed motion along a path, and the semantic space of manner is highly differentiated. For V-language speakers, manner is much less salient and attention is focused on changes of location and the settings in which motion occurs. The determining linguistic factor seems to be the availability of a main-verb slot for manner verbs in S-languages, in contrast to a main-verb slot for path verbs in V-languages.[11] S-language speakers are thereby habituated to making frequent online decisions about the type of manner involved in motion events. A number of phenomena indicate that manner is a salient and differentiated conceptual field for such speakers, in comparison with speakers of V-languages. In summary, for S-language speakers:

• Manner verbs are easily accessed in a listing task.

• Manner verbs are frequently used in conversation, oral narrative, and written narrative.

• Speakers readily access many different types of manner verbs, attending to fine-grained distinctions between similar manners of movement.

• A large portion of the manner-verb lexicon is used in the preschool period, requiring learners to differentiate between types of manner.

• Meanings of manner verbs are readily extended for purposes of evaluation and metaphorical descriptions of events and processes.

- Listeners and readers tend to build up detailed mental images of manner of movement in reported events.

## 7.5  Spatial Descriptions

Similar evidence of linguistic influences on online attention is provided by the rich collection of studies of spatial relations carried out by members of the Cognitive Anthropology Research Group of the Max Planck Institute for Psycholinguistics in Nijmegen (e.g., Levinson, 1996a,b; Pederson et al. 1998). One component of this research distinguishes between languages that rely on *relative* versus *absolute* orientation in describing locations of objects. Relative systems are familiar to speakers of European languages, who tend to locate objects by reference to the position and orientation of the viewer of a scene (e.g., *to the left of the house, in front of the tree*). In absolute systems, reference is made to a fixed bearing, such as compass points or landscape features (e.g., *west of the house, north of the tree*).[12] Perhaps a third of the world's languages use absolute systems, in which, for example, one would say, 'There's a rabbit north of the tree', or 'seaward from the tree', rather than 'behind the tree'. In order to use an absolute system, you always have to know where you are in relation to the fixed external referent points. That is, online production and interpretation of utterances requires attention to those points, and users of such languages must constantly update their locations accordingly. This is perhaps one of the most powerful thinking-for-speaking effects that has been demonstrated. Even when you are in a windowless room, or traveling in a bus in the dark, you must know your location relative to the fixed points in order to talk about events and locations.[13] As we will see, online attention of this sort also has consequences for cognitive processes that occur outside of acts of speaking or understanding.

## 7.6  Memory for Reported Events

It is unlikely that people experience events in their lives differently because of the language they speak. But events quickly become part of a personal narrative, and then language can begin to shape those memories. As pointed out above, many of the events that we remember were encountered *only* through narrative; that is, human beings are voracious producers and consumers of news and stories. The mental representations that are built up in the process of "listening/reading for understanding" are likely to bear the traces of the language in which the event was reported, giving rise to effects such as those in the mental imagery experiment. It has long been known that verbal instructions and questions can influence recall, as shown most dramatically in research on eyewitness testimony (e.g., Loftus 1996). In fact, people can have vivid memories of events that they experienced only in the form of a verbal account. Piaget provided a particularly graphic case of what he called "memories which depend on other people" (1962, 187–188). He described a vivid and detailed childhood memory in which his nurse had prevented a man from kidnapping him. However, when he was 15, the nurse confessed that she had made up the story of the kidnap attempt. Piaget concluded, "I therefore must have heard, as a child, the account of this story, which my parents believed, and projected it into the past in the form of a visual memory, which was a memory of a memory, but false. Many real memories are doubtless of the same order." Research on "source monitoring" by Johnson and her collaborators (e.g., Johnson, Hashtroudi, and Lindsay 1993) provides a detailed picture of the factors that determine people's ability to assess the sources of their memories, knowledge, and beliefs. As Johnson, Hashtroudi, and Lindsay point out, "Movies, television, books, magazines, newspapers—all are sources of fictional information that may, under some circumstances, be treated as reliable information" (p. 13). It is quite likely that the language in which information is presented—both fictional and documentary—plays a role in the ways in which information is stored and evaluated. However, we still lack crosslinguistic research on such issues as eyewitness testimony and source monitoring, so the question of linguistic relativity in memory for reported events remains open.

## 7.7   Memory for Events for Later Reporting

In order to report an event, you must have paid attention to linguistically relevant components of that event while you experienced it. At first glance, this seems trivially obvious. When you report an encounter with a friend in a language with gender pronouns, you must have remembered the sex of the friend. But, of course, you would remember that aspect regardless of your language. However, when reporting an encounter in English, you may not remember if your friend approached you from the south, or from the direction of a distant landmark such as a mountain or the sea, as you would if you spoke a language that required this sort of absolute orientation. That is, you can only include those elements in the verbal account that you noticed while experiencing the reported situation. As Gumperz and Levinson have pointed out (1996, 27), "[T]hinking in a special way for speaking will not be enough. We must mentally encode experiences in such a way that we can describe them later, in the terms required by our language." Thus, those event components that must be attended to in thinking for speaking must also be mentally stored for future speaking. As noted earlier, thinking for *present* speaking becomes part of *potential* speaking. Here we have evidence for the classical Whorfian quest for covert effects of language on nonverbal cognition. The Nijmegen research has rigorously demonstrated such effects in a large number of nonlinguistic tasks, carried out across a range of linguistic and cultural communities. Pederson et al. (1998) make this point forcefully:

Far more than developing simple habituation, use of the linguistic system, we suggest, actually forces the speaker to make computations he or she might otherwise not make. Any particular experience might need to be later described, and many are. Accordingly many experiences must be remembered in such a way as to facilitate this. Since it seems, based on our findings, that the different frames of reference cannot be readily translated, we must represent our spatial memories in a manner specific to the socially normal means of expression. That is, the linguistic system is far more than just an *available* pattern for creating internal representations: to learn to speak a language successfully *requires* speakers to develop an appropriate mental representation which is then available for nonlinguistic purposes. (p. 586)

## 7.8    A Framework for Thinking-for-Speaking Research

Spatial conceptualization has provided a rich arena for research on possible linguistic effects on online thinking and memory.[14] Space turns out to be a domain that can be construed in quite different ways in different languages, although there are clearly underlying universals. Temporality is another such domain. For example, frog-story research shows different patterns of attention to such temporal factors as duration, boundedness, and simultaneity (Aksu-Koç and von Stutterheim 1994; Slobin 1996a). We have yet to determine the range and types of domains that are susceptible to online linguistic shaping of the sort proposed here. Diversity in linguistic coding provides the basic data for speculations about relativity, and habitual use of linguistic forms (see Fuchs and Robert 1997). That is, in the online tasks of producing and interpreting messages, attention is directed to the necessary analysis and categorization of experience. Most of the data presented in this chapter rely on an inferential argument: speakers of typologically different languages vary in their linguistic construals of events, across a wide range of situations of language use. There seem to be quite clear differences in habitual ways of talking about the sorts of events that all human beings experience and care about. More elusive have been clear demonstrations that these sorts of online attention may also have long-term and pervasive effects on mental representation and conceptual processes. The most successful attempts, thus far, come from research on absolute orientation (Pederson et al. 1998), number (Lucy 1992), deixis (Bickel 2000; Danziger 1994; Hanks 1990, 1996), and motion (summarized in this chapter). What is needed for a full picture of linguistic relativity and determinism is systematic exploration of areas of mental life in which thinking for speaking can be demonstrated as having effects on how people experience those events that they are likely to talk about later ("anticipatory effects"), matched with demonstrations of cognitive effects after events have been experienced ("consequential effects"). Schematically, there are three time frames that must be considered in a full research program:

• *Experience time:* This is the time of prelinguistic or nonlinguistic coding, when *anticipatory effects* of language may play a role. That is, the individual must attend to those event dimensions that are relevant for linguistic coding.

• *Speaking time:* This is the time of *thinking for speaking* and *listening for understanding*—that is, the time in which linguistically codable dimensions must be accessed and attended to.

• *Testing time:* This is the time for nonlinguistic assessment of attention to codable dimensions—that is, the testing of *consequential effects*: tests of recall, recognition, and inference.

Crosslinguistic and typological analysis provides candidates for research, but the challenge is to select those coded dimensions that are likely to have anticipatory and consequential effects. Only parts of the full scheme have been sketched out, and only with regard to a few domains of experience. However, I have argued here that—while researchers work at filling in the larger picture of anticipatory and consequential effects of language—the effects at speaking time present the critical interface between language and cognition.

### 7.9   Speaking, Thinking, and Cultural Practice

The various thinking-for-speaking phenomena summarized in this chapter seem to be independent of culture. The division between S-languages and V-languages is based entirely on lexicalization patterns. For example, France and Spain would seem to be closer, culturally, to England and Germany than to Turkey and Japan, yet the findings reported here make the opposite grouping. Similarly, Chinese does not group with Korean and Japanese, but rather with Germanic and Slavic languages with regard to salience of manner of motion. The Nijmegen research on spatial orientation also points to linguistic rather than cultural determinants. For example, two Mayan languages (Tzeltal, Tzotzil) use absolute orientation, while two other Mayan languages (Mopan, Yucatec) do not. The research also excludes geographical determinism, because the various orientation types are scattered across a range of terrains. For example, Belhare, spoken in the Himalayas, has a different spatial system than Swiss German, spoken in the Alps (Bickel 2000).

Examples such as these are methodologically appealing, in that they make it possible, to some extent, to collapse across cultures. However, acts of communication always take place in a cultural context, and cultural practices are part of the online processes that include thinking and speaking. Anyone who has lived in more than one language knows that each language is not only a system for coding objects and events, but also a system that—in its use—constitutes interpersonal and intrapersonal values, expectations, and dispositions. Ervin-Tripp (Ervin 1964) has provided a rare empirical demonstration that bilinguals reveal different "personalities" in using each of their languages—or at least that "a shift in language [may be] associated with a shift in social roles and emotional attitudes" (p. 506). She gave a personality test (the Thematic Apperception Test) to fluent French-English bilinguals. The TAT elicits stories in response to pictures, and subjects told stories about each picture in both French and English. Ervin-Tripp found that bilinguals provided significantly different personality profiles when responding to the same picture in French versus English. For example, French stories showed more withdrawal and autonomy, whereas English stories showed greater need for achievement. Here we go far beyond individual components of a language, finding that use of a language, as a whole, may invoke the cultural norms and practices in which it is embedded.

An important and growing body of work in anthropological linguistics provides more fine-grained demonstrations of ways in which culture and language co-constitute each other in ongoing processes of speaking and engaging in cultural practices. I will cite just a few of many such path-breaking studies.

Hanks has studied *deixis*, writing a book with a title that provides a clear picture of the approach: *Referential Practice: Language and Lived Space among the Maya* (1990). Using both linguistic and ethnographic data, he shows that

Maya deixis is related in basic and very significant ways to a range of other orientational systems in the Maya world. These include cultural understandings of the human body, the social organization of the household and domestic space, cardinal point orientation, agricultural practices whereby the land is transformed and goods produced, and the ritual enactments corresponding to all of the foregoing. (p. 8)

Bickel (1997, 2000), working on deixis in a quite different linguistic and cultural context, also deals with "the grammar of space and socio-cultural practice" (2000, 176). He documents grammaticization of spatial deixis throughout Belhare grammar, as well as demonstrating central roles of spatial location and orientation in a range of cultural practices, including design of houses and social relations. Bickel notes that thinking-for-speaking phenomena should not be sought in individual minds alone:

Correlations between language and cognition often attest to a unidirectional link from public language to private thinking. Correlations between linguistic and cultural patterns, however, suggest mutual influence, since both speaking and social behavior are publicly shared activities that are transmitted across generations. Thus, language and nonlinguistic practice together construct a relativized cognitive ground. From this perspective, Whorfian effects do not obtain between modules of isolated minds, but are fundamentally embedded in a *habitus* of public practice. (2000, 185)

Danziger (1996) shows that the Mopan Maya use similar frames of reference in spatial language and kinship relations. She points out that particular grammatical structures apply to both domains, emphasizing that "the experience of using language in social interaction therefore helps to engender culturally-specific modes of thinking" (p. 67). That is, thinking for speaking in similar fashion across domains—spatial and cultural—reinforces habitual ways of thinking about relations in general.

Finally, Gumperz (e.g., 1982, 1996) has long argued that uses of specific linguistic forms in conversation serve as contextualization cues to the presuppositions and ideologies that are inherent in any conversational exchange. He and Levinson conclude, "It follows that we cannot think of a 'world-view' as inherent in a language, somehow detached from all the practices established for its use" (Gumperz and Levinson 1996, 230).

The attempt to find thinking-for-speaking effects of particular linguistic forms is thus part of a much larger framework of online communication, negotiation, and action. What all of these processes have in common, however, is that they are *processes*—that is, they unfold in time and are shaped in use. It is difficult, in a language like English, to conceptualize dynamic interactions of ever-changing forces that nevertheless exhibit distinct patterns. In fact, note that all of the available terms seem to be nouns. With effort, we may be able to go beyond this sort of English speaking for thinking, as we attempt to develop dynamic models of "language, thought, and culture."

## Notes

1. I have presented thinking-for-speaking data on motion events in a number of places, and I give only schematized findings here. More detailed discussion of data on manner of movement can be found in Slobin 2000, on path and land-

marks in Slobin 1997, and on child language in Berman and Slobin 1994. A full list of references includes Batra 2001; Chouinard 1997; Dukhovny and Kaushanskaya 1998; Hsiao 1999; Jovanović and Kentfield 1998; Jovanović and Martinović-Zić, in press; Martinović-Zić and Jovanović, in press; Mucetti 1997; Özçalışkan 2000, in preparation; Özçalışkan and Slobin 1999, 2000a,b,c; Slobin 1987, 1996a,b; Slobin and Hoiting 1994.

2. The Latinate form of (1b) is available in English, but it is not the everyday expression. Thinking-for-speaking research is concerned with the habitual means of encoding used by speakers of a language.

3. Where there is no citation to a written report, reference is made to unpublished data that I have gathered together with students at the University of California at Berkeley and in collaboration with Harriet Jisa in Lyon, France, and Aura Bocaz in Chile.

4. The following verbs were listed by the students: *amble, barge, bike, bounce, bound, canter, caravan, careen, charge, chase, climb, coast, crawl, creep, dance, dart, dash, dawdle, dive, drag, drift, drive, edge, fall, flit, flitter, float, fly, gallop, glide, hike, hop, hurry, inch, jaunt, jet, jog, jump, leap, limp, lollygag, lope, march, meander, mosey, pace, pedal, plod, pony, prance, promenade, race, ramble, ride, roll, rollerblade, run, rush, sail, sashay, saunter, scale, scamper, scoot, scurry, scuttle, shoot, shuffle, skate, ski, skip, skitter, slide, slink, slip, slither, somersault, speed, spin, sprint, stalk, step, stomp, stride, stroll, strut, stumble, swagger, sweep, swim, swing, thrust, tiptoe, toboggan, traipse, trap, trot, truck, tumble, twirl, waddle, walk, waltz, wander, wiggle, zip, zoom.*

5. Similar results come from ongoing research in which speakers are asked to label videoclips of human movement. Thus far, English, Spanish, and Basque data are available (in Batra 2001, and from ongoing research by Slobin and Ibarretxe). For example, a clip of someone moving about in a slow, tired manner elicited a range of verbs from a group of 26 English speakers (*loaf, meander, mope, pace, saunter, slouch, slump, stroll, sulk, trudge, walk, wander*) but only three Spanish verbs with fairly general meanings of 'walk' (*andar, caminar, pasear*). The stimuli are currently being used in Spain, Turkey, Korea, and Thailand, eliciting manner verbs in Spanish, Basque, Turkish, Korean, and Thai— with the expectation that those languages will demonstrate a lower level of lexical diversity than English.

6. The following 34 types of manner verbs were used in English conversations, again indicating the availability of this domain: *clamber, climb, crawl, dash, dive, drag oneself, drift, drive, flee, float, flop, fly, glide, hike, jump, leap, march, plunge, poke, run, rush, slide, sneak, stagger, step, stride, stumble, toddle, totter, trot, trudge, walk, wander, zoom.*

7. For a discussion of intratypological differences in attention to manner of motion, see Slobin, in preparation.

8. This sample was picked to cut across language families: Romance, Turkic, Germanic, Slavic. From each novel, 20 trajectories were selected at random,

defined as a description of the motion of a protagonist from a resting position until coming to rest at a new position where a plot-advancing event takes place. The novels represented in the table are as follows: *Spanish:* Allende, Carpentier, Cela, Donoso, García Márquez, Muñoz Molina, Rulfo, Sabato, Vargas Llosa; *Turkish:* Atay, Başar, Fürüzan, Karasu, O. Kemal, Y. Kemal, Livaneli, Pamuk, Tekin; *English:* Anaya, Byatt, Derbyshire, du Maurier, Fowles, Hemingway, Lessing, McCullers, Steinbeck; *Russian:* Aksenov, Dostovskij, Gorbunov, Gorkij, Neznanskij, Vainer and Vainer.

9. The English novels were Anaya, Fowles, Hemingway, Lessing, McCullers, Steinbeck; the Spanish novels were Allende, Cela, Donoso, García Márquez, Sabato, and Vargas Llosa. Similar patterns appear in a smaller sample of translations between English (Hemingway, McCullers, Steinbeck) and Turkish (Karasu, Y. Kemal, Pamuk): 68% of English manner verbs were retained in Turkish translation, while 80% of Turkish manner verbs were retained in English translation. Engish translators, working from either Spanish or Turkish originals, often replaced V-language manner verbs with more expressive or dynamic manner verbs in English (47% of translated manner verbs from Spanish, 35% of translated manner verbs from Turkish); by contrast, Spanish and Turkish translators never amplified English manner verbs in translation. Similar findings are related for a sample of Spanish translations of 50 novels written in English (Mora Gutiérrez 1998). In brief, translations into English "up the ante" for manner expression, while translations out of English reduce the level of manner description.

10. In related research, Naigles and co-workers are finding evidence for typological preferences in the learning of new words in experimental contexts. English- and Spanish-speaking adults were presented with novel motion verbs in situations in which the verb could refer to either path or manner of motion. Naigles and Terrazas (1998) found that English speakers were more likely to attribute manner meanings, while Spanish speakers were more likely to attribute path meanings. Hohenstein (2001) has replicated these findings for monolingual English- and Spanish-speaking 7-year-olds (but not for 3-year-olds). These findings suggest that, in learning a language, the child develops expectations about the dominant lexicalization patterns of the language and uses these expectations as the basis of acquiring the meanings of new lexical items. Naigles et al. (1998, 547) suggest that language-specific lexicalization patterns should enable children "to *fast-map*, or quickly and accurately associate a new verb with its meaning."

11. this is somewhat of a simplification, because manner verbs are allowed for some kinds of path descriptions in V-languages, but are excluded from paths that cross a boundary or terminate in a change of state (Aske 1989; Slobin 1996b, 1997; Slobin and Hoiting 1994). What is important for the present argument is that there are no such restrictions on the use of manner verbs in S-languages, resulting in different habitual styles of event description for the two language types.

12. For simplicity of presentation, I omit the third system of spatial description—*intrinsic* orientation—which makes use of inherent properties of objects, such as fronts and backs.

13. Similar crosslinguistic, typological differences are reported for the use of *gestures* that accompany speech, showing differential attention to relative and absolute spatial relations, according to the type of language spoken, as well as differential attention to manner and path in S- and V-languages (Kita, Danziger, and Stolz, in press; Levinson, in press; McNeill, McCullough, and Duncan, in press; Özyürek and Kita 1999; Özyürek and Özçalışkan 2000; and chapters in McNeill 2000).

14. The framework outlined here was formulated in a discussion at the Max Planck Institute for Psycholinguistics in Nijmegen in 1993. The participants were Penny Brown, Pim Levelt, Steve Levinson, John Lucy, Dan Slobin, and David Wilkins.

## References

Aksenov, V. (2000). *Apel'siny iz Marokko*. Moscow: Izograf EKSMO Press.

Aksu-Koç, A. A., and von Stutterheim, C. (1994). Temporal relations in narrative: Simultaneity. In R. A. Berman and D. I. Slobin, *Relating events in narrative: A crosslinguistic developmental study* (pp. 393–456). Hillsdale, NJ: Erlbaum.

Allende, I. (1982). *La casa de los espíritus*. Barcelona: Plaza and Janes. [English transl. M. Bogin (1985). *The house of the spirits*. New York: Knopf.]

Anaya, R. (1972). *Bless me, Última*. New York: Warner Books. [Spanish transl. anon. (1992). *Bendíceme, Última*. New York: Warner Books.]

Aske, J. (1989). Path predicates in English and Spanish: A closer look. *Proceedings of the Berkeley Linguistics Society*, *15*, 1–14.

Atay, O. (1971). *Tutunamayanlar*. Ankara: Sinan Yayınları.

Başar, K. (1992). *Sen olsaydın yapmazdın, biliyorum*. Istanbul: AFA Yayınları.

Batra, R. R. (2001). *e-Motion: Using digitized video clips to explore the semantic fields of manner verbs*. Unpublished senior honors thesis, Program in Cognitive Science, University of California, Berkeley.

Berman, R. A., and Slobin, D. I. (1994). *Relating events in narrative: A crosslinguistic developmental study*. Hillsdale, NJ: Erlbaum.

Bickel, B. (1997). Spatial operations in deixis, cognition, and culture: Where to orient oneself in Belhare. In J. Nuyts and E. Pederson (Eds.), *Language and conceptualization* (pp. 46–83). Cambridge: Cambridge University Press.

Bickel, B. (2000). Grammar and social practice: On the role of "culture" in linguistic relativity. In S. Niemeier and R. Dirven (Eds.), *Evidence for linguistic relativity* (pp. 161–192). Amsterdam: John Benjamins.

Bowerman, M. (1985). What shapes children's grammars? In D. I. Slobin (Ed.), *The crosslinguistic study of language acquisition: Vol. 2. Theoretical issues* (pp. 1257–1319). Hillsdale, N.J.: Erlbaum.

Bowerman, M., and Choi, S. (2001). Shaping meanings for language: Universal and language-specific in the acquisition of spatial semantic categories. In M. Bowerman and S. C. Levinson (Eds.), *Language acquisition and conceptual development* (pp. 475–511). Cambridge: Cambridge University Press.

Brown, R. (1958). *Words and things.* Glencoe, IL: Free Press.

Byatt, A. S. (1990). *Possession: A romance.* New York: Random House.

Carpentier, A. (1983). *El siglo de las luces.* Barcelona: Editorial Seix Barral.

Cela, C. J. (1942). *La familia de Pascual Duarte.* Madrid: Editorial Aldecoa. [English transl. A. Kerrigan (1964). *The family of Pascual Duarte.* Boston: Little, Brown.]

Choi, S., and Bowerman, M. (1991). Learning to express motion events in English and Korean: The influence of language-specific lexicalization patterns. *Cognition, 41,* 83–121.

Chouinard, M. M. (1997). *Speaking of motion…: How do children acquiring their first language learn to properly express motion events?* Unpublished senior honors thesis, Department of Psychology, University of California, Berkeley.

Danziger, E. (1994). Out of sight, out of mind: Person, perception, and function in Mopan Maya spatial deixis. *Linguistics, 32,* 885–907.

Danziger, E. (1996). Parts and their counterparts: Spatial and social relationships in Mopan Maya. *The Journal of the Royal Anthropological Institute, 2,* 67–82.

Derbyshire, J. (1996). *Seeing Calvin Coolidge in a dream.* New York: St. Martin's Griffin.

Donoso, J. (1958). *Coronación.* Barcelona: Editorial Seix Barral. [English transl. J. Goodwin (1965). New York: Knopf.]

Dostoevskij, F. (1880/1970). *Brat'ja Karamazovy.* Leningrad: Izd-vo Xudožestvennaja Literatura.

Dukhovny, E., and Kaushanskaya, M. (1998). *Russian verbs of motion.* Unpublished paper, Department of Psychology, University of California, Berkeley.

du Maurier, D. (1938). *Rebecca.* New York: Modern Library. [Spanish transl. F. Calleja (1959). *Rebeca.* Barcelona: Plaza and Janes.]

Ervin, S. M. (1964). Language and TAT content in bilinguals. *Journal of Abnormal and Social Psychology, 68,* 500–507.

Fowles, J. (1969). *The French lieutenant's woman.* Boston: Little, Brown. [Spanish transl. A. M. de la Fuente (1981). *La mujer del teniente francés.* Barcelona: Editorial Argos Vergara.]

Fuchs, C., and Robert, S. (Eds.). (1997). *Diversité des langues et représentations cognitives.* Paris: OPHRYS. [English transl. (1999). *Language diversity and cognitive representations.* Amsterdam: John Benjamins.]

Fürüzan. (1974). *47'liler*. Ankara: Bilgi Yayınevi.

Fürüzan. (1974). *Parasız yatılı*. Ankara: Bilgi Basımevi.

García Márquez, G. (1982). *Cien años de soledad*. Madrid: Espasa-Calpe. [English transl. G. Rabassa (1970). *One hundred years of solitude*. New York: Harper and Row.]

Goldberg, A. E. (1995). *Constructions: A Construction Grammar approach to argument structure*. Chicago: University of Chicago Press.

Gorbunov, V. (1994). *Krov na podramnike*. Moscow: Nadežda.

Gorkij, M. (1913/1958). *Detstvo*. Moscow: Goslitizdat.

Gumperz, J. J. (1982). *Discourse strategies*. Cambridge: Cambridge University Press.

Gumperz, J. J., and Levinson, S. C. (Eds.). (1996). *Rethinking linguistic relativity*. Cambridge: Cambridge University Press.

Hanks, W. F. (1990). *Referential practice: Language and lived space among the Maya*. Chicago: University of Chicago Press.

Hanks, W. F. (1996). Language form and communicative practices. In J. J. Gumperz and S. C. Levinson (Eds.), *Rethinking linguistic relativity* (pp. 232–270). Cambridge: Cambridge University Press.

Hemingway, E. (1941). *For whom the bell tolls*. London: Jonathan Cape. [Spanish transl. L. de Aguado (1973). *Por quién doblan las campanas*. Barcelona: Editorial Planeta.] [Turkish transl. N. Özyürek (1966). *Çanlar kimin için çalıyor*. Istanbul: Varlık Yayınlar.]

Hohenstein, J. M. (2001). *Motion event similarities in English- and Spanish-speaking children*. Unpublished doctoral dissertation, Yale University.

Hsiao, A. H.-H. (1999). *Holding the frog in place: Linguistic typology of Mandarin Chinese*. Unpublished senior honors thesis, Department of Psychology, University of California, Berkeley.

Johnson, M. K., Hashtroudi, S., and Lindsay, D. S. (1993). Source monitoring. *Psychological Bulletin, 114*, 3–28.

Jovanović, J., and Kentfield, M. (1998). *Manifold manner: An exploratory analysis of French and English verbs of motion*. Unpublished paper, Department of Psychology, University of California, Berkeley.

Jovanović, J., and Martinović-Zić, A. (in press). Why manner matters: Contrasting English and Serbo-Croatian typology in motion descriptions. In C. Moder and A. Martinović-Zić (Eds.), *Discourse across languages and cultures*. Amsterdam: John Benjamins.

Karasu, B. (1985). *Gece*. Istanbul: Metis Yayınları. [English transl. G. Gün and B. Karasu (1994). *Night*. London: Louisiana State University Press.]

Kemal, O. (1960). *El kızı*. Istanbul: Ak Kitabevi.

Kemal, Y. (1970). *Ağrıdağı efsanesi*. Istanbul: Cem Yayınevi. [English transl. T. Kemal (1975). *The legend of Ararat*. London: Collins and Harvill.]

Kita, S., Danziger, E., and Stolz, C. (in press). Cultural specificity of spatial schemas as manifested in spontaneous gestures. In M. Gattis (Ed.), *Spatial schemas in abstract thought*. Cambridge, MA: MIT Press.

Lessing, D. (1952). *A proper marriage*. New York: New American Library. [Spanish transl. F. Parcerisas and A. Samons (1979). *Un casamiento convencional*. Barcelona: Editorial Argos Vergara.]

Levelt, W. J. M. (1989). *Speaking: From intention to articulation*. Cambridge, MA: MIT Press.

Levinson, S. C. (1996a). Frames of reference and Molyneux's question: Cross-linguistic evidence. In P. Bloom, M. A. Peterson, L. Nadel, and M. F. Garrett (Eds.), *Language and space* (pp. 109–169). Cambridge, MA: MIT Press.

Levinson, S. C. (1996b). Relativity in spatial conception and description. In J. J. Gumperz and S. C. Levinson (Eds.), *Rethinking linguistic relativity* (pp. 177–202). Cambridge: Cambridge University Press.

Levinson, S. C. (in press). *Space in language and cognition: Explorations in cognitive diversity*. Cambridge: Cambridge University Press.

Livaneli, Z. (1979). *Arafatta bir çocuk*. Istanbul: Cem Yayınevi.

Loftus, E. F. (1996). *Eyewitness testimony*. Cambridge, MA: Harvard University Press.

Lucy, J. (1992). *Grammatical categories and cognition: A case study of the linguistic relativity hypothesis*. Cambridge: Cambridge University Press.

Lucy, J. (1996). The scope of linguistic relativity: An analysis and review of empirical research. In J. J. Gumperz and S. C. Levinson (Eds.), *Rethinking linguistic relativity* (pp. 37–69). Cambridge: Cambridge University Press.

Lucy, J. (2000). Introductory comments. In S. Niemeier and R. Dirven (Eds.), *Evidence for linguistic relativity* (pp. ix–xxi). Amsterdam: John Benjamins.

Martinović-Zić, A., and Jovanović, J. (in press). Conceptualization of motion and language-specific constraints in first-language acquisition. *MIT working papers in linguistics, 26*.

Mayer, M. (1969). *Frog, where are you?* New York: Dial Press.

McCullers, C. (1946). *The member of the wedding*. Boston: Houghton Mifflin. [Spanish transl. J. Silva (1982). *Frankie y la boda*. Barcelona: Bruguera.] [Turkish transl. I. Kantemir (1991). *Düğünün bir üyesi*. Istanbul: Remzi Kitabevi.]

McNeill, D. (Ed.). (2000). *Language and gesture: Window into thought and action*. Cambridge: Cambridge University Press.

McNeill, D., McCullough, K.-E., and Duncan, S. D. (in press). An ontogenetic universal and how to explain it. In C. Müller and R. Posner (Eds.), *The semantics and pragmatics of everyday gestures*. Berlin: Verlag Arno Spitz.

Mora Gutiérrez, J. P. (1998). *Directed motion in English and Spanish*. Unpublished doctoral dissertation, University of Seville, Spain.

Mucetti, R. (1997). *Thinking and speaking about movement: How parents and their children talk about motion events in English, Spanish, and Italian during the early stages of language acquisition.* Unpublished senior honors thesis, Department of Psychology, University of California, Berkeley.

Muñoz Molina, A. (1992). *Los misterios de Madrid.* Barcelona: Editorial Seix Barral.

Naigles, L. R., Eisenberg, A. R., Kako, E. T., Highter, M., and McGraw, N. (1998). Speaking of motion: Verb use in English and Spanish. *Language and Cognitive Processes, 13,* 521–549.

Naigles, L. R., and Terrazas, P. (1998). Motion-verb generalizations in English and Spanish: Influences of language and syntax. *Psychological Science, 9,* 363–369.

Narayanan, S. (1997). *Knowledge-based action representations for metaphor and aspect (KARMA).* Unpublished doctoral dissertation, University of California, Berkeley.

Neznanskij, F. (1984). *Jarmarka v Sokol'nikax.* Frankfurt am Main: Posev.

Ohara, K. H. (2000). Cognitive and structural constraints on motion descriptions: Observations from Japanese and English. *Proceedings of the 2nd International Conference on Cognitive Science and the 16th Annual Meeting of the Japanese Cognitive Science Society (Joint Conference),* 994–997.

Özçalışkan, Ş. (2000, August). *Contrastive effect of narrative perspective vs. typological constraints in encoding manner of motion: A developmental look.* Paper presented at the 7th International Pragmatics Conference, Budapest.

Özçalışkan, Ş. (2002). *Metaphors we move by: A crosslinguistic analysis of motion event metaphors in English and Turkish.* Unpublished doctoral dissertation, University of California, Berkeley.

Özçalışkan, Ş., and Slobin, D. I. (1999). Learning "how to search for the frog": Expression of manner of motion in English, Spanish, and Turkish. *Proceedings of the Boston University Conference on Language Development, 23,* 541–552.

Özçalışkan, Ş., and Slobin, D. I. (2000a). *Climb up* vs. *ascend climbing*: Lexicalization choices in expressing motion events with manner and path components. *Proceedings of the Boston University Conference on Language Development, 24,* Vol. 2, 558–570.

Özçalışkan, Ş., and Slobin, D. I. (2000b, August). *Codability effects on the expression of manner of motion in Turkish and English.* Pater presented at the 10th International Conference on Turkish Linguistics, Istanbul. [to appear in the conference proceedings, ed. by S. Özsoy]

Özçalışkan, Ş., and Slobin, D. I. (2000c). Expression of manner of movement in monolingual and bilingual adult narratives: Turkish vs. English. In A. Göksel and C. Kerslake (Eds.), *Studies on Turkish and Turkic languages.* Wiesbaden: Harrassowitz.

Özyürek, A., and Kita, S. (1999). Expressing manner and path in English and Turkish: Differences in speech, gesture, and conceptualization. *Proceedings of the Cognitive Science Society, 21,* 507–512.

Özyürek, A., and Özçalışkan, Ş. (2000). How do children learn to conflate manner and path in their speech and gestures? *Proceedings of the Stanford Child Language Research Forum, 30,* 77–85.

Pamuk, O. (1990). *Kara kitap.* Istanbul: Can Yayınlari. [English transl. G. Gün (1994). *The black book.* New York: Farrar Straus Giroux.]

Pederson, E., Danziger, E., Wilkins, D., Levinson, S., Kita, S., and Senft, G. (1998). Semantic typology and spatial conceptualization. *Language, 74,* 557–589.

Piaget, J. (1962). *Play, dreams and imitation in childhood.* New York: Norton. [Transl. of (1946) *La formation du symbole chez l'enfant: Imitation, jeu et rêve, image et représentation.* Neuchâtel: Delachaux et Niestlé.]

Pinker, S. (1989). *Learnability and cognition: The acquisition of argument structure.* Cambridge, MA: MIT Press.

Pinker, S. (1994). *The language instinct: How the mind creates language.* New York: Morrow.

Rulfo, J. (1953). *Pedro Páramo.* Barcelona: Editorial Planeta.

Sabato, E. (1950). *El túnel.* Barcelona: Editorial Seix Barral. [English transl. M. S. Peden (1988). New York: Ballantine Books.]

Slobin, D. I. (1987). Thinking for speaking. *Proceedings of the Berkeley Linguistics Society, 13,* 435–444.

Slobin, D. I. (1996a). From "thought and language" to "thinking for speaking." In J. J. Gumperz and S. C. Levinson (Eds.), *Rethinking linguistic relativity* (pp. 70–96). Cambridge: Cambridge University Press.

Slobin, D. I. (1996b). Two ways to travel: Verbs of motion in English and Spanish. In M. Shibatani and S. A. Thompson (Eds.), *Grammatical constructions: Their form and meaning* (pp. 195–217). Oxford: Oxford University Press.

Slobin, D. I. (1997). Mind, code, and text. In J. Bybee, J. Haiman, and S. A. Thompson (Eds.), *Essays on language function and language type: Dedicated to T. Givón* (pp. 437–467). Amsterdam: John Benjamins.

Slobin, D. I. (2000). Verbalized events: A dynamic approach to linguistic relativity and determinism. In S. Niemeier and R. Dirven (Eds.), *Evidence for linguistic relativity* (pp. 107–138). Amsterdam: John Benjamins.

Slobin, D. I. (in preparation). The many ways to search for a frog: Linguistic typology and the expression of motion events. In S. Strömqvist and L. Verhoeven (Eds.), *Relating events in narrative: Typological and contextual perspectives.* Mahwah, NJ: Erlbaum.

Slobin, D. I., and Hoiting, N. (1994). Reference to movement in spoken and signed languages: Typological considerations. *Proceedings of the Berkeley Linguistics Society, 20,* 487–505.

Steinbeck, J. (1947). *The pearl*. New York: Viking. [Spanish transl. F. Baldiz (1980). *La perla*. Barcelona: Balaguer.] [Turkish transl. A. Selver (1995). *İnci*. Istanbul: Oda Yayınlar.]

Strömqvist, S., and Verhoeven, L. (Eds.). (in preparation). *Relating events in narrative: Typological and contextual perspectives*. Mahwah, NJ: Erlbaum.

Talmy, L. (1991). Path to realization: A typology of event conflation. *Proceedings of the Berkeley Linguistics Society, 17*, 480–519.

Talmy, L. (2000). *Toward a cognitive semantics*. Cambridge, MA: MIT Press.

Tekin, L. (1990). *Berci Kristin çöp masalları*. Istanbul: Metis Yayınları. [English transl. R. Christie and S. Paker (1993). *Berji Kristin: Tales from the Garbage Hills*. New York: Marion Boyars.]

Vainer, A., and Vainer, G. (1972). *Vizit k minotavru*. Moscow: Molodaja Gvardija.

Vargas Llosa, M. (1977). *La tía Julia y el escribidor*. Barcelona: Editorial Seix Barral. [Spanish transl. H. R. Lane (1982). *Aunt Julia and the script-writer*. New York: Avon Books.]

Yu, N. (1998). *The contemporary theory of metaphor: A perspective from Chinese*. Amsterdam: John Benjamins.

_I am hoping this is more pertinent to where I am going_

# IV

## Languages as Tool Kit: Does the Language We Acquire Augment Our Capacity for Higher-Order Representation and Learning?

_Y: scaffolding: if there's a word, there's possibly a new concept to grasp._

A man-made object designed to
symbolize and ~~facilitate~~ *pander to* human
motives ~~for~~ ~~sitting~~ being seated.

# 8

# Why We're So Smart

Dedre Gentner

## 8.1 Introduction

Human cognitive abilities are remarkable. Our mental agility has allowed us to adapt to a vast range of environments, and even to adapt our environments to suit ourselves. We've been clever enough to eradicate most of our competitors and to spread over most of the earth. Indeed, we now find ourselves in the ironic position of striving to preserve a few of our formerly fearsome predators.

What is the nature of this ability? A list of the cognitive skills that distinguish us would include

• The ability to draw abstractions from particulars—to generalize experience and store regularities across vastly different cases

• The ability to maintain hierarchies of abstraction, so that we can store information about Fido, about dachshunds, about dogs, or about living things

• The ability to concatenate assertions and arrive at a new conclusion

• The ability to reason outside of the current context—to think about different locations and different times and even to reason hypothetically about different possible worlds

• The ability to compare and contrast two representations to discover where they are consistent and where they differ

• The ability to reason analogically—to notice common relations across different situations and project further inferences

• The ability to learn and use external symbols to represent numerical, spatial, or conceptual information

*[handwritten margin note: What is a chair?]*

*[handwritten margin note: metaphor]*

Our language abilities are equally outstanding. They include our ability to learn a generative, recursive grammar, as well as a set of semantic-conceptual abilities:

· The ability to learn symbols that lack any iconic relation to their referents

· The ability to learn and use symbols whose meanings are defined in terms of other learned symbols, including even recursive symbols such as the set of all sets

· The ability to invent and learn terms for abstractions as well as for concrete entities

· The ability to invent and learn terms for relations as well as things

To what do we owe these powers? Are they multiple separate abilities, or is there a core set of abilities that engenders them all? At least three sources of our superiority have been proposed. One is innate domain theories: perhaps our starting knowledge state is qualitatively superior to that of other animals. Another possibility is innate processing abilities: we might possess larger processing capacity and/or more powerful learning mechanisms than other animals. A third possibility is that it is participation in human language and culture that gives us our edge. I will argue for the latter two possibilities. This is not to deny the considerable evidence that human infants are born with built-in attentional capacities and tacit expectations about the physical world and about social inter-actions. However, it's likely that many of those capacities are shared with other higher animals, particularly social animals.[1] The question here is what makes us smarter than the rest.

My thesis is this: what makes humans smart is (1) our exceptional ability to learn by analogy, (2) the possession of symbol systems such as language and mathematics, and (3) a relation of mutual causation between them whereby our analogical prowess is multiplied by the pos-session of relational language. My argument has three parts. First, rela-tional concepts are critical to higher-order cognition, but relational concepts are both nonobvious in initial learning and elusive in memory retrieval. Second, analogy is the mechanism by which relational knowl-edge is revealed. Third, language serves both to invite learning relational concepts and to provide cognitive stability once they are learned. In short, analogy is the key to conceptual learning, and relational language is the key to analogy.

*[handwritten margin note: Simplistic. It may already be there]*

My case for the importance of language rests on an account of higher-order learning that my colleagues and I have been developing for the last two decades. I begin by laying out a general account of cognitive development, emphasizing what we have called "the career of similarity" (Gentner and Rattermann 1991). I then discuss the symbiotic development of analogy and relational language.

## 8.2    The Career of Similarity

In his career-of-similarity hypothesis, Quine (1960) proposed that over development, children move from perceiving only "brute" perceptual similarity to perceiving more sophisticated likenesses—"theoretical" similarity. The career of similarity has wide ramifications. Virtually every cognitive process, from categorization to transfer, is influenced by explicit or implicit similarity comparisons.

*[handwritten margin note: No? Is it justmore tenuous?]*

Gentner and Rattermann (1991) amplified this account to propose a developmental progression (1) from simply responding to overall similarity to attending to selective similarity; and (2) within selective similarity, from a focus on object similarity to a focus on relational similarity, and from perceptual commonalities to conceptual commonalities. We reviewed evidence to suggest that a major driver of this relational shift in similarity is changes in children's knowledge—particularly the acquisition of higher-order relational knowledge.

On this account, the career of similarity exists in a relation of mutual causation with the nature of children's representations. Children's initial knowledge representations differ from adult representations in being (1) more situation-specific, (2) more perceptual, and (3) more variable. There is abundant evidence for the claim that early representations contain relatively more situation-specific perceptual information than do adult representations (e.g., Rovee-Collier and Fagen 1981; Landau, Smith, and Jones 1988). The third claim, early variability, requires some explanation. What I mean is that early representations are highly variable across contexts, even within the same child. That is, different representations will be invoked at different times for situations that an

*different*
*Weather, different time, different*
*different chemical to approach*
*balance is*
*unfamiliar*

adult would encode in like terms. I hypothesize that even something as "stable" in adult life as the neighbor's dog coming to the fence may be represented differently on different occasions by a very young child.

These representational claims have implications for the career of similarity. The instability of early representations implies that children's earliest similarity matches should be highly conservative: that is, babies should perceive similarity only when there is a large degree of overlap. This is often stated as the claim of holistic similarity in babies and thought to arise from perceptual specificity. I suggest that the holistic similarity arises only in part from early perceptual specificity—it mainly results from the variability of early representations. For if different construals are possible even for the same object, then only if there is an extremely high degree of potential overlap will the child's representations overlap enough for him to perceive similarity.

There is considerable evidence for the claim of early conservative similarity (Gentner and Medina 1998; Gentner and Rattermann 1991; Smith 1989). For example, Chen, Sanchez, and Campbell (1997) found that 10-month-old infants could learn to pull on a cloth to reach a toy, but they failed to transfer to a new pulling situation unless it was highly similar to the previously experienced situation. By 13 months, infants were able to transfer with less concrete similarity. In studies of infants' causal reasoning, Oakes and Cohen (1990) found evidence both for early conservatism and for an early focus on objects over relations. They investigated 6- and 10-month-old infants' perception of launching events by varying spatial and temporal features that should render such events either causal or noncausal. The results showed that infants at 10 months, but not 6 months, discriminated the events on the basis of causal relations. The younger infants appeared to respond on the basis of the individual objects in the events, but not the causal relationship between objects. Their results suggest that infants' perception of causal relations appears gradually and that it is initially very conservative—that is, specific to the kinds of objects included in the event.

The claim that infants are extremely conservative learners may seem wildly implausible in view of the rapidity of human learning. I suggest that far from being a disadvantage, early conservatism is necessary in order for humans to be appropriately flexible learners. The fact that early comparisons are extremely conservative allows for emergent abstractions. This brings me to the second part of the causal interaction: the influence of similarity comparisons on representation.

I began by stating that analogical processing is central in human cognition. By "analogical processing" I do not mean only the perception of distant similarity in which only the relations match. Rather, I include the kind of mundane similarity comparisons that involve common entities as well as common relations. Such comparisons are a driving force in children's learning. The course of emergent abstractions depends crucially on the way structure-mapping operates: on which similarity matches are relatively easy and inevitable, and on the results of carrying out comparisons. I will give a brief review of structure-mapping in section 8.3, but for now I focus on three key points.

First, the structure-mapping process is sensitive to both object similarity and relational similarity, but favors common relational structure because of a tacit preference for systematicity (connectivity) and depth in the matching process. Second, the same process of structural alignment and mapping is used for mundane literal similarity as for analogy. Literal similarity (overall similarity) comparisons are easy to compute, because the object and relational matches are all mutually supportive. Analogical matches are more difficult, because the relational correspondences are not supported by object matches, and may even be opposed by them.[2] Third, carrying out any comparison—even a literal similarity comparison—tends to render common relations more salient; thus, even a literal comparison facilitates carrying out a later analogy that is based on the same relational structure.

Overall (literal) similarity matches are the easiest matches to notice and process. Because both object correspondences and relation correspondences enter into the one consistent alignment, such matches can readily be aligned even early in learning, when representational variability is high. This, I believe, is the underlying reason that young children rely on holistic similarity. When representations are variable, only a rich, overdetermined match has the redundancy necessary to guarantee finding an alignment, and hence strong overall matches constitute the earliest reliable similarity matches (Kemler 1983; Smith 1989). The privileges of overall literal similarity do not end with childhood. There is evidence that adults also process literal similarity matches faster than purely relational matches (Gentner and Kurtz, in preparation; Kurtz and Gentner 1998) and high-similarity matches faster than low-similarity matches (Wolff and Gentner 2000). Further, rich concrete matches, such as two identical dachshunds, are perceived as more similar than sparse concrete matches, such as two identical circles, by both children and adults (Gentner and Rattermann 1991; Tversky 1977).

Comparison processes can be prompted in several ways. Some comparisons are invited explicitly, when likenesses are pointed out by adults: for example, "That's a wolf. It's like a dog, except it's wilder." Some comparisons are invited by the fact that two situations have a common linguistic label (e.g., "These are both lamps"). Some arise from the child's spontaneous noticing of similarity. Some are engineered by the child, as in the circular reaction (Piaget 1952). An infant notices something interesting and then tries to repeat it again and again. This fascination with immediate repetition, I suggest, is a manifestation of comparison in learning. Such close repetition with variation may provide an ideal learning experience for infants.

Although comparison is an inborn process, its manifestation—whether a sense of sameness is perceived for a given pair of potential analogues—depends on how the situations are represented, and this in turn depends on experience. The conservative learning thesis implies that most of children's early spontaneous comparisons are mundane by adult lights. Early in learning, comparisons are made only between situations that match overwhelmingly. These close comparisons yield small insights; they render small differences between the situations salient; and they result in marginally more abstract representations that can then participate in more distant comparisons. As similarity comparisons evolve from being perceptual and context bound to becoming increasingly sensitive to common relational structure, children show an increasing capacity to reason at the level of abstract commonalities and rules.

Comparison is a major means by which children go beyond their early situated representations. Comparisons among exemplars—initially concrete, but progressively more abstract—promote abstraction and rule learning. Such learning provides a route by which children learn the theory-like relational information that informs adult concepts. For example, children come to know that both tigers and sharks are carnivores, while deer and hippopotamuses are herbivores, that tigers prey on deer, and so on; they learn that a taxi is not defined as a yellow car but as a vehicle that can be hired (Keil and Batterman 1984). The structure-mapping process is central in this evolution in part because it allows learners to discover commonalities. More importantly, as noted above, the structure-mapping process promotes relational commonalities over common object properties. This is important because objects are more cognitively and perceptually salient than relations in the information structure of the perceived world (Gentner 1982; Gentner and Boroditsky 2001). Objects (or more precisely, complex structural objects) are relatively easy to individuate; they are learned early; and even adults are swayed by object matches in contexts where relational matches would clearly be more useful. The great value of analogy—and of structure-mapping processes even when applied to literal comparisons—lies in creating a focus on common relational systems and thus lifting a relational pattern away from its object arguments.

I have argued so far (1) that relational learning is important to the development of cognition and (2) that it proceeds via structure-mapping processes. Because many of the specific processing claims made here require an understanding of structure-mapping, before turning to the role of language I review the theory and simulation here.

## 8.3   Structure-Mapping: A Brief Review

Structure-mapping theory postulates that the comparison process is one of alignment and mapping between structured conceptual representations (Falkenhainer, Forbus, and Gentner 1989; Gentner 1983, 1989; Gentner and Markman 1997; Goldstone 1994; Goldstone and Medin 1994; Markman and Gentner 1993; Medin, Goldstone, and Gentner 1993). The commonalities and differences between two situations are found by determining the maximal structurally consistent alignment between their representations. A structurally consistent alignment is characterized by one-to-one mapping (i.e., an element in one representation can correspond to at most one element in the other representation) and parallel connectivity (i.e., if elements correspond across the two representations, then the elements they govern must correspond as well). When more than one structurally consistent match exists between two representations, contextual relevance and the relative systematicity of the competing interpretations are used. All else being equal, the richest and deepest relational match is preferred (the systematicity principle). The alignment process favors deep systems over shallow systems, even if they have equal numbers of matches (Forbus and Gentner 1989). Finally, predicates connected to the common structure in the base, but not initially present in the target, are proposed as candidate inferences in the target. Because these inferences are the structural completion at the best match between the terms, and because the best match is highly likely to be a deep relational match, the candidate inferences are often causally informative. Thus, structure-mapping processes can lead to spontaneous but informative inferences.

Sentences (1)–(5) show different kinds of similarity matches:

(1)  The dog chased the cat.

(2)  The coyote chased the lynx.

(3)  The shark chased the mackerel.    *chasing*

(4)  Amalgamated Tire Co. made a takeover bid for Racine Ironworks.

(5)  The cat chased the mouse.

Because matches at all levels enter into the alignment process, the easiest comparisons should be those of rich overall (literal) similarity. A concrete match like {(1) and (2)}—in which both the objects and the relations match—is intuitively easier to process than a less similar abstract match like {(1) and (3)}, or—yet more challengingly—{(1) and (4)}. For pairs like (1) and (2), the comparison process is easy, because the matches are mutually supporting, yielding one clear dominant interpretation. As noted above, overall similarity matches—in which the object match and the relational matches are mutually supporting—are easier to process than purely analogical matches like {(1) and (3)}, in which there are often stray object-attribute matches that are inconsistent with the maximal relational match. A particularly difficult case is a cross-mapped analogy like {(1) and (5)}. A cross-mapped analogy (Gentner and Toupin

1986) contains an object match (e.g., cat → cat) that is inconsistent with the relational match. Such matches are more difficult for children to map than either literal similarity matches or standard analogies, because there are competing modes of alignment. However, despite the greater difficulty of a cross-mapping, older children and adults normally resolve them in favor of the relational match—evidence of a tacit preference for systematicity in analogical alignment (Gentner and Toupin 1986; Markman and Gentner 1993).[3] Even adults often choose the object match when asked to state correspondences in cross-mapped pictorial scenes (Markman and Gentner 1993), especially under a high processing load (Kubose, Holyoak, and Hummel, in preparation). Finally, Goldstone (1994) found evidence that local matches dominate early and relational matches later in processing cross-mapped matches. A computational model of analogical mapping, the Structure-Mapping Engine (SME), provides a model of the processes of alignment and mapping.

This process model has important implications for learning and development. SME's alignment process, taken as a model of human processing, suggests that the act of carrying out a comparison promotes structural alignment and renders the common structure, especially relational structure, more salient (Gentner and Bowdle 2001; Markman and Gentner 1993; Wolff and Gentner 2000). It is also important that structure-mapping is accomplished with a process that begins blind and local. Achieving a deep structural alignment does not require advance knowledge of the point of the comparison. (If it did, it would be relatively useless as a developmental learning process.)

There are at least five ways in which the process of comparison can further the acquisition of knowledge: (1) highlighting and schema abstraction; (2) projection of candidate inferences—inviting inferences from one item to the other; (3) re-representation—altering one or both representations so as to improve the match (and thereby, as an important side effect, promoting representational uniformity); (4) promoting attention to relevant differences; and (5) restructuring—altering the domain structure of one domain in terms of the other (Gentner and Wolff 2000). These processes enable the child to learn abstract commonalities and to make relational inferences.

Highlighting commonalities may seem like a rather trivial learning process, but this is not true in the case of common relations. Considerable evidence shows that the process of promoting common relational structure invited by mutual alignment between closely similar items promotes learning and transfer. Because the alignment process renders common relational structure more salient, structural alignment promotes the disembedding of hitherto nonobvious common relational systems (Gentner and Namy 1999; Gick and Holyoak 1983; Loewenstein, Thompson, and Gentner 1999). Indeed, I suggest that comparison—that is, the process of structural alignment and mapping—is a learning mechanism powerful enough to acquire structured rulelike knowledge (Gentner and Medina 1998).

## 8.4   Why Relational Language Matters

Relational terms invite and preserve relational patterns that might otherwise be fleeting.[4] Consider the terms in table 8.1, which range from spatial relations to causal relations to social communicative relations. A language lacking such terms would be unimaginably impoverished. In such a language, it would be prohibitively cumbersome to express complex predictions, conjectures, dichotomous chains of thought, hypothetical arguments, and so on—not to mention counterfactuals such as "If this language lacked relational terms, it would be more difficult to communicate ideas like this one."

The sample of relational terms in table 8.1 suggests the range and utility of relational language. It includes verbs and prepositions—members of classes that are dedicated to conveying relational knowledge and that contrast with object reference terms on a number of grammatical and informational dimensions (Gentner 1981). However, it also includes a large number of relational nouns (e.g., *weapon, conduit,* and *barrier*), and these pose an interesting learning problem to which I return below.

However, although relational concepts are important, they are often not obvious. One reason that relational language is important in higher mental life is that, unlike object concepts, relational concepts are not automatically learned. Relational concepts are not simply given in the

**Table 8.1**
Some relational terms    *stone (n) is not relational.*

Relational nouns

| *General relation terms* | *Terms incorporating similarity and logical relatedness* |
|---|---|
| cause | twin |
| prevention | equivalence |
| source | identity |
| result | converse |
| advantage | inverse |
| bane | prediction |
| ally | contradiction |
| accident | |
| *Terms of communication* | *Terms that range from concrete to abstract usage* |
| threat | weapon |
| lie | gift |
| promise | target |
| excuse | haven |
| pretext | screen |
| dispute | filter |
| | barrier |
| | conduit |
| | leeway |

Verbs, prepositions, and general connectives

| | |
|---|---|
| cause | however |
| prevent | nevertheless |
| foster | therefore |
| engender | accordingly |
| permit | contrary |
| inhibit | except |
| deter | |
| accelerate | |
| force | |

*All are relational!!    this is too fluffy. transitive verbs*

**Table 8.2**
Relational versus object-referential terms in the domain of biology

| Relational terms | Object-reference terms |
| --- | --- |
| carnivore *very dubious* | tiger |
| scavenger | snail |
| prey | deer |
| parent | gorilla |
| weed | dandelion |
| parasite | flea |

*meat it eats*

natural world: they are culturally and linguistically shaped (Bowerman 1996; Talmy 1975). This malleability is expressed in the relational relativity principle—that the parsing of the perceptual world into a relational lexicon differs more across languages than does that for object terms (Gentner 1982; Gentner and Boroditsky 2001). To bring home this second point, table 8.2 contrasts relational nouns with ordinary referential nouns within the domain of biology.

If relational language bears a nonobvious relation to the world, it follows that relational terms should be harder to learn than terms such as concrete nominals whose referential relations are more transparent. Indeed, there is considerable evidence that relational terms are hard to learn. One indication of the relative difficulty of learning relations is that verbs and prepositions enter children's vocabularies later than do concrete nouns (Gentner 1982; Gentner and Boroditsky 2001; Goldin-Meadow, Seligman, and Gelman 1976). Another indication is that the full meanings of verbs and other relational terms are acquired relatively slowly (Bowerman 1996; Olguin and Tomasello 1993). Words like *if* and *because* (Byrnes 1991; Scholnick and Wing 1982) or *buy*, *sell*, and *pay* (Gentner 1978) may not be fully understood until 8 or 9 years of age.

The difficulty of learning relational terms relative to object terms can be seen not only across form class—in the advantage of nouns over verbs—but also *within* the nominal class, in the acquisition of relational nouns. Relational nouns sometimes denote relations directly: for example, *symmetry*. More commonly, they denote categories whose membership is determined by a particular relation (either temporary or enduring) that category members have with another entity or category: for example, *gift, weapon, friend, sister,* and *home.* Children often initially interpret relational terms as object reference terms, and only later come to appreciate the relational meaning (Gentner and Rattermann 1991). For example, kinship terms are often understood initially in terms of characteristics of individuals, and only later in terms of relational roles (Clark 1993). Likewise, Keil and Batterman (1984) found that 4-year-olds conceive of an *island* as a place with sand and palms, and of an *uncle* as a nice man with a pipe. Only later do they learn the relational descriptors, that an *island* is a body of land surrounded by water, and an *uncle*, any male in a sibling relationship with one's mother or father. Hall and Waxman (1993) found that $3\frac{1}{2}$-year-olds had difficulty learning novel relational nouns denoting concepts like "passenger." Even when they were explicitly told (for example), "This one [referring to a doll] is a *blicket* BECAUSE IT IS RIDING IN A CAR," children tended to interpret the novel noun as referring to the object category and extended it to a similar-looking doll.

Gentner and Klibanoff (in preparation) tested preschool children's ability to learn relational meanings, using a combination of comparison and labeling to underscore the relational structure. In this study, 3-, 4-, and 6-year-olds were shown picture cards and heard a novel relational noun used in two parallel contexts: for example, "The knife is the *blick* for the watermelon, and the ax is the *blick* for the tree." Then they were asked to choose the *"blick"* in a third context: for example, "What would be the *blick* for the paper?" The children chose among three picture cards: *same relation* (correct; e.g., a pair of scissors), *thematic* (e.g., a pencil), and *same nominal category* (e.g., another piece of paper). Both 4- and 6-year-olds correctly chose the *same relation* card. However, 3-year-olds performed at chance in this task, despite the extensive guidance.

However, although relational language is hard to learn, the benefits outweigh the difficulty. Gentner and Loewenstein (2002) discuss several specific ways in which relational language can foster the learning and retention of relational patterns:

• *Abstraction.*   Naming a relational pattern helps to abstract it—to de-situate it from its initial context. This increases the likelihood of seeing the pattern elsewhere in another situation. We have obtained this effect in studies of mapping, as discussed later (Gentner and Rattermann 1991; Loewenstein and Gentner 1998, 2002; Rattermann and Gentner 1998, 2002).

• *Initial registration.*   Hearing a relational term applied to a situation invites children to store the situation and its label, even before they fully understand the term's meaning. This is just to say that Roger Brown's "language as an invitation to form concepts" applies to relational concepts as well as to object concepts. Then, when further exemplars with the same label are encountered, there is a chance that comparison with the prior instance may promote a relational meaning, even when none was initially obvious. Hearing a relational term used across contexts invites abstracting its meaning. By giving two things the same name, we invite children to compare them, whether or not they occur in experiential juxtaposition. Thus, relational language creates symbolic juxtapositions that might not occur in the physical world.

• *Selectivity.*   Once learned, relational terms afford not only abstraction but also selectivity. We focus on a different set of aspects and relations when we call a cat a *pet* from when we call him a *carnivore*, or a *good mouser*, or a *lap warmer*. Selective linguistic labeling can influence the construal of a situation. For example, a labeling manipulation can influence the degree of "functional fixedness" in an insight task (Glucksberg and Danks 1968; Glucksberg and Weisberg 1966).

• *Reification.*   Using a relational term can reify an entire pattern, so that new assertions can be stated about it. A named relational schema can then serve as an argument to a higher-order proposition. For example, consider this sentence from the *New York Times Book Review*: "The economic adversity caused by droughts or floods far exceeds the direct impact on the food supply." The economy of expression made possible by the relational nouns *adversity, drought, flood,* and *impact,* as well as the higher-order connecting relations *cause* and *exceed,* makes it possible to state a complex embedded proposition compactly. Expressing such complex assertions as the above would be prohibitively awkward without such relational compaction.

• *Uniform relational encoding.*   Habitual use of a given set of relational terms promotes uniform relational encoding, thereby increasing the probability of transfer between like relational situations (Forbus, Gentner, and Law 1995). When a given domain is encoded in terms of a stable set of relational terms, the likelihood of matching new examples with stored exemplars that share relational structure is increased. Thus, habitual use of a stable system of relational language can increase the probability of relational reminding. In instructional situations, it can foster appropriate principle-based reminding and transfer, and mitigate the perennial bugaboos of retrieval: inert knowledge and surface-based retrieval. The growth of technical vocabulary in experts reflects the utility of possessing a uniform relational vocabulary.

### 8.4.1   Uniform Relational Structure, Retrieval, and Transfer

The claim that uniform relational language aids analogical retrieval is important, because analogical retrieval is generally quite poor. People routinely fail to be reminded of past experiences that are relationally similar to current experiences, even when such remindings would be useful in their current task, and even when it can be demonstrated that they have retained the prior knowledge (Gentner, Rattermann, and Forbus 1993; Gick and Holyoak 1980; Keane 1988; Ross 1989). There is evidence from studies in mathematics that this "inert knowledge" problem is less severe for experts than for novices (Novick 1988). Although Novick did not investigate the encoding vocabulary of the two groups, other studies of similarity-based retrieval have found a relation between the quality of the encoding (as assessed in participants' summaries of the materials) and the likelihood of relational retrieval (Gick and Holyoak 1983; Loewenstein, Thompson, and Gentner 1999). These results are consistent with the conjecture that one benefit of expertise is better, less idiosyncratic relational representations, which, as noted above, would promote relational retrieval.

More direct evidence that uniform relational language promotes transfer comes from studies by Clement, Mawby, and Giles (1994), who gave adults passages to read and later gave them new passages that were structurally similar but different in their specific characters and actions—the classic situation in which poor retrieval abilities have been demonstrated. For some learners, the parallel structure in the two matching passages was expressed using relational terms that had the same meanings (e.g., X *ate* Y and A *consumed* B). For others, the parallel structure was expressed using nonsynonymous relational pairs (e.g., X *munched on* Y and A *gobbled up* B). This was a fairly subtle manipulation; the differing relational pairs were partly overlapping in meaning, so that they could readily have been aligned had the passages been seen together. However, even this minimal manipulation made a difference: people who received synonymous terms—such as *ate* and *consumed*—were more likely to retrieve the initial passage given the probe than those who received nonsynonymous pairs. Clement, Mawby, and Giles concluded that the use of common relational encoding can promote analogical retrieval in adults.

Does language—especially, use of uniform relational language—influence children's memory retrieval? Some researchers have suggested that conversations with adults might be important in shaping children's memories (Nelson 1996). Herbert and Hayne (2000) studied 18-month-old infants in a deferred imitation task. Children were shown how to rattle by putting a ball into a cup and shaking it. The key variable was what kind of language children heard during the first session: empty narration (e.g., "Let's have a look at this …"), actions only (e.g., "Push the ball into the cup …"), goals only (e.g., "We can use these things to make a rattle. Let's have a look at this …"), or actions plus goals (e.g., "We can use these things to make a rattle. Push the ball into the cup …"). The latter two groups also received a prompt before the test, reminding them that they could use these things to make a rattle. After four weeks, children were retested to see if they could still reproduce the actions. Only the group that heard action-plus-goal language was able to reproduce the action at above-baseline rates.

### 8.4.2   Relational Language in Cognitive Development

Relational language both invites comparison and preserves the results as a (relational) abstraction. Jeff Loewenstein, Mary Jo Rattermann, and I have sought empirical evidence for this claim. We have focused on spatial relations like *on*, *in*, and *under* (Loewenstein and Gentner 1998) and *symmetry* and *monotonicity* (Kotovsky and Gentner 1996; Rattermann and Gentner 1998, 2002). These kinds of spatial terms satisfy three criteria for an arena in which to investigate possible effects of language on cognitive development: (1) they show substantial crosslinguistic variation, (2) they lend themselves to objective testing, and (3) they are accessible to children. The logic of our studies is first, to establish a challenging spatial relational task, and then to test whether language for spatial relations can improve children's performance.

Rattermann and I tested the power of relational labels to promote relational insight, using a very simple mapping task (Gentner and Rattermann 1991; Rattermann and Gentner 1998, 2002). Children aged 3, 4, and 5 saw two triads of objects, the child's set and the experimenter's set, both arranged in monotonically increasing order according to size. As in DeLoache's (1987, 1995) search studies, children watched as the experimenter hid a sticker under an object in the experimenter's triad; they were told that they could find their sticker by looking "in the same place" in their triad. The correct response was always based on relational similarity: that is, the child had to find the object of the same relative size and position (smallest → smallest; middle → middle; etc.). Children were always shown the correct response after making their guess.

When the two sets were literally similar, 3-year-old children readily learned the mapping. But when the objects were shifted to a cross-mapped pattern, as in figure 8.1, so that the object matches were inconsistent with the best relational alignment (Gentner and Toupin 1986), the children had great difficulty grasping the relational match, particularly  when the objects were rich and detailed. Indeed, in the rich-object cross-mapped versions of the task, 3- and 4-year-old children performed at chance (32%) even though they were shown the correct response on every trial (14 trials total).

Having thus established a difficult relational task, we then investigated whether providing relational language could help children perform this relational alignment. Before children carried out the cross-mapping task, they were provided with a brief training session in which we modeled using the labels *daddy*, *mommy*, and *baby* (or in other studies, *big*, *little*, *tiny*) for the characters in the two triads. We chose these family labels because they are often used spontaneously by preschool children to mark monotonic change in size (Smith 1989). The reasoning was that applying these labels to the three members of each triad would invite the child to

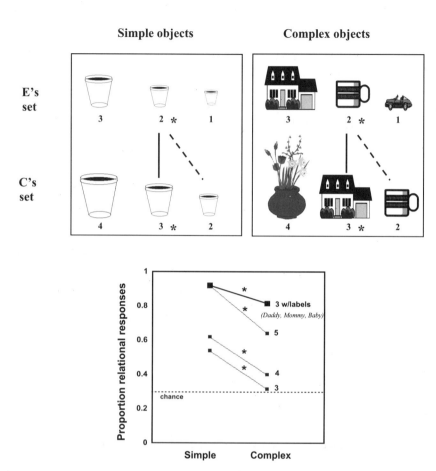

**Figure 8.1**
Materials and results for the Rattermann and Gentner spatial mapping task with cross-mapped objects, in which object matches compete with relational matches. In the top figures (*top*), asterisks and the solid line denote the correct match; the dashed line denotes the incorrect object match. The graph (*bottom*) shows the results for 3-, 4-, and 5-year-old children in the baseline condition and for 3-year-old children given the relational labels *daddy*, *mommy*, *baby*.

highlight the higher-order relational pattern of monotonic increase that forms the essential common system to align.

The results of the labeling manipulation were striking. The 3-year-olds given relational language performed well in the cross-mapping task on both the sparse (89% relational responding) and rich (79% relational responding) stimuli, as compared to performance rates of 54% and 32% without relational language. In fact, 3-year-olds given relational language performed on a par with 5-year-olds in the baseline condition. Further, 3-year-old children were fairly able to transfer their learning to new triads with no further use of the labels by the experimenters. That the improvement was specific to relational labels and was not just some general attentional effect of using language is shown by the fact that other relational labels denoting monotonic size-change (e.g., *big*, *little*, *tiny*) also improved performance, while neutral object labels (e.g., *jiggy*, *gimli*, *fantan* or *Freddy*, *Max*, *Bobby*) did not. Finally, when the children were brought back to the laboratory four to six weeks later, the group with relational language experience continued to show benefits of having represented the higher-order relational structure; they were better able to carry out the mapping task than their counterparts without relational language training. We suggest that the use of common relational labels prompted children to notice and represent the common higher-order relation of monotonic increase—in other words, that this facilitated making the relational alignment.

More evidence that language can foster higher-order relational structure comes from research by Loewenstein and Gentner (1998, 2002). We tested the effects of spatial language on spatial mapping ability, using the spatial prepositions *on*, *in*, and *under*—three particularly early spatial terms (Bowerman 1989; Clark 1974; Johnston 1988)—as well as the locatives *top*, *middle*, and *bottom*. As in the Rattermann and Gentner studies, we first established a difficult spatial analogy task and then tested whether labeling the relevant relations would improve performance. The child was shown two identical tall boxes, a hiding box and a finding box. Each box had a shelf in the middle so that it had three salient placement locations, as shown in figure 8.2: on top, in the middle, and under the box. Each box had three identical plastic cards, one in each

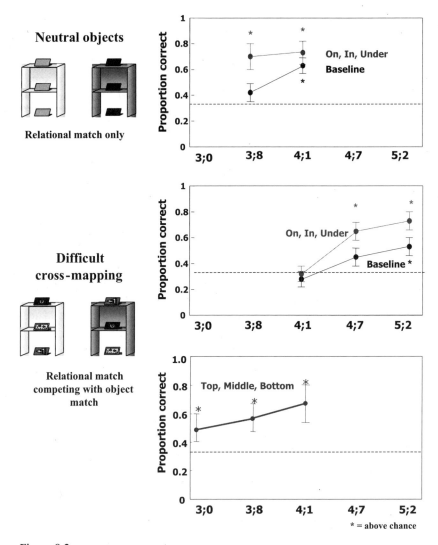

**Figure 8.2**
Results of the Loewenstein and Gentner spatial mapping studies, showing benefits of overt spatial language that diminish with age but reappear for more difficult tasks

position. One card had a star on its back, making it the "winner." Preschool children were shown the location of the winner at the hiding box and had to find the winner in the corresponding location at the finding box.

In some respects, the task is a relatively easy version of the search task used in DeLoache's (1987, 1995) and in our own (Loewenstein and Gentner 2001) model-room studies. The hiding and finding models are nearly identical and are placed close together so that they can be viewed simultaneously. However, the box task is considerably more difficult than the standard model-room task in one key respect: it cannot be solved by object correspondences. Because all the cards look alike, to solve the task the child must find corresponding spatial relations between the hiding box and the finding box.

For half the children, spatial relational language was used to describe the initial hiding event (e.g., "I'm putting this *on* the box"). For the other half (the control condition), the experimenter simply said as he placed the winner in its spot, "I'm putting it *here*." In both cases, the child was asked, "Can you find the winner in the very same place in the finding box?" The experimenter put the winner at one of the three locations in the hiding box as the child watched, and the child searched for the corresponding winner in the finding box.

Loewenstein and I noted five predictions that should follow if spatial relational language leads to forming articulated spatial representations that support the relational mapping process: (1) young children should perform better when overt spatial relational language is used; (2) older children, who have internalized the relational system, will not need overt language; (3) if the task is made more difficult, older children will again show benefits from language; (4) the benefits of language should be predictable from the semantics of the terms (as opposed to there being some general attentional effect of labeling); and (5) the benefits should be retained over time. These predictions were borne out. At age 3;6, children who had heard the box locations described in terms of the spatial relations *on*, *in*, and *under* performed substantially better on the mapping task than control children, who performed at levels just better than chance. By age 4;0, children no longer needed to hear the relational language to succeed at the mapping task (figure 8.2, top panel). However, if cross-mapped objects were used, placing object similarities in competition with the current relational correspondences, then 4-year-olds performed at chance in both conditions. With this more difficult task, in keeping with prediction (3), still older children (ages 4;7 and 5;2) showed significant benefits of relational language (figure 8.2, middle panel).

To test the claim of semantic specificity, we compared the terms *top/middle/bottom* (which form a connected relational system) with the terms *on/in/under* (which each express a separate relation between a figure and a ground). If children's representations reflect the semantics of the terms, then they should be better able to maintain a relational mapping with the deeper relational system conveyed by *top/middle/bottom*. Indeed, this was the outcome: even 3-year-olds were able to carry out the relational mapping when the connected system of *top/middle/bottom* was used. Thus, hearing relational language facilitated children's ability to encode and map on the basis of spatial relations. The benefits of language-guided encoding were maintained when children were brought back to the laboratory a few days later and asked to "play the game again" (with no mention of the spatial terms). It appears that the language experience led to a genuinely different encoding (and not to some momentary attentional benefit). This result is evidence that overt use of relational language can invite children to represent and use higher-order relational structure.

## 8.5    Symbol Use in Other Primates

Studies of the role of language in human thought are hampered by the fact that there is no comparison group of otherwise normal humans who lack a language. However, there is an indirect approach. We can compare nonhuman primates who have been taught symbol systems to otherwise matched animals who have not (Gentner and Rattermann 1991; Kuczaj and Hendry, this volume). There are several ways in which language appears to make a difference. I focus on two arenas: numerical competency and relational matching.

### 8.5.1    Number
Boysen and her colleagues have carried out an intriguing set of studies of quantity judgments among chimpanzees (Boysen and Berntson 1995;

Boysen et al. 1996). In their studies, a chimpanzee is shown two arrays of candy differing in quantity (e.g., one vs. three candies). The animal points to one of the arrays and then is given the other. Clearly, the best strategy is to point to the smaller number of candies, thereby garnering the larger set. This strategy turned out to be extremely difficult for the chimpanzees, even though all the animals tested had been given cognitive training with number symbols.[5] Even after many trials, they continued to fail the task, repeatedly pointing to the larger amount and receiving the smaller amount. Not surprisingly, they readily succeeded when the task was simply to point to the array they wanted; but they could not master the reverse strategy of pointing to the array they did not want.

However, the situation changed when the same chimpanzees were tested with numerical symbols. In this case, they readily selected the smaller Arabic numeral, thus garnering the (larger) quantity of candies represented by the unselected numeral. In subsequent trials, they consistently mastered the correct strategy with numerals and failed it with actual arrays. Why do the animals perform so much better with numerals? The numbers do not add new quantity information—indeed, the animals are responding all too strongly to the quantity difference in the concrete situation. It appears that the advantage of abstract symbols is that they allow the chimpanzees to process the quantities at a level of abstraction removed from the rich sensory power of the actual food.

*obviously!*

This pattern is reminiscent of studies of human development. In the Rattermann and Gentner mapping task, children are better able to resist a tempting (incorrect) object match when the objects are perceptually sparse than when the objects are richly detailed and thus far more compelling as similarity matches. Likewise, DeLoache has found that preschoolers do better in a model-room mapping task when given photographs rather than three-dimensional models. In the case of the chimpanzees, numerals served as the ultimate "abstract objects." Using numerals allowed them to select and compare only the property of magnitude, leaving behind the sensory qualities that were their undoing in the concrete choice task.

### 8.5.2 Relational Labeling and Relational Matching

Across species, relational matching is an uncommon ability. While many animals can succeed in learning a match-to-sample task with objects such as that shown in (6), the ability to succeed at a relational matching task like the one shown in (7)—that is, at analogical matching—is much rarer (Premack 1983):

(6)    A

    A    B

(7)    AA

    BB    CD

Oden, Thompson, and Premack (2001) have carried out a fascinating set of studies that suggests that symbol training is crucial to relational matching (see Kuczaj and Hendry, this volume). When chimpanzees were taught to choose a particular symbol for two identical objects and another symbol for two nonidentical objects—that is, symbols for *same* and *different*—they readily generalized these symbols to relations between objects (Thompson, Oden, and Boysen 1997). For example, having learned to choose *same* for A/A and *different* for A/B, they can then solve a relational match-to-sample task. That is, when given triad (7), they can choose BB if asked to choose the *same* one, and CD if asked to choose the *different* one. To do this, the chimpanzee must apply *same/different* at the relational level as well as the object level. It is as though the chimp succeeds only when she can construct representations with relational predicates, yielding the triad in (8):

(8)        *same*(A,A)

    *same*(B,B)        *different*(C,D)

Symbol training appears to be necessary for success on the relational matching task. However, it is not sufficient. There are species differences in the ability to learn relational similarity, even when symbols are given. Macaque monkeys given the same training with *same* and *different* symbols as the chimpanzees were eventually able to master object matching, but not relational matching (Washburn, Thompson, and Oden 1997). Interestingly, infant chimpanzees—but not infant macaques—show a kind of implicit relational matching. After handling a series of pairs of identical objects, they show more interest in a nonidentical

comparators again

pair, and vice versa (Oden, Thompson, and Premack 2001). Thus, infant chimpanzees show an implicit capacity that can become an explicit cognitive ability with the support of symbols.

Premack (1983; see also Oden, Thompson, and Premack 2001) interprets such findings in terms of two codes: an imaginal code closely tied to the perceptual properties of objects and a propositional code. He suggests that only animals who have learned a symbolic communication system use a propositional code. Chimpanzees are born with the capacity for implicit relational matching, but whether they ever realize their full potential for analogical thinking depends on whether they learn relational language.

## 8.6 Summary and Discussion

To the question I began with—"What makes humans so smart relative to other species?"—I have given two answers: (1) analogical ability, (2) language. First, humans are endowed with a greater degree of analogical ability than other species. Although we are not the only animal with analogical ability, the difference in degree of ability is so great that it stands as a qualitative difference. We are roughly similar to other intelligent species in our ability to form associations and to engage in statistical learning. Indeed, in many arenas, such as navigation and spatial memory, our powers are inferior to those of other animals. Structure-mapping processes are where we most differ from other species in our cognitive powers.

The second contributor to our intelligence is language and other cultural systems, which multiply our cognitive resources. Language augments our cognition in a number of ways. Externally, it allows each new generation to learn from and build further on the knowledge of past generations. Internally, as argued in this chapter, language provides cognitive tools. It augments the ability to hold and manipulate concepts and sets of concepts—in particular, systems of relations. Thus, although structure-mapping may be a species-wide innate ability, its deployment is influenced by language and culture. The results reviewed here suggest that the acquisition of relational language is instrumental in the development of analogy. It follows, then, that the acquisition of relational language contributes importantly to the development of cognition.

*written*

*is it? V? ... es relational touch with connections. relational language simply put us back in touch with older memories and synaptic connections.*

### 8.6.1   Structural Alignment and the Career of Similarity

Are structure-mapping processes innate? Evidence provided by Gomez and Gerken (1999) and Marcus et al. (1999) suggests that the answer is yes: the ability to notice and abstract relational regularities across exemplars is in place even in 7- and 8-month-olds. In Marcus et al.'s studies, infants received 16 three-syllable strings with the same pattern—either ABA (e.g., *pa-ti-pa, go-di-go*) or ABB. After three repetitions of these 16 strings, the infants were tested on strings consisting of new syllables— half in the trained pattern, half in the nontrained pattern. Infants dishabituated significantly more often to sentences in the nontrained pattern than to sentences in the trained pattern, indicating that they had abstracted the common structure from the training set.

My colleagues and I have successfully modeled Marcus et al.'s results using a system (SEQL) that compares examples (via SME) and sequentially abstracts their common structure (Gentner, Kuehne, and Forbus, in preparation; Kuehne, Gentner, and Forbus 2000; Skorstad, Gentner, and Medin 1988). Unlike most simulations of these findings, it requires only the set of 48 sentences given to infants (whereas some connectionist simulations require thousands of trials). These findings are consistent with the possibility that structure-mapping processes are responsible for the infants' grammar-learning process.

At this point, a challenge might reasonably be raised: if structure-mapping processes are present at birth, then why is the normal course of development so slow? Or to put it another way, how can the same process explain both the results of the infant grammar studies, in which babies show rapid structural abstracting, and the lengthy process of normal children's grammar learning? The resolution lies in when and whether comparisons are made. Structural alignment processes are extremely powerful at aligning and revealing common relations *when they are brought to bear.* Even adults miss many potential comparisons. As noted earlier, in memory experiments, adult participants routinely fail to retrieve past exemplars that are analogous to current exemplars. We are often not reminded of prior experiences that are potentially analogous to current experiences, and this is particularly true for novices, whose representations are more idiosyncratic and less likely to match each other than those of experts. Children's early representations are highly idiosyncratic and context specific. Thus, in order to notice a match, they require either very high overall similarity or very close temporal juxtaposition—ideally, both. In the infant grammar studies, the babies receive the latter—repeated close comparisons that allow progressive alignment of the common structure.

In habituation experiments like Marcus et al.'s studies, babies receive an optimal learning experience, from the vantage of structure-mapping theory.[6] In the ordinary course of learning, the application of structure-mapping processes is largely constrained by the luck of environmental juxtapositions. In habituation experiments, luck is in the hands of a benevolent experimenter, who can guarantee optimal juxtapositions.

### 8.6.2   Are Symbols Necessary?

Several recent schools of thought—including dynamic systems theory, situated cognition, and distributed connectionism—have generated an interest in subsymbolic or nonsymbolic representations.[7] In the extreme, some theorists have argued that symbolic representation, or structured representation, or even representation in general, has no role in human cognition. The evidence presented here suggests that human cognition arises not only from the world as directly perceived, but also from learned symbol systems that facilitate the apprehension of relational structure.

I reviewed two lines of evidence for the claim that learned symbol systems contribute to cognitive ability. The first line examines the effects of acquiring language. In our studies, children's performance on mapping tasks benefited from hearing the terms *top, middle, bottom* (Loewenstein and Gentner 1998, 2002) or the terms *daddy, mommy, baby* (Rattermann and Gentner 1998, 2002). In our studies, the overt use of relational language aids children's performance on analogical mapping tasks across a wide range of age and task difficulty. These findings are most naturally explained by assuming (1) that symbolic relations are used in carrying out analogical mapping tasks, and (2) that the acquisition of relational language plays a role in the development of symbolic representations.

The above line of argument has the disadvantage that all normal children can eventually perform the tasks in our studies without the overt use of relational language. This fact is not necessarily inconsistent with my claims—for example, it could be that older children have internalized relational symbols learned from language—but it raises the possibility that the effects of language in our task are transient and perhaps epiphenomenal. However, there is a second line of evidence for the importance of symbols that cannot be explained away in this manner—namely, studies comparing other great apes who either do or do not possess symbol systems. Boysen's chimps can master the task of pointing to the nondesired pile of candy if and only if they have a symbolic code for numbers that lets them rise above the concrete situation. It is only when the perceptual-motor affordances of real foods are replaced by abstract symbols that the animals can reason clearly enough to choose the best strategy. Direct perception in this case is working against them; it is abstraction that allows them to succeed.

To ask whether similar benefits accrue in human learning, one avenue of inquiry is the acquisition of technical language. Because any given technical vocabulary is learned by some but not all humans, we can compare "haves" with "have nots" as in the chimpanzee studies. There is some evidence that the acquisition of technical language can confer new cognitive possibilities. Koedinger, Alibali, and Nathan (in preparation) argue that the acquisition of algebraic notation allows children to move from concretely grounded representations of word problems to symbolic representations; and further, that although grounded representations are more effective for simple problems, symbolic representations are better for complex problems.

All this suggests that although situated or embodied cognition may be a natural mode of human processing, there are many cases where what is needed is the opposite: representations that are de-situated or disembodied. Symbolic representations lose some of the richness of embodied cognition, but they open possibilities that cannot be imagined without them. One function of language may be to augment natural modes of cognition with an alternative representational scheme that permits abstract cognition.

### 8.6.3 Language and Thought

It is useful to contrast the view taken here with other views on language and thought. The strong version of the Sapir-Whorf hypothesis holds that (1) languages vary in their semantic partitioning of the world; (2) the structure of one's language influences the manner in which one perceives and understands the world; (3) therefore, speakers of different languages will perceive the world differently. Past efforts to demonstrate the strong version of the Whorfian position have produced mostly negative results (Pinker 1994; however, see Hunt and Agnoli 1991; Kay and Kempton 1984; Lucy 1994; Lucy and Shweder 1979). Current research continues to find mixed results, as demonstrated by the chapters in this volume.

Vygotsky's (1962) theory also gives language a major role in cognition. However, his theory focuses chiefly on the general effects of learning a language, rather than on the specific conceptual construals invited by a given language. According to Vygotsky, with the advent of language children augment their prelinguistic cognitive abilities—reactive attention, associative learning, and sensorimotor intelligence—with new capacities for focused attention, deliberate memory, and symbolic thought (see also Dennett 1993). On this view, acquiring a language gives the child control over his own mental processes: the ability to direct attention, to choose a course of thought, and to formulate mental plans.

Thus, the Sapir-Whorf view has it that the grammatical structure of a language shapes its speakers' perception of the world, and the Vygotskian view emphasizes that possessing an internal language permits speakers to guide their own mental processes. I am suggesting a third, hybrid position: that learning specific relational terms and systems provides representational resources that augment our cognitive powers. On this account, language is neither a lens through which one forever sees the world, nor a control tower for guiding cognition, but a set of tools with which to construct and manipulate representations.

Whereas tests of the Whorfian hypothesis have generally involved between-language comparisons, the cognitive tools view can be tested within a language. We can compare outcomes when different subsets of symbolic terms are provided to different groups (as in our studies) or are acquired by different populations (as in the case of technical vocabularies). Of course, the cognitive resources view I espouse also suggests possible crosslinguistic differences. Languages that have different lexicalizations of relational information offer their speakers different options for representation and reasoning. Indeed, relational terms are the most likely arena in which to find linguistic influences on thought, for two reasons. First, relational terms are more variable crosslinguistically than object reference terms (as discussed earlier). Obviously, semantic differences are necessary (though not sufficient) for there to be resulting cognitive differences. Second, relational terms—including spatial relational terms and verbs—provide framing structures for the encoding of situations and events. Hence, semantic differences in these categories could reasonably be expected to have cognitive consequences.

But despite the obvious importance of crosslinguistic studies, I have argued here that there are important issues that apply within a single language. Relational labels invite the child (or adult) to notice, represent, and retain structural patterns of elements, and therefore to transfer relational patterns and to reason fluently over combinations of relations. Even within a single language, the acquisition of relational terms provides both an invitation and a means for the learner to modify her thought.

### 8.6.4    Challenges and Limitations

First, a few clarifications are in order. I am not suggesting that all culturally learned concepts are relational; concepts like "fruit" and "shard" are counterexamples (for different reasons). I am also not claiming that all abstract concepts are relational. Counterexamples include concepts like "idea" and "entity." (However, I'd guess that a large percentage of abstract terms are relational.) There are also many abstract concepts whose representations include both relational information and intrinsic information—for example, "mammal" and "reptile," which are abstract. Another important clarification is that although I have focused on language, there are other acquired systems that make us smart—among them, numbers (Carey 1998; Spelke, this volume), maps (Uttal 2000), and other artifacts (Norman 1993).

Turning to a deeper issue, the proposal that learning language can invite new conceptual representations runs immediately into a classic objection. Fodor's circularity challenge is that "... one cannot learn a language unless one has a language. In particular, one cannot learn a first language unless one already has a system capable of representing the predicates in that language *and their extensions*" (1975, 64; italics

Familiarity/similarity comparator says "1". A hit.

[sense do not
have to make
sense at first
but become
familiar? = make
sense?]

[yes. but
not conceived.]

original). Thus, we can't learn a word's meaning unless we already have the representational resources necessary to understand the concepts to which it refers. The learning hypothesis might still be saved by making strong assumptions about the innate set of representational resources— for example, by assuming that we begin with a set of primitives out of which semantic representations are built. However, although the empirical evidence concerning semantic primitives can be debated, this is clearly a troublesome move, particularly in the absence of a viable candidate set of primitives. Thus, Fodor concludes that learning cannot give us new concepts. He therefore proposes that humans are born with an innate language of thought, in terms of which they learn the overt language of their community.

This is the kind of argument that makes psychologists want to say, "Oh, go away—can't you see we're busy doing experiments?" But the question of what we start with is important. The challenge, then, is that *learners need a prior conceptual understanding of what a word means in order to attach a word to that meaning.* I do not have a complete answer. But I believe one part of the answer lies in the distinction between implicit and explicit understanding. Learning words provides explicit internal labels for ideas that were previously merely implicit, and this gain in explicitness has cognitive consequences. Likewise, carrying out an analogy lays bare common structure that was previously invisible, embedded in the richness of particular exemplars. In Boysen's studies of chimpanzees, infant chimpanzees show implicit sensitivity to identicality relations between objects. But they cannot cash in this sensitivity, even as adults, without language training. Only if they are given symbols for *same* and *different* can they reliably detect sameness and difference over relations. I suggest (1) that the relational symbols invite explicit representation of the relations, and (2) that this explicitness makes the *same/different* relations more portable—it allows the chimpanzees to go beyond object matches to a new level of application between relations.

Extrapolating to humans, this suggests that one result of language learning may be to change the internal language from a restricted implicit system to a more powerful explicit system. A reasonable question at this point is whether there are other relations, besides same/different, that might be implicitly present in humans prior to language learning.

[by whose
usage]

Crosslinguistic patterns suggest that some relational terms are particularly easy to acquire (Choi and Bowerman 1991); although more remains to be done, this work may provide clues as to which relational concepts are implicitly formed prelinguistically.

Once some relational concepts are extracted, learning more words can occur by conceptual combination. For example, *forget* can be learned as not-remember, or *trade* as a reciprocal giving relation: x gives something to y and y gives something to x. Another way of deriving new meanings from old is by analogy. For example, suppose a child is told that fish breathe water with their *gills* (a new word). She is invited to map a causal chain from (8) to (9) (humans to fish):

(8)  PERMIT(EXTRACT(lungs(people), oxygen, air),
     BREATHE(people, air))

(9)  PERMIT(EXTRACT(gills(fish), oxygen, water), BREATHE(fish,
     water))

*[handwritten margin note: The handing down of prior knowledge is clearly psst ling but not entirely so.]*

Of course, this is only the beginning. At this point, the child knows only the functional role of gills, not what they look like or how they work—but she has delineated the concept of gills and perhaps become curious to know more. That kind of focused curiosity is part of what makes language a potent force in learning.

Finally, the relational concepts provided by language and other cultural systems are a key starting set. But speakers are not limited to the set of existing lexicalized relations. As Bowerman (1981) and Clark (1993) have observed, children regularly invent new relational terms. Indeed, the propensity to invent symbols is a striking difference between humans and other apes. Further, new relational concepts can arise in a language through mechanisms such as metaphorical abstraction, by which concrete terms are extended into abstract meanings (see table 8.1) (Gentner and Bowdle 2001; Glucksberg and Keysar 1990; Kittay and Lehrer 1981; Wolff and Gentner 2000). Speakers constantly go beyond the current resources of their language to develop new relational abstractions. Extensions into progressively higher-order relational terms have characterized the history of science and mathematics. However, I suggest that systems of currently lexicalized relations frame the set of new ideas that can be readily noticed and articulated.

### 8.6.5 Conclusions

General learning mechanisms have come under heavy fire in the last few decades. Children's learning is seen as far too rapid to be accounted for by a general learning process. Further, children seem primed for learning in certain domains, such as mechanical causation, biology, and theory of mind. This has suggested to many researchers that humans possess special faculties for learning in privileged domains. By analogy with grammar, these other privileged domains are assumed to have built-in representations and processes that facilitate acquisition.

In the above account, the human advantage is a cognitive head start over other species. I suggest another perspective. The great evolutionary advantage of the human species is adaptability. We are at home in the tropics or in the Arctic. To design a superbly adaptable species, one might best create one that begins with few biases beyond those necessary for mammalian life, that has a powerful general learning mechanism that abstracts significant commonalities and differences, and that has a species-wide method of capture—namely, language—with which to preserve important cognitive discoveries so that they can be combined generatively and passed to the young.

I am not suggesting that humans are born without constraints. We appear to come equipped with the basic mammalian starting set of attentional biases and learning propensities, as well as others that stem from being social animals. There also appear to be attentional biases evolved specifically for language, such as a readiness to learn the voiced-nonvoiced distinction (Saffran 2001). But in contrast to theories that postulate that humans have more built-in knowledge and theory than other species, I suggest the reverse: if anything, we have less. Whereas the frog comes programmed to jump for looming shade and to flick its tongue for small moving objects, we come prepared to learn what is dangerous and what is edible. Far from being a disadvantage, our relatively unbiased initial state allows us to learn whatever comes our way.

This "less is more" proposal for the human endowment is not new, of course. It has a long history in evolutionary anthropology. But for the most part, general learning as an explanation for cognitive development has been out of favor in the last two decades of cognitive theorizing. In part, this resulted from the limitations of purely behaviorist approaches to learning. But we now know of learning mechanisms that go beyond mere association and perceptual generalization. Structure-sensitive comparison processes, which occur even in infancy, can invite alignment and progressive abstraction of relational structures.

Finally, learning language is crucial to the development of~~whose~~cognition. Learned relational symbols provide representational tools with which to structure knowledge. These learned relational tools amplify the human capacity for structural alignment and mapping. For example, if a pattern discovered by analogy is named, it becomes easier to see as part of yet another analogy. This process of extracting relations via analogy and then preserving them via language acts to bootstrap learning and to create the structured symbolic representations essential for higher-order cognition.

### Notes

The research on spatial relational terms reported here was supported by NSF-ROLE grant 21002/REC–0087516. The research on analogical learning and the development of the computer simulation of analogical processing were supported by ONR grant N00014–92-J–1098. I thank Susan Goldin-Meadow and Arthur Markman for comments on this chapter; Jeff Loewenstein, Mary Jo Rattermann, Ken Kurtz, and Arthur Markman for valuable discussions of these issues; and Kathleen Braun and Michelle Osmondson for help with the research.

1. It is surely not a coincidence that the species that show the most impressive cognitive abilities are social animals: apes, dogs, dolphins, crows, parrots.

2. Another factor is that there are typically multiple relational structures within any one representation. In literal similarity, most of these relational structures can be placed in correspondence, again strengthening the match. In analogy, typically only one or perhaps two relational structures match, so the maximal match must typically be discerned from among many local relational matches, most of which must eventually be discarded.

3. Younger children often make the object match instead of the relational match, presumably because they lack sufficiently elaborated relational representations to yield a relational alignment deep enough to prevail against the object match (Gentner and Rattermann 1991; Gentner and Toupin 1986).

4. *Relational terms* are terms that convey a relation: that is, a proposition taking at least two arguments. First-order relations take entities as their arguments. Nth order relations have at least one $(N - 1)$th relation as arguments.

5. Space does not allow a full description of chimpanzees' number achievements. However, Boysen and her colleagues have trained one animal, Sheba, to

point to a number on a screen to express the cardinality of a set of objects (up to at least five). In number tasks, Sheba often partitions objects and touches them sequentially, as do children learning to count. Matsuzawa (1991) taught a female chimpanzee (Ai) to name the number of items from one to six. Ai was able to transfer this skill to new objects.

6. Consideration of comparison processes also points up an important issue in the interpretation of habituation results. It is fair to conclude that the generalizations infants arrive at in habituation experiments are within their power to learn, but not that the knowledge was present before the experience of habituation. Thus, conclusions of the form "The babies understand that ..." should in many cases be replaced by "The babies can readily learn that ..."

7. See Markman 1999 and Markman and Dietrich 1999, 2000, for extended discussions of this point.

## References

Bowerman, M. (1981). The child's expression of meaning: Expanding relationships among lexicon, syntax and morphology. In H. Winitz (Ed.), *Native language and foreign language acquisition* (Vol. 379, pp. 172–189). New York: New York Academy of Sciences.

Bowerman, M. (1989). Learning a semantic system: What role do cognitive predispositions play? In M. L. Rice and R. L. Schiefelbusch (Eds.), *The teachability of language* (pp. 133–168). Baltimore: Brookes.

Bowerman, M. (1996). Learning how to structure space for language: A cross-linguistic perspective. In P. Bloom, M. A. Peterson, L. Nadel, and M. F. Garrett (Eds.), *Language and space* (pp. 385–436). Cambridge, MA: MIT Press.

Boysen, S. T., and Berntson, G. G. (1995). Responses to quantity: Perceptual versus cognitive mechanisms in chimpanzees (*Pan troglodytes*). *Journal of Experimental Psychology: Animal Behavior Processes, 21*, 82–86.

Boysen, S. T., Berntson, G. G., Hannan, M. B., and Cacioppo, J. T. (1996). Quantity-based interference and symbolic representations in chimpanzees (*Pan troglodytes*). *Journal of Experimental Psychology: Animal Behavior Processes, 22*, 76–86.

Byrnes, J. P. (1991). Acquisition and development of *if* and *because*: Conceptual and linguistic aspects. In S. A. Gelman and J. P. Byrnes (Eds.), *Perspectives on language and thought: Interrelations in development* (pp. 3–27). Cambridge: Cambridge University Press.

Carey, S. (1998). Knowledge of number: Its evolution and ontogenesis. *Science, 242*, 641–642.

Chen, Z., Sanchez, R. P., and Campbell, T. (1997). From beyond to within their grasp: The rudiments of analogical problem solving in 10- and 13-month-olds. *Developmental Psychology, 33*, 790–801.

Choi, S., and Bowerman, M. (1991). Learning to express motion events in English and Korean: The influence of language-specific lexicalization patterns. *Cognition, 41,* 83–121.

Clark, E. V. (1974). Non-linguistic strategies and the acquisition of word meanings. *Cognition, 2,* 161–182.

Clark, E. V. (1993). *The lexicon in acquisition.* Cambridge: Cambridge University Press.

Clement, C. A., Mawby, R., and Giles, D. E. (1994). The effects of manifest relational similarity on analog retrieval. *Journal of Memory and Language, 33,* 396–420.

DeLoache, J. S. (1987). Rapid change in the symbolic functioning of very young children. *Science, 238,* 1556–1557.

DeLoache, J. S. (1995). Early understanding and use of symbols: The model model. *Current Directions in Psychological Science, 4*(4), 109–113.

Dennett, D. C. (1993). Learning and labeling. *Mind and Language, 8,* 540–548.

Falkenhainer, B., Forbus, K. D., and Gentner, D. (1989). The structure-mapping engine: Algorithm and examples. *Artificial Intelligence, 41,* 1–63.

Fodor, J. A. (1975). *The language of thought.* New York: Crowell.

Forbus, K. D., and Gentner, D. (1989). Structural evaluation of analogies: What counts? *Proceedings of the Cognitive Science Society, 11,* 341–348.

Forbus, K. D., Gentner, D., and Law, K. (1995). MAC/FAC: A model of similarity-based retrieval. *Cognitive Science, 19,* 141–205.

Gentner, D. (1978). On relational meaning: The acquisition of verb meaning. *Child Development, 49,* 988–998.

Gentner, D. (1981). Some interesting differences between nouns and verbs. *Cognition and Brain Theory, 4,* 161–178.

Gentner, D. (1982). Why nouns are learned before verbs: Linguistic relativity versus natural partitioning. In S. A Kuczaj (Ed.), *Language development: Vol. 2. Language, thought, and culture* (pp. 301–334). Hillsdale, NJ: Erlbaum.

Gentner, D. (1983). Structure-mapping: A theoretical framework for analogy. *Cognitive Science, 7,* 155–170.

Gentner, D. (1989). Mechanisms of analogical learning. In S. Vosniadou and A. Ortony (Eds.), *Similarity and analogical reasoning* (pp. 199–241). Cambridge: Cambridge University Press.

Gentner, D., and Boroditsky, L. (2001). Individuation, relativity and early word learning. In M. Bowerman and S. C. Levinson (Eds.), *Language acquisition and conceptual development* (pp. 215–256). Cambridge: Cambridge University Press.

Gentner, D., and Bowdle, B. F. (2001). Convention, form, and figurative language processing. *Metaphor and Symbol, 16,* 223–247.

Gentner, D., and Klibanoff, R. S. (in preparation). *On acquiring gifts: The development of the ability to learn relational nouns.*

Gentner, D., Kuehne, S., and Forbus, K. (in preparation). *A model of infant grammar learning using structural alignment.*

Gentner, D., and Kurtz, K. J. (in preparation). *The mechanisms of mapping: Evidence from on-line analogy judgments.*

Gentner, D., and Loewenstein, J. (2002). Relational language and relational thought. In J. Byrnes and E. Amsel (Eds.), *Language, literacy, and cognitive development* (pp. 87–120). Mahwah, NJ: Erlbaum.

Gentner, D., and Markman, A. B. (1997). Structure-mapping in analogy and similarity. *American Psychologist, 52,* 45–56.

Gentner, D., and Medina, J. (1998). Similarity and the development of rules. *Cognition, 65,* 263–297.

Gentner, D., and Namy, L. (1999). Comparison in the development of categories. *Cognitive Development, 14,* 487–513.

Gentner, D., and Rattermann, M. J. (1991). Language and the career of similarity. In S. A. Gelman and J. P. Byrnes (Eds.), *Perspectives on language and thought: Interrelations in development* (pp. 225–277). Cambridge: Cambridge University Press.

Gentner, D., Rattermann, M. J., and Forbus, K. D. (1993). The roles of similarity in transfer: Separating retrievability from inferential soundness. *Cognitive Psychology, 25,* 524–575.

Gentner, D., and Toupin, C. (1986). Systematicity and surface similarity in the development of analogy. *Cognitive Science, 10,* 277–300.

Gentner, D., and Wolff, P. (1997). Alignment in the processing of metaphor. *Journal of Memory and Language, 37,* 331–355.

Gick, M. L., and Holyoak, K. J. (1980). Analogical problem solving. *Cognitive Psychology, 12,* 306–355.

Gick, M. L., and Holyoak, K. J. (1983). Schema induction and analogical transfer. *Cognitive Psychology, 15,* 1–38.

Glucksberg, S., and Danks, J. H. (1968). Effects of discriminative labels and of nonsense labels upon the availability of novel function. *Journal of Verbal Learning and Verbal Behavior, 7,* 72–76.

Glucksberg, S., and Keysar, B. (1990). Understanding metaphorical comparisons: Beyond similarity. *Psychological Review, 97,* 3–18.

Glucksberg, S., and Weisberg, R. W. (1966). Verbal behavior and problem solving: Some effects of labeling in a functional fixedness problem. *Journal of Experimental Psychology, 71,* 659–664.

Goldin-Meadow, S., Seligman, M. E., and Gelman, R. (1976). Language in the two-year-old. *Cognition, 4,* 189–202.

Goldstone, R. L. (1994). Similarity, interactive activation, and mapping. *Journal of Experimental Psychology: Learning, Memory, and Cognition, 20,* 3–28.

Goldstone, R. L., and Medin, D. L. (1994). Time course of comparison. *Journal of Experimental Psychology: Learning, Memory, and Cognition, 20*, 29–50.

Gomez, R. L., and Gerken, L. (1999). Artificial grammar learning by 1-year-olds leads to specific and abstract knowledge. *Cognition, 70*, 109–135.

Hall, D. G, and Waxman, S. R. (1993). Assumptions about word meaning: Individuation and basic-level kinds. *Child Development, 64*, 1550–1570.

Herbert, J., and Hayne, H. (2000). The ontogeny of long-term retention during the second year of life. *Developmental Science, 3*, 50–56.

Hunt, E., and Agnoli, F. (1991). The Whorfian hypothesis: A cognitive psychology perspective. *Psychological Review, 98*, 377–389.

Johnston, J. R. (1988). Children's verbal representation of spatial location. In J. Stiles-Davis and M. Kritchevsky (Eds.), *Spatial cognition: Brain bases and development* (pp. 195–205). Hillsdale, NJ: Erlbaum.

Kay, P., and Kempton, W. (1984). What is the Sapir-Whorf hypothesis? *American Anthropologist, 86*, 65–79.

Keane, M. T. (1988). *Analogical problem solving*. New York: Halsted Press.

Keil, F. C., and Batterman, N. (1984). A characteristic-to-defining shift in the development of word meaning. *Journal of Verbal Learning and Verbal Behavior, 23*, 221–236.

Kemler, D. G. (1983). Holistic and analytical modes in perceptual and cognitive development. In T. J. Tighe and B. E. Shepp (Eds.), *Perception, cognition and development: Interactional analysis* (pp. 77–102). Hillsdale, NJ: Erlbaum.

Kittay, E. F., and Lehrer, A. (1981). Semantic fields and the structure of metaphor. *Studies in Language, 5*, 31–63.

Koedinger, K. R., Alibali, M. W., and Nathan, M. J. (in preparation). *Trade-offs between grounded and abstract representations: Evidence from algebra problem solving.*

Kotovsky, L., and Gentner, D. (1996). Comparison and categorization in the development of relational similarity. *Child Development, 67*, 2797–2822.

Kubose, T. T., Holyoak, K. J., and Hummel, J. E. (2002). The role of textual coherence in incremental analogical mapping. *Journal of Memory and Language, 47*(3), 407–435.

Kuehne, S. E., Gentner, D., and Forubs, K. D. (2000). Modeling infant learning via symbolic structural alignment. *Proceedings of the Cognitive Science Society, 22*, 286–291.

Kurtz, K. J., and Gentner, D. (1998, November). *The mechanisms of mapping: Evidence from on-line judgments of analogy.* Poster presented at the meeting of the Psychonomic Society, Dallas, TX.

Landau, B., Smith, L., and Jones, S. (1988). The importance of shape in early lexical learning. *Cognitive Development, 3*, 299–321.

Loewenstein, J., and Gentner, D. (1998). Relational language facilitates analogy in children. *Proceedings of the Cognitive Science Society, 20*, 615–620.

Loewenstein, J., and Gentner, D. (2001). Spatial mapping in preschoolers: Close comparisons facilitate far mappings. *Journal of Cognition and Development, 2,* 189–219.

Loewenstein, J., and Gentner, D. (2002). *Relational language fosters relational encoding and mapping.* Manuscript submitted for publication.

Loewenstein, J., Thompson, L., and Gentner, D. (1999). Analogical encoding facilitates knowledge transfer in negotiation. *Psychonomic Bulletin and Review, 6,* 586–597.

Lucy, J. A. (1994). *Grammatical categories and cognition.* Cambridge: Cambridge University Press.

Lucy, J. A., and Shweder, R. A. (1979). Whorf and his critics: Linguistic and nonlinguistic influences on color memory. *American Anthropologist, 81,* 581–618.

Marcus, G. F., Vijayan, S., Bandi, R. S., and Vishton, P. M. (1999). Rule-learning in seven-month-old infants. *Science, 283,* 77–80.

Markman, A. B. (1999). *Knowledge representation.* Mahwah, NJ: Erlbaum.

Markman, A. B., and Dietrich, E. (1999). Whither structured representations? *Behavioral and Brain Sciences, 22,* 626–627.

Markman, A. B., and Dietrich, E. (2000). In defense of representation. *Cognitive Psychology, 40,* 138–171.

Markman, A. B., and Gentner, D. (1993). Structural alignment during similarity comparisons. *Cognitive Psychology, 25,* 431–467.

Matsuzawa, T. (1991). Nesting cups and metatools in chimpanzees. *Behavioral and Brain Sciences, 14,* 570–571.

Medin, D. L., Goldstone, R. L., and Gentner, D. (1993). Respects for similarity. *Psychological Review, 100,* 254–278.

Nelson, K. (1996). *Language in cognitive development: The emergence of the mediated mind.* Cambridge: Cambridge University Press.

Norman, D. A. (1993). *Things that make us smart.* Reading, MA: Addison-Wesley.

Novick, L. R. (1988). Analogical transfer, problem similarity, and expertise. *Journal of Experimental Psychology: Learning, Memory, and Cognition, 14,* 510–520.

Oakes, L. M., and Cohen, L. B. (1990). Infant perception of a causal event. *Cognitive Development, 5,* 193–207.

Oden, D. L., Thompson, K. R., and Premack, D. (2001). Can an ape reason analogically? Comprehension and production of analogical problems by Sarah, a chimpanzee (*Pan troglodytes*). In D. Gentner, K. J. Holyoak, and B. N. Kokinov (Eds.), *The analogical mind: Perspectives from cognitive science* (pp. 471–498). Cambridge, MA: MIT Press.

Olguin, R., and Tomasello, M. (1993). Twenty-five-month-old children do not have a grammatical category of verb. *Cognitive Development, 8,* 245–272.

Piaget, J. (1952). *The origins of intelligence in children.* New York: Norton.

Pinker, S. (1994). *The language instinct.* New York: Morrow.

Premack, D. (1983). The codes of man and beasts. *Behavioral and Brain Sciences, 6,* 125–167.

Quine, W. V. O. (1960). *Word and object.* Cambridge, MA: MIT Press.

Rattermann, M. J., and Gentner, D. (1998). The effect of language on similarity: The use of relational labels improves young children's performance in a mapping task. In K. Holyoak, D. Gentner, and B. Kokinov (Eds.), *Advances in analogy research: Integration of theory and data from the cognitive, computational, and neural sciences* (pp. 274–282). Sopfhia: New Bulgarian University.

Rattermann, M. J., and Gentner, D. (2002). *The effect of language on similarity: The use of relational labels improves young children's analogical mapping performance.* Manuscript submitted for publication.

Ross, B. H. (1989). Distinguishing types of superficial similarities: Different effects on the access and use of earlier problems. *Journal of Experimental Psychology: Learning, Memory and Cognition, 15,* 456–468.

Rovee-Collier, C. K., and Fagen, J. W. (1981). The retrieval of memory in early infancy. In L. P. Lipsett (Ed.), *Advances in infancy research* (Vol. 1, pp. 225–254). Norwood, NJ: Ablex.

Saffran, J. R. (2001). The use of predictive dependencies in language learning. *Journal of Memory and Language, 44,* 493–515.

Scholnick, E. K., and Wing, C. S. (1982). The pragmatics of subordinating conjunctions: A second look. *Journal of Child Language, 9,* 461–479.

Skorstad, J., Gentner, D., and Medin, D. (1988). Abstraction processes during concept learning: A structural view. *Proceedings of the Cognitive Science Society, 10,* 419–425.

Smith, L. B. (1989). From global similarities to kinds of similarities: The construction of dimensions in development. In S. Vosniadou and A. Ortony (Eds.), *Similarity and analogical reasoning* (pp. 146–178). New York: Cambridge University Press.

Talmy, L. (1975). Semantics and syntax of motion. In J. Kimball (Ed.), *Syntax and semantics* (Vol. 4, pp. 181–238). New York: Academic Press.

Thompson, R. K. R., Oden, D. L., and Boysen, S. T. (1997). Language-naive chimpanzees (*Pan troglodytes*) judge relations between relations in a conceptual matching-to-sample task. *Journal of Experimental Psychology: Animal Behavior Processes, 23,* 31–43.

Tversky, A. (1977). Features of similarity. *Psychological Review, 84,* 327–352.

Uttal, D. H. (2000). Seeing the big picture: Map use and the development of spatial cognition. *Developmental Science, 3,* 247–286.

Vygotsky, L. (1962). *Thought and language.* Cambridge, MA: MIT Press. (Original work published 1934.)

Washburn, D. A., Thompson, R. K. R., and Oden, D. L. (1997, November). *Monkeys trained with same/different symbols do not match relations.* Paper presented at the meeting of the Psychonomic Society, Philadelphia, PA.

Wolff, P., and Gentner, D. (2000). Evidence for role-neutral initial processing of metaphors. *Journal of Experimental Psychology: Learning, Memory, and Cognition, 26,* 529–541.

# 9

## Does Language Help Animals Think?

Stan A. Kuczaj, II, and Jennifer L. Hendry

### 9.1 Introduction

The biggest obstacles in the study of the relationship between language and thought are the gaps in our understanding of language and thought themselves. The past century witnessed both remarkable discoveries and thought-provoking theories about the nature of language and the nature of thought, but there is still much to learn about both phenomena. Although the relationship between language and thought might remain a mystery until they are better understood as individual entities, it seems more likely that a complete understanding of language and a complete understanding of thought will depend on determining the manner(s) in which the two systems interact. Of course, this is easier said than done.

Specifying the relation between language and thought is a complex task, as evidenced by the chapters in this book. On the one hand, we have suggestions that language is important for thought. For example, de Villiers and de Villiers consider the possibility that language may facilitate children's understanding of others' knowledge and beliefs, Gentner emphasizes the role of language in the understanding of abstract relational information (see also Gentner and Loewenstein 2002), and Spelke suggests that language helps children to integrate spatial information. On the other hand, Munnich and Landau argue that language does not influence thought in any meaningful way. In a very real sense, then, the chapters in this book mirror the history of this topic.

## 9.2   Some Historical Background

The notion that language influences thought has a long history. Approximately 250 years ago, the German philosopher Herder proposed that language shapes human cognition (Herder 1768), a hypothesis that has been advocated by a number of theorists in the intervening years (e.g., Darwin 1871; Humboldt 1907; Sapir 1931; Whorf 1956). This hypothesis has obvious implications for the ontogeny of language and thought, and was considered by two of the most influential developmental psychologists of the past century, Jean Piaget and Lev Vygotsky.

Although Piaget (1968) recognized the reciprocal nature of language development and cognitive development, he minimized the role of language in cognitive development. In fact, Piaget emphasized that language was made possible only by the representational capabilities of cognition:

Language and thought are linked in a genetic circle where each necessarily leans on the other in an interdependent formation and continuous reciprocal action. *In the last analysis, both depend on intelligence itself, which antedates language and is independent of it.* (Piaget 1968, 98; emphasis added)

For Piaget, then, cognitive development interacts with language development, but the leader in this dance is always cognition. Thus, even though Piaget (1968; Piaget and Inhelder 1969) acknowledged that language may be necessary for the development of logical reasoning, he also believed that language plays a minor role compared to the cognitive capacity that allows the mental manipulation of mental representations.

Vygotsky (1962) argued for a much more interactive relationship between language development and cognitive development. Although Vygotsky acknowledged the independence of early cognitive development and early language development, he emphasized the interdependence of language and thought in subsequent development and suggested that "learning to direct one's own mental processes with the aid of words or signs is an integral part of the process of concept formation" (1962, 59). Luria aptly summarized Vygotsky's views:

*Only Consciously*

In [Vygotsky's] view, language is the most decisive element in systematizing perception; insofar as words are themselves a product of sociohistorical development, they become tools for formulating abstractions and generalizations, and facilitate the transition from unmediated sensory reflection to mediated, rational

thinking.... "Categorical thinking" and "abstract orientation" are the consequences of a fundamental reorganization of cognitive activity that occurs under
the impact of a new, social factor—a restructuring of the role that language plays
in determining psychological activity. (Luria 1976, 49–50)

## 9.3 Some Ontogenetic Considerations

Our brief consideration of Piaget's and Vygotsky's views demonstrates
that, from a developmental perspective, it is necessary to distinguish two
representational systems: (1) the system that provides the foundation for
the nonlinguistic conceptual system, and (2) the system that underlies
language. Infants acquire and manipulate concepts prior to the acquisition of language (Haith and Benson 1998; Mandler 1998), demonstrating the existence of a nonlinguistic conceptual system. As children learn
language, they continue to construct an increasingly rich and complex
representational system. Part of this process involves the integration of
the nonlinguistic representational system and the representational system
that results from language acquisition. It seems likely that the distinction
between these two representational systems becomes fuzzier as children
attempt to make sense of the words that they hear. By filling in the gaps
in their lexicon, children structure both their linguistic representational
system and their understanding of their world (Kuczaj 1999; Kuczaj,
Borys, and Jones 1989). Thus, the general developmental picture is one
in which children begin to interpret and categorize their experience
before they learn language, but the process of making sense of the world
is facilitated by language as children acquire their mother tongue. At the
very least, language acquisition influences the representational nature of
thought because it provides valuable cues about ways in which information can be organized and manipulated. In fact, language may provide
necessary cues about abstract information (e.g., hypothetical events and
constructs; Kuczaj and Daly 1979) and manipulations of abstract information (e.g., analogies and relational thought; Gentner and Loewenstein
2002). As Kuczaj (1999) notes:

It is possible that being exposed to a new word that denotes a hypothetical construct, an unobservable entity, or a mental state is necessary for the acquisition of
the concepts that represent the hypothetical construct, the unobservable entity,
or the mental state. The words that denote such concepts may be the best clues

for the existence of the non-concrete referents, and so may play crucial roles in directing the child's efforts to comprehend abstract properties of the world. (p. 154)

The facilitative effect of language continues throughout the lifespan. Adults find it easier to form concepts and solve many problems when they are able to use language (Cabrera and Billman 1996; Hunt and Agnoli 1991; Simons 1996). However, the effects of language on cognitive performance depend at least in part on the type of information being processed. Simons (1996) found that adults were better able to remember objects that had verbal labels, but that memory for the spatial configuration of objects was independent of such labels. This finding is important, for it demonstrates that the manner in which language and thought interact depends on the nature of the information that is processed.

## 9.4    Some Phylogenetic and Comparative Considerations

What can the study of nonhuman animals contribute to the study of the relationship between language and thought? At first blush, the answer would seem to be "nothing at all." After all, only humans possess the complex productive symbolic communication system that is human language, a system that is not even approximated among the known communication systems of other species (Hauser 1997; Kuczaj and Kirkpatrick 1993). Obviously, the cognitive capabilities of organisms that lack language (human infants and nonhuman species) do not depend on language. Consequently, specifying these capabilities can provide clear evidence about the sorts of cognitive accomplishments that are independent of language. Thus, both the study of human infants and the study of nonhuman animals are important to the issues at hand.

Throughout the remainder of this chapter, the term *language* will be used to refer to both the artificial symbolic systems that humans have attempted to teach various species and the communication systems that animals spontaneously employ in their natural habitat. We recognize that these systems are not equivalent to human language (Kuczaj and Kirkpatrick 1993), and use the term *language* as convenient shorthand. No nonhuman species has created or learned a symbolic system that rivals human language, although members of various species have evidenced abilities that suggest "languagelike" competencies. The most common such competency involves the association of symbols with objects, actions, and events in production or comprehension (and sometimes both), although the size of an animal's "vocabulary" is always minuscule compared to that of even young human children (Kuczaj 1999) and is also much more likely to focus on the here and now than that of young children (Kuczaj and Daly 1979). Evidence for syntax and flexible conversational interchanges is at best controversial (e.g., Kako 1999; Shanker, Savage-Rumbaugh, and Taylor 1999). Nonetheless, comparing the cognitive repertoires of animals with different "language" experiences may help to determine the manner in which different aspects of language (both natural and trained) influence different aspects of cognition. Such comparisons are important if we are to have an evolutionary theory of language and thought to complement our developmental theories.

## 9.5 Some Possible Differences between Humans and Animals

Although humans often behave irrationally and sometimes fail to accomplish relatively simple tasks (such as accurately tallying ballots in presidential elections), we are capable of sophisticated forms of reasoning and complex problem solving far beyond that evidenced by any other species. Although some nonhuman primate species and some cetacean species have impressive cognitive abilities, these abilities are primarily concerned with the here and now, oftentimes the attainment of some concrete goal. In contrast, even young human children spontaneously engage in dialogues concerning hypothetical events (Kuczaj and Daly 1979). One important difference between human and animal cognition, then, may be the extent to which possible and even impossible events and objects can be represented and considered.

Humans are also able to reason about abstract relational concepts, an ability that Gentner and Loewenstein (2002) consider the sine qua non of human cognition. Precious little evidence exists to suggest that other species possess this ability, and so another difference between animal and human cognition may concern the extent to which abstract relational concepts can be represented and manipulated. Gentner and Loewenstein also argue that the capacity for analogical learning and reasoning is essential for the development of relational thinking. Moreover, they suggest that relational language is a powerful tool for promoting and consolidating "insights of analogical abstraction." As we shall see, these considerations are important for the comparative study of relational thinking.

In addition to the gulf that separates animal cognition and human cognition, as noted earlier there is a great chasm between the language abilities of humans and other species. Presaging recent controversies and arguments, many of Darwin's contemporaries doubted that any species other than humans possessed a capacity for language (e.g., Lyell 1863; Muller 1870). Muller (1864) argued that "the one great barrier between brute and man is language" (p. 367), a notion that has considerable support among contemporary theorists (e.g., Chomsky 1988; Macphail 1996; Pinker 1995).

The fact that the human cognitive repertoire and the human linguistic symbolic system have no counterparts in the animal realm is one reason that many scholars have suggested that the two systems are intimately connected. For example, Darwin speculated about the phylogenetic relationship of the two systems in his musings about human evolution.

The mental powers of some early progenitor of man must have been more highly developed than in any existing ape, before even the most imperfect form of speech could have come into use; but we may confidently believe that the continued use and advancement of this power would have reacted upon the mind by enabling and encouraging it to carry on long trains of thought. A long and complex train of thought can no more be carried on without words, whether spoken or silent, than a long calculation without the use of figures or algebra. (Darwin 1871, 57)

Darwin's speculations on the evolution of language and thought emphasized the necessity of some form of "highly developed" cognitive abilities for language to emerge, and the subsequent role of language in expanding these abilities into even more sophisticated cognitive powers. In Darwin's view, cognitive abilities and linguistic structure coevolved as a natural consequence of continued efforts to communicate more effectively. Theoretically, then, any species that possessed sufficient basic cognitive abilities and communicative needs might evolve increasingly complex cognitive and communicative powers as cognition and language reciprocally influence one another's evolution.

## 9.6 Animal Language

### 9.6.1 Language in the Wild

Numerous species have been shown to possess communication systems of varying degrees (see Hauser 1997 and Bradbury and Vehrencamp 1998 for detailed and considered reviews). For example, alarm calls have been observed in a variety of species (Gouzoules, Gouzoules, and Tomasczcki 1998; Gyger, Marler, and Pickert 1987; Lawson and Lanning 1980; Macedonia 1990; Sherman 1977; Yamashita 1987). However, it is sometimes difficult to determine whether these signals are under the volitional control of the animals that produce them or automatically produced in response to environmental stimuli (Smith 1998). For example, a ground squirrel is more likely to trill when it detects a predator if close relatives are near (Sherman 1977). Although it is possible that the squirrel controls its vocalizations and so purposely decides to trill when relatives are near and not to trill when only nonrelated squirrels are near, it is also possible that squirrels automatically produce alarm signals when they sense a predator. The close proximity of relatives may increase monitoring behavior, which in turn increases the likelihood of spying a predator. Thus, the increase in trills when in proximity to close relatives might reflect increased monitoring rather than volitional decisions about whether to trill. However, for at least some species, such as vervet moneys, animals are less likely to produce an alarm call if they are alone when they spy a predator (Cheney and Seyfarth 1990b), which demonstrates that the calls are not automatically elicited by the presence of a predator.

At least some alarm calls involve referential meaning. Vervet monkeys use different alarm calls to designate the presence of specific predators (e.g., eagles, leopards, snakes), and listeners react appropriately to these different calls (Seyfarth and Cheney 1997). For example, monkeys hearing an eagle alarm call tend to look up and scurry into the bush, while monkeys hearing a snake alarm call tend to look down and avoid tall grass and dense bush. Further support for the referential nature of at

least some alarm calls comes from a study of diana monkeys (Zuberbühler, Cheney, and Seyfarth 1999). Female and male diana monkeys
both give alarm calls to indicate the presence of predators, and each
gender has a different call for eagles than for leopards. However, each
gender has a distinct call for each predator. Thus, the male alarm call
for "leopard" is acoustically distinct from the female alarm call for
"leopard." Nonetheless, if a female hears a male "leopard" alarm, she
will produce her "leopard" alarm rather than some other sound, such as
an "eagle" alarm. In addition, monkeys who have heard an alarm call do
not respond as strongly to subsequent predator vocalizations. This finding suggests that they had interpreted the earlier alarm call as indicative
of the predator's presence, and either see no need for further arousal or
remain silent in order to avoid calling attention to themselves when they
subsequently hear the predator's vocalizations. This pattern of results is
consistent with the notion that the monkeys respond to the semantic information contained in the calls and the context in which the calls occur
rather than solely to the absolute acoustic characteristics of the calls.

Given all this, vervet monkeys are remarkably insensitive to external
cues concerning predators (Cheney and Seyfarth 1990b). For example,
vervets seem unconcerned about the presence of a gazelle carcass in a
tree even though such a scenario is positively correlated with the presence of a leopard. Similarly, they do not avoid python tracks. On the
contrary, one group of monkeys followed the tracks into the bush, and
then were startled when they encountered the python. Vervets' failure to
react to such external cues suggests that they do not associate these
visual cues with danger, even when they have had opportunities to observe a leopard dragging a carcass into a tree or a python leaving a trail
in the sand. Cheney and Seyfarth suggest that this failure reflects an
inability to understand cause-and-effect relationships, an inability that
prohibits the realization that the presence of a gazelle carcass in a tree
might predict the presence of a leopard even if no leopard is in sight or
that a python trail in the sand might predict the presence of a snake even
though no snake is in view (see Tomasello 1998 and Povinelli 2000
for additional evidence that nonhuman primates' understanding of the
world is limited).

### 9.6.2 Language Enculturation

Attempts to teach animals some form of language have typically involved introducing the animals to labels associated with objects, actions, and even emotions (Gardner and Gardner 1969; Herman, Kuczaj, and Holder 1993; Premack 1971; Rumbaugh 1977). In many of these studies, animals were explicitly reinforced for correctly using a symbol. In several more recent studies, traditional operant conditioning techniques were abandoned in favor of implicit label "teaching." In these studies, the symbolic system was modeled in the presence of the animal but no attempt was made to train the animal to make correct individual responses. Instead, humans used the system to interact with other humans as well as the target animal. As a consequence, symbols were acquired through observation and association rather than through direct reinforcement for correct use. For example, a bonobo took "walks in the woods" with humans, during which times symbols were used to refer to objects and actions (Savage-Rumbaugh and Lewin 1994). The bonobo also learned symbols through his daily observations of language sessions between humans and his mother (Rumbaugh, Savage-Rumbaugh, and Washburn 1996). The bonobo's acquisition of symbols demonstrates that explicit training is not necessary for animals to learn a symbolic communication system. In fact, implicit teaching produced results far superior to those that occurred in studies that employed operant methods. The bonobo was also observed to practice with his keyboard when humans were not present, suggesting that this symbolic system was intrinsically rewarding to him. Unlike earlier studies in which language was most likely to occur when the animals were prompted by humans, relatively few (approximately 11%) of the bonobo's utterances were imitations or responses to prompts from humans. However, 96% of the bonobo's utterances were requests of some sort (Greenfield and Savage-Rumbaugh 1990), demonstrating that the primary function of language for this animal was instrumental.

Another example of this sort of language teaching involved an African gray parrot. The parrot received his exposure to labels by watching two humans interact, one of whom served as the teacher and one of whom adopted the role of a parrot "student" (Pepperberg 1993, 1998).

The parrot soon began to participate in this dialogue. His speech eventually included labels for objects and concepts such as shape, color, and numbers.

Comparing the accomplishments of the above-mentioned bonobo and parrot with those of other language-trained animals demonstrates that the type of language experience provided to animals strongly influences the extent to which they learn the target symbolic system. Experience that includes social interaction and clear indications of the referential nature of the symbols is most likely to yield positive results (Pepperberg 1998). However, it is important to remember that even the most striking accomplishments reported for language-enculturated animals pale in comparison to the language acquisition of human children. Nonetheless, it is still possible that an animal's experience with a symbolic communication system influences its thought.

## 9.7    Possible Effects of Language Enculturation

### 9.7.1    Visual Processing Strategies

One effect of exposure to symbols may be a heightened awareness of the features that are important for discriminating the symbols from one another. Shyan and Wright (1993) argue that the salience of features of visual symbols changes as animals gain experience with the symbols in a "language-training" context. Specifically, Shyan and Wright suggest that experience with symbols during language training causes animals to abandon a "global" perceptual strategy in favor of one that focuses on salient individual features. For example, two dolphins that had been trained over a six-year period to respond to gestures produced by humans had learned to comprehend approximately 40 gestures that consisted of hand and arm movements (Shyan 1985; Shyan and Herman 1987). One dolphin had learned to respond to individual symbols only and was never shown combinations of signs. This dolphin had heard combinations of sounds that were intended to represent elementary syntactic relations in an attempt to teach her a simple acoustic language. The other dolphin was not trained to respond to combinations of sounds, but had learned to respond to combinations of gestures that represented a simple syntax (Herman, Kuczaj, and Holder 1993; Herman, Richards, and Wolz 1984). Thus, the two dolphins' experience with the target gestures differed in one important aspect. One dolphin experienced the gestures individually, while the other saw both individual gestures and combinations of gestures. The dolphin that was trained with only individual gestures did experience combinations of sounds. The combinations of gestures and the combinations of sounds were presented to the dolphins in the context of language training, and so we will refer to one dolphin as the *gestural language* dolphin and the other dolphin as the *acoustic language* dolphin. Aspects of 15 gestures were manipulated in order to ascertain the features of the gestures that affected the dolphins' comprehension (Shyan 1985; Shyan and Herman 1987). The gestural language dolphin was most sensitive to changes in a gesture's location relative to the producer's body, next most sensitive to the overall unfolding pattern of the gesture, less sensitive to the direction of the gesture's motion and gross-motor motions, and least sensitive to fine-motor motion, shape of the hand, and hand orientation. In comparison, the acoustic language dolphin did not focus on the individual features of the gestures but instead used a more global recognition strategy. As a result, this dolphin's responses were more easily disrupted by gestural modifications. In a sense, then, it appears that experience with visual symbols may affect information-processing strategies. Apes and humans are prone to focus on the global structure of visual stimuli (Fagot and Tomonaga 1999), while monkeys are more likely to process individual features (Fagot and Deruelle 1997). If dolphins are more like apes and humans than they are like monkeys, the tendency to focus on global structure is overcome by experience with visual symbols during language training, perhaps because these stimuli obtain a unique representational status as symbols.

### 9.7.2 Categorization

Many animals are able to form categories using a variety of properties. At least in this sense, then, these animals are able to identify and compare relationships that hold among the properties of stimuli. The ability to classify information into categories makes it easier for animals to process and make sense of the information they encounter and to compare present experiences with previous ones (e.g., Schusterman,

Reichmuth, and Kastak 2000). The ability to categorize parts of one's experience provides obvious evolutionary advantages, not the least of which is the facilitation of more rapid and accurate responses.

Language enculturation is not necessary for categorization. Pigeons can learn to discriminate photographs containing trees from those that do not, and they can generalize this ability to novel photographs. When pigeons make mistakes, they tend to incorrectly categorize photographs containing objects that closely resemble trees (e.g., stalks of celery) as if they were trees (Herrnstein and Loveland 1964; Herrnstein, Loveland, and Cable 1976). Pigeons are also able to distinguish photographs containing people from photographs without people, suggesting that they can classify disparate objects such as trees and people into categories that they are able to use to decide if novel instances are members of the category.

Premack (1983) has argued that the ability of many species to form concepts is based on their use of an *imaginal code*. Such a code is closely tied to the perceptual properties of objects. Given this reliance on readily perceived perceptual attributes, classification based on an imaginal code need not depend on any sort of symbolic label (although such labels might facilitate classification—see de Rose 1996; Horne and Lowe 1996; Stromer and MacKay 1996 for discussions of the role of labels in classification by animals). In contrast, relational judgments (such as *same* and *different*) require an abstract code since such judgments sometimes require the ability to abstract a relationship from a variety of perceptual situations that may not share any readily perceived features. According to Premack, only humans and animals that have had experience with a symbolic communication system use an abstract code. If so, the ability of nonhuman animals to engage in relational thinking depends on language enculturation.

Even if most animals are limited to imaginal codes, as Premack suggests, it is possible that there are species-specific differences in the ability to recode the information obtained via direct perception. Recoding involves the mental transformation of information into another code or format (Ashcroft 1994). For humans, language facilitates information processing, including the recoding of information. However, language is not necessary for recoding. For example, language-naive bottlenose dolphins are able to correctly choose targets in match-to-sample tasks when the target and the choices are presented in different modalities (Harley 1993; Harley, Roitblat, and Nachtigall 1996; Herman, Pack, and Hoff-mann-Kuhnt 1998; Pack and Herman 1995). Objects presented to the dolphins visually are readily identified echoically from a multitarget array. The inverse also held true: dolphins easily identify echoically presented stimuli in subsequent visual target arrays. These findings suggest that dolphins represent information in a sufficiently abstract way to allow for use in a variety of modalities, and that they can recode representations from one sensory system in order to make judgments about information presented in another sensory system.

The cross-modal matching ability of nonhuman primates may be facilitated by language training, specifically the use of symbols to refer to objects. Two such language-enculturated chimpanzees successfully matched a visual lexigram to an object they could not see but could feel (Savage-Rumbaugh, Sevcik, and Hopkins 1988). Another chimpanzee was more accurate in matching targets across visual and tactile modes if she had previously learned to label the objects (Rumbaugh 1997). These findings suggest that experience with symbols enhanced the animals' abilities to solve tasks involving cross-modal perception, perhaps because the symbols resulted in more abstract representations of the objects (Rumbaugh 1997).

The fact that some animals can recode information suggests that these animals are able to represent information in some form that is at least somewhat independent of the absolute perceptual properties themselves. Otherwise, animals should fail all cross-modal tasks. However, even if animals are capable of representing information in some sort of abstract code that allows recoding, this is not relational thinking in the most common sense of the term. Relational thinking typically refers to the ability to compare relations that exist among sets of stimuli rather than the ability to recognize a stimulus as a previously experienced one. The data concerning recoding suggest that object recognition may involve more abstract representations than Premack supposed, but they do not demonstrate that animals are capable of relational thinking.

Savage-Rumbaugh et al. (1980) tested the categorization skills of two chimpanzees that had been trained to use visual symbols to refer to objects (Savage-Rumbaugh 1986). These symbols typically concerned food or tools that could be used to obtain food. In the categorization task, the chimpanzees were trained to sort objects into either a food or a tool category. They learned to sort the objects, photographs of the objects, and the symbols for the objects. The chimpanzees were also taught superordinate symbols for the general categories of food and tool. Once they had learned the task, both chimpanzees were able to sort new tools and foods correctly and to respond to new objects with the appropriate symbol. The fact that they could sort symbols as well as objects into the appropriate categories suggests that the symbols were associated with representations of the objects themselves. Another chimpanzee that had also learned to use visual symbols to refer to objects proved able to sort an initial set of six objects as tools or food and to associate each general category with an appropriate symbol. However, this chimpanzee did not correctly apply these symbols to new tools and foods. This suggests that this chimpanzee's language training had resulted in the acquisition of a series of specific associations that were not linked to representations that could be manipulated. In fact, she had learned to associate individual symbols with specific objects during her language training, and she had limited interactive experience with other sentient beings. The other chimpanzees had experienced a more interactive language environment and seemed to have learned to use symbols as representations of classes of objects, and so were better able to relate the symbols, representations, and objects. The categorization behaviors of these chimpanzees suggest the use of a representational code that goes beyond perceptual similarity, and so may be considered as support for Premack's claim that language enculturation changes the representational nature of thought. However, the results also suggest that the type of language enculturation may mediate the effects of language enculturation on cognitive performance.

Most of the evidence to evaluate Premack's hypothesis about relational thinking comes from captive chimpanzees, although there is evidence that other species can engage in some forms of relational thinking. Pepperberg and Brezinsky (1991) report that an African gray parrot with significant amounts of language enculturation understood relative size, and could indicate whether two objects were the same size and whether one object was larger or smaller than a comparison object. Two bottlenose dolphins' ability to learn and generalize the concepts of *same* and *different* suggested that language enculturation may have played a role in the dolphins' performance (Herman, Pack, and Wood 1994; Mercado et al. 2000). One dolphin had considerable experience with gestural symbols and readily comprehended short multigesture sequences (Herman, Kuczaj, and Holder 1993). This dolphin generalized her *same/different* concepts more readily than did the dolphin that lacked such enculturation. However, the comparison between the two dolphins is not a straightforward one. The language-enculturated dolphin had considerably more experience with problem-solving tasks and was generally viewed as the dolphin at this facility that was most likely to succeed on any task (personal experience of first author). It is possible, then, that her ability to generalize *same* and *different* reflected aspects of her experience (including human expectations) other than exposure to gestural symbols.

Nonhuman primates tend to learn the *same/different* concept with relative ease (Oden, Thompson, and Premack 1988). The ability to extend this concept to other domains is much more pronounced in apes (and humans) than in other species. Thompson, Oden, and Boysen (1997) taught chimpanzees to choose one symbol when they saw two identical objects and another symbol when they saw two objects that were not identical. These animals readily generalized their use of the *same* and *different* symbols to relations that held between pairs of objects. For example, a chimpanzee might see one object set that consisted of two identical triangles (and so were the same) and another object set consisting of two identical circles (and so were also the same). In such a case, chimpanzees responded with the *same* symbol even though the objects in the two pairs were different, demonstrating that they were comparing the relations that held within and between the sets of objects. In contrast, macaque monkeys that were trained to use *same* and *different* symbols to compare objects with one another proved unable to reliably compare the relations of sets of objects (Washburn, Thompson, and Oden 1997). The monkeys were able to learn to express whether the two objects in a set were the same or different, but they never learned to compare the relations that held within and between two sets of objects.

Recall that Gentner and Loewenstein (2002) suggest that the ontogeny of relational thinking is strongly influenced by analogical learning and reasoning, and that relational language plays an important role in this developmental phenomenon. Analogies involve processing information about the relations between relations, and as such they involve more sophisticated representations than do judgments of *same* or *different* (Gentner 1998; Holyoak and Thagard 1997; Vosniadou and Ortony 1989). Gillan, Premack, and Woodruff (1981) tested the ability of a language-trained chimpanzee to solve analogical reasoning tasks. One type of task required the chimpanzee to match the perceptual relationship of pairs of objects. For example, the chimpanzee might see a large sawtooth shape and a small sawtooth shape paired together (Aa), a symbol that represented the relationship *same as*, and a large triangle with a dot in the center (B). The chimpanzee's task was to choose between a small triangle with a dot in the center (b) or a large triangle without a dot (B'). The chimpanzee was most likely to choose the objects (in our example, the small triangle with the dot) that resulted in the same relationship as the target pair of objects, consistent with the notion that she understood the analogical relationships that held among the objects. Another task required the chimpanzee to match more conceptual relationships. For example, the chimpanzee might see a lock paired with a key, the symbol that indicated *same as*, and a can. The task was to choose between a can opener and a paint brush. The chimpanzee was most likely to choose the object that completed the same functional relationship as the target pair. Thus, she would choose the can opener in our example because the can opener could be used to open the can just as the key could be used to open the lock.

Many years later, this same chimpanzee was presented with another set of analogical problems (Oden, Thompson, and Premack 2001). The chimpanzee was asked to complete analogies, as in Gillan, Premack, and Woodruff's (1981) study. She was also asked to construct analogies, a much more challenging task than the completion task. For the construction tasks, the chimpanzee was given a board divided into four squares that had the *same as* symbol in place. In one condition, she was given four objects that could be arranged to create an analogy. In another condition, she was given five objects, only four of which could be used to create an analogy. The chimpanzee proved able to construct analogies in both these conditions, demonstrating an ability to determine relations among stimuli even when the nature of these relations had not been specified in advance. Oden, Thompson, and Premack suggest that the chimpanzee's success was based on her previous experience with symbols that represented abstract *same* and *different* relations (see also Thompson, Oden, and Boysen 1997), just as children's analogical reasoning is facilitated by relational language (Gentner and Loewenstein 2002; Rattermann and Gentner 1998). However, experience with these sorts of symbols is not sufficient to produce analogical judgments in all species (Thompson and Oden 2000). Old-world macaque monkeys that had been trained to use symbols for *same* and *different* to judge the similarity of pairs of objects failed analogy tasks (Washburn, Thompson, and Oden 1997). Some minimal level of cognitive sophistication is required if exposure to relational symbols is to facilitate the perception and consideration of analogical relations. In this sense, there is an interaction between cognitive ability and experience with language, as hypothesized by Darwin, Vygotsky, and others. According to Thompson and Oden (1993, 2000), this interaction culminates in propositional representations that can be encoded and manipulated by apes and humans, but not by less cognitively adept species.

### 9.7.3 Cultural Transmission

There is considerable debate about the extent to which nonhuman primates and cetaceans possess even rudimentary types of cultural knowledge, cultural variability, and cultural transmission within and between generations (e.g., Byrne and Russon 1998; Heltne and Marquardt 1989; Kuczaj 2001; Russon 1999; Tomasello 1998; Whiten et al. 1999). However, there is a consensus that the transmission of knowledge from individual to individual and from generation to generation is a defining feature of culture (see, e.g., Bonner 1980; Greenfield et al. 2000; Kuczaj 2001; Rendell and Whitehead 2001). Greenfield et al. (2000) argue that the evolution of learning and teaching mechanisms results in behavioral flexibility for the individual and cultural change for the group. In their words, "the phylogenetic evolution of learning and teaching mechanisms creates a biologically based potential for cultural change" (p. 239).

Bonner (1980) suggests that from a phylogenetic perspective, knowledge transmission progresses from observational learning to simple forms of teaching to more complex forms of instruction (e.g., the type that humans engage in when they do things such as write chapters for books).

Although Bonner considers observational learning to be one of the easier forms of information transmission, there is considerable controversy about the ability of nonhuman animals to learn in this manner (e.g., Byrne and Russon 1998; Kuczaj, Gory, and Xitco 1998; Tomasello 1996b). Tomasello and his colleagues (Call and Tomasello 1996; Tomasello and Call 1997; Tomasello, Savage-Rumbaugh, and Kruger 1993) suggest that chimpanzees can emulate goals that they have observed others obtain, but that they cannot actually imitate the specific actions that they have observed unless they have benefited from some form of human enculturation. Apes that have experienced language enculturation do sometimes more readily imitate the actions of others than do apes that lack language enculturation (Rumbaugh 1997). For example, two chimpanzees that had received considerable amounts of language training learned to use joysticks to play a video game by observing and imitating humans. In contrast, neither of two language-naive chimpanzees learned to play the game through observation. Subsequent attempts to explicitly teach these chimpanzees how to play the video game also failed. The two language-naive animals never learned that the joystick moved the on-screen cursor and so never learned to play the game (Savage-Rumbaugh 1986). Other examples of language-enculturated apes imitating behaviors are more anecdotal. These include an orangutan that spontaneously imitated some of the actions of his keepers, including behaviors such as "cooking" (Miles, Mitchell, and Harper 1996), and a bonobo that learned to make his own flint flakes after observing a human flint-knapper doing the same (Rumbaugh, Savage-Rumbaugh, and Washburn 1996; Savage-Rumbaugh and Lewin 1994). According to the definitions adopted by Tomasello, these latter behaviors would be considered emulations rather than imitations because the apes evidenced little concern with replicating the exact behaviors of the models.

A different view is offered by Greenfield et al. (2000). They report that young chimpanzees paid close attention to the ways in which sticks were used to fish for termites as well as to the termites themselves. Perhaps laboratory studies of imitation (e.g., Nagell, Olguin, and Tomasello 1993) underestimate the imitative capacity of animals because the laboratory tasks do not truly engage the animals' abilities. If so, naturalistic studies of imitation (Boesch 1996; Greenfield et al. 2000) are more likely to reveal an animal's imitative competence. Of course, the lack of control in the naturalistic situation makes it difficult (but not impossible) to determine whether or not imitation has actually occurred (Kuczaj 2001).

In fact, much of the evidence for cultural transmission in non-language-enculturated animals comes from observations of the spontaneous behavior produced by wild animals (e.g., Byrne and Russon 1998). For example, Boesch (1991, 1993) observed chimpanzee mothers  helping their offspring learn to use a hammer and anvil to crack nuts. Mothers with infants are more likely than other chimpanzees to leave an intact nut in the hollow of a tree-root anvil with a stone hammer on top of it. This situation provides infants with the opportunity to open (or at least try to open) the nut by pounding on it with the hammer. Mothers are also more likely to leave a nut and hammer for infants that are old enough to successfully wield the hammer than for younger infants. These behaviors are consistent with the notion that chimpanzee mothers are facilitating the acquisition of tool use in their infants. Boesch (1993) also reports an incident in which a mother corrected her son's nut-opening behavior. The son had placed a nut in a haphazard position on the just-used anvil. Before he could strike it with his hammer, the mother intervened by taking the nut in her hand, cleaning the anvil, and replacing the nut in the correct position on the anvil. While the mother watched, the son successfully opened the nut. This anecdote, though striking, is unusual. In general, there is little evidence to support the notion that adult animals deliberately teach their young (Cheney and Seyfarth 1990a).

There is even less evidence that animals use language to teach another animal, even one of their offspring. Species that use referential alarm calls do not use these calls as teaching tools. Young vervet monkeys overgeneralize their alarm calls, and so might produce an eagle alarm call in response to a harmless bird or even a leaf (Cheney and Seyfarth 1990b). Older vervets learn to ignore infants' calls because of the high number of false alarms that are produced, but adults do not correct the infant or purposely demonstrate the correct use of the call. Instead, vervet young are thought to learn the correct extension of their calls by observing both the correct calls of others and other monkeys' reactions to the young vervets' calls.

### 9.7.4   Theory of Mind

One major difference between animals and humans concerns the ability to recognize what others see, believe, know, or want, an ability that most animals lack (Povinelli 2000; Seyfarth and Cheney 1997; Tomasello 1996a). Evidence for animal understanding of others' mental states is rare. One possible example of such understanding comes from the use of gestures to communicate. Even juvenile chimpanzees are sensitive to the perceptual readiness of the receiver of their message (Tomasello et al. 1997). For example, if the receiver has its back turned to a juvenile chimpanzee, the juvenile uses a noise-making "ground slap" rather than a gesture to get the receiver's attention. This suggests that juvenile chimpanzees are able to consider another's perspective and that this ability does not depend on language enculturation. Of course, it is possible that the chimpanzees have learned that others must be facing them in order for their gestures to produce the desired effect, and so restrict their use of gestures to such contexts even though they do not understand the perceiver's mental state (see Povinelli 2000 for expanded arguments about how primates might solve problems in ways that make them appear smarter than they really are).

Call and Tomasello (1998) suggest that language enculturation may facilitate the ability to understand others' mental lives. Understanding the point of view of others requires relational thinking, and so this prediction is consistent with Premack's contention that language enculturation enables a form of thinking not available to language-naive organisms (although the behavior of the juvenile chimpanzees suggests that at least some form of this ability exists in animals that have not experienced language enculturation). There is some support for Call and Tomasello's hypothesis. Chimpanzees that had experienced language training cooperated with one another by using their language keyboard to solve problems (Savage-Rumbaugh 1986). Dolphins that were exposed to an artificial symbolic communication system spontaneously engaged in pointing behavior that seemed to be intentionally produced in

 Conflation

order to direct the attention of others (Xitco, Gory, and Kuczaj 2001). Perhaps language enculturation enables animals to express their theory of mind in ways they might otherwise not make use of.

Reviewing the available literature on deception and concealment in great ape species, Mitchell (1999) speculates that the capacity for deception might be enhanced by language enculturation and even involve the communicative symbol system to which the animal has been exposed. For example, apes that have been taught sign language have been reported to use signs to denote falsehoods, including an item's presence, the animal's interest in an object, and whether the animal was engaging in an activity or going somewhere (Miles 1986). Of course, it is often difficult to reliably determine the intent to deceive (Kuczaj et al. 2001), and so the effects of language enculturation in this domain are unclear.

### 9.8 What Can Animals Do without Language Enculturation?

In the previous section, we have considered a number of areas in which language enculturation might facilitate animal thought. Before we summarize these findings and speculations, we should note that animals possess a number of cognitive abilities that are clearly not dependent on language enculturation (de Waal 1998; Roberts 1998).

#### 9.8.1 Memory
Animals are able to represent various aspects of their experience in memory (Balda, Pepperberg, and Kamil 1998; Pearce 1997). Many species can correctly choose a target stimulus from an array following delays between presentation of the target stimulus and the choice array (D'Amato and Worsham 1972; Herman and Thompson 1982; Langley and Riley 1993). Todt and Hultsch (1998) hypothesize that the vocal development of birds involves the hierarchical organization of memory, which facilitates the acquisition and use of large amounts of information. Consistent with Miller's (1956) pioneering suggestion that humans are able to increase their working memory capacity by "chunking" information into meaningful units, Todt and Hultsch also suggest that birds use "chunking" to learn longer vocal sequences, the song being the chunkable unit. Pigeons also benefit from information presented in a way

that enhances chunking opportunities (Terrace 1991), and rats seem able to chunk information about spatial locations (Dallal and Meck 1990; Macuda and Roberts 1995). Many birds can recognize individuals on the basis of their calls or songs (Batista, Nelson, and Gaunt 1998; Gnam 1988; Saunders 1983). The use of sounds in individual recognition has also been found in a number of other species, including vervet monkeys (Cheney and Seyfarth 1990b) and dolphins (Caldwell, Caldwell, and Tyack 1990; Janik 2000). These findings are consistent with the notion that these species can store information about individual sounds and use these representations for individual recognition. All of the above behaviors depend on mnemonic representations of the original stimulus that can be recalled and used to make the subsequent choice, demonstrating that language enculturation is not necessary for such representations.

A number of species are able to remember the spatial relations that exist among objects. Bees are able to remember and communicate the location of bountiful pollen sources relative to their home hive, and they appear to use some form of cognitive map to do so (Gould 1986; von Frisch 1946). Octopuses can learn the relative location of open burrows and retain this information about spatial relationships for up to one week (Boal et al. 2000). Spatial memory has also been demonstrated in birds (Clayton and Krebs 1994; Hurley and Healy 1996), domestic dogs (Gagnon and Dore 1993), rats (Morris 1981; Tolman, Ritchie, and Kalish 1946), turtles (Lopez et al. 2000), and primates (Menzel 1996; Tinklepaugh 1932; Tomasello 1998). Given these findings, and Simons's (1996) report that human spatial memory does not depend on language, it seems clear that language is not necessary for spatial learning and memory.

### 9.8.2 Counting and Transitive Inference

Some animals can discriminate quantities and even count, numerical abilities that might be improved by language enculturation but certainly do not depend on it (Boysen and Berntson 1989; Capaldi 1993; Gallistel 1993; Rumbaugh, Savage-Rumbaugh, and Hegel 1987; Thomas, Fowlkes, and Vickery 1980; but see Davis and Perusse 1988 for an opposing viewpoint). Other work has demonstrated understanding of transitive relations (if $A > B$, and $B > C$, is $A$ greater or less than

C?) in squirrel monkeys (McGonigle and Chalmers 1977), chimpanzees (Boysen et al. 1993), pigeons (von Ferson et al. 1991), and rats (Davis 1992). These findings suggest that language is not necessary for at least some forms of transitive "reasoning." However, it is possible that in at least some cases the animals solve the task without transitive "reasoning." Instead, the animals may have learned to make correct transitive decisions through the principles of associative learning (Couvillon and Bitterman 1992; Steirn, Weaver, and Zentall 1995). In contrast, human children can generalize their understanding of transitive relations to hypothetical situations, and they may even overgeneralize this knowledge to inappropriate relations. For example, some children erroneously conclude that if a boy loves a dog, and the dog loves a girl, then the boy loves the girl (Kuczaj and Donaldson 1982), a clear demonstration that their understanding of transitive relations does not depend on direct experience with the relevant entities.

### 9.8.3 Insight and Problem Solving

Some species seem able to solve problems in insightful ways. For example, Kohler's (1925) apes learned to stack boxes on top of one another in order to obtain bananas that were out of reach. As noted earlier, some wild chimpanzees use stick tools to gather termites (Goodall 1986), and others use a hammer and anvil to crack nuts (Sakura and Matsuzawa 1991). However, nonhuman primates do not always show insightful solutions to problems. Visalberghi and Limongelli (1994) found that capuchin monkeys could not correctly solve a task that required them to ascertain that a tube contained a trap that had to be avoided if the prize contained in the tube was to be obtained. Limongelli, Boysen, and Visalberghi (1995) presented the same problem to five chimpanzees. Only two of the chimpanzees were able to solve the problem. Neither of these apes had experience with language, demonstrating that language enculturation was not necessary to successfully solve this problem. In fact, one of the chimpanzees that failed the task had considerable experience with language. Thus, experience with language is neither necessary nor sufficient for successful performance on the tube-trap problem. Limongelli, Boysen, and Visalberghi's results illustrate the need for caution when we compare cognitive performances across species, for there are clearly both individual differences and species differences to consider. This becomes particularly important when we deal with studies in which only one or two members of a species are available for testing.

Our final example of insight/problem solving concerns a language-enculturated chimpanzee's knowledge of the physical world. Premack and Woodruff (1978) showed the chimpanzee videotapes depicting a human attempting to obtain bananas that were out of reach. After watching each 30-second videotape, the chimpanzee was given two cards. One card showed the human performing a behavior that would not result in obtaining the bananas. The other card depicted the human using a tool to solve the problem. The chimpanzee chose the card that would result in the problem's being solved on 21 of 24 trials. In other tests, the chimpanzee was initially shown videotapes of a person doing a variety of things, such as trying to play a phonograph when it was not plugged in, use a hose that was not connected to the faucet, or escape from a locked cage. When shown two photographs, the chimpanzee chose the photograph that resulted in the problem being solved in all such trials. Although it is impossible to determine whether the chimpanzee's experience with language or her experience with human activities allowed her to represent the correct solutions to these problems (Savage-Rumbaugh, Rumbaugh, and Boysen 1978), it is clear that she understood more about the workings of the physical world than do most other captive chimpanzees (see Povinelli 2000 for details concerning chimpanzees' failures of understanding concerning the physical domain).

## 9.9   Conclusions

The answer to the question posed in the title of this chapter seems to be yes. Language does help animals to think. But exactly how does language enculturation affect animal thought? Language enculturation has been hypothesized to produce quantitative changes by enhancing existing abilities and qualitative changes by providing a necessary framework for new abilities. There are data that can be interpreted as support for each of these notions. The facilitating effect of language enculturation on existing abilities has the most support, both empirically and theoretically. For example, in a recent consideration of this problem, Langer

(2000) concludes that language enculturation produces quantitative but not qualitative changes in chimpanzees' cognitive repertoires.

Part of the problem with the claim that language enculturation produces new forms of thinking is that it is difficult to demonstrate that an animal lacks a particular cognitive ability (Tyack 1993). Language enculturation may provide investigators with different ways to assess existing abilities (e.g., by using learned symbols such as *same* and *different* to test understanding of these concepts) as well as provide animals new means with which to express existing abilities. Or language enculturation may be a trigger that releases cognitive potentials that would otherwise remain unrealized. Distinguishing these possibilities presents the largest challenge to the study of the effects of language experience on animal thought.

We are left, then, with a relatively unsettled state of affairs. Experience with meaningful symbols and meaningful two-way communication systems does appear to enhance animals' cognitive capabilities, but the nature of this enhancement is unclear. On the one hand, enculturation may be limited to quantitative changes in existing abilities, as suggested by Langer (2000). Moreover, human enculturation may simply produce changes that would normally result from the animal's enculturation by members of its own species (Russon 1999). On the other hand, language enculturation may result in qualitative changes in thought, as suggested by Darwin (1871), Premack (1983), and Thompson and Oden (2000).

We suspect that the final answers to these questions will depend on both the nature of the language enculturation and the cognitive ability being considered. For example, animals do not need language enculturation to categorize objects. However, experience with object labels might result in an animal creating object categories that it would otherwise not form, resulting in a quantitative change in categorization. But an animal that lacked relational concepts, such as *same* and *different* (ideally, we could test this without the use of symbols), might learn these concepts through the use of the symbols in some language-enculturated environment. This would result in a qualitatively different mode for organizing aspects of the world. Or an animal might understand *same* and *different*, but lack the ability to use these concepts to judge abstract information concerning relations. If language enculturation resulted in an ability to use *same* and **different** to reason about abstract information as well as concrete objects, then a qualitative change in thought would have occurred.

A significant part of the problem is how little we know about the cognitive capabilities of species other than our own. Our select survey of the literature on animal cognition revealed that animals possess a wide array of cognitive abilities, many of which clearly do not depend on any form of natural animal language or human-based language encultura-tion. However, we still know relatively little about animal cognition compared to animal learning or human cognition. Our incomplete understanding of animal cognition makes it difficult to assess the effects of language on cognition. Unless we know the extent to which animals possess a cognitive ability, we cannot reliably determine the manner in which language enculturation enhances or even creates the ability. For example, experience with visual symbols makes these symbols more salient and may even affect the manner in which information about the symbols is processed (Shyan and Wright 1993). However, it is impos-sible to determine if this shift in processing strategy occurs solely as a result of experience with symbols as part of a communication system. Perhaps any experience that yielded a similar increase in the salience of symbol discrimination would produce a similar pattern of results.

Even if language enculturation does result in enhanced and different strategies for discriminating and categorizing the symbols that make up the communication system, this is not a change in the nature of thought. But if language enculturation changes the nature of the representational code, as Premack (1983) suggests, then language does have the capacity to produce qualitative changes in thought. Although there are precious few data with which to assess Premack's hypothesis, the data that do exist are consistent with the notion that language-enculturated animals outperform language-naive animals. The capacity to learn from watching others and the understanding of others' mental states may both be enhanced by language enculturation. The ability to learn to indicate whether a stimulus is the same as or different from another stimulus is also enhanced by experience with symbols that denote *same* and **differ-ent**. The more complex comparisons of relations with relations seem to require language enculturation, as suggested by Premack. Only language-enculturated chimpanzees have been found to recognize that members of one pair of objects (AA) have the same relationship to one another as members of another pair of objects (BB), even though the objects in pair AA are different from the objects in pair BB. Even more striking, one language-enculturated chimpanzee evidenced analogical ability, both in terms of completing analogies and in terms of constructing analogies. However, no animal (language-enculturated or not) has demonstrated an ability to understand more complex relationships. For example, comparing the relationship between AA and BB and the relationship between XX and YY seems to be too difficult for any nonhuman animal. There are different levels of abstract thought, and the ability to represent and manipulate complex relationships may reflect significant differences in the abstract thinking of different species.

Much of the available evidence regarding the influence of language on animal thought concerns heightened awareness of objects (including other animals) and object relations in the animal's world. Language enculturation may influence animal thought by increasing the number of possibilities that the animals are able to consider. According to Jackendoff (1992), the significance of information relates directly to the possible interpretations available to the organism receiving the information. Human children are able to consider multiple possibilities at a relatively early age, an ability that among other things allows them to evaluate hypothetical situations (Kuczaj and Daly 1979). Perhaps language enculturation changes animal thought in the sense that it provides animals with their first hints that information may be interpreted in a number of ways, which in turn might lead to the representation and manipulation of multiple possibilities. The ability to reflect on multiple possibilities opens the door for relational thinking in both the physical and the social realm, thereby enabling animals to solve problems and consider things that would otherwise evade them. If this scenario is true, then language enculturation does change the nature of animal thought.

We close with one final caveat. It is not possible to make a silk purse out of a sow's ear. No matter how talented and determined an investigator might be, it is impossible to teach a symbolic system to an animal that lacks the ability to represent and manipulate symbols. Similarly, language enculturation will affect animal cognition only to the extent that the animals possess sufficient cognitive architecture to benefit from this type of experience. For example, chimpanzees benefited from experience with symbols for *same* and **different** to a much greater extent than did monkeys. But even more cognitively sophisticated animals such as chimpanzees and dolphins do not seem to benefit as much as humans from experience with language. The finding that humans and chimpanzees share approximately 98% of their proteins and DNA is typically interpreted as evidence for the close similarity of the two species (Weiss 1987). The shared genetic similarity between the two species is remarkable, but the more important message would seem to be that a relatively small difference in genetic material can produce significant phenotypic differences. Chimpanzees may be our closest living genetic relatives (based on shared genotypes), but the differences between the two species are vast. We suspect that the same pattern will hold for comparisons of animal and human cognition. As we improve our techniques for assessing animal cognition, we will discover more and more humanlike abilities in animals, and so find that animal and human cognition are more similar than we once thought. However, the similarities will continue to be dwarfed by the differences between animal and human cognition. The human capacity for abstract rational thought is not even approximated by any other species, and it is likely to remain so regardless of the richness that language enculturation adds to any animal's cognitive life.

## References

Ashcroft, M. H. (1994). *Human memory and cognition.* New York: Harper Collins.

Balda, R. P., Pepperberg, I. M., and Kamil, A. C. (Eds.). (1998). *Animal cognition in nature: The convergence of psychology and biology in laboratory and field.* San Diego, CA: Academic Press.

Batista, L. F., Nelson, D. A., and Gaunt, S. L. (1998). Cognitive processes in avian vocal acquisition. In R. P. Balda, I. M. Pepperberg, and A. C. Kamil (Eds.), *Animal cognition in nature: The convergence of psychology and biology in laboratory and field* (pp. 245–274). San Diego, CA: Academic Press.

Boal, J. G., Dunham, A. W., Hanlon, R. T., and Williams, K. T. (2000). Experimental evidence for spatial learning in octopuses (*Octopus bimaculoides*). *Journal of Comparative Psychology, 114,* 246–252.

Boesch, C. (1991). Teaching among wild chimpanzees. *Animal Behaviour, 41*, 530–532.

Boesch, C. (1993). Aspects of tool-use transmission in wild chimpanzees. In K. R. Gibson and T. Ingold (Eds.), *Tools, language and intelligence* (pp. 171–183). Cambridge: Cambridge University Press.

Boesch, C. (1996). Three approaches for assessing chimpanzee culture. In A. E. Russon, K. A. Bard, and S. T. Parker (Eds.), *Reaching into thought: The minds of the great apes* (pp. 404–429). Cambridge: Cambridge University Press.

Bonner, J. T. (1980). *The evolution of culture in animals*. Princeton, NJ: Princeton University Press.

Boysen, S. T., and Berntson, G. G. (1989). Numerical competence in a chimpanzee (*Pan troglodytes*). *Journal of Comparative Psychology, 103*, 23–31.

Boysen, S. T., Berntson, G. G., Shreyer, T. A., and Quigley, K. S. (1993). Processing of ordinality and transitivity by chimpanzees (*Pan troglodytes*). *Journal of Comparative Psychology, 107*, 208–216.

Bradbury, J. W., and Vehrencamp, S. L. (1998). *Principles of animal communication*. Sunderland, MA: Sinauer.

Byrne, R. W., and Russon, A. E. (1998). Learning by imitation: A hierarchical approach. *Behavioral and Brain Sciences, 21*, 667–721.

Cabrera, A., and Billman, D. (1996). Language-driven concept learning: Deciphering Jabberwocky. *Journal of Experimental Psychology: Learning, Memory, and Cognition, 22*, 539–555.

Caldwell, M. C., Caldwell, D. K., and Tyack, P. L. (1990). Review of the signature whistle hypothesis for the Atlantic bottlenose dolphin. In S. Leatherwood and R. R. Reeves (Eds.), *The bottlenose dolphin* (pp. 199–234). San Diego, CA: Academic Press.

Call, J., and Tomasello, M. (1996). The effect of humans on the cognitive development of apes. In A. E. Russon, K. A. Bard, and S. T. Parker (Eds.), *Reaching into thought: The minds of the great apes* (pp. 371–403). Cambridge: Cambridge University Press.

Call, J., and Tomasello, M. (1998). Distinguishing intentional from accidental actions in orangutans (*Pongo pygmaeus*), chimpanzees (*Pan troglodytes*), and human children (*Homo sapiens*). *Journal of Comparative Psychology, 112*, 192–206.

Capaldi, E. J. (1993). Animal number abilities: Implications for a hierarchical approach to instrumental learning. In S. T. Boysen and E. J. Capaldi (Eds.), *The development of numerical competence: Animal and human models* (pp. 191–209). Hillsdale, NJ: Erlbaum.

Cheney, D. L., and Seyfarth, R. M. (1990a). Attending to behavior versus attending to knowledge: Examining monkeys' attribution of mental states. *Animal Behaviour, 40*, 742–753.

Cheney, D. L., and Seyfarth, R. M. (1990b). *How monkeys see the world: Inside the mind of another species.* Chicago: University of Chicago Press.

Chomsky, N. (1988). *Language and problems of knowledge: The Managua lectures.* Cambridge, MA: MIT Press.

Clayton, N. S., and Krebs, J. R. (1994). Memory for spatial and object-specific cues in food-storing and nonstoring birds. *Journal of Comparative Psychology, 174,* 371–379.

Couvillon, P. A., and Bitterman, M. E. (1992). A conventional conditioning analysis of "transitive inference" in pigeons. *Journal of Experimental Psychology: Animal Behavior Processes, 18,* 308–310.

Dallal, N. L., and Meck, W. H. (1990). Hierarchical structures: Chunking food type facilitates spatial memory. *Journal of Experimental Psychology: Animal Behavior Processes, 16,* 69–84.

D'Amato, M. R., and Worsham, R. W. (1972). Delayed matching in the capuchin monkey with brief sample durations. *Learning and Motivation, 3,* 304–312.

Darwin, C. (1871). *The descent of man and selection in relation to sex.* London: Murray.

Davis, H. (1992). Transitive inference in rats (*Rattus norvegicus*). *Journal of Comparative Psychology, 106,* 342–349.

Davis, H., and Perusse, R. (1988). Numerical competence in animals: Definitional issues, current evidence, and a new research agenda. *Behavioral and Brain Sciences, 11,* 561–615.

de Rose, J. C. (1996). Controlling factors in conditional discriminations and tests of equivalence. In T. R. Zentall and P. M. Smeets (Eds.), *Stimulus class formation in humans and animals* (pp. 253–278). Amsterdam: Elsevier.

de Waal, F. (1998). *Chimpanzee politics: Power and sex among apes.* Baltimore: The Johns Hopkins University Press.

Fagot, J., and Deruelle, C. (1997). Processing of global and local visual information and hemispheric specialization in humans (*Homo sapiens*) and baboons (*Papio papio*). *Journal of Experimental Psychology: Human Perception and Performance, 23,* 429–442.

Fagot, J., and Tomonaga, M. (1999). Global and local processing in humans (*Homo sapiens*) and chimpanzees (*Pan troglodytes*): Use of a visual search task with compound stimuli. *Journal of Comparative Psychology, 113,* 3–12.

Gagnon, S., and Dore, F. Y. (1993). Search behavior of dogs (*Canis familiaris*) in invisible displacement problems. *Animal Learning and Behavior, 21,* 246–254.

Gallistel, C. R. (1993). A conceptual framework for the study of numerical estimation and arithmetic reasoning in animals. In S. T. Boysen and E. J. Capaldi (Eds.), *The development of numerical competence: Animal and human models* (pp. 211–223). Hillsdale, NJ: Erlbaum.

Gardner, R. A., and Gardner, B. T. (1969). Teaching sign language to a chimpanzee. *Science, 165*, 664–672.

Gentner, D. (1998). Analogy. In W. Bechtel and G. Graham (Eds.), *A companion to cognitive science* (pp. 107–113). Malden, MA: Blackwell.

Gentner, D., and Loewenstein, J. (2002). Relational language and relational thought. In J. Byrnes and E. Amsel (Eds.), *Language, literacy, and cognitive development* (pp. 87–120). Mahwah, NJ: Erlbaum.

Gillan, D. D., Premack, D., and Woodruff, G. (1981). Reasoning in the chimpanzee: I. Analogical reasoning. *Journal of Experimental Psychology: Animal Behavior Processes, 7*, 1–17.

Gnam, R. (1988). Preliminary results on the breeding biology of Bahama amazon. *Parrot Letter, 1*, 23–26.

Goodall, J. (1986). *The chimpanzees of Gombe: Patterns of behavior*. Cambridge, MA: Harvard University Press.

Gould, J. L. (1986). The locale map of honey bees: Do insects have cognitive maps? *Science, 232*, 861–863.

Gouzoules, H., Gouzoules, S., and Tomasczcki, M. (1998). Agonistic screams and the classification of dominance relationships: Are monkeys fuzzy logicians? *Animal Behaviour, 55*, 51–60.

Greenfield, P. M., Maynard, A. E., Boehm, C., and Schmidtling, E. Y. (2000). Cultural apprenticeship and cultural change: Tool learning and imitation in chimpanzees and humans. In S. T. Parker, J. Langer, and M. L. McKinney (Eds.), *Biology, brains, and behavior: The evolution of human development* (pp. 237–277). Sante Fe, NM: School of American Research Press.

Greenfield, P. M., and Savage-Rumbaugh, E. S. (1990). Grammatical combination in *Pan paniscus*: Processes of learning and invention in the evolution and development of language. In S. T. Parker and K. A. Gibson (Eds.), *"Language" and intelligence in monkeys and apes: Comparative developmental perspectives* (pp. 540–578). New York: Cambridge University Press.

Gyger, M., Marler, P., and Pickert, R. (1987). Semantics of an avian alarm call system: The male domestic fowl, *G. domesticus*. *Behaviour, 102*, 15–40.

Haith, M. M., and Benson, J. B. (1998). Infant cognition. In D. Kuhn, R. S. Siegler (Vol. Eds.), and W. Damon (Ed.), *The handbook of child psychology: Cognition, perception, and language* (5th ed., Vol. 2, pp. 199–254). New York: Wiley.

Harley, H. E. (1993). *Object representation in the bottlenosed dolphin (Tursiops truncatus): Integration and association of visual and echoic information*. Unpublished doctoral dissertation, University of Hawaii.

Harley, H. E., Roitblat, H. L., and Nachtigall, P. E. (1996). Object representation in the bottlenosed dolphin (*Tursiops truncatus*): Integration of visual and echoic information. *Journal of Experimental Psychology, 22*, 164–174.

Hauser, M. D. (1997). *The evolution of communication*. Cambridge, MA: MIT Press.

Heltne, P. G., and Marquardt, L. A. (Eds.). (1989). *Understanding chimpanzees*. Cambridge, MA: Harvard University Press.

Herder, J. (1768). *Fragmente über die neuere deutsche Literatur. Abänderungen und Zusätze der zweiten Ausgabe der Fragmente. Erste Sammlung.* Gustav Hempel, Berlin: Author. (Original work published by Herders Werke.)

Herman, L. M., Kuczaj, S. A., II, and Holder, M. D. (1993). Responses to anomalous gestural sequences by a language-trained dolphin: Evidence for processing of semantic relations and syntactic information. *Journal of Experimental Psychology, 122,* 184–194.

Herman, L. M., Pack, A. A., and Hoffmann-Kuhnt, M. (1998). Seeing through sound: Dolphins (*Tursiops truncatus*) perceive the spatial structure of objects through echolocation. *Journal of Comparative Psychology, 112,* 292–305.

Herman, L. M., Pack, A. A., and Wood, A. M. (1994). Bottlenose dolphins can generalize rules and develop abstract concepts. *Marine Mammal Science, 10,* 70–80.

Herman, L. M., Richards, D. G., and Wolz, J. P. (1984). Comprehension of sentences by bottlenosed dolphins. *Science, 16,* 129–219.

Herman, L. M., and Thompson, R. K. (1982). Symbolic identity and probed delayed matching of sounds in the bottlenosed dolphin. *Animal Learning and Behavior, 10,* 22–34.

Herrnstein, R. J., and Loveland, D. H. (1964). Complex visual concept in the pigeon. *Science, 146,* 549–551.

Herrnstein, R. J., Loveland, D. H., and Cable, C. (1976). Natural concepts in pigeons. *Journal of Experimental Psychology: Animal Behavior Processes, 2,* 285–301.

Holyoak, K. J., and Thagard, P. (1997). The analogical mind. *American Psychologist, 52,* 35–44.

Horne, P. J., and Lowe, C. F. (1996). On the origins of naming and other symbolic behavior. *Journal of the Experimental Analysis of Behavior, 65,* 185–241.

Humboldt, W. (1907). *Gesammelte Schriften.* Berlin: Author.

Hunt, E., and Agnoli, F. (1991). The Whorfian hypothesis: A cognitive psychology perspective. *Psychological Review, 98,* 377–389.

Hurley, T. A., and Healy, S. D. (1996). Memory for flowers in rufous hummingbirds: Location or visual clues? *Animal Behaviour, 51,* 1149–1157.

Jackendoff, R. (1992). *Languages of the mind: Essays on mental representation.* Cambridge, MA: MIT Press.

Janik, V. M. (2000). Whistle matching in wild bottlenosed dolphins (*Tursiops truncatus*). *Science, 289,* 1355–1357.

Kako, E. (1999). Elements of syntax in the systems of three language-trained animals. *Animal Learning and Behavior, 27,* 1–14.

Kohler, W. (1925). *The mentality of apes.* London: Routledge and Kegan Paul.

Kuczaj, S. A., II. (1999). The world of words: Thoughts on the development of a lexicon. In M. Barrett (Ed.), *The development of language: Studies in developmental psychology* (pp. 133–160). East Sussex, UK: Psychology Press.

Kuczaj, S. A., II. (2001). Cetacean culture: Slippery when wet. *Behavioral and Brain Sciences, 24,* 340–341.

Kuczaj, S. A., II, Borys, R. H., and Jones, M. (1989). On the interaction of language and thought: Some thoughts and developmental data. In A. Gellatly, D. Rogers, and J. Slaboda (Eds.), *Cognition and social worlds* (pp. 168–189). Oxford: Oxford University Press.

Kuczaj, S. A., II, and Daly, M. (1979). The development of hypothetical reference in the speech of young children. *Journal of Child Language, 6,* 563–580.

Kuczaj, S. A., II, and Donaldson, S., II. (1982). If the boy loves the girl and the girl loves the dog, does the boy love the dog? The overgeneralization of verbal transitive inference skills. *Journal of Psycholinguistic Research, 11,* 197–206.

Kuczaj, S. A., II, Gory, J. D., and Xitco, M. J., Jr. (1998). Using programs to solve problems: Imitation versus insight. *Behavioral and Brain Sciences, 21,* 695–696.

Kuczaj, S. A., II, and Kirkpatrick, V. M. (1993). Similarities and differences in human and animal language research: Toward a comparative psychology of language. In H. L. Roitblat, L. M. Herman, and P. E. Nachtigall (Eds.), *Language and communication: Comparative perspectives* (pp. 45–63). Hillsdale, NJ: Erlbaum.

Kuczaj, S. A., II, Tranel, K., Trone, M. and Hill, H. M. (2001). Are animals capable of deception or empathy? Implications for animal consciousness and animal welfare. *Animal Welfare, 10,* 161–174.

Langer, J. (2000). The descent of cognitive development. *Developmental Science, 3,* 361–378.

Langley, C. M., and Riley, D. A. (1993). Limited capacity information processing and pigeon matching-to-sample: Testing alternative hypotheses. *Animal Learning and Behavior, 21,* 226–232.

Lawson, R. W., and Lanning, D. V. (1980). Nesting and status of the Maroon-fronted parrot (*Rhynchopsitta terrisi*). In R. F. Pasquier (Ed.), *Conservation of new world parrots* (pp. 385–392). ICBP Technical Publication No. 1.

Limongelli, L., Boysen, S. T., and Visalberghi, E. (1995). Comprehension of cause-effect relations in a tool-using task by chimpanzees (*Pan troglodytes*). *Journal of Comparative Psychology, 109,* 47–51.

Lopez, J. C., Rodriguez, F., Gomez, Y., Vargas, J. P., Broglio, C., and Salas, C. (2000). Place and cue learning in turtles. *Animal Learning and Behavior, 28,* 360–372.

Luria, A. R. (1976). *Cognitive development: Its cultural and social foundations.* Cambridge: Cambridge University Press.

Lyell, C. (1863). *The geological evidences of the antiquity of man.* London: Murray.

Macedonia, J. M. (1990). What is communicated in the antipredator calls of lemurs: Evidence from playback experiments with ring-tailed and ruffed lemurs. *Ethology, 86,* 177–190.

Macphail, E. M. (1996). Cognitive function in mammals: The evolutionary perspective. *Cognitive Brain Research, 3,* 279–290.

Macuda, T., and Roberts, W. A. (1995). Further evidence for hierarchical chunking in rat spatial memory. *Journal of Experimental Psychology: Animal Behavior Processes, 21,* 20–32.

Mandler, J. M. (1998). Representation. In D. Kuhn, R. S. Siegler (Vol. Eds.), and W. Damon (Ed.), *Handbook of child psychology: Cognition, perception, and language* (5th ed., Vol. 2, pp. 255–308). New York: Wiley.

McGonigle, B. O., and Chalmers, M. (1977). Are monkeys logical? *Nature, 267,* 694–696.

Menzel, C. (1996). Structure-guided foraging in long-tail macaques. *American Journal of Primatology, 38,* 117–132.

Mercado, E., III, Killebrew, D. A., Pack, A. A., Macha, I. V. B., and Herman, L. M. (2000). Generalization of "same-different" classification abilities in bottle-nosed dolphins. *Behavioural Processes, 50,* 79–94.

Miles, H. L. (1986). How can I tell a lie? Apes, language and the problem of deception. In R. W. Mitchell and N. S. Thompson (Eds.), *Deception: Perspectives on human and nonhuman deceit* (pp. 245–266). Albany: State University of New York Press.

Miles, H. L., Mitchell, R. W., and Harper, S. (1996). Simon says: The development of imitation in an enculturated orangutan. In A. E. Russon, K. A. Bard, and S. T. Parker (Eds.), *Reaching into thought: The minds of the great apes* (pp. 278–298). Cambridge: Cambridge University Press.

Miller, G. A. (1956). The magical number seven, plus or minus two: Some limits on our capacity for processing information. *Psychological Review, 63,* 81–97.

Mitchell, R. W. (1999). Strategic script violation in great apes and humans. In S. T. Parker, R. W. Mitchell, and H. L. Miles (Eds.), *The mentalities of gorillas and orangutans* (pp. 295–315). Cambridge: Cambridge University Press.

Morris, R. G. (1981). Spatial localization does not require the presence of local cue. *Learning and Motivation, 12,* 239–260.

Muller F. M. (1864). *Lectures on the science of language delivered at the Royal Institution of Great Britain in February, March, April, and May, 1863.* London: Longman, Green, Longman, Roberts, and Green.

Muller, F. M. (1870). The science of language. *Nature, I,* 256–259.

Nagell, K., Olguin, K., and Tomasello, M. (1993). Processes of social learning in the tool use of chimpanzees and human children. *Journal of Comparative Psychology, 107,* 174–185.

Oden, D. L., Thompson, R. K., and Premack, D. (1988). Spontaneous transfer of matching by infant chimpanzees (*Pan troglodytes*). *Journal of Experimental Psychology: Animal Behavioral Processes, 14,* 140–145.

Oden, D. L., Thompson, R. K. R., and Premack, D. (2001). Can an ape reason analogically? Comprehension and production of analogical problems by Sarah, a chimpanzee (*Pan troglodytes*). In D. Gentner, K. J. Holyoak, and B. N. Kokinov (Eds.), *The analogical mind: Perspectives from cognitive science* (pp. 471–498). Cambridge, MA: MIT Press.

Pack, A. A., and Herman, L. M. (1995). Sensory integration in the bottlenosed dolphin: Immediate recognition of complex shapes across the senses of echolocation and vision. *Journal of the Acoustical Society of America, 98,* 722–733.

Pearce, J. M. (1997). *Animal learning and cognition.* East Sussex, UK: Psychology Press.

Pepperberg, I. M. (1993). Cognition and communication in an African gray parrot (*Psittacus erithacus*): Studies on a nonhuman, nonprimate, nonmammalian subject. In H. L. Roitblat, L. M. Herman, and P. E. Nachtigall (Eds.), *Language and communication: Comparative perspectives* (pp. 221–248). Hillsdale, NJ: Erlbaum.

Pepperberg, I. M. (1998). The African gray parrot: How cognitive processing might affect allospecific vocal learning. In R. P. Balda, I. M. Pepperberg, and A. C. Kamil (Eds.), *Animal cognition in nature: The convergence of psychology and biology in laboratory and field* (pp. 381–409). San Diego, CA: Academic Press.

Pepperberg, I. M., and Brezinsky, M. V. (1991). Acquisition of a relative class concept by an African gray parrot (*Psittacus erithacus*): Discriminations based on relative size. *Journal of Comparative Psychology, 105,* 286–294.

Piaget, J. (1968). *Six psychological studies.* New York: Vintage Books.

Piaget, J., and Inhelder, B. (1969). *The psychology of the child.* New York: Basic Books.

Pinker, S. (1995). Facts about human language relevant to its evolution. In J. P. Changeux and J. Chavaillon (Eds.), *Origins of the human brain* (pp. 262–285). Oxford: Clarendon Press.

Povinelli, D. J. (2000). *Folk physics for apes.* Oxford: Oxford University Press.

Premack, D. (1971). On the assessment of language competence in the chimpanzee. In A. M. Schrier and F. Stollnitz (Eds.), *Behavior of nonhuman primates* (Vol. 4, pp. 185–228). New York: Academic Press.

Premack, D. (1983). Animal cognition. *Annual Review of Psychology, 34,* 351–362.

Premack, D., and Woodruff, G. (1978). Does the chimpanzee have a theory of mind? *Behavioral and Brain Sciences, 4,* 515–526.

Rattermann, M. J., and Gentner, D. (1998). The effect of language on similarity: The use of relational labels improves young children's performance in a mapping task. In K. Holyoak, D. Gentner, and B. Kokinov (Eds.), *Advances in analogy research: Integration of theory and data from the cognitive, computational, and neural sciences* (pp. 274–282). Sofia: New Bulgarian University.

Rendell, L., and Whitehead, H. (2001). Culture in whales and dolphins. *Behavioral and Brain Sciences, 24,* 309–323.

Roberts, W. A. (1998). *Principles of animal cognition.* New York: McGraw Hill.

Rumbaugh, D. M. (1977). *Language learning by a chimpanzee: The LANA project.* New York: Academic Press.

Rumbaugh, D. M. (1997). Competence, cortex, and primate models: A comparative primate perspective. In N. A. Krasnegor, G. R. Lyon, and P. S. Goldman-Rakic (Eds.), *Development of the prefrontal cortex: Evolution, neurobiology, and behavior* (pp. 117–139). Baltimore: Brookes.

Rumbaugh, D. M., Savage-Rumbaugh, E. S., and Hegel, M. T. (1987). Summation in the chimpanzee *(Pan troglodytes). Journal of Experimental Psychology: Animal Behavior Processes, 13,* 107–115.

Rumbaugh, D. M., Savage-Rumbaugh, E. S., and Washburn, D. A. (1996). Toward a new outlook on primate learning and behavior: Complex learning and emergent processes in comparative perspective. *Japanese Psychological Research, 38(3),* 113–125.

Russon, A. E. (1999). Naturalistic approaches to orangutan intelligence and the question of enculturation. *International Journal of Comparative Psychology, 12(4),* 181–202.

Sakura, O., and Matsuzawa, T. (1991). Flexibility of wild chimpanzee nut-cracking behavior using stone hammers and anvils: An experimental analysis. *Ethology, 87,* 237–248.

Sapir, E. (1931). Conceptual categories in primitive languages. *Science, 74,* 578.

Saunders, D. A. (1983). Vocal repertoire and individual vocal recognition in the short-billed white-tailed Black cockatoo, *Calyptorhynchus fenereus latirostris. Australian Wildlife Research, 10,* 527–536.

Savage-Rumbaugh, E. S. (1986). *Ape language: From conditioned response to symbol.* New York: Columbia University Press.

Savage-Rumbaugh, E. S., and Lewin, R. (1994). *Kanzi: The ape at the brink of the human mind.* New York: Wiley.

Savage-Rumbaugh, E. S., Rumbaugh, D. M., and Boysen, S. T. (1978). Sarah's problems in comprehension. *Behavioral and Brain Sciences, 1,* 555–557.

Savage-Rumbaugh, E. S., Rumbaugh, D. M., Smith, S. T., and Lawson, J. (1980). Reference: The linguistic essential. *Science, 210,* 922–924.

Savage-Rumbaugh, E. S., Sevcik, R. A., and Hopkins, W. D. (1988). Symbolic cross-modal transfer in two species of chimpanzees. *Child Development, 59,* 617–625.

Schusterman, R. J., Reichmuth, C. J., and Kastak, D. (2000). How animals classify friends and foes. *Current Directions in Psychological Science*, 9, 1–6.

Seyfarth, R. M., and Cheney, D. L. (1997). Behavioral mechanisms underlying vocal communication in nonhuman primates. *Animal Learning and Behavior*, 25, 249–267.

Shanker, S. G., Savage-Rumbaugh, E. S., and Taylor, T. J. (1999). Kanzi: A new beginning. *Animal Learning and Behavior*, 27, 24–25.

Sherman, P. W. (1977). Nepotism and the evolution of alarm calls. *Science*, 197, 1246–1253.

Shyan, M. R. (1985). Methodological note: Analyzing signs for recognition and feature salience. *Sign Language Studies*, 46, 87–92.

Shyan, M. R., and Herman, L. M. (1987). Determinants of recognition of gestural signs in an artificial language by Atlantic bottle-nosed dolphins (*Tursiops truncatus*) and humans (*Homo sapiens*). *Journal of Comparative Psychology*, 101, 112–125.

Shyan, M. R., and Wright, A. A. (1993). The effects of language on information processing and abstract concept learning in dolphins, monkeys, and humans. In H. L. Roitblat, L. M. Herman, and P. E. Nachtigall (Eds.), *Language and communication: Comparative perspectives* (pp. 385–401). Hillsdale, NJ: Erlbaum.

Simons, D. J. (1996). In sight, out of mind: When object representations fail. *Psychological Science*, 7, 301–305.

Smith, W. J. (1998). Cognitive implications of an information-sharing model of animal communication. In R. P. Balda, I. M. Pepperberg, and A. C. Kamil (Eds.), *Animal cognition in nature: The convergence of psychology and biology in laboratory and field* (pp. 227–244). San Diego, CA: Academic Press.

Steirn, J. N., Weaver, J. E., and Zentall, T. R. (1995). Transitive inference in pigeons: Simplified procedures and a test of value transfer theory. *Animal Learning and Behavior*, 23, 76–82.

Stromer, R., and MacKay, H. (1996). Naming and the formation of stimulus classes. In T. R. Zentall and P. M. Smeets (Eds.), *Stimulus class formation in humans and animals* (pp. 221–252). Amsterdam: Elsevier.

Terrace, H. S. (1991). Chunking during serial learning by a pigeon: I. Basic evidence. *Journal of Experimental Psychology: Animal Behavior Processes*, 17, 81–93.

Thomas, R. K., Fowlkes, D., and Vickery, J. D. (1980). Conceptual numerousness judgments by squirrel monkeys. *American Journal of Psychology*, 93, 247–257.

Thompson, R. K., and Oden, D. L. (1993). "Language training" and its role in the expression of tacit propositional knowledge in chimpanzees (*Pan troglodytes*). In H. L. Roitblat, L. M. Herman, and P. E. Nachtigall (Eds.), *Language and communication: Comparative perspectives* (pp. 365–384). Hillsdale, NJ: Erlbaum.

Thompson, R. K., and Oden, D. L. (2000). Categorical perception and conceptual judgments by nonhuman primates: The paleological monkey and the analogical ape. *Cognitive Science, 24*, 363–396.

Thompson, R. K., Oden, D. L., and Boysen, S. T. (1997). Language-naive chimpanzees (*Pan troglodytes*) judge relations between relations in an abstract matching task. *Journal of Experimental Psychology: Animal Behavior Processes, 23*, 31–43.

Tinklepaugh, O. L. (1932). Multiple delayed reaction with chimpanzees and monkeys. *Journal of Comparative Psychology, 8*, 197–236.

Todt, D., and Hultsch, H. (1998). Hierarchical learning, development and representation. In R. P. Balda, I. M. Pepperberg, and A. C. Kamil (Eds.), *Animal cognition in nature: The convergence of psychology and biology in laboratory and field* (pp. 275–304). San Diego, CA: Academic Press.

Tolman, E. C., Ritchie, B. F., and Kalish, D. (1946). Studies in spatial learning: I. Orientation and the short-cut. *Journal of Experimental Psychology, 36*, 12–24.

Tomasello, M. (1996a). Chimpanzee social cognition. Commentary for *Monographs of the Society for Research in Child Development, 61*(3).

Tomasello, M. (1996b). Do apes ape? In B. G. Galef, Jr., and C. M. Heyes (Eds.), *Social learning in animals: The roots of culture* (pp. 319–346). New York: Academic Press.

Tomasello, M. (1998). Uniquely primate, uniquely human. *Developmental Science, 1*, 1–30.

Tomasello, M., and Call, J. (1997). *Primate cognition.* New York: Oxford University Press.

Tomasello, M., Call, J., Warren, J., Frost, T., Carpenter, M., and Nagel, K. (1997). The ontogeny of chimpanzee gestural signals: A comparison across groups and generations. *Evolution of Communication, 1*, 1–19.

Tomasello, M., Savage-Rumbaugh, E. S., and Kruger, A. C. (1993). Imitative learning of actions on objects by children, chimpanzees, and enculturated chimpanzees. *Child Development, 64*, 1688–1705.

Tyack, P. L. (1993). Animal language research needs a broader comparative and evolutionary framework. In H. L. Roitblat, L. M. Herman, and P. E. Nachtigall (Eds.), *Language and communication: Comparative perspectives* (pp. 115–152). Hillsdale, NJ: Erlbaum.

Visalberghi, E., and Limongelli, L. (1994). Lack of comprehension of cause-effect relationships in tool-using capuchin monkeys (*Cebus apella*). *Journal of Comparative Psychology, 108*, 15–22.

von Ferson, L., Wynne, C. L., Delius, J. D., and Staddon, J. R. (1991). Transitive inference in pigeons. *Journal of Experimental Psychology: Animal Behavior Processes, 17*, 334–341.

von Frisch, K. (1946). Dialects in the language of the bees. *Scientific American, 207*, 78–87.

Vosniadou, S., and Ortony, A. (Eds.). (1989). *Similarity and analogical reasoning*. Cambridge: Cambridge University Press.

Vygotsky, L. S. (1962). *Thought and language*. Cambridge, MA: MIT Press. (Original work published 1934.)

Washburn, D. A., Thompson, R. K. R., and Oden, D. L. (1997). *Monkeys trained with same/different symbols do not match relations*. Paper presented at the meeting of the Psychonomic Society, Philadelphia, PA.

Weiss, M. (1987). Nucleic acid evidence bearing on hominoid relationships. *Yearbook of the American Journal of Physical Anthropology, 30*, 41–74.

Whiten, A., Goodall, J., McGrew, W. C., Nishida, T., Reynolds, V., Sugiyama, Y., Tutin, C. E. G., Wrangham, R. W., and Boesch, C. (1999). Cultures and chimpanzees. *Nature, 399*, 682–685.

Whorf, B. L. (1956). *Language, thought, and reality* (J. B. Carroll, Ed.). Cambridge, MA: MIT Press.

Xitco, M. J., Jr., Gory, J. D., and Kuczaj, S. A., II. (2001). Spontaneous pointing in bottlenose dolphins. *Animal Cognition, 4*, 115–123.

Yamashita, C. (1987). Field observations and comments on the Indigo macaw (*Anodorhynchus leari*), a highly endangered species from northeastern Brazil. *Wilson Bulletin, 99*, 280–282.

Zuberbühler, K., Cheney, D. L., and Seyfarth, R. M. (1999). Conceptual semantics in a nonhuman primate. *Journal of Comparative Psychology, 113*, 33–42.

# 10

# What Makes Us Smart? Core Knowledge and Natural Language

Elizabeth S. Spelke

## 10.1 Introduction

*the 98% DNA !* [handwritten annotation]

When we compare the sensory and motor capacities of humans to those of other primates, we discover extensive similarities. Human visual and auditory capacities closely resemble those of rhesus monkeys, for example, as do the neural mechanisms that subserve these capacities (e.g., Felleman and van Essen 1991). Human locomotion and other actions also depend on systems shared by many animals (e.g., Thelen 1984). These similarities strongly suggest that the psychology of humans is continuous with that of nonhuman animals and depends on a common set of mechanisms.

When we compare the cognitive achievements of humans to those of nonhuman primates, however, we see striking differences (table 10.1). All animals have to find and recognize food, for example, but only humans develop the art and science of cooking. Many juvenile animals engage in play fighting, but only humans organize their competitive play into structured games with elaborate rules. All animals need to understand something about the behavior of the material world in order to avoid falling off cliffs or stumbling into obstacles, but only humans systematize their knowledge as science and extend it to encompass the behavior of entities that are too far away or too small to perceive or act upon. As a final example, all social animals need to organize their societies, but only humans create systems of laws and political institutions to interpret and enforce them.

What is it about human cognition that makes us capable of these feats? In this chapter, I consider two possible answers to this question.

**Table 10.1**
Some unique feats of human cognition

| Cooking | Theater | Science |
|---------|---------|---------|
| Music | Architecture | Politics |
| Sports | Tool manufacture | Law |
| Games | Mathematics | Religion |

The first answer guided my research for 20 years, but I now believe that it is wrong. The second answer is just beginning to emerge from research conducted over the last decade, and I think it has a chance of being right. Both answers center on the concept of core knowledge, which I can best introduce by turning to the first answer.

## 10.2   What Makes Us Smart? Uniquely Human, Core Knowledge Systems

According to the first answer, the cognitive capacities of any animal depend on early-developing, domain-specific systems of knowledge. Just as infant animals have specialized perceptual systems for detecting particular kinds of sensory information and specialized motor systems guiding particular kinds of actions, infant animals have specialized, task-specific cognitive systems: systems for representing material objects, navigating through the spatial layout, recognizing and interacting with other animals, and the like. These specialized systems provide the core of all mature cognitive abilities, and so whatever is unique to human cognition depends on unique features of our early-developing, core knowledge systems. At the root of our capacities to construct and learn physics, for example, may be a distinctive core system for representing material objects and their motions; at the root of human mathematics may be uniquely human core systems for representing space and number; and at the root of human politics, law, and games may be distinctive systems for representing people and their social arrangements.

This thesis supports a particular research agenda: to understand what is special about human cognition, we should study core knowledge systems as they emerge in infants and young children. Such studies have been conducted over the last 30 years, and they indeed suggest that human infants are equipped with core knowledge systems. Nevertheless, the systems found in young infants do not appear to distinguish us from many nonhuman animals.

### 10.2.1 Object Mechanics

Consider, for example, the core system for representing material objects. Research over the last two decades provides evidence that infants have a system for perceiving objects and their motions, for filling in the surfaces and boundaries of an object that is partly hidden, and for representing the continued existence of an object that moves fully out of view. Evidence for these abilities comes from studies using both reaching methods and preferential looking methods (see Spelke 1998, for review). An experiment by Wynn (1992a) serves as an example of the latter.

Wynn (1992a; figure 10.1) presented 5-month-old infants with a puppet stage on which she placed a single puppet. Then a screen was introduced, concealing the puppet, and a second puppet appeared from the side of the display and disappeared behind the screen. Finally, the screen was lowered to reveal one or two puppets on the stage, and infants' looking time at these displays was measured and compared. If infants failed to represent the existence and the distinctness of the two puppets behind the screen, then the outcome display presenting one puppet should have looked more familiar to them, because they had only ever seen a single puppet on the stage at a time. Because infants tend to look longer at displays that are more novel, infants therefore should have looked longer at the display of two puppets. In contrast, if infants represented the continued existence of the first puppet behind the screen, the distinct identity of the second puppet when it was introduced from the side, and the continued existence of the second puppet behind the screen, then the outcome display presenting only a single puppet should have looked more novel to them, because it suggested that one of the puppets had mysteriously disappeared. Infants indeed looked longer at the one-puppet outcome, providing evidence that they perceived and represented two puppets in this event.

Wynn's experiment has enjoyed many replications and extensions (see Wynn 1998, for review). Notably, it has been replicated in studies that control for infants' representations of the features and spatial locations

**Figure 10.1**
Schematic depiction of displays for a study of infants' representations of persisting, numerically distinct objects using a preferential looking method. (After Wynn 1992a.)

Reaching task

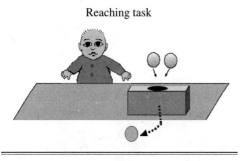

Locomotor choice task

**Figure 10.2**
Schematic depiction of displays for studies of object representation using reaching and locomotor choice methods. (After Feigenson, Carey, and Hauser 2002; Van de Walle, Carey, and Prevor 2001.)

of the objects (respectively, Simon, Hespos, and Rochat 1995; Koechlin, Dehaene, and Mehler 1998): infants look longer at arrays presenting the wrong number of objects, even when the shapes, colors, and spatial locations of the objects in both displays are new. Wynn's findings also have been replicated with older infants in experiments using two different methods, each focusing on a different response system: manual search in a single, opaque box containing one or two objects, and locomotor choice between two such boxes (Feigenson, Carey, and Hauser 2002; Van de Walle, Carey, and Prevor 2001; figure 10.2). In studies using the latter method, for example, infants who have just begun to locomote independently are shown two cookies placed in succession into one opaque box and one cookie placed into a second box, and then they are allowed to crawl toward one or the other box. Infants were found

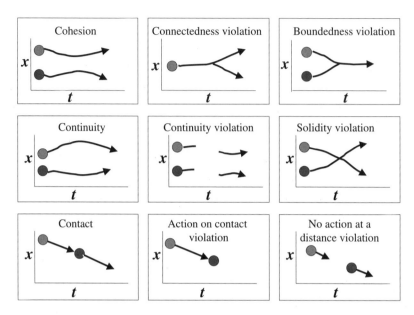

**Figure 10.3**
Principles of object representation in human infancy. (After Spelke 1990.)

to crawl preferentially to the box with the greater number of cookies (Feigenson, Carey, and Hauser 2002). These converging findings from three paradigms suggest that infants have robust abilities to represent the persistence and the distinctness of hidden objects.

Summarizing these and other studies, I have proposed that human infants represent objects in accord with three spatiotemporal constraints on object motion (figure 10.3). Infants represent objects as cohesive bodies that maintain both their connectedness and their boundaries as they move, as continuous bodies that move only on connected, unobstructed paths, and as bodies that interact if and only if they come into contact. Despite some controversy in the field, I believe these conclusions are well supported (Spelke 1998). Nevertheless, there is no reason to think that the core system for representing objects, centering on the constraints of cohesion, continuity, and contact, is unique to humans. Representational abilities that equal or exceed those of human infants have been found in a variety of nonhuman animals, including both adult monkeys and newly hatched chicks.

*[handwritten margin note: the sub-atomic illusion]*

Hauser has presented Wynn's task to adult free-ranging rhesus monkeys, using all three methods used with infants: preferential looking, manual search, and locomotor choice (Hauser, Carey, and Hauser 2000; Hauser, MacNeilage, and Ware 1996). With all three methods, the performance of adult monkeys equaled or exceeded that of human infants. Humans evidently are not the only creatures to represent objects as spatiotemporally continuous bodies.

The monkeys in Hauser's experiments were adults, but capacities to represent objects have been found in infant animals as well. Indeed, they have been found in chicks who are only 1 day old. Investigators in two laboratories have used an imprinting method in order to present newly hatched chicks with some of the object representation tasks used with human infants (e.g., Lea, Slater, and Ryan 1996; Regolin, Vallortigara, and Zanforlin 1995). As is well known, chicks who spend their first day of life in isolation with a single moving inanimate object will tend to approach that object in preference to other objects in any stressful situation. In a variety of studies, this approach pattern has been used to assess chicks' representations of the hidden object. In one set of studies, for example, chicks who spent their first day of life with a center-occluded object were placed on their second day of life in an unfamiliar cage (a moderately stressful situation) with two versions of the object at opposite ends, in which the previously visible ends of the object either were connected or were separated by a visible gap. Chicks selectively approached the connected object, providing evidence that they, like human infants, had perceived the imprinted object to continue behind its occluder (Lea, Slater, and Ryan 1996; see also Regolin and Vallortigara 1995; figure 10.4). In further studies, chicks were presented with events in which the imprinted object became fully occluded. Even after an extended occlusion period, the chicks selectively searched for the occluded object, providing evidence that they represented its continued existence (Regolin and Vallortigara 1995).

These findings suggest that a wide range of vertebrates have early-developing capacities to represent objects. The core system for representing objects found in human infants does not appear to be unique to us and so cannot in itself account for later-developing, uniquely human abilities to reason about the physical world.

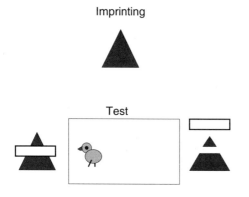

**Figure 10.4**
Schematic depiction of an experiment on object representation in 2-day-old chicks using an imprinting method. (After Regolin and Vallortigara 1995.)

### 10.2.2   Number Sense

Perhaps studies of object representations fail to reveal uniquely human capacities, because object representations are so close to perception and so fundamental to many animals. Our human capacities for science and technology, however, depend greatly on the development and use of mathematics. Moreover, formal mathematics is a uniquely human accomplishment. Perhaps a core system for representing number distinguishes human cognition from that of nonhuman animals and serves as the basis for the development of mathematics, technology, and science.

Research on normal human adults and on neurological patients provides evidence that representations of number and operations of arithmetic depend in part on "number sense": a sense of approximate numerical values and relationships (Dehaene 1997; Gallistel and Gelman 1992). The performance of this system is characterized by Weber's law: as numerosity increases, the variance in subjects' representations of numerosity increases proportionately, and therefore discriminability between distinct numerosities depends on their difference ratio. Does this number sense derive from a core cognitive system that is present in infants?

Recently, Fei Xu, Jennifer Lipton, and I have addressed this question through studies of 6-month-old infants' abilities to discriminate between large numerosities. In our first studies (Xu and Spelke 2000b), infants

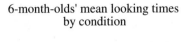

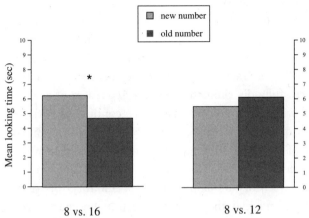

6-month-olds' mean looking times
by condition

**Figure 10.5**
Looking times to displays presenting a novel number of dots, in experiments testing for discrimination of 8 from 16 or 12 dots. * indicates a significant difference. (After Xu and Spelke 2000b.)

were presented with visual arrays of dots on a succession of trials. On different trials, the dots appeared in different sizes and at different positions, but there were always 8 dots in the array for half the infants and 16 dots for the others. To control for display brightness and size, the dots in the more numerous arrays were half the size, on average, of those in the less numerous array and appeared at twice the density. Dot arrays were presented until infants' spontaneous looking time to the arrays declined to half its initial level. Then infants were presented with new arrays of 8 and 16 dots in alternation, equated for density and dot size. If infants responded to any continuous properties of the dot arrays, they should have looked equally at the two test numerosities, because those variables were equated either across the familiarization series or across the test series. In contrast, if infants responded to numerosity and discriminated the arrays with 8 versus 16 elements, they were expected to look longer at the array with the novel numerosity. That looking preference was obtained, providing evidence for numerosity discrimination at 6 months of age (figure 10.5).

In subsequent studies using this method, infants failed to discriminate between arrays of 8 versus 12 dots (Xu and Spelke 2000b), providing evidence that their sense of number is imprecise. Moreover, infants successfully discriminated 16 from 32 dots and failed to discriminate 16 from 24 dots (Xu and Spelke 2000a), providing evidence that discriminability accords with Weber's law for infants, as it does for adults, and that the critical Weber fraction for infants lies between 1.5 and 2. Finally, infants successfully discriminated between sequences of 8 versus 16 tones, presented with the same controls for the continuous variables of the duration and quantity of sound, and they failed to discriminate between sequences of 8 versus 12 tones (Lipton and Spelke in press). These findings provide evidence that numerosity representations are not limited to a particular sensory modality (visual or auditory) or format (spatial vs. temporal), and that the same Weber fraction characterizes discriminability across very different types of arrays. The sense of number found in adults therefore appears to be present and functional in 6-month-old infants.

Does a core sense of number account for our uniquely human capacity to develop formal mathematics? If it did, then no comparable evidence for number sense should be found in any nonhuman animals. In fact, however, capacities to discriminate between numerosities have been found in nearly every animal tested, from fish to pigeons to rats to primates (see Dehaene 1997 and Gallistel 1990 for reviews, and figure 10.6 for evidence from a representative experiment). Like human infants, animals are able to discriminate between different numerosities even when all potentially confounding continuous variables are controlled, they discriminate between numerosities for both spatial arrays and temporal sequences in a variety of sensory modalities, and their discrimination depends on the ratio difference between the numerosities in accord with Weber's law. Humans' early-developing number sense therefore fails to account, in itself, for our uniquely human talents for mathematics, measurement, and science.

### 10.2.3   Natural Geometry

Before abandoning my first account of what makes humans smart, I will consider one last version of this account, inspired by Descartes (1647).

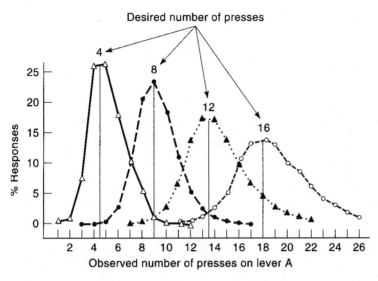

**Figure 10.6**
In this experiment, rats obtain food by pressing one lever (A) a predetermined number of times and then pressing a second lever. The number of presses on A matches approximately the required number, and responses become increasingly variable as the numbers get larger. (After Mechner 1958.)

Descartes famously proposed that humans are the only animals who are endowed with reason and that human reason is the source of all our distinctive cognitive achievements. Many of Descartes's examples of the use of reason come from the domain of geometry. Descartes invited us to consider the case of a blind man who holds two sticks that cross at a distance from himself (figure 10.7, top). Because the man is blind, he lacks any distal sense for apprehending the distance of the sticks' crossing point (c). Nevertheless, Descartes suggested, the man can use "natural geometry" to infer the location of this crossing point from knowledge of the distance and angular relation between his two hands at the points at which they grasp the sticks (a and b). Systematic use of Euclidean geometric principles not only allows the blind man to perceive objects at a distance, it also allows the development of the sciences of astronomy, optics, and physics (Descartes 1647). Perhaps, then, natural geometry is the core knowledge system that accounts for our uniquely human cognitive capacities.

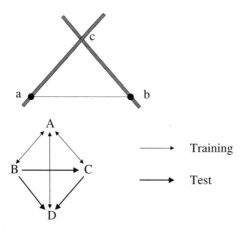

**Figure 10.7**
*Top*: schematic representation of the blind man's problem. (After Descartes 1647.) *Bottom*: schematic depiction of a task presented to blind and to blindfolded young children. (After Landau, Spelke, and Gleitman 1984.)

Almost 20 years ago, Barbara Landau, Henry Gleitman, and I attempted to test Descartes's conjecture by presenting a version of his triangulation problem to young blind and blindfolded children (Landau, Spelke, and Gleitman 1984; figure 10.7, bottom). Children were introduced into a room containing objects at four stable locations, and they were walked between the objects on specific paths. For example, a child might be walked from her mother seated in a chair (location A) to a table (location B), a box of toys (location C), and a mat (location D). Then the child was asked to move independently from one object to another on a path she had not previously taken (e.g., she might be asked to take a toy from the box and put it on the table, traversing the novel path from C to B). Note that the same principles of Euclidean geometry that allow solution of the blind man's stick problem should, in principle, allow solution of this triangle problem. Both blind and blindfolded children solved the problem reliably, providing evidence for Descartes's thesis that humans are endowed with natural geometry.

Does this endowment account for uniquely human reasoning abilities? Once again, studies of navigation in other animals are pertinent to this claim, and they provide resounding evidence against it. An exceedingly wide range of animals have been observed and tested in navigation tasks like the one Landau, Spelke, and Gleitman (1984) presented to young children. In every case, the performance of nonhuman animals has equaled or exceeded the performance of young children.

The most dramatic evidence for natural geometry in a nonhuman animal comes from studies of navigating desert ants (Wehner and Srinivasan 1981; figure 10.8). These ants leave their nest in the nearly featureless Tunisian desert in search of animals that may have died and can serve as food, wending a long and tortuous path from the nest until food is unpredictably encountered. At that point, the ants make a straight-line path for home: a path that differs from their outgoing journey and that is guided by no beacons or landmarks. If the ant is displaced to novel territory so that all potential landmarks are removed, its path continues to be highly accurate: within 2 degrees of the correct direction and 10 percent of the correct distance. This path is determined solely by the geometric relationships between the nest location and the distance and direction traveled during each step of the outgoing journey. Ants therefore have a "natural geometry" that appears to be at least equal to, if not superior to, that of humans.

To summarize, humans indeed have early-developing core knowledge systems, and these systems permit a range of highly intelligent behaviors and cognitive capacities including the capacity to represent hidden objects, to estimate numerosities, and to navigate through the spatial layout. In each case, however, nonhuman animals have been found to have capacities that equal or exceed those of human infants. The core knowledge systems that have been studied in human infants so far therefore do not account for uniquely human cognitive achievements. It remains possible, of course, that other core knowledge systems *are* unique to humans and account for unique aspects of our intelligence. In the absence of plausible candidate systems, however, I will turn instead to a different account of uniquely human cognitive capacities.

## 10.3   What Makes Us Smart? Uniquely Human Combinatorial Capacities

The suggestion I now explore begins with the thesis that humans and other animals are endowed with early-developing, core systems of knowl-

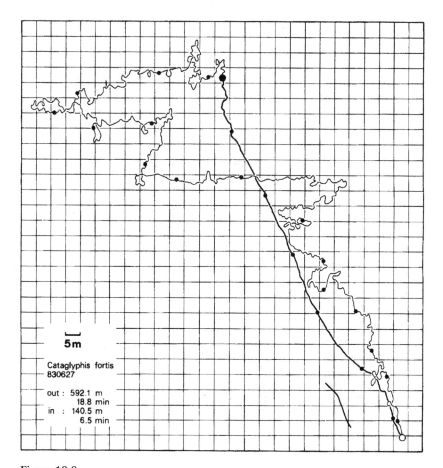

**Figure 10.8**
Path taken by a desert ant during its outward (thin line) and homeward (thick line) journey in familiar territory. (After Wehner and Srinivasan 1981.) Very similar behavior was observed after a displacement that removed all local spatial cues.

edge but that these systems are limited in four respects. First, the systems are *domain specific*: each serves to represent only a subset of the entities in the child's surroundings. Second, the systems are *task specific*: the representations constructed by each system guide only a subset of the actions and cognitive processes in the child's repertoire. Third, the systems are relatively *encapsulated*: the internal workings of each system are largely impervious to other representations and cognitive processes. Fourth, the representations delivered by these systems are relatively *isolated* from one another: representations that are constructed by distinct systems do not readily combine together.

The core knowledge systems found in human infants exist throughout human life, and they serve to construct domain-specific, task-specific, encapsulated, and isolated representations for adults as they do for infants. With development, however, there emerges a new capacity to combine together distinct, core representations. This capacity depends on a system that has none of the limits of the core knowledge systems: it is neither domain nor task specific, for it allows representations to be combined across any conceptual domains that humans can represent and to be used for any tasks that we can understand and undertake. Its representations are neither encapsulated nor isolated, for they are available to any explicit cognitive process. This system is a specific acquired natural language, and the cognitive endowment that gives rise to it is indeed unique to humans: the human language faculty. Natural languages provide humans with a unique system for combining flexibly the representations they share with other animals. The resulting combinations are unique to humans and account for unique aspects of human intelligence.

To illustrate this suggestion, I will briefly describe the two lines of research that led to its emergence. First, I present a series of studies on children's developing navigation and spatial memory, conducted in collaboration with Linda Hermer-Vazquez, Ranxiao Frances Wang, and Stephane Gouteux. Then, I discuss a larger body of research on children's developing concepts of number undertaken by Susan Carey and myself, with numerous collaborators and students.

### 10.3.1 Space
Although animals are endowed with rich and exquisitely precise mechanisms for representing and navigating through the spatial layout, the

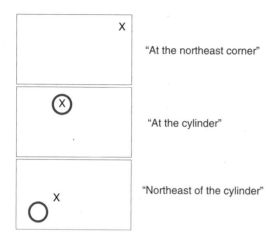

**Figure 10.9**
Schematic and simplified depiction of three tasks presented to rats. (After Biegler and Morris 1993, 1996.)

navigation of nonhuman animals sometimes shows interesting limits. In experiments by Biegler and Morris (1993, 1996; figure 10.9), for example, rats learned quite readily to locate food by searching in a particular geocentric position (e.g., the northeastern corner of the test chamber) or by searching near a particular landmark (e.g., in the vicinity of a white cylinder), but they had more difficulty learning to search in a particular geocentric relationship to a particular landmark (e.g., northeast of the white cylinder). Although rats evidently could represent that food was located "northeast of the room" or "at the cylinder," they could not readily combine these representations so as to represent that food was located "northeast of the cylinder."

A similar limit has appeared in experiments by Cheng and Gallistel (Cheng 1986; Gallistel 1990; Margules and Gallistel 1988). In their studies, rats were shown the location of food, then were disoriented, and finally were allowed to reorient themselves and search for the food. Rats readily reoriented themselves in accord with the shape of the room, but not in accord with the brightness of its walls, even though experiments dating back to Lashley show that rats can learn to respond selectively to white versus black walls directly. Although the rats' reorientation system evidently represented that food was located "at a corner with a *long* wall

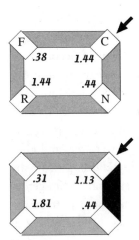

**Figure 10.10**
Tasks and performance of young children tested in a version of Cheng's (1986) reorientation task in which a toy was hidden and searching was measured at the correct location (C), the geometrically equivalent location (R), and the near and far, geometrically distinct locations (N and F). (After Hermer and Spelke 1984.)

on the left," it did not readily represent that food was located "at a corner with a *white* wall on the left." Like Biegler and Morris's studies, these studies suggest a limit to the combinatorial capacities of rats in navigation tasks.

Hermer-Vazquez and I sought to determine whether the same limit exists in children; to our surprise, we found that it did. In our studies, 1.5 to 2-year-old children were tested in a situation similar to Cheng's, in which they saw an object hidden in a corner of a rectangular room, they were disoriented, and then they searched for the object (Hermer and Spelke 1994, 1996; figure 10.10). Like Cheng's rats, children reoriented themselves in relation to the shape of the room but not in relation to the coloring of its walls. In subsequent experiments, children failed to reorient in accord with wall coloring even when it was made highly familiar (through experience over several sessions), when it was highly stable, when it was a successful direct cue for children in a task not involving reorientation, and when the distinctive wall coloring was presented in a cylindrical room with no geometrically distinctive shape (Gouteux and Spelke 2001; Wang, Hermer-Vazquez, and Spelke 1999).

Research in other laboratories confirms that children are highly predisposed to reorient in accord with the shape of their surroundings, and that under many circumstances children fail to reorient in accord with nongeometric information (Learmonth, Nadel, and Newcombe, in press; Learmonth, Newcombe, and Huttenlocher, in press; Stedron, Munakata, and O'Reilly 2000). Both rats and children do show sensitivity to nongeometric information in some circumstances, however (e.g., Cheng and Spetch 1998; Dudchenko et al. 1997; Learmonth, Newcombe, and Huttenlocher, in press; Stedron, Munakata, and O'Reilly 2000), possibly by means of a mechanism that circumvents geocentric navigation altogether and locates food by matching specific views of the environment to stored "snapshots" (e.g., Cartwright and Collett 1983; see Collett and Zeil 1998, for discussion).

In brief, both children and rats can learn to search to the left or right of a geometrically defined landmark, and they can learn to search directly at a nongeometrically defined landmark, but they do not readily combine these two sources of information so as to search left or right of a nongeometrically defined landmark. In contrast, human adults tested under similar circumstances show this ability quite readily (Gouteux and Spelke 2001; Hermer and Spelke 1994). What accounts for this difference?

Developmental research by Hermer-Vazquez, Moffett, and Munkholm (2001) suggested that the transition to more flexible navigation is closely related to the emergence of spatial language. In cross-sectional research, the transition was found to occur at about 6 years of age, around the time that children's language production shows mastery of spatial expressions involving *left* and *right*. Further studies of children at this transitional age revealed that performance on a productive language task with items involving the terms *left* and *right* was the best predictor of success on the reorientation task. Spatial language and flexible navigation therefore are correlated, but are they causally related?

In an initial attempt to address this question, Hermer-Vazquez, Spelke, and Katsnelson (1999; figure 10.11) returned to studies of human adults, using a dual-task method. If spatial language is causally involved in flexible navigation, we reasoned, then any task that interferes with subjects' productive use of language should interfere with their navigation

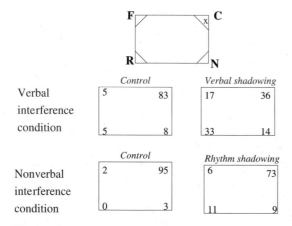

**Figure 10.11**
Tasks and performance of adults tested in the reorientation task used with children, under conditions of no interference (left) or of verbal or nonverbal interference (right). (After Hermer-Vazquez, Spelke, and Katsnelson 1999.)

as well. Accordingly, adults were tested in Hermer's reorientation task while performing one of two simultaneous interference tasks: a verbal shadowing task that interferes specifically with language production, or a nonverbal, rhythm shadowing task that is equally demanding of attentional and memory resources but does not involve language. Although rhythm shadowing caused a general impairment in performance, subjects in that condition continued to show a flexible pattern of reorientation in accord with both geometric and nongeometric information. In contrast, subjects in the verbal shadowing condition performed like young children and rats, reorienting in accord with the shape of the room but not in accord with its nongeometric properties. These findings provide preliminary evidence that language production is causally involved in flexible performance in this reorientation task.

Why might language make humans more flexible navigators? One possible answer relies on the combinatorial properties of language. Perhaps the most remarkable property of natural language is its compositionality: once a speaker knows the meanings of a set of words and the rules for combining those words together, she can represent the meanings of new combinations of those words the very first time that she hears them. The compositionality of natural languages explains how it is possible for people to understand what they hear or read, when virtually every sentence they encounter is new to them. Once a speaker knows the syntactic rules of her native language and the meanings of a set of terms, she will understand the meanings of any well-formed expressions using those terms the first time that she hears them, and she will be able to produce new expressions appropriately without any further learning.

Although the compositional semantics of a natural language is intricate and not fully understood, one thing is clear: the rules for combining words in a sentence apply irrespective of the core knowledge system that constructs the representations to which each word refers. Once a speaker has learned the expression *left of X* and a set of terms for people, places, numbers, events, objects, collections, emotions, and other entities, she can replace X with expressions that refer to entities from any and all of these domains (e.g., *left of the house where the happy old man cooked a 14-pound turkey for his family last Thanksgiving*). Natural language therefore can serve as a medium for forming representations that transcend the limits of domain-specific, core knowledge systems.

More specifically, the navigation experiments of Cheng and Hermer suggest that humans and other animals have a core system for representing geometric properties of the spatial layout (in the terms of Cheng and Gallistel, a "geometric module"). Left-right relationships are distinguished in this system: a rat or a child who has seen an object hidden left of a long wall searches reliably to the left of that wall rather than to its right. Children therefore may learn the meaning of the term *left* by relating expressions involving that term to purely geometric representations of the environment. Studies of the visual system suggest further that children also have relatively modular systems for representing information about colors and other properties of objects, and these systems may permit children to learn the meanings of terms for colors such as *blue* and for environmental features such as *wall*. Once they have learned these terms, the combinatorial machinery of natural language allows children to formulate and understand expressions such as *left of the blue wall* with no further learning. This expression cannot be formulated readily outside of language, because it crosscuts the child's encapsulated core domains. Thanks to the language faculty, however, this expression serves to represent this conjunction of information quickly and flexibly. Such use may underlie adults' flexible spatial performance.

### 10.3.2   Number

So far, I have suggested that natural language allows humans, and only humans, to represent combinations of information such as "left of the blue wall." Does language also allow humans to construct new systems of knowledge? Research on children's changing concepts of number is beginning to suggest that it may.

I have already described two lines of research providing evidence that human infants and other animals represent numerical information. First, experiments by Wynn and others reveal that infants and nonhuman primates can represent the numerical identity of each object in a scene, the numerical distinctness of distinct objects, and the effects of adding or subtracting one object. Second, experiments by Xu and others reveal that infants and many nonhuman animals can represent the approximate numerosity of a set of objects or events. These two capacities, however, appear to depend on distinct systems: human infants and adult non-human primates do not spontaneously combine them into a system of knowledge of natural number.

Evidence for the distinctness of core representations of small numbers of objects, on one hand, and of approximate numerical magnitudes, on the other hand, comes from four types of experimental findings. First, representations of numerically distinct objects show a set size limit of about 3 for infants (4 for adult humans and for nonhuman primates), whereas representations of approximate numerosities are independent of set size: infants and nonhuman primates can discriminate equally well between sets of 8 versus 16 and 16 versus 32, for example (Xu and Spelke 2000a,b). Second, representations of large approximate numerosities show a Weber fraction limit between 1.5 and 2 for 6-month-old infants, between 1.2 and 1.5 for 9-month-old infants, and about 1.15 for adult humans (e.g., Lipton and Spelke, in press; van Oeffelen and Vos 1982), whereas representations of numerically distinct objects do not: infants can discriminate 2 from 3 objects, even though the Weber fraction is below their threshold. These contrasting limits create a double

**Table 10.2**
Dissociations between human infants' representations of individuals and their numerical distinctness, and of sets and their cardinal values

|  | Individuals | Sets |
|---|---|---|
| *a. Limits to discrimination* | | |
| Set size limit of 3–4 | + | − |
| Weber limit of 1.5–2 | − | + |
| *b. Robustness over stimulus variations* | | |
| Variation in visibility | + | − |
| Variation in element size | − | + |

dissociation between representations of small numbers of objects and representations of sets (table 10.2a).

A third finding that differentiates between representations of objects and sets concerns the effects of occlusion: representations of numerically distinct objects are robust over occlusion, whereas representations of approximate numerosities are not. Although human infants and monkeys who witness the successive introduction of individual objects into an opaque box can represent that a box with 3 objects has more objects than a box with 2, they fail to represent that a box with 8 objects has more objects than a box with 4, even though the ratio difference between these numerosities is above their Weber limit (Feigenson, Carey, and Hauser 2002; Hauser, Carey, and Hauser 2000).

A fourth difference concerns the effects of variations in properties of the items to be enumerated such as their size and spacing: representations of large approximate numerosities are robust over such variations, whereas representations of objects are not. Human infants discriminate 8 from 16 items on the basis of numerosity when item size, item density, filled area, and total area are varied—findings that provide evidence that they represent large numbers of items as forming a set with an approximate cardinal value. In contrast, infants fail to discriminate 1 item from 2 or 2 items from 3 on the basis of numerosity under these conditions (Clearfield and Mix 1999; Feigenson, Carey, and Spelke 2002; Xu and Spelke 2000a). This latter finding suggests that infants represent small numbers of objects as distinct individuals but not as forming a set, whose cardinal value can be compared to the cardinal values of sets composed of other, numerically distinct objects. The third and fourth findings constitute a second double dissociation between representations of small numbers of objects and representations of large approximate numerosities (table 10.2b).

Considerable evidence therefore suggests that human infants are endowed with two distinct systems for representing numerosity. One system represents small numbers of persisting, numerically distinct individuals exactly and takes account of the operation of adding or removing one individual from the scene. It fails to represent the individuals as a set, however, and therefore does not permit infants to discriminate between different sets of individuals with respect to their cardinal values. A second system represents large numbers of objects or events as sets with cardinal values, and it allows for numerical comparison across sets. This system, however, fails to represent sets exactly, it fails to represent the members of these sets as persisting, numerically distinct individuals, and therefore it fails to capture the numerical operations of adding or subtracting one. Infants therefore represent both "individuals" and "sets," but they fail to combine these representations into representations of "sets of individuals."

The concept "set of individuals" is central to counting, simple arithmetic, and all natural number concepts. If infants lack this concept, they should have trouble understanding natural number terms such as *two*. Moreover, young children should miss the point of the verbal counting routine, even if they learn to mimic this routine. A rich body of research provides evidence that preschool children have both these problems (Fuson 1988; Griffin and Case 1996; Wynn 1990, 1992b).

Most children begin verbal counting in their second or third year of life. For months or years thereafter, however, they fail to understand the meaning of the routine or of the words that comprise it. Research by Wynn (1990, 1992b) provides evidence that children's understanding develops in four steps (table 10.3). At stage 1, when they first begin counting, children understand that *one* refers to "an object": if they are shown a picture of one fish and a picture of three fish and are asked for *one fish*, they point to the correct picture; if they are allowed to count an array of toy fish and then are asked to give the experimenter *one fish*, they offer exactly one object. At this stage, children also

**Table 10.3**
The development of children's understanding of number words and the counting routine. (After Wynn 1990, 1992b.)

| Age | Understanding of number words and counting routine |
| --- | --- |
| 2–2.5 years | *One* designates "an individual."<br>*Two, three,..., six,...* designate "a set." |
| 2.5–3.25 years | *One* designates "an individual."<br>*Two* designates "a set composed of an individual and another individual."<br>*Three,..., six,...* designate "a set other than *two*." |
| 3.25–3.5 years | *One* designates "an individual."<br>*Two* designates "a set composed of an individual and another individual."<br>*Three* designates "a set composed of an individual, another individual, and still another individual."<br>*Four,..., six,...* designate "a set other than *two* or *three*." |
| 3.5–adult | Each number word designates "a set of individuals." The set designated by each number word contains "one more individual" than the set designated by the previous word in the counting routine. |

understand that all other number words apply to arrays with more than one object. They never point to a picture of one object when asked to point to *two fish* or *six fish*, and they never produce just one object when asked for more than one.

Nevertheless, stage 1 children have very limited understandings of the meanings of the words in their counting routine. When they are shown pictures of two fish and of three fish and are asked to point to the picture with *two fish*, they point at random. Moreover, when they are allowed to count an array of objects and then are asked to give the experimenter one of the numbers of objects designated by a word in their own counting routine, they grab a handful of objects at random (Wynn 1990, 1992b). At this stage, children do not even understand that the applicability of specific number words changes when the numerosity of a set is changed by addition or subtraction: if children are allowed to count a pile of eight fish and then are told that the pile contains eight fish, they will continue to maintain that the pile has eight fish after four fish are removed (Condry, Spelke, and Xu 2000). For stage 1 children, *one* appears to refer to "an individual" and all other number words appear to refer to "some individuals" (in the informal sense of "more than one").

After about nine months of counting experience, on average, Wynn's children work out the meaning of the word *two*. At this stage, children correctly point to or produce two objects when asked for two, and they point to or produce arrays of more than two objects when asked for any larger number. Three further months suffice for children to learn the meaning of *three*. Finally, children show comprehension of all the words in their counting routine, and they use counting when they are asked for larger numbers of objects. On average, it takes children about 1–1.5 years of experience with counting before they achieve this understanding.

Why does it take children so long to learn the meanings of words like *two*? I suggest that *two* is difficult to learn because it refers to a "set of individuals," and such a concept can only be represented by combining information across distinct core knowledge systems. Children readily learn part of the meaning of *one* by relating this word to representations constructed by their core system for representing objects: they learn that *one* applies just in case the array contains an object. Children also readily learn part of the meanings of the other number words by relating each word to representations of sets constructed by their core system of number sense: they learn that (e.g.) *six* applies just in case the array contains a set with an approximate cardinal value. To learn the full meaning of *two*, however, children must combine their representations of individuals and sets: they must learn that *two* applies just in case the array contains a set composed of an individual, of another, numerically distinct individual, and of no further individuals (figure 10.12). The lexical item *two* is learned slowly, on this view, because it must be mapped simultaneously to representations from two distinct core domains.

Children eventually are able to learn the meanings of *two* and *three*, because the sets of individuals to which these terms refer are within both the set size limit of their system for representing objects and the Weber fraction limit of their system for representing sets. Larger numbers, however, exceed both these limits. How do children progress from Wynn's stage 3 to stage 4 and work out the meanings of the terms for the larger numbers within their counting routine?

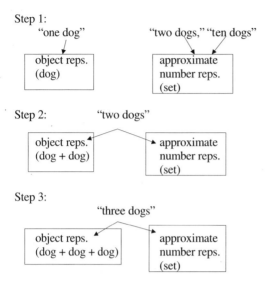

**Figure 10.12**
Hypothesized linkages between number words and core systems of representation at the first three steps in children's developing understanding of counting, number words, and the natural numbers

The above analysis suggests a possible answer. Once children have mapped *two* and *three* both to their system for representing individuals and to their system for representing sets, they are in a position to notice two things. First, relating the counting routine to the system of object representation reveals that the progression from *two* to *three* in the counting routine is marked by *the addition of one individual* to the set. Second, relating the counting routine to the system of number sense reveals that the progression from *two* to *three* is marked by *an increase in the cardinal value* of the set. Children may come to understand both the workings of the counting routine and the meanings of all the words it encompasses by generalizing these discoveries to all other steps in the counting routine. That is, children may achieve stage 4 when they realize that every step in the counting routine is marked by the successive addition of one individual so as to increment the cardinal value of the set of individuals. Because these representations exceed the limits of all the child's core knowledge systems, these realizations depend on elaborate conceptual combinations. Those combinations, in turn, may depend on the natural language of number words and of the counting routine.

Studies of children's learning of number words and counting therefore are consistent with the thesis that language serves as a medium for combining core representations of numerosity and constructing natural number concepts. To test this thesis, however, we must go beyond the present, correlational evidence with children. One way to do this is to ask whether the counting words of a specific natural language are causally involved in number representations in adults. Research with Sanna Tsivkin and Gail O'Kane suggests that they are (O'Kane and Spelke 2001; Spelke and Tsivkin 2001; figure 10.13).

This research used a bilingual training method. Adults who were proficient in two languages (Russian and English or Spanish and English) were taught different sets of number facts. In some studies, the facts were in the domain of arithmetic: for example, adults might be taught to memorize the exact answer to a two-digit addition problem. In other studies, the facts appeared in stories and concerned the age of a character, the number of people or objects in a scene, the date at which something occurred, or some measured dimension of an object. In each study, subjects learned some facts in one of their languages and some facts in the other. In each language, a given fact could concern a large exact numerosity, a large approximate numerosity, or a small exact number of objects. Study materials were presented until subjects could retrieve all the information correctly and easily.

After learning each fact in just one language, subjects were tested on all the facts in both their languages, and the amounts of time needed to retrieve facts in the trained and untrained language were compared. For facts about approximate numerosities or small numbers of objects, there was little or no advantage to performance in the trained language, relative to the untrained language. These findings suggest that large approximate and small exact number facts were represented independently of language for adults, as they must be for infants and nonhuman animals. In contrast, for facts about large exact numbers, there was a distinct advantage to performance in the language in which a fact was trained. This finding suggests that subjects drew on a specific natural language in

Reaction time

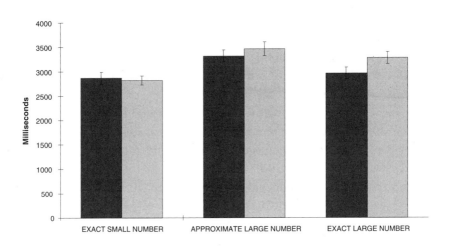

Accuracy

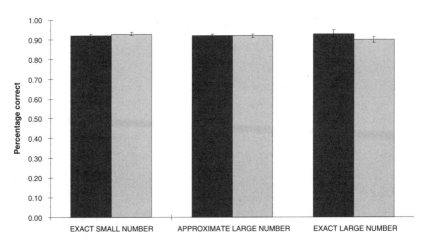

■ Trained language

Untrained language

**Figure 10.13**
Performance of bilingual adults when tested for knowledge of small exact, large approximate, and large exact numbers in the language of training versus the untrained language. (After O'Kane and Spelke 2001.)

learning facts about large, exact numbers: the language in which those facts were presented.

These findings and others (see especially Dehaene et al. 1999) begin to suggest that human number representations have at least three components (see Dehaene 1997 and Spelke 2000 for more discussion). For very small numbers, these representations depend in part on what is often called a "subitizing" system (Mandler and Shebo 1982; Trick and Pylyshyn 1994): a system for representing small numbers of objects (up to four). For large approximate numerosities, number representations depend in part on a system for representing approximate numerical magnitudes (Dehaene 1997; Gallistel and Gelman 1992). For large exact numerosities, number representations depend in part on each of these systems and in part on a specific natural language.

## 10.4   Thought and Language

I have considered two possible answers to the question, What makes humans smart? According to the first answer, human intelligence depends on a biological endowment of species-specific, core knowledge systems. According to the second answer, human intelligence depends both on core knowledge systems that are shared by other animals and on a uniquely human combinatorial capacity that serves to conjoin these representations to create new systems of knowledge. The latter capacity, I suggest, is made possible by natural language, which provides the medium for combining the representations delivered by core knowledge systems. On the second view, therefore, human intelligence depends both on a set of core knowledge systems and on the human language faculty. Recent research on human infants, nonhuman primates, and human adults now seems to me to favor this view.

In closing, I attempt to situate this view in the context of debates over the relation of language and thought. Does this view imply that many of our concepts are learned? Does learning a natural language change the set of concepts that we can entertain? Do people who learn different languages have different conceptual repertoires? To approach these questions, I begin with one a priori objection that is commonly raised against all these possibilities.

### 10.4.1   The Nativist's Objection: Learnability of Natural Languages

Natural languages are learned by children who hear people talk about the things and events around them. In order for this learning to be possible, however, children must be able to conceptualize the things and events around them in the right ways: children won't, for example, learn the meaning of *cow* unless they can relate the utterance of the word to the presence of an object in the extension of the kind "cow." The latter representation is only possible if the child already has a workable concept of cows and a workable procedure for identifying instances of that concept. Thus, it would seem that language gives us a vehicle for expressing our concepts but doesn't provide a means to expand our concepts: we don't learn new concepts by learning a natural language.

My response to this argument is to grant it. Children learn many of the words of their language by relating those words to preexisting concepts: the concepts that are made explicit by their core knowledge systems. In particular, children learn the term *left* in relation to the preexisting concept "left" that is provided by their geometric system of representation. This concept, which is shared by rats, is surely independent of language, as are the child's concepts "blue" and "thing," which allow her to learn the words *blue* and *thing*. Moreover, children cannot learn, through language or any other means, any concepts that they cannot already represent. If children cannot represent the concept "left of the blue thing," as Hermer's research suggests, then they cannot learn to represent it.

Natural languages, however, have a magical property. Once a speaker has learned the terms of a language and the rules by which those terms combine, she can represent the meanings of all grammatical combinations of those terms without further learning. The compositional semantics of natural languages allows speakers to know the meanings of new wholes from the meanings of their parts. Although a child lacking the concept "left of the blue thing" cannot learn it, she does not need to. Having learned the meanings of *left*, *blue*, and *thing*, she knows the meaning of the expression *left of the blue thing*. Thanks to their compositional semantics, natural languages can expand the child's conceptual repertoire to include not just the preexisting core knowledge concepts but also any new well-formed combination of those concepts.

## 10.4.2   A Whorfian Research Program

If the compositionality of natural language semantics gives rise to uniquely flexible human cognition, then the thesis that language produces new concepts cannot be ruled out on logical grounds, and both this thesis and the possibilities that follow from it become open to empirical test. One much-discussed possibility that can be pursued in this context is Whorf's thesis that the members of different cultures and language groups have different repertoires of concepts. Note that no evidence or arguments in this chapter support Whorf's thesis. If the combinatorial properties of language that produce new concepts are universal across human languages, then uniquely human conceptual capacities will be universal as well. Questions about the existence of cultural differences in human conceptual capacities therefore hinge in part on questions about the origins and nature of compositional semantics. How does compositional semantics work? Is there a single, universal compositional semantics that applies to all languages, or do languages vary in their combinatorial properties? How do children develop the ability to use the compositional semantics of natural languages?

Although I cannot answer any of these questions, I close with a final suggestion. Studies of cognition in nonhuman animals and in human infants, and studies of cognitive development in human children, may shed light both on our remarkable capacity for combining word meanings into complex expressions and on our corresponding capacity to combine known concepts into new ones. Two difficult questions faced by linguists and other cognitive scientists are (1) what are the primitive building blocks of complex semantic representations? and (2) what are the basic combinatorial processes by which these building blocks are assembled? Research from the fields discussed here suggests a general approach to these questions. The building blocks of all our complex representations are the representations that are constructed from individual core knowledge systems. And the basic processes that combine them are the processes that children use in constructing their first new concepts. Studies of cognition in nonhuman animals, in human infants, and in developing children therefore may shed light on central aspects both of our uniquely human capacity for language and of our uniquely human capacity for building new systems of knowledge.

## Note

Thanks to Lori Markson for comments on this chapter and to Stanislas Dehaene, Pierre Jacob, Uta Frith, Tim Shallice, and members of the Institut Jean Nicod (Paris) and the Institute for Cognitive Neuroscience (London) for discussion. Supported by grants from NIH (HD23103) and NSF (REC 0196471) and by a Fogarty Senior International Fellowship (TW 02373).

## References

Biegler, R., and Morris, R. G. M. (1993). Landmark stability is a prerequisite for spatial but not discrimination learning. *Nature, 361,* 631–633.

Biegler, R., and Morris, R. G. M. (1996). Landmark stability: Studies exploring whether the perceived stability of the environment influences spatial representation. *The Journal of Experimental Biology, 199,* 187–193.

Cartwright, B. A., and Collett, T. S. (1983). Landmark learning in bees. *Journal of Comparative Physiology, 151,* 521–543.

Cheng, K. (1986). A purely geometric module in the rat's spatial representation. *Cognition, 23,* 149–178.

Cheng, K., and Spetch, M. L. (1998). Mechanisms of landmark use in mammals and birds. In S. Healy (Ed.), *Spatial representation in animals* (pp. 1–17). Oxford: Oxford University Press.

Clearfield, M. W., and Mix, K. S. (1999). Number versus contour length in infants' discrimination of small visual sets. *Psychological Science, 10,* 408–411.

Collett, T. S., and Zeil, J. (1998). Places and landmarks: An arthropod perspective. In S. Healy (Ed.), *Spatial representation in animals* (pp. 18–53). Oxford: Oxford University Press.

Condry, K., Spelke, E. S., and Xu, F. (2000, June). *From the infant's number concepts to the child's number words.* Poster presented at the International Conference on Infant Studies, Brighton, UK.

Dehaene, S. (1997). *The number sense: How the mind creates mathematics.* Oxford: Oxford University Press.

Dehaene, S., Spelke, E., Pinel, P., Stanescu, R., and Tsivkin, S. (1999). Sources of mathematical thinking: Behavioral and brain-imaging evidence. *Science, 284,* 970–974.

Descartes, R. (1647). *Discourse on method and essays.* (Numerous translations are available.)

Dudchenko, P. A., Goodridge, J. P., Seiterle, D. A., and Taube, J. S. (1997). Effects of repeated disorientation on the acquisition of spatial tasks in rats: Dissociation between the appetitive radial arm maze and aversive water maze. *Journal of Experimental Psychology: Animal Behavior Processes, 23,* 194–210.

Feigenson, L., Carey, S., and Hauser, M. (2002). The representations underlying infants' choice of more: Object files vs. analog magnitudes. *Psychological Science, 13,* 150–156.

Feigenson, L., Carey, S., and Spelke, E. S. (2002). Infants' discrimination of number vs. continuous extent. *Cognitive Psychology, 44,* 33–36.

Felleman, D. J., and van Essen, D. C. (1991). Distributed hierarchical processing in the primate cerebral cortex. *Cerebral Cortex, 1,* 1–47.

Fuson, K. C. (1988). *Children's counting and concepts of number.* New York: Springer-Verlag.

Gallistel, C. R. (1990). *The organization of learning.* Cambridge, MA: MIT Press.

Gallistel, C. R., and Gelman, R. (1992). Preverbal and verbal counting and computation. *Cognition, 44,* 43–74.

Gouteux, S., and Spelke, E. S. (2001). Children's use of geometry and landmarks to reorient in an open space. *Cognition, 81,* 119–148.

Griffin, S., and Case, R. (1996). Evaluating the breadth and depth of training effects, when central conceptual structures are taught. In R. Case and Y. Okamoto (Eds.), The role of central conceptual structures in the development of children's thought (pp. 83–102). *Monographs of the Society for Research in Child Development* (Serial No. 246).

Hauser, M., Carey, S., and Hauser, L. (2000). Spontaneous number representation in semi-free-ranging rhesus monkeys. *Proceedings of the Royal Society, London, 267,* 829–833.

Hauser, M., MacNeilage, P., and Ware, M. (1996). Numerical representations in primates. *Proceedings of the National Academy of Sciences, 93,* 1514–1517.

Hermer, L., and Spelke, E. S. (1994). A geometric process for spatial reorientation in young children. *Nature, 370,* 57–59.

Hermer, L., and Spelke, E. S. (1996). Modularity and development: The case of spatial reorientation. *Cognition, 61,* 195–232.

Hermer-Vazquez, L., Moffett, A., and Munkholm, P. (2001). Language, space, and the development of cognitive flexibility in humans: The case of two spatial memory tasks. *Cognition, 79,* 263–299.

Hermer-Vazquez, L., Spelke, E. S., and Katsnelson, A. (1999). Sources of flexibility in human cognition: Dual-task studies of space and language. *Cognitive Psychology, 39,* 3–36.

Koechlin, E., Dehaene, S., and Mehler, J. (1998). Numerical transformations in five-month-old human infants. *Mathematical Cognition, 3,* 89–104.

Landau, B., Spelke, E. S., and Gleitman, H. (1984). Spatial knowledge in a young blind child. *Cognition, 16,* 225–260.

Lea, S. E. G., Slater, A. M., and Ryan, C. M. E. (1996). Perception of object unity in chicks: A comparison with the human infant. *Infant Behavior and Development, 19,* 501–504.

Learmonth, A. E., Nadel, L., and Newcombe, N. S. (in press). Reorientation, landmark use and size: The fate of a geometric module. *Psychological Science.*

Learmonth, A. E., Newcombe, N. S., and Huttenlocher, J. (in press). Toddlers' use of metric information and landmarks to reorient. *Journal of Experimental Child Psychology.*

Lipton, J. S., and Spelke, E. S. (in press). Origins of number sense: Large number discrimination in human infants. *Psychological Science.*

Mandler, G., and Shebo, B. J. (1982). Subitizing: An analysis of its component processes. *Journal of Experimental Psychology: General, 11,* 1–22.

Margules, J., and Gallistel, C. R. (1988). Heading in the rat: Determination by environmental shape. *Animal Learning and Behavior, 16,* 404–410.

Mechner, F. (1958). Probability relations within response sequences under ratio reinforcement. *Journal of the Experimental Analysis of Behavior, 1,* 109–121.

O'Kane, G. C., and Spelke, E. S. (2001, November). *Language dependence in representations of number, space, and time.* Poster presented at the meeting of the Psychonomic Society, Orlando, FL.

Regolin, L., and Vallortigara, G. (1995). Perception of partly occluded objects by young chicks. *Perception and Psychophysics, 57,* 971–976.

Regolin, L., Vallortigara, G., and Zanforlin, M. (1995). Object and spatial representations in detour problems by chicks. *Animal Behaviour, 49,* 195–199.

Simon, T. J., Hespos, S. J., and Rochat, P. (1995). Do infants understand simple arithmetic? A replication of Wynn 1992a. *Cognitive Development, 10,* 253–269.

Spelke, E. S. (1990). Principles of object perception. *Cognitive Science, 14,* 29–56.

Spelke, E. S. (1998) Nativism, empiricism, and the origins of knowledge. *Infant Behavior and Development, 21,* 181–200.

Spelke, E. S. (2000). Core knowledge. *American Psychologist, 55,* 1233–1243.

Spelke, E. S., and Tsivkin, S. (2001). Language and number: A bilingual training study. *Cognition, 78,* 45–88.

Stedron, J. M., Munakata, Y., and O'Reilly, R. C. (2000, July). *Spatial reorientation in young children: A case of modularity?* Poster presented at the International Conference on Infant Studies, Brighton, UK.

Thelen, E. (1984). Learning to walk: Ecological demands and phylogenetic constraints. In L. P. Lipsitt and C. Rovee-Collier (Eds.), *Advances in infancy research* (Vol. 3). Norwood, NJ: Ablex.

Trick, L., and Pylyshyn, Z. W. (1994). Why are small and large numbers enumerated differently? A limited capacity preattentive stage in vision. *Psychological Review, 101,* 80–102.

Van de Walle, G., Carey, S., and Prevor, M. (2001). Bases for object individuation in infancy: Evidence from manual search. *Journal of Cognition and Development, 1,* 249–280.

van Oeffelen, M. P., and Vos, P. G. (1982). A probabilistic model for the discrimination of visual number. *Perception and Psychophysics, 32,* 163–170.

Wang, R. F., Hermer-Vazquez, L., and Spelke, E. S. (1999). Mechanisms of reorientation and object localization by human children: A comparison with rats. *Behavioral Neuroscience, 113,* 475–485.

Wehner, R., and Srinivasan, M. V. (1981). Searching behavior of desert ants, genus *Cataglyphis* (Formicidae, Hymenoptera). *Journal of Comparative Physiology, 142,* 315–338.

Wynn, K. (1990). Children's understanding of counting. *Cognition, 36,* 155–193.

Wynn, K. (1992a). Addition and subtraction by human infants. *Nature, 358,* 749–750.

Wynn, K. (1992b). Children's acquisition of the number words and the counting system. *Cognitive Psychology, 24,* 220–251.

Wynn, K. (1998). Psychological foundations of number: Numerical competence in human infants. *Trends in Cognitive Sciences, 2,* 296–303.

Xu, F., and Spelke, E. S. (2000a, July). *Large number discrimination in infants: Evidence for analog magnitude representations.* Paper presented at the International Conference on Infant Studies, Brighton, UK.

Xu, F., and Spelke, E. S. (2000b). Large number discrimination in 6-month-old infants. *Cognition, 74,* B1–B11.

# 11

## Conceptual and Linguistic Factors in Inductive Projection: How Do Young Children Recognize Commonalities between Animals and Plants?

Kayoko Inagaki and Giyoo Hatano

### 11.1 Introduction

In contrast to the large number of studies on deduction, induction has not been a popular topic in experimental cognitive psychology (Holland et al. 1986). This is probably because there is no logically correct answer for induction, and whether one's answer is appropriate depends on one's goal, prior knowledge, and context. For example, although an argument is generally considered to be stronger when its premises are diverse than when they are similar (Osherson et al. 1990; Sloman 1993), this does not always hold: some people do not evaluate argument strength using premise diversity but by "aptly" relying on their rich specific knowledge (Coley et al. 1999; Proffitt, Coley, and Medin 2000).

However, this characteristic makes induction tasks highly useful for assessing reasoners' knowledge, as well as possible influences of language on their reasoning. How far reasoners project a property observed in an entity often depends on the salient category they possess to which the entity belongs. Even when the property attribution seems based on similarity to the observed entity, the judgment of similarity may be structural or relational (Gentner 1983). In other words, it is greatly influenced by conceptual categories that the reasoners possess. For example, if reasoners who possess a concept of fish learn that a goldfish has a heart, they are likely to infer that a tunny or a killifish also has a heart, though both of them look different. Most humans are expected to be equipped with the basic reasoning ability that allows them to project a target property to other members of the category the exemplar belongs to. Thus, their specific patterns of projection can be attributed primarily to which categories are salient during the induction. We suggest that such category salience is influenced by language use, and also by goals and contexts that interact with how a property is linguistically encoded.

Induction is an apt area in which to investigate language effects: that is, how reasoning performance varies depending on ways in which entities involved in the argument are encoded. We suggest that whether a property asserted of one category will be asserted of another category is determined by how the property is described—reasoners are willing to conclude from the premise "dogs love their young," through inductive inference, that "cats love their young," but may hesitate to conclude that "cats love their puppies" from the premise "dogs love their puppies."

Such a role for language in influencing patterns of induction would be of great importance in cognition, for induction is a central process in expanding knowledge. More specifically, starting from the given pieces of information, induction allows people to offer a new argument, to form a new category, and to derive new rules and regularities. As Holland et al. (1986) claim, induction not only is guided by prior knowledge, but also produces new knowledge. Reasoners may recognize commonalities among new entities through perceiving or projecting a set of properties to these entities, and come to treat them as belonging to the same newly constructed category. For example, reasoners may construct a new primitive category of mollusks including an octopus and a nautilus after applying to (as well as perceiving in) them properties such as living in the sea, having a soft body, and moving on the bottom of the sea.

We discuss below two types of inductive reasoning: *inductive projection* and *analogy*. These inferential processes are similar because both are used to derive new pieces of information about the less familiar entity (which is called the *target*) from knowledge about the more familiar one (the *source* or *base*) on the basis of the perceived similarity between the two entities. In inductive projection, reasoners infer that if the source has a property X, a target that is highly similar to the source also has that property. Similarity is determined in terms of either feature overlap (Sloman 1993) or categorical inclusion (Osherson et al. 1990). In analogy, reasoners infer that if the source has a property X, the target has another property Y, so that the relationship between the source and X and that between the target and Y is structurally the same (Gentner

a genetic construct which ~~and blood~~ /renewing blood/ may at some stage be capable locomotion, /reproduction/ ^be^ capable

1983). In other words, inductive projection can be regarded as a special case of structure alignment in which the source and the target are so similar that properties X and Y are almost identical. The boundary between inductive projection and analogy is not distinct, however. Since exactly the same property is seldom owned by another entity, the property needs to be tuned, modified, or replaced by another property even in inductive projection. To illustrate, the property of "moving on its own" refers to different actions depending on whether the entity is a human, a dog, a pigeon, a carp, or a grasshopper. Likewise, even if the property is expressed by a well-specified identical word, it many not be identical in source and target: for example, even if both are said to "have a heart," the size of the heart is expected to vary depending on whether the target is large (e.g., an elephant) or small (e.g., an ant). Such modulations are based on our ability to "carry out fluent, apparently effortless, structural alignment and mapping" (Gentner and Markman 1997, 53).

How might language influence these two processes? A critical difference between the two processes is that, unlike in analogy, in inductive projection the property can be applied as far as it is given the same label, though some metaphorical extension is permitted. For this reason, linguistic factors may well constrain inductive projection more than they do analogy, though language influences analogical reasoning as well (Gentner and Rattermann 1991; Rattermann and Gentner 1998). To put it differently, patterns of projection may vary considerably depending on how the target property is expressed. Each predicate has its own scope, outside of which it is anomalous (e.g., Keil 1979). Animals can be taken ill, and so can plants; but machines can be in trouble but cannot be taken ill. The property of taking food can be extended to all animals if it is for survival, but should be limited to humans and a small number of other advanced animals if it is seen as a snack. This dependence on linguistic cues occurs partly because, since how much similarity justifies the extension of the property is not specified, reasoners are willing to use such linguistic cues as additional constraints.

Machines can be 'sick,'

In this chapter, we examine young children's inductive projection in the domain of naive biology—more specifically, in relation to their grasp of commonalities between animals and plants. We will show that children's inductions are influenced by the language used to describe the property.

More specifically, we present studies showing that, if the property to be projected is properly described and given in an appropriate context, young children can not only (1) use the concept of living things to constrain inductive projection, but also (2) be helped to grasp the concept explicitly through inductively projecting a few human properties to both animals and plants. Through projecting human properties common to both animals and plants, young children can be better prepared to map the knowledge of animals to that of plants in forced analogy. We will focus on direct and indirect language effects as well as effects of providing biological context.

## 11.2   Inductive Projection of Biological Properties

In young children's understanding of biological phenomena, we assume, they often rely on personification—that is, an inference from humans to other living entities. This is because they tend to map any target onto the most familiar source—in most cases, humans (Inagaki and Hatano 1991). Since young children are so familiar with humans, while necessarily being ignorant of most other animate objects, they use knowledge about humans as the source for making inductive-projective or analogical predictions or explanations. For example, after having experienced growing flowers, one 5-year-old girl spontaneously used the person analogy for flowers, saying, "Flowers are like people. If flowers eat nothing [are not watered], they will fall down of hunger. If they eat too much [are watered too often], they will be taken ill" (Motoyoshi 1979). When asked, "A tulip is dead tired and not lively. Will it become fine if we leave it as it is?" a 5-year-old boy answered as follows: "A tulip is the same as a person only in that point. (E: In what point?) If we leave the tulip as it is ... if we water it a little bit and give it a rest, it will become fine again" (Inagaki and Hatano 1987). These two examples indicate that children can rely on person analogies based on relational and causal similarity, not perceptual similarity, in predicting or explaining behaviors of plants in everyday situations.

However, previous studies on inductive projection from humans have reported that young children fail to attribute to plants those properties that all living things possess. In assessing whether young children possess a combined category of living things, Carey (1985) examined whether children's induction of a given property would be constrained by the biological category. Children 6 years of age were taught a novel property on dogs and bees, on dogs and flowers, or only on flowers; that is, they were told that Xs had *golgi*—tiny, curly things that could not be seen without a microscope. The children were asked later whether other animals and nonanimals (including astronomical ones) would also have *golgi*. The results indicated no evidence that the concept of living things constrained their induction; children who were taught on dogs and flowers tended to attribute the novel property more widely than those who were taught on dogs and bees or only on flowers, but they often overattributed the property even to nonliving things.

These results, however, need not be taken as showing that young children have not acquired a concept of living things that includes both animals and plants. It is possible for young children not to use categories they have in attributing properties simply because they tend to rely on similarity-based inferences (Inagaki and Sugiyama 1988). It is also possible that the children in Carey's (1985) study failed to use biological boundaries in inductive projection not because they lacked the concept of living things, but because they failed to activate this concept when asked about the novel and incomprehensible property of golgi. Gutheil, Vera, and Keil's (1998) study, which primarily concerned the concept of animals, in part supports this line of reasoning. They showed that when given biological contexts consisting of brief explanations about the functions of animal properties, 4-year-olds produced extended and accurate projections of those properties to various animals; moreover, they did so to the same extent as the 7-year-olds in Carey's (1985) study, where such contexts were not given. This suggests that giving some information about biological functions of properties helps young children activate and use the biological categories they have.

Inductive projection may also be influenced by linguistic variables as mentioned above—that is, how the property is described. When the property is described in forms readily applicable to both animals and plants (e.g., using verbs that refer to functional or emerging processes such as *get better* or *discharge*), it is more likely to be applied to plants as well as animals than when it is described using verbs that refer to external action such as *look at* or *defecate*. Gutheil, Vera, and Keil (1998) failed to induce the attribution of given properties to plants in part because they used action verbs, such as *eat*, *sleep*, or *have a baby*. Moreover, in their study, human-favored expressions were used to give contexts (e.g., "If the person doesn't eat, he will *get skinnier and skinnier* and he will die," or "This person has a heart which pumps *blood* around his body"; emphasis added), which also might lead the children not to extend the given property to plants.

In what follows, we examine contributions of conceptual, contextual, and linguistic factors to reasoning by analyzing patterns of inductive projection, taking examples from young children's extension of human properties to nonhuman entities. We used humans as the exemplar because young children's biology is human centered (Carey 1985; Inagaki and Hatano 1987), and projection ought to be maximal from the familiar and prototypical exemplar (Carey 1985; Rips 1975). We were especially interested in demonstrating that even young children are able to use the category of living things in inductive projection, particularly when contextual and linguistic cues can assist them. We also wanted to investigate whether projecting a set of properties common to different members of a category would make the category more salient—more specifically, whether children could be made more conscious of commonalities between animals and plants through the experience of inductively projecting human properties to both animals and plants.

## 11.3   Can Young Children Project Biological Properties to Animals and Plants? Influences of Similarity, Context, and Language

We consider below whether young children can inductively project some biological properties that humans have to both animals and plants, but not to nonliving things. As described earlier, previous studies have reported that young children failed to attribute to plants those properties that all living things possess. We believe that this failure might be attributed to the lack of salience of this biological category. Some animals look very different from humans, but plants are even more dissimilar; for example, they do not have a face, eyes, arms, and so on. The category of living things that includes perceptually diverse members may not be activated unless prompted by contexts.

Linguistic factors may also influence inductive projection to plants. The English word *animate* easily reminds us of an animal. The Hebrew word corresponding to English *animal* is very close to the Hebrew words corresponding to *living* and *alive*, but the word corresponding to *plant* has no obvious relation to these terms (Stavy and Wax 1989). The Japanese verb corresponding to *be* has two forms, *iru* and *aru*; *iru* is applied to humans and other animals, whereas *aru* is applied to plants and nonliving things. In the typical induction task, information given to children is conceptually too limited to map it aptly to proper objects. Hence, they may be easily obstructed by the linguistic barriers, and they may fail to extend human properties to plants.

It is plausible that young children will be able to extend human properties to plants in the inductive projection if they are given both contextual and linguistic help. By "contextual help," we mean that the children's attention is drawn to the biological significance of the property that is to be projected. We appeal to the children's sense of vitalistic biology. In a previous study (Inagaki and Hatano 1993), we found that children aged 5–6 years tend to understand biological phenomena in terms of vitalism. More specifically, young children seem to consider that living things, including humans, take in vital power from food/water to maintain vigor and that a surplus of the vital power induces their growth. Thus, by giving descriptions about functions of properties in terms of vitalism, we expect children to activate their general biological knowledge and to be able to extend human properties to plants in inductive projection. Our hypothesis is that this biological context will help children notice functional or causal similarity between humans and other living entities (including plants) in terms of ways of living and organic constructions.

By "linguistic help," we mean that properties are described in linguistic forms that are readily (literally) applicable to both animals and plants. The properties animals possess can be described either (1) by using action verbs that refer to externalized behaviors (such as *eat* or *excrete*) that are applicable to animals but not to plants, or (2) by using verbs that refer to functional or emerging processes (such as *need nutrients* or *become bigger*). Using the latter type of verb may help children to recognize that these properties are not limited to animals. In a sense, this could be seen as the removal of linguistic barriers for extension rather than as a help.

We conducted two experiments in study 1, but in what follows we discuss both experiments together because they are similar. (For details, see Inagaki and Hatano 1996, experiments 2 and 2a.) Two conditions were set up in both experiments: the context condition and the no-context condition. In the context condition, we gave short vitalistic descriptions about the function of the target property for a person that referred to taking in or exchanging vital power or energy. In the no-context condition, we did not give such descriptions. If giving vitalistic accounts of properties for a person enhances children's use of the concept of living things in their inductive projection, we could infer that children consider both animals and plants to be biological entities with the same underlying mechanisms.

Fifty-two 5-year-old Japanese-speaking kindergarten children participated in experiment 1 and 40 5-year-olds participated in experiment 2. (The instructions, questions, and answers were all in Japanese, but their English translations will be given below.) The children were randomly assigned to either the context condition or the no-context condition. Chronological age and gender were equated in both conditions. As the target properties, we used growth and being taken ill in experiment 1, and needing food and water and being taken ill (in another phrasing) in experiment 2. These are properties that animals and plants share. We also asked about filler (animal) properties, namely, breathing, eating, and defecating. These were included to check whether children attributed the target property just mechanically. Breathing and eating have analogous properties among plants, but the specific action verbs we used, *eats* and *breathes*, are applicable to animals alone.

What follows are example descriptions of properties given to the children. The italicized parts were given only to children in the context condition.

Grows: A person becomes bigger and bigger *by taking in energy from food and water*. Then, does X become bigger and bigger? (Exp. 1)

Needs food/water: A person needs water and/or food. *If he does not take in energy or vital power from water and/or food, he will die.* Then, does X need water and/or food? (Exp. 2)

Is taken ill: A person is sometimes taken ill *because his energy or vital power is gradually weakened by germs going into his body.* Then, is X sometimes taken ill? (Exp. 1)

Is taken ill: A person is sometimes taken ill *because his energy or vital power is gradually weakened when he feels too cold or too hot.* Then, is X sometimes taken ill? (Exp. 2) (We found that a mixture of the vitalistic explanation and the germ explanation in experiment 1 might not have accurately represented children's biological beliefs. Thus, we modified the description into the diminution of vital power due to a loss of balance in experiment 2.)

Properties described using action verbs were used as fillers.

Breathes: A person breathes *in order to take in vital power from fresh air.* Then, does X breathe? (Exp. 1)

Eats: A person eats food every day. *If he doesn't eat food and cannot take in energy or vital power from it, he will die.* Then, does X eat something? (Exp. 1)

Defecates: A person poops. *He gets rid of matter that is no longer useful inside the body as feces.* Then, does X poop? (Exp. 2)

There were nine target objects, three each from animal, plant, and nonliving thing categories: a squirrel, alligator, grasshopper, tulip, dandelion, pine tree, stone, pencil, and chair. Each property question was asked about all of the objects before the inquiry proceeded to another property. The target objects were randomly ordered for each participant, but the property questions were asked in a fixed order.

We counted individual children's numbers of "Yes" responses to three instances each of animals, plants, and nonliving things. Then we classified their patterns of induction into four patterns: an animal-and-plant pattern ("Yes" responses to all three instances of animals and plants but not to any of the nonliving things); an animal pattern ("Yes" responses only to animals), a human pattern (no "Yes" responses), and "others" (patterns not satisfying any of the previous criteria). We allowed one unexpected response; for example, 3/2/0 or 3/3/1 was classified as an animal-and-plant pattern.

With respect to the performances in the two conditions, we expected to find the second of these three possible results:

1. If children respond on the basis of their object-specific knowledge (what they know specifically about each object), children in both the context and the no-context condition will often show the animal-and-plant pattern, and thus there will be no difference between the context and no-context conditions.

2. If children possess a concept of living things but the concept is not salient and is fragile, children in the context condition will show the animal-and-plant pattern more often than those in the no-context condition.

3. If children do not possess a concept of living things, children in both the context and the no-context condition will seldom show the animal-and-plant pattern, and thus there will be no difference between the context and the no-context conditions.

Figure 11.1 shows occurrence rates of the animal-and-plant pattern for each property in the context and no-context conditions. The inductive projections from humans were extended up to plants by a majority of the children in the context condition for growth, needing food/water, and being taken ill when these were phrased properly. Children in the context condition displayed animal-and-plant patterns for the four target properties 63% of the time on average, whereas children in the no-context condition did so 33% of the time. For the three target properties excluding being taken ill (poorly phrased), the corresponding percentages were 77% versus 42%. The second of the above three possibilities is supported, as expected. That is, the present findings strongly suggest that the children already possessed the concept of living things, because the given description was too brief for them to acquire the concept. This excluded the third possibility. The first possibility was also rejected. If our participants had responded on the basis of their object-specific knowledge, there would have been no difference in the frequency of the animal-and-plant patterns between the two conditions.

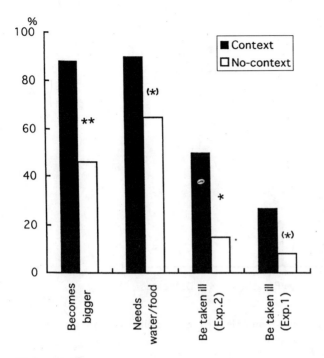

**Figure 11.1**
Occurrence rates of the animal-and-plant pattern for each property in the context and no-context conditions

For the filler properties, percentages of animal-and-plant patterns were generally low (figure 11.2). There was no effect of context. It is clear that the children did not give "Yes" responses mechanically.

The results also provide evidence for language effects, as can be seen by contrasting figure 11.1 with figure 11.2. When the description of properties involved specific action verbs (figure 11.2), the projection was seldom extended to plants. Even when the contextual information that emphasized the biological significance of the properties was given, very few animal-and-plant patterns occurred.

Most striking was the contrast between *eating* and *needing food/ water*. As discussed earlier, *eating* is an action verb that is specific to animals, whereas *needing food/water* uses a general verb indicating a functional or emerging process. These different descriptions of highly

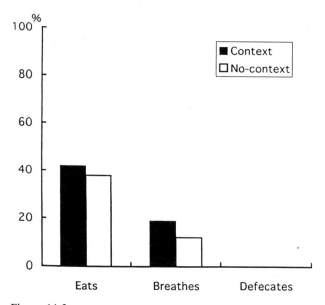

**Figure 11.2**
Occurrence rates of the animal-and-plant pattern for filler (animal) properties in the context and no-context conditions

similar properties produced very different patterns of projections. See figure 11.3 for the proportion of "Yes" responses to animals, plants, and nonliving things. For the property of eating, quite a number of the children hesitated to answer "Yes" or "No" in attributing eating to plants. Nine children said, "It drinks water," without answering "Yes" or "No." These responses (19 in all) were counted as "Yes." In spite of this, animal patterns were most dominant for the property of eating.

It should be noted that the children who showed the animal-and-plant pattern for one property often showed the same pattern for other properties in the context condition; more than half (13) of the 23 children who showed the animal-and-plant pattern for growth showed the same pattern at least once for other properties—7 for being taken ill and 10 for eating—in experiment 1, and about half of the children in experiment 2 showed this pattern of overlap for both needing food/water and being taken ill. This strongly suggests that these children possessed not a collection of simple associations, but a more or less coherent set of properties that animals and plants share.

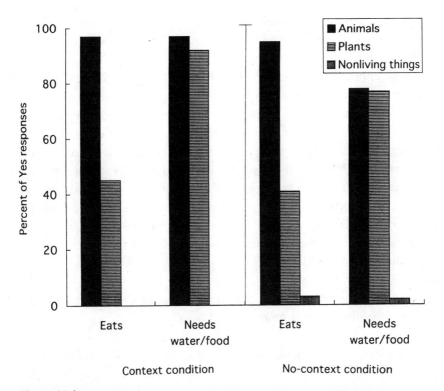

**Figure 11.3**
Percentages of "Yes" responses to animals, plants, and nonliving things for "eating" and "needing food/water" in the context and no-context conditions

In sum, children as young as 5 years of age, at least potentially, consider humans, other animals, and plants as biological entities with the same underlying mechanisms—more specifically, as entities staying vigorous by taking in vital power from food and water and growing in size by using the vital power surplus. Animals and plants are perceptually so different (e.g., in terms of spontaneous movement) that young children's use of the concept of living things requires the context that draws their attention to the biological processes that animals and plants share. The idea of taking in vital power from food and water and growing in size by using the vital power surplus is appealing to children who lack knowledge about photosynthesis, and it helps them recognize commonalities between animals and plants.

A supportive context alone does not always suffice to enable children to use the concept of living things in inductive projection. The results also show effects of the language used to describe the properties. When the target property is described with a specific action verb, the children's concept of living things is less likely to be triggered, as suggested by the children's performance on the filler items in our present experiments and in Gutheil, Vera, and Keil's (1998) study. Thus, we can summarize that young children have a concept of living things, but this concept is not salient and is fragile in the sense that both contextual and linguistic aids are necessary for them to use it. The idea that using general terms may facilitate projection of properties between different specific members of a category is related to the idea that uniform relational vocabularies may contribute to relational mapping across different sets of objects (Gentner and Rattermann 1991).

## 11.4   Projecting the Same Properties Helps Young Children Recognize Commonalities between Animals and Plants

In this section, we consider whether inductive projection can help children form a new category or at least grasp a category more explicitly. Is young children's recognition of commonalities between animals and plants enhanced through mediating "person analogies" or activated recognition of commonalities between humans and other nonhuman entities? To answer this question, in study 2 we gave another group of children both the inductive projection task with contexts and the forced analogy task. The inductive projection task involved almost the same procedure as the context condition in the experiments of study 1 mentioned earlier. That is, 5-year-olds were given the inductive projection task with a biological context for three properties: needing food/water (from experiment 2), becoming bigger (experiment 1), and being taken ill (experiment 2), in this order. The properties used in the induction task were described by general, functional terms that could comfortably be applied to plants as well as animals. Thus, this particular inductive task might facilitate performance in three different ways: by using living-thing properties only, by setting an appropriate conceptual context, and by using general language. If this ideal induction task is given to children before the analogical task, will they show greater analogical insight?

Immediately after this induction task, the children were given the forced analogy task. They were directly asked whether plants or non-living things would manifest phenomena similar to those observed for animals, always referring to two examples of each category. This was the strategy we adopted after exploring a few alternative methods of directly asking children about commonalities between animals and plants (experiment 3 in Inagaki and Hatano 1996). The use of generic terms like *animals* and *plants* is desirable (e.g., "What do animals and plants have in common?"), but is not possible with our participants, mainly because the term corresponding to English *plants (shokubutsu* in Japanese) is incomprehensible to most of them. Asking children about the commonalities between an example of the category "animal" and an example of the category "plant" often induced local comparisons that were not applicable to these categories in general. The only method that proved to work was asking children whether a few examples of plants or of nonliving things would display phenomena similar to those observed for a few examples of animals. Thus, after being asked to identify each drawing of the six examples of animals, plants, and nonliving things, the child was told that certain animals (a squirrel and an alligator) reveal such and such a phenomenon and was then asked whether plants (a tulip and a pine tree) or nonliving things (a chair and a public telephone) would reveal a similar one. When the child replied, "Yes," he or she was asked what it was. (Two instances of artifacts were used as examples of non-living things because asking young children to recognize a similar phenomenon for an apparently mixed category of artifacts and nonliving natural kinds seemed too demanding.)

The biological phenomena used in the forced analogy task were those that had not been dealt with in the induction task: overfeeding, being ill fed, breathing, and growing in number. For these phenomena, only 50% or fewer of the children recognized commonalities between animals and plants in the experiment reported in Inagaki and Hatano 1996. The following are example questions used in the forced analogy task in this experiment.

Overfeeding: A squirrel or an alligator becomes ill when it eats too much food. *Do you think anything similar to this occurs with a tulip or a pine tree/with a chair or a pay phone?*

Growing in number: A squirrel or an alligator gradually increases in number by having babies or laying eggs. (The above italicized part was repeated.)

Children who had been given the forced analogy task immediately after the inductive projection task were compared with those who were given the forced analogy task alone (experiment 3 in Inagaki and Hatano 1996) in terms of their recognition of commonalities between animals and plants in the forced analogy task. We expected that, after recognizing that (1) animals have some human properties and that (2) plants have the same human properties in inductive projection, the children would be able to infer that (3) animals and plants share some other properties.

As shown in table 11.1, for being ill fed and overfeeding, and to a lesser extent for breathing, the children who had been given the induction task in advance grasped commonalities between animals and plants significantly more often than those who had not. For growing in number, such a tendency was not found at all. In other words, through the mediating inductive projection of human properties, which activated the recognition of commonalities between humans and plants as well as between humans and animals, the children recognized some features in plants functionally equivalent (or structurally mapped) to the selected animal properties. However, we must add that this effect of the "mediating"

**Table 11.1**
Percentages of applying animal analogy to plants (P) or nonliving things (N)

| | Being ill fed | | Overfeeding | | Breathing | | Growing in number | |
|---|---|---|---|---|---|---|---|---|
| | P | N | P | N | P | N | P | N |
| Preceded by inductive projection task | 95** | 0 | 60* | 0 | 60 | 0 | 45 | 2 |
| Not preceded by inductive projection task | 50** | 0 | 33* | 3 | 45 | 0 | 50 | 5 |

*Note:* The two percentages were significantly different, $*p < .05$, $**p < .01$.

projection of human properties was limited to phenomena related to taking nutriment. This could be because young children's first biology emerges around taking nutriment and individual growth, or perhaps because the contexts given to the children in the present study emphasized the biological nature of needing food/water and growing in size only.

At first glance, this experiment did not deal with language effects. However, it seems plausible that the clear context effects found here are attributable in part to the effects of language. Children who were given the inductive projection task before the forced analogy task grasped commonalities between animals and plants more often in the forced analogy task than did those who had not, even when the forced analogy task used an action verb (e.g., *breathing*). We believe that children's enhanced performance on the analogy task may be attributable to linguistic variables in the inductive projection task—in other words, to indirect language effects. Imagine another condition, in which the inductive projection task involved specific action verbs: *eats and drinks* instead of *needs food/water*, *breaks a bone* instead of *is taken ill*, and so on. In this hypothetical condition, few animal-and-plant patterns would have been produced. It seems very unlikely that such an induction task could have enhanced the grasp of commonalities between animals and plants in the following forced analogy task. We suggest that the inductive projection task facilitated animal-plant analogies later because the former task used language readily applicable to both animals and plants.

## 11.5   How Language Effects Are Produced in Inductive Projection

Our experiments have demonstrated that inductive projection can be influenced by linguistic variables—that is, by how the property is described. When a general functional term is used, the property is more likely to be applied to plants as well as animals than when an "action" term is used. How is this difference produced? Do young children try to project the property in the same way irrespective of descriptive terms, and reject the conclusion that plants have that property when its description is anomalous as a predicate for plants? Processes through which language effects are produced cannot be that simple. This is because (1) the scope of a predicate is not always defined in an all-or-nothing fashion, (2) some metaphorical extension is permitted even for a descriptive term applied to humans or animals only, and (3) whether the property is projected to the target depends on its recognized similarity to the source as well. In fact, in our study 1, a substantial number of young children hesitantly applied *eating* to plants, indicating that a property may be applied even when it is anomalous, if respondents strongly believe that the target has a functionally equivalent property. Some other children, who did not project this property to plants, added, "A tulip (or dandelion or pine tree) drinks water, though." This shows, we suggest, that they were tempted to extend this biologically essential property of taking nutriment and wondered if they could rephrase the property. Young children seem to consider both the similarity between the source and the target, on one hand, and whether the description of the property can be applied to the target "comfortably," on the other.

If such complex cognitive processes are involved in inductive projection, we must doubt our presumption at the beginning of this chapter that linguistic factors constrain inductive projection more strongly than they constrain analogy. Language effects may be produced in these two types of reasoning in a more or less similar fashion. Gentner and Rattermann (1991; Rattermann and Gentner 1998) assert that, in analogies, language (e.g., a common relational term) invites reasoners to notice and maintain particular patterns of relationships. It has also been found that analogical retrieval of prior scenarios is facilitated by the use of common relational terms between the initial scenario and the probe story (Clement, Mawby, and Giles 1994). General, functional terms describing properties in inductive projection may also have such "invitational" effects. To put it differently, these terms not only enable but also encourage reasoners to retrieve and hold particular conceptual categories that the source belongs to, and thus particular similarity metrics for assessing the distance between the source and the target.

Generally speaking, we believe, language influences thinking primarily by activating and holding salient some of the representations of entities and their transformations. We do not believe that language is indispensable for acquiring representations. For example, the formation of conceptual categories does not presuppose learning the corresponding label, at least for taxonomic categories for natural kinds. Those biological categories are constructed much earlier than the corresponding words are learned. For example, the category "living things" is available to young children long before they learn a difficult word in Japanese, *seibutsu* or *ikimono*, during school years. Young children's category of living things might be, if verbalized, "something like humans, needing food/water and growing." Yet it can be used to constrain the process of inductive projection to plants even when the children do not possess its concise label.

Needless to say, typically the descriptive term and the category develop hand in hand. The use of a general term for describing a particular entity's property presupposes some preliminary grasp of the category including the entity; by activating the category, the general term will be retrieved promptly. In this sense, language and conceptual understanding must be mutually facilitative.

## 11.6  Conclusion

We can draw the following conclusion concerning children's inductive projection from humans: if children are given a context directing their attention to the biological function of the target properties that humans possess, and at the same time the properties are described in functional, general terms to remove language barriers for extension, they can go beyond perceptual or global similarity in the inductive projection. In other words, they can recognize relational and causal similarity between humans and plants as well as between humans and animals. Children's inductive projection of human properties serves as a "mediation" or "bridge" that facilitates the explicit grasp of commonalities between nonhuman animals and plants.

Our experimental results have implications for research and theory on inductive projection and also reasoning in general. First, reasoning, especially induction, is heavily constrained by a reasoner's knowledge, but this does not mean that the reasoner's performance always reveals the knowledge he or she possesses. It is true that inductive projection is constrained by categorical knowledge, but categories are not simply either possessed or not—they may be salient or latent, even when possessed. Sometimes it is necessary to provide reasoners with contextual and/or linguistic help to evoke the pattern of induction that reflects their knowledge accurately. We should not prematurely conclude that reasoners do not possess the knowledge from their pattern of projection unless sufficient contextual and linguistic cues are provided.

Second, inductive projection, especially among children, is strongly influenced by linguistic factors: how the target property is phrased, how its significance is explained, and so on. Reasoners seem to be sensitive to these factors, because so-called reasoning tasks require additional, linguistic cues to derive plausible answers. That people do not solve deduction problems in purely logical ways has been demonstrated repeatedly (Cheng and Holyoak 1985; Johnson-Laird 1983). However, induction tasks may require even more reliance on extralogical cues. We should keep in mind that even a very subtle linguistic cue may affect the process of reasoning.

Third, the acquired knowledge not only is used in reasoning such as inductive projection and analogy, but also can be elaborated in the process. Inductive reasoning as a domain-general mechanism plays an important role in the development of core domains of thought such as naive biology, and the acquisition of core domains of thought in turn constrains the process of reasoning. Little is known about this reciprocal process of knowledge use and elaboration, but it is an important research topic if we want to understand the dynamic nature of cognitive growth.

## References

Carey, S. (1985). *Conceptual change in childhood*. Cambridge, MA: MIT Press.

Cheng, P. W., and Holyoak, K. J. (1985). Pragmatic reasoning schemas. *Cognitive Psychology, 17*, 391–416.

Clement, C. A., Mawby, R., and Giles, D. E. (1994). The effects of manifest relational similarity on analog retrieval. *Journal of Memory and Language, 33*, 396–420.

Coley, J. D., Medin, D. L., Proffitt, J. B., Lynch, E., and Atran, S. (1999). Inductive reasoning in folkbiological thought. In D. L. Medin and S. Atran (Eds.), *Folkbiology* (pp. 205–232). Cambridge, MA: MIT Press.

Gentner, D. (1983). Structure-mapping: A theoretical framework for analogy. *Cognitive Science, 7*, 155–170.

Gentner, D., and Markman, A. B. (1997). Structure-mapping in analogy and similarity. *American Psychologist, 52*, 45–56.

Gentner, D., and Rattermann, M. J. (1991). Language and the career of similarity. In S. A. Gelman and J. P. Byrnes (Eds.), *Perspectives on language and thought: Interrelations in development* (pp. 225–277). New York: Cambridge University Press.

Gutheil, G., Vera, A., and Keil, F. C. (1998). Do houseflies think? Patterns of induction and biological beliefs in development. *Cognition, 66*, 33–49.

Holland, J. H., Holyoak, K. J., Nisbett, R. E., and Thagard, P. R. (1986). *Induction*. Cambridge, MA: MIT Press.

Inagaki, K., and Hatano, G. (1987). Young children's spontaneous personification as analogy. *Child Development, 58*, 1013–1020.

Inagaki, K., and Hatano, G. (1991). Constrained person analogy in young children's biological inference. *Cognitive Development, 6*, 219–231.

Inagaki, K., and Hatano, G. (1993). Young children's understanding of the mind-body distinction. *Child Development, 64*, 1534–1549.

Inagaki, K., and Hatano, G. (1996). Young children's recognition of commonalities between animals and plants. *Child Development, 67*, 2823–2840.

Inagaki, K., and Sugiyama, K. (1988). Attributing human characteristics: Developmental changes in over- and underattribution. *Cognitive Development, 3*, 55–70.

Johnson-Laird, P. N. (1983). *Mental models*. Cambridge: Cambridge University Press.

Keil, F. C. (1979). *Semantic and conceptual development: An ontological perspective*. Cambridge, MA: Harvard University Press.

Motoyoshi, M. (1979). *Essays on education for day care children: Emphasizing daily life activities*. Tokyo: Froebel-kan. [in Japanese]

Osherson, D. N., Smith, E. E., Wilkie, O., and Lopez, A. (1990). Category-based induction. *Psychological Review, 97*, 185–200.

Proffitt, J. B., Coley, J. D., and Medin, D. L. (2000). Expertise and category-based induction. *Journal of Experimental Psychology: Learning, Memory, and Cognition, 26*, 811–828.

Rattermann, M. J., and Gentner, D. (1998). The effect of language on similarity: The use of relational labels improves young children's performance in a mapping task. In K. Holyoak, D. Gentner, and B. Kokinov (Eds.), *Advances in analogy research: Integration of theory and data from the cognitive, computational, and neural sciences* (pp. 274–282). Sofia: New Bulgarian University.

Rips, L. J. (1975). Induction about natural categories. *Journal of Verbal Learning and Verbal Behavior, 14*, 665–681.

Sloman, S. A. (1993). Feature-based induction. *Cognitive Psychology, 25*, 231–280.

Stavy, R., and Wax, N. (1989). Children's conceptions of plants as living things. *Human Development, 32*, 88–94.

# 12

# Language for Thought: Coming to Understand False Beliefs

Jill G. de Villiers and Peter A. de Villiers

## 12.1 Propositional Attitudes

*Propositional attitudes* is the term used by philosophers of mind to label those hypothetical states of mind in which we formulate our lay theories of psychology and explanations of action, both for ourselves and for others. We say that we *know* that today is Friday, or that we *believe* that the train leaves at 2 p.m., or that we *worry* that the deadline is near, or that we *hope* that the editor is forgiving. We explain others' behavior and traits in like terms: Frances *worries* that her daughter is growing up too fast; Stephen *believes* he is likely to win promotion; Harold *knows* that he has to pay that bill. This past century has seen the field of psychology struggle with the need for such terms: Can they be dispensed with, in a purely functional analysis of behavior? Can they be dispensed with, in a mature neuroscience? We are not addressing these deeper issues in this chapter, though if asked, we would answer no. We ask simply, how does the child develop a theory of propositional attitudes, and is there any evidence that such a theory is more than talk? That is, does the child's conception of mind play any mediating role in how the child acts toward other people, or in predicting how other people will act?

On one account, the child might come to act toward others, or predict how they will act, without benefit of any "theory" couched in propositional attitude terms. Over time, the child comes to describe why he acted in such a way, or why he predicted such and such a behavior, in the culturally prescribed way, in terms of beliefs, fears, knowledge, desires, and the like. On this account, children should show implicit understanding of other people's actions before they can explicitly describe why they acted in that way or predict their actions on such an explanatory basis. Obviously, the implicit understanding of action might then be something we share with other social primates, who might lack the means of expressing propositional attitudes, but not the fundamental understanding of why others act as they do. Perhaps such an implicit theory is based on empathy, or simulation of what I myself would do if faced with such a set of circumstances. None of this would require the language of propositional attitudes: that is only necessary for explicit reasoning. A young child might understand others implicitly, and then over time come to formulate an explicit theory based on the language of the culture around him.

We have no doubt that the above account is partly true. In particular, we consider the evidence compatible with such a position in the case of such elementary propositional attitudes as *intend to, desire for*, and probably simple emotions such as *fear of*. There is evidence from the developmental psychology literature and from animal behavior that nonverbal infants and primates (at least) can figure out what another conspecific is *intending* to do, what he *wants*, and what he is *afraid of*— provided that those attitudes are premised on a shared world view (see, e.g., Cheney and Seyfarth 1990; Meltzoff, Gopnik, and Repacholi 1999; Tomasello 1996) But the case of *belief* is another story, as has been recognized for several decades. Dennett (1983) and Premack and Woodruff (1978) argued convincingly that the real test that a creature has a "theory of mind" rests on the ability to understand that another person or animal has a *false* belief. In such a case, the person being observed is behaving under a false premise: he is acting in a way that is inconsistent given what the observer perceives to be true of the world. For example, a person is looking fruitlessly in the wrong place for something he wants, or he is acting in a way oblivious to a danger the observer can see, or he is acting toward an object in a bizarre way as if it were something else entirely. Instead of writing off such an individual as crazy, or being puzzled and revising our conception of the world as we know it, we might typically say, respectively, "Oh, he doesn't know his wife moved his sandwich," or "Oops, he doesn't realize that chair is broken," or "He mustn't know that it's a candle, not a real apple."

Having a "theory of mind" entails using such propositional attitude ascriptions in our understanding of the individual's behavior, and by "understanding" we mean predicting how the individual will act, explaining why the individual acted like that, or just describing the behavior in psychological terms rather than purely behavioral ones. The latter two features are restricted to language-using creatures, but "prediction" need not be verbal: the holder of an implicit theory of mind might move in anticipation to the place where the deluded individual will go, or take evasive action if danger will result from the impending mistake. Thinking up such scenarios and their behavioral consequences is the occupation of creative-minded ethologists who take Dennett (1983) seriously on the question of assessment of intentionality expressed by other creatures, but ambiguity in interpreting an animal's behavior is still endemic. The point is that in the arena of false beliefs, the particular content of the propositional attitude ascription is critical to the understanding, because it is content that is not simply reflected in the observer's own world view. The observer and the observed do not share a simple object of desire, of fear, or of belief, such that the observer can simply empathize. Instead, the observed individual has a *mis*apprehension, a *mis*perception, a belief at variance with the observer's world view, and that must be represented as such for the observer to proceed to predict.

Does the language that we use to describe our understanding of others' behavior fool us into thinking that we use such an explicit theory as we watch these events? Ryle (1949) and Skinner (1974) thought so. If so, the language of propositional attitudes is just so much ad hoc justification, and in another culture, or in a different psychology, it could easily be formulated some other way.

However, if the language of propositional attitudes is capturing some truth of the matter about how we reason about false beliefs, then the predictions are entirely different. On this less obvious account, if propositional attitudes capture the reasoning we use to figure out why people act when they hold a false belief, then only creatures with sufficient reasoning ability could make successful predictions about others' actions. What is "sufficient reasoning ability"? On some accounts, it is representational, couched in the inner calculus of thought, perhaps as Fodor (1979) calls it, the "language of thought." For Fodor, thinking is necessarily propositional and symbolic even in animals and infants, and logically prior to natural language but equally complex in its capacity for representing meanings. For Fodor, then, a nonverbal creature could also formulate a theory of mind using the propositional attitudes as internal representations for predicting how others act. Nevertheless, Fodor (1992) acknowledges that there may be processing limitations that restrict either animals or younger humans from reaching a mature reasoning about false beliefs: limitations that are external to the representational system itself.

Alternatively, and controversially, not only are propositional attitudes the appropriate way to describe our internal representations, but "sufficient reasoning ability" is defined by having language of the appropriate degree of complexity: mental verbs, with tensed complements expressing propositions about the world (J. G. de Villiers and P. A. de Villiers 2000; Segal 1998). On this view, an individual with less language or no language would not be able to formulate the appropriate representation of another person holding a false belief and hence would have no basis for reasoning about that person's actions. Such an individual not only would fail to give adequate explanations of why someone acted strangely (lacking the terms in which to express it to our satisfaction), but also would fail to show evidence of understanding why that person acted the way he did. In other words, no *prediction* would be possible.

Why on earth would people hold such a view? First, the empirical evidence might have driven them to it, and we will try to excuse ourselves on that basis, though of course the interpretation of empirical evidence is never beyond question. Theoretical persuasions and background also pave the way. So, second, such a view might just be defensible within a computational theory of the mind in which language plays an enabling role for representations. This view has been formulated in a variety of ways by theorists as diverse as Bickerton (1995), Carruthers (1996), Jackendoff (1996), and Karmiloff-Smith (1992), though not as specifically as we do here.

In what follows, we try to formulate this position as clearly as we can, in the *belief* that precision is what leads to progress, and in the *fear* that it might also lead to an immortal place in the Hall of Fame of laughable and easily debunked ideas. We start with some empirical background and some alternative ways of interpreting the data, before we return to the specific account that we favor.

## 12.2   Children's Theory-of-Mind Development

Our goal in this chapter is thus to describe some new findings relating language and thought in the area of false-belief reasoning. Children are said to achieve a representational theory of mind when they have the ability to understand that other people might have false beliefs, beliefs that do not coincide with their own or with external reality as they see it. For example, if a character in a story does not see a desired object moved to a new location, where will he then search for this object upon his return? Or, if this character is seen searching in the old location, why is he doing that? The classic finding is that 3-year-olds predict that the character will go to where the object now is, neglecting the role that his false belief plays in accounting for his behavior (Wimmer and Perner 1983). By 4 years of age, most children predict the character's false belief and use it to predict and explain his subsequent actions. A minor industry of research on theory of mind has sprung up over the past 20 years, and many fascinating and clever experiments have revealed aspects of children's conceptual and social reasoning that were previously unknown (for reviews see, e.g., Astington 1993; Lewis and Mitchell 1994; Mitchell 1996; Mitchell and Riggs 2000). A theory of mind is considered central to children's conception of the social world and to their predictions and explanation of others' behavior. This extends to mastery of narrative discourse skills, since a child who has an immature theory about characters in a story will fail to appreciate, or tell, satisfying stories, being caught in the landscape of "action" rather than that of "consciousness" (Bruner 1986). A failure to reach a mature theory of mind is also considered a ground-breaking analysis of the core problem in autism (Baron-Cohen 1995; Baron-Cohen, Leslie, and Frith 1985; Baron-Cohen, Tager-Flusberg, and Cohen 2000; Leslie 1991).

Explanations for the changes in the child's theory of mind are just slightly less numerous than the studies undertaken within this framework, but they generally fall into four types. One approach stresses the modular properties of a special-purpose theory of mind mechanism

(ToMM) that matures during the first two to three years of life (Leslie 1994) and can be selectively damaged in disorders such as autism. Having a theory of mind is essentially innate, and the emergence of children's reasoning based on those concepts reflects the interaction between maturation of the ToMM and a variety of other developing cognitive skills (see also Fodor 1992, for a similar argument for the innateness of theory of mind). In particular, Leslie (1994) suggests that the ToMM works in conjunction with a more general-purpose selection processor (SP) that feeds information or premises to the reasoning about mental states. Thus, performance on the standard false-belief tasks is interpreted as primarily a function of the demands that those tasks make on executive functioning (in particular, the inhibition of a bias to respond to the false-belief questions with reality).

A second approach, simulation theory, emphasizes children's privileged access to their own mental states. It is suggested that as children develop an understanding of both the separation from and the similarity between themselves and other people, they come to understand others' mental states and consequent actions by analogy to what they themselves experience and do in similar situations—by simulation (e.g., Harris 1992). It is the abstractness and complexity of the simulation required—for example, appreciating the sources of causation of mental states—that determines the point at which children can master reasoning tasks about other people's false beliefs.

A third major class of theories proposes that a basic conceptual change in children's representation of mental states occurs around the age of 4 and is tapped by the standard false-belief tasks. A cluster of reasoning tasks that require metarepresentation of mental states (i.e., children's ability to reflect on or represent the content of their own and others' representations of events) are mastered at this point in cognitive development (Astington and Gopnik 1991; Perner 1991b; Wellman 1990). A subset of these accounts of theory-of-mind development are termed "theory-theory," because they take seriously the analogy of the child's development in this domain to theory building in other knowledge domains, such as the sciences (see, e.g., Gopnik and Wellman 1992, 1994). The child is seen as forming a network of connected concepts about hypothetical entities (mental processes and representations) on the basis of evidence from observing behavior in social and communicative interaction. These "theories" of mind change as different types of evidence are perceived and need to be accommodated and as the child's cognitive capacities grow.

Finally, the fourth approach finds that the term *theory* is too strong or that it carries too much excess conceptual baggage from its colloquial usage. It stresses nontheoretical, direct interpersonal or social knowledge (Hobson 1991). This knowledge about others' minds is elaborated as the child interacts socially and communicatively, but it is not abstract or theory-like. Conceptual development is seen as more continuous and context sensitive, and the idea of a stagelike or general conceptual change around age 4 is rejected. Instead, the cultural- and experience-specificity of the child's knowledge and reasoning is emphasized. Nelson (1996) criticizes the emphasis on studies of false-belief reasoning, claiming the experimental tasks are far from representative of everyday interpersonal problems children must deal with daily in their social world with familiar adults and children. She objects that the standard tasks tend to be relatively object oriented: where something is placed; what is in a box; how someone is predicted to behave with respect to objects, not in social settings with respect to people.

Empirical tests that clearly distinguish among these alternative theories are sparse. So researchers' allegiance to any one of them seems to be based largely on commitments to general theories of child development and learning, or on epistemological preferences concerning the nature of cognitive representations in children and the need to postulate innate constraints on development. The different theoretical accounts are also somewhat short on specific processes or mechanisms for the change in children's reasoning in the prototypical false-belief reasoning tasks that seems to occur around age 4. Hence, there has been a great deal of recent interest in two processes that may play a central role in that change: the development of executive functions for the planning and control of behavior, and the acquisition of language in which to encode and communicate mental state concepts.

Executive functions are basically problem-solving skills that consist of three principal components: working memory to enable the problem to be represented and kept in mind; flexible selection between, and following of, embedded rules; and inhibitory control to reflect on the options before producing the first response that comes to mind. These processes would seem to be good candidates for the major task-demand features of the classic tests of false-belief understanding. And indeed each has been found in various studies to be significantly correlated with preschoolers' performance on those tasks, even when the effects of age and/or IQ are partialed out (Carlson, Moses, and Hix 1998; Davis and Pratt 1995; Frye, Zelazo, and Palfai 1995; Gordon and Olson 1998; Hughes 1998). However, each of these components has also been claimed to be the *real* underlying causal variable while the others are derivative. The problem is that the correlations come and go from study to study depending on how many and which particular set of false-belief and executive function tests are used, and on how widely the children's scores vary on the different tasks. Many of these skills change considerably in this period of preschool development, so it is not surprising that significant correlations are found among them, but it is very difficult to tease them apart in the usual cross-sectional developmental research paradigm. We will address some possible solutions to these methodological problems in later sections in which we describe our research on the possible roles of language.

## 12.3   A Causal Role for Language of the Mind?

Since the earliest work on theory of mind, researchers have been intrigued by the relationship between theory-of-mind achievements and language development. Around the same time that children are acquiring the ability to monitor others' knowledge and beliefs and desires, they are also using language about mental states, such as verbs of desire, belief, and knowledge. Such talk is generally absent from 2-year-olds' conversation but increasingly common among 3-year-olds (Bartsch and Wellman 1995; Bretherton and Beeghly 1982; Shatz, Wellman, and Silber 1983). If language reflects preoccupations and cognitive achievements in other domains, this would not be too surprising, but the timing is odd: children seem to be engaged in such talk before they pass the classic tasks (Bartsch and Wellman 1995). Two possibilities emerge for reconciling this discrepancy:

1. The children's spontaneous language is actually not as rich as the language required in the tasks. Bartsch and Wellman take this possibility very seriously and divide up the children's spontaneous speech into genuine references to mental state, in particular false beliefs, and other references to true beliefs, or "opinion markers" such as "I think I'll have an apple." Even with these qualified analyses, there is evidence in at least some children for false-belief references about one year earlier than the classic false-belief tasks are normally passed. Unfortunately, these children were not tested on reasoning about false beliefs, because their transcripts (in the computerized CHILDES database) were often collected decades earlier.

2. The tasks make other cognitive demands, and these demands are not present when children spontaneously describe false beliefs in their natural environments. It seems evident that in spontaneous speech children choose the moment, and when we choose it, as experimenters, their performance is less adequate.

Other studies have tried to link language and false-belief performance in the same children studied over time. Could language be a prerequisite rather than a reflection of cognitive change? In a longitudinal study of toddlers, Farrar and Maag (1999) found that language abilities at 24 and 27 months of age (vocabulary size and grammatical complexity on the MacArthur Communicative Development Inventory) were significantly correlated with theory-of-mind performance on the standard unseen-location-change and unexpected-contents tasks by the same children at 48 months. The correlations remained significant when the effects of age, vocabulary at 48 months (on the Peabody Picture Vocabulary Test), and verbal memory were statistically controlled for. Farrar and Maag suggest that the emergence of language may provide the linguistic tools to understand language about mental states, and so facilitate formation of those concepts. But they also note that the children who were linguistically more advanced at age 2 could also have been more advanced in their general social-cognitive development at that point in time, so the design of their study does not allow any firm conclusions about the causal role of language.

In a much stronger study, Astington and Jenkins (1999) report that levels of syntactic and semantic development (on the Test of Early Language Development) around age 3 predicted later performance on the standard tests of false-belief reasoning around age 4. However, earlier performance on the theory-of-mind tests did not predict later performance on the language test.

Another approach to studying the impact of language acquisition on theory-of-mind development is to look at the effects of language delay on false-belief reasoning. In this approach, deaf children provide a critical test. Many deaf children have significantly delayed language acquisition, but they have age-appropriate nonverbal intelligence and active sociability. Studying their theory-of-mind reasoning can therefore tease out the effects of language acquisition from those of cognitive maturation and engagement in social interaction—of course, to the extent that the latter do not themselves depend on language acquisition. A subgroup of deaf children who have deaf parents are exposed to a full language from birth in the form of a natural sign language, so their language acquisition follows the normal timetable. They therefore provide a control for any effects of deafness per se. If language acquisition plays a central role in theory-of-mind development, then deaf children with delayed language will experience corresponding delays in their understanding and reasoning about mental states.

Several studies of deaf children have reported just such effects:

1. Deaf children with language delay (oral or signing) show a delay of up to several years in their reasoning about the cognitive states (thoughts, beliefs, and knowledge) of others (J. G. de Villiers and P. A. de Villiers 2000; Gale et al. 1996; Peterson and Siegal 1995, 1997, 1999; Steeds, Rowe, and Dowker 1997).

2. Deaf children show comparable levels of performance on highly verbal tests of false-belief reasoning (e.g., the unexpected-contents task) and much less verbal or essentially nonverbal tests of reasoning about cognitive states (J. G. de Villiers and P. A. de Villiers 2000; Gale et al. 1996). So the delayed performance on standard tests of false-belief reasoning does not just result from the language demands of the task itself—the need to follow a narrative or the complexity of the question asked, for example.

3. Deaf children's delay in theory-of-mind reasoning is specific to the representation of cognitive states that do or do not correspond to per-

ceived reality. They do not have general problems with metarepresentation or being able to judge the contents of a physical represention that no longer reflects the scene that is in front of them (P. A. de Villiers, Pyers, and Salkind 1999; Peterson and Siegal 1998).

4. Deaf children who acquire a natural sign language from an early age (because they have a signing deaf relative in the home) are far less delayed in theory-of-mind development compared to deaf children with hearing parents (Peterson and Siegal 1997, 1999). In fact, some studies find that natively signing deaf children with deaf parents are not delayed at all in their understanding of false beliefs (Courtin 2000; Deleau 1996).

## 12.4   Why Might Language Help? Sociocultural Accounts

Here again there are several views that are tantalizingly intertwined. A social/cultural theorist is inclined to see the story in straightforward terms: the child is acquiring the cultural theories about minds, and these include the ways of talking about minds. However, at least three different interpretations are possible here:

1. Language about the mind is the best and quickest avenue of evidence for the child to build a theory about mind and the right explanation of behavior (Perner 2000). Waiting to witness behaviors and make inferences about their causes without hearing an accompanying linguistic description is laborious and unreliable. Language is the best tool for conveying this theory, just as language is traditionally argued to be a successful vehicle for elders to convey the accumulated wisdom of the species to the young, so they don't have to repeat mistakes of the past (only a nonparent could believe this!). On this view, *language is very useful, but not strictly prerequisite*, as it plays no special role in thought itself. It is just the source of evidence. For example, a bright primate might be able to figure some things out with enough experience of social beings, a position that might be adopted by simulation theory, for example. Interestingly, such a view makes it not language itself but experience that needs to accumulate: the language is a means, a vehicle, for conveying the culture's theories, and the child is presumed adept at processing the language to grasp these ideas. So such a view is potentially in keeping with a strong nativist view about language, that it develops

early and that the child reaches adult competence at a young age with no particular need for specialized input or nurturance. The situations that provide the key evidence for others' mental contents need to arise labeled and interpreted by a competent language user, to build the conceptual theory. The conceptual theory, however, is paramount: language is how we talk about it.

Nelson (1996) argues that "the representational potential of interpretive discourse about complex events [is] an important influence on the child's developing understanding of the social world" (p. 304). She proposes a role of language in the development of the "culturally mediated mind," in which the child uses language to re-represent understandings that were first established on the level of direct experience. On her view, the cultural system reflected in adults' ideas about others' mental states (i.e., their collective "folk psychology") becomes available to children as they participate as language users in cultural activities such as games, routines, and especially storytelling. Because thinking is opaque to an observer, the linguistic explanations and interpretation provided by other members of the culture are critical for understanding these "hidden causes" of behavior.

However, on Nelson's account, it is not enough for the child to simply be exposed to the language of mental states in relevant situations to come to an understanding of mental states. The child must have already constructed a model, a system of interpretations, from observations of actions, reactions, and interactions, as well as language uses.

Carruthers and Boucher (1998) distinguish two views of the role of language. The above account maps onto their *communicative* conception of language, in which language is an adjunct to belief and thought, and its purpose is primarily for communicating thoughts from mind to mind. On the other hand is the *cognitive* conception of language, in which language is critically implicated in human thinking. Consider two minor variants of this possibility next.

2. The child is learning to think for speaking, to use an apt expression of Slobin's (1991, this volume). That is, particular cultures have particular ways of talking about the mind and behavior, and the child is learning to think in those acceptable ways as he hears the language used by

others. He comes to use the language and it embodies the cultural theory of mind. His thoughts (at least those he gives voice to) are constrained by these ways of talking, just as they are in his expressions of spatial relations if he is a Tzeltal speaker (Levinson 1996). On this view, *language is a mesh through which the world is viewed*, and whenever tasks require talk about such matters, the child will express the talk in these culturally confined ways. Could there be other ways of thinking? Of course, and they are embodied in other languages. Can we shake off our linguistic mesh and use these ways of thinking? Probably only with difficulty and conscious attention, rather like learning a different phonology. Whether nonlinguistic thinking proceeds under the same constraints is a controversial question from this standpoint, though it certainly seems a possibility, especially if that thinking were to be engaged implicitly, unconsciously. Investigating this question is the emphasis of the present volume, as it was for Benjamin Lee Whorf: can evidence be found of fundamental differences in categorization, or reasoning, by virtue of the conceptualizations embodied in different languages? As we discuss below, the evidence that people have fundamentally different theories of mind by virtue of speaking different languages is controversial.

On this view, the *learning* of language is more prominent, with adherents seeing language learning as the development of a cultural skill, one developed within the framework of social discourse and nurtured by others. Language is intricately entwined with the meanings and concepts it conveys, and the emphasis is on learning by doing. On this view, the idea of a conceptual theory of mind *before* or *without* a particular language makes little sense. This view has echoes of debates in philosophy of science concerning the radical incommensurability of theoretical paradigms (Kuhn 1962; Scheffler 1982). In other words, there is always a language, a set of categories, a symbolic theory, through which one comes to partition and understand the world, and speakers of different languages, like holders of different scientific theories, cannot find a neutral ground because there is no such thing.

3. There is a third alternative, one that dissolves the distinction between thought and language even more completely, by calling thought "inner speech." Vygotsky (1962) suggests that the child acquires lan-

*[handwritten: 10 year old child: unfamiliar = a cold hug, red hug with erratic rhythm.]*

guage and speech through social interaction, and when that speech has been acquired it moves inward to become complex thought:

> The child begins to perceive the world not only through his eyes, but also through speech. As a result, the immediacy of "natural" perception is supplanted by a complex mediated process; as such, speech becomes an essential part of the child's cognitive development. (Vygotsky 1978, 32)

Vygotsky argues that the child goes through a stage that he calls "naive psychology":

*[handwritten left margin: parrot]*

> This phase is very clearly defined in the speech development of the child. It is manifested by the correct use of grammatical forms and structures before the child has understood the logical operations for which they stand. The child may operate with subordinate clauses … long before he really grasps causal, conditional or temporal relations. He masters the syntax of speech before the syntax of thought. (Vygotsky 1962, 46)

Thus, the child acquires language of the mind first because he needs to master it before he can reason about the mind, *using that language as his inner mode of thought* (Garfield, Peterson, and Perry 2000). A child without mastery of the public language about the mind would be unable to reason about such matters as false beliefs, presumably even in non-linguistic tasks.

Implicit or unconscious reasoning raises an interesting question for a Vygotskian. Presumably if language is inner thought, such thought might pass out of the focus of conscious attention, but one should always be able to shift back to it and "hear" it going on. According to this view, one might predict that prediction of behavior should follow explanation or description of false beliefs, because to predict is to engage in explicit (internal language) description and then computation of the behavioral consequences. In fact, Bartsch and Wellman (1989) report just such a priority for mental explanations of the causes of behavior over the classic prediction of what an ignorant or misled character will do. In their study, a puppet character placed an object in one location and then left the scene. While the puppet was gone, the object was moved to another location. When the puppet returned, either the child was asked where he would look for the object (the classic task), or the puppet went to the place where he had put the object (now the "wrong" place) and the child was asked why he was looking there. Preschoolers could explain the

*[handwritten: perceived unfolding threat evokes 'oh!' or a scream. The mind is working faster than it can form grammatical expression.]*

reasons for the action before they could predict it. However, the generality of this result has been questioned (Perner 1991a), and we have been unable to replicate it in our longitudinal research with preschoolers (J. G. de Villiers and Pyers 1997).

Of course, these three theories are starkly described to highlight differences in emphasis among them, and they do not exhaust the possible ways that language as social tool might enable reasoning. Many contemporary theorists have fine-tuned them (Carruthers and Boucher 1997; Garfield, Peterson, and Perry 2001; Nelson 1996; Nelson, Plesa, and Hensler 1998), and it is possible to imagine even more alternatives. For example, the first type of theorist might deny being a nativist about language acquisition; the second type might deny that implicit reasoning can occur; and the third type might say that inner speech can become completely unconscious. But all see language as embedded first and foremost in culture and social discourse, and thereby as the means by which the theory of the mind gets conveyed. The first theorist considers language of the mind to be the source of explicit evidence about mental states; the second argues that the conventional way of talking about minds constrains the language that the child acquires; and the third, that the way society talks becomes the way children talk to themselves internally.

## 12.5 Improving on Sociocultural Accounts

What can possibly improve on such theories? Theorists of almost any stripe can find something appealing here, so why are we dissatisfied? Of course, this is a psychological question, and Freudians would look to our early training: behaviorists converted to cognitive science. What is dissatisfying is that we need a specific account, one that explains just how learning language can enable children to think in ways they couldn't before or without it. We need an account that explains why 4-year-olds typically pass false-belief tasks and 2- to 3-year-olds don't, and why children seem to grasp nonverbal tasks requiring monitoring another's beliefs at the same time as verbal tasks that require overt linguistic responses. If such an account also makes sense of exactly what is out of reach of our primate relatives, who have very good social intelligence but

*there are no lies in the womb.*

so far seem to lack a human-style theory of mind (i.e., one that can accommodate the apprehension of others' false beliefs), so much the better.

In thinking about these questions, we asked, What about language might make it a prerequisite rather than a reflection of cognitive change? Once we know that, we can be more specific in our predictions and in our tests. We contended that vocabulary wasn't likely to be the key, because it doesn't have enough representational structure to capture a false belief in sufficient detail. Suppose there was a word for someone holding a false belief. In fact, there is: "The man is *deluded*." Would that help us reason about what he would do? No, because it fails to capture the *content* of his delusion, and the content matters for prediction and understanding. Could we add something: "The man is deluded about the candle"? Perhaps, but that emphasizes only the focus of his delusion, and again, the content is missing—how do we know he will eat said candle? We know that once we find a way to represent a proposition like "The man thinks the candle is an apple." Now not only might we predict that he will eat the candle—we also know he won't light it, and we might even expect him to try slicing it or coring it. Notice the language that is required: it consists of a mental verb with a tensed complement; and the complement, the embedded proposition, is false.

The candle is an apple.

Such false statements are legitimate when embedded under propositional attitude verbs, or intentional verbs: *think, believe, know, worry,* and so on. In fact, complements have a special status in that the complement can be a false proposition without making the proposition expressed by the whole sentence false. While it is *false* that

The candle is an apple,

it is *true* that

He thinks *the candle is an apple.*

Other types of clauses—for example, adjuncts that are not embedded in the same hierarchical manner under a verb—must contain true propositions or derail the truth of the entire sentence:

He is crying because *the candle is an apple.*

Only language of this degree of structural complexity—namely, a distinction between the complements and adjuncts of complex clauses—is representationally rich enough to capture false beliefs. We reasoned that children should only show appropriate false-belief reasoning once they had acquired the syntax that underlies this distinction. Other evidence of sophisticated vocabulary or other kinds of sophisticated syntax—relative clauses, for example, which involve embedding but not the crucial syntactic/semantic property above—should be irrelevant.

But then we have to be careful not to impale ourselves on the horns of a dilemma: we risk making the result either trivially true or conceptually incoherent.

Consider the dilemma:

1. Suppose we design tasks that call upon linguistic reasoning, such as asking for descriptions or explanations of persons acting under false beliefs, and we give credit only if the child uses false-belief ascriptions. Obviously, complex language is needed for the task, and we have made the result trivially true.

2. We could design the language requirement to encourage false-complement usage in such a way as to require children to understand and formulate a sentence about false belief, but it is conceptually incoherent for them to do so without understanding false beliefs first.

Fortunately, we had some solutions to this dilemma before we began. To solve the first part, we choose false-belief tasks that do not require children to respond by using explicit linguistic complements. For example, we can use "Where will he look?" predictions, or accept "Because he put it there" as an explanation, or, as discussed later, develop tasks that do not require verbal stories or linguistic responses at all.

To solve the second part, we can do two things. First, we can design a task that requires processing or understanding a complement construction in a minimal way, without entailing the ascription or understanding of a false belief. We simply see if children can repeat what they are told when it is couched in the form of a mental verb with a false complement: what we call the *memory for complements* task (J. G. de Villiers and Pyers 1997). Second, we can see if children have mastered false complements with nonmental verbs, such as verbs of communication, that require precisely the same complement structures syntactically and semantically as mental verbs, but with none of the reference to invisible mental events:

He said the candle was an apple.

As J. G. de Villiers (1995b) has argued, communication verbs and their false complements might provide an essential step in the mastery of false complements with mental verbs.

If we can show that mastery of false-complement structures with nonmental verbs, or the ability to hold in memory a mental verb with a false complement, precedes the ability to predict or give nonmental (but adequate) explanations for behavior premised on a false belief, we have avoided being impaled on the horns of the dilemma but have established our case for linguistic prerequisites.

## 12.6   Empirical Research Testing Our Account

These conditions were met in the longitudinal study of 3- and 4-year-olds reported by J. G. de Villiers and Pyers (1997) and J. G. de Villiers and Pyers (in press). In that study, two cohorts of 19 and 9 preschoolers were given a battery of false-belief tasks (of the standard variety, requiring the following of a story in which a character, or the child, has a false belief) and a set of tasks assessing their language. The children were tested four times over the course of a year, beginning between 3 and 3½ years of age and with approximately four months between testing sessions. The linguistic tasks included a few designed to encourage the use of false complements, including simply repeating something communicated or thought by a character couched in terms of a complement. For example:

This girl thinks she has a hole in her pants. But look, it's just a label! *Point back to original picture:* What did the girl think?

Children between ages 3 and 5 get gradually better at answering such questions correctly: for example, "She had a hole in her pants" or "It was a hole." The criterion for passing the task was to answer 10 out of 12 such questions correctly. Notice the task does not require children to "read" a character's mind or to predict or explain action: processing the language and treating the complement as an embedded form is all that is

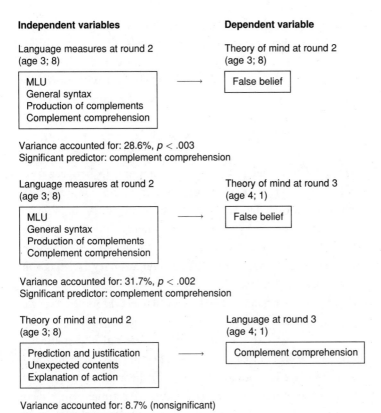

**Independent variables**          **Dependent variable**

Language measures at round 2          Theory of mind at round 2
(age 3; 8)                            (age 3; 8)

| MLU |
| General syntax |
| Production of complements |
| Complement comprehension |

⟶   | False belief |

Variance accounted for: 28.6%, $p < .003$
Significant predictor: complement comprehension

Language measures at round 2          Theory of mind at round 3
(age 3; 8)                            (age 4; 1)

| MLU |
| General syntax |
| Production of complements |
| Complement comprehension |

⟶   | False belief |

Variance accounted for: 31.7%, $p < .002$
Significant predictor: complement comprehension

Theory of mind at round 2          Language at round 3
(age 3; 8)                         (age 4; 1)

| Prediction and justification |
| Unexpected contents |
| Explanation of action |

⟶   | Complement comprehension |

Variance accounted for: 8.7% (nonsignificant)
Significant predictor: None

**Figure 12.1**
Linear regression analyses of predictors of false-belief reasoning in a longitudinal study of 28 preschoolers tested over the course of a year from age 3; 4 to age 4; 5. Language predicts false-belief reasoning but not vice versa.

required, not mind reading. The results of several types of analyses, but in particular, linear regressions, showed that being able to process false complements was the best predictor of how children performed on false-belief tasks at a later point in time, but not vice versa (see figure 12.1). Furthermore, the linguistic ability was specific to complements, not to mastery of other complex sentence forms revealed in the children's spontaneous speech.

Hence, the data from normally developing children are at least consistent with the claim that mastery of syntactic complementation, specifically *that* clauses that permit a false complement, is a prerequisite for, and the best predictor of, understanding false beliefs. Of course, this is only the beginning of the story. We have to ask, This may be the way it is in mainstream American culture, and in English, and with normally developing 4-year-olds. But could it be otherwise? We take two further paths at this point: our work looking at older children who are language delayed but otherwise normal, and other work looking at variations across cultures.

For some years we have been studying the relationship between language and oral deaf children's reasoning about emotions, desires, false beliefs, and states of knowledge (J. G. de Villiers and P. A. de Villiers 2000; P. A. de Villiers et al. 1997; P. A. de Villiers and Pyers 2001; Gale et al. 1996). We have now extended those studies to deaf children acquiring American Sign Language (ASL) as their primary language in preschool and early school years.

In collaboration with Brenda Schick and Robert Hoffmeister, we undertook a comprehensive study of theory-of-mind reasoning in deaf children aged 4 to 8 years from a variety of educational and linguistic backgrounds (P. A. de Villiers et al. 2001). The subjects were 86 deaf children from oral-only educational settings with hearing teachers, and 90 deaf children from intensive ASL educational settings with deaf teachers. Hearing loss for all of the children was prelingual, and they all scored in the normal range on three different tests of nonverbal intelligence. All except two of the oral children had hearing parents. Among these children, unaided hearing losses varied from 47 to 120 dB (mean = 92 dB): 53 of them wore hearing aids while the remaining 33 had cochlear implants. Forty-nine of the signing children had deaf parents and 41 had hearing parents. Among these children, unaided hearing loss ranged from 45 to 120 dB (mean = 90 dB). The children with different parental and educational backgrounds were approximately equally distributed across the four age levels: 4, 5, 6, and 7 years.

The children were tested on a battery of nonverbal intelligence, theory-of-mind, and language assessments in several sessions over a two-week span. The theory-of-mind tasks included several versions of the standard verbal tests of false-belief reasoning widely used with hearing children (we will call these the *high-verbal* tasks). First, there were three picture-supported unseen-object-location-change stories (Wimmer and Perner 1983; as revised by Gale et al 1996 for use with deaf children) in which the children were asked both where an uninformed character would first look for the moved object and why the character would look there. Second, for two familiar containers with unexpected contents the children were asked both to recall their own initial false belief before they looked in the box, and to judge what a friend would first think was in the box before looking in it (Perner, Leekam, and Wimmer 1987).

In addition, the children participated in two games with considerably fewer verbal requirements that were designed to tap into their reasoning about states of knowledge/ignorance and the beliefs or expectations of a character (we will call these the *low-verbal* tasks). One of these was a sticker-hiding game in which the children had to decide whose advice to take about the location of a sticker that had been hidden (out of sight of the child) in one of four identical boxes (see P. A. de Villiers and Pyers 2001; Gale et al. 1996). On each trial, the question was, did the child choose the box pointed to by an adult who had watched where the sticker was hidden or the one pointed to by an adult who had been sitting, blindfolded, on the child's side of the screen that obscured the hiding? If children understood that seeing leads to knowing, and that knowing translates into accurate advice, they should always choose to follow the adult who did the watching.

The second game consisted of sequences of six pictures telling a simple story about two characters (the pictures very clearly related the events so that no verbal narrative was needed). A key character either watched an unusual object being substituted for the familiar contents of a distinctive container (e.g., a Crayola crayon box) or did not see the substitution made. The child's task was to complete the final picture in the sequence by choosing which face (on a transparent overlay) to put on the key character when he opened the container and revealed the unusual object. Depending on the character's expectations, he could either be "surprised" (a face with a characteristically surprised expression) or "not surprised" (a neutral face). This low-verbal task was therefore modeled after the standard high-verbal unexpected-contents task. Our earlier research showed that these two low-verbal tasks were passed at about the same age and were significantly correlated with performance on the standard verbal false-belief reasoning tasks for both hearing children and oral deaf children (P. A. de Villiers and Pyers 2001; Gale et al. 1996).

Spoken-language assessments for the oral deaf children included one-word vocabulary comprehension (on the Peabody Picture Vocabulary Test–Revised) and production (on the Expressive One-Word Picture Vocabulary Test), as well as a standardized test of the understanding of spoken English sentence syntax (the Comprehensive Evaluation of Language Function Preschool Sentence Structure subtest). Short videoclips of people (and a dog) engaged in a variety of actions and interactions were used to elicit production of sentences with verbs of desire (*want*) and cognitive states (*think* and *know*). The children were asked to describe what happened in the video and also why characters did what they did (especially when they made mistakes out of ignorance or having a false belief) (P. A. de Villiers and Pyers 2001). Processing of false-complement clauses was assessed in the simple procedure described above in which the children were asked to repeat what a pictured character had thought or said even though it had been revealed that the character was mistaken about the represented event or object (J. G. de Villiers and Pyers 1997). Finally, two short narratives were elicited with silent videotaped cartoons, both of which incorporated instances of mistakes and deception.

The ASL production and comprehension of the deaf children from the intensive signing educational settings were also extensively assessed. This assessment included sign vocabulary comprehension, comprehension and production of classifiers, and comprehension of various other features of ASL syntax. The signing children also produced ASL sentences with references to communication and mental states. Two narratives were elicited with the same pictures and videoclips used with the oral children. Finally, the children's processing of embedded false-complement clauses in ASL was assessed with a translation of the complement-sentence-processing procedure described above.

Thus, three different aspects of the language of both the oral and the signing children were evaluated: their vocabulary development, their general syntactic comprehension, and more specifically their processing and production of false-complement clauses with verbs of communication and cognition.

Several key features of the study represent considerable improvements over prior research on theory of mind in deaf children. First, we tested a substantial sample of young deaf children comparable in age to the hearing children tested in previous research. Second, the various theory-of-mind reasoning tasks were all translated into ASL by native signers, and all of the testing of the signing deaf children was carried out directly by deaf researchers using fluent ASL, not through an interpreter. Third, we used both the standard verbal false-belief reasoning tasks and much less verbal (or nonverbal) tasks to assess the children's theory-of-mind development. The use of low-verbal tasks allows the effects of the language requirements of the tasks themselves to be isolated and controlled for. Finally, most previous studies of theory of mind in deaf children have taken only general and inadequate measures of the children's language skill, or none at all. Our study included extensive assessments of the children's language and specifically tested the children's receptive and expressive mastery of embedded false-complement clauses.

Three major results from the study argue that language plays a fundamental role in the conceptual development of the deaf children in this domain of social cognition:

1. The performance of the ASL-signing children with deaf parents (ASL-DoD) on the standard false-belief reasoning tasks was comparable to that of hearing preschoolers of the same age (Wellman, Cross, and Watson 1999). These deaf children had early natural language input and had acquired fluent complex ASL by age 4 to 5 years.

2. The reasoning about false beliefs of the ASL-signing children with hearing parents (ASL-DoH) and of the oral deaf children, both of which groups were delayed in their language development, was significantly worse than that of hearing preschoolers on the same tasks. This was true both for the standard tasks that involve complex language in their administration—such as the unexpected-contents task—and for the surprised-face game that had very low verbal task demands but required the same reasoning about expectations and beliefs. On each of these tasks, the native-signing ASL-DoD group performed significantly better than the other two groups of deaf children, for whom language acquisition was delayed, although the groups were well matched in age, hearing

**ASL (DoD) vs. ASL (DoH) vs. Oral (DoH) -- Verbal FB scores**

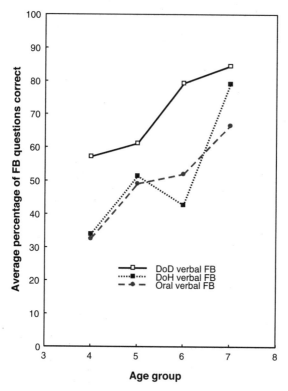

**Figure 12.2**
Comparisons on various measures of false-belief (FB) and other theory-of-mind (ToM) reasoning between three groups of deaf children varying in language background. DoD children have deaf parents; DoH children have hearing parents. (From P. A. de Villiers et al. 2001.)

loss, and nonverbal IQ and memory measures. Figure 12.2 compares the three groups of deaf children on two measures of their theory-of-mind reasoning: the percentage of false-belief questions answered correctly (out of seven false-belief questions that were asked across the verbal tasks), and the average number of theory-of-mind tasks that the children passed at each age. The latter measure included five theory-of-mind tasks: the unseen-location-change stories, two versions of the unexpected-contents task (own belief and a friend's belief), the sticker-hiding game, and the surprised-face game.

**ASL (DoD) vs. ASL (DoH) vs. Oral (DoH) -- Number of ToM tasks passed**

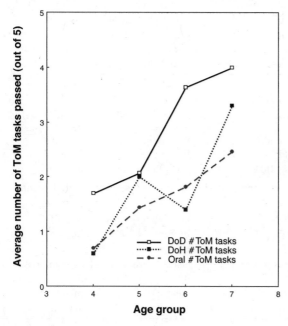

**Figure 12.2**
(continued)

3. Third, multiple regression analyses were carried out separately for the ASL-signing children and the oral English-speaking deaf children to determine which of various independent measures were significant independent predictors of performance on the theory-of-mind tasks. Tables 12.1 and 12.2 show that there were remarkable similarities in the predictors of theory-of-mind reasoning for the two groups of children despite the differences in syntax and modality between ASL and spoken English. For both signing and oral children the most reliable predictors of theory-of-mind reasoning were language measures—in particular, vocabulary size and the processing of embedded false-complement clauses. For both groups, hearing loss, nonverbal IQ, and basic syntactic skills (not including complements) were never significant independent predictors of theory of mind.

These data suggest a crucial role for language in the development of a mature theory of mind, particularly false-belief understanding. It must be

**Table 12.1**
Linear multiple regressions predicting theory-of-mind measures for oral deaf children. Predictor variables: age, hearing loss, nonverbal IQ on the DAS Pattern Construction, sequence memory on the Knox's Cubes test, one-word expressive vocabulary (EOWPVT), basic sentence syntax comprehension (CELF-Preschool), and processing of embedded complements. (From P. A. de Villiers et al. 2001.)

|  | Total verbal false-belief score /7 | Number of low-verbal tasks passed /2 | Total number of theory-of-mind tasks passed /5 |
|---|---|---|---|
| Linear multiple regression | $r^2 = .48$ $F(7,67) = 8.8$ $p < .001$ | $r^2 = .34$ $F(7,67) = 4.8$ $p < .001$ | $r^2 = .61$ $F(7,67) = 17.5$ $p < .001$ |
| Significant predictors | complements $(p = .02)$ vocabulary $(p = .000)$ | complements $(p = .015)$ vocabulary $(p = .013)$ | complements $(p = .005)$ vocabulary $(p = .000)$ |
| Nonsignificant measures | age hearing loss IQ memory syntax | age hearing loss IQ memory syntax | age hearing loss IQ memory syntax |

said that this does *not* mean that language-delayed deaf children are like autistic children, because these two groups exhibit very significant differences in early theory of mind. Deaf children are sociable and interested in people, gesture readily, and follow eye-gaze to establish joint referencing (J. G. de Villiers et al. 1993; Goldin-Meadow and Mylander 1984), unlike autistic children (Baron-Cohen 1995). What is absent in deaf children with limited exposure to language is the syntactic device of complementation, found to be the most consistent predictor of their failure on all the false-belief tasks.

Let us evaluate what this might mean for the various theories. If these tasks require merely a linguistically expressed theory about the mind for explanation and justification, it might be argued that the deaf children have had limited exposure to talk rich enough to grasp that theory (Peterson and Siegal 1999). It should be noted that the vocabulary measure could be considered a proxy for how much linguistic input the children have taken in, and it indeed predicts their success at false-belief tasks.

**Table 12.2**
Linear multiple regressions predicting theory-of-mind measures for ASL-signing deaf children. Predictor variables: age, hearing loss, nonverbal IQ on the DAS Pattern Construction, sequence memory on the Knox's Cubes test, one-word receptive vocabulary, basic sentence syntax, and processing of embedded complements. (From P. A. de Villiers et al. 2001.)

| | Total verbal false-belief score /7 | Number of low-verbal tasks passed /2 | Total number of theory-of-mind tasks passed /5 |
|---|---|---|---|
| Linear multiple regression | $r^2 = .48$ $F(7, 78) = 10.4$ $p < .001$ | $r^2 = .52$ $F(7, 78) = 12.0$ $p < .001$ | $r^2 = .65$ $F(7, 78) = 20.1$ $p < .001$ |
| Significant predictors | complements $(p = .039)$ vocabulary $(p = .005)$ | complements $(p = .004)$ age $(p = .012)$ | complements $(p = .000)$ vocabulary $(p = .002)$ |
| Nonsignificant measures | age hearing loss IQ memory syntax | hearing loss IQ memory syntax vocabulary | age hearing loss IQ memory syntax |

But the complement measure independently predicts how the children perform on the verbal and nonverbal tasks, suggesting that performance on those tasks is also mediated by some linguistic or linguistically triggered representation. If language were merely the best source of evidence for a theory of mind, we might expect some delay in acquisition if children have to work it out without much language, but we would not expect the tight relation between their performance and the specific language skill of mastering false complements.

Furthermore, the children's low-verbal and high-verbal task performances are generally highly correlated, so it does not seem to be the case that some children have figured out the theory nonverbally but still can't express it, and other children have figured out how to talk the talk but don't yet use it in prediction or to control their choices on less verbal tasks. Instead, the data are just what one would expect if the acquisition of complementation in language—in particular, the mastery of false complements—made possible the representation of certain relationships, those holding between people's minds and states of affairs, that were inaccessible or incomplete before.

Two challenges emerge for our account: the potential for implicit reasoning in the absence of language, and cross-cultural variation in developing theories of mind.

## 12.7    The Possibility of Implicit Reasoning

The obvious and essential questions to address concern the potential for implicit reasoning in the absence of language, reasoning that might escape these requirements of linguistic propositional representation. Notice that we have failed to find such evidence in our studies of the deaf children, despite the use of low-verbal procedures in which one might have expected implicit reasoning to show up. There are a small number of deaf children in our studies with virtually no use of complex language who passed the sticker-hiding task by our criterion; however, since those same children failed the other low-verbal task, the surprised-face task, it is possible that their performance is to be expected from a normal distribution around chance responding. For example, another small number of children got fewer than 2 out of 10 right on the same task, that is, below chance! But it is also possible that these children hit on a partial solution to the task that falls short of full theory-of-mind reasoning. The task requires the child to pay attention to who knows and who doesn't know where the sticker is hidden, and to take the knower's advice on where to find it. It does not require computation of false beliefs, strictly speaking, just that seeing leads to knowing and knowing leads to good advice. But it is also possible to use a simpler strategy, if you catch on quickly enough over the first few trials, such as "The blindfold is always wrong." The two solutions can be distinguished with enough controls, such as changing the blindfold to a paper bag, or having the ignorant adult leave the room while the sticker is hidden. Chimpanzees who were successful on this task after extensive training proved to be using the more stimulus-bound strategy and had to learn the task all over again when the circumstances changed (Heyes 1993; Povinelli, Nelson, and Boysen 1990). Thus, they could not be said to be computing something as abstract as "He sees, therefore he knows, where the object is hidden." We did not put our child subjects through this more rigorous test.

Clements and Perner (1994) report implicit false-belief reasoning in children just before they pass the standard tasks and, at least theoretically, before they have the linguistic prerequisites, though language was not assessed. It is worth considering this result because it is also mirrored in a task carried out in the laboratory by Hauser (1999) with tamarin monkeys, a suspiciously ill-equipped species for high-level reasoning, and no candidate at all for language. The results point to some important precursors to a mature theory of mind that must be taken into account, as well as useful cautions about interpretation and controls.

Clements and Perner's study combined a highly verbal task with a nonverbal behavioral measure of false-belief understanding. Unlike our study, where both the "story" and the performance demands are nonverbal, Clements and Perner's study presented children with a highly structured verbal story—containing lines like "So she picked up the cheese and walked, fully visible, across the hill to the other mouse hole where she put the cheese"—as well as an acted-out scenario of the classic unseen-location-change task. In the explicit response version of the story, they asked the standard question, "Which box will the mouse look in for his cheese?" (the mouse being the unknowing character, and the cheese having been moved by another character). On this task, the children showed the classic result, with the majority passing around 4 years of age. However, with the same children they also used an implicit, nonverbal response version of the task. In this version of the task, Clements and Perner said simply, "Here comes the mouse. I wonder where he will look for his cheese?" They then videotaped the child's eye-gaze to see which mousehole the child looked at first, one near the place where the cheese used to be, or one near the box containing the newly moved cheese. By this nonverbal performance measure, children at a much younger age (2; 11) were likely to gaze at the mousehole where the mouse would emerge, given his false belief.

Because this is an important result, it is worth examining closely. In fact, the children did not look at the box where the mouse would look for his cheese, but at the entrance to one of two tunnels from which they expected the mouse to emerge (above the box where he placed his cheese). As it happens, this was also the place where the mouse last disappeared, so alternative explanations might arise. Fortunately, the experimenters had a clever control (the important SEE control promoted by Leslie (1994)): namely, a situation in which the mouse watched the cheese get moved to the new location before he went into his house. In that condition, the children did not look at where the mouse last went, but where they expected him to come out, near the new location of the cheese. Together, then, the results belie the counterexplanation. Surely the children could only succeed if their eye-gaze was being driven by their expectations, which in turn could only be being driven by their understanding where the mouse should emerge given his beliefs. Dienes and Perner (1999) contend that this is an example of implicit knowing: the reasoning is entirely below conscious understanding and only capable of driving fundamental actions such as gaze direction, not explicit action such as answering questions. The latter awaits a full representational maturity, about a year later.

If this is so, the position we have taken about the causal role of language in the development of false-false belief reasoning must be considerably weakened, to refer not to *any* reasoning but only to explicit answering. Then why does the sticker-hiding game not call upon the same implicit understanding—just because the child commits with a pointing/reaching gesture to the box that hides the sticker?

Consider in addition the results Hauser (1999) obtained with his definitely nonverbal tamarin monkeys. Obviously, the scenario they witnessed had to be entirely nonlinguistic. The tamarin watched an experimenter (A) take a bite of an apple (a desired object). He gave the monkey a piece of the apple and then placed the rest of it in a covered box. Experimenter A then left the room and experimenter B moved the apple to a second covered box. Experimenter A then returned and went either to the first box or to the second. The measure taken of the tamarins' expectations is not prediction, but excitement/attention measured by differential looking time to the two conditions. The basic finding is that the monkeys look longer when experimenter A's behavior is unexpected to us—for example, looking in the place where the apple now is, rather than where the experimenter left it. On the face of it, this looks again like implicit false-belief understanding, this time indexed through looking time, not direction. Again, Hauser used a SEE control in which experimenter A was present and watching when experimenter B moved the apple. In the SEE control condition, the monkeys were more attentive when experimenter A looked in the empty box, which was now counter to expectations based on his knowledge of the apple's whereabouts.

At first blush, this is a troubling finding for our theory that complex language is a prerequisite for false-belief reasoning. However, further experimental conditions studied by Hauser question the extent to which the tamarins were really computing the experimenter's beliefs or states of knowledge. The monkeys showed a paradoxical stimulus-boundness similar to that of Povinelli's chimpanzees (see also Povinelli and Giambrone, in press, for a broader analysis of the failure of primates to infer states of knowledge). Conditions in which experimenter A stayed in the room but was blindfolded or turned his back elicited the same results as the SEE control condition, as if the tamarins paid no attention to experimenter A's state if he was present. Hauser argues that something short of full false-belief reasoning is going on here: he suggests that the tamarins are able to monitor "behavioral/attentional focus" and that they apparently use this focus to drive their expectations. Much work is currently being done in this area that points to the importance of careful controls, especially when something as fragile as looking time is the measure in a relatively unconstrained situation. One possibility raised by Hauser's results is this: When a tamarin encounters an individual, it evaluates that individual's states of desire/intention. This is particularly important if these states coincide with the tamarin's own state, and in this case that coincidence was emphasized, as experimenter A fed the tamarin a piece of the apple before placing it in the box. When experimenter A leaves the room and the apple is moved, the tamarin follows the actions with interest but they do not require updating the mental "file card" representing what experimenter A desired/intended. When experimenter A returns, the tamarin reactivates that file card and expects certain behavior consistent with it—namely, moving to the apple's old location. In the SEE control, the apple is moved in full view of both experimenter and monkey, and the tamarin notes the new focus of experimenter A's interest. But when experimenter A stays in the room but

not accounted for:

SB-e
Smell
eye
Teeth

is denied access to the information, the tamarin fails to monitor his knowledge state at all. Perhaps this is just processing overload caused by monitoring experimenter B as well, though both are also present during the SEE control.

Suppose the children in Clements and Perner's study were operating under a similar set of attentional guidelines, that is, "Remember where people last directed their behavior, and expect them to maintain it during an absence." This would drive eye-gaze toward the last place the mouse directed his own eye-gaze/behavior, coinciding with the right answer as the setup was arranged. But what an odd psychology that would be! It's not a bad start, but it can very easily go awry—for instance, if the individual's physical presence is considered enough to count as seeing, an assumption the tamarins apparently fell for. The fact that the children were told a richly linguistic story, with minimal puppets playing the role of the characters, makes the comparison between the two studies more difficult to make.

In our own laboratory, we have struggled with a much less verbal version of Clements and Perner's task conveyed by human actors on videotape, also measuring eye-gaze direction. Our goal was to develop a version that could be used with nonverbal deaf children, so we minimized the verbal story support by having live-action humans hamming it up. Unfortunately, we misunderstood Clements and Perner's original finding, on the basis of, for example, this statement by Perner:

Additional evidence against executive function problems in the false belief task is provided by the finding that children show awareness of the false belief *by looking at the correct location where the protagonist thinks the object is*, before they can answer explicitly with the correct location (Clements and Perner, 1994). (Perner 1998, 297; italics ours)

We mistakenly believed that the children in their study were differentially gazing at the box where the mouse might look, and we thought it was important to separate that clearly from the place where the mouse emerged. We therefore arranged for the (human) mouse to come out in a central location before moving to the box. While the mouse was still behind the scenes, we said, "Here comes the mouse! I wonder where he's gonna look?" and we measured the child's eye-gaze in one or the other direction. The results were quite disappointing. Children's eye-gaze following this prompt was no more correct than was their explicit pointing to the boxes following the subsequent question "Where's he gonna look for his cheese?" In addition, the children failed to process the story on the video, so that getting them to pass the control memory questions (e.g, "Where did the mouse first put the cheese?") was like pulling teeth. Either Hauser has the right idea with a tasty piece of live-action apple, or Clements and Perner do with a richly verbal story structure. It was hardly the case that the 42 children in our doomed pilot were inattentive: their eyes were glued to the screen, but we have no idea where their minds were.

We are apparently not alone in our misunderstanding of Clements and Perner's result: Hauser (1999) also misdescribes it in his paper (p. 183). Dienes and Perner (1999) describe the finding only slightly less ambiguously in saying, "A majority of these children look (visual orienting response) *in anticipation of the protagonist at the empty location* where the protagonist mistakenly thinks the object is" (p. 748; italics ours). But why would the children be able to look expectantly at the point of the mouse's reemergence, but not at the box where he might look? Dienes and Perner (1999) argue that the eye-gaze reveals a purely behavioral expectation: implicit knowing, not the result of explicit computation across representations. They take the stance that implicit understanding falls short of a theory of belief and is based purely on observing behavioral regularities. They suggest that the child has learned that certain events go together. That is, a statistical patterning of possible combinations produces associative expectations without explicit predication: it is not *about* anything. So the child can *anticipate* correctly where the protagonist will go to get the desired object without explicitly *representing* that he will go there. This "anticipatory pattern completion" can trigger a nonreflective action schema or guide visual orientation. This implicit knowing is replaced by a theory of belief that incorporates a causal understanding that is flexibly available across scenarios, agents, and so forth. Once the theory of belief emerges, the representational content becomes available for counterfactual reasoning.

Goldin-Meadow and Alibali (1999) provide an important discussion of the difference between eye-gaze and gesturing as signs of implicit knowledge. They argue that gestures lie on a continuum, with one extreme being totally implicit. For example, in moving a pointing hand to a target (visually guided movement) there need be no explicit predication or factuality: the gesture is not *about* anything, and the gesture can be unconscious. Other gestures can be both predication and factuality explicit: for example, knowingly pointing to an object, or to a location to indicate where an object is. Thus, Dienes and Perner (1999) can argue that the visual orienting responses in Clements and Perner's study are both factuality and predication implicit—they are not about anything. Despite appearances, the eye-gaze is not directed to the goal; it is not an answer to the rhetorical question "I wonder where he will look?" but simply an anticipation of the protagonist's path. However, the children's pointing gestures in our nonverbal sticker-hiding game are explicit indications of their beliefs about the location of the sticker, and therefore are unlike the spontaneous eye movements.

Dienes and Perner (1999) connect their distinctions to the levels of knowing discussed by Karmiloff-Smith (1992), who also places implicit, purely procedural knowledge at one extreme and conscious, verbally accessible and reportable knowledge at the other. For us, the question revolves around how sophisticated the procedural knowledge can get. Karmiloff-Smith permits a level of knowing called "Explicit I" in which the information originally available only as limited procedural knowledge becomes accessible to other processing systems, though still not conscious or verbalizable. In Dienes and Perner's terms, this level is called predication explicit, but factuality implicit.

The question that arises is whether such *flexible* reasoning about beliefs is possible without the representational change made possible by complex language. Such reasoning would require explicit predication on Dienes and Perner's model. To summarize the evidence so far:

1. Clements and Perner's young subjects could shift eye-gaze to the potential path of the protagonist, contingent on his past behavior, his desires, and possibly his belief state.

2. In a later experiment, the subjects could (only if quickly and "nonreflectively") move a mat to the place where a protagonist might emerge, again contingent on his past behavior, his desires, and possibly his belief state.

3. Hauser's tamarins gazed longer at a protagonist who did something out of keeping with his past behavior, his desires, and possibly, but only primitively, his belief state.

4. In our pilot study, children did not look selectively at the goal place in anticipation of the protagonist's moving there, a failure also found by others (J. Perner, personal communication).

5. Pointing to the place where the protagonist will look shows no advantage over answering verbally: implicit knowing does not support pointing.

6. Ruffman (2000) trained children to place bets on an outcome (i.e., how probable it was that the protagonist would look in one place or another), but implicit knowing did not support betting.

7. In our sticker-hiding task, neither hearing nor deaf children below the critical language level could choose a hiding place contingent on a protagonist's knowledge state.

Given the data surveyed, it seems improbable that younger children's (or other less verbal beings') procedural theory of beliefs extends to the level that can be called "predication explicit" (Dienes and Perner 1999), entailing that the goal be represented in a flexible manner accessible to reasoning and action. At best, the form of implicit knowledge of beliefs that emerges early in children and is seen in other primates may drive eye-gaze and/or looking time connected to the protagonist's expected behavior, but not to the subjects' action schemas such as reaching, pointing, betting, or choosing, all of which pattern with verbal responses. The one possible exception to this rule is the observation (2, above) that children will move a mat in anticipation of the protagonist's path.

So the results on implicit false-belief reasoning are tantalizing, but controls are essential. Refinement of these in both animal studies and studies of young children may help to clarify just what is implicit knowledge in this domain, and in which ways it is less sophisticated than the more explicit kind of knowledge that emerges reliably in children several months later. It would also be extremely useful to have detailed linguistic measures on the same children: Clements and Perner's "implicitly knowing" children are the same age as that given for the first reports of genuine complements with mental verbs in Bartsch and Wellman's (1995) studies of spontaneous speech. Perhaps understanding in each domain first emerges at this earlier age, with reliable performance solidifying several months later.

Let us raise the possibility that we are completely wrong, and we are merely trying to downplay the importance of implicit reasoning. Suppose the social theorists of language are right. Everybody, including social creatures like tamarins who can read humans, develops an implicit theory of mind that is noncomputational and procedural rather than declarative. In addition, and overlaid on this, we humans—at least those of us who have appropriate access to language as our culture uses it—acquire a way of talking that embodies this particular lay psychology. This explicit theory augments and partly enhances the implicit understanding, making it more reliably available and resistant to distraction and confusion (e.g., Nelson 1996). Then further questions arise:

1. Is implicit knowing always a prerequisite? Suppose autistic children fail to develop the procedural knowledge, being inattentive or unable to make sense of behavioral regularities of others. If such children were to learn enough language to support reasoning by explicit description of beliefs, could they succeed via that route? (Tager-Flusberg 1999)

2. Why are language-delayed children so poor at the nonverbal tasks? Why do deaf children not simply maintain their grasp on implicit reasoning? In fact, why don't they show steady improvement, given that they need to monitor visual social cues so carefully? Can procedural knowledge become flexible and predication explicit through practice alone?

3. What if the culture doesn't have a lay psychology like ours? Is any linguistic encoding enough to reach explicit knowledge? That brings us to the issue central to this volume: cultural variation.

## 12.8 Cultural Variation

This chapter should not be included in a volume of this sort if we do not face up to the Whorfian challenge and ask, are there significant cross-linguistic differences in false-belief reasoning as a function of the languages spoken in particular cultures? Lillard (1998) and Vinden and

Astington (2000) provide interesting reviews of the range of cultural interpretations of mind and behavior, many of which differ greatly from our standard Western lay-psychology conceptions of internal mental states mediating causally between environment and action. For example, many people in the Pacific islands group give a purely externalist account of behavior, referring not to mental states as explanations but to environmental causes. Other cultures invoke internalist explanations having to do with possession by witches or spirits. If children acquire their fledgling theories of mind by learning to talk the talk of their particular culture, then variation should be the norm and there should be little evidence of universality. On the other hand, if there is some universal core of understanding of the mind, such as reading intentions, desires, and false beliefs, then one might expect universality in these matters to the extent that the tasks themselves do not invoke explanatory concepts of a higher order. These higher-level explanatory concepts might be a cultural overlay, much like the variety of theories in psychology revealed in the past 500 years of writing on the subject in Western culture. Whether we follow Locke or Freud or Skinner or Frege on the nature of mental states may not influence where we, or 4-year-old children around the world, expect Maxi to look for his chocolate. The explanations we give for Maxi's choice, however, may vary depending on our larger psychological or epistemological theory.

What does cross-cultural evidence suggest? Unfortunately, little on which we can hang a conclusion, primarily because the data are sparse. Ideally, a relevant study would include (1) assessment of the child subject's language development and (2) theory-of-mind tasks with varying language requirements, from prediction through explanation. Though the existing studies have taken extraordinary pains to make the tasks culturally appropriate through choice of materials, use of native speakers as experimenters, careful translation of instructions, and so forth, they still fall short of the ideal.

There is little enough cross-cultural work on false-belief reasoning, and even less that speaks to the role of language, or the properties of the language, in those cultures that have been studied. For example, early work by Avis and Harris (1991) on the Baka people in Cameroon using a culturally modified version of the unseen-location-change task revealed that children in that culture master the relation between false belief and emotions at the same general age as children in Western literate cultures. Unfortunately, we know nothing about the Baka's language for mental events or the lay psychology of the culture. Two major types of questions emerge about language variation in this domain, one pertinent to the social/cultural theory, the other to the universality of complementation for representation.

For example, might there be cultures that hold no special theories of the mind—no reference to internal events, intentions, desires, or beliefs? If such a culture exists, it would provide a very interesting test of the present hypotheses, because surely there would be no means by which children could develop the representational structures for reasoning about the mind, on anybody's theory except perhaps Leslie's (1994) or Fodor's (1992). Vinden and Astington (2000) review some evidence from non-Western cultures like those of Samoa and the Baining people of Papua New Guinea in which external causes of behavior are invoked in place of internal causes specific to an individual. Vinden (1996) points also to the lack of internal state descriptions among speakers of Junin Quechua in Peru, one of several Quechua languages that have no separate words for mental states like belief; instead of a word corresponding to *believe*, they use the Junin Quechua counterpart of *say* (Adelaar 1977). Vinden also contends that little conversation in the culture concerns intentions, desires, and beliefs, and that the speakers of Junin Quechua may operate in daily life in the landscape of events that Bruner (1986) describes as prior to the landscape of consciousness in Western children's narrative thought. Vinden's work among the Junin Quechua suggests a significant delay in the acquisition of false-belief understanding. A majority of the children were still failing the (culturally modified) classic false-belief tasks (unexpected contents) at 8 years old, although they commanded the appearance-reality distinction at a considerably younger age. Vinden (1999) also found evidence of significantly delayed false-belief reasoning in other non-Western cultures, from Cameroon to Papua New Guinea. In the absence of more information about the languages and about conversations between adults and children in natural circumstances, and without either language measures or nonverbal tasks, it is premature to interpret this finding within our framework. It remains possible that there are cultures that do not offer the linguistic input necessary to support false-belief reasoning, or at least offer it so infrequently as to prolong the stages of acquisition. We find this unlikely, but we may be suffering from ethnocentrism. Vinden and Astington (1999) mention Warren (1995) as reporting that the Kaqchikel Mayans say that others' motivations and feelings are unknowable, using the phrase "Each mind is a world." But is this so far from possible-world semantics in current Western linguistics?

More weakly, suppose there are cultures in which it is just "not done" or impolite to refer to others' beliefs, thoughts, desires, and so forth. How could a child develop an understanding of the mind through language in such a culture? Japan is purportedly such a culture, yet the data collected by Matsuo and Hollebrandse (1999) and Hasegawa (2000) suggest that 4-year-old Japanese speakers are able to pass the classic false-belief tasks at ages comparable to those of children in the United States and that they readily understand and use references to others' states of mind.

More particularly, there is linguistic controversy over the status of complements in other languages. For example, the adjunct/complement distinction is debated in Japanese (Matsuo and Hollebrandse 1999); and there may exist languages in which there is no structural equivalent to complementation, but only "direct speech" under a verb of communication. These crosslinguistic issues are deeply important, but very little is known for certain. Researchers in the Chomskian tradition take it as given that languages all have equivalent structural and semantic complexity—in particular, that all languages have to have the special semantics that occur under intentional verbs (Wierxbicka 1992, cited in Bartsch and Wellman 1995). Frankly, rather little is known about the syntax of complex clauses in languages that are very different from English. That is in part why we are so interested in ASL: complementation in sign languages seems markedly different from complementation in English, and we may make progress on some of these very tricky issues through studying ASL learners. For example, ASL permits "role shifting," a device rather like direct speech quotation, to mark an utterance (or a belief) as belonging to another character. Yet early reports suggest role shifting is not a device that children adopt at the start: they prefer the more orthodox structure consisting of communication/mental verb + content (J. Pyers, personal communication). Japanese has adverbs corresponding to English *unintentionally* and *mistakenly*, and children learn them quite early, but apparently not until after they learn embedding under mental verbs (Hasegawa 2000). This constitutes only a flimsy basis for arguing for the universality of our account, and we hope to see much more work that addresses these issues cross-culturally and cross-linguistically.

We need to demonstrate that although languages, cultures, and subcultures vary in kind of talk and amount of talk about mental events/explanations of behavior, in all cases the key ingredient is present in the language to which children are exposed, hence buffering them against the vagaries of such variation for developing this critical human skill (Allen, de Villiers, and François 2001). We are as yet in no position to defend the possible universality of such a claim.

## 12.9    Back to Theories

We have argued that language provides humans with something more than a means of expressing culturally acquired theories about mental states and behavior. We contend that the linguistic structures of embedded complements have the right degree of representational richness for capturing false beliefs, and this representational advantage pertains to reasoning, not just justification and explanation. We have used data from normally developing children and from language-delayed deaf children to make our case, though several empirical findings remain unsettled and much experimentation remains to be done. We will turn now to a theoretical exposition by Jackendoff (1996) that we find congenial to our point and that nicely illustrates how the social and cognitive accounts of the role of language might intersect.

Jackendoff (1996) expresses a theory of the relationship between language and thinking that is very close to the one we are developing, though his is broader in scope. He contends that language provides a "scaffolding" that makes possible certain varieties of thought more complex in nature than those available to our nonverbal cousins in the animal kingdom. Like us, he completely agrees that complex chains of

Vygotsky

reasoning can occur without linguistic expression, and in nonverbal creatures (Fodor 1975). But he also attempts to analyze what conscious-ness is, and he wishes to argue that language is conscious while thought is not. That is, thinking proceeds in an unconscious realm, and when it is manifest in linguistic form it becomes conscious—that is, when we catch ourselves in the act of thinking. Thus, the form of conscious experience is driven by the forms of language. Jackendoff accepts that much of the mind is modular, but argues that interface modules must do the translation between thoughts and linguistic form, or visual imagery and thought. Since these translations are not perfect, we do not experience (have con-scious access to) everything we think.

*recollection or image is thought.*

But none of that requires language to do anything more special than influencing our conscious experience. It does not play any role in the reasoning itself. Jackendoff goes on to make a stronger claim: that in three particular ways, language also helps thinking. The first way reflects the social-constructivist arguments above: namely, that language, in its role as the means of communicating, permits the sharing of past history and current gossip and scientific and social theories, all of which are in-accessible to creatures that are limited to the here and now (Nelson 1996).

The second way that Jackendoff claims language influences thinking derives from his theory that conscious experience is made possible through linguistic expression, so that an animal, let's say a monkey, has no experience of the chains of abstract reasoning, no inner voice, no ability to plot. Jackendoff gives an example based on behavioral ethology work by Cheney and Seyfarth (1990), who demonstrated that a monkey that is attacked will often retaliate by attacking a monkey related to the attacker. But the conscious reasoning that might accompany this act in a human must be lacking from the monkey's experience. For example, Jackendoff argues there can be no nonlinguistic representation of doing some act "for a reason"—the notion of causation is available to us humans only linguistically, not through a visual image for example. This is an extremely interesting and controversial argument that we will not pursue further here. But it still involves no particular influence of language on thought. It is just a variant of the traditional account of language giving voice to existing thoughts. However, Jackendoff goes on to claim that because language provides a way to bring to consciousness abstract parts of thought that are inaccessible through other means, it can then focus attention on such aspects and bring higher-power processing to bear on them. The linguistic expression then serves as a handle for focused attention:

> Language is the only modality of consciousness in which the abstract and relational elements of thought are available as separable units. By becoming conscious, these elements of thought become available for attention. Attention in turn refines them, both by anchoring and drawing out details, and also by concretizing or reifying conceptual units that have no stable perceptual base. (1996, 24)

The third aspect of Jackendoff's theory is equally relevant to our arguments. He argues that humans subject percepts to valuations:

Did I see that before or is it new?    *comparators*

Was that a dream or did it really happen?    *interesting. What about sleep-walking*

Did I mean to do that or was it an involuntary movement?

Through language, we can give the valuations that accompany perception and action some palpable form, and we can embed them:

Why do I think that was a dream?

If I believe that, shouldn't I also revise my position on such and such a theory?

Metareasoning of this sort, given form by linguistic expressions attached to valuations, opens up realms of thinking and reasoning inaccessible to nonverbal beings. In particular, language becomes a means of attaching a truth or a certainty value to our beliefs. Echoes of the same view are found in different forms in the work of Bickerton (1995), who emphasizes how language opens up the new possibility of reflective or "offline" thinking. And a sociocultural theorist such as Nelson (1996) allows that complex language provides a way to represent contrast between reality and nonreality, both in communicating with others and in eventually understanding one's own mental states.

So Jackendoff shares our conception that language provides a means of representation of abstract relations, and he also provides a glimpse of a model that might connect language in important ways to consciousness and attention. Let us make concrete how it would connect to theory-of-mind reasoning.

As mentioned above, for Jackendoff, the first role of language in thinking maps onto the social theorist's view that language embodies the cultural views of the mind and explanations of behavior. This other members of the community convey to children through linguistic communication, just as they transmit theories of the cosmos or of biology or religion.

The second is very similar to the view we have presented in which language makes possible the representation of a world that is counter to the world that corresponds to our perceptual experience: the world in which propositions we find false can be held as true by another person. This is the embedding of propositions in the form of complements under mental verbs, the syntactic structure of which is the same as the embedding of propositions under verbs of speech, and which could be acquired through that less opaque medium.

This makes more specific the position advocated by Karmiloff-Smith (1992). In Karmiloff-Smith's theory, cognitive development proceeds in stages, from purely procedural knowledge to implicit knowledge to explicit (conscious) knowledge, usually verbal. An explicit theory-of-mind equivalent to Perner's (1991b) metarepresentational stage is the outcome of a process of "redescription" into different representational formats. Karmiloff-Smith argues that the acquisition of the terms themselves for mental states, desires, and so forth, may be essential to this redescription process because the linguistic representations provide a privileged format for encoding propositional attitudes. Language is crucial because it "scaffolds" the symbolic representation. Thus, 3-year-olds fail at standard tasks because their rudimentary symbolic representations are not sufficient to override "experience-based" interpretations. All we would add is that it is not just symbols for the terms that change this representational capacity: it is crucially the syntax of complementation that increases the power.

The third or evaluative use of language in thinking is the one that theory-of-mind tasks call upon when they ask such questions as "How do you know?"; but it may be required even in such tasks as unseen-location-change, if the child proceeds by conscious reasoning about why the character will act the way he does and gives a suitable justification. Of course social theorists can claim this as their own too: it could be argued that we humans learn what is an acceptable justification and explanation via our shared culture, and do not construct it for ourselves.

The very interesting questions that remain concern trying to identify the contribution of each of these types of linguistic "assistance" in a given task, and much experimental ingenuity will be needed to do so. The ideal demonstration would show that providing children with the critical linguistic ingredient makes a sudden change in their reasoning abilities, a finding not predictable by the accretion of experience/learning by doing/learning to talk that way. A training study by Hale and Tager-Flusberg (2000) approximates this ideal. Their 3-year-old subjects changed from failing to passing false-belief tasks after a short amount of training on processing complements with communication, not mental, verbs. However, the children in their study who trained directly on false-belief tasks also improved, so the result is far from conclusive.

In sum, significant questions remain about how language influences false-belief reasoning. We have proposed a specific prerequisite, but how it achieves its effects is still unclear. It is also very evident that more work is needed on implicit false-belief reasoning and exactly where it falls short of an explicit theory of mind. Crosslinguistic work on styles of talk about the mind and specific encoding of intentional terms is also a significant area of need. But the direct assistance that language provides to thinking in this domain of social cognition seems hard to deny.

## Note

Preparation of this chapter was supported by NIH grants R01 HD32442 and R01 DC02872 to the authors.

## References

Adelaar, W. F. H. (1977). *Tarma Quechua*. Lisse: Peter de Ridder Press.

Allen, B. A., de Villiers, J. G., and François, S. (2001). Deficits versus differences: African American children's linguistic paths towards a theory of mind. In M. Almgren, A. Barreña, M.-J. Ezeizabarrena, I. Idiazabal, and B. MacWhinney (Eds.), *Research on child language acquisition: Proceedings of the 8th conference of the International Association for the Study of Child Language.* Somerville, MA: Cascadilla Press.

Astington, J. (1993). *The child's discovery of the mind.* Cambridge, MA: Harvard University Press.

Astington, J., and Gopnik, A. (1991). Theoretical explanations of children's understanding of the mind. *British Journal of Developmental Psychology, 9*, 7–31.

Astington, J., and Jenkins, J. (1999). A longitudinal study of the relation between language and theory-of-mind development. *Developmental Psychology, 35*, 1311–1320.

Avis, J., and Harris, P. (1991). Understanding reasoning among Baka children: Evidence for a universal conception of mind. *Child Development, 62*, 460–467.

Baron-Cohen, S. (1995). *Mindblindness.* Cambridge, MA: MIT Press.

Baron-Cohen, S., Leslie, A., and Frith, U. (1985). Does the autistic child have a Theory of Mind? *Cognition, 21*, 37–46.

Baron-Cohen, S., Tager-Flusberg, H., and Cohen, D. J. (Eds.). (2000). *Understanding other minds: Perspectives from developmental cognitive neuroscience* (2nd ed.). Oxford: Oxford University Press.

Bartsch, K., and Wellman, H. M. (1989). Young children's attribution of action to beliefs and desires. *Child Development, 60*, 946–964.

Bartsch, K., and Wellman, H. M. (1995). *Children talk about the mind.* New York: Oxford University Press.

Bickerton, D. (1995). *Language and human behavior.* Seattle: University of Washington Press.

Bretherton, I., and Beeghly, M. (1982). Talking about internal states: The acquisition of an explicit theory of mind. *Developmental Psychology, 18*, 906–921.

Bruner, J. (1986). *Actual minds, possible worlds.* Cambridge, MA: Harvard University Press.

Carlson, S. M., Moses, L. J., and Hix, H. R. (1998). The role of inhibitory processes in young children's difficulties with deception and false belief. *Child Development, 69*, 672–691.

Carruthers, P. (1996). *Language, thought and consciousness: An essay in philosophical psychology.* Cambridge: Cambridge University Press.

Carruthers, P., and Boucher, J. (1998). *Language and thought: Interdisciplinary themes.* Cambridge: Cambridge University Press.

Cheney, D. L., and Seyfarth, R. M. (1990). Attending to behaviour versus attending to knowledge: Examining monkeys' attribution of mental states. *Animal Behaviour, 40*, 742–753.

Clements, W. A., and Perner, J. (1994). Implicit understanding of belief. *Cognitive Development, 9*, 377–395.

Courtin, C. (2000). The impact of sign language on the cognitive development of deaf children: The case of theories of mind. *Journal of Deaf Studies and Deaf Education, 5,* 266–276.

Davis, H., and Pratt, C. (1995). The development of children's theory of mind: The working memory explanation. *Australian Journal of Psychology, 47,* 25–31.

Dennett, D. (1983). Intentional systems in cognitive ethology: The "Panglossian paradigm" defended. *Behavioral and Brain Sciences, 6,* 343–355.

Deleau, M. (1996). L'attribution d'états mentaux chez les enfants sourds et entendants: Une approche du rôle de l'expérience langagière sur une Théorie de l'Esprit. *Bulletin de Psychologie, 3,* 1–20.

de Villiers, J. G. (1995a). Questioning minds and answering machines. *Proceedings of the Boston University Conference on Language Development, 19,* 20–36.

de Villiers, J. G. (1995b). *Steps in the mastery of sentence complements.* Paper presented at the meeting of the Society for Research in Child Development, Indianapolis, IN.

de Villiers, J. G., Bibeau, L., Ramos, E., and Gatty, J. (1993). Gestural communication in oral deaf mother-child pairs. *Journal of Applied Psycholinguistics, 14,* 319–347.

de Villiers, J. G., and de Villiers, P. A. (2000). Linguistic determinism and the understanding of false beliefs. In P. Mitchell and K. Riggs (Eds.), *Children's reasoning and the mind.* Hove, UK: Psychology Press.

de Villiers, J. G., and Pyers, J. (1997). Complementing cognition: The relationship between language and theory of mind. In *Proceedings of the Boston University Conference on Language Development, 21,* 136–147.

de Villiers, J. G., and Pyers, J. (in press). Complements to cognition: A longitudinal study of the relationship between complex syntax and false-belief understanding. *Cognitive Development.*

de Villiers, P. A., de Villiers, J. G., Schick, B., and Hoffmeister, R. (2001). *Theory of mind development in signing and non signing deaf children: The impact of sign language on social cognition.* Poster presented at the meeting of the Society for Research in Child Development, Minneapolis, MN.

de Villiers, P. A., Hosler, E., Miller, K., Whalen, M., and Wong, J. (1997). *Language, theory of mind, and reading other people's emotions: A study of oral deaf children.* Poster presented at the meeting of the Society for Research in Child Development, Washington, DC.

de Villiers, P. A., and Pyers, J. (2001). Complementation and false belief representation. In M. Almgren, A. Barreña, M.-J. Ezeizabarrena, I. Idiazabal, and B. MacWhinney (Eds.), *Research on child language acquisition: Proceedings of the 8th conference of the International Association for the Study of Child Language.* Somerville, MA: Cascadilla Press.

de Villiers, P. A., Pyers, J., and Salkind, S. (1999). *Language delayed deaf children understand "false" photographs but not false beliefs.* Poster presented at the meeting of the Society for Research in Child Development, Albuquerque, NM.

Dienes, Z., and Perner, J. (1999). A theory of implicit and explicit knowledge. *Behavioral and Brain Sciences, 22,* 735–808.

Farrar, M. J., and Maag, L. (1999). *Early language development and the later emergence of a theory of mind.* Poster presented at the meeting of the Society for Research in Child Development, Albuquerque, NM.

Fodor, J. A. (1975). *The language of thought.* New York: Crowell.

Fodor, J. A. (1992). Discussion: A theory of the child's theory of mind. *Cognition, 44,* 283–296.

Frye, D., Zelazo, P. D., and Palfai, T. (1995). Theory of mind and rule-based reasoning. *Cognitive Development, 10,* 483–527.

Gale, E., de Villiers, P., de Villiers, J., and Pyers, J. (1996). Language and theory of mind in oral deaf children. *Proceedings of the Boston University Conference on Language Development, 20,* Vol. 1, 213–224.

Garfield, J. L., Peterson, C., and Perry, T. (2001). Social cognition, language acquisition and the development of the theory of mind. *Mind and Language, 16,* 494–541.

Goldin-Meadow, S., and Alibali, M. (1999). Does the hand reflect implicit knowledge? Yes and no. *Behavioral and Brain Sciences, 22,* 766–767.

Goldin-Meadow, S., and Mylander, C. (1984). Gestural communication in deaf children: The effects and non-effects of parental input on early language development. *Monographs of the Society for Research in Child Development, 49,* 1–121.

Gopnik, A., and Wellman, H. (1992). Why the child's theory of mind really is a theory. *Mind and Language, 7,* 145–171.

Gopnik, A., and Wellman, H. (1994). The 'theory theory'. In L. Hirschfeld and S. Gelman (Eds.), *Mapping the mind: Domain specificity in culture and cognition.* New York: Cambridge University Press.

Gordon, A. C., and Olson, D. R. (1998). The relation between acquisition of a theory of mind and the capacity to hold in mind. *Journal of Experimental Child Psychology, 68,* 70–83.

Hale, C. M., and Tager-Flusberg, H. (2000). Will training on language influence theory of mind development? *Proceedings of the Boston University Conference on Language Development, 24,* Vol. 2, 391–398.

Harris, P. L. (1992). From simulation to folk psychology: The case for development. *Mind and Language, 7,* 120–144.

Hasegawa, C. (2000). *Acquisition of theory of mind in Japanese children.* Unpublished B.A. honors thesis, Smith College.

Hauser, M. D. (1999). Primate representation and expectations: Mental tools for navigation in a social world. In P. D. Zelazo, J. W. Astington, and D. R. Olson (Eds.), *Developing theories of intention*. Mahwah, NJ: Erlbaum.

Heyes, C. M. (1993). Anecdotes, training, trapping and triangulating: Do animals attribute mental states? *Animal Behaviour, 46*, 177–188.

Hobson, R. (1991). Against the theory of "Theory of Mind." *British Journal of Developmental Psychology, 9*, 33–51.

Hughes, C. (1998). Executive function in preschoolers: Links with theory of mind and verbal ability. *British Journal of Developmental Psychology, 16*, 233–253.

Jackendoff, R. (1996). How language helps us think. *Pragmatics and Cognition, 4*, 1–34.

Karmiloff-Smith, A. (1992). *Beyond modularity: A developmental perspective on cognitive science*. Cambridge, MA: MIT Press.

Kuhn, T. (1962). *The structure of scientific revolutions*. Chicago: University of Chicago Press.

Leslie, A. M. (1991). The theory of mind impairment in autism: Evidence for a modular mechanism of development? In A. Whiten (Ed.), *Natural theories of mind: Evolution, development and simulation of everyday mindreading*. Oxford: Blackwell.

Leslie, A. M. (1994). Pretending and believing: Issues in the theory of ToMM. *Cognition, 50*, 211–238.

Levinson, S. C. (1996). Frames of reference and Molyneux's question: Cross-linguistic evidence. In P. Bloom, M. Peterson, L. Nadel, and M. Garrett (Eds.), *Language and space*. Cambridge, MA: MIT Press.

Lewis, C., and Mitchell, P. (Eds.). (1994). *Children's early understanding of mind: Origins and development*. Hillsdale, NJ: Erlbaum.

Lillard, A. (1998). Ethnopsychologies: Cultural variations in theories of mind. *Psychological Bulletin, 123*, 3–32.

Matsuo, A., and Hollebrandse, B. (1999). The acquisition of sequence of tense in Japanese. *Proceedings of the Boston University Conference on Language Development, 23*, Vol. 2, 431–442.

Meltzoff, A. N., Gopnik, A., and Repacholi, B. M. (1999). Toddler's understanding of intentions, desires, and emotions: Explorations of the dark ages. In P. D. Zelazo, J. W. Astington, and D. R. Olson (Eds.), *Developing theories of intention: Social understanding and self-control*. Nahwah, NJ: Erlbaum.

Mitchell, P. (1996). *Acquiring a conception of mind*. Hove, UK: Psychology Press.

Mitchell, P., and Riggs, K. J. (Eds.). (2000). *Children's reasoning and the mind*. Hove, UK: Psychology Press.

Nelson, K. (1996). *Language in cognitive development: The emergence of the mediated mind*. New York: Cambridge University Press.

Nelson, K., Plesa, D., and Hensler, S. (1998). Children's theory of mind: An experiential interpretation. *Human Development, 41,* 7–29.

Perner, J. (1991a). On representing that: The asymmetry between belief and desire in children's theory of mind. In D. Frye and C. Moore (Eds.), *Children's theories of mind.* Hillsdale, NJ: Erlbaum.

Perner, J. (1991b). *Understanding the representational mind.* Cambridge, MA: MIT Press.

Perner, J. (1998). The meta-intentional nature of executive functions and theory of mind. In P. Carruthers and J. Boucher (Eds.), *Language and thought: Interdisciplinary themes.* Cambridge: Cambridge University Press.

Perner, J. (2000). About + belief + counterfactual. In P. Mitchell and K. Riggs (Eds.), *Children's reasoning and the mind.* Hove, UK: Psychology Press.

Perner, J., Leekam, S., and Wimmer, H. (1987). Three-year-olds' difficulty with false belief: The case for a conceptual deficit. *British Journal of Developmental Psychology, 5,* 125–137.

Peterson, C. C., and Siegal, M. (1995). Deafness, conversation and theory of mind. *Journal of Child Psychology and Psychiatry, 36,* 459–474.

Peterson, C. C., and Siegal, M. (1997). Domain specificity and everyday biological, physical, and psychological thinking in normal, autistic, and deaf children. In H. M. Wellman and K. Inagaki (Eds.), *The emergence of core domains of thought: Children's reasoning about physical, psychological, and biological phenomena.* San Francisco, CA: Jossey-Bass.

Peterson, C. C., and Siegal, M. (1998). Changing focus on the representational mind: Deaf, autistic, and normal children's concepts of false photos, false drawings, and false beliefs. *British Journal of Developmental Psychology, 16,* 301–320.

Peterson, C. C., and Siegal, M. (1999). Representing inner worlds: Theory of mind in autistic, deaf, and normal-hearing children. *Psychological Science, 10,* 126–129.

Povinelli, D. J., and Giambrone, S. (in press). Inferring other minds: Failure of the argument by analogy. *Philosophical Topics.*

Povinelli, D. J., Nelson, K. E., and Boysen, S. T. (1990). Inferences about guessing and knowing by chimpanzees. *Journal of Comparative Psychology, 104,* 203–210.

Premack, D., and Woodruff, G. (1978). Does the chimpanzee have a theory of mind? *Behavioral and Brain Sciences, 4,* 515–526.

Ruffman, T. (2000). Nonverbal theory of mind: Is it important, is it implicit, is it simulation, is it relevant to autism? In J. Astington (Ed.), *Minds in the making: Essays in honor of David Olson.* Oxford: Blackwell.

Ryle, G. (1949). *The concept of mind.* London: Hutchinson.

Scheffler, I. (1982). *Science and subjectivity.* (2nd ed.). Indianapolis, IN: Hackett.

Segal, G. (1998). Representing representations. In P. Carruthers, and J. Boucher (Eds.). *Language and thought: Interdisciplinary themes.* Cambridge: Cambridge University Press.

Shatz, M., Wellman, H., and Silber, S. (1983). The acquisition of mental verbs: A systematic investigation of first references to mental state. *Cognition, 14,* 301–321.

Skinner, B. F. (1974). *About behaviorism.* New York: Knopf.

Slobin, D. I. (1991). Learning to think for speaking: Native language, cognition, and rhetorical style. *Pragmatics, 1,* 7–26.

Steeds, L., Rowe, K., and Dowker, A. (1997). Deaf children's understanding of beliefs and desires. *Journal of Deaf Studies and Deaf Education, 2,* 185–195.

Tager-Flusberg, H. (2000). Language and understanding minds: Connections in autism. In S. Baron-Cohen, H. Tager-Flusberg, and D. Cohen (Eds.), *Understanding other minds: Perspectives from developmental cognitive neuroscience.* (2nd ed.). Oxford: Oxford University Press.

Tomasello, M. (1996). Chimpanzee social cognition. *Monographs of the Society for Research in Child Development, 61,* 161–173.

Vinden, P. G. (1996). Junin Quechua children's understanding of mind. *Child Development, 67,* 1707–1716.

Vinden, P. G. (1999). Children's understanding of mind and emotion: A multicultural study. *Cognition and Emotion, 13,* 19–48.

Vinden, P., and Astington, J. (2000). Culture and understanding other minds. In S. Baron-Cohen, H. Tager-Flusberg, and D. Cohen (Eds.), *Understanding other minds: Perspectives from development cognitive neuroscience.* (2nd ed.). Oxford: Oxford University Press.

Vygotsky, L. S. (1962). *Thought and language.* Cambridge, MA: MIT Press. (Original work published 1934.)

Vygotsky, L. S. (1978). *Mind in society* (M. Cole, Ed.). Cambridge, MA: Harvard University Press.

Warren, K. (1995). Each mind is a world: Dilemmas of feeling and intention in a Kaqchikel May community. In L. Rosen (Ed.), *Other intentions.* Santa Fe, NM: School of American Research Press.

Wellman, H. M. (1990). *The child's theory of mind.* Cambridge, MA: MIT Press.

Wellman, H., Cross, D., and Watson, J. (1999). *A meta-analysis of theory of mind development: The truth about false belief.* Poster presented at the meeting of the Society for Research in Child Development, Albuquerque, NM.

Wierzbicka, A. (1992). *Semantics, culture, and cognition.* Oxford: Oxford University Press.

Wimmer, H., and Perner, J. (1983). Beliefs about beliefs: Representation and constraining function of wrong beliefs in young children's understanding of deception. *Cognition, 13,* 103–128.

# V

Language as Category Maker: Does the Language We Acquire Influence Where We Make Our Category Distinctions?

# 13

# Space under Construction: Language-Specific Spatial Categorization in First Language Acquisition

Melissa Bowerman and Soonja Choi

## 13.1 Introduction

Does language influence nonlinguistic cognition, and do different languages influence it in different ways? Testing these classical Whorfian questions presupposes speakers who are old enough to have mastered the relevant aspects of their language. For toddlers in the very early stages of linking meanings to language forms, we need to ask another question: do the concepts initially associated with language arise solely through nonlinguistic cognitive development, or are they formulated, at least in part, under linguistic guidance?

Establishing where children's early meanings come from—the relative contributions of nonlinguistic cognition and exposure to language—is important to the debate about the Whorfian hypothesis because it provides clues to how flexible—hence how potentially malleable—children's cognitive structuring of their physical and social world is. If the concepts children bring to the language acquisition task are so salient and prepotent that language is simply molded around them, linguistic influences on nonlinguistic cognition seem less likely. Put differently, the more robustly children organize their world according to certain categories of meaning and not others, independently of language, the more resistance language would have to overcome to bring about any restructuring of mental life. On the other hand, if children readily take on the structuring of meaning displayed in the input language, this suggests a receptivity to patterns of conceptual organization introduced from outside that makes Whorfian effects more plausible.

*The push and shove of Whorfian theory.*

*my ideas are under attack!*

Until recently, opinion among developmentalists came down almost unanimously on the side of nonlinguistic cognition as the driving force behind children's early word meanings. The dominance of this position is due in part to its compatibility with the universalist/cognitivist climate *What about* that has reigned more generally in psychology and linguistics over the *w* *pre-birth?* last 30 years (see Bowerman 1989, 2000, for an overview). During the

*feelings* prelinguistic period, children have been portrayed as busy establishing a *light* repertoire of basic notions of objects, actions, causality, and spatial rela-*sounds* tions. As they begin to want to communicate, they are seen as searching *tastes* for the linguistic forms that allow them to express their ideas (e.g., Nel-*smells* son 1974; Slobin 1973). Alternatively (a more recent trend), they are depicted as trying to discover which concept, from among those already available to them, is the one an adult intends by her use of a word (e.g., Gleitman 1990). Within this universalist/cognitivist perspective, there is little room for Whorf.

In the last decade, however, new ways of thinking about the relationship between language and cognition have emerged. Most basically, long-standing arguments for semantic universals—which had been a cornerstone of the universalist/cognitivist approach—have been challenged by a renewed interest in language diversity. Languages are undoubtedly constrained in their expression of meaning, but they are by no means uniform: in every conceptual domain, there are significant differences in the categories of meaning to which words, bound morphemes, and grammatical patterns are linked. Where languages differ, human cognition must be correspondingly flexible, and there is no reason to suppose that just one mode of construal is easiest or most obvious for children (Brown 1965, 317). Indeed, as we will discuss, recent comparisons of children learning different languages show that children adopt language-specific principles of categorization by as early as the one-word stage. Evidence for early mastery of language-specific categories does not, of course, show that the linguistic categories, once acquired, exert an influence on nonlinguistic cognition, but it does set the stage for this possibility. Consistent with this, studies over the last few years have offered new evidence for a variety of Whorfian effects, as discussed in some of the chapters of this volume.

*ling*
*post-birth*
*non-ling*
*Prebirth*

In this chapter, we explore developmental perspectives on the Whorfian hypothesis in the domain of spatial cognition and language. Space may seem like an unpromising domain in which to investigate crosslinguistic semantic variation and its effects on children: spatial words have in fact often been used as prime evidence for the claim that early words map directly to prelinguistic concepts (e.g., Slobin 1973), and the human ability to perceive and mentally represent spatial relationships is undeniably supported and constrained by a host of universal influences, both biological and environmental (e.g., vision, posture, front-back body asymmetry, and gravity—Clark 1973). Recent research shows, however, that languages diverge strikingly in the way they organize spatial meanings—for example, in the spatial frames of reference they use (Levinson 1996, this volume; Pederson et al. 1998) and in how many and what kinds of spatial relationships they recognize (Ameka 1995; Bowerman 1989, 1996a,b; Bowerman and Choi 2001; Bowerman and Pederson, in preparation; Brown 1994; Choi and Bowerman 1991; Wilkins and Hill 1995).

This variation raises challenging questions for developmentalists. By the time toddlers learn their first words, they already have a practical grasp of many aspects of space, including when objects will fall, what objects can contain other objects, and the path objects can follow in moving from one place to another (Baillargeon 1995; Needham and Baillargeon 1993; Spelke et al. 1992). They are also sensitive to certain categories of spatial relationships, such as left-right, above-below, and between (Antell and Caron 1985; Behl-Chadha and Eimas 1995; Quinn 1994, in press; Quinn et al. 1999). What happens, then, when they are confronted with a language-specific organization of space? Do powerful prelinguistic concepts of space initially hold sway, causing children to use the spatial words of their language in accordance with universal "child basic" spatial meanings (Slobin 1985)? Or do children take on the imprint of the local language from the beginning? Thinking for speaking

As with most starkly drawn conflicts between nature and nurture, the answer is not simple: both nonlinguistic cognition and language seem to influence early spatial semantic development, often in interaction. In the following sections, we first briefly summarize evidence for the contribution of nonlinguistic cognition. We then review recent crosslinguistic findings suggesting a role for the linguistic input as well: children use and understand spatial words according to language-specific categories from a very young age. Early sensitivity to linguistic organization might mean that children can construct semantic categories on the basis of the input, but in itself it is not decisive: perhaps it means only that children are good at choosing among alternative concepts made available by non-linguistic cognition. Further evidence for the existence of a construction process, however, comes from error data: patterns of correct and incorrect usage of spatial words differ across languages, and they do so systematically, in ways that suggest that children try to make sense of the distribution of the words in the speech they hear. Category construction of course requires a learning mechanism, and some raw perceptual or conceptual building materials for the mechanism to work on. Our discussion of these elements brings us back to the Whorfian question, and we present evidence from a new study showing that learning a language can affect nonlinguistic spatial cognition by selectively maintaining or discouraging sensitivity to spatial distinctions that are, or are not, relevant to that language. We conclude with a brief sketch of a plausible learning process that could lead to these effects.

## 13.2   Universality and Language Specificity in Early Spatial Semantic Development

### 13.2.1   Evidence for the Role of Cognition

All around the world, children's first spatial words are applied to the same kinds of events: putting things into containers and taking them out, separating things and trying to put them back together, piling things up and knocking them down, donning and doffing clothing, opening and closing objects, climbing on and off laps and furniture, being picked up and put down, and posture changes like standing up and sitting down. Consistent with these preferred topics, early-acquired spatial words revolve around relationships of containment (e.g., for English, *in*, *out*), accessibility (*open*, *close*, *under*), contiguity and support (*on*, *off*), verticality (*up*, *down*), and posture (*sit*, *stand*). Only later come words for proximity (*next to*, *between*, *beside*), and still later words for projective relationships (*in front of*, *behind*) (Bowerman and Choi 2001; Bowerman, de León, and Choi 1995; Choi and Bowerman 1991; Johnston and Slobin 1979; Sinha et al. 1994). This sequence of development is consistent with the order of emergence of spatial concepts established through nonlinguistic testing by Piaget and Inhelder (1956), and this correspondence led to the hypothesis that cognitive development sets the pace in spatial semantic development. The idea was that as new spatial concepts mature, children look for linguistic forms to express them with (Johnston and Slobin 1979; Parisi and Antinucci 1970; Slobin 1973).

Further evidence for the role of nonlinguistic spatial cognition has come from children's under- and overextensions of spatial forms. Words that in adult speech can be used for both motion and static relationships (e.g., *up*, *down*, *in*, *out*) tend at first to be restricted to motion (Smiley and Huttenlocher 1995). Words for the relationships "in front of" and "behind" are initially applied only to things in front of or behind the child's own body; later they are extended to a wider range of reference objects with inherent fronts and backs (e.g., *behind the car*); and still later they are extended to nonfeatured objects (*behind the bottle*) (Johnston 1984). Words applied to actions involving separation are often broadly overextended (e.g., *open* for pulling two Frisbees apart) (Bowerman 1978; Bowerman, de León, and Choi 1995; Clark 1993). Researchers have assumed that systematic deviations from adult usage patterns indicate that children are relying on their *own* concepts, since— to the extent that they are guided by concepts introduced through *adult* speech—their usage should be more or less correct (see Clark 2001 on the reasoning). Later on (section 13.3) we will argue that comparisons of error patterns across languages in fact provide strong evidence for the construction of categories under linguistic guidance. But when children do make errors, their generalizations often proceed along shared cognitive "fault lines"; for example, overextended words for separation in different languages converge on rather similar classes of events.

### 13.2.2 Evidence for the Role of Language

Although on first impression children learning different languages seem to approach spatial encoding in a similar way, closer inspection reveals significant differences. Much of the evidence for crosslinguistic variation in early semantic categorization comes from our work comparing children learning English and Korean (Bowerman and Choi 2001; Choi and Bowerman 1991; Choi et al. 1999). Before showing examples, we must sketch some important differences in how English and Korean classify space. We focus first on "topological" path words applied to motions "in," "out," "on," "off," and so on, and, within this domain, we restrict ourselves to caused rather than spontaneous motion. Later we will look also at the expression of paths "up" and "down." Following Talmy (1985), we refer to the moving or moved object as the *figure* and the object with respect to which it moves as the *ground*.

**13.2.2.1 Spatial Categorization in Adult English and Korean**   In talking about placement of one object with respect to another, English speakers make a fundamental distinction between putting a figure into an enclosure, container, or volume of some kind (*put [throw, stuff, etc.] IN*) and putting it into contact with an exterior (i.e., flat or convex) surface of the ground object (*put [set, smear, etc.] ON*). This classification is illustrated in figure 13.1. The same semantic space is partitioned differently in Korean (figure 13.2).[1] Notice in particular that *kkita* (see middle of figure 13.2), a very early-learned verb, picks out a path category having to do with bringing three-dimensional objects with complementary shapes into an interlocking, tight-fit relationship (a comparison of figure 13.2 with figure 13.1 shows that *kkita* crosscuts the categories of *put in* and *put on*, and extends to some situations that are considered neither "putting in" nor "putting on"). This everyday verb has no English counterpart.[2]

The crosscutting of the domain of *put in* by *kkita* means that what English treats as a unified category of "containment" events is, for speakers of Korean, subdivided (see bottom of figure 13.2): tight-fit containment events like putting a book into an exactly matching box-cover, described with *kkita*, are treated as a different class of actions from loose-fit containment events like putting an apple into a bowl or a book into a bag, described with *nehta*.[3] The category of *nehta* encompasses not only loose containment events but also loose encirclement events, such as putting a loose ring on a pole (not shown). Just as Korean breaks down the category of English *put in*, it also subdivides the domain of *put*

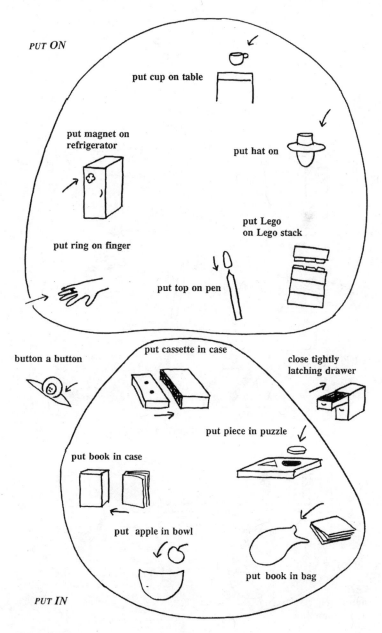

**Figure 13.1**
Categorization of some spatial events in English

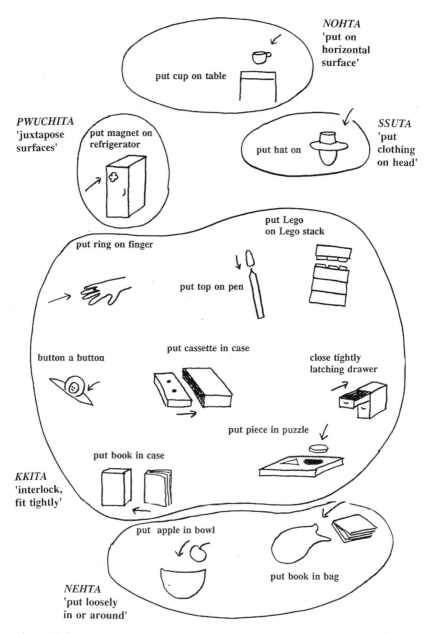

**Figure 13.2**
Categorization of some spatial events in Korean

*on* (top of figure 13.2). Here, the partitioning is more extensive: attaching a figure to the exterior surface of a ground object with a complementary three-dimensional shape (e.g., putting a top on a pen or a Lego block on a stack of Legos) falls into the "tight-fit" category of *kkita*, while juxtaposing objects with flat surfaces (e.g., magnet on refrigerator) is *pwuchita*, depositing a figure on a roughly horizontal surface (e.g., cup on table) is *nohta*, and putting a clothing item on the head is *ssuta* (distinguished from putting clothing on the trunk—*ipta*, and feet—*sinta*).

Notice that all the words shown in figures 13.1 and 13.2 are applied to *topological* relationships—situations of the sort encoded in English by words like *in*, *on*, *together*, and *around* or their opposites—but they focus on topological properties of different kinds. For instance, *put* IN requires the figure to end up in an interior space or volume of the ground, but is indifferent to whether the fit between figure and ground is tight or loose. *Kkita*, in contrast, cares centrally about the fit between a figure and a ground with complementary shapes, but is indifferent to whether this fit is obtained by insertion, covering, surface attachment, or encirclement.

### 13.2.2.2  Spatial Categorization in the Spontaneous Speech of Learners of English and Korean

If children initially associate spatial words with a universal set of basic concepts of space, these differences between English and Korean should not matter: learners of the two languages should interpret and categorize the spatial events of their world in a similar way. But in a study of the spontaneous speech of children age 1–3 years, we found that language-related differences such as those shown in figures 13.1 and 13.2 were in place by as early as 17–20 months (Choi and Bowerman 1991). As soon as the children used the words productively for both familiar and novel situations,[4] learners of English distinguished systematically between actions involving containment (*in*) and those involving surface contact/support (*on*), regardless of fit, while learners of Korean ignored this distinction in favor of a discrimination between tight fit and various loose-fit and loose contact events along the lines shown in figure 13.2. The Korean-speaking children also distinguished, like adults, between putting clothing on the head, the trunk, and the feet—all *(put)* ON for the learners of English. Although figures 13.1 and 13.2 show only acts of "joining" objects (putting in, on, etc.), acts of separation are also treated differently in adult English and Korean, and the children showed sensitivity to these distinctions as well: for example, learners of English discriminated between *out* of a container and *off* a surface, while learners of Korean used *ppayta* 'remove from tight fit' (the opposite of *kkita*), *kkenayta* 'remove from loose containment' (the opposite of *nehta*), and *pesta* 'remove clothing item' (from any body part). In short, when the children talked about spatial events, they classified them in language-specific ways. (Of course, this does not mean that they never made errors from the adult point of view. Errors will be discussed in section 13.3.)

**13.2.2.3 Elicited Production**    Spontaneous speech data offer valuable clues to children's early semantic categories, but comparisons across children and across languages are often indirect, since children do not talk about exactly the same events. To allow for more exact crosslinguistic comparisons and quantitative analysis, we designed an elicited production study to examine how speakers of English, Korean, and an additional language, Dutch, encode actions of joining and separating objects (Bowerman 1996a; Choi 1997). In a playlike setting, we elicited descriptions of a wide range of actions from 10 adult speakers of each language and 10 children in each of three age groups ranging from 2 to 3½ years. The actions included putting objects into tight and loose containers and taking them out, attaching and detaching things in various ways, putting objects down on surfaces, opening and closing, hanging and "unhanging," buttoning and unbuttoning, and putting on various clothing items and taking them off.

To compare the linguistic classification systems of speakers from different language and age groups, we examined which actions they used the same expressions for and which ones they distinguished. The logic is like that used in analyzing sorting task data: actions described in the same way are like stimuli sorted into the same pile; actions described in different ways are like stimuli sorted into different piles. The data can be represented in similarity matrices (for all actions taken pairwise: does the person use the same expression? different expressions?), and these can be analyzed with techniques suitable for similarity data, such as multi-dimensional scaling or cluster analysis (see Bowerman 1996a). If language learners initially map spatial words onto a universal set of basic spatial notions, children at least in the youngest age group (2–2$\frac{1}{2}$ years) could be expected to classify events more like same-age children learning other languages than like adult speakers of their own language. If they classify more like same-language adults, this means that their word use is guided by categories that are already language specific, even though perhaps not yet entirely adultlike.

The outcome of the analyses was clear: from the youngest age group on up, the children grouped and distinguished the actions significantly more like adult speakers of their own language than like same-age children learning the other two languages. As in their spontaneous speech, the children learning English, like the adults in this study, distinguished systematically between events of containment (e.g., putting toys into a suitcase, small cars into a box, and a piece into a puzzle, all described as *[put]* IN) and events of contact/support/surface attachment (e.g., putting a suitcase on a table, a Lego on a Lego stack, a ring on a pole, and clothing onto various body parts, all called *[put]* ON). In contrast, the children learning Korean—also as in their spontaneous speech and like the adults in this study—subdivided events of containment depending on whether they were loose (e.g., toys into suitcase, cars into box: *nehta* 'put loosely in/around') or tight (e.g., piece into puzzle: *kkita* 'interlock, fit tightly'), and they grouped tight containment events with tight surface attachment or encirclement events (e.g., joining Legos, putting a cap on a pen or a close-fitting ring on a pole) (all *kkita*). They also used different verbs, as is appropriate, for putting clothing on the head, trunk, and feet. This study shows that by at least 2 to 2$\frac{1}{2}$ years of age, children learning different languages classify space in strikingly different ways for purposes of talking about it.

**13.2.2.4 Early Comprehension** The studies just discussed establish that learners achieve language specificity very early. But how early? Do they discover the spatial semantic categories of their language only in the early phases of actually *producing* spatial words, or do they begin to work on them even earlier, in pre-production language *comprehension*?

To explore this question, we designed a crosslinguistic preferential looking study to compare very young children's comprehension of two
early-learned words with overlapping denotations: *put in* for learners
of English and *kkita* 'interlock, fit tightly' for learners of Korean (Choi
et al. 1999). This study showed that children understand these categories language-specifically at least by 18 to 23 months (the only age
group tested): hearing *put in* (embedded in various carrier phrases) directed our English-learning subjects' attention toward events involving
containment, regardless of tightness of fit, whereas hearing *kkita* pulled
our Korean-learning subjects' attention toward events involving tight
fit, regardless of containment. This looking pattern is illustrated in figure
13.3 for two of the four event pairs used.

Most of the children were not yet producing the target word for their
language, according to parental report, which suggests that sensitivity to
language-specific spatial categories begins to develop in comprehension
even before production sets in. This finding allows us to reconcile two
observations that have previously seemed to conflict. On the one hand,
children often generalize spatial words rapidly to a wide range of referents in their production—a finding that has been taken as evidence that
the words express meanings that originate in nonlinguistic cognition
(e.g., McCune-Nicolich 1981; Nelson 1974). On the other hand, as soon
as children use spatial words productively, they use them to pick out
language-specific categories of meaning—a finding that suggests guidance from the input language. How can both things be true? The results
of our comprehension study suggest that generalization in early production can be both rapid and language specific because children start to
work out the categories in comprehension before production begins.

### 13.2.2.5  Additional Evidence for Language Specificity in Early Spatial Language

Containment and support are not the only spatial domains
that are treated differently by children learning different languages. Another important area of diversity is the expression of *vertical motion*. In
English, the commonality among diverse events involving motion "up"
and "down" is captured with the path particles *up* and *down*, which can
be combined with many different verbs (e.g., *go/climb/slide* UP/DOWN,
*pick* UP, *put* DOWN, *sit/stand* UP, *sit/lie* DOWN, *look* UP/DOWN). English-

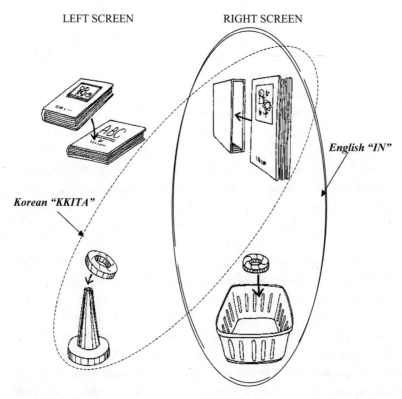

LEFT SCREEN          RIGHT SCREEN

*English "IN"*

*Korean "KKITA"*

**Figure 13.3**
Two pairs of scenes used to test comprehension of English *put in* and Korean *kkita* in Choi et al. 1999, showing the language-specific looking patterns obtained

speaking children grasp the abstract spatial meaning of these morphemes very early. *Up* and *down* figure among their first relational words, emerging sometimes by as early as 12 to 14 months and typically by 16 to 17 months (Bloom 1973; Choi and Bowerman 1991; Gopnik 1980; Greenfield and Smith 1976; Nelson 1974; Smiley and Huttenlocher 1995). Some children restrict them initially to spontaneous and caused movements of their own body, while others generalize them immediately across a wide range of referents (see Choi and Bowerman 1991, 100ff., for discussion); by the end of the second year of life, however, children typically use them freely for a variety of "vertical motion" events, both familiar and novel. A few examples from a little girl between 13 and 16 months: *down* as she tried to climb down from a counter and as a request to be taken down from it, while she sat at the top of a slide preparing to slide down, when dumping yarn into a wagon, when setting books on the floor, and when trying to take a small chair down from on top of a low table (Choi and Bowerman 1991).

Korean lacks all-purpose "up" and "down" morphemes, and the encoding of events involving vertical motion develops very differently in learners of this language (Choi and Bowerman 1991). Children learning Korean talk about events involving vertical motion using a large variety of verbs, which enter their speech piecemeal between the ages of about 17 and 24 months and are used appropriately for relatively specific categories of action, either spontaneous (intransitive verbs) or caused (transitive verbs): for example, first *anta* 'hold/carry in arms' and *epta* 'hold/carry on back' as requests to be picked up, and *ancta* 'assume a sitting posture' (either 'up' or 'down'), *nwupta* 'lie down', and *ileseta* 'stand up' for posture changes; later *ollita* 'cause to ascend' and *naylita* 'cause to descend' for putting objects on a raised surface or taking them down; still later *olla kata* 'ascend go' (= go up) and *naylye kata* 'descend go' (= go down) for spontaneous vertical movements like negotiating stairs or climbing on and off furniture. If learners of Korean recognize a common element of vertical motion "up" or "down" across these events, this is not apparent in their word use; for example, they do not overextend *ollita* 'cause to ascend' to requests to be picked up or helped to stand up.

Like children learning Korean, children learning Tzeltal and Tzotzil, sister Mayan languages spoken in the Chiapas highland of Mexico, use no all-purpose words for vertical motion "up" or "down," but distinguish a variety of posture changes, ways of being picked up and carried, and falling. They are also quick to get the hang of a number of verbs that distinguish language-specific categories of positioning: for example, *nuj* 'be located face down/upside down', *kot* 'be located standing on all fours', *pak'* 'be located on the ground', and *kaj* 'be located on a high surface' (Tzotzil), and *pach* 'be located, of an upright bowl-shaped object' (Tzeltal) (Brown 2001; de León 1999, 2001). A favorite early verb for children learning Tzotzil is *xoj*, which specifies actions in which an elongated object ends up encircled by a ring- or tube-shaped object. This

These early things and knowledges are active but beyond formal recollection

verb—which picks out a topological category different again from those of English *put in* and *put on* and Korean *kkita*—is used appropriately at a very young age for actions that result in a "ring-and-pole" configuration regardless of whether it is the "ring" or the "pole" that is moved: for example, putting a ring on a pole or a pole through a ring, an arm in a sleeve, a leg in a trouser-leg, a head through an opening in a shawl, a chick in a blouse pocket, and a coil of rope over a peg (Bowerman, de León, and Choi 1995).

### 13.2.3  Summary: Universality and Language Specificity

Previous work has suggested that early spatial concepts are universal, with children mapping the spatial morphemes of their language directly to such presumably basic notions as containment, contact and support, and vertical motion "up" and "down," after these become available in the course of nonlinguistic cognitive development. It is true that children initially concentrate on words for various kinds of topological relationships and for events involving vertical motion, and this focus is presumably conditioned by cognitive factors. But within these bounds, the meanings of children's early spatial words are by no means universal, and the ways they differ are consistent with differences in the target languages' partitioning of these semantic domains.

### 13.3  Do Children Construct Semantic Categories of Space? Evidence from Error Patterns

Does early language-specific variation in children's semantic categorization of space mean that learners are capable of using linguistic input to actively construct spatial categories that they might otherwise not have had? This is one possible explanation for the findings, but it is not the only one. An alternative is that children's early nonlinguistic repertoire of spatial concepts is more extensive than has been assumed, including not only the notions of containment and support corresponding to English *in* and *on*, but also a notion of tight fit or interlocking corresponding to Korean *kkita*, and presumably further concepts corresponding to the categories of early-learned spatial words in other languages (Mandler 1992, 1996; see Bloom 2000, 250–254, for discussion).

Under this scenario, children's task would not be to construct a concept to account for a word's pattern of use in the input, but to select, from among the concepts already available to them, the one that adult speakers intend when they use the word (see Gleitman 1990 for similar assumptions about the early acquisition of verb meanings).

As Bloom notes, "this alternative is plausible only to the extent that one doesn't have to posit a new set of nonlinguistic spatial notions for every language we look at; the variation that exists should be highly constrained"; ideally, there should also be "evidence for these putatively nonlinguistic spatial categories in babies" (2000, 252). At present, spatial semantic development has been investigated in too few languages to establish just how constrained the list of notions would be (although it is worth noting that so far, each new language examined has turned up new candidates, such as Tzotzil *xoj* 'put into a "ring-and-pole" configuration', and Tzeltal *pach* 'be located, of an upright bowl-shaped object'). Evidence on babies' spatial categorization will be discussed in section 13.5.

Interesting additional clues to whether language learners simply choose from among preexisting concepts, or can actively construct semantic categories from early on, come from errors in children's use of spatial words (Bowerman 1996a; Bowerman and Choi 2001; Choi 1997). Recall, for example, that children often overextend words for "separating" objects. These errors have typically been interpreted as evidence for a direct reliance on nonlinguistic concepts of space—that is, on children's sense that events of certain kinds are so similar that they should be described with the same word even though adults may describe them using different words (Bowerman 1978; Griffiths and Atkinson 1978; McCune and Vihman 1997). If this view were correct, we could expect a very strong convergence across children learning different languages on the makeup of the categories picked out by their early uses of "translation equivalent" words. But this is not the case: whether or not children overextend a particular word, and the exact shape of their extension patterns, turn out to differ across languages in ways that are closely related to semantic and statistical properties of the target language.

Errors with *open* and its translation equivalents provide a good illustration. These errors have been reported in children's spontaneous speech in English and several other European languages (Bowerman 1978; Clark 1993). Typical are examples from a child who used *open* between about 16 and 21 months not only for canonical actions on doors, windows, boxes, and the like, but also for separating two Frisbees, unscrewing a plastic stake from a block, spreading the handles of nail scissors apart, taking the stem off an apple, a piece out of a jigsaw puzzle, a handle off a riding toy, and a shoe off a foot, and also for turning on an electric typewriter, a light, and a water faucet (Bowerman 1978). Similar errors occurred in our crosslinguistic elicited production study (section 13.2.2.3): children from 2 to $3\frac{1}{2}$ years learning English or Dutch often overextended *open* (Dutch *open[-maken]* 'open[-make]') to actions like pulling Pop-beads and Lego blocks apart, undoing a Velcro fastening, and taking the top off a pen or a shoe off a foot.

Children learning Korean, in contrast, scarcely make this error. In our elicited production study, there was only one such overextension (*yelta* 'open' for unhooking two train cars); and in the spontaneous speech data examined in Choi and Bowerman (1991), there were none. How to explain this difference? A plausible answer points to differences in the breadth and makeup of the categories in the "opening" domain in Korean versus English (and Dutch) (Dutch *open* 'open' has an extension similar to that of English *open*). As shown in figure 13.4, actions that fall uncontroversially into the *open* category in English are split up in Korean into a number of more specific categories, many of which include events that would not be described as "opening" in English: opening doors, boxes, bags, and the like (*yelta*, the verb most similar to *open*); opening objects with two parts that separate symmetrically (a clamshell, a mouth, a pair of shutters or sliding doors) (*pellita*); opening things that spread out flat (a book, hand, or fan) (*phyelchita*); and so on.

The possible effect of these differences on learners is suggested by a simple experiment by Landau and Shipley (1996), which tested how children generalize names for novel objects. Two different novel objects —the "standards"—were placed in front of 2- and 3-year-old children. Children in the same label condition heard the same name applied to

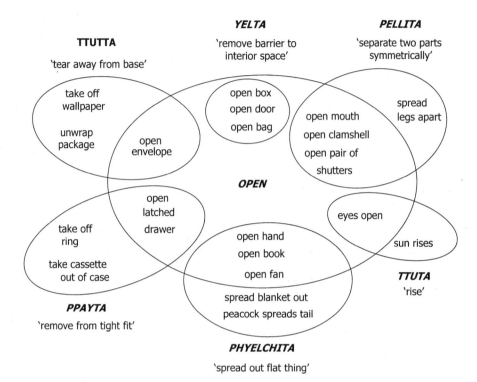

**Figure 13.4**
Categorization of "opening" in English and Korean

both standards ("This is a blicket ... and this is a blicket"). Children in the different label condition heard different names ("This is a blicket ... and this is a steb"). Now the children were shown, one by one, four test objects, which had been "morphed" so that they were intermediate in shape along a continuum between the two standards. When asked, for each test object, "Is this a blicket?," children in the same label condition accepted *blicket* at ceiling for all test objects, but children in the different label condition accepted it decreasingly as the test objects grew less like the first standard and more like the second. Landau and Shipley conclude that hearing identical labels can induce children to "'fill in' the gap between even very different exemplars, probably guided by the assumption that members lying on the hypothetical similarity line between standards

lowest common denominator = dictionary
definition = chair.
" The chairs are bolted to the floor!" " It belongs to the dentist
" The Dentist's chair." No special label.
" Reclining chair"
" An erecting bed"

are also members of the category" (p. 446). Hearing different labels, in contrast, leads children to set up a boundary somewhere on the gradient between the two exemplars.

To apply the logic of this experiment to the treatment of candidate "opening" actions, children learning English and Dutch are in the same label condition: they are invited, on hearing *open* applied to so many different kinds of actions, to generalize very broadly;[5] object details like having symmetrically moving parts or being able to spread out flat are taken to be irrelevant to the meaning of the word. Children learning Korean, on the other hand, are in the different label condition: hearing a different word at every juncture dampens the inclination to generalize *yelta*, the word for the most prototypical "open" events.

But Korean learners do have another word, also shown in figure 13.4, that they overgeneralize to many events of "separation": *ppayta* 'un-interlock; remove from tight fit' (this is the opposite of *kkita* 'interlock, fit tightly', although it is more tolerant in what it counts as a "tight fit"). Is this then simply another word for the same concept to which learners of English and Dutch (over)extend *open*? It is not. Critically, although the extensions of Korean *ppayta* and English or Dutch *open* overlap in children's speech, they show clear language-related differences (Bowerman and Choi 2001); this is especially obvious in the distribution of responses in our elicited production task.

Learners of Korean who participated in this task, like the adults, used *ppayta* most frequently and consistently for *separating fitted, meshed, or interlocked objects with a bit of force* (e.g., pulling Pop-beads or Lego blocks apart, taking the top off a pen, prying an audiocassette out of its case). From this core meaning, they sometimes overextended it to separations involving other objects or object parts that were somehow "engaged" with each other, even if not tightly fitted (e.g., opening a box or suitcase, taking Legos out of a bag, "unsticking" adhering and magnetized objects, and taking off clothing); in these uses, however, *ppayta* competed with other, more appropriate words in the children's speech.

In contrast, uses of *open* by learners of English and Dutch in this task—as in the speech of the adult participants—centered on *separation as a means of making something accessible* (e.g., opening a box, suitcase, or cassette case to get at something inside; cf. also the predominant uses in children's spontaneous speech for opening doors, windows, etc.— Bowerman 1978). From this core, *open* was extended relatively rarely to separating objects such as Pop-beads or Legos and to taking off clothing (these actions were much more often called *[take]* OFF by the learners of English), or to taking things out of containers (much more often called *[take]* OUT). Spontaneous speech data (Bowerman 1978; Clark 1993) show that English learners also overextend *open* to events where something is made accessible with little or no separation of "engaged" elements, such as turning on an electrical appliance or water faucet, pulling a chair away from a table, bending a knee to reveal a toy hidden behind it, and sliding a T-shirt up to peek at the belly beneath. Korean learners do not use *ppayta* for these events, presumably because its primary use in adult speech has to do with the physical disconnection of engaged elements, and not (in contrast to adult English *open*) with making something accessible.

Examples like these suggest that even very young children are closely attuned to the way words are distributed across events in the speech they hear, and that their word meanings can be influenced by factors such as the number and semantic makeup of competing forms, the frequency and consistency with which a form is used for events of various types, and (not illustrated here, but see Bowerman 1996a) the presence or absence of polysemy in a word's meaning. These are the kinds of factors that have been singled out in "usage-based" approaches to language, which stress the dynamic properties of linguistic knowledge and posit that speakers of all ages can induce schemas and continually restructure them in response to (possibly shifting) patterns in the linguistic input (e.g., Bybee 1985, 1991; MacWhinney 1987). This view of category construction lends itself well to computational modeling of schema induction, and indeed, Regier (1997) has successfully modeled some of the differences between young learners of English and Dutch in the elicited production study discussed here and in section 13.2.2.3.

Category construction of course requires both a learning mechanism and raw materials (perceptual or conceptual sensitivities) that can be structured into new configurations. Let us consider these requirements in turn.

## 13.4    Mechanisms of Category Construction

In an earlier era, when it was more usual to suppose that different languages make use of different concepts and that language input has something to do with the formation of new concepts, Roger Brown described the process of lexical development as "the Original Word Game." In this game,

> the tutor names things in accordance with the semantic custom of his community. The player forms hypotheses about the categorial nature of the things named. He tests his hypotheses by trying to name new things correctly. The tutor compares the player's utterances with his own anticipations of such utterances, and, in this way, checks the accuracy of fit between his own categories and those of the player. He improves the fit by correction. (1958, 194)

In this formulation of the learning process, one of the critical problems that Brown was trying to solve was the fact that "everything in the world is susceptible of multiple categorizations" (1958, 225). This means that even if children know what a word refers to in a particular context (i.e., have solved "Quine's problem" of identifying the referent), they cannot be certain how to identify additional instances of the same category. The ambiguity is reduced when the word is encountered again in other contexts: "a speech invariance is a signal to form some hypothesis about the corresponding invariance of referent" (1958, 228). In today's intellectual climate, we would resist the implication that children formulate and test their hypotheses consciously, or that improving the fit between hypothesis and target category requires explicit correction. Still, Brown's characterization of how children could form categories under linguistic guidance retains a strong intuitive appeal. What is lacking, however, is an explicit specification of the learning procedure.

A modern approach to learning with the potential to capture Brown's insights more precisely is *structure-mapping* (Gentner 1983, this volume; Gentner and Loewenstein 2002; Gentner and Markman 1997; Gentner and Namy 1999; Gentner and Rattermann 1991). Structure-mapping theory, which focuses on the acquisition of relational concepts by learners of any age, posits that relational abstractions can emerge in the course of *comparing* exemplars. In the process of comparing, the learner tries to align structured conceptual representations with each other and to identify the ways in which they are similar and different. Alignments are typically shallow at first, suggests Gentner, based primarily on similarities in the objects that play a role in the situations being compared (we come back to this shortly). But with successive opportunities to compare situations in which the objects vary, alignments based on more abstract similarities in the *relationships* among the objects are discovered. Studies have suggested that the process of comparing can call attention to abstract relational similarities that otherwise go unnoticed (Kotovsky and Gentner 1996; Loewenstein and Gentner 2001).

In experiments, comparisons leading to relational abstractions have been stimulated in a variety of ways—for example, by presenting subjects with successive exemplars of a candidate relationship or explicitly asking them to compare instances (Gentner and Loewenstein 2002; Gentner and Namy 1999). Gentner hypothesizes that one stimulant to comparison with tremendous importance for children's development is *hearing the same word applied to different situations* (cf. Brown 1958, 210: repetitions of a word across contexts "will orient the player toward contemporaneous stimuli and will tell him when the important nonlinguistic stimuli recur"). Note that specific instantiations of the concepts encoded by words typically occur at different times, often embedded in very different contexts, and are in no other way flagged as being somehow "the same." Being prompted to compare situations that are called by the same word—for example, events labeled *open* or *take off*, or behaviors described as *cruel* or *generous*—could lead learners to search for and extract cross-situational commonalities that are considered important in their society. The word that promotes the comparison of instances, suggests Gentner, also provides a convenient label for the relationship that the flagged situations share, and this makes the relationship more accessible the next time it is relevant.

Notice that in our earlier discussion (section 13.3) of why children learning English and Dutch overextend their word for prototypical "opening" events, while children learning Korean do not, we already made an implicit appeal to a process of comparison. There, we suggested that in using the word *open*, English-speaking adults in essence invite children to generalize broadly: by flagging a set of events as diverse as opening a door, opening the eyes, and opening a book, they implicitly prompt children to *compare* them in search of some commonality. Depending on the semantic categories of the language, the set of events singled out for comparison will differ, so the scope of the learner's final categories will differ. For example, to arrive at a concept that accounts for the distribution of *open* in English, learners must ignore the identity and many of the properties of the objects involved in the events labeled *open*, and bring into focus an abstract relationship that has to do with making something accessible. In contrast, to grasp the meanings of the "opening" verbs in Korean, children must recognize that certain object information is critical—for example, that uses of *pellita* all involve objects with two parts that are separated symmetrically (mouth, clam-shell, sliding doors that meet in the middle, pair of legs) and that uses of *phyelchita* all involve objects that can be spread out flat (book, hand, fan, picnic cloth) (see figure 13.4).

Many of Gentner's experiments in domains other than language acquisition have suggested that it is difficult for learners to disregard object information in favor of a relational commonality—that abstraction proceeds stepwise, first to situations that are closely similar to the original exemplars and only later to situations involving very different kinds of objects. Counter to this, we have often been impressed, in our work on the acquisition of relational words, at how quickly children make conceptual leaps to contexts quite different from those in which a word has been modeled (see, e.g., the broad overextensions of *off*, *open*, and other relational words discussed in Bowerman 1978, 1980). In our view, the learning of relational words can proceed in either direction: either by stepwise extension from known exemplars (abstraction; expanding the domain of an initially underextended word) or by adding critical information that was initially overlooked (differentiation; narrowing the domain of an initially overextended word).[6] Regardless of directionality, what is crucial is the process of comparison, and it seems plausible that language—here, the way spatial words are distributed across referent events in the speech children hear—guides learners in discovering what needs to be compared, and so can influence the final makeup of learners' semantic categories.

## 13.5  Raw Ingredients for Category Construction: What Are Infants' Spatial Sensitivities?

Obviously, a serious theory of learning cannot conjure up concepts out of nothing. Even a theory like structure-mapping, which posits that deep relational structures that are not known a priori can be disembedded over time from a morass of surface detail, must presuppose that learners have the wherewithal to set up initial representations of situations and that they are sensitive to certain properties and dimensions along which situations can be compared. Establishing exactly what these building materials consist of (e.g., domain-general sensitivities to perceptual properties? domain-specific sensitivities, such as "semantic primitives" for space? more abstract inborn conceptual knowledge?) is one of the most challenging and controversial questions facing developmentalists today (see, e.g., Fodor 1975; Landau and Jackendoff 1983; Mandler 1992, 1996; Spelke et al. 1992, for some different views on the problem). In the domain of space, one critical source of evidence for investigating these issues is information about what kinds of spatial distinctions and similarities are salient to infants *before* they acquire spatial words.[7]

### 13.5.1  Containment, Support, and Tight Fit

Casasola and Cohen (2002) have recently examined the prelinguistic status of three categories of central interest to us: CONTAINMENT (English *in*), SUPPORT (English *on*, encompassing both support from beneath, as in *Put the cup on the table*, and surface attachment, as in *Put this Lego block on that one*), and the INTERLOCKING/TIGHT-FIT category associated with Korean *kkita*, which crosscuts "in" and "on" relations. Two groups of infants from an English-speaking environment, 9–11 months (prelinguistic stage) and 17–19 months old (early linguistic stage), were habituated to four videotaped actions showing events of putting varied objects into either a containment, a support, or a tight-fit relation.[8] Four test trials followed: (1) familiarized objects being put into the familiar relation (one of the habituation events again), (2) familiarized objects put into a novel relation, (3) novel objects put into the familiarized relation, and (4) novel objects put into a novel relation.

At both ages, infants who had been habituated to the containment relation discriminated reliably (as determined by assessing which events caused their attention to revive) between this relation and another (a support event) regardless of whether the objects depicting the relation were familiar or novel. But at neither age did the babies who had been habituated to the support or tight-fit relation discriminate between the familiar relation and the novel relation (a tight containment event for the support condition and a loose containment event for the tight-fit condition). The younger babies in the support and tight-fit conditions reacted only to the novel objects, not to the relationships. The older babies discriminated between familiar objects in the novel versus familiar relation, but they did not look longer at novel objects in the novel relation than at novel objects in the familiar relation; apparently they had not picked up on the support or tight-fit property shared by all the habituation events they had witnessed.

In sum, this study provides evidence that prelinguistic infants are sensitive to a category of "containment" events, but not to the categories of "support" and "tight-fit" events, at least as operationalized here. Of course, further studies using other techniques may still reveal such sensitivities. But for the moment—as also noted by Casasola and Cohen—this outcome leaves open the possibility that these two categories are constructed in the course of learning the meaning of English *on* or Korean *kkita*.[9]

### 13.5.2   Tight versus Loose Containment

Discovering a shared property of "tight fit" that transcends containment events requires being able to distinguish, *within* the containment category, between putting things into containers that fit tightly (e.g., a book into a fitted box-cover: Korean *kkita*) versus into containers that fit loosely (e.g., an apple into a bowl: Korean *nehta*; see figure 13.2). To explore whether prelinguistic infants are sensitive to these subcategories of containment, McDonough, Choi, and Mandler (in press) tested infants 9, 11, and 14 months of age from both English- and Korean-speaking environments.

The study employed a modified version of the familiarization-novelty preference procedure used by Behl-Chadha and Eimas (1995) and Quinn

(1994) to study the categorization of left-right and above-below in young infants. Babies were first shown six pairs of videotaped scenes of putting one object into another. Half were familiarized with *tight-fit* containment events (the tight-IN condition), and the other half with *loose-fit* containment events (loose-IN); in both conditions, a wide range of figure and ground objects were used. After familiarization, two test trial pairs were shown, identical for children in the two conditions: one member of each test pair showed putting yet another novel object into yet another tight-fitting container (a novel relation for children in the loose-IN condition); the other member showed putting this same novel object into a loose-fitting container (a novel relation for children in the tight-IN condition).[10]

Infants from both language environments and in all three age groups (9, 11, and 14 months) looked longer at the test scenes showing an additional instance of the *familiar* relation than at the test scenes showing an instance of the *novel* relation, regardless of which relation—tight-IN or loose-IN—they had been familiarized on.[11] These results show that babies in this age range can discriminate between tight and loose containment events. Thus, sensitivity to the tightness of a containment event—handy if you happen to be growing up in a Korean-speaking environment—is accessible to preverbal children.[12]

### 13.5.3 Summary on Infant Spatial Sensitivities, and a Caveat

To summarize, studies of infant cognition using the habituation/familiarization paradigms show that already in the first year of life, babies are sensitive to three categories of spatial events that are relevant to the spatial words we have been considering: "containment" (Casasola and Cohen 2002; section 13.5.1) and two subcategories of containment, "tight" versus "loose" (McDonough, Choi, and Mandler, in press; section 13.5.2). There is as yet no evidence for sensitivity to a *kkita*-style category of "tight three-dimensional fit" that encompasses both tight-fit containment and events of surface attachment/covering/encircling, nor for an *on*-style category of support that encompasses both placing things loosely on surfaces and juxtaposing surfaces by attachment, covering, or encirclement.

*resurrected !*

It is important to recognize that although these studies show a prelin-guistic sensitivity to certain categories, they do not establish just when or how the categories emerged. The infants' grasp of the categories might already have been firmly in place before the experiments began—available when needed. Also possible, however, is that the infants became sensitized to the categories *in the course of the experiment*.

Recall that, according to structure-mapping theory (Gentner, this volume; Gentner and Namy 1999), an appreciation for an abstract relational similarity often emerges through the process of *comparing* situations and trying to align them with one another. Language is, by hypothesis, one good way to prompt comparison, but it is not the only one. Assuming that infants have attained a certain minimal level of cognitive "readiness" (also of course necessary before the language-guided learning of a new category could take place), being shown successive actions all instantiating the same candidate event category (e.g., "containment" or "tight containment") during the familiarization phase of an experiment might prompt babies to discover an abstract relational similarity they had not previously recognized.

Results from the domain of early speech perception (Maye, Werker, and Gerken 2002) show that babies are in fact astonishingly sensitive to the statistical distribution of the stimuli they encounter in the familiarization/habituation phase of a study. Babies 6 and 8 months old were exposed for only 2.3 minutes to one of two frequency distributions of the same set of speech sounds ranging along a continuum from /ta/ to /da/: a *bimodal* distribution (the most frequently presented sounds were clustered at the /ta/ and /da/ ends of the continuum, with fewer from in between) and a *unimodal* distribution (the most frequently presented sounds were the ones intermediate on the continuum, with fewer from either pole). On the test phase of the study, only the infants in the bimodal condition discriminated tokens from the endpoints of this same continuum; babies in the unimodal condition did not.

Applying the reasoning to the "containment" studies, we can imagine that familiarization/habituation to a set of containment events that are all "tight" or all "loose," as in McDonough, Choi, and Mandler's study, may—analogously to the bimodal condition used by Maye, Werker, and

Gerken—cause the child to (temporarily?) set up a relatively narrow category (either tight or loose containment), thereby promoting discrimination of these events from events of the opposing degree of fit. In contrast, familiarization/habituation to a range of containment events that encompasses *both* tight and loose instances, as in Casasola and Cohen's study, may—analogously to the unimodal distribution—lead to formation of a single, more abstract category, which can be discriminated as a whole from events belonging to still another category, such as support.

Clearly, more research is needed to determine how much the categories to which preverbal infants show sensitivity can be manipulated by changing the exact makeup of the familiarization stimuli: high malleability would suggest a strong potential for rapid online learning, while low malleability would suggest that children rely in this experimental paradigm on category distinctions that are already available to them.

### 13.6  Does Learning Language-Specific Spatial Semantic Categories Affect Nonlinguistic Cognition?

Let us now return to the Whorfian question: does learning the spatial semantic categories of our native language influence how we think about space? If the requirement to learn the meanings of the words in their language causes children to form concepts of space that they would not otherwise have had, then in this minimal sense language can be said to affect cognition. But inquiries into the Whorfian hypothesis usually rightly hold out for more: for evidence that even when people are *not* talking or listening to speech, the structure of their language influences their cognition—for example, their perceptual sensitivities, their non-linguistic similarity judgments, their recall accuracy, or their problem-solving strategies.

It is by no means necessary that the semantic spatial categories of a language affect the way its speakers deal with space nonlinguistically. In a domain other than space, Malt et al. (1999) showed that when speakers of English, Spanish, and Chinese were asked to label a set of containers (bottles, jars, etc.), the three language groups classified very differently from one another, but when they were asked to compare objects and judge how similar they were to one another, their classifications were much more alike. Whorfian effects have, however, been documented in tasks having to do with space (see the frame-of-reference studies discussed in Levinson 1996, this volume; Pederson et al. 1998) and for nonlinguistic categorization in domains other than space (Lucy 1992; Lucy and Gaskins 2001, this volume). So the potential for Whorfian effects on nonlinguistic spatial categorization remains open.

To explore whether the spatial semantic categories of English versus Korean affect speakers' nonlinguistic sensitivities, McDonough, Choi, and Mandler (in press) extended the familiarization-novelty preferential looking task described in section 13.5.2, which tested tight and loose containment, to *adult* speakers of these languages. The adults were simply asked to watch the video scenes. Their gaze behavior, like that of the babies, was videotaped, and the amount of time they spent watching the familiar versus novel events on the test trials was compared. Recall that 9- to 14-month-old babies in both language communities looked significantly longer at the test scenes showing the relation they had been familiarized on, regardless of whether it was tight or loose containment, thereby showing that they are sensitive to this distinction. Adult speakers of Korean behaved in exactly the same way. Adult speakers of English, in contrast, looked equally long at the two members of each test pair; they showed no sensitivity to the distinction between tight and loose containment. These data suggest that the distinction between tight and loose containment events, if English speakers recognize it at all, is far less salient to them than it is to Korean speakers. This is a real Whorfian effect.[13]

Even if English-speaking adults do not notice the distinction between tight and loose containment events in the course of casual viewing, could they do so if prompted to compare and contrast the events more explicitly? Immediately after participating in the preferential looking task just described, the adult subjects in McDonough, Choi, and Mandler's study took part in an oddity task. Four of the actions they had just seen on the looking task were acted out for them with real objects: three came from the familiarization trials and one was a test pair action depicting the novel relation. For example, participants who had just been in the tight containment familiarization condition were now presented with three instances of tight containment events (putting a Lego person in a Lego car, a book in a matching box-cover, and a cork in a bottle) and one instance of a loose containment event (putting sponge letters in a large bowl). The experimenter performed the four actions one by one, just as in the video scenes, and then asked the participant, "Which is the odd one?" After making their selection, participants were asked to explain it.

Across the two conditions, significantly more Korean- than English-speaking adults based their choice on degree of fit (80% vs. 37%). Almost two-thirds (63%) of the English speakers selected on the basis of object properties (e.g., texture, size, or function of the object)—for example, "This one is made of glass," "This is a tall object." Thus, even when they were explicitly asked to compare a set of events all involving containment, the English speakers were relatively insensitive to the tight-versus loose-fit distinction; their attention was drawn much more to the properties of the objects.

These differences in sensitivity to tight versus loose containment of course mirror the differences in the semantic categories of the two languages. When talking about putting one thing into another, Korean speakers must assess how tight the containment relationship is so that they can choose appropriately between *kkita* 'interlock, fit tightly' and *nehta* 'put loosely in/around'. English speakers *can*, of course, also talk about this distinction if it is really important to do so (as we have been doing throughout this chapter, with the aid of imprecise translations plus examples to illustrate what we mean), but they rarely need to worry about it: for everyday purposes, an all-encompassing *(put)* IN is sufficient.

## 13.7    Conclusions

Taken together, the studies discussed in sections 13.4–13.6 suggest a developmental sequence in the acquisition of language-specific categories of space that goes something like this. (Of course, there is no reason to suppose that space is the only conceptual domain in which this process is at work.)

Before embarking on the language acquisition task, infants notice many different properties of specific spatial situations. Some of these properties may already take a relatively abstract form and so immediately be recognized as applying to a number of different situations ("containment" might be a case in point). Other properties may be more embedded in the contexts in which they occur (e.g., "attachment in the Lego fashion" might be seen as distinct from "attachment in the cap-on-pen fashion," so that infants are slow to recognize potential cross-contextual similarities among these situations unless they are prompted in some way to compare them.

In cases like this, an important stimulant to comparison can be hearing the same word. As the child encounters successive uses of the word, she "tries" (although this process is presumably rarely if ever conscious) to align the referent situations and work out what they have in common. Sometimes she may already have a suitable concept in her cognitive tool kit, but may simply not have noticed that it is applicable to some of the situations. Other times there is no existing concept that does the job, and the child has to construct a new one to account for the distribution of the word. (The qualifications mentioned in note 5 of course apply here too.)

As semantic categories are formed, the speaker becomes increasingly skilled at making the rapid automatic judgments they require; for example, Korean speakers implicitly monitor how tight the fit is in contexts of putting one object into contact with another, since the choices they have to make when talking about such events depend on it. These linguistically relevant sensitivities achieve and maintain a high degree of standing readiness (see also Slobin, this volume). Sensitivities that are not needed for the local language may diminish over time (although presumably they do not always do so). Loss of sensitivity seems especially likely in the case of distinctions that not only are irrelevant to the lexical and grammatical distinctions of the local language, but also crosscut the distinctions that *are* relevant, since attending to linguistically irrelevant distinctions might interfere with developing the automaticity that is needed for the linguistically relevant ones.

This sketch of semantic development, based on the research reviewed in this chapter, has some striking parallels to the view of early speech sound perception that has been built up over the last couple of decades. In the first months of life, infants have been shown to be sensitive to a large variety of phonetic distinctions, both those that play a role in their language and those that do not. By the end of their first year, infants have reorganized their pattern of speech sound discrimination around the phonetic structure of their native language, and they have lost sensitivity to some of the contrasts their language does not use (Best, McRoberts, and Sithole 1988; Kuhl et al. 1992; Polka and Werker 1994; Streeter 1976; Werker and Tees 1984, 1999). Though loss of sensitivity to phonetic contrasts has been the phenomenon most thoroughly documented and discussed, there is also evidence that linguistic experience can *increase* sensitivity to certain distinctions (Aslin et al. 1981; Polka, Colantonio, and Sundara 2001).

Just how deep the parallels go between early speech perception and the early development of semantic categories is not yet clear. For instance, does the decline in English speakers' sensitivity to the distinction between tight and loose containment demonstrated by McDonough, Choi, and Mandler (in press) come about quickly, as soon as language-specific principles of categorizing containment in English are learned, or does this happen only later? Are declines in sensitivity to semantic distinctions as persistent, even in the face of new experience, as declines in phonetic sensitivity, or are they easily reversed? There is clearly much work to be done here. One thing, however, is becoming clear: just as infants are geared from the beginning to discover underlying phonological regularities in the speech stream, so too are they born to zero in on language-specific patterns in the organization of meaning.

## Notes

We thank Jürgen Bohnemeyer and Dan Slobin for helpful comments on earlier drafts of this chapter, and Jürgen Bohnemeyer for suggesting the title "Space under Construction."

1. In Talmy's (1985, 1991) typological classification of the characteristic ways languages express path meanings, English is a "satellite-framed" language—a language that expresses path meanings primarily through particles, prepositions, or affixes (cf. *go* IN/OUT/UP/DOWN/ACROSS and *put* IN/ON/TOGETHER, *take* OUT/ OFF/APART). In contrast, Korean is a "verb-framed" language—a language that expresses path primarily through verbs with meanings suggested by English verbs such as *enter, exit, ascend, descend, insert, extract* (these verbs are not "native" to English, but are borrowed from Romance, where they represent the dominant pattern).

2. Sometimes *fit* is suggested to us as the English counterpart of *kkita*, but *fit* does not fit: in one way it is too general and in another too specific. Too general because for *kkita*, but not *fit*, figure and ground must have complementary shapes *before* the action is carried out, and the fit requires at least a slight degree of three-dimensional engagement (thus, *kkita* cannot be used in contexts like "Does this belt fit?" or "This bandage is too small to fit over the wound"). Too specific because *fit* is typically used only when the degree of fit is the point at issue, and not for actions like putting a cassette into its cassette case or the cap on a pen. Relatively low frequency English words like *interlock*, *mesh*, *couple*, or *engage* come a bit closer, but the first two suggest the involvement of more than one projecting part from each object, and the second two evoke the notion of a connecting link between two entities, such as train cars, so it is absurd to use them for putting a book into a tight box-cover or a cap on a pen—perfectly normal uses for *kkita*. The meaning of *kkita* can, of course, be approximated in English by combining words into phrases such as *tight fit*, as we have done in this chapter, but such phrases are inexact and cumbersome, and, as ad hoc compositions, they are not part of the permanent stock of semantic categories of English.

3. Conversely, of course, from the Korean point of view, the English insistence on honoring containment relations wherever applicable means that a commonality is missed between diverse events involving snug fit, regardless of whether the figure ends up "in," "on," or in some other relation to the ground.

4. It is important to look for evidence of productivity (e.g., uses of a word for novel referents, including referents for which adults would not use it). This is to rule out an interpretation for early language-specific word use that does not require crediting children with knowledge of language-specific categories: that children simply repeat what they have often heard adults say in particular contexts. (See Choi and Bowerman 1991, 110, for discussion.)

5. The range of exemplars across which generalization can take place is presumably constrained by both the child's level of cognitive development and the conceptual "stretch" required to bridge the gap. For instance, the meaning associated with *in front of* and *behind* will not at first include projective relationships based on speaker perspective (as in *The glass is in front of the plate*), even though uses for such relations occur in the input, because the child cannot yet understand them (Johnston 1984). And the meaning of *on* for young English speakers is unlikely to encompass both spatial applications and manipulations with lights and other electric appliances; more probably, these uses of *on* are acquired independently.

6. See Regier 1997 for relevant discussion of how a semantic category can initially be formulated too broadly but later narrowed. In a computational model of the learning of some of the spatial words used by learners of English and Dutch in the elicited production study discussed in sections 13.2.2.3 and 13.3, Regier shows that words that are initially overextended will gradually retreat to their conventional adult boundaries if the learning model is equipped with a weak sensitivity to the Principle of Mutual Exclusivity (Markman 1989): the idea that a referent object or event should have only one name.

unfamiliar

7. A number of important studies have explored infants' ability to *reason* about spatial situations of the kind we are interested in—for example, whether they show surprise when confronted with impossible events of containment or support (e.g., Baillargeon 1995; Caron, Caron, and Antell 1988; Hespos and Baillargeon 2001; Needham and Baillargeon 1993). But this research does not fundamentally address how infants *categorize* these events—for example, which events they perceive as "the same" even when they are instantiated with different objects. In the following discussion, we will focus on studies of spatial categorization.

8. For example, children in the *containment* condition repeatedly saw four containment events, two "loose" (putting an animal into a basket, putting a car into a container) and two "tight" (candle into same-shaped cookie-cutter, green peg into yellow block), until they reached the habituation criterion. Children in the *support* condition similarly saw two "loose" and two "tight" habituation events. For children in the *tight fit* condition, the four habituation events comprised the two "tight" containment events used in the containment condition and the two "tight" support events used in the support condition; these events would all be described in Korean with the verb *kkita*. The study thus tested sensitivity to crosscutting event categories.

9. One reason why the tight-fit category of *kkita* might be difficult to form is suggested by the results of a study by Baillargeon and Wang (2002). These authors compared infants' ability to reason about "containment" versus "covering" events, both of which involved the same objects: a short, snug container and a cylindrical object taller than the container. In the containment event, the infant watched as the cylinder was lowered into the container until it could no longer be seen; in the covering event, the container, shown in an inverted position, was lowered over the cylinder until the cylinder could no longer be seen. Both events are impossible, and for the same reason: the container is shorter than the cylinder. But children do not apply the same reasoning when faced with the two scenarios: they show surprise at the impossible containment event already by $7\frac{1}{2}$ months, but they are not surprised by the impossible covering event until 12 months. What babies know about containment events, then, does not initially transfer to covering events, and this means, conclude Baillargeon and Wang, that "containment" and "covering" are, for them, distinct event categories. Intriguingly, *both* Baillargeon and Wang's containment and covering events would be described with the Korean verb *kkita*, as long as the cylinder and container fit each other precisely. If babies indeed see events of the two types as strictly different, it may be hard for them to spontaneously spot a property they can share, such as snug three-dimensional fit in the case of the cylinder and container. Perhaps here is a place where linguistic input—hearing the same word applied to seemingly disparate events—can prompt toddlers to discover a commonality that might otherwise go unnoticed. That is: children would try to align events whose initial representations are disparate, revolving around "containment" versus "covering," to discover what they have in common, and in so doing they would discover "three-dimensional tight fit."

10. The children in the tight-IN condition saw actions of putting (1) nesting cups into nesting cups, (2) shapes into matching holes in a shape box, (3) Lego people into fitted niches in cars, (4) toy keys into locks, (5) books into fitted box-covers, (6) corks into bottles. The children in the loose-IN condition saw actions of putting (1) Lego people into the bed of a truck, (2) shapes into jewelry boxes, (3) pom-poms into candy molds, (4) pencils into a pencil cup, (5) shapes into a long basket, (6) Bristle-blocks into a cloth bag. The test pairs were (a) putting sponge letters into matching holes in foam mats versus into loose bowls, and (b) putting pegs into tight niches in variously shaped blocks versus into loose containers. The figure was held constant across the two scenes of each test pair to minimize the possibility that children would look longer at one of the scenes than the other because they preferred its figure, rather than because they preferred the relationship depicted; the color, size, and shape of the ground objects were also held as constant as possible.

11. Given the typical preference pattern found in studies with similar designs (e.g., Behl-Chadha and Eimas 1995; Quinn 1994), it may seem surprising that the infants looked longer at the familiarized relation than at the novel one. Hunter and Ames (1988) have shown that preference for familiarity over novelty is related to both task complexity and familiarization time: the more complex the task and/or the shorter the familiarization time, the greater the preference for familiarity; conversely, the easier the task and/or the longer the familiarization time, the greater the preference for novelty. The progression through a familiarity-to-novelty preference sequence is independent of age, although older participants may shift from familiar to novel with relatively more complex stimuli or relatively shorter familiarization times than younger participants. The experiment comparing tight and loose containment differed from those mentioned above in both task complexity and duration of familiarization time. The stimuli were far more complex (dynamic events rather than static pictures, with objects that changed from scene to scene in color, size, shape, and texture), and babies were familiarized to these stimuli for a preset number of trials, rather than habituated (i.e., shown instances of the same relation until they lose interest). Discovering what the familiarization scenes had in common may thus have been difficult, and babies may still have been intrigued to detect yet another new event that fit the category they were busy with.

12. Hespos and Spelke (2000) demonstrate sensitivity to a distinction between tight and loose containment even earlier (5 months). However, the containment scenes used in their study all involved simple containers and contained objects that—aside from the difference in tightness—were identical, so it is unclear whether babies of this age can yet generalize the distinction across objects as diverse as those used in McDonough, Choi, and Mandler's stimuli. (See Casasola and Cohen 2002 and Quinn, in press, for evidence that, in habituation/familiarization studies of infant spatial categorization, babies at first distinguish a novel spatial relation from a familiarized one only when the objects in the novel-relation test trials are the *same objects* they saw in the familiarization phase; only later can they discriminate between the two relations even when the objects change. Only the latter behavior is evidence for sensitivity to a spatial *category*.)

13. Studies purporting to show Whorfian effects are often criticized because, even though the task is ostensibly nonlinguistic, subjects might covertly be using language: for example, when asked to make judgments about the similarities and differences among stimuli, they might decide to group things together that they call by the same name. This explanation is not cogent for this experiment, however. Subjects were simply asked to watch the videos, and they were not expecting any memory tests or judgments about what they had seen; it is unlikely that they were covertly labeling the events they were shown and deciding to look longer at events with one label than at events with another.

## References

Ameka, F. (1995). The linguistic construction of space in Ewe. *Cognitive Linguistics, 6*, 139–181.

Antell, S. E. G., and Caron, A. J. (1985). Neonatal perception of spatial relationships. *Infant Behavior and Development, 8*, 15–23.

Aslin, R. N., Pisoni, D. B., Hennessy, B. L., and Perey, A. J. (1981). Discrimination of voice onset time by human infants: New findings and implications for the effects of early experience. *Child Development, 52*, 1135–1145.

Baillargeon, R. (1995). A model of physical reasoning in infancy. In C. Rovee-Collier and L. P. Lipsitt (Eds.), *Advances in infancy research* (Vol. 9, pp. 305–371). Norwood, NJ: Ablex.

Baillargeon, R., and Wang, S. (2002). Event categorization in infancy. *Trends in Cognitive Sciences, 6*, 85–93.

Behl-Chadha, G., and Eimas, P. D. (1995). Infant categorization of left-right spatial relations. *British Journal of Developmental Psychology, 13*, 69–79.

Best, C. T., McRoberts, B. W., and Sithole, N. M. (1988). Divergent developmental patterns for infants' perception of two nonnative speech contrasts. *Infant Behavior and Development, 18*, 339–350.

Bloom, L. (1973). *One word at a time: The use of single word utterances before syntax*. The Hague: Mouton.

Bloom, P. (2000). *How children learn the meanings of words*. Cambridge, MA: MIT Press.

Bowerman, M. (1978). The acquisition of word meaning: An investigation into some current conflicts. In N. Waterson and C. Snow (Eds.), *The development of communication* (pp. 263–287). New York: Wiley.

Bowerman, M. (1980). The structure and origin of semantic categories in the language-learning child. In M. L. Foster and S. H. Brandes (Eds.), *Symbol as sense: New approaches to the analysis of meaning* (pp. 277–299). New York: Academic Press.

Bowerman, M. (1989). Learning a semantic system: What role do cognitive predispositions play? In M. L. Rice and R. L. Schiefelbusch (Eds.), *The teachability of language* (pp. 133–168). Baltimore: Brookes.

Bowerman, M. (1996a). Learning how to structure space for language: A cross-linguistic perspective. In P. Bloom, M. Peterson, L. Nadel, and M. Garrett (Eds.), *Language and space* (pp. 385–436). Cambridge, MA: MIT Press.

Bowerman, M. (1996b). The origins of children's spatial semantic categories: Cognitive vs. linguistic determinants. In J. J. Gumperz and S. C. Levinson (Eds.), *Rethinking linguistic relativity* (pp. 145–176). Cambridge: Cambridge University Press.

Bowerman, M. (2000). Where do children's meanings come from? Rethinking the role of cognition in early semantic development. In L. P. Nucci, G. Saxe, and E. Turiel (Eds.), *Culture, thought, and development* (pp. 199–230). Mahwah, NJ: Erlbaum.

Bowerman, M., and Choi, S. (2001). Shaping meanings for language: Universal and language-specific in the acquisition of spatial semantic categories. In M. Bowerman and S. C. Levinson (Eds.), *Language acquisition and conceptual development* (pp. 475–511). Cambridge: Cambridge University Press.

Bowerman, M., de León, L., and Choi, S. (1995). Verbs, particles, and spatial semantics: Learning to talk about spatial actions in typologically different languages. *Proceedings of the Child Language Research Forum*, 27, 101–110.

Bowerman, M., and Pederson, E. (in preparation). *Cross-linguistic perspectives on topological spatial relationships*.

Brown, P. (1994). The INs and ONs of Tzeltal locative expressions: The semantics of static descriptions of location. *Linguistics*, 32, 743–790.

Brown, P. (2001). Learning to talk about motion UP and DOWN in Tzeltal: Is there a language-specific bias for verb learning? In M. Bowerman and S. C. Levinson (Eds.), *Language acquisition and conceptual development* (pp. 512–543). Cambridge: Cambridge University Press.

Brown, R. (1958). *Words and things*. Glencoe, IL: Free Press.

Brown, R. (1965). *Social psychology*. New York: Free Press.

Bybee, J. L. (1985). *Morphology: A study of the relation between meaning and form*. Amsterdam: John Benjamins.

Bybee, J. L. (1991). Natural morphology: The organization of paradigms and language acquisition. In T. Heubner and C. A. Ferguson (Eds.), *Crosscurrents in second language and linguistic theories* (pp. 67–93). Amsterdam: John Benjamins.

Caron, A. J., Caron, R. F., and Antell, S. E. (1988). Infant understanding of containment: An affordance perceived or a relationship conceived? *Developmental Psychology*, 24, 620–627.

Casasola, M., and Cohen, L. B. (2002). Infant categorization of containment, support and tight-fit spatial relationships. *Developmental Science*, 5, 247–264.

Choi, S. (1997). Language-specific input and early semantic development: Evidence from children learning Korean. In D. I. Slobin (Ed.), *The crosslinguistic study of language acquisition: Vol. 5. Expanding the contexts* (pp. 41–434). Hillsdale, NJ: Erlbaum.

Choi, S., and Bowerman, M. (1991). Learning to express motion events in English and Korean: The influence of language-specific lexicalization patterns. *Cognition, 41*, 83–121.

Choi, S., McDonough, L., Bowerman, M., and Mandler, J. (1999). Early sensitivity to language-specific spatial categories in English and Korean. *Cognitive Development, 14*, 241–268.

Clark, E. V. (1993). *The lexicon in acquisition.* Cambridge: Cambridge University Press.

Clark, E. V. (2001). Emergent categories in first language acquisition. In M. Bowerman and S. C. Levinson (Eds.), *Language acquisition and conceptual development* (pp. 379–405). Cambridge: Cambridge University Press.

Clark, H. H. (1973). Space, time, semantics, and the child. In T. E. Moore (Ed.), *Cognitive development and the acquisition of language* (pp. 27–64). New York: Academic Press.

de León, L. (1999). Verbs in Tzotzil early syntactic development. *International Journal of Bilingualism, 3*, 219–240.

de León, L. (2001). Finding the richest path: Language and cognition in the acquisition of verticality in Tzotzil (Mayan). In M. Bowerman and S. C. Levinson (Eds.), *Language acquisition and conceptual development* (pp. 544–565). Cambridge: Cambridge University Press.

Fodor, J. (1975). *The language of thought.* New York: Crowell.

Gentner, D. (1983). Structure-mapping: A theoretical framework for analogy. *Cognitive Science, 7*, 155–170.

Gentner, D., and Loewenstein, J. (2002). Relational language and relational thought. In E. Amsel and J. P. Byrnes (Eds.), *Language, literacy, and cognitive development* (pp. 87–120). Mahwah, NJ: Erlbaum.

Gentner, D., and Markman, A. B. (1997). Structure-mapping in analogy and similarity. *American Psychologist, 52*, 45–56.

Gentner, D., and Namy, L. L. (1999). Comparison in the development of categories. *Cognitive Development, 14*, 487–513.

Gentner, D., and Rattermann, M. J. (1991). Language and the career of similarity. In S. A. Gelman and J. P. Byrnes (Eds.), *Perspectives on language and thought: Interrelations in development* (pp. 225–277). Cambridge: Cambridge University Press.

Gleitman, L. (1990). The structural sources of verb meanings. *Language Acquisition, 1*, 3–55.

Gopnik, A. (1980). *The development of non-nominal expressions in 12–24-month-old children.* Unpublished doctoral dissertation, Oxford University.

Greenfield, P., and Smith, J. (1976). *The structure of communication in early language development.* New York: Academic Press.

Griffiths, P., and Atkinson, M. (1978). A "door" to verbs. In N. Waterson and C. Snow (Eds.), *The development of communication* (pp. 311–319). New York: Wiley.

Hespos, S. J., and Baillargeon, R. (2001). Reasoning about containment events in very young infants. *Cognition, 78,* 207–245.

Hespos, S. J., and Spelke, E. S. (2000). *Conceptual precursors to spatial language: Categories of containment.* Paper presented at the meeting of the International Society on Infant Studies, Brighton, UK.

Hunter, M., and Ames, E. W. (1988). A multifactor model of infant preferences for novel and familiar stimuli. In C. Rovee-Collier and L. P. Lipsitt (Eds.), *Advances in infancy research* (Vol. 5, pp. 69–95). Norwood, NJ: Ablex.

Johnston, J. R. (1984). Acquisition of locative meanings: Behind and in front of. *Journal of Child Language, 11,* 407–422.

Johnston, J. R. and Slobin, D. I. (1979). The development of locative expressions in English, Italian, Serbo-Croatian and Turkish. *Journal of Child Language, 6,* 529–545.

Kotovsky, L., and Gentner, D. (1996). Comparison and categorization in the development of relational similarity. *Child Development, 67,* 2797–2822.

Kuhl, P., Williams, K. A., Lacerda, F., Stevens, K. N., and Lindblom, B. (1992). Linguistic experience alters phonetic perception in infants by 6 months of age. *Science, 255,* 606–608.

Landau, B., and Jackendoff, R. (1993). "What" and "where" in spatial language and spatial cognition. *Behavioral and Brain Sciences, 16,* 217–238.

Landau, B., and Shipley, E. (1996). Object naming and category boundaries. *Proceedings of the Boston University Conference on Language Development, 20.2,* 443–452.

Levinson, S. C. (1996). Frames of reference and Molyneux's question: Cross-linguistic evidence. In P. Bloom, M. Peterson, L. Nadel, and M. Garrett (Eds.), *Language and space* (pp. 109–169). Cambridge, MA: MIT Press.

Loewenstein, J., and Gentner, D. (2001). Spatial mapping in preschoolers: Close comparisons facilitate far mappings. *Journal of Cognition and Development, 2,* 189–219.

Lucy, J. A. (1992). *Grammatical categories and cognition: A case study of the linguistic relativity hypothesis.* Cambridge: Cambridge University Press.

Lucy, J. A., and Gaskins, S. (2001). Grammatical categories and the development of classification preferences: A comparative approach. In M. Bowerman and S. C. Levinson (Eds.), *Language acquisition and conceptual development* (pp. 257–283). Cambridge: Cambridge University Press.

MacWhinney, B. (1987). The competition model. In B. MacWhinney (Ed.), *Mechanisms of language acquisition* (pp. 249–308). Hillsdale, NJ: Erlbaum.

Malt, B. C., Sloman, S. A., Gennari, S., Shi, M., and Wang, Y. (1999). Knowing versus naming: Similarity and the linguistic categorization of artifacts. *Journal of Memory and Language, 40*, 230–262.

Mandler, J. (1992). How to build a baby: II. Conceptual primitives. *Psychological Review, 99*, 587–604.

Mandler, J. (1996). Preverbal representation and language. In P. Bloom, M. Peterson, L. Nadel, and M. Garrett (Eds.), *Language and space* (pp. 365–384). Cambridge, MA: MIT Press.

Markman, E. (1989). *Categorization and naming in children: Problems of induction.* Cambridge, MA: MIT Press.

Maye, J., Werker, J. F., and Gerken, L. (2002). Infant sensitivity to distributional information can affect phonetic discrimination. *Cognition, 82*, B101–B111.

McCune, L., and Vihman, M. (1997). *The transition to reference in infancy.* Unpublished manuscript.

McCune-Nicolich, L. (1981). The cognitive bases of relational words in the single-word period. *Journal of Child Language, 8*, 15–34.

McDonough, L., Choi, S., and Mandler, J. (in press). Understanding spatial relations: Flexible infants, lexical adults. *Cognitive Psychology.*

Needham, A., and Baillargeon, R. (1993). Intuitions about support in 4.5-month-old infants. *Cognition, 47*, 121–148.

Nelson, K. (1974). Concept, word, and sentence: Interrelations in acquisition and development. *Psychological Review, 81*, 267–285.

Parisi, D., and Antinucci, F. (1970). Lexical competence. In G. B. Flores d'Arcais and W. J. M. Levelt (Eds.), *Advances in psycholinguistics* (pp. 197–210). Amsterdam: North-Holland.

Pederson, E., Danziger, E., Wilkins, D., Levinson, S. C., Kita, S., and Senft, G. (1998). Semantic typology and spatial conceptualization. *Language, 74*, 557–589.

Piaget, J., and Inhelder, B. (1956). *The child's conception of space.* London: Routledge and Kegan Paul.

Polka, L., Colantonio, C., and Sundara, M. (2001). A cross-language comparison of /d/~/ð/ perception: Evidence for a new developmental pattern. *Journal of the Acoustical Society of America, 109*, 2190–2201.

Polka, L., and Werker, J. F. (1994). Developmental changes in perception of nonnative vowel contrasts. *Journal of Experimental Psychology: Human Perception and Performance, 20*, 421–435.

Quinn, P. C. (1994). The categorization of above and below spatial relations by young infants. *Child Development, 65*, 58–69.

Quinn, P. C. (in press). Concepts are not just for objects: Categorization of spatial relational information by infants. In D. H. Rakison and L. M. Oakes (Eds.), *Early category and concept development: Making sense of the blooming, buzzing confusion.* Oxford: Oxford University Press.

Quinn, P. C., Norris, C. M., Pasko, R. N., Schmader, T. M., and Mash, C. (1999). Formation of a categorical representation for the spatial relation between by 6- to 7-month-old infants. *Visual Cognition*, 6, 569–585.

Regier, T. (1997). Constraints on the learning of spatial terms: A computational investigation. In R. L. Goldstone, P. G. Schyns, and D. L. Medin (Eds.), *Psychology of learning and motivation* (Vol. 36, pp. 171–217). San Diego, CA: Academic Press.

Sinha, C., Thorseng, L. A., Hayashi, M., and Plunkett, K. (1994). Comparative spatial semantics and language acquisition: Evidence from Danish, English, and Japanese. *Journal of Semantics*, 11, 253–287.

Slobin, D. I. (1973). Cognitive prerequisites for the development of grammar. In C. A. Ferguson and D. I. Slobin (Eds.), *Studies of child language development* (pp. 175–208). New York: Holt, Rinehart and Winston.

Slobin, D. I. (1985). Crosslinguistic evidence for the language-making capacity. In D. I. Slobin (Ed.), *The crosslinguistic study of language acquisition: Vol. 2. Theoretical issues* (pp. 1157–1256). Hillsdale, NJ: Erlbaum.

Smiley, P., and Huttenlocher, J. (1995). Conceptual development and the child's early words for events, objects, and persons. In M. Tomasello and W. Merriman (Eds.), *Beyond names for things: Young children's acquisition of verbs* (pp. 21–61). Hillsdale, NJ: Erlbaum.

Spelke, E. S., Breinlinger, K., Macomber, J., and Jacobson, K. (1992). Origins of knowledge. *Psychological Review*, 99, 605–632.

Streeter, L. A. (1976). Language perception of two-month-old infants shows effects of both innate mechanism and experience. *Nature*, 259, 39–41.

Talmy, L. (1985). Lexicalization patterns: Semantic structure in lexical forms. In T. Shopen (Ed.), *Language typology and syntactic description: Vol. 3. Grammatical categories and the lexicon* (pp. 57–149). Cambridge: Cambridge University Press.

Talmy, L. (1991). Path to realization: A typology of event conflation. *Proceedings of the Berkeley Linguistics Society*, 17, 480–519.

Werker, J. F., and Tees, R. C. (1984). Cross-language speech perception: Evidence for perceptual reorganization during the first year of life. *Infant Behavior and Development*, 7, 49–63.

Werker, J. F. and Tees, R. C. (1999). Experiential influences on infant speech processing: Toward a new synthesis. *Annual Review of Psychology*, 50, 509–535.

Wilkins, D. P., and Hill, D. (1995). When "go" means "come": Questioning the basicness of basic motion verbs. *Cognitive Linguistics*, 6, 209–259.

# 14

# Reevaluating Linguistic Relativity: Language-Specific Categories and the Role of Universal Ontological Knowledge in the Construal of Individuation

Mutsumi Imai and Reiko Mazuka

## 14.1 Introduction

*[handwritten margin note: sand and statues]*

Within the domain of concrete entities, objects and substances have very different properties. Objects are individuated, whereas substances are nonindividuated. Thus, the two kinds of entities have fundamentally different criteria for the notion of identity or sameness. When we say that two objects are *identical* or *the same*, we are referring to "two objects in their entirety" and not to "two distinctive parts of a single object." In contrast, when we say that two substances are *identical* or *the same*, there is no notion of wholeness. Substances are of "scattered existence," and there is no such thing as "whole sand," "whole water," or "whole clay" (see Quine 1969). This portion of sand is identical to that portion of sand, as long as the two portions consist of the same physical constituents. This difference in identity or sameness between objects and substances leads to fundamentally different extension principles for determining category membership across the two ontological kinds. For example, the label *cup* is applied to whole objects of a similar "cup" shape that can potentially contain liquid, regardless of their color and material components. If a "cup" is broken into pieces, each porcelain piece no longer constitutes a "cup." In contrast, the word *clay* is extended to any portion of clay, regardless of shape. One can divide a portion of clay into many small pieces, and each piece is still clay.

Not surprisingly, this ontological distinction with respect to individuation is grammatically marked in many languages around the world. For example, in English, object kinds are linguistically marked as count nouns, while substance kinds are marked as mass nouns. However, there is substantial crosslinguistic variation. For example, classifier languages have been noted as having a drastically different system for linguistically marking individuation (Imai 2000; Imai and Gentner 1997; Lucy 1992). In English, individuated entities (typically concrete objects) are referred to by count nouns, while nonindividuated entities (typically substances) are referred to by mass nouns, and whenever a noun is used, its count/mass status must be specified (Wierzbicka 1988). Unlike English, classifier languages in general do not mark a noun's count/mass status. That is, nouns referring to individuated objects and those referring to nonindividuated substances are not syntactically distinguished. (A more detailed structural comparison of English-type languages and classifier languages is provided later.)

Given this crosslinguistic difference in marking individuation in grammar, an important question immediately arises. Does language influence the formation of these ontological concepts at all? This question can be asked in two forms. The first form directly concerns linguistic relativity. Do crosslinguistic variations in marking ontological categories yield different construals of the ontological categories across speakers of different languages? If so, in what form and to what degree? The second form of the question arises from a developmental perspective. How do children come to possess ontological concepts? Are ontological categories acquired independently of language, or are they acquired through language learning?

In this chapter, we will explore these questions. We first briefly review two competing views on this issue: the linguistic relativity view and the universal ontology view. We then report a series of crosslinguistic developmental studies comparing English speakers and Japanese speakers, which were conducted to address these issues. Given the findings from these studies, we argue that, in contrast to these views, the answer lies in the middle ground and cannot be stated in a simple black-and-white fashion.

## 14.2   Review of the Two Dominant Views

### 14.2.1   Linguistic Relativity View

Roughly speaking, there are two competing views about whether differences in the structural treatment of individuation across different languages yield any significant psychological consequences. The so-called linguistic relativity view advocates that structural differences in language produce significantly different construals of the world (Whorf 1956). Interestingly, there are two major variations within the linguistic relativity view. The philosopher Quine (1960, 1969) asserts that children come to understand the ontological distinction between objects and substances only after learning the count/mass distinction. This is a very strong version of linguistic relativity, since the extreme interpretation of Quine's assertion would lead to the prediction that speakers of a language that does not grammatically mark this ontological distinction may never come to understand the fundamental ontological difference between objects and substances.

The linguistic anthropologist Lucy (1992) also advocates the linguistic relativity position, but his version is somewhat different from Quine's. In his comparative analysis of English and Yucatec Maya (a classifier language), the greatest difference between English-type languages and classifier languages is revealed in the domain of inanimate, discrete entities (Lucy 1992; Lucy and Gaskins 2001). In his view, a unit of individuation is presupposed in the meanings of English count nouns, while no unit of individuation is included in the meanings of mass nouns. In contrast, all nouns in classifier languages are lexically equivalent to English mass nouns, lacking the specification of a unit in their meanings and referring to the substance or material composition of an object. Lucy argues that this structural difference between English and Yucatec should lead speakers of the two languages to pay attention to different perceptual aspects of entities in the world, especially for inanimate, discrete entities. He asserts that a unit of individuation is best indicated by the shapes of objects, and this should lead native speakers of English to pay habitual attention to shape. In contrast, native speakers of a classifier language should develop habitual attention to material composition over shape:

For lexical nouns referring to objects which have a well-defined shape and are composed of a single material, the contrast between the two languages can be especially salient. Use of the English lexical items routinely draws attention to the shape of a referent insofar as its form is the basis for incorporating it under some lexical label. Use of the Yucatec lexical items, by contrast, routinely draws attention to the material composition of a referent insofar as its substance is the basis for incorporating it under some lexical label. Thus in cases where *English lexical structure routinely draws attention to shape, Yucatec lexical structure routinely draws attention to material.* If these linguistic patterns translate into general sensitivity to these properties of referents, then *English speakers should attend relatively more to the shape of objects* and *Yucatec speakers should attend relatively more to the material composition of objects* in other cognitive activities ... (Lucy 1992, 89; emphasis original)

Lucy (1992) tested this conjecture by comparing the classification behavior of speakers of American English and speakers of Yucatec. He showed Yucatec-speaking adults and English-speaking adults a standard stimulus (e.g., a sheet of paper). He then showed them two alternatives, one the same shape as the standard (e.g., a sheet of plastic) and the other a different kind of object made of the same material as the standard (e.g., a book). He asked which of the two alternatives was more similar to the standard. He found that Yucatec-speaking adults showed a reliable bias toward material alternatives and English-speaking adults a reliable bias toward shape alternatives. These results were taken to suggest that language influences whether people use shape or material composition in judging the similarity of objects.

Note that Lucy's and Quine's proposals may make somewhat different predictions about the learning process of speakers of classifier languages. As previously stated, the extreme interpretation of Quine's view would lead to the prediction that children speaking a classifier language will never learn the ontological difference between objects and substances. On the other hand, if we take Lucy's view to an extreme (although he may not be willing to go this far), we may predict that children learning a classifier language will construe any discrete inanimate entity as a chunk/lump of substance. Nonetheless, the two theorists' views are similar in that both claim that the ontological distinction between objects and substances is not a universal property of human cognition, and that the distinction between object kinds and substance kinds—which English speakers regard as the "fundamental ontological dichotomy"—is merely a reflection of their language's particular form of linguistic categorization. According to Lucy (Lucy and Gaskins, this volume), because there is no universal ontology, children learning a language that does not grammatically mark the ontological distinction do not need to learn the ontological distinction regarding individuation in order to acquire the lexicon of this language. In fact, Lucy and Gaskins claim that the presence of the ontological distinction would interfere with lexical acquisition (sec. 15.4).

### 14.2.2   Universal Ontology View

In contrast to those holding linguistic relativity views (particularly Quine's version of relativity), the developmental psychologists Soja, Carey, and Spelke (1991) have argued that children are endowed with an innate appreciation of the ontological distinction between objects and substances.[1] They have shown that English-speaking 2-year-olds who have not yet acquired the count/mass syntax are able to constrain meanings of novel words using the ontological distinction between objects and substances: hearing a novel noun in association with a solid, discrete entity (i.e., an object ), they extended the word on the basis of shape; and hearing a novel noun in association with a nonsolid substance, they extended the word on the basis of material identity, ignoring shape. As a natural consequence of the conclusion that the ontological distinction is available prior to language acquisition, Soja, Carey, and Spelke argue that this knowledge is universally present, whether or not a child's native language marks the distinction in grammar.

### 14.2.3   Empirical Data Concerning the Two Positions

As noted above, there is a substantial discrepancy in the literature with respect to the relation between language and the ontological concepts regarding individuation. In particular, how should we evaluate the linguistic relativity and universal ontology positions, given Lucy's (1992) empirical results supporting the former and Soja, Carey, and Spelke's (1991) results supporting the latter?

In spite of the elegance of these studies, neither study's results are unambiguously conclusive. Mazuka and Friedman (2000), for example, question Lucy's interpretation of his results, saying that they might be better explained in terms of sociocultural factors, that is, in terms of the vast difference in the cultural and educational backgrounds of the American subjects and the Yucatec subjects. They conducted a study similar to Lucy's using English-speaking American college students and Japanese college students, and in fact did not replicate Lucy's results with the Japanese subjects.

Soja, Carey, and Spelke's results are not definitive either, because, as Imai and Gentner (1997) point out, the possibility cannot be ruled out that the 2-year-olds they tested had already been influenced by language. To make sure that the children's word extensions reflected early knowledge of the ontological concepts rather than knowledge of syntax, Soja, Carey, and Spelke measured the children's productive command of count/mass syntax and found no correlation between productive control and children's performance on the task. However, the production task they had conducted might not have been sensitive enough to capture all that the 2-year-olds knew about count/mass grammar. In fact, the results were somewhat different when Soja (1992) later presented novel words in the "ontologically wrong" syntax (i.e., when mass noun syntax was used in the object trials and count noun syntax was used in the substance trials). If children determine the projection of word meanings solely on the basis of ontological knowledge without being influenced by syntax at all, there should be no difference in their performance when novel words are presented in the "ontologically correct" syntax and when they are presented in the "ontologically incorrect" syntax. However, Soja found that the 2-year-olds' performance was affected by syntax, although the magnitude of the effect of syntax was not strong enough to change the default construal of the named entities.

Furthermore, a massive body of developmental research, most of which has investigated conceptual development within a single language community (rather than in a cross-cultural/crosslinguistic context), reports a powerful influence of language on cognition. In particular, it is well known that children tend to form more consistent, adultlike categories when asked to determine the extension of a novel label than when asked to determine the "same" or "most similar" object without invocation of any labels (e.g., Imai, Gentner, and Uchida 1994; Landau, Smith, and Jones 1988; Markman and Hutchinson 1984; Subrahmanyam, Landau, and Gelman 1999; Waxman and Gelman 1986; Waxman and Kosowski 1990). This influence of language on category formation and appreciation of "kinds," which of itself may be considered a variant of the Whorfian effect (e.g., Byrnes and Gelman 1991), has been observed as early as 12 months of age (Waxman and Markow 1995; Xu 1999). Given this evidence for an impact of language on conceptual development in infants much younger than those tested by Soja, Carey, and Spelke (1991), together with some effect of syntax reported by Soja (1992), it is difficult to exclude the possibility that the appreciation for the ontological distinction between objects and substances demonstrated by English-speaking 2-year-olds is a consequence of, or at least is influenced by, early language learning.

The ideal test should involve children whose native language does not have a linguistic apparatus for marking individuation. Also, to minimize the possibility of attributing the crosslinguistic difference to differences in sociocultural background rather than linguistic factors, the two language groups being compared should have comparable socioeconomic and educational backgrounds (see Mazuka and Friedman 2000). Since Japanese provides an ideal case for this purpose, we conducted a series of studies to directly address the problems facing Soja, Carey, and Spelke's (1991) and Lucy's (1992) studies. However, before we report our results, a comparison of the structural treatment of individuation in Japanese and in English is in order, since the interpretation of the results hinges on the structural analysis of the two languages.

## 14.3 Structural Analysis of Individuation in English and Japanese

### 14.3.1 Marking Individuation in English
As stated earlier, English and Japanese differ sharply in *how*, and in particular, *how systematically*, individuation is marked. English obligatorily marks the status of an entity with respect to individuation. For example, when introducing an entity named by a common noun, English speakers always syntactically distinguish whether the entity is individuated (by using a count noun) or nonindividuated (by using a mass noun). English also makes a singular/plural distinction such that when speakers refer to multiple distinct individuals of the same type, they use a plural noun. Native English speakers also appear to know implicitly the count/mass status of nouns in their lexicon, not only for concrete entities but also for nonconcrete, intangible entities such as events and abstract concepts. For example, most speakers would probably judge that *I've come up with a conclusion* and *many conclusions* sound natural but that *I've come up with conclusion* and *much conclusion* sound awkward. Hence,

they implicitly know that the abstract term *conclusion* is a count noun. Likewise, on the basis of analogous judgments, English speakers probably know that the aggregate *lentils* is a count noun but the aggregate *gravel* is a mass noun, that the superordinate *vehicle* is a count noun but the superordinate *clothing* is a mass noun, and so forth. Of course, context may alter the count/mass status of a noun, and some nouns may have dual status (e.g., *chocolate*). However, English speakers appear to view most nouns primarily as either count or mass nouns.

### 14.3.2    Marking Individuation in Japanese

Japanese treats individuation quite differently from English. Several observations suggest that Japanese is much less likely to explicitly mark the status of an entity with respect to individuation. Japanese speakers typically do not introduce an entity in this way (as English speakers do). For example, if $X$ denotes a noun, then in the sentence *Kore (this) wa (topic-marking particle) X desu (IS-polite)* 'This is X,' $X$ can (among other things) refer to either an object or a substance. Japanese also does not make the singular/plural distinction. In the absence of context, someone hearing the sentence above would not know whether it refers to one individual or more than one; (see also Imai 1999; Imai and Haryu 2001).

*Only in quantifying contexts* does Japanese individuate nouns, using classifiers and a few quantifiers. The way individuation is realized, however, is much the same as the way English individuates mass nouns. In English, nonindividuated entities are quantified by explicitly providing a unit of quantification (e.g., two *glasses* of water, two *bottles* of water). Classifiers provide a similar function in numeral classifier languages (Craig 1994). Importantly, this numeral + classifier construction is not limited to the English sense of mass nouns. It is required in quantifying *any* noun including those denoting apparently individuated entities such as people, animals, cars, chairs, and so on.

Even though individuated and nonindividuated entities are not apparently distinguished by different syntactic constructions, one might wonder if there is a strong correlation between individuation and classifier classes. That is, if we know that the noun $X$ is associated with the classifier $Y$, might we be able to predict that $X$ belongs to the class of individuals or that of nonindividuals? By and large, the answer is no. Many classifiers, including shape classifiers such as *ko* (for three-dimensionally salient things), *hon* (for long, thin things), and *mai* (for flat things) and measuring classifiers such as *hai* (a cup/glass/bowl of), *yama* (a heap of), and *hako* (a box/carton of), can appear with both objects and substances. For example, *hon*, one of the most frequently used classifiers (see Lakoff 1987), typically appears with long, thin objects such as pencils and chopsticks, so it is usually characterized as a classifier for long, thin *objects*. However, on closer inspection, what is crucial to the meaning of *hon* is the long and thin (i.e., one-dimensionally salient) *shape* per se. That is, class members do not need to be objects. *Hon* (and other shape classifiers such as *ko* and *mai*) can appear with typical substances such as butter, water, and wine; in these cases, the classifier indicates the shape of the portion of the given substance or the shape of the container the substance appears in. These observations suggest that the conceptual distinction regarding individuation is not a crucial factor for determining membership for each classifier class.

### 14.3.3 Comparison of Japanese and Yucatec

Being a classifier language, Japanese shares many structural characteristics with Yucatec. For example, there is no obligatory marking for individuation in either language; and in both, all nouns require a classifier when quantified, whether they refer to an object or to a substance. However, there is at least one important difference between Japanese and Yucatec. We will briefly discuss this below, since not every aspect of Lucy's (1992) structural analysis of Yucatec necessarily applies to Japanese (or other classifier languages), and this in turn may suggest that Lucy's prediction for how speakers of Yucatec construe individuation may not be applied to speakers of classifier languages in general.

Lucy notes that in Yucatec, a noun referring to a substance is often extended to refer to different objects that are made of that substance by attaching different shape classifiers. For example, the word *che* 'wood' is used to refer not only to the material itself, but also to a variety of objects that are composed of wood and have distinctive shapes, such as 'tree, stick, board' (1992, 74). Also, a single noun can be used to refer to different parts of an entity, which are denoted by different names in

English. For example, depending on the accompanying classifier, the single word *ha'as* refers to the fruit of the banana plant (i.e., what English speakers call *banana*), the leaf, the plant itself (i.e., the tree), a bunch of the fruit, and so forth. This pattern does not hold for Japanese nouns.

In Japanese, just as in English,[2] the name of an object is not usually related to the name of the material it is made of, either semantically or morphologically. Also, a part of an object usually has a name that is lexically independent of the name of the object itself. For example, wood, sticks, trees, boards, and leaves are all denoted by different names that are not morphologically related. This linguistic property makes Japanese more suitable than Yucatec to test Lucy's argument that it is the structural (i.e., grammatical) rather than lexical property of classifier languages that leads the speaker's "habitual attention" to the material component of the entity. Because of the particular lexical property of Yucatec—that many object names were extended from material names— it is difficult to determine whether the material bias shown by Yucatec speakers should indeed be attributed to the grammatical property or to the lexical property, if indeed the difference between the Yucatec and American English speakers can be attributed to linguistic factors in the first place. On the other hand, if Japanese speakers display the same material bias, we can more comfortably attribute it to the structural (i.e., grammatical) property of the language, since object names are not derived from material names in Japanese and since the sociocultural and educational background of Japanese speakers is more compatible with that of English speakers living in the United States.

## 14.4   Japanese-English Crosslinguistic Studies

In this section, we will report two crosslinguistic studies conducted by Imai and her colleagues (Imai and Gentner 1997; Imai and Mazuka 1997; Imai 2000). To give a brief overview, we first discuss whether Japanese-speaking children and adults project noun meanings differently for objects and substances following ontological principles. We then report how Japanese- and English-speaking children and adults construe a range of entities as individuated or nonindividuated in a nonlinguistic context. We compare people's classification behavior in linguistic and nonlinguistic contexts, and we discuss how language (here, the presence of novel labels) might influence speakers' construals of entities. Later (section 14.6), we report follow-up studies that were conducted to clarify some questions raised by the results of the main crosslinguistic studies.

### 14.4.1   How Do Speakers of English and Japanese Project Word Meanings?

Imai and Gentner (1997) extended Soja, Carey, and Spelke's (1991) studies crosslinguistically, comparing English speakers and Japanese speakers at various levels of development, including four age groups: early 2-year-olds, late 2-year-olds, 4-year-olds, and adults. Following Soja, Carey, and Spelke's procedure, Imai and Gentner introduced a novel label in association with an entity children had never seen before. For English speakers, the labels were introduced in such a way that the noun's syntactic count/mass status was not revealed (e.g., "Look at this *dax*. Can you point to the tray that also has the *dax* on it?"). The structure of Japanese does not reveal the noun's status of individuation (e.g., "Kore (this) wa (topic-marking particle) *dax* desu (IS). Dochira (which) no (genitive) sara (tray) ni (locative particle) *dax* ga (subject-marking particle) aru (exist)?").

In constructing the stimulus materials, Imai and Gentner set up three different types of entities so that the stimuli reflected the individuation continuum within the realm of inanimate concrete entities, including both solid objects and nonsolid substances. Unlike Lucy (1992), Imai and Gentner thought that even within this domain (i.e., [−animate, +discrete] in Lucy's terms), some entities, such as those that have complex and cohesive structures, are more naturally individuated than ones that have simple structures (see also Gentner 1982; Gentner and Boroditsky 2001). Thus, the first type, the *complex objects*, consisted of real objects that had fairly complex shapes and distinct functions, although the functions were unknown to the children in the studies. In contrast, the second type, the *simple objects*, had very simple structures with no distinct parts. They were made of a solid substance such as clay or wax, formed into a very simple shape (e.g., the shape of a kidney). The third type, the *substances*, consisted of nonsolid materials such as sand or hair-setting gel, arranged in distinct, interesting shapes.

At a global level (i.e., when we compared the overall response patterns across the three entity types between the two language groups), Imai and Gentner's results support the universal ontology position across all age groups tested. Just like English-speaking children and adults, Japanese speakers, from 2 years of age through adulthood, clearly showed distinct (and ontologically correct) word meaning projection patterns across the complex object trials and the substance trials.

However, when English and Japanese speakers' categorization behavior was examined more closely by comparing the behavior of the two language groups within each trial type, there was a marked crosslinguistic differences in the simple object and substance trials. In the substance trials, while Japanese speakers projected the word meaning onto material, English speakers responded randomly. In the simple object trials, while English speakers treated these simple-shaped solid, discrete entities in the same way as the complex objects and projected the word meaning onto shape, Japanese-speaking children overall showed random performance. (In fact, Japanese-speaking adults projected the word meaning onto material significantly above chance.)

In summary, Imai and Gentner's (1997) results supported the universal ontology position at a global level, refuting Quine's version of linguistic relativity. However, at the same time, Imai and Gentner found noteworthy crosslinguistic differences between the two language groups that were partly consistent with Lucy's proposal. Given these results, it would be interesting to see if the crosslinguistic differences found in the word meaning projection task are replicated in a no-word classification task, where people are asked to determine which of two test stimuli is the "same" as the standard. Because the novel noun's syntactic status was ambiguous in Imai and Gentner's word extension paradigm, the results in principle should reflect the subject's construal of the labeled entity as individuated or nonindividuated. Nonetheless, it is possible that categorization behavior is different across a word extension context and a no-word context, as many studies have reported. Children tend to form more adultlike, consistent categories when asked to determine the extension of a novel label than when asked to determine the "same" or "most similar" object without invocation of any labels (e.g., Imai, Gentner, and Uchida 1994; Landau, Smith, and Jones 1988; Markman and

Hutchinson 1984; Waxman and Gelman 1986; Waxman and Kosowski 1990).

This dissociation between categorization in naming and nonnaming contexts has been found with adults as well. Malt et al. (1999) conducted a series of categorization tasks with English speakers, Spanish speakers, and Chinese speakers. When participants were asked to categorize a variety of containers on the basis of names, the three language groups categorized rather differently; but when they were asked to categorize on the basis of overall similarity or functional similarity, the cross-cultural agreement was much higher (see also Malt, Sloman, and Gennari, this volume). Thus, there are some grounds to suspect that the crosslinguistic differences found in Imai and Gentner's study may not hold for similarity judgment/categorization that does not involve naming. In particular, it is possible that English speakers and Japanese speakers categorize much more similarly in a no-word classification task. Thus, to further evaluate the universal ontology view and the linguistic relativity view, we conducted a no-word classification task with English-speaking and Japanese-speaking children and adults (Imai and Mazuka 1997).

### 14.4.2   Crosslinguistic Comparison in a No-Word Categorization Task

Monolingual Japanese-speaking and English-speaking 4-year-olds and adults who had not participated in the previous label extension studies participated in a no-word classification task. The stimuli and the procedure were the same as in the previous label extension studies, except that no labels were provided. The subject was presented with a standard entity and two alternatives, and was asked to select "what is the same as" the standard entity. The English instruction was "Show me what's the same as this," and the Japanese instruction was "Kore (this) to (with) onaji-nano (same) wa (topic-marking particle) docchi (which) desuka (IS-question)?"

### 14.4.2.1   Adults' Classification Behavior in the No-Word Task   The crosslinguistic difference between English speakers and Japanese speakers in the word extension task found by Imai and Gentner (1997) was replicated in the no-word categorization task for adults. As in the word extension task, the adults in both language groups matched the shape

alternative to the standard in the complex object trials. However, the marked crosslinguistic differences found in the simple object and the substance trials in the word extension task were also found here. In the simple object trials, the adults in the two language groups showed the opposite construals: while the English speakers regarded the shape alternative as the "same" as the standard entity, the Japanese speakers regarded the material alternative as the same. In the substance trials, while the Japanese speakers unanimously selected the material alternative, showing the substance construal for these entities, the English speakers responded randomly.

Response patterns in the no-word categorization task were plotted together with those observed in the word extension task for each language-age group (see figure 14.1). For both language groups, the adults in each group showed almost identical response patterns across the two tasks (see figures 14.1(b) and 14.1(d)).

**14.4.2.2  Children's Classification Behavior in the No-Word Task**   In contrast to the adult's performance, children's classification behavior in the no-word task did not converge to their age-mates' behavior in the word extension task. In particular, the English-speaking children's behavior differed drastically across the two classification contexts (see figure 14.1(a)). While the English-speaking children in the word extension task showed virtually the same response patterns as the English-speaking adults, their age-mates in the no-word categorization task performed at chance level in all three trial types.

**14.4.2.3  Correspondence Analysis**   The comparison of English speakers and Japanese speakers indicates that the children's response patterns were very similar to those of the adults in their own language group *in the word extension task*, already exhibiting the language-specific categorization bias. In contrast, in the no-word classification task, this language-specific bias was not observed as clearly. In fact, a correspondence analysis revealed that the English-speaking children behaved more like the Japanese-speaking children than like the English-speaking adults. Correspondence analysis is a graphical technique for analyzing two-way contingency data, whose goal is to describe the relationships between

(a) English-speaking 4-year-olds

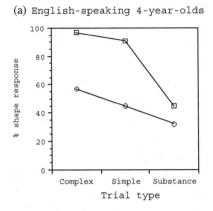

(b) English-speaking adults

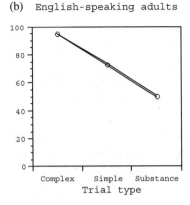

-□- Word
-○- No Word

(c) Japanese-speaking 4-year-olds

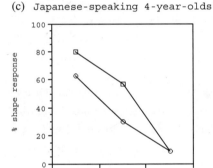

(d) Japanese-speaking adults

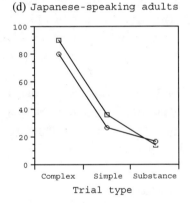

**Figure 14.1**
Subject's classification behavior in the (neutral-syntax) word extension task and in the no-word classification task: (*a*) English-speaking 4-year-olds, (*b*) English-speaking adults, (*c*) Japanese-speaking 4-year-olds, and (*d*) Japanese-speaking adults

two variables in a correspondence table in a low-dimensional space, while simultaneously describing the relationships between the categories for each variable (Greenacre 1984).

In our case, the first variable was Subject Group (Japanese-speaking adults, Japanese-speaking children, English-speaking adults, English-speaking children) and the second variable was Stimulus Type (Complex Object, Simple Object, Substance). The distances between category points in a plot reflect the relationship between the categories, with similar categories plotted close to each other. For readability, only the four categories of the Subject Group variable were plotted. In the word extension case (figure 14.2(a)), the two language groups made two distinct clusters, with adults and children within each language group close to each other. In contrast, in the no-word classification case (figure 14.2(b)), while the Japanese-speaking children and the Japanese-speaking adults were close to each other, the English-speaking adults and the English-speaking children were far apart. In fact, the English-speaking children were much closer to the Japanese-speaking children than to the English-speaking adults.

### 14.4.2.4 Summary of the Results of the Japanese-English Crosslinguistic Comparative Studies    Let us summarize the findings of the Japanese-English crosslinguistic comparative studies reported thus far.

1. Adults' classification behavior was almost identical across the word extension task (with ambiguous count/mass syntax) and the no-word classification task. In contrast, for both language groups, the children's classification behavior between the word extension and no-word classification tasks did not converge as closely. In particular, a clear dissociation between the two tasks was found among the English-speaking children.

2. In both word extension and no-word classification tasks, adults honored the ontological distinction between objects and substances. When the standard entity was a solid object with a complex structure, they selected the match on the basis of shape. When the standard entity was a nonsolid substance, the proportion of shape choices greatly decreased and the proportion of material choices increased.

(a) Word condition

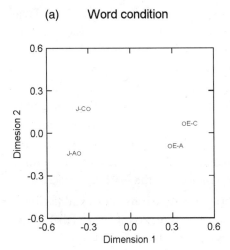

(b) No-word condition

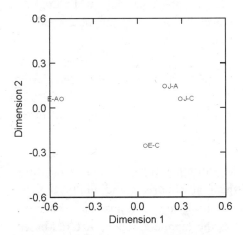

**Figure 14.2**
Plot of responses by Japanese-speaking children (J-C), Japanese-speaking adults (J-A), English-speaking children (E-C), English-speaking adults (E-A) in a correspondence analysis: (*a*) word condition; (*b*) no-word condition

3. There were also noteworthy crosslinguistic differences between Japanese speakers and English speakers in both the word extension and the no-word classification tasks. In the simple object trials, English-speaking adults selected the match on the basis of shape, suggesting that they construed the standard entity as an individuated "object." In contrast, Japanese-speaking adults selected the match on the basis of material, suggesting that they construed the standard entity as a nonindividuated "substance." In the substance trials, Japanese-speaking adults uniformly selected the match on the basis of material identity, while English-speaking adults were split between the shape choice and the material choice.

4. Children showed response patterns very similar to those of adults in the same language group only in the word extension task. Given a label whose syntactic count/mass status was ambiguous, both English-speaking and Japanese-speaking children extended it on the basis of shape in the complex object trials. In the simple object trials, while English-speaking children extended the label on the basis of shape, Japanese-speaking children showed chance-level performance. In the substance trials, while English-speaking children showed chance-level performance, Japanese-speaking children clearly extended the label on the basis of material.

## 14.5   Puzzling Questions

Some of the findings from the crosslinguistic research reported above leave us with puzzling questions and demand further clarification and explanation. For example, how should we account for the crosslinguistic difference in the simple object and substance trials? In particular, how should we interpret the English-speaking children's and adults' chance-level performance in the substance trials and the Japanese children's chance-level performance as well as the Japanese adults' material-based responses in the simple object trials? How should we account for the difference in the English-speaking children's behavior across the word extension and no-word classification tasks? In particular, how should we interpret their chance-level, ontology-indifferent classification behavior in the no-word task? Obviously, these questions are all related to one another, but we will deal with them in order.

### 14.5.1   What Does the Crosslinguistic Difference Mean?

Given the marked crosslinguistic difference in adult's responses in the simple object trials, we might wonder whether the results in the simple object trials mean that English speakers and Japanese speakers construe the same entities in fundamentally different ways. A strong linguistic relativity position would endorse this hypothesis. As stated earlier, Quine (1969) conjectured that this is the case. Lucy (1992, 2000) also explicitly casts doubt on the view that the distinction between objects and substances is a universal and ontological dichotomy, arguing that it is instead "a discourse property assigned to entities in different ways in each language" (2000, xvii).

The findings reported here suggest that this is not a plausible answer, however. As stated earlier, had Lucy's strong linguistic relativity position been correct, Japanese speakers should have selected the material choice for all three types of entities in both the word extension and the no-word classification tasks. Similarly, had Quine been correct, Japanese speakers should have shown ontology-indifferent responses; but the fact that Japanese-speaking children and adults projected word meanings differently for complex-structured objects and nonsolid substances suggests that the ontological contrast between individuated objects and nonindividuated substances is honored independent of language.

But then, how should we interpret the crosslinguistic difference? The data we have reported so far certainly argue for a universally present ontological distinction at a global level. At the same time, however, we think it is quite possible that language influences the *boundary* of the two ontological classes, biasing the preferred construal of a particular type of entity in one way or the other. If true, this phenomenon constitutes a piece of evidence for linguistic relativity. Specifically, we conjecture that the criteria for determining the class membership of a given entity may be influenced by a bias developed as a result of learning a particular language, and that the influence of this language-specific bias is maximized when the entity's perceptual properties are ambiguous and allow "dual" construals. Thus, the Japanese-speaking children's chance-level performance in the simple object trials and the adults' material-based classification do not necessarily mean that they fail to understand that those simple-shaped solid lumps of substances would follow principles of physical objects such as the principle of common fate, the principle of cohesion, and so forth (Spelke 1990). We think that the Japanese speakers were able to see that the entities used for the simple object trials *could be* construed as objects, but for some reason (we will come back to this) they were biased toward construing them as portions of nonindividuated substances while English speakers were biased toward construing them as members of object kinds. Likewise, we believe that the English speakers were able to tell that the entities used for the substance trials were instances of substance kinds. To demonstrate this, we conducted additional studies, to which we now turn.

## 14.6    Follow-up Experiments

### 14.6.1    Two Follow-up Studies with English Speakers

In a further study, we examined to what extent a change in a noun's syntactic status would cause English speakers to shift the default categorization bias (Imai and Mazuka 1997). It is known that from a very young age, English speakers are aware of how the count/mass syntax maps onto the corresponding ontological classes (e.g., Bloom 1994; Soja 1992; Wisniewski, Imai, and Casey 1996). We reasoned that, if a noun's syntactic status strongly conflicted with English speakers' construal of the referred entity, they would be confused and respond randomly. In contrast, if English speakers were aware that the simple-shaped discrete entities used for the simple object trials could be construed as portions of nonindividuated substance and that the entities used for the substance trials were really nonindividuated substances, they would easily change their construals for these entities according to the syntax. We tested English-speaking 4-year-olds and adults to examine this.

The same 12 sets (4 sets in each trial type) used in the word extension (with ambiguous syntax) and no-word classification tasks were used for this study. Participants were asked to select one of the two alternatives that they considered the "same" as the standard. However, in this study, a novel noun was associated with the standard in an explicit syntactic frame. Participants in the count syntax condition heard novel nouns embedded in count syntax throughout the 12 trials. Likewise, participants in the mass syntax condition heard novel nouns embedded in mass syntax throughout the 12 trials. The instruction used in the count syntax condition was "Look! This is *a* X (pointing to the standard). Can you point to *another* X?" The instruction used in the mass syntax condition was "Look! This is X. Can you point to *some more* X?"

When novel nouns were presented in the mass noun syntactic frame, the default classification patterns were largely changed by the syntax (see figures 14.3(a) and 14.3(c)). Specifically, in the mass syntax condition, the adults responded exactly as predicted. They responded randomly in the complex object trials (48%), presumably because complex objects very strongly invite the "object construal" and the syntax conflicts with this strong default response. In contrast, they chose the material alternative in the simple object trials (85% material response). This suggests that, despite a strong bias toward construing a simple-shaped solid lump of substance as an individuated object, the English-speaking adults did have dual construals for these entities; that is, they were fully aware that these entities can also be construed as a portion of substance. In the substance trials, they again selected the material alternative greatly above chance level (87%).

Overall, the children's response pattern in the mass syntax condition was very similar to the adults' pattern: they responded randomly in the complex object trials and gave strong material responses in the substance trials (59% and 19.6% shape response, respectively). However, unlike the adults, the 4-year-olds performed at chance level in the simple object trials (46% shape response). Recall that in the ambiguous syntax case, their shape response level had been very high (91%)—in fact, almost as high as for the complex objects (95%). Even though they performed at chance level in the simple object trials using the mass noun syntactic frame, their shape responses decreased by 45% from the ambiguous syntax case. Thus, English-speaking 4-year-olds definitely knew that mass noun syntax flags nonindividuation (see also Bloom 1994; Subrahmanyan, Landau, and Gelman 1999 for similar findings). However, because they were so strongly biased toward construing any discrete entities as individuated objects (Bloom 1994, 2000; see also Shipley and Shepperson 1990), it must have been difficult for them to construe the entities used in the simple object trials as portions of nonindividuated

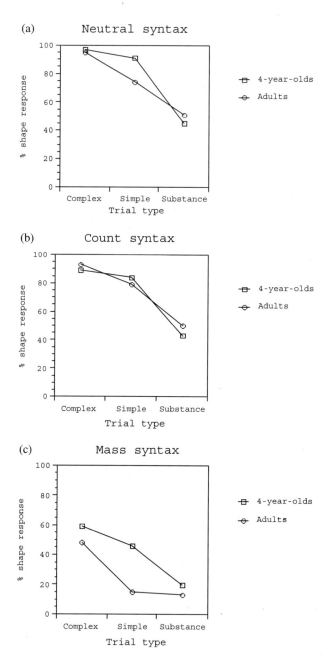

**Figure 14.3**
English speakers' classification behavior in the (*a*) neutral syntax condition, (*b*) count syntax condition, and (*c*) mass syntax condition

substances, overcoming this bias. As in the complex object trials, the mass noun syntax thus strongly conflicted with their construal of the entities; hence, their responding fell to chance level.

For both age groups, the response pattern in the count syntax condition was almost identical to the pattern found in the ambiguous syntax word extension task: participants showed a very high rate of shape responding (see figure 14.3(b)). This is no surprise for the complex and simple object trials, because the rates of shape responding in these two trial types were already at ceiling in the ambiguous syntax case. For the substance trials, we had expected to see an increase in shape responding in the count syntax condition, since count syntax indicates that the entity referred to is individuated. Surprisingly, however, both the children and the adults responded randomly, just as in the ambiguous syntax case.

It may be that the English speakers assumed the novel nouns presented in the ambiguous syntactic frame indeed to be count nouns. Because the count/mass syntax is obligatory in English, perhaps the English speakers in Imai and Gentner's (1997) study did not (or perhaps more accurately, could not) encode ambiguously presented nouns as having a "neutral" syntactic status. Even though the nouns' syntactic status was made ambiguous, the children may have assumed that the nouns were count nouns rather than mass nouns, possibly because the count interpretation is unmarked for *the/this/that* X. Even though articles such as *the, this,* and *that* can appear with either a count noun or a mass noun, children hear count nouns more frequently than mass nouns (Samuelson and Smith 1999).

However, it remains puzzling why the English speakers, especially the adults, performed at chance level in the substance trials even in the no-word classification task. Why did they not give material responses for these items? As mentioned earlier, the fact that they were able to give substance responses with the mass noun syntax suggests that they could construe those entities as nonindividuated substances. Why, then, did the English speakers respond randomly even in the no-word classification task? One possibility is that, besides having a bias toward assuming a novel noun to be a count noun when its syntactic status is not explicitly given, seeing two substances in the same distinct shape may have led the

English speakers to think that identity of shape might be significant, even though they were well aware that the standard entities were nonsolid substances and hence that their shapes had little to do with their essence.

This possibility was confirmed by an additional follow-up experiment, in which only the standard entity was presented and English-speaking adults determined whether the label for it should be a count noun or a mass noun (Imai 2000). Monolingual English-speaking adults who had not taken part in the earlier studies were tested. The stimulus materials were the 12 standard entities used by Imai and Gentner (1997). Each standard entity was presented alone without the two test alternatives. Two cards were placed next to the standard entity. A nonsense count noun phrase was written on one card (e.g., *a fep*), and a nonsense mass noun phrase on the other card (e.g., *some fep*). The experimenter asked the participants to select the card on which the label for the entity was given in the appropriate syntax.[3] As in earlier studies, the English-speaking adults showed a strong "object" construal for the standard entities used in the complex object trials and the simple object trials (100% and 83%, respectively). In contrast, unlike in earlier studies, the English speakers now exhibited a strong "substance" construal for the standard entities in the substance trials, selecting the mass noun labels 80% of the time. Thus, the English speakers did construe the entities in the substance trials as nonindividuated substances, and the chance-level performance in the substance trials in the previous studies was most likely a consequence of seeing two identically shaped substances next to each other. Note that it is still important that juxtaposition of two identically shaped substances affected only the English speakers, not the Japanese speakers. However, the two findings—(1) English speakers were able to make the substance construals very easily when the labels were embedded in the mass syntax and (2) English speakers judged that the mass syntax was appropriate for the labels when the standard entities were presented alone—suggest that this crosslinguistic difference does not in itself mean that the ontological distinction between objects and substances is language relative, contrary to Quine (1969) and Lucy (1992, 2000).

Of course, one may rightly ask, "Then what does the crosslinguistic difference really mean?" We will come back to this question. First, however, we report another follow-up study with Japanese-speaking children, which examined the meaning of their chance-level performance in the simple object trials.

### 14.6.2   Japanese-Speaking Children's Construal of Simple Objects

Japanese-speaking children consistently performed at chance level in the simple object trials both in the word extension task and in the no-word classification task. How should we interpret this? It could be that the difference in classification behavior across the complex object and substance trials was a matter of perceptual salience of the target entities and had little to do with ontological appreciation. That is, children may have based their judgment of sameness on the most salient perceptual property, be it color, texture, or shape. They may have chosen the same-shape item in the complex object trials simply because shape was more salient than color/texture in the entities they saw in those trials, and likewise for the substances they saw in the substance trials. They may have responded randomly in the simple object trials because neither the shape nor the color/texture of the entities in those trials particularly stood out. To examine this possibility, a study was conducted.

Imai (2000) examined Japanese-speaking 3-year-olds' classification behavior in a word extension task and a no-word classification task. In contrast to the previous studies, which employed a forced-choice paradigm (Imai and Gentner 1997; Imai and Mazuka 1997), this study allowed children to select more than one object. This paradigm is possible because not only does Japanese lack a count/mass distinction, it also lacks a singular/plural distinction. From the instruction "*X* o (accusative-marking particle) totte (give-imperative)" 'Give me *X*', it was thus totally ambiguous whether one or more than one object should be selected (see also Imai and Haryu 2001). As in the previous studies, the stimuli included real artifacts with complex structures and simple-shaped entities handmade out of a solid substance. The standard entities were all unfamiliar to the children. Each set consisted of four test items: a same-shape item, a same-material item, and two distractor items. The children were randomly assigned to either the word extension condition or the no-word classification condition. In the word extension condition, a child was presented with the standard entity, which was given a novel label *X*.

The child was then shown all four test items in the first set and was asked which of the test items was also X. When the child made a selection, whether he or she selected one or more than one item, the experimenter asked whether there was/were any more X. When the child said "No" to the prompt, the experimenter proceeded to the next set. In the no-word classification condition, a child was first presented with the standard entity, and then with the four test items. The experimenter said to the child, "Kore (this) to onaji (same)-no (genitive-marking particle) o (accusative-marking particle) totte (give-imperative)" 'Give me what's the same as this'.

We were particularly interested in the children's responses for the simple object trials. If children do not appreciate the ontological distinction, depending solely on perceptual saliency, they should select *both* the same-shape item and the same-material item, because both dimensions are equally salient for those simple-structured entities. In contrast, if they indeed honor the ontological distinction, they should select either the same-shape item or the same-material item, but not both, although the selection may be evenly divided between the two.

It turned out that the Japanese-speaking children showed the latter pattern in the word extension condition, but the former pattern in the no-word classification condition. In both the word extension and the no-word classification conditions, among the four test items, the children rarely selected the distractors. In the word extension condition, the children selected *only* the same-shape item 55% of the time, and *only* the same-material item 44% of the time. Remember, this was not a forced-choice task, and children could have selected *both* items. However, 12 children out of 15 selected only one test item for all sets, and the average number of selected items per set was 1.02. In contrast, in the no-word classification condition, the children selected the same-shape item 69% of the time, and the same-material item 73% of the time. The average number of selected items per set was 1.56. That is, children in the no-word classification condition selected *both* items about half of the time.

In the complex object trials, the children again selected only one item in extending novel labels. The average number of selected items per set was again 1.02. This time, however, the children clearly extended the label on the basis of shape, selecting only the same-shape item 82% of the time. In contrast, in the no-word condition, children were more willing to select the same-material item (55%) *in addition to* the same-shape item (82%). The average number of selected items per set was 1.4.

The fact that Japanese-speaking children did not extend a novel label to both the same-shape item and the same-material item at the same time while they were willing to select both items in a no-word classification context is important. It strongly suggests that Japanese-speaking children understand that, even though the two types of nouns were syntactically undistinguished, there *are* two types of nouns (i.e., nouns denoting individuated objects and nouns denoting nonindividuated substances) and that the two types of nouns are governed by different extension principles. That is, they appear to know implicitly that a noun denotes *either* a kind of object *or* a kind of substance, but not a disjunctive category of the form "things having shape X, *or* things consisting of substance Y." Like English speakers, Japanese-speaking children understand that the entities used in the simple object trials can be construed either as individuated objects or as portions of a nonindividuated substance. Unlike English-speaking children, who are strongly biased toward the "object" construal, Japanese-speaking children have no particular preference between the two possible construals. However, very importantly, once having determined that a given entity is an object (or a substance), a child does not generalize the label across the boundary of the two ontological kinds.

But then, how should we explain the fact that children made disjunctive categories that bluntly violated the ontological distinction in the no-word classification condition? We will discuss this issue next.

## 14.7    Accounting for the Dissociation between Behavior in the Word Extension Task and Behavior in the No-Word Classification Task

The fact that children showed unprincipled classification behavior in the no-word context is consistent with the results of the previous studies reported earlier, as well as a body of developmental literature (e.g., Imai, Gentner, and Uchida 1994; Landau, Smith, and Jones 1988; Markman and Hutchinson 1984; Subrahmanyam Landau, and Gelman 1999; Waxman and Gelman 1986; Waxman and Kosowski 1990). But does this mean that children do not in general understand that there are two distinct ontological categories, and that only in the context of label extension does this understanding somehow mysteriously emerge? This is a vexing question, especially given that well before learning their first word, infants may distinguish objects and substances with respect to individuation and numerosity (Huntley-Fenner and Carey 1995).

We offer the following possible account. Things can be similar in many ways and thus there is more than one way of grouping them. For example, things can be grouped on the basis of similarity in one perceptual dimension such as shape, texture, or color; on the basis of a thematic relation; or on the basis of nonperceptual, deeper similarity based on ontological/taxonomic kinds. Since there are many ways in which objects can be similar, even though children have a rudimentary understanding of the ontological distinction between objects and substances, they may not yet have learned which way of grouping is considered the "norm" in their culture—in other words, how adults in their community (culture) classify things in the world *by default* when a particular goal or context is not specified. Language is one powerful tool for leading children to form a bias toward paying attention to the kinds of categories that are the norm in their culture, that is, categories that are agreed to signal deeper commonalities.

Thinking this way, we can explain the dissociation in Japanese- and English-speaking children's classification behavior between the word extension context and the no-word classification context. In the context of label extension, both Japanese- and English-speaking children were able to apply the ontologically correct extension principle once they determined whether a given entity was an individuated object or a nonindividuated substance (although they may have divided the individuated-nonindividuated continuum differently). In contrast, in the context of no-word classification, they violated the ontological principles not because they lacked those principles but because they did not know that ontology-based classification was what was expected among other possible ways of grouping entities.

Here, the following two facts are particularly worth noting: (1) adults within each language group showed virtually identical classification behavior across the word extension and the no-word classification contexts; (2) both Japanese-speaking and English-speaking children showed the language-specific bias exhibited by the adults in their own language group in the simple object and substance trials only in the word extension context. These two facts suggest that children become attentive to the criteria for similarity and categorization honored by the adults in their culture first in a linguistic context. This bias toward a particular kind of classification then gradually becomes part of habitual thinking in everyday cognitive activities that do not directly involve language. The bias toward language-specific categories in word-learning contexts seems to emerge very early, most likely before the age of 2 (see also Choi and Bowerman 1991). However, it takes some time for this language-specific bias to penetrate into nonlinguistic cognitive domains such as similarity judgment or classification.

## 14.8 Reevaluating Linguistic Relativity

Given the commonalities and differences between Japanese speakers and English speakers, how should we evaluate linguistic relativity? On the one hand, we have argued for universal early appreciation of ontological concepts. On the other hand, the crosslinguistic difference in the simple object and substance trials in the reported studies indicates that the boundary between the ontological categories—that is, the classes of individuals and nonindividuals—is influenced by language. Specifically, the crosslinguistic difference lies in the perceptual process by which class membership is determined under the influence of language, but not in the ontological distinction per se. Japanese speakers and English speakers both know that objects and substances belong to distinct conceptual classes that are governed by fundamentally different principles from very early on, most likely prior to language learning. However, language-specific grammatical categorization in each language leads speakers to form habits of attending to a particular set of perceptual attributes that are most relevant and useful for determining a given entity's grammatical class.

English requires its speakers to determine whether a given entity is individuated and hence should be denoted by a count noun or whether it is nonindividuated and hence should be denoted by a mass noun, even if the entity's perceptual affordance for the class membership is weak and ambiguous.[4] Thus, English speakers may have developed simple perceptual heuristics, which can be instantly applied even when they have very little knowledge about the target entity. Because solidity and boundedness are very good indicators of individuation, English speakers may have developed a bias toward construing any solid, bounded entity (including simple-structured entities that could well be construed as chunks of rigid substances) as an individuated object. Also, because complex shape is another good indicator for individuation (Gentner and Boroditsky 2001; see also Lucy 1992), English speakers may have formed a stronger sensitivity to shape, and this may have led the English speakers in our studies to think that the complex shapes formed by nonsolid substances indicated individuation, even though they could see that those entities were indeed portions of nonindividuated substances.

In contrast, Japanese does not grammatically specify an entity's individuation status and hence may not lead its speakers to place special weight on solidity and shape in determining whether a given entity should be construed as individuated or nonindividuated. Thus, when the entity's perceptual affordance is weak and ambiguous (and hence the dual construal is allowed), as with the entities used in the simple object trials, Japanese-speaking children do not have a systematic bias toward one construal over the other, yielding chance-level performance.

Although we argue that the ontological concepts are universal, we would like to emphasize that the difference in classification behavior between Japanese and English speakers should not be dismissed as unimportant to human cognition. As perception and attention are important elements of human cognition, if language-specific categorizations indeed lead English speakers and Japanese speakers to form different attentional biases toward certain perceptual attributes, then we should retain a version of linguistic relativity (see Hunt and Agnoli 1991 for a similar view).

Importantly, in this light, our evaluation of Lucy's view of linguistic relativity is twofold. It appears to us that Lucy's written statements (Lucy 1992, 2000) allow three slightly different forms of linguistic relativity: (1) Because all nouns in classifier languages are equivalent to mass nouns, speakers of a classifier language should construe any inanimate discrete entity as some material that is transformed to its current form for a certain function or purpose. (2) Ontology is language relative and the ontological distinction realized in English does not necessarily reflect universal ontology. (3) Upon seeing inanimate discrete entities, English speakers exhibit stronger attentional bias toward shape than speakers of a classifier language; conversely, speakers of a classifier language exhibit stronger attentional bias toward the material constituent of entities.

Of course, these three versions are closely related. Nonetheless, our evaluation of Lucy's position in light of our empirical data differs depending on which version of linguistic relativity he is taking. Version (1) is clearly incorrect because Japanese speakers construed complex-structured objects as individuated objects in both word extension and no-word classification tasks. Version (2), which is the same as Quine's view, is also incorrect because Japanese speakers do appreciate the ontological distinction and honor the ontological principle in word extension. We would also note that Lucy and Gaskins's (this volume) claim about the role of the ontological distinction in Japanese children's lexical acquisition is mistaken. They say that "an ontologically 'given' distinction between objects and substances (or preindividuated and nonindividuated entities) cannot help a child acquiring Japanese lexicon because the language doesn't mark the contrast lexically" (sec. 15.4). Contrary to this claim, precisely because the language doesn't mark the ontological distinction, ontological knowledge is necessary for Japanese children to build up a lexicon. Recall that, unlike the lexicon of Yucatec, the Japanese lexicon contains both nouns denoting discrete objects and nouns denoting substances, and they are not morphologically related. Lacking count/mass syntax, if there were no ontological distinction regarding individuation, Japanese-speaking children would have no way of knowing how the names of things such as cups, bottles, balls, clay, sand, butter, and so on, should be generalized.

Version (3), however, is consistent with our data in that English speakers gave shape responses at a higher rate than Japanese speakers. However, slightly deviating from Lucy's prediction, we found this pattern with only one type of discrete object (i.e., simple objects), as well as with nonsolid substances.

Lastly, like other theorists, we would like to emphasize the role of language in shaping concepts in light of concept acquisition (e.g., Byrnes and Gelman 1991; Gentner and Medina 1997; Gentner and Rattermann 1991; Imai, Gentner, and Uchida 1994; Waxman and Kosowski 1990; Xu 1999). Even though there seem to be some building blocks of concepts that exist prior to language learning (e.g., Carey 1997), language provides children with a tool to bootstrap themselves into coherent, integrated, abstract concepts, by integrating fragmentary representational resources and highlighting the kinds of similarity and ways of categorization that are most emphasized in their culture (e.g., Gentner and Medina 1997; Hermer-Vazquez, Spelke, and Katsnelson 1999; Xu 1999). In our view, this itself is direct and strong evidence for the general Whorfian hypothesis—in other words, evidence that language plays a direct and strong role in shaping thought. Interestingly, however, the influence of language on cognitive development seems to derive largely from the lexical rather than grammatical level, contra Quine's (1969) and Lucy's (1992) claims.

## 14.9   Interactions among the Structure of the World, Universal Conceptual Constraints, and Language-Specific Categories

It is important to note that the ontological concept of individuation is not the sole factor that is responsible for the similar classification behavior of Japanese speakers and English speakers in the tasks reported here. The world is structured to form natural clusters, inviting humans to categorize entities according to these natural divisions (e.g., Berlin 1992; Rosch 1978). Entities located at the center of each cluster are considered to be "better members" than others located near the boundary of an adjacent cluster (Rosch and Mervis 1975). In our case, the objects used in the complex object trials are better members of the class of "object kinds" than those used in the simple object trials, and indeed, people's classification behavior was greatly affected by how stronlgy the perceptual nature of the target entity invites humans to place it into a particular category. When the perceptual affordance of a given entity strongly suggests the entity's status of individuation, then there is little room for language to affect people's default construal for that entity (cf. Gentner 1982). It is when the entity's perceptual affordance is weak and ambiguous that language exerts its maximum influence. Human cognition is neither absolutely universal nor absolutely diverse (Gentner and Boroditsky 2001; Malt 1995; Medin et al. 1997). To fully understand human cognition, we need to investigate how universal cognitive disposition and/or universally possessed knowledge interact with language-specific linguistic properties, and how these two factors interact with the way the world is structured and presents itself to humans.

## Notes

1. It should be noted that there is another important line of thought, which endorses Soja, Carey, and Spelke's view that the ontological distinction between objects and substances is universal, but does not agree with their account for the universality. While Soja, Carey, and Spelke attribute children's early sensitivity to the ontological distinction to innate knowledge about ontology, Gentner and Boroditsky (2001) argue that infants start out with no ontological concepts. What infants have is a gradually increasing set of differentiations. With this, a distinction between readily individuated complex objects and self-individuating animates first breaks off from the rest of the material world, and this distinction bootstraps children into ontological concepts (see Samuelson and Smith 1999 for a similar view). Unfortunately, we cannot address which view is correct, since we do not have data from children younger than 24 months. Thus, we do not differentiate the two views here, calling them both simply the "universal ontology position."

2. This pattern occurs occasionally in English (e.g., the word *glass* can be used both as a mass noun and as a count noun), but it is far more common in Yucatec than in English.

3. The experimenter said to the participant, "Suppose you are teaching a child a label for this entity in some foreign language. Would you say this is 'a *dax*' or 'some *dax*'?"

4. *Affordance* is the degree to which a certain categorization is allowed, based on the salience of the perceptual properties of an entity, given humans' predisposition to conceive of entities in terms of that categorization.

## References

Berlin, B. (1992). *Ethnobiological classification: Principles of categorization of plants and animals in traditional societies*. Princeton, NJ: Princeton University Press.

Bloom, P. (1994). Possible names: The role of syntax-semantics mappings in the acquisition of nominals. *Lingua, 92*, 297–329.

Bloom, P. (2000). *How children learn the meaning of words.* Cambridge, MA: MIT Press.

Carey, S. (1997). Do constraints on word meanings reflect prelinguistic cognitive architecture? *Cognitive Studies: Bulletin of the Japanese Cognitive Science Society, 4,* 35–58.

Byrnes, J. P., and Gelman, S. (1991). Perspectives on thought and language: Traditional and contemporary views. In S. Gelman and J. P. Byrnes (Eds.), *Perspectives on language and thought.* Cambridge: Cambridge University Press.

Choi, S., and Bowerman, M. (1991). Learning to express motion events in English and Korean: The influence of language-specific lexicalization patterns. *Cognition, 41,* 83–121.

Craig, C. G. (1994). Classifier languages. In R. E. Asher (Ed.), *The encyclopedia of language and linguistics.* Oxford: Pergamon Press.

Gentner, D. (1982). Why nouns are learned before verbs: Linguistic relativity versus natural partitioning. In S. A. Kuczaj (Ed.), *Language development: Vol. 2. Language, thought, and culture.* Hillsdale, NJ: Erlbaum.

Gentner, D., and Boroditsky, L. (2001). Individuation, relativity and early word learning. In M. Bowerman and S. C. Levinson (Eds.), *Language acquisition and conceptual development.* Cambridge: Cambridge University Press.

Gentner, D., and Medina, J. (1997). Comparison and the development of cognition and language. *Cognitive Studies: Bulletin of the Japanese Cognitive Science Society, 4,* 112–149.

Gentner, D., and Rattermann, M. J. (1991). Language and the career of similarity. In S. Gelman and J. P. Byrnes (Eds.), *Perspectives on language and thought.* Cambridge: Cambridge University Press.

Greenacre, M. J. (1984). *Theory and applications of correspondence analysis.* London: Academic Press.

Hermer-Vazquez, L., Spelke, E., and Katsnelson, E. (1999). Sources of flexibility in human cognition: Dual-task studies of space and language. *Cognitive Psychology, 39,* 3–36.

Hunt, E., and Agnoli, F. (1991). The Whorfian hypothesis: A cognitive psychology perspective. *Psychological Review, 98,* 377–389.

Huntley-Fenner, G., and Carey, S. (1995). *Individuation of objects and portions of non-solid substances: A pattern of success (objects) and failure (non-solid substances).* Poster presented at the meeting of the Society for Research in Child Development, Indianapolis, IN.

Imai, M. (1999). Constraint on word learning constraints. *Japanese Psychological Research, 41,* 5–20.

Imai, M. (2000). *Universality and cross-linguistic difference in the construal of individuation.* Paper presented at the Language and Thought Symposium conducted at Thinking 2000, Durham, UK.

Imai, M., and Gentner, D. (1997). A crosslinguistic study of early word meaning: Universal ontology and linguistic influence. *Cognition, 62,* 169–200.

Imai, M., Gentner, D., and Uchida, N. (1994). Children's theories of word meaning: The role of shape similarity in early acquisition. *Cognitive Development, 9,* 45–75.

Imai, M., and Haryu, E. (2001). How do Japanese children learn proper nouns and common nouns without clues from syntax? *Child Development, 72,* 787–802.

Imai, M., and Mazuka, R. (1997). *A crosslinguistic study on the construal of individuation in linguistic and non-linguistic contexts.* Paper presented at the meeting of the Society for Research in Child Development, Washington, DC.

Lakoff, G. (1987). *Women, fire, and dangerous things: What categories reveal about the mind.* Chicago: University of Chicago Press.

Landau, B., Smith, L. B., and Jones, S. S. (1988). The importance of shape in early lexical learning. *Cognitive Development, 3,* 299–321.

Lucy, J. A. (1992). *Grammatical categories and cognition: A case study of the linguistic relativity hypothesis.* Cambridge: Cambridge University Press.

Lucy, J. A. (2000). Introductory comments. In S. Niemeier and R. Dirven (Eds.), *Evidence for linguistic relativity.* Amsterdam: John Benjamins.

Lucy, J. A., and Gaskins, S. (2001). Grammatical categories and the development of classification preferences: A comparative approach. In M. Bowerman and S. C. Levinson (Eds.), *Language acquisition and conceptual development.* Cambridge: Cambridge University Press.

Malt, B. C. (1995). Category coherence in cross-cultural perspective. *Cognitive Psychology, 29,* 85–148.

Malt, B. C., Sloman, S., Gennari, S., Shi, M., and Wang, Y. (1999). Knowing versus naming: Similarity and the linguistic categorization of artifacts. *Journal of Memory and Language, 40,* 230–262.

Markman, E. M., and Hutchinson, J. E. (1984). Children's sensitivity to constraints on word meaning: Taxonomic versus thematic relations. *Cognitive Psychology, 16,* 1–27.

Mazuka, R., and Friedman, R. (2000). Linguistic relativity in Japanese and English: Is language the primary determinant in object classification? *Journal of East Asian Linguistics, 9,* 353–377.

Medin, D. L., Lynch, E. B., Coley, J., and Atran, S. (1997). Categorization and reasoning among tree experts: Do all roads lead to Rome? *Cognitive Psychology, 32,* 49–96.

Quine, W. V. O. (1960). *Word and object.* Cambridge, MA: MIT Press.

Quine, W. V. O. (1969). *Ontological relativity and other essays.* New York: Columbia University Press.

Rosch, E. (1978). Principles of categorization. In E. Rosch and B. B. Lloyd (Eds.), *Cognition and categorization*. Hillsdale, NJ: Erlbaum.

Rosch, E., and Mervis, C. B. (1975). Family resemblances: Studies in the internal structure of categories. *Cognitive Psychology, 7*, 573–605.

Samuelson, L. K., and Smith, L. B. (1999). Early noun vocabularies: Do ontology, category organization and syntax correspond? *Cognition, 73*, 1–33.

Shipley, E. E., and Shepperson, B. (1990). Countable entities: Developmental changes. *Cognition, 34*, 109–136.

Soja, N. N. (1992). Inferences about the meanings of nouns: The relationship between perception and syntax. *Cognitive Development, 7*, 29–45.

Soja, N. N., Carey, S., and Spelke, E. S. (1991). Ontological categories guide young children's inductions of word meaning: Object terms and substance terms. *Cognition, 38*, 179–211.

Spelke, E. S. (1990). Principles of object perception. *Cognitive Science, 14*, 29–56.

Subrahmanyam, K., Landau, B., and Gelman, R. (1999). Shape, material and syntax: Interacting forces in the acquisition of count and mass nouns. *Language and Cognitive Processes, 14*, 249–281.

Waxman, S. R., and Gelman, R. (1986). Preschoolers' use of superordinate relations in classification and language. *Cognitive Development, 1*, 139–156.

Waxman, S. R., and Kosowski, T. D. (1990). Nouns mark category relations: Toddlers' and preschoolers' word learning biases. *Child Development, 61*, 1461–1473.

Waxman, S. R., and Markow, D. (1995). Words as invitations to form categories: Evidence from 12- to 13-month-old infants. *Cognitive Psychology, 29*, 257–302.

Whorf, B. L. (1956). *Language, thought, and reality* (J. B. Carroll, Ed.). Cambridge, MA: MIT Press.

Wierzbicka, A. (1988). *The semantics of grammar*. Amsterdam: John Benjamins.

Wisniewski, E., Imai, M., and Casey, L. (1996). On the equivalence of superordinate concepts. *Cognition, 60*, 269–298.

Xu, F. (1999). Object individuation and object identity in infancy: The role of spatiotemporal information, object property information, and language. *Acta Psychologica, 102*, 113–136.

# 15

## Interaction of Language Type and Referent Type in the Development of Nonverbal Classification Preferences

John A. Lucy and Suzanne Gaskins

### 15.1 Introduction

We have argued for the utility of a comparative developmental approach to exploring the relation between language diversity and thought (Lucy and Gaskins 2001). In this chapter, we elaborate the importance of taking a structure-centered approach to such comparative-developmental research (Lucy 1997a). A structure-centered approach begins with an analysis of language structure and then moves to an operational characterization of reality implicit in it, rather than the other way around (Lucy 1992b, 273–275; 1997a). This contrasts with prevailing domain-centered approaches that begin with a characterization of some domain of reality and then consider how language structure responds to it. Ideally, a structure-centered approach entails a comparison of *patterns* (or configurations) of cognitive response across language-internal structural variations (Lucy 1992a, 86–91). Such a comparison of patterns of language-thought association escapes many of the interpretive difficulties inherent in the comparison of absolute levels of performance across vastly different cultures and assessment conditions.

Although our earlier comparative-developmental work did implement a structure-centered approach, it did not fulfill this ideal of providing evidence of cognitive patterning across language-internal structural variation. Here we extend that earlier work so as to compare configurations of linguistic and cognitive behaviors rather than absolute responses. We begin by discussing the general importance and nature of a structure-centered approach. We then present a case study relating specific language-based predictions to parallel cognitive-experimental work with adults and children. We conclude by comparing the results of this approach with some related contemporary work.

## 15.2    A Structure-Centered Approach

### 15.2.1    A Whorfian Approach: From Language to Reality

Contemporary research into the influence of language type on thought takes the work of Benjamin Lee Whorf (1956) as its point of departure—whether or not the actual substance and significance of that work are well understood by those who invoke it. This is not the place to revisit Whorf's arguments in detail (for that see Lucy 1985, 1992b, in press), but one key aspect, namely, his views about the mutual relation of language and reality, deserves mention since it lies at the heart of his comparative approach and motivates the one developed here.

Whorf's approach to the relation of language and reality emphasizes the equal value of diverse languages as referential devices. This view, part of the heritage of Boasian anthropology, contrasts with previous hierarchical views wherein some languages were regarded as intrinsically superior at representing reality and hence as vehicles for thought (Lucy, in press). The grounds used to establish the nature of reality under the hierarchical views have been quite various—religious, aesthetic, practical, scientific. But the recurrent theme in such views is that reality is given and knowable independently of language such that different languages can then be judged as capable of representing it more or less adequately.[1] But once we entertain the alternative view that diverse languages represent reality equally well, then the hierarchical views and the various assumptions they depend upon (about the specific nature of reality as well as its givenness and knowability) are necessarily called into question.

Although the egalitarian view of languages officially prevails in contemporary scholarly discussion, the hierarchical view lives on unofficially. It appears in the folk belief that one's own language conveys reality better or with more precision than do other languages. And it emerges in language research in the persistent (if unwitting) tendency to privilege the investigator's own language categories and their construal of reality both in theoretical works and in crosslinguistic description and comparison. Any linguistic investigator examining how diverse languages construe reality must, therefore, constantly be on guard to represent reality and undertake comparison in a way that is neutral or fair to all the systems being compared. To do this effectively, the researcher needs a set of formal procedures for developing such descriptions since good intentions rarely suffice when deep, pervasive biases are at issue.

One common approach to developing a neutral basis of comparison attempts to characterize some domain of reality independently of any language, usually through the use of some purportedly neutral technical or scientific metalanguage. However, such *domain-centered* approaches (Lucy 1997a), built as they are from our own language and culture, still risk rendering reality in terms of our own categories and finding that other languages fail to measure up in complexity and accuracy.[2] This has been, for example, the fate of research on the differential encoding of color in language. Color term "systems" are developed for various languages by grouping together various lexical forms in each language referring to the domain of color (in this case, a set of standardized color samples developed for art and commerce). These systems are taken as functionally equivalent to our own even though they may lack any structural unity within the other languages and have dramatically different semantic implications. These "systems" are then ordered into an evolutionary hierarchy largely according to how closely they match our own system, which conveniently serves as the unspoken telos for the whole project (Lucy 1997b).

An alternative, *structure-centered* approach to comparison, as first envisioned by Whorf (1956; Lucy 1997a), begins with an analysis and comparative typology of language structures and their semantics, developing thereby a rendering of reality as it appears through the "window of language" (Lucy 1992b, 275). In this approach, the collective tendencies of many languages are pooled to form a comparative grid within which each individual contrast can be made. Here there is no pretense, at least for now, of a final rendering of reality—rather, only of a provisional rendering adequate to the task of fair comparison of languages. Operationally, such an approach to comparison through language centers on careful analysis of actual systems of language category meanings within a typological framework. It characterizes the implications of these meanings for the interpretation of reality and for nonlinguistic behavior with respect to it. Ultimately, it aims to understand how diverse linguistic renderings of the world arise and what effects they have on thought about reality. But it does not, indeed cannot, presuppose a language-independent access to reality at the outset.

### 15.2.2    Previous Research: From Language to Cognition

The present study continues a line of research assessing the correspondence of linguistic structures with patterns of cognitive behavior. The original research (Lucy 1992a) explored the ways structural differences between American English and Yucatec Maya (an indigenous language of Mexico) related to the cognition of adult speakers of those languages. Specifically, the research focused on the patterned relationship between grammatical number marking and responses on memory and classification tasks involving pictures and objects.

The linguistic portion of the research compared the languages in terms of a formal, crosslinguistic typological characterization supplemented by frequency-of-use data. This linguistic analysis revealed three noun phrase types relevant to the English-Yucatec comparison. Each type can in turn be characterized by a semantic feature bundle drawn from a larger set manifest crosslinguistically in number-marking systems (Lucy 1992a, 56–61, 79–82). Associated with each semantic feature bundle is a set of actual referents, some of which will be relevant to the experimental work to follow. These referents were characterized notionally as Animals, Implements, and Substances,[3] where these are to be understood as rough labels of certain extensional sets and not intentional criteria for assignment to the language categories.[4]

The cognitive portion of the research demonstrated that where the two languages agreed in their treatment of a given referent type (Animals and Substances), the nonverbal cognitive responses were similar; and where the two languages diverged in their treatment of a given referent type (Implements), the nonverbal cognitive responses also differed. This result appeared most clearly in a series of tasks using picture stimuli that represented the various referent types and assessed attentiveness to their number.[5] Insofar as both groups perform alike in certain respects, we have assessment-internal evidence that the two groups see the task in the same way, increasing our confidence that the observed differences are real differences. Further, even when there is no specific match in absolute response pattern (perhaps due to differential cultural familiarity with the assessment procedure), the comparison of *patterns* of response across the referent types remains valid. Indeed, the pattern of results is the real phenomenon, not the absolute preference score on any individual item. And it is this pattern (i.e., the relative ordering of responses with respect to different referent types) that any alternative explanation will have to account for.

A second task series focused more narrowly on just object referents, the point of major contrast between the two languages, and used actual physical items for stimuli. These tasks revealed a relative classification bias toward shape on the part of English speakers and toward material on the part of Yucatec speakers, in line with the expectations based on the language analysis. This work has since been replicated with a wider and more carefully controlled array of stimuli and extended to trace out the developmental emergence of the contrast in young children (Lucy and Gaskins 2001). But this research with actual physical stimuli lacked an internal comparison among types of stimuli—primarily because the presupposed unit (and hence the cognitive predictions) seemed to vary across noun phrase types in a way difficult to address experimentally (see discussion Lucy 1992a, 88–90).

The new research reported below extends the cognitive assessment procedure using actual stimulus objects by exploring responses to referents closer to the material type of referent, where the two languages, and hence cognitive responses, should be in rough agreement. The primary aim is to assess whether the nonverbal cognitive responses of speakers agree where the languages agree (i.e., for materials), just as they differ where the languages differ (i.e., for objects). In this way, the work reported here brings to the tasks using physical objects the overall design logic adopted in the previous work using the picture tasks, with its attendant benefits in terms of predicting both similarities and differences between languages and patterns of response within languages. The new work should also forestall the tendency in some quarters to misconstrue the shape or material bias as general over all referent types. A secondary aim of the current work is to explore how children respond to these referent types. This will help resolve a number of questions left open by the previous developmental work regarding the extent of children's early classification preferences for shape. Here again, it is the pattern of response across ages that is central rather than the particular absolute rates.

## 15.3    Empirical Study

### 15.3.1    Language Contrast: Number-Marking Semantics

As background for the cognitive assessment, we first need to describe the language contrast. Yucatec Maya and American English differ in their nominal number-marking patterns.

First, the two languages contrast in the way they signal plural for nouns. English exhibits a *split* pattern whereby speakers obligatorily signal plural for nouns semantically marked as referring to discrete [+discrete] objects (e.g., *car*, *chair*) but not for those referring to amorphous [−discrete] materials (e.g., *sugar*, *mud*).[6] Yucatec exhibits a *continuous* pattern whereby speakers are never obliged to signal plural for any referent, although they may opt to do so if they wish.

Second, the two languages contrast in the way they enumerate nouns. English is again split such that for [+discrete] nouns, numerals directly modify their associated nouns (e.g., *one candle, two candles*) whereas for [−discrete] nouns, an appropriate unit (or *unitizer*) must be specified, which then takes the number marking (e.g., *one clump of dirt, two cubes of sugar*). Yucatec is again continuous such that all numerals must be supplemented by a special form, usually referred to as a *numeral classifier*, which typically provides crucial information about the shape or material properties of the referent of the noun (e.g., *'un-tz'íit kib'* 'one **long thin** candle', *ká'a-tz'íit kib'* 'two **long thin** candle'). Numeral classifiers of this type are a well-known grammatical phenomenon with wide area distribution, though probably best known from the languages of Asia, such as Chinese, Japanese, and Thai.

Since many classifiers have to do with the shape or form of a referent, one common interpretation of them is that they represent a special emphasis on these concepts in a language's semantics in contrast to languages such as English. This claim would be more plausible if the classifiers were optional, occurred in many morphosyntactic contexts, and appeared only in a few languages. But in fact they are obligatory, they are confined to a single morphosyntactic context, and they are fairly common among the world's languages—all of which suggests that they do not represent merely an emphasis but rather an indispensable solution to a formal referential difficulty characteristic of languages of a certain morphosyntactic type.

So why have numeral classifiers? What problem do they solve? The need for them reflects the fact that *all nouns in Yucatec are semantically unspecified as to quantificational unit*—almost as if they referred to unformed substances. So, for example, the semantic sense of the Yucatec word *kib'* in the example cited above is better translated into English as 'wax' (i.e., 'one **long thin** wax')—even though, when occurring alone without a numeral modifier in conditions other than enumeration, the word *kib'* can routinely refer to objects with the form and function that we would call candles (as well as to other wax things). Once one understands the quantificational neutrality of the noun, it becomes clearer why one must specify a unit (i.e., use a form such as a classifier) when counting, since expressions such as *one wax* apparently do not make quantificational sense in this language, much as they do not in English. By contrast, many nouns in English include the notion of quantificational "unit" (or "form") as part of their basic meaning—so when we count these nouns, we can simply use the numeral directly without any classifier (e.g., *one candle*). In essence, then, whereas English requires such a unitizing construction only for some nouns, Yucatec requires one for all of its nouns.

The patterns of plural marking and numeral modification just described are closely related to each other and form part of a unified number-marking pattern evidenced across many languages. In particular, languages with rich, obligatory plural marking such as Hopi tend not to have obligatory unitizing constructions such as numeral classifiers, and those with a rich, obligatory use of numeral classifiers such as Chinese tend not to have plural marking. Languages at these extremes are essentially continuous in their number-marking pattern over the entire spectrum of noun phrase types. However, many languages have both types

**Table 15.1**
Obligatory number-marking patterns: contrast for stable and malleable referent
types for continuous (e.g., Yucatec) and split (e.g., English) type languages

| | Referent type | |
| --- | --- | --- |
| Language type | Stable | Malleable |
| Continuous (Yucatec) | unitizer | unitizer |
| Split (English) | plural | unitizer |

of marking; that is, both pluralization and unitization are present. In
such languages, the lexicon tends to be internally split such that noun
phrases requiring plural marking with multiple referents tend not to require unitizers for counting, and those requiring unitizers for counting
tend not to require plurals when used with multiple referents. More
specifically, there is an ordering relationship such that, across languages,
it is more common for some referents to have plural marking and
others to have unitizer marking. (Again, see Lucy 1992a, 61–71, for
fuller discussion.)

Yucatec exhibits the continuous pattern requiring unitizers in the form
of numeral classifiers for all nouns and not requiring plurals for any of
them. English exhibits the split pattern; it requires plurals but not
unitizers for nouns referring to ordinary discrete objects, and it requires
unitizers but not plurals for nouns referring to amorphous entities. This
contrasting pattern is displayed graphically in table 15.1. However, it
should be emphasized that the label *unitizer* employed here to indicate
the crosslanguage functional similarity should not be overinterpreted in
terms of structural-semantic meaning. Even where these languages look
similar, there are important differences in syntactic structure and hence in
semantic value for the various form classes. In particular, quantification-
neutral Yucatec nouns are not structurally identical to quantification-
neutral English nouns (so-called mass nouns) since the Yucatec nouns do
not enter into a systematic contrast relation with quantification-marked
nouns (so-called count nouns).[7] Likewise, their actual cognitive construal
remains an empirical question.

### 15.3.2 Cognitive Hypotheses and Predictions

To assess whether traces of these contrasting verbal patterns appear in speakers' cognitive activities more generally, we need first to draw out the implications of these grammatical patterns for the general interpretation of experience. We have seen that English encodes quantificational unit (or some equivalent) in a large number of its lexical nouns whereas Yucatec does not. It is difficult to form a single generalization about the meaning value of such patterns because the kind of unit presupposed apparently varies across the spectrum of lexical noun types both within and across languages. What might be a good default presupposition may well differ dramatically for an animate referent, an object, a material, and so on. But if we focus first on the denotational meaning of nouns referring to objects—that is, discrete concrete referents with *stable* form —then certain regularities exist from which cognitive implications can be drawn.[8]

The quantificational unit presupposed by English nouns referring to discrete objects of this type is frequently the shape of the object. Hence, use of these English lexical items routinely draws attention to the shape of a referent as the basis for incorporating it under some lexical label and assigning it a number value. Yucatec nouns of this type, lacking such a specification of quantificational unit, do not draw attention to shape and, in fact, fairly routinely draw attention to the material composition of a referent as the basis for incorporating it under some lexical label. If these linguistic patterns translate into a general cognitive sensitivity to these properties of referents of the discrete type, then *Yucatec speakers should attend relatively more to the material composition of objects (and less to their shape), whereas English speakers should attend relatively less to the material composition of discrete objects (and more to their shape).*

We can develop a second prediction about material referents. Any concrete material referent must appear at any given moment in time with some spatial configuration, that is, in some shape or arrangement.[9] We will confine our interest here to those materials that retain their contiguity without the assistance of a container, what we will term *malleable* objects.[10] For these referents, a temporary (or accidental) shape is available at the moment of reference, but it could be otherwise for it is highly contingent on the current state of affairs.

Since *both* Yucatec and English nouns referring to such material referents *lack* a presupposed quantificational unit, their semantics should ignore the temporary shape and, in fact, should routinely draw attention to the material composition of a referent as the basis for incorporating it under a lexical label. If these linguistic patterns translate into a general cognitive sensitivity to these properties of referents of the material type, then *both Yucatec and English speakers should attend relatively more to the material composition of such malleable objects (and less to their shape)*.

The two sets of predictions can be brought together into a unified prediction for these two types of objects. English and Yucatec should disagree on their treatment of discrete stable objects in line with the differences in their grammatical treatment of them, but the two languages should agree on their treatment of malleable objects in line with the similarity in their grammatical treatment of them. Alternatively, looking within each language, we can predict that English will show a cognitive split vis-à-vis the two types of objects whereas Yucatec will show cognitive continuity across them. These predictions are displayed in table 15.2. Notice that the predictions are relative rather than absolute; that is, they contrast patterns, not absolute values.

### 15.3.3   Cognitive Contrast: Shape versus Material Preference
These language-based cognitive predictions were tested with speakers from both languages by developing several experimental assessments.

**Table 15.2**
Predicted relative attentiveness to material versus shape: contrast for stable and malleable referent types for speakers of continuous (e.g., Yucatec) or split (e.g., English) type languages

| | Referent type | |
|---|---|---|
| Language type | Stable | Malleable |
| Continuous (Yucatec) | material | material |
| Split (English) | shape | material |

**15.3.3.1 Adult Differences** The initial step was to compare the performance of adults in both groups. One would expect the maximal contrast among adult speakers, and the adult contrast also provides the baseline for developmental comparisons that follow.

**Stable Objects** The first prediction tested was that for stable objects. (These results are described more fully in Lucy and Gaskins 2001.) Adult speakers were shown triads of naturally occurring objects familiar to both groups. Each triad consisted of an original *pivot* object and two *alternate* objects, one of the same shape as the pivot and one of the same material as the pivot. So, for example, speakers were shown a plastic comb with a handle as a pivot and asked whether it was more like a wooden comb with a handle or more like a plastic comb without a handle. The expectation was that English speakers would match the pivot to the other comb with a handle whereas the Yucatec speakers would match it to the other comb made of plastic. Informants were shown a large number of such triads, which, across the stimulus set, controlled for size, color, function, wholeness, and familiarity. Examples appear in figure 15.1.

The predicted classification preference was strongly confirmed, with 12 English speakers choosing the material alternate only 23% of the time and 12 Yucatec speakers favoring it 61% of the time. Clearly, the two groups classify these objects differently and in line with the expectations based on the underlying lexical structures of the two languages. Notice that both patterns of classification are reasonable and neither can be described as inherently superior to the other.

Manipulations of color, size, and wholeness did not affect the basic shape or material preference. Unfamiliar objects—that is, objects made of an unknown material or in an uninterpretable shape—tended to produce consternation and to lower the Yucatec preference for material choices. The case with function, in the sense of the typical use of an object, was more complicated. The results just reported obtain when function is neutralized by having all three objects share a function or differ in function. But when function coincided with either shape or material, this tended to alter the responses for both groups (see Lucy and Gaskins 2001).[11]

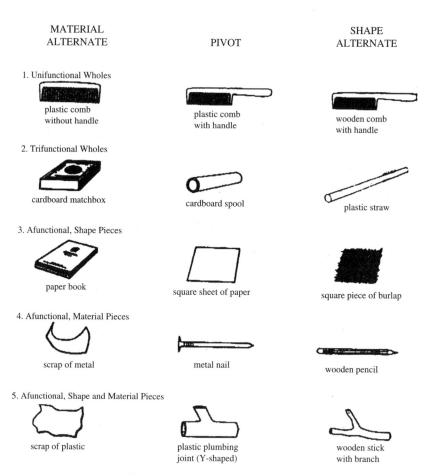

**Figure 15.1**
Examples of triad stimuli for stable objects. (Excerpted from figure 9.1 in Lucy and Gaskins 2001, 266.)

**Malleable Objects**    The prediction for material referents in the form of malleable objects was also tested with adult speakers from both languages, again using a triads classification task. Informants were shown six triads such that each pivot and its alternates were composed of different sorts of materials such as foams, creams, gels, pastes, powders, particles, or granules, each formed temporarily into distinctive shapes (see figure 15.2). Although both the materials and shapes were selected to be familiar to both sets of informants, the individual *combinations* of

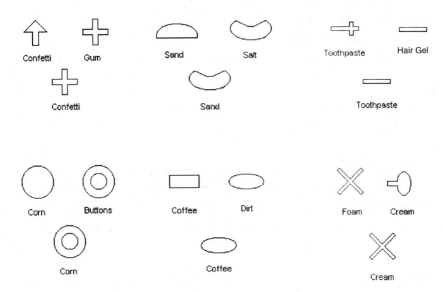

**Figure 15.2**
Examples of triad stimuli for malleable objects

shape and material were relatively novel for everyone. Size and color were controlled in these triads. Function was also controlled in the sense that each malleable object taken as a whole had no clear function.[12]

It is perhaps worth mentioning that the transitory properties of these objects made the assessment itself difficult, especially in the Mexican field conditions. For example, arranging beads, toothpaste, and the like into fixed shapes was intrinsically difficult in both settings; and working with shaving cream and instant coffee in the Yucatec setting—that is, in a house open to tropical humidity and occasional breezes—was especially difficult. Just at this practical level it was obvious that these were "objects" in a different sense than those used in the first study.

The results show both groups making a substantial number of material choices as expected, with Yucatec speakers favoring material choices 53% of the time and English speakers favoring them 34% of the time. However, clearly English speakers still favor shape overall. Although the direction of contrast is similar to that found for stable objects, the group difference was not statistically reliable with these materials.

**Summary**    Essentially, the results are in line with the predictions. Where the two languages agree in their treatment of malleable objects, there is no difference in their degree of preference for material classification. Where the two languages disagree in their treatment of stable objects, there are divergent preferences for material or shape classification as a function of the language difference. The full import of these results will only become clear in the light of the developmental data reported next.

**15.3.3.2  Developmental Patterns**    As part of an effort to unpack the mechanisms and linkages at work, we next explored the developmental emergence of these preferences. Assessments using the same triad materials described above were made of 12 English-speaking and 12 Yucatec-speaking children at ages 7 and 9.

**Stable Objects**    With stable object stimuli, English-speaking and Yucatec-speaking 7-year-olds showed an identical early bias toward shape—choosing material alternates only 12% of the time. By age 9, the English-speaking children continued to favor shape, choosing material alternates only 18% of the time. But by this age, the Yucatec-speaking children were choosing material alternates 42% of the time, a result contrasting significantly with the English-speaking children and much like that of adult Yucatec speakers. Thus, the same kind of language-group difference found among adult speakers is also found in children by age 9—and the result is statistically reliable. Again, the manipulations of color, size, and wholeness did not affect the results. Further, shifts in the alignment of function did not produce the big deflections characteristic of the adult groups. The adult and developmental data are jointly displayed in figure 15.3. (For full discussion see Lucy and Gaskins 2001.)

**Malleable Objects**    With malleable object stimuli, both English-speaking and Yucatec-speaking 7-year-olds showed a substantial number of material choices. English-speaking children choose the material alternate 42% of the time and Yucatec-speaking children choose the material alternate 46% of the time. This contrasts strongly with the 7-year-old pattern of choosing material for stable objects only 12% of the time and resembles the preference pattern shown by older Yucatec speakers with

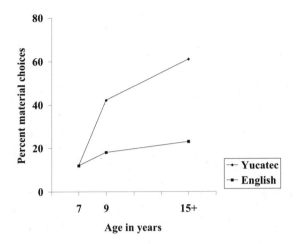

**Figure 15.3**
Developmental pattern for English and Yucatec classification preferences with stable objects: material versus shape. (Excerpted from figure 9.3 in Lucy and Gaskins 2001, 274.)

stable objects. At age 9, there is essentially no change: English-speaking children choose material alternates 43% of the time and Yucatec-speaking children choose them 50% of the time. Thus, the similarity of response found among adult speakers for objects of this type also appears in children. And again, the manipulations of color, size, and wholeness did not affect the results. The adult and developmental data are jointly displayed in figure 15.4. Viewed in contrast to the developmental data, the adult results appear more strongly differentiated in a manner reminiscent of the stable object results—which perhaps suggests some general transfer of effect from the latter category.

**Summary**    On the basis of these results, consolidated in figure 15.5, we can draw three conclusions about the development of language-related classification preferences for these types of referents.

First, all things being equal, 7-year-olds show marked sensitivity to referent type independently of language group membership.[13] They show a relative preference for material as a basis of classification with malleable objects and a relative preference for shape as a basis of classification with stable objects. Both bases of classification respond to stimulus

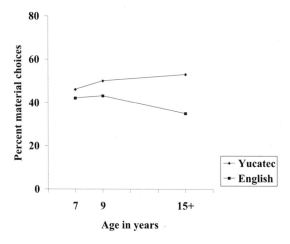

**Figure 15.4**
Developmental pattern for English and Yucatec classification preferences with malleable objects: material versus shape

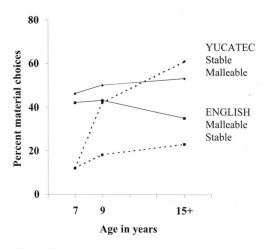

**Figure 15.5**
Developmental pattern for English and Yucatec classification preferences with both stable and malleable objects: material versus shape

properties and are fully available to and used by both groups. Apparently, referent type but not language type is the dominant factor in these nonverbal cognitive tasks at this age.

Second, 9-year-olds show differential sensitivity to referent type as a function of language group membership. Their preferences differ where the languages differ and correspond where the languages correspond. Essentially, 9-year-old English-speaking children continue to differentiate the two types of referents, a pattern that accords well with the split pattern in English. By contrast, 9-year-old Yucatec-speaking children begin to give up their relative shape preference with stable objects in favor of more material-based classifications, a pattern that accords well with the unified or continuous treatment of these referents by the adult language. Apparently, both referent type and language type affect cognition by age 9.

Third, in the context of the developmental data, we can see that there is some trend in the adult responses toward consolidation into a dominant pattern for each group. The Yucatec responses converge toward material choices and the English responses toward using shape. The split-marking pattern in English obviously makes the erasure of the distinction difficult in that language; that is, this trend remains subordinate to the main effect of cognition aligning with the specific linguistic treatment of a referent type. We can summarize by saying that *the two groups begin by grouping distinct referent types in the same way and end by regrouping same referent types in quite distinct ways as a function of language type.*

## 15.4 Discussion

The results reported here confirm the patterns found in earlier work. Overall, number-marking patterns in the two languages correspond to patterns of adult cognitive preference. Where the languages agree, so does the cognition, and where the languages disagree, so does the cognition. This holds true not only for plural-marking patterns in relation to attentiveness to number using picture stimuli (Lucy 1992a, in preparation) but now also for number-marking patterns in relation to preference for shape or material using object stimuli. The results show that the cognitive responses to particular referent types depend on the treatment of those referent types in each language. Neither language type nor referent type alone is sufficient to predict the results.

Several factors converge to suggest that language is the organizing force in these correspondences. First, the language patterns allow prediction of adult cognitive patterns, but not vice versa. The grammatical patterns allow us to predict both global cognitive differences (e.g., relative overall attentiveness to number or material across a range of stimuli) and local patterns of response as a function of grammatical distinctions among referent types. Knowing what stimuli are in play, what task is in use, or what sorts of cognitive responses are "natural" to humans will not allow equivalently precise prediction of adult language use. The remaining alternative would be to claim that these highly specific response patterns are somehow shaped by other aspects of culture and then the language patterns fall into place. However, the developmental results with stable objects undermine this view: 7-year-olds show the language contrast before they show the cognitive one. And it is not at all clear what cultural factor(s) would explain just this pattern of results across referent types.

The argument for the primacy of language (rather than culture) can be further bolstered by evidence from other languages associated with markedly different cultures. Fortunately, similar assessments of shape and material preference have now been made with Japanese speakers (Imai 2000; Imai and Mazuka, this volume). The Japanese language is similar to Yucatec in that it rarely marks plural and obligatorily uses classifiers in count constructions. In a comparison with English, therefore, we would expect adult Japanese speakers to perform more like Yucatec speakers in showing a relative preference for material over shape overall and in showing the strongest contrast for stable objects. The Japanese-English results are presented in table 15.3 along with the comparable Yucatec-English results from the present project.

Although the stimuli, tasks, and goals of the Japanese study were quite different,[14] the relevant results were very similar. First, across all referent types, the Japanese speakers favored material choices more than did the English speakers.[15] Second, for simple object referents (the set most equivalent to our stable objects), where we would expect a marked contrast between the two groups, Japanese speakers strongly favored mate-

**Table 15.3**
Percentage of adult English, Japanese, and Yucatec classification choices showing preferences for material as a basis for object classification. (Adapted from table 9.3 in Lucy and Gaskins 2001, 269, and figure 3 in Imai 2000, 155.)

| | Object type | |
| --- | --- | --- |
| Language | Stable | Malleable |
| Imai | | |
| Japanese | 73 | 83 |
| English | 28 | 50 |
| (Difference) | (45) | (33) |
| Lucy and Gaskins | | |
| Yucatec | 61 | 53 |
| English | 23 | 35 |
| (Difference) | (38) | (17) |

rial and English speakers strongly favored shape. Third, for substance referents (the set most equivalent to our malleable objects), where we would expect more similarity, the Japanese speakers continue to favor material at about the same level, but English speakers now show a significant number of material choices, leading to a somewhat narrower gap between the two groups. Crucial here are the patterns: Japanese speakers show a relative preference for material when compared with English speakers performing the same task, and the group difference is relatively larger for stable objects, where the languages contrast maximally, than for malleable objects, where they contrast minimally. In the context of substantial cultural, task, and procedural differences, these results conform remarkably well to the predictions based on the grammatical analysis and lend further credibility to the argument that language is the decisive factor.[16]

The Japanese research also explored children's responses on these tasks, although with 4-year-olds rather than 7- and 9-year-olds. The Japanese 4-year-old results are presented in table 15.4 along with the comparable results for 7-year-olds from the present project. Here, given the findings reported above, we would expect to find differential responses to the referent types for these age groups, but we would not expect to find overall differences between the two language groups. The

**Table 15.4**
Percentage of children's English, Japanese, and Yucatec classification choices showing preferences for material as a basis for object classification. (Adapted from table 9.3 in Lucy and Gaskins 2001, 269, and figure 3 in Imai 2000, 155.)

| | Object type | |
| --- | --- | --- |
| Language | Stable | Malleable |
| Imai | | |
| Japanese (4-year-olds) | 70 | 92 |
| English (4-year-olds) | 55 | 74 |
| (Difference) | (15) | (18) |
| Lucy and Gaskins | | |
| Yucatec (7-year-olds) | 12 | 46 |
| English (7-year-olds) | 12 | 42 |
| (Difference) | (0) | (4) |

first expectation is borne out in that both groups prefer material choices more for malleable objects than for stable ones. But the second expectation, that the two groups will look roughly similar, is not borne out: the Japanese speakers show a stronger overall preference for material than do the English speakers.[17] In itself this might suggest some global language-specific effect. However, the overwhelming preponderance of material choices in all the Japanese subgroups contrasts so strongly with the results of the Yucatec-English study that it suggests there is some fundamental difference in the assessment task or materials.

One way to interpret these differences, and reconcile the two sets of results, is to regard the children's data in each case as the baseline or default for speakers working with the specific task and materials used. From this vantage, in the Japanese-English study, speakers find the stable object stimuli used in the task somewhat material biased. Adult Japanese speakers apparently find this material bias congenial because they also tend to show it in their responses. Adult English speakers, however, find their language out of sync with this material bias and opt for more shape-based choices, more or less evenly across referent types. Applying the same sort of reasoning to the Yucatec-English comparison, speakers find the stable object stimuli used in the study somewhat shape biased. Adult English speakers seem to find this congenial overall and show the

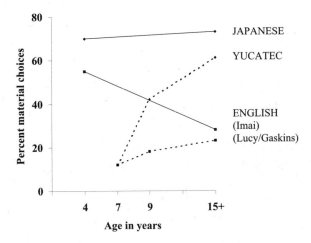

**Figure 15.6**
Developmental pattern for English, Yucatec, and Japanese classification preferences with stable objects: material versus shape

same basic response pattern. Adult Yucatec speakers, however, find the
shape bias out of sync with their language and opt for more material-
based choices. The malleable objects are more or less neutral in childhood (consistent, actually, with their lexical semantic marking) for both
studies, and the two groups show modest deflections in the direction of
their overall preference. In short, even though the two experiments appear to have quite different baseline response biases as indicated by the
choices of the children, the adults shift from these baselines in a way
consistent with an interpretation in terms of a language influence. For the
crucial stable object referent group, figure 15.6 displays graphically the
deflections in classification preference that occur from childhood baseline
toward an adult pattern in line with the structure of each language.[18]

Although, when interpreted in this way, the Japanese-English comparative findings support the main conclusions of the Yucatec-English
research, they emerge from a distinct research tradition with different
goals and assumptions. That tradition embraces the notions that certain
nonlinguistic experiences are ontologically privileged and that linguistic
forms referring to them should be learned earlier. So, for example, nouns
are thought to be easier to learn than verbs (Gentner 1982) and object
names easier than substance names (Gentner and Boroditsky 2001, 221).

The conceptual and empirical viability of these claims remains controversial but need not concern us here.

What requires emphasis is that the present research project neither makes nor requires equivalent claims about ontological privilege. Rather, the referent types defined here have been developed through linguistic comparison within a typological framework. Insofar as they have a notional interpretation as linguistic forms,[19] they do not directly reflect nonlinguistic reality or the perception of it; rather, they reflect speech-centric categories deriving from the self-reflexive capacity of language (see Lucy 1992a, 70–71, for an explanation, which follows Silverstein 1981 in this regard).[20] Although many such categories may well turn out to correspond in interesting ways to pre- or nonlinguistic category biases, it is not necessary or even desirable to assume this at the outset. Inversely, there is nothing in this research that precludes the presence of pre- or nonlinguistic universals of categorization. In short, the research reported here focuses on the impact of language on thinking, and the analysis neither depends on nor aims to establish claims regarding universal nonlinguistic ontology.

From this vantage, the division of nouns in English into two classes (i.e., lexically unitized or not) is a linguistic fact that we can use to delimit two types of referents. We can then look at how these referent types are treated in Yucatec. But there is no expectation that these referent types have, as types, a language-independent ontological status, or that Yucatec speakers will mark them, or, if they don't mark them, that they in fact "actually" have the distinction and then have somehow to learn to "overlook" or "suppress" them in their language. Rather, the claim is the following: if the distinction in referent types turns out to be relevant or irrelevant for their language, then their cognition should reflect this in some detectable way.

By contrast, research on linguistic relativity arising out of an acquisition paradigm tends to take a different approach. This research, based largely on English, seeks to establish that an object/substance (or individuated/nonindividuated) distinction is ontologically given to all children prior to learning language on the view that this will then help explain how the child learns the count/mass distinction (e.g., Soja, Carey, and Spelke 1991). Evaluating this proposal has proven difficult, however, because English-speaking children are constantly exposed to the count/mass distinction in their language even if they don't produce or comprehend it, raising the possibility that the distinction arises from this language exposure (this position attributed to Quine 1960, 1969). Cross-linguistic comparison with Japanese, which lacks a count/mass distinction, was undertaken precisely to eliminate these confounding effects of early exposure (Imai and Gentner 1997). But notice that the original language acquisition arguments no longer make much sense from this comparative perspective. An ontologically "given" distinction between objects and substances (or preindividuated and nonindividuated entities) cannot help a child acquiring the Japanese lexicon because the language doesn't mark the contrast lexically. So the presence of the distinction certainly cannot aid acquisition—if anything, it would interfere with it. Despite this, the comparative acquisition research continues to focus on evaluating the ontological givenness of this English distinction even among Japanese speakers.[21] This perhaps accounts for the tendency to frame research on linguistic relativity in terms of an opposition with universal ontology even though these two notions need not necessarily be in opposition.[22] It also illustrates the common tendency in comparative research to privilege certain language categories in characterizing how domains of reality are encoded. The apparently neutral characterization of reality already contains within it the categories of one of the languages.

In sum, the approach advocated and exemplified in the current study remains resolutely Whorfian by focusing on contrasts in linguistic structure and minimizing a priori commitments about the nature of reality. Analysis begins with close description of linguistic structure, follows this with systematic linguistic comparison, frames the contrast typologically, and then characterizes differences in referential tendency. It is the latter differences that provide the basic hypotheses for the psychological research rather than any a priori assumptions about what in reality must be encoded, about universals of human cognition, or about how infant perceptual patterns implicate adult ontological commitments. In short, rather than beginning with a somehow-already-known reality and asking how different languages manage to cope with it, the approach advocated here takes the characterization of reality itself as problematic and therefore begins with language structures and induces the implicit construals of reality emergent in them. Careful analysis of these patterns should lead in time to a vision of reality as it emerges through the "window of language," that is, reality as it gets utilized in human discursive activity. This in turn would provide the foundation for asking deeper questions about the extent to which our *conception* of reality can be independent of our language.

## Notes

Basic financial support for the comparative and developmental research reported here was provided by the Spencer Foundation (Chicago). The project received additional support from the Cognitive Anthropology Research Group of the Max Planck Institute for Psycholinguistics, The Netherlands. For the object-sorting tasks, Christine Kray assisted with the Yucatec sample and Kathy Mason assisted with the English sample. For the materials-sorting task, Deborah Augsburger helped with both Yucatec and English samples. We especially thank Jim Johnson, principal, and the children of Harvey C. Sabold Elementary School, Springfield, Pennsylvania, and the parents and children in Yucatan, Mexico, all of whom helped us with cheerful good humor. An earlier version of this chapter was presented to the Whither Whorf Workshop, Northwestern University, 29 May 1998.

1. Whorf occasionally espoused similar views about the relative "fit" between individual languages and reality before fully embracing the egalitarian view (Lucy 1992b, 32–36).

2. Nearly all research that sees language acquisition as a "mapping" of a single known reality runs afoul of this bias.

3. Implements were of two types, tools and containers. In later work, we use the term *Material* instead of *Substance* when speaking of experimental stimuli (versus semantic value).

4. So, for example, referents marked semantically as [+animate] need not be animate or living from a biological point of view, and vice versa. What is crucial, rather, is the degree to which the referent approaches the maximally presupposed referents in speech. See Silverstein 1981 and discussion in Lucy 1992a, 68–71.

5. In the picture study, the three referent types were operationalized as Animals, Implements, and Substances, respectively. The original study used only adult male subjects. The finding has now been replicated with a sample including adult women (Lucy, in preparation).

6. Lucy (1992a, 56–83) explains the features used here as well as the frequent, yet optional marking of plural in Yucatec for the [+animate] subset of [+discrete] entities.

7. See discussion below regarding "mass" and "count" nouns.

8. When we call an object "stable," we mean only that the current shape would hold steady under many actions (moving it, setting another object on it, etc.). We do not mean that it would remain stable under all imaginable actions or conditions or even that the current shape is canonical in some way. A metal spoon, a wooden stick, or a sheet of paper would all be stable by this criterion even though each can be cut or bent and might be encountered in a variety of specific shapes. Whether an object is regarded as stable (or malleable) ultimately depends on the predicate at issue in the discourse; we have chosen exemplars where the presuppositions run strongly in one direction such that the discrete form of the referent can generally be presupposed for predication. See note 10.

9. The impossibility of presenting the referent of a noun referring to material without *some* shape was one of the reasons this referent type was not assessed in Lucy 1992a. Here the problem of representing the semantics of these nouns operationally in the cognitive tasks is "solved" by using objects whose shapes, although distinctive enough to allow a shape designation, neither are durable nor have any intrinsic connection with the materials. See also notes 8 and 10. The deeper point is that the meaning of any lexeme (or lexical class) is never adequately represented by one of its referents. In experimental work, we are always using approximations.

10. When we call an object "malleable," we mean to highlight the highly contingent nature of its shape such that practically any action or change of conditions will alter its configuration unless some outside force conserves it. Thus, the discrete form of the referent cannot generally be presupposed for predication. We did not use liquids or vapors in this study primarily because their use generally would require introducing a second, containing object into the tasks to give them shape. See note 8.

11. When function aligned against a group's preferred classification preference, it led to choices against the usual pattern. Specifically, the Yucatec preference for material dropped from 61% on the function-neutral triads to 39% when function was aligned with shape, and the English preference for material rose from 23% for the function-neutral triads to 72% when function was aligned with material, both statistically reliable shifts. It appears that when function matches are available, they can affect the results and need to be carefully controlled when assessing a relative shape versus material classification preference (see Lucy and Gaskins 2001).

12. In the terminology of Lucy and Gaskins 2001, these stimuli were comparable to the "afunctional pieces."

13. It is perhaps worth emphasizing that just as the English-speaking children have substantial command of the plural by age 7, so too do the Yucatec-speaking children have substantial command of the numeral classifier system by this age. Seven-year-old Yucatec-speaking children reliably use classifiers when counting, draw appropriate semantic distinctions among them in comprehension tasks, and will judge a number construction lacking them as faulty. However, they fall far

short of having command of the full range of classifiers in comprehension and their range in production is narrower still. In short, they have the basic structural implications straight but do not yet have the full lexical range of an adult. Hence, to the extent that these cognitive results derive from these basic structural characteristics of the language rather than mastery of specific lexical items, there is no reason they could not appear at age 7. That they do not do so suggests that some rather specific reorganizations in the relation between language and thought take place between ages 7 and 9.

14. Regarding the stimuli, in addition to simple objects and substances (our stable and malleable objects), the Japanese-English comparative work also used complex objects—that is, "factory-made artifacts having complex shapes and specific functions" (Imai and Gentner 1997, 179; cf. Imai 2000, 146). The results for these complex object stimuli cannot be directly compared with our results because there was no formal counterbalancing of the coincidence of function with shape and material alternatives in the Japanese-English comparison. However, the extremely high number of shape choices for these object types relative to other object types in both groups is quite consistent with our findings that the coincidence of function with shape sharply increases the number of shape choices (Lucy and Gaskins 2001, 269; also see note 11 above). The instructions in the Japanese-English work asked whether the shape or material alternative was "the same" as the pivot rather than which was "more like" it. In our experience, use of the term *the same* in certain constructions can prompt more material choices, which may account for the greater absolute number of material choices found in Imai's tasks. Finally, regarding the differences in goals, these relativity studies are rooted in a paradigm concerned with what shapes a child's acquisition. As will be pointed out later in the discussion, this leads to a consistent preoccupation with universal prelinguistic ontology (seeing this as the opposite of relativity) even when the comparative cases chosen have effectively rendered this concern irrelevant (since the ontological distinction can be of little help in acquiring a language that does not honor it). As indicated in the introduction, the present approach resists making such prior, language-independent commitments about ontology or reality.

15. The Japanese-English study elicited more material responses in every cell. This difference is discussed below.

16. These responses were also shown to be in very tight alignment with characteristic word extension patterns elicited experimentally in the two languages. See note 21.

17. It is not clear whether this difference is statistically reliable.

18. Mazuka and Friedman (2000) report adult Japanese speakers showing a preference for shape over material using a similar assessment. The results are difficult to evaluate because they did not control for function (see note 11). Their explanation for the preference in terms of "cultural" or "educational" factors, always tenuous since no substantive evidence was ever given for them, now seems even less tenable in light of the new Japanese and Yucatec developmental data.

19. The notional characterizations referred to here have to do with semantic and pragmatic meaning. They should not be confused with the notional approximations used to pick stimuli for the cognitive research.

20. The hierarchy of noun phrase types developed by Lucy (1992a, 56–83) should not, therefore, be termed an "animacy" hierarchy (cf. Gentner and Boroditsky 2001, 229) since this suggests a completely nonlinguistic basis for the categories and elides the essentially discursive (or pragmatic) basis for the ordering. This hierarchy based on an empirical comparison of language structures also produces orderings distinct from those postulated employing other criteria (e.g., Gentner and Boroditsky 2001, 215, 230).

21. Since the acquisition of the Japanese language cannot in itself show the effects of the ontological distinction in ordinary use, the usual measure of effect is experimentally induced word extension. When these extensions align with the grammar, they are taken to show the influence of language on thinking; when they don't align, they are taken to show the influence of thinking on language. Conceptually, then, these word extension patterns hover somewhere between language and thought: a measure of both yet not quite a measure of either. On the one hand, the Japanese-English comparative data show contrasting extension patterns among words that are treated alike grammatically—even in adulthood. So the extensions cannot be used as an exact measure of having acquired the grammar. On the other hand, such extensions really cannot be construed as a nonlinguistic measure either since they involve judgments about verbal meaning. In this respect, they are silent on the question of linguistic relativity proper, that is, on the question of the influence of language on thinking more generally. Indeed, this limitation prompted Imai (2000) to supplement these word extension tasks with nonlinguistic (or "no-word") classification tasks precisely to allow her to examine the relation of language to nonverbal classification preferences as had been done in the Yucatec-English research.

22. Insofar as there exist some universal aspects of ontology, they may be irrelevant to language (hence not marked), relevant but optionally encoded, or universally exploited. And even if universally exploited, they need not be lexically encoded but rather signaled grammatically or discursively. So no necessary relation can be assumed. It seems more sensible then to work forward from what languages *do* encode than to presume what they *must* encode.

# References

Gentner, D. (1982). Why nouns are learned before verbs: Linguistic relativity versus natural partitioning. In S. A. Kuczaj (Ed.), *Language development: Vol. 2. Language, thought, and culture* (pp. 301–334). Hillsdale, NJ: Erlbaum.

Gentner, D., and Boroditsky, L. (2001). Individuation, relativity, and early word learning. In M. Bowerman and S. C. Levinson (Eds.), *Language acquisition and conceptual development* (pp. 215–256). Cambridge: Cambridge University Press.

Imai, M. (2000). Universal ontological knowledge and a bias toward language-specific categories in the construal of individuation. In S. Niemeier and R. Dirven (Eds.), *Evidence for linguistic relativity* (pp. 139–160). Amsterdam: John Benjamins.

Imai, M., and Gentner, D. (1997). A cross-linguistic study of early word meaning: Universal ontology and linguistic influence. *Cognition, 62*, 169–200.

Lucy, J. A. (1985). Whorf's view of the linguistic mediation of thought. In E. Mertz and R. Parmentier (Eds.), *Semiotic mediation: Sociocultural and psychological perspectives* (pp. 73–97). Orlando, FL: Academic Press.

Lucy, J. A. (1992a). *Grammatical categories and cognition: A case study of the linguistic relativity hypothesis.* Cambridge: Cambridge University Press.

Lucy, J. A. (1992b). *Language diversity and thought: A reformulation of the linguistic relativity hypothesis.* Cambridge: Cambridge University Press.

Lucy, J. A. (1997a). Linguistic relativity. *Annual Review of Anthropology, 26*, 291–312.

Lucy, J. A. (1997b). The linguistics of "color." In C. Hardin and L. Maffi (Eds.), *Color categories in thought and language* (pp. 320–346). Cambridge: Cambridge University Press.

Lucy, J. A. (in press). Afterword: The power of an idea. In J. B. Carroll (Ed.), *Language, thought, and reality: Selected writings of Benjamin Lee Whorf* (2nd ed.). Cambridge, MA: MIT Press.

Lucy, J. A. (in preparation). Language related diversity in adult classification preferences. Manuscript.

Lucy, J. A., and Gaskins, S. (2001). Grammatical categories and the development of classification preferences: A comparative approach. In M. Bowerman and S. C. Levinson (Eds.), *Language acquisition and conceptual development* (pp. 257–283). Cambridge: Cambridge University Press.

Mazuka, R., and Friedman, R. (2000). Linguistic relativity in Japanese and English: Is language the primary determinant in object classification? *Journal of East Asian Linguistics, 9*, 353–377.

Quine, W. V. O. (1960). *Word and object.* Cambridge, MA: MIT Press.

Quine, W. V. O. (1969). *Ontological relativity and other essays.* New York: Columbia University Press.

Silverstein, M. (1981). Case-marking and the nature of language. *Australian Journal of Linguistics, 1*, 227–244.

Soja, N., Carey, S., and Spelke, E. (1991). Ontological categories guide young children's inductions of word meaning: Object terms and substance terms. *Cognition, 38*, 179–211.

Whorf, B. L. (1956). *Language, thought, and reality: Selected writings of Benjamin Lee Whorf* (J. B. Carroll, Ed.). Cambridge, MA: MIT Press. (Original works written 1927–1941.)

# 16

## Thought before Language: Do We Think Ergative?

Susan Goldin-Meadow

### 16.1 Introduction

Languages around the globe classify experience in different ways. Benjamin Whorf (1956) first popularized the notion that linguistic classifications might influence not only how people talk but also how they think. More specifically, Whorf suggested that the relentless use of a particular linguistic categorization might, at some point, also affect how speakers categorize the world even when they are not talking.

This provocative hypothesis is most often explored by comparing the nonlinguistic performance of speakers whose languages differ systematically in the way they categorize experience. In this chapter, however, I take a different approach: I observe people who have had no exposure to any conventional language whatsoever. The thoughts of these individuals cannot possibly have been shaped by language. As a result, whatever categories they express reveal thoughts that *do not* depend on language—thought before language. I begin by demonstrating that individuals who are not exposed to language are nevertheless able to communicate ideas with others. Moreover, I show that these communications are structured in linguistically regular patterns. I focus, in particular, on how patients and actors are treated in spontaneous communication that has not been shaped by a language model.

Before describing this work, I briefly review a study that is often taken to bear directly on the Whorfian hypothesis: a comparison of the categories expressed by speakers of languages that differ in the way they mark number. The example is instructive because it provides insight into the kind of role that language may play in shaping thought, the kinds of *two = one for each hand = familiar*

domains in which language may have its effect, and the kinds of experiments that are often taken as evidence of that effect.

## 16.2  Language Can Shift Where Boundaries Are Drawn along a Continuum: An Example from Number Marking

All languages mark number. As an example, English speakers indicate whether a noun refers to one or many by producing it in a singular or plural form (e.g., *cat* vs. *cats*, *broom* vs. *brooms*). However, while they are obligated to mark plurals for some entities (animates, implements), English speakers do not mark plurals for others (e.g., substances—English speakers say *mud*, not *muds*, whether they are talking about one puddle or many). In this sense, English speakers group animates and implements together, and distinguish them from substances, with respect to number marking. Lucy (1992) provides evidence that English speakers make the same groupings even when they are *not* talking. Lucy presented English speakers with a picture recall task and determined whether they paid attention to changes in the number of items in the picture. Lucy found that English speakers did notice when the number of animates and implements in the picture had changed (i.e., when the number of animates or implements varied from the original, they correctly said this was not the picture they had seen previously). In contrast, these same English speakers failed to notice a difference when the number of substances in the picture was changed (they erroneously accepted as correct pictures in which the number of mud puddles varied from the original).

Lucy then extended this paradigm to address the Whorfian hypothesis by presenting the same pictures to speakers of Yucatec Maya. Yucatec is a language that marks numbers of objects a bit differently from English (Lucy 1992, 58). At the extremes, like English, Yucatec marks plurals for animates and does not mark plurals for substances. However, the languages differ in the way they deal with the number of implements. In English, implements take plural marking and thus are treated like animates (e.g., *brooms*). In Yucatec, implements do not take plural marking and thus are treated like substances (i.e., the equivalent of saying *some broom*).

The Whorfian hypothesis would predict that after many years of speaking Yucatec, Mayans ought to perform differently from English speakers when recalling pictures of implements, even when not talking about them. And they did. As expected, speakers of both languages noticed when the number of animates in the picture changed, and they failed to notice when the number of substances changed (Lucy 1992). However, as Whorf might have predicted, Yucatec speakers did not notice changes in the number of implements, while English speakers did.

Note that the number-marking linguistic system is an ideal context in which to explore questions of language and thought. There is a continuum (ranging from animate objects to substances) along which these two languages—indeed, according to Lucy (1992), all languages—are organized. One end of the continuum is always treated as categorically different from the other end, thus establishing a basic framework within which differences among speakers can be detected (see Imai and Gentner 1997). Within this framework, languages differ with respect to where along the continuum they draw the categorical boundary. Implements can be thought of in terms of their form and thus categorized with animates, the English pattern. Alternatively, implements can be thought of in terms of their substance and thus categorized with substances, the Yucatec pattern. The crucial question revolves around whether speakers follow the patterns set by their language when categorizing exemplars from the middle of the continuum in a nonlinguistic context.

In this chapter, I examine another linguistic system, also organized around a continuum. The focus will again be on where boundaries are drawn when exemplars in the middle are categorized.

## 16.3  Language and Thought When There Is No Model for Language

Lucy's work suggests that language can influence thought, even languageless thought, at least after language has been well learned and become habitual. Here, I ask a slightly different question in a very different way. My work addresses what happens to thought when language is still a novel skill. Will language exert an influence on thought or, alternatively, will thought affect the way language itself is learned?

*I think the latter. (metaphor + colour prefs and effects, etc.*

Kick! — always yes = me control
Kick! → stroke sometimes = not me control = other.

496    Goldin-Meadow

If thought drives the way language is learned, we might expect the initial stage of language learning to be comparable around the globe—perhaps revealing a basic child grammar of the sort that Slobin (1985) proposed. In fact, commonalities can be found at the very early stages of language learning. For example, children around the globe express the same basic semantic relations in their two-word utterances (Brown 1973). However, even at this early stage, we can see effects of the language model to which a child is exposed. As an example, children's earliest utterances reflect the word order patterns prevalent in their parents' talk (e.g., Bowerman 1973), and they display morphological devices if those devices are transparent in the adult language (e.g., as in Turkish; Aksu-Koç and Slobin 1985).

Thus, and perhaps not surprisingly, the language model to which a child is exposed has an immediate impact on at least some aspects of the language the child acquires (see also Berman and Slobin 1994; Choi and Bowerman 1991). Does this mean that children's thoughts are, from the start, molded by the languages they learn? Not necessarily. In fact, Lucy's own work indicates that before age 9, and long after they have acquired the Yucatec number-marking system in their language, Yucatec-speaking children display the *English* nonlinguistic number-marking pattern (focusing not on the substance of implements, but on their form) rather than the Yucatec pattern shown by adult speakers of their language (Lucy and Gaskins 2001, this volume). This finding suggests that if language does have an impact on thought, its effect may not be felt until the linguistic system has been routinely used for many years—until middle childhood. *layer on layer*

What are the implications of these findings for language learning? Although children learn very early the particular forms of the language to which they are exposed, these forms may not influence thought until later in development. Why not? Perhaps children come to the language-learning situation with biases of their own. These biases may have to be overridden by a language model, but they clearly do not get in the way of language learning (and indeed may even facilitate the process). But how are we to discover these biases? We cannot take the early words and sentences children produce as an uncontaminated view of their biases simply because children's words are, from the very first, heavily influenced by the language to which they are exposed. The most straightforward approach is to look at what children do when they are not exposed to a model of a conventional language. Such situations, although rare, do arise.

Deaf children born to hearing parents are, at times, not exposed to a conventional sign language until adolescence. Moreover, if their hearing losses are so severe as to preclude the acquisition of spoken language, they are unable to profit from the conventional spoken language that surrounds them. Despite their lack of access to a usable conventional language model, these deaf children invent gesture systems to communicate with the hearing individuals in their worlds. The gestures have syntactic (Feldman, Goldin-Meadow, and Gleitman 1978; Goldin-Meadow and Feldman 1977; Goldin-Meadow and Mylander 1984, 1998), morphologic (Goldin-Meadow, Mylander, and Butcher 1995), and lexical (Goldin-Meadow et al. 1994) structure and thus have many of the rudimentary properties of natural language.

I explore in this chapter how deaf children creating their own gesture systems deal with one particular structural aspect of natural language that bears importantly on the issue of language and thought: typological variation in how actors and patients are marked in transitive and intransitive sentences. This system, like number marking, is organized around a continuum, with languages agreeing on how they treat the endpoints, but differing on where they mark the categories in the middle. All languages distinguish (syntactically, morphologically, or both) patients from actors in transitive relations. In English, for example, transitive actors precede the verb, patients follow (*John hit Sam*); in addition, transitive actors are replaced by pronouns in the nominative case, patients by pronouns in the accusative case (*He hit him*). What distinguishes languages along this dimension is how they treat exemplars from the middle category, the intransitive actor.

Some languages, English among them, are called "accusative" languages and mark intransitive actors like transitive actors. For example, both precede verbs (*John ran home, John hit the cat*) and both take nominative case when replaced by pronouns (e.g., *He ran home, He hit the cat*). Moreover, patients are distinguished from both types of actors: patients follow verbs (*The cat hit John*) and take accusative case when replaced by a pronoun (*The cat hit him*). In this way, the initiator properties of the intransitive actor are highlighted (the fact that John initiates the running, as opposed to his being affected by the running). Other languages, called "ergative" languages, align intransitive actors with patients rather than with transitive actors (Dixon 1979; Silverstein 1976). If English were ergative, intransitive actors would follow verbs as patients do (*Ran John*) and would be replaced by the same pronoun as patients (*Ran him*). The ergative pattern highlights the affectee properties of the intransitive actor (the fact that John is affected by the running, as opposed to initiating the running).

In short, as with the number-marking devices examined by Lucy (1992), there are two categories that are distinguished from one another in all languages (transitive actor vs. patient) and a third category (intransitive actor) that is aligned with one category in one set of languages (transitive actor in accusative languages) and with the other category in the other set of languages (patient in ergative languages).

Children have no difficulty learning either accusative or ergative languages (Ochs 1982; Slobin 1985). Thus, on the basis of language learning in typical situations where children are exposed to accusative versus ergative language models, we might guess that children have no bias whatsoever as to how intransitive actors are to be treated. But, as already mentioned, it is difficult to identify children's predispositions from their early language. The most straightforward way to discover their biases is to examine children who have not yet been exposed to a language model: for example, deaf children creating their own gesture systems without linguistic input. I ask here whether, in their gesture systems, deaf children treat intransitive actors like transitive actors or like patients; that is, do these children (and, by inference, do all children) come to the language-learning situation with a bias for categorizing intransitive actors as either initiators or affectees? First, let us consider some necessary background on deafness and language learning.

## 16.4   Background on Deafness and Language Learning

Deaf children born to deaf parents and exposed from birth to a conventional sign language such as American Sign Language (ASL) acquire that language naturally; that is, these children progress through stages in acquiring sign language similar to those of hearing children acquiring a spoken language (Newport and Meier 1985). However, 90% of deaf children are not born to deaf parents who can provide early exposure to a conventional sign language. Rather, they are born to hearing parents who, quite naturally, tend to expose their children to speech (Hoffmeister and Wilbur 1980). Unfortunately, it is extremely uncommon for deaf children with severe to profound hearing losses to acquire the spoken language of their hearing parents naturally—that is, without intensive and specialized instruction. Even with instruction, deaf children's acquisition of speech is markedly delayed when compared either to the acquisition of spoken language by hearing children of hearing parents or to the acquisition of sign language by deaf children of deaf parents. By age 5 or 6, and despite intensive early training programs, the average profoundly deaf child has only limited linguistic skills in speech (Conrad 1979; Mayberry 1992; Meadow 1968). Moreover, although some hearing parents of deaf children send their children to schools in which one of the manually coded systems of English is taught, other hearing parents send their deaf children to "oral" schools in which sign systems are neither taught nor encouraged. Thus, these deaf children are not likely to receive input in a conventional sign system, or to be able to use conventional oral input.

The children I have studied are severely (70–90 dB bilateral hearing loss) to profoundly (> 90 dB bilateral hearing loss) deaf, and their hearing parents chose to educate them using an oral method. At the time of our observations, the children ranged in age from 1;2 to 4;10 (years; months) and had made little progress in oral language, occasionally producing single words but never combining those words into sentences. In addition, at the time of our observations, the children had not been exposed to a conventional sign system of any sort (e.g., ASL or a manual code of English). As preschoolers in oral schools for the deaf, the children spent very little time with the older deaf children in the school who might have had some knowledge of a conventional sign system (i.e., the preschoolers attended school only a few hours a day and were not on the playground at the same time as the older children). In addition, the children's families knew no deaf adults socially and interacted only with other hearing families, typically those with hearing children.

We coded all of the gestures that the children produced during these spontaneous play sessions. In order for a manual movement to be considered a gesture, it must be produced with the intent to communicate. The difficulty lies in discriminating acts that communicate indirectly (e.g., pushing a plate away, which indicates that the eater has had enough)— acts we did not want to include in our study—from acts whose sole purpose is to communicate symbolically (e.g., a "stoplike" movement of the hands produced in order to suggest to the host that another helping is not necessary). Lacking a generally accepted behavioral index of deliberate or intentional communication, we decided that a communicative gesture must meet the following two criteria (Feldman, Goldin-Meadow, and Gleitman 1978; Goldin-Meadow and Mylander 1984). First, the movement must be directed to another individual. This criterion is satisfied if the child attempts to establish eye contact with the communication partner. Since manual communication cannot be received unless the partner is looking, checking for a partner's visual attention is a good sign that the child intended the movement to be seen. Second, the movement must not be a direct act on the other person or relevant object. As an example, if the child attempts to twist open a jar, that act is not considered a gesture for OPEN, even if the act does inform others that help is needed in opening the jar. If, however, the child makes a twisting motion in the air, with eyes first on the other person to establish contact, the movement is considered a communicative gesture. In sum, behaviors are included in our analyses only if they are produced with the intent to communicate. They thus reflect thoughts that have been recruited for this purpose.

## 16.5　Marking Actors and Patients in Transitive and Intransitive Gesture Sentences: An Ergative Pattern

The "lexicon" of the deaf children's gesture systems contained both pointing gestures and characterizing gestures. Pointing gestures were used to index or indicate objects, people, places, and the like, in the surroundings. Characterizing gestures were stylized pantomimes whose iconic forms varied with the intended meaning of each gesture (e.g., a C-hand rotated in the air to indicate that someone was twisting open a jar).

Gestures of this sort, particularly pointing gestures but also some characterizing gestures, are produced by hearing children (Acredolo and Goodwyn 1988; Butcher, Mylander, and Goldin-Meadow 1991). However, the deaf children's use of these gestures was unique in that their gestures fit into a structured system, while hearing children's gestures do not (Goldin-Meadow and Morford 1985; Morford and Goldin-Meadow 1992).

The deaf children combined their gestures into sentences. The boundaries of a gesture sentence were determined on motoric grounds. If the child produced one gesture and then, without pausing or relaxing the hand, produced a second gesture, those two gestures were considered part of the same sentence. If, however, the two gestures were separated by a pause or relaxation of the hand, each was considered a separate unit. I use the term *sentence* loosely and only to suggest that the deaf children's gesture strings share some structural properties with early sentences in child language. I focus on two properties here, beginning with data from the most prolific of the deaf children we have studied (David) to do so: (1) production probability, the likelihood that a particular semantic element will be gestured in a two-gesture sentence when it is permissible in that sentence; and (2) gesture order, the likelihood that the gesture for a particular semantic element will be produced in first or second position in a two-gesture sentence.

*based on observations & causality*

### 16.5.1  Production Probability

When we first observed David, he was in what might be called a "two-gesture" period, akin to a young hearing child's two-word period—a time when his utterances for the most part contained at best two gestures. If such a child wants to communicate an idea with three semantic elements, he will be forced to leave one of these elements out of the surface structure of his two-gesture sentences. For example, if describing a mouse eating cheese, David could not produce gestures for the eater (mouse), the eating action, and the eaten (cheese) in a two-gesture sentence. He might drop out elements randomly, producing gestures for each element a third of the time. However, this was not the strategy David adopted.

David was quite systematic in the elements he included and excluded from his two-gesture transitive sentences: he produced gestures for patients (the eaten-cheese) and omitted gestures for transitive actors (the eating-mouse). Thus, like all natural languages, David's gesture system made a distinction between actors and patients in transitive sentences, a distinction based on patterns of occurrence and nonoccurrence. — *hole*

What about intransitive actors, such as a mouse running to its hole? *dative* Figure 16.1 (top) presents the probability of production for transitive actors, intransitive actors, and patients in David's two-gesture sentences that could, in theory, contain any two of these three elements (e.g., transitive sentences with an underlying structure of actor-act-patient, and intransitive sentences with an underlying structure of actor-act-goal). Note that David produced gestures for the intransitive actors (the running-mouse) as often as for patients (the eaten-cheese)—and far more often than for transitive actors (the eating-mouse). In this sense, then, David's gestures pattern like ergative languages: intransitive actors and patients are treated alike (produced), whereas transitive actors are treated differently (omitted).

— *top thing on mind = subject*

### 16.5.2  Gesture Order

Where did David place his gestures in a two-gesture sentence, once he had produced them? Even at the two-word stage, children exposed to conventional languages tend to place words (or signs; see Newport and Ashbrook 1977) in privileged positions in their sentences, and the orders they follow tend to be the predominant orders used by adult speakers of the language. Thus, for example, an English-learning child would likely produce *Mouse eat*, *Eat cheese*, or *Mouse cheese* for the transitive renditions or *Mouse run* for the intransitive renditions—in each case, actors (both transitive and intransitive) occur in first position of a two-word sentence, and patients occur in second position.

David too followed particular order patterns, but in gesture. Interestingly, his gesture orders were distinct from the canonical word order of the English that was spoken around him. Figure 16.1 (bottom) presents the probability that transitive actors, intransitive actors, or patients would be the first gesture produced in a two-gesture sentence. Note first that David tended to produce gestures for patients in first position of his two-gesture sentences (CHEESE-EAT) and gestures for transitive actors in

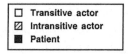

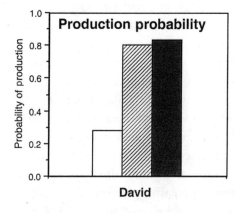

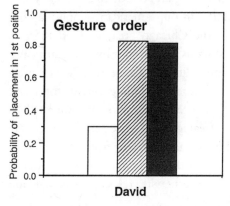

**Figure 16.1**
The likelihood that David will produce gestures for transitive actors, intransitive actors, and patients in two-gesture sentences that permit each of these elements (*top*); and that he will produce gestures for transitive actors, intransitive actors, and patients in the first position of a two-gesture sentence (*bottom*)

second position (EAT-*MOUSE*), thus distinguishing between actors and patients in transitive sentences not only in terms of production probability but also in terms of gesture order. Second, David tended to produce gestures for intransitive actors in first position (*MOUSE*-RUN)—precisely the same position in which patients occur (*CHEESE*-EAT) and distinct from the habitual position of transitive actors (EAT-*MOUSE*). Thus, David followed an ergative pattern (treating intransitive actors and patients alike) with respect to gesture order as well as production probability.

Was David unique? We might expect that deaf children left to their own devices might invent gesture systems with patterns found in all natural languages (e.g., they might all distinguish between transitive actors and patients), but their systems might vary in just the areas where languages vary (e.g., some children might align intransitive actors with patients as David did, thus reflecting an ergative pattern; others might align them with transitive actors, reflecting an accusative pattern). When we examine the 9 other deaf children in our American sample, 5 from the Philadelphia area and 4 from the Chicago area, we find that, as expected, all of the children did distinguish between transitive actors and patients in terms of production probability (see figure 16.2, which presents data from the 6 Philadelphia children, including David (top), and the 4 Chicago children (middle); Goldin-Meadow and Mylander 1984). Moreover, all 9 of the children also treated intransitive actors in precisely the same way that they treated patients, and different from the way they treated transitive actors. Thus, all 10 of the deaf children in our American sample displayed an ergative pattern with respect to production probability.

In terms of gesture order, like David, 8 of the 9 children tended to produce gestures for patients before acts (Donald 26 of 41, Dennis 10 of 11, Mildred 19 of 27, $p$'s < .05; Karen 17 of 25, Tracy 7 of 8, $p$'s < .10; Marvin 21 of 33, Kathy 8 of 12, Chris 6 of 10; and the exception, Abe 11 of 23). Although they produced fewer relevant sentences, many also showed a tendency to produce intransitive actors before acts as well (Abe 6 of 6, Tracy 7 of 7, Donald 7 of 10, Karen 5 of 6, Marvin 4 of 6, Kathy 2 of 3; Mildred and Chris were the exceptions, both 2 of 5; and Dennis produced no relevant combinations). Again, many of the children treated intransitive actors like patients. However, David was the only child who

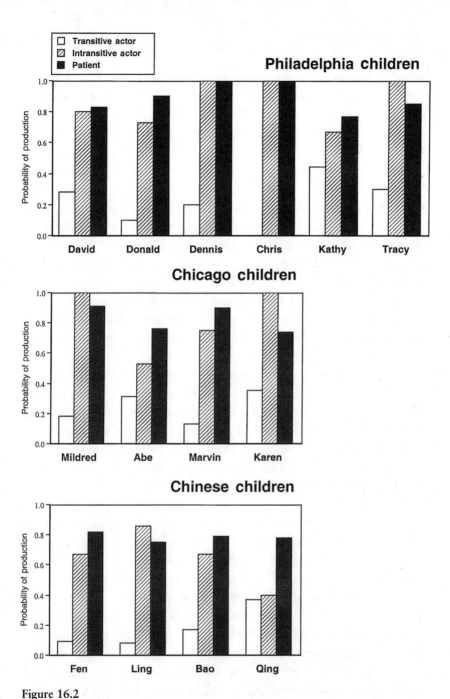

**Figure 16.2**
The likelihood that the American deaf children from Philadelphia (*top*) or Chicago (*middle*) and the Chinese deaf children from Taipei (*bottom*) will produce gestures for transitive actors, intransitive actors, and patients in two-gesture sentences that permit each of these elements

produced a sufficient number of transitive actors to determine a consistent order. As a result, it was impossible to determine whether transitive actors were distinguished from both patients and intransitive actors in terms of gesture order as well as production probability for the 9 other American children.

The ergative pattern in the deaf children's gestures could reflect a tendency to see objects as affected by actions rather than as initiators of action. In the sentence *You go to the corner*, the intransitive actor *you* has a double meaning. On the one hand, *you* refers to the goer, the actor, the initiator of the going action. On the other hand, *you* refers to the gone, the patient, the affectee of the going action. At the end of the action, *you* both "have gone" and "are gone," and the decision to emphasize one aspect of the actor's condition over the other is arbitrary. By treating intransitive actors like patients, the deaf children are highlighting the affectee properties of the intransitive actor over the initiator properties.

It is important to note that the deaf children really are marking thematic role, and not just producing gestures for the most salient or most informative element in the context. One very sensible (albeit wrong) possibility is that the deaf children produce gestures for intransitive actors and patients more often than for transitive actors because intransitive actors and patients tend to be new to the discourse more often than transitive actors (cf. DuBois 1987). In other words, the production probability patterns seen in figure 16.2 could be an outgrowth of a semantic element's status as "new" or "old" in the discourse. If the novelty of a semantic element is responsible for how often that element is gestured, we would expect production probability to be high for all "new" elements (regardless of role) and low for all "old" elements (again, regardless of role). We find no evidence for this hypothesis (Schulman, Mylander, and Goldin-Meadow 2001; see also Goldin-Meadow and Mylander 1984, 49). Rather, we find an ergative production probability pattern for "new" elements when analyzed on their own, as well as for "old" elements when analyzed on their own, as we would expect if thematic role, rather than novelty, determines how often an element is gestured.

## 16.6   Is the Ergative Pattern Unique to American Deaf Children? A Look at Chinese Deaf Children

All of the American deaf children whose gestures we have examined display, not only a distinction between transitive actors and patients, but also a tendency to treat intransitive actors like patients rather than transitive actors (i.e., an ergative pattern). Where does this ergative pattern come from? One possibility is that subtle differences in the way the children's hearing parents interact with them might influence the structure of their gestures. For example, Bruner (1974/75) has suggested that the structure of joint activity between a hearing mother and her hearing child exerts a powerful influence on the structure of the child's communication. To determine whether the ergative structure in the deaf children's gestures is a product of the way in which mothers and children jointly interact in their culture, we studied deaf children of hearing parents in a second culture, a Chinese culture.

We chose Chinese culture as a second culture in which to explore the spontaneous communication systems of deaf children because literature on socialization (Miller, Mintz, and Fung 1991; Young 1972), on task-oriented activities (Smith and Freedman 1982), and on academic achievement (Chen and Uttal 1988; Stevenson et al. 1990) suggests that patterns of mother-child interaction in Chinese culture differ greatly from those in American culture, particularly those in white, middle-class American culture. In addition, our own studies of the interaction between hearing mothers and their deaf children in Chinese and American families replicate these differences (Goldin-Meadow and Saltzman 2000; Wang 1992; Wang, Mylander, and Goldin-Meadow 1995).

We have examined 4 deaf children of hearing parents in Taipei, Taiwan, each observed twice between the ages of 3;8 and 4;11 (Goldin-Meadow and Mylander 1998). The children had hearing losses so severe that they could not acquire the spoken language of their parents even with intensive instruction. Moreover, their hearing parents had not yet exposed them to a conventional sign system (e.g., Mandarin Sign Language, Taiwanese Sign Language, Signed Mandarin). All 4 of the children were found to use gestures spontaneously to communicate with the hearing individuals in their worlds. Moreover, all 4 combined gestures into gesture strings characterized by production probability and gesture order regularities.

Figure 16.2 (bottom) displays the production probability patterns for the 4 Chinese deaf children. Note that all 4 children produced gestures for patients considerably more often than they produced gestures for transitive actors. Moreover, 3 of the 4 produced gestures for intransitive actors as often as for patients, and far more often than they produced gestures for transitive actors; that is, they displayed an ergative pattern identical to the American deaf children's pattern. One child, Qing, was an exception. Qing produced gestures for intransitive actors at the same low rate as she produced gestures for transitive actors, considerably less often than she produced gestures for patients. In this sense, Qing displayed an accusative pattern.

With respect to gesture order, all 4 of the Chinese children produced gestures for patients before gestures for acts (CHEESE-EAT): Ling 11 of 12, Bao 26 of 29, Fen 9 of 11, Qing 29 of 29 ($p$'s $\leq$ .03, binomial test on each child). Moreover, 3 of the 4 produced gestures for intransitive actors before gestures for acts (MOUSE-GO): Ling produced 14 of 15 relevant sentences conforming to this pattern, Qing 17 of 19, Bao 12 of 15 ($p$'s $\leq$ .02); Fen was an exception (1 of 4). Only Qing produced enough sentences containing transitive actors to explore order regularities for this semantic element. She produced gestures for transitive actors in first position of her two-gesture sentences (MOUSE-EAT, 8 of 8, $p \leq$ .004), thus displaying neither an ergative nor an accusative pattern with respect to gesture order. She did, however, reliably produce gestures for patients before gestures for transitive actors when the two were produced in a single sentence (CHEESE-MOUSE, 6 of 7, $p \leq$ .06), thus continuing to maintain a distinction between patients and transitive actors in gesture order as well as production probability.

Note that, in principle, it is possible for a child to produce gestures for intransitive actors at a rate completely different from gestures for either patients or transitive actors. Thus, the children need not have conformed to either an accusative or an ergative pattern with respect to production probability. Nevertheless, the patterns displayed in the gestures of 13 of the 14 children observed thus far, American and Chinese, followed one of the two predominant patterns found in natural languages. Indeed, 13 of the 14 children displayed an ergative pattern (i.e., intransitive actors are treated like patients and distinct from transitive actors), even though neither English nor Mandarin is an ergative language.

Why might this be? Of the two patterns, ergative structure is much less common in the world's languages than accusative structure. Why does almost every deaf child we have observed seem to find it so natural? One possibility is that the gesture production probability patterns reflect the way that *children* view the world before their thoughts have been molded by a language model. Children may have a bias to see scenes in terms of outcomes rather than initiating forces—a patient bias. Thus, when seeing intransitive actors—runners, for example—children may focus on their being affected by the running, rather than on their initiating the running. If so, we might expect the gesture patterns we have found thus far to be unique to children. We explore this possibility by examining the gestures that adults produce in two situations: the spontaneous gestures adults produce along with their talk, and the intentional gestures adults produce when asked to communicate without using their mouths.

## 16.7 Is the Ergative Pattern Unique to Children?

### 16.7.1 Spontaneous Gestures Adults Produce As They Talk

We examined the spontaneous gestures of a subset of the hearing mothers of the deaf children in our studies. We used precisely the same techniques for determining gesture sentences and the semantic elements contained within those sentences as we used for the deaf children—we viewed the mothers' videotapes with the sound off, as though they too were deaf. The production probability results are presented in figure 16.3 (top graph for the 6 American mothers who were on the tapes long enough for us to explore their gestures, data from Goldin-Meadow and Mylander 1984; bottom graph for the Chinese mothers, data from Goldin-Meadow and Mylander 1998).

The first point to note is that there was no uniformity across the mothers, either within one culture or across cultures. It is difficult to abstract a single pattern from these sets of gestures. However, as a group,

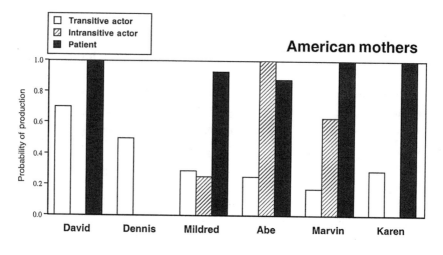

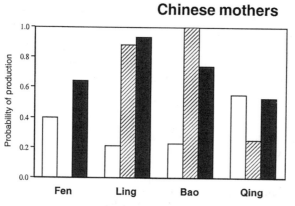

**Figure 16.3**
The likelihood that the hearing mothers of the American deaf children (*top*) or Chinese deaf children (*bottom*) will, in the spontaneous gestures that accompany their speech, produce gestures for transitive actors, intransitive actors, and patients in two-gesture sentences that permit each of these elements

the mothers did produce more gestures for patients than for transitive actors, thus distinguishing between the two, as did their children. But it is where *intransitive actors* are situated relative to transitive actors and patients that determines the typology of a language, and here mothers and children differed: the mothers showed no reliable patterning of gestures for intransitive actors, whereas their children produced gestures for intransitive actors at a rate significantly different from gestures for transitive actors but not different from gestures for patients, thus displaying an ergative pattern.

In terms of gesture order, Chinese mothers tended to order their gestures within sentences in the same way as their children, placing patients before acts (mothers Bao 16 of 21, Fen 14 of 16, Ling 11 of 11, $p$'s $< .01$) and intransitive actors before acts (mothers Bao 5 of 5, Fen 7 of 7, Qing 6 of 6, $p$'s $< .02$; Ling 9 of 12, $p < .07$), with the exception that Qing's mother showed no patient-act order (6 of 12) and no patient–transitive actor order (2 of 5) while her child did. American mothers produced very few gesture sentences at all. In the few they did produce, 5 mothers produced gestures for patients before acts (mothers Abe 5 of 6, Karen 4 of 5, Marvin 4 of 5, Dennis 1 of 1, Mildred 5 of 9; and the exception, mother David 1 of 4); but only 1 produced a gesture for an intransitive actor before a gesture for an act (mother Mildred 1 of 1), and 2 displayed the opposite order (mothers Marvin and Abe, 3 of 4; Goldin-Meadow and Mylander 1984).

Overall, the mothers' gestures did not show a consistent ergative pattern in the way that their deaf children's gestures did. Why not? The mothers' gestures were qualitatively different from their children's in that they were routinely accompanied by speech (all of the mothers were committed to oral education and thus spoke when communicating with their children). The mothers' gestures thus served a different function from the deaf children's gestures. While the deaf children's gestures were forced to fulfill all of the functions of communication, the hearing mothers' gestures shared that communicative function with speech. The lack of a stable pattern in the mothers' gestures is likely due to the fact that we analyzed their gestures *without* speech. However, the mothers' gestures were produced *with speech* and form an integrated system with that speech when analyzed in context (see Goldin-Meadow, McNeill, and Singleton 1996; McNeill 1992). Moreover, the mothers' gesture patterns are likely to be influenced by the speech they accompany (neither English nor Mandarin is an ergative language). If the adults found themselves in a situation in which they too had to rely solely on gesture to communicate, it is at least possible that a consistent, perhaps ergative, pattern would emerge. The next section explores this possibility.

### 16.7.2    Intentional Gestures Adults Produce without Talk

Two college students, both native English speakers who had no knowledge of sign language, participated in the study (Goldin-Meadow, Gershkoff-Stowe, and Yalabik 2000). We showed these adults videotaped vignettes from the battery designed by Supalla et al. (in press) to assess knowledge of ASL. The adults were asked to describe each event depicted on the videotape without using speech and using only their hands. Neither the gesturer nor the "listener" was permitted to talk. The two adults took turns gesturing and alternated playing the roles of gesturer and listener during the session (see Gershkoff-Stowe and Goldin-Meadow 1998 for further details on the basic experimental procedure). Because we were interested in whether there might be changes in the gestures over time, we arranged for the two adults to meet twice a week for several weeks.

We used the same system of analysis for the adults as we did for the deaf children and their hearing parents. For this analysis, we looked at gesture strings that could have contained three semantic elements but, in fact, contained only two (e.g., transitive sentences with an underlying structure of actor-act-patient, and intransitive sentences with an underlying structure of actor-act-goal). Figure 16.4 displays the probability that each of the adults produced a gesture for a transitive actor, an intransitive actor, or a patient in a two-gesture sentence. To determine whether the adults would display a consistent pattern immediately or needed time to evolve a pattern, we divided the data into three parts (the first three sessions, the second three, and the last three). Note that both gesturers produced gestures for intransitive actors as often as they produced gestures for patients, and far more often than they produced gestures for transitive actors—and did so from the very beginning of the

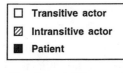

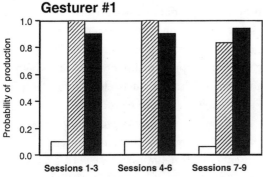

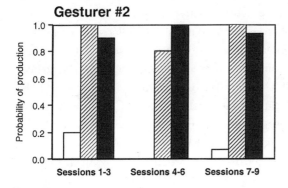

**Figure 16.4**
The likelihood that two adult English speakers, when asked to gesture without speaking, will produce gestures for transitive actors, intransitive actors, and patients in two-gesture sentences that permit each of these elements. The data are divided into three parts: the first three sessions in which the two gesturers participated, the second three, and the last three.

study. In other words, they immediately displayed the same ergative pattern seen in the deaf children's gestures.

In some of the vignettes, humans performed the action; in others, mechanical toys did the deed. To determine whether the animacy of the actor had any influence on production probability, we divided each adult's data into descriptions of scenes containing human actors versus toy actors and recalculated production probability scores. Figure 16.5 presents the data. The ergative pattern is apparent for both adults whether they described human or toy actors (although it is cleaner for the first gesturer when she described actions involving human actors).

In terms of gesture order, both adults tended to produce gestures for intransitive actors in first position of their two-gesture sentences (e.g., MOUSE RUNS; 94% of 51 sentences for one gesturer, 91% of 47 for the other). This result is hardly surprising, as the pattern parallels typical word order for intransitive actors in English. Neither adult produced many gestures for transitive actors (four for one, five for the other), which made it impossible to determine an order preference for this semantic element. More interestingly, both gesturers tended to produce gestures for patients in first position of their two-gesture sentences (CHEESE EAT; 84% of 81 sentences for one gesturer, 73% of 73 for the other). Not only is this pattern identical to the deaf children's gesture order for patients, but it is also different from the pattern typically found in English (i.e., *eat cheese* see also Hammond and Goldin-Meadow 2002). Thus, the patient-first pattern is particularly striking in English-speaking adults' gesturing.

The deaf children often (although not always; see Goldin-Meadow et al. 1994) used deictic pointing gestures to convey patients. The adults were not able to take advantage of this strategy simply because there were no objects in the room at which they could point. The adults were forced to invent an iconic gesture for their patients; for example, a smoking movement at the mouth to refer to an ashtray, which was then followed by a gesture representing the action that was done on that ashtray (e.g., a throwing action). Even though they used iconic rather than pointing gestures to refer to patients, the adults followed the same ordering patterns as the deaf children (see Yalabik 1999 for additional details on the adults' gesture productions).

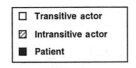

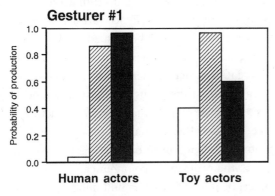

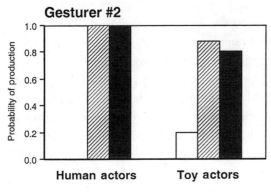

**Figure 16.5**
The likelihood that two adult English speakers, when asked to gesture without
speaking, will produce gestures for transitive actors, intransitive actors, and
patients in two-gesture sentences that permit each of these elements. The data are
partitioned according to the scene described (scenes with human actors vs. toy
actors).

## 16.8    The Ergative Pattern Is More Pervasive than Might First Appear

We have found the ergative pattern to be robust in communication situations. Deaf children of hearing parents who are inventing their own gesture systems tend to organize their gesture sentences around an ergative pattern. Equally striking, we found that when asked to describe a series of action vignettes using their hands rather than words, English-speaking adults invented an ergative structure identical to the one developed by the deaf children, rather than the accusative pattern found in their spoken language. These findings suggest that ergative structure is not unique to child language-creators. Rather than reflecting a childlike way of organizing information for communication, the ergative pattern may reflect a robust solution to the problem of communicating information from one mind to another, be it an adult or a child mind.

Even hearing children, who have a solution to the communication problem at their disposal in the form of a language model, often fall back on an ergative pattern. For example, children who are learning English and thus acquiring an accusative structure display an ergative pattern at the early stages of language learning, particularly when deciding which semantic elements to explicitly mention in words. Goldin-Meadow and Mylander (1984, 62–64) reanalyzed the data from 4 hearing children in the two-word period and showed that each child tended to produce words for intransitive actors and for patients at the same rate, and both at a higher rate than for transitive actors. Similarly, children learning Korean (Choi 1999; Clancy 1993), Inuktitut (Allen and Schroder, in press), and Samoan (Ochs 1982) go through a period during which their transitive verbs typically occur with a single argument, the patient, and intransitive verbs occur with the actor—an ergative pattern despite the fact that, although Inuktitut and Samoan are ergative, Korean is not. In fact, DuBois (1987) has suggested that ergativity underlies all languages, including accusative languages, at least at a discourse level.

Taken together, these observations suggest that the ergative pattern is robust in communication situations involving both adults and children. Does the patient focus found in ergative systems arise in noncommunicative situations as well? In our current work, we are exploring this question by asking adults to reconstruct an intransitive scene with pic-

*familiar sound to pregnant mum recurs only after fetus gains hearing – eg mismatch uncle with Klaxon – mum may feel distress not know why. It is the baby's chemicals – not he*

tures that represent objects playing different semantic roles in both communicative and noncommunicative situations (in the communicative situation, the adults, all English speakers, were asked to talk while selecting the pictures). Our initial results suggest that, even in noncommunicative situations, adults select pictures in a particular order (even though the task does not require them to do so). Moreover, while the order in which adults select the pictures resembles English word order in the communicative situation (moving object–action–stationary object), it resembles the order found in their own spontaneously created gestures in the noncommunicative situation (stationary object–moving object–action) (Gershkoff-Stowe and Goldin-Meadow, in press). Our future work will explore whether pictures for patients occupy a privileged position in reconstructions of transitive scenes, as our gesture findings suggest they might.

Recent findings from a very different type of study (Griffin and Bock 2000) suggest that focusing on the patient may, in fact, be a "natural" way of viewing an action. Griffin and Bock monitored eye movements under several conditions: adults described a simple event shown in a picture (with or without the opportunity to prepare their speech; speech conditions); adults viewed the picture with the goal of finding the person or thing being acted on in each event (patient condition); adults viewed the picture without any specific task requirements (inspection condition). From the perspective of our studies, the most interesting finding is that the adults' eye movements were skewed toward the patient early in the viewing, not only in the patient condition, but also in the inspection condition. In other words, when given no instructions, the adults' first inclination was to focus on the patient—the semantic element that typically occupies the initial position in the gesture sentences created by the deaf children and hearing adults in our studies. In contrast, when asked to describe the scene in speech, the adults skewed their eye movements to the agent, the semantic element that typically occupies the subject position of an English sentence.

Our data, taken with Griffin and Bock's (2000) findings, suggest that focusing on patients may be a default bias found in both processing and acquisition tasks. When asked only to view a scene, adults focus their attention on the patient. This attentional bias is abandoned when the adults are asked to talk about the scene in a conventional language whose syntactic structure does not match the bias. In a similar fashion, when not exposed to a usable conventional language model, children display a patient bias in their self-generated communication systems. This bias is abandoned when the children are exposed to a language model whose syntactic structures do not match the bias. Thus, the biases that we discover in our studies of the gesture systems generated by deaf children may have relevance beyond children and acquisition to human thought in general.

Whatever the outcome of future studies of noncommunicative situations, it is clear that the ergative pattern is resilient in communicative situations. Why then is it relatively infrequent in the syntax and morphology of the world's languages? If a patient focus is such a natural way of taking in a scene, why don't most of the world's languages design their structures to take advantage of what would appear to be an easily processed format?

*The parent is the actor. The baby is the patient. The baby is done to. It knows it and does not like it, So it cries.*

We don't know, but we do have some guesses. Slobin (1977) has suggested that languages face several pressures simultaneously: pressures to be clear, processible, quick, easy, and expressive. Importantly, Slobin points out that these pressures do not necessarily all push language in the same direction. For example, the pressure to be semantically clear often conflicts with pressures to be processed quickly or to be rhetorically expressive. The need to be clear may pressure languages to adopt structures that reinforce the patient bias; however, at the same time, the need to be quick and expressive may pressure languages toward structures that do not have a patient focus. If the bias toward patients is as fundamental as Griffin and Bock's (2000) and the spontaneous gesture data suggest, it may be overridden only at a cost: there may greater cognitive costs involved in processing sentences that do not organize around the patient than sentences that do.

*Speculation*

We have now come full circle. How robust the patient focus is in the face of a habitually used language that does not organize around patients is a Whorfian question. Can using a non-patient-focus language day after day, year after year, alter what appears to be a natural focus on the patient? If so, this would be a Whorfian effect: after enough habitual use, it is likely that there would be little or no cognitive cost to processing such a language (e.g., no cost to processing an accusative language such as English that overrides the patient focus). If, however, habitually using a language that overrides the patient focus does not alter this focus (a noneffect from the Whorfian point of view), there ought to be some sort of cognitive cost involved in processing a non-patient-focus language of this sort.

Whatever the answer, this set of questions is one that we are able to pose only after having explored the thoughts children communicate before they have been molded by a language model. Moreover, our findings underscore the robustness of ergative structure: children do not need a language model to focus consistently on the patient and adopt an ergative pattern in their language (or thought)—but they may well need one to adopt an accusative pattern.

## Note

The work described in this chapter was supported by grant RO1 DC00491 from NIDCD. I thank my many collaborators, Lila Gleitman, Heidi Feldman, Carolyn Mylander, Lisa Gershkoff-Stowe, Elif Yalabik, for their help over the years in developing these ideas, and the children and their families for their continued cooperation and friendship.

## References

Acredolo, L. P., and Goodwyn, S. W. (1988). Symbolic gesturing in normal infants. *Child Development, 59,* 450–466.

Aksu-Koç, A. A., and Slobin, D. I. (1985). The acquisition of Turkish. In D. I. Slobin (Ed.), *The crosslinguistic study of language acquisition: Vol. 1. The data* (pp. 839–878). Hillsdale, NJ: Erlbaum.

Allen, S. E. M., and Schroder, H. (in press). Preferred argument structure in early Inuktitut spontaneous speech data. In J. D. DuBois, L. Kumpf, and W. Ashby (Eds.), *Preferred argument structure: Grammar as architecture for function.* Amsterdam: John Benjamins.

Berman, R. A., and Slobin, D. I. (1994). *Relating events in narrative: A cross-linguistic developmental study.* Hillsdale, NJ: Erlbaum.

Bowerman, M. (1973). *Early syntactic development: A cross-linguistic study with special reference to Finnish.* Cambridge: Cambridge University Press.

Brown, R. (1973). *A first language.* Cambridge, MA: Harvard University Press.

Bruner, J. (1974/75). From communication to language: A psychological perspective. *Cognition, 3,* 255–287.

Butcher, C., Mylander, C., and Goldin-Meadow, S. (1991). Displaced communication in a self-styled gesture system: Pointing at the non-present. *Cognitive Development*, 6, 315–342.

Chen, C., and Uttal, D. H. (1988). Cultural values, parents' beliefs, and children's achievement in the United States and China. *Human Development*, 31, 351–358.

Choi, S. (1999). Early development of verb structures and caregiver input in Korean: Two case studies. *The International Journal of Bilingualism*, 3, 241–265.

Choi, S., and Bowerman, M. (1991). Learning to express motion events in English and Korean: The influence of language-specific lexicalization patterns. *Cognition*, 41, 83–121.

Clancy, P. (1993). Preferred argument structure in Korean acquisition. *Proceedings of the Child Language Research Forum*, 25, 307–314.

Conrad, R. (1979). *The deaf child*. London: Harper and Row.

Dixon, R. M. W. (1979). Ergativity. *Language*, 55, 59–138.

DuBois, J. D. (1987). The discourse basis of ergativity. *Language*, 63, 805–855.

Feldman, H., Goldin-Meadow, S., and Gleitman, L. (1978). Beyond Herodotus: The creation of language by linguistically deprived deaf children. In A. Lock (Ed.), *Action, symbol, and gesture: The emergence of language* (pp. 351–414). New York: Academic Press.

Gershkoff-Stowe, L., and Goldin-Meadow, S. (1998). The role of a communication partner in the creation of a gestural language system. *Proceedings of the Boston University Conference on Language Development*, 22, 246–256.

Gershkoff-Stowe, L., and Goldin-Meadow, S. (in press). Is there a natural order for expressing semantic relations? *Cognitive Psychology*.

Goldin-Meadow, S., Butcher, C., Mylander, C., and Dodge, M. (1994). Nouns and verbs in a self-stled gesture system: What's in a name? *Cognitive Psychology*, 27, 259–319.

Goldin-Meadow, S., and Feldman, H. (1977). The development of language-like communication without a language model. *Science*, 197, 401–403.

Goldin-Meadow, S., Gershkoff-Stowe, L., and Yalabik, E. (2000). The rsilience of ergative structure in language created by children and by adults. *Proceedings of the Boston University Conference on Language Development*, 24, 343–353.

Goldin-Meadow, S., McNeill, D., and Singleton, J. (1996). Silence is liberating: Removing the handcuffs on grammatical expression in the manual modality. *Psychological Review*, 103, 34–55.

Goldin-Meadow, S., and Morford, M. (1985). Gesture in early child language: Studies of deaf and hearing children. *Merrill-Palmer Quarterly*, 31, 145–176.

Goldin-Meadow, S., and Mylander, C. (1984). Gestural communication in deaf children: The effects and non-effects of parental input on early language development. *Monographs of the Society for Research in Child Development*, 49, 1–121.

Goldin-Meadow, S., and Mylander, C. (1998). Spontaneous gesture systems created by deaf children in two cultures. *Nature, 391,* 279–281.

Goldin-Meadow, S., Mylander, C., and Butcher, C. (1995). The resilience of combinatorial structure at the word level: Morphology in self-styled gesture systems. *Cognition, 56,* 195–262.

Goldin-Meadow, S., and Saltzman, J. (2000). The cultural bounds of maternal accommodation: How Chinese and American mothers communicate with deaf and hearing children. *Psychological Science, 11,* 311–318.

Griffin, Z. M., and Bock, K. (2000). What the eyes say about speaking. *Psychological Science, 11,* 274–279.

Hammond, A. J., and Goldin-Meadow, S. (2002). The robustness of non-English sequences in created gesture systems. *Proceedings of the Boston University Conference on Language Development, 26,* 278–289.

Hoffmeister, R., and Wilbur, R. (1980). Developmental: The acquisition of sign language. In H. Lane and F. Grosjean (Eds.), *Recent perspectives on American Sign Language* (pp. 61–78). Hillsdale, NJ: Erlbaum.

Imai, M., and Gentner, D. (1997). A crosslinguistic study of early word meaning: Universal ontology and linguistic influence. *Cognition, 62,* 169–200.

Lucy, J. A. (1992). *Grammatical categories and cognition: A case study of the linguistic relativity hypothesis.* New York: Cambridge University Press.

Lucy, J. A., and Gaskins, S. (2001). Grammatical categories and the development of classification preferences: A comparative approach. In M. Bowerman and S. C. Levinson (Eds.), *Language acquisition and conceptual development* (pp. 257–283). Cambridge: Cambridge University Press.

Mayberry, R. I. (1992). The cognitive development of deaf children: Recent insights. In S. Segalowitz and I. Rapin (Eds.), *Child neuropsychology: Vol. 7. Handbook of neuropsychology* (pp. 51–68). Amsterdam: Elsevier.

McNeill, D. (1992). *Hand and mind: What gestures reveal about thought.* Chicago: University of Chicago Press.

Meadow, K. (1968). Early manual communication in relation to the deaf child's intellectual, social, and communicative functioning. *American Annals of the Deaf, 113,* 29–41.

Miller, P. J., Mintz, J., and Fung, H. (1991, October). *Creating children's selves: An American and Chinese comparison of mothers' stories about their toddlers.* Paper presented at the meeting of the Society for Psychological Anthropology.

Morford, M., and Goldin-Meadow, S. (1992). Comprehension and production of gesture in combination with speech in one-word speakers. *Journal of Child Language, 9,* 559–580.

Newport, E. L., and Ashbrook, E. F. (1977). The emergence of semantic relations in American Sign Language. *Papers and Reports on Child Language Development, 13,* 16–21.

Newport, E. L., and Meier, R. P. (1985). The acquisition of American Sign Language. In D. I. Slobin (Ed.), *The crosslinguistic study of language acquisition: Vol. 1. The data* (pp. 881–938). Hillsdale, NJ: Erlbaum.

Ochs, E. (1982). Ergativity and word order in Samoan child language. *Language*, 58, 646–671.

Schulman, B. W., Mylander, C., and Goldin-Meadow, S. (2001). Ergative structure at sentence and discourse levels in a self-generated communication system. *Proceedings of the Boston University Conference on Language Development*, 25, 815–824.

Silverstein, M. (1976). Hierarchy of features and ergativity. In R. M. W. Dixon (Ed.), *Grammatical categories in Australian languages* (pp. 112–171). Canberra: Australian Institute of Aboriginal Studies.

Slobin, D. I. (1977). Language change in childhood and history. In J. Macnamara (Ed.), *Language learning and thought* (pp. 185–214). New York: Academic Press.

Slobin, D. I. (1985). Introduction: Why study acquisition crosslinguistically? In D. I. Slobin (Ed.), *The crosslinguistic study of language acquisition: Vol. 1. The data* (pp. 3–24). Hillsdale, NJ: Erlbaum.

Smith, S., and Freedman, D. (1982). *Mother-toddler interaction and maternal perception of child development in two ethnic groups: Chinese-American and European-American.* Paper presented at the meeting of the Society for Research in Child Development, Detroit, MI.

Stevenson, H. W., Lee, S.-L., Chen, C., Stigler, J. W., Hsu, C.-C., and Kitamura, S. (1990). Contexts of achievement. *Monographs of the Society for Research in Child Development*, 55, No. 221.

Supalla, T., Newport, E. L., Singleton, J. L., Supalla, S., Metlay, D., and Coulter, G. (in press). *Test battery for Amrican Sign Language morphology and syntax.* Burtonsville, MD: Linstok Press.

Wang, X-l. (1992). *Resilience and fragility in language acquisition: A comparative study of the gestural communication systems of Chinese and American deaf children.* Unpublished Doctoral dissertation, University of Chicago.

Wang, X-l., Mylander, C., and Goldin-Meadow, S. (1995). The resilience of language: Mother-child interaction and its effects on the gesture systems of Chinese and American deaf children. In K. Emmorey and J. Reilly (Eds.), *Language, gesture, and space* (pp. 411–433). Hillsdale, NJ: Erlbaum.

Whorf, B. L. (1956). *Language, thought and reality: Selected writings of Benjamin Lee Whorf* (J. B. Carroll, Ed.). Cambridge, MA: MIT Press.

Yalabik, E. (1999). *From deaf children to hearing adults: What is common (or different) in their self-created gestures?* Unpublished Master's thesis, University of Chicago.

Young, N. F. (1972). Socialization patterns among the Chinese of Hawaii. *Amerasia Journal*, 1(4), 31–51.

# Index